CW01650269

Queen Sālote *of* Tonga

ELIZABETH WOOD-ELLEM

Queen Sālote *of* Tonga

THE STORY OF AN ERA
1900–1965

AUCKLAND UNIVERSITY PRESS

First published 1999
Reprinted 1999 (May, October)

Auckland University Press
University of Auckland
Private Bag 92019
Auckland
New Zealand

© Elizabeth Wood-Ellem 1999

ISBN 1 86940 205 7

This book is copyright. Apart from fair dealing for the purpose of private study, research, criticism or review, as permitted under the Copyright Act, no part may be reproduced by any process without the prior permission of the publisher.

Front cover photograph: Courtesy Adrienne Kaeppler
Back cover photograph: *New Zealand Herald*

Cover design by Christine Hansen

Printed by South Wind Production, Singapore

"The objective that is ever before me and which inspires all my thoughts is to unify and consolidate at this time the Kingdom of Tonga, that we may really achieve the reputation that is credited to us in the world outside: There is not in the world a little Kingdom like Tonga, peaceful, contented and happy."

Queen Sālote, speech at the Opening of Parliament, 15 June 1937.
Tonga Government Gazette, 17 (19 Aug. 1937) 136.

To the memory of my parents, Olive and Harold Wood,
and of my "other mother", Nusi Havea.

Contents

Preface

Queen Sālote Tupou III of Tonga was the great figure of my childhood, a myth in her own lifetime. That myth both inspired and proved a stumbling block in the process of writing this history: the imperative was to understand how such a myth was created, the difficulty was that I was myself so affected by the myth and I had to search long and hard for the human being that was Queen Sālote. In the years since her death in 1965, Queen Sālote had become an icon for Tongans and *papālangi* (people of European descent) alike.

How then did I come to write this history? Queen Sālote wished a history of Tonga to be written to include her own reign, and chose Elizabeth Bott Spillius to undertake the task. Elizabeth's career took another path, so the mantle fell on me. Without Elizabeth's preliminary work, I could not have written this book. Then my own connection with Tonga, since my birth and childhood in Tonga, was stimulated by eight visits over the last 24 years and by the knowledge that it would be difficult for a Tongan to write about such a chief, a chief who achieved the sacred *mana* (see Glossary).

Elizabeth Bott Spillius knew Queen Sālote in her twilight years, when it was the highest duty of the Tongan people to anticipate her wishes. My other prime informants, my parents (Rev. Dr Harold and Dr Olive Wood), had known her in the 1920s and 1930s, and my father gave the oration at the Queen's funeral in 1965. My parents were faithful to the myth, with that loyalty one owes to an admirable person upon whose survival depends the welfare of many; for the "peace and unity" so earnestly sought by the Queen were extremely fragile.

In 1973 my father asked me to assist with research for an article about the Queen for Noel Rutherford's *Friendly Islands: a history of Tonga*. That article embodied the myth of the unchallengeable and unchallenged ruler. I subsequently decided to take Queen Sālote and her consort as the subject of my doctoral thesis, focusing on their leadership in the period 1918–41. In the 1990s I was offered two fellowships so I could complete the study of the whole of Queen Sālote's life.

If I had known the difficulties I would encounter, I might not have begun the task. The major difficulty was the lack of written records and their distant locations. The Western Pacific High Commission records, for example, were removed from Suva and taken to Milton Keynes, England, for no very good reason, between the first and second stages of this project. Since Pacific scholars live in the Pacific, there are better locations than Milton Keynes.

Secondly, the more I read the documents and talked with Tongans, the clearer it became that I could not write just a biography. Not only does one need a context in which see the significance of a life, but other published sources on the period 1900–65 are fragmentary. I would have to commit myself to studying the society and politics of Queen Sālote's lifetime. Hence the subtitle to this book: *the story of an era*. Having begun, the task proved to be an education in the way an individual and a country are shaped by circumstances and by each other.

The third difficulty was that although Queen Sālote is most famous among *papālangi* for her warmth and graciousness at the coronation of Queen Elizabeth II in 1953, Tongans saw a very different person: tough, hard-working, just, ambitious. I was, as a *papālangi*, inadequate for the task ahead. On the other hand, no Tongan appeared likely to attempt it, and since Queen Sālote's death in 1965 a new generation of Tongans has grown up who do not know the Queen, and who (judging by school projects and the like) are increasingly curious about her.

The fourth difficulty was the temptation of superficiality. Other writers have written books in which the words "Queen Sālote" appear in the title, but they have found the task of extensive research too daunting. It seemed to me that I could best contribute to Tongan historiography by writing a detailed account of 65 years, and allow others to use it as a springboard for later work, using sources not available to me. In particular, I hope that Tongan scholars will take advantage of their fluency in the language and their family connections to use oral sources before they all disappear, particularly those of Ha'apai, Vava'u, and the Niuas.

The portrait I have attempted to draw of Queen Sālote is of a human being, not without flaws (which she would be last to deny), but of someone who rose to the responsibilities that life brought her. Her responses to different challenges in her life underlie each chapter in this book.

My clearest memory of Queen Sālote comes from when I was five years of age. There had been a choir competition, in which 37 choirs from all over Tonga had come to compete. After the competition, all the choirs (accompanied by their relations) went to the Palace to sing for the Queen. The Queen sat crosslegged in the doorway, facing the big space at the back of the Palace that saw and would see so many dances, presentations, and other celebrations. On that back verandah, at a respectful distance from the Queen, sat half-a-dozen of her *kau matāpule* (see *matāpule* in Glossary). Because it was a *papālangi* occasion, my father, the conductor of the choirs, was permitted to breach protocol, not only by turning his back on the Queen, but by standing on a box that would elevate him above the Queen's head. The grounds were packed with people who were singing for an audience of one.

Indelible in my mind also is the sound of her car starting up with the first bar of the National Anthem at the end of a church service. By the end of the Anthem, the car and her attendants were ready at the door to take her away. To a child the sound of the car and the Anthem conveyed that the reverence for the Queen was of the same quality as reverence for the God we had just worshipped.

Sometimes Sālote did not leave Nafualu (where we lived) immediately after the service, but came and had morning tea with my parents. My parents were ready to send me and my siblings away, but, given half an opportunity, the Queen would utter those words she addressed to many children: "Come and sit by me."

By the time I began my research (1974), the Queen had been dead for nine years. Nevertheless I was aware that for all Tongans the Queen's *mana* was still powerful, and that it was difficult for them to speak of someone who was essentially still present. Casual references were (I was assured) likely to result in some disturbance of the natural order of things. This suggested to me that the *'ofa* (love) the people felt for their sovereign was tinged with a degree of fear, but not the fear of retribution, rather the fear of offending someone who could hardly control her supernatural powers, even after death.

In spite of difficulties, the research for this job has given me much enjoyment, partly because of the pleasure of research and writing about something so intrinsically interesting as Queen Sālote and her kingdom, and partly because of the many friendships that have come out of the work.

My doctoral thesis (1981) contains of a list of the names of people who assisted me during that first period of my research. I need to repeat some of those acknowledgements and add others. To HM Tāufa'āhau Tupou IV, who gave me permission to undertake the research. To HM Halaevalu Mata'aho and HRH Tu'ipelehake for gracious conversations. To HRH Prince 'Ulukālala-Lavaka-Ata and HRH Princess Nanasipau'u for support and advice, and for reading sections of the book in typescript. To The University of Melbourne, The Australian National University, The University of Auckland, and the Macmillan Brown Centre (University of Canterbury) for scholarships and fellowships; and to the History Department of The University of Melbourne, where I am currently a research associate. To the Myer Foundation for financial assistance during two field trips. To my parents, Rev. Dr Harold and Dr Olive Wood (now deceased), for generously assisting with the early stages of my research. To Professor Emeritus Greg Dening, the supervisor of my doctoral thesis, for his patience, and to him and Donna for their continuing friendship. To Dr Elizabeth Bott Spillius and James Spillius for making their 1958–60 papers available, and to Elizabeth for many discussions. To Rev. Dr S. 'Amanaki Havea, Dr Melenaite Taumoefolau, Tilisi Faupula Bryce, Dilys Rowlands, Helen Taliai, Rev. Dr Toa Fīnau, for translations. To the late Manu Faupula for copies of Queen Sālote's letters to Rev. Sau Faupula. To the late Halaevalu Maile, Ve'ehala (Leilua), and Nānisi Helu; and to Tupou Posesi Fanua, Moala Simiki, Kakala Taumoefolau, and other informants. To the late Tavi (Preben Kauffmann), who helped me understand the underlying logic of the social structure of Tonga. To the late A. C. (Archie) Reid and to Mary and the late Rodger Page the younger, for reminiscences. To Rev. Lopeti and Mele Taufa and Barbara and Dr 'Epeli Hau'ofa for insights. To Dr Adrienne Kaeppler for her generosity and for reading an early draft of this book, for many conversations during field trips, and for her publications; to Dr Ian Campbell for reading an even earlier draft. To Rev. Dr H. G. Cummins, Dr Phyllis Herda, and Associate Professor Judith Huntsman for encouragement. To Rev. Siupeli and Helen Taliai and Rev. Howard and Janet Secomb for answering questions. To Futa Helu for the sheer enjoyment of his papers on Tongan custom. To Rebecca Maxwell, who listened while all 19 chapters were read aloud to her and made encouraging comments. To Sir David Attenborough for generously giving me photographs taken on his 1959 visit to Tonga. To numerous librarians and archivists in Fiji, Australia, and New Zealand for help over the two periods of research, 1974–81 and 1994–97.

Notes on Tongan Spelling and on Chiefly Titles

Prior to 1943 the letter g stood for the sound ng, and the Wesleyan schools used the letter b where the Catholic schools used p; j had earlier been largely abandoned in favour of s. In 1943 HRH Prince Tupouto'a, newly appointed Minister for Education (now HM Tāufa'āhau Tupou IV), approved the substitution of ng for g and enjoined uniformity in the use of p and s (eliminating b and j entirely), divided words that were formerly one word, and standardized the use of the glottal stop (*fakau'a*) in written texts where the sound occurred in spoken speech. A macron was later added to indicate the long vowel. The reformed alphabet was used by C. M. Churchward in his *Tongan Grammar* (1953) and *Tongan Dictionary* (1959). The Tongan alphabet now consists of the letters

a, ā, e, ē, f, h, i, ī, k, l, m, n, ng, o, ō, p, s, t, u, ū, v, ' (*fakau'a*).

In order to minimize confusion for the reader, the modern spelling has been used throughout this book, with the exception of quotations and titles of older works listed in the bibliography. A glossary has been included to facilitate understanding of those Tongan words used in the text. However, lists in this book that require alphabetical order have, for practical reasons, disregarded the *fakau'a*.

Plurals

In everyday speech *papālangi* and Tongans speaking English often make plurals by adding "s" to a Tongan word. However, the plural is correctly indicated by the use of a plural word as a prefix, the most common being *kau*, *ngaahi*, *fanga*, and *'u* (*ongo* indicates two). Thus *matāpule* becomes *kau matāpule*, and *kāinga* becomes *ngaahi kāinga*. The plural indicator chosen can determine the meaning: *kau malanga* meaning "preachers" and *ngaahi malanga* meaning "sermons". Some words have a distinctive plural. Thus *'eiki* (chief) becomes *hou'eiki* (aristocrats) and *tehina* (younger brother of man) becomes *fototehina*.

Homonyms abound, and the intended meaning is indicated by the choice of pronoun. Every noun may be used as a verb, adjective, or adverb.

Names

Surnames were unknown in Tonga prior to the setting up of mission schools in Tonga and were not widely used until the expansion of secondary education in the late 1940s. Nowadays most Tongans have a Tonganized *papālangi* name (e.g. Sione = John; Melenaite = Mary Knight; ʻIlaisaane = Eliza Anne), plus a Tongan personal name (e.g. Fīnau, Manu, Kakala, Toa), and a surname. See below for more examples of names.

Titles and rank

When a chief succeeds to a title, he is no longer referred to by any of these names, but only by his title, except when it is necessary to distinguish between him and his predecessors or successors. Thus Uiliami or Viliami (William) Tupoulahi was known by his chiefly title of Tungī from 1909. The additional nickname Mailefihi distinguishes him from his grandfather Tungī (Halatuituia) and from his successor. Whether in such cases the personal name follows or precedes the title has not been standardized, but in order to avoid making the use of titles and personal names too complicated the practice in this book has been to use the personal name after the title whenever the personal name is required, but in parentheses – for example, Tuʻivakanō (Polutele) – except in a few cases where custom dictates otherwise, such as Tungī Mailefihi.

In some cases the personal name of a chief has become the title of a descendant. For example, Kalanivalu was a personal name of a son of the last Tuʻi Tonga, and became a title only when his grandson succeeded in 1935. ʻUlukālala was the personal name of chiefs of a particular line, but did not become a title until Haʻamea succeeded his father in 1938. Tupoutoʻa was the personal name of the Tuʻi Kanokupolu of the early nineteenth century and became the title of his great-grandson, and thereafter of the Crown Prince.

The aristocrats (*houʻeiki*) of Tongan society trace their descent from the Tuʻi Tonga or sacred ruler. Their status is assured regardless of titleholding. In the eighteenth century there were many titles (indicating control of land-and-people). Only a few of these titleholding chiefs were given the status of hereditary estateholder (*nōpele* or *matāpule maʻu tofiʻa*) by Tupou I (in 1875, 1880, and 1882), by Tupou II (1894 and 1903), and by Sālote Tupou III (1921). Chiefly titles are divided into *haʻa* (clan groups or lineages), with titles being "sons" or "younger brothers" to the most senior title of that *haʻa*. The *haʻa*, formerly the basis of military alliances and still defining ritual obligations, gradually became less important in the twentieth century.

Many titles died out (except when someone appears to represent them in the *kava* ceremony), for without *fonua* (land-and-people) and an heir born of a chiefly woman, the title loses its *raison d'être*. Titles of *kau matāpule* have survived (whether they had land or not) if they function as ceremonial attendants to their chiefs. But chiefs have to provide material support for their *kau matāpule*, and the number declined when chiefs who were not made hereditary estateholders could not support attendants.

"Rank is everything", said Queen Sālote, but rank is sometimes absolute (personal or blood rank) and sometimes relative (*kāinga* rank or rank by title). Personal or blood rank is based on the sum total of the rank of one's ancestors, the most elevated rank being direct descent from the Tu'i Tonga, and even more from the Tu'i Tonga Fefine (eldest sister of the Tu'i Tonga) or Tamahā (daughter of the Tu'i Tonga Fefine). Relative or *kāinga* rank applies on ceremonial occasions, such as funerals, where relationships through a certain person (the corpse in the case of a funeral) determines whether one is "high" (*'eiki*) or "low" (*tu'a*) on that occasion. A person whose absolute rank was high might not eat at a feast if she or he is "low" on that occasion; for example, "low" is descended from the grandfather while "high" is descended from that grandfather's sister. (Sisters always outrank brothers.) Rank by title is less ambiguous than the other systems of ranking, for the prestige of the title depends, first, on its antiquity and, secondly, on the achievements of its holders (in war, marriage, landholding, and so on).

From the class of lesser chiefs (the *'eiki si'i*) were drawn (in Queen Sālote's time) many of the district officers and town officers, who ruled a district or a village when the hereditary estateholder was an absentee landlord. The chief of that village represented the hereditary estateholder in the day-to-day affairs of the village and made recommendations about allocation of farming and town allotments (*'api tukuhau* and *'api kolo*).

More about names

Some Tongan names are not gender-specific, e.g. Tupou and Manu. The following are some of the frequently used names that were originally *papālangi* names:

'Alipate = Albert
'Ana = Anna
'Ēseta/'Esetia = Esther
Haloti = Harold
'Ikani = Egan
Lesieli = Rachel
Mele = Mary

Melenaite = Mary Knight
Molitoni = Moulton
Motekiai = Mordecai
Nānisi = Nancy (not to be confused with Nanasi, which is short for Nanasipau'u)
Sālote = Charlotte
Samisoni = Samson
Seini = Jane
Sela = Sarah
Sēmisi = James
Siaki = Jack
Siaosi = George
Sioape = Joab
Sioeli = Joel
Sione = John
Siosiua = Joshua
Sisilia = Cecilia
Tēvita = David
Uiliami or Viliami = William

Other names (e.g. Lavinia) are spelt in the same way as in English, but the syllables are given equal emphasis (La-vi-ni-a).

List of Illustrations

List of Figures

Abbreviatons used in Figures

TH Tu'i Ha'atakalaua
TK Tu'i Kanokupolu
TT Tu'i Tonga
TTF Tu'i Tonga Fefine

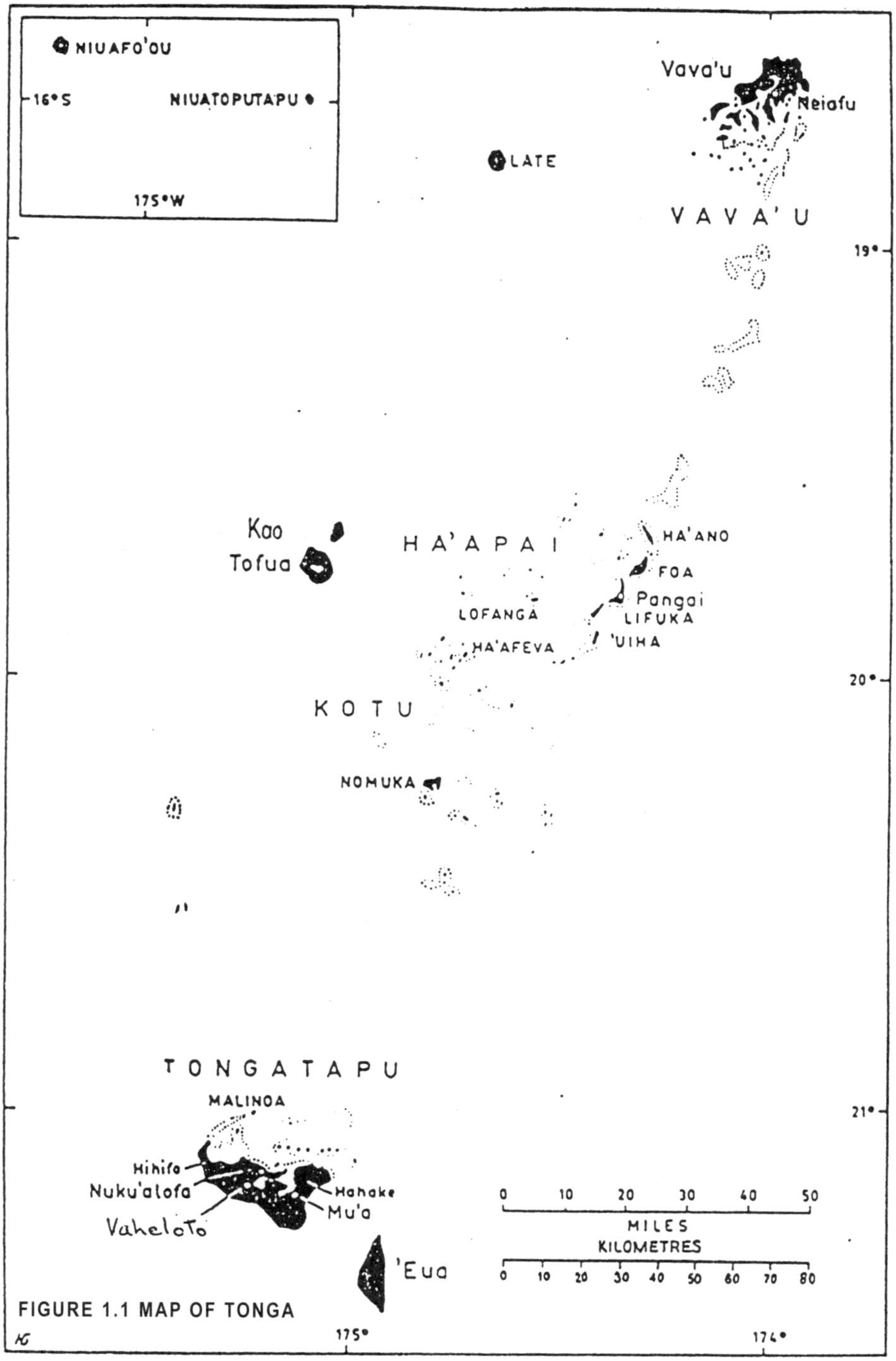

FIGURE 1.1 MAP OF TONGA

FIGURE 1.2 PLAN OF NUKU‘ALOFA, *c.*1921

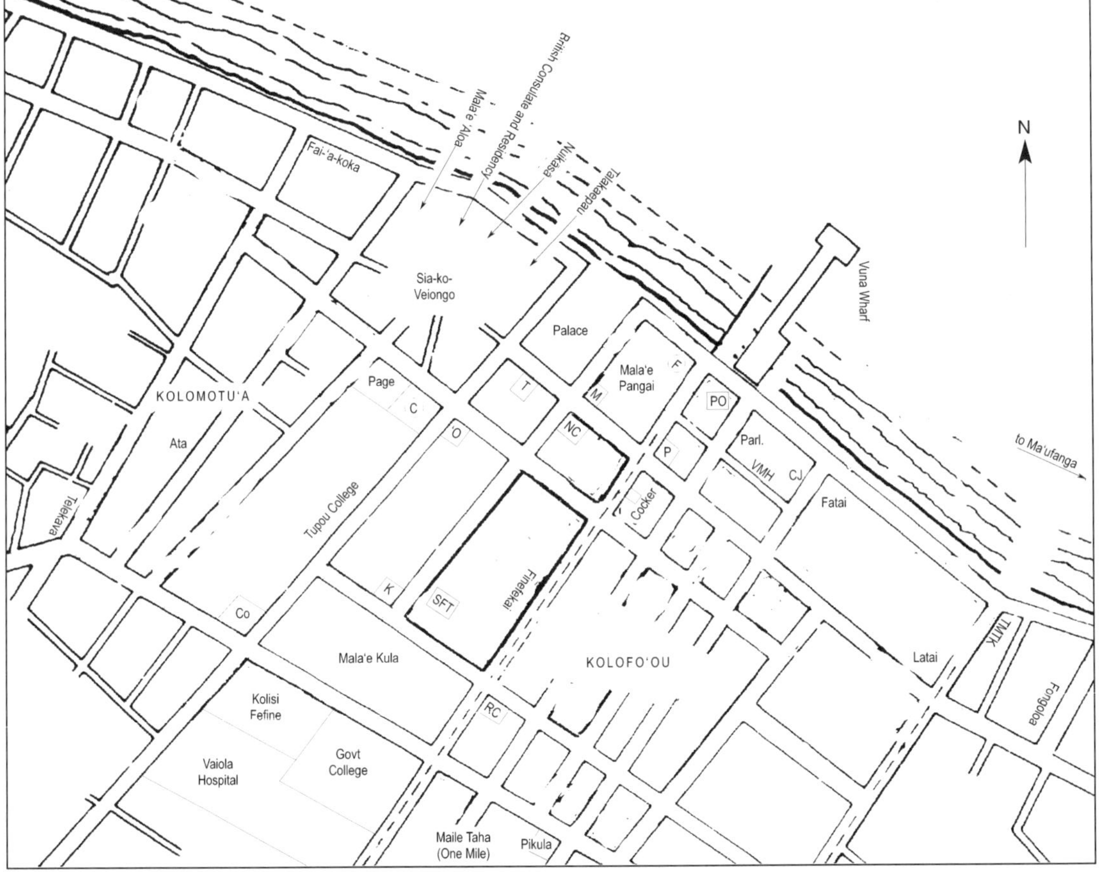

Key:
C = Church
CJ = Chief Justice
Co = Collocott
F = flagpole
K = Kaitangi
M = Mapu-‘a-fuiva
NC = Nuku‘alofa Club
‘O = ‘Otualea
P = Premier
Parl. = Parliament
PO = Treasury and Post Office
RC = Roman Catholic Church
SFT = Sione Filipe Tongilava
T = Tu‘ivakanō
TMTK = Tonga Ma‘a Tonga Kautaha
VMH = Victoria Memorial Hall

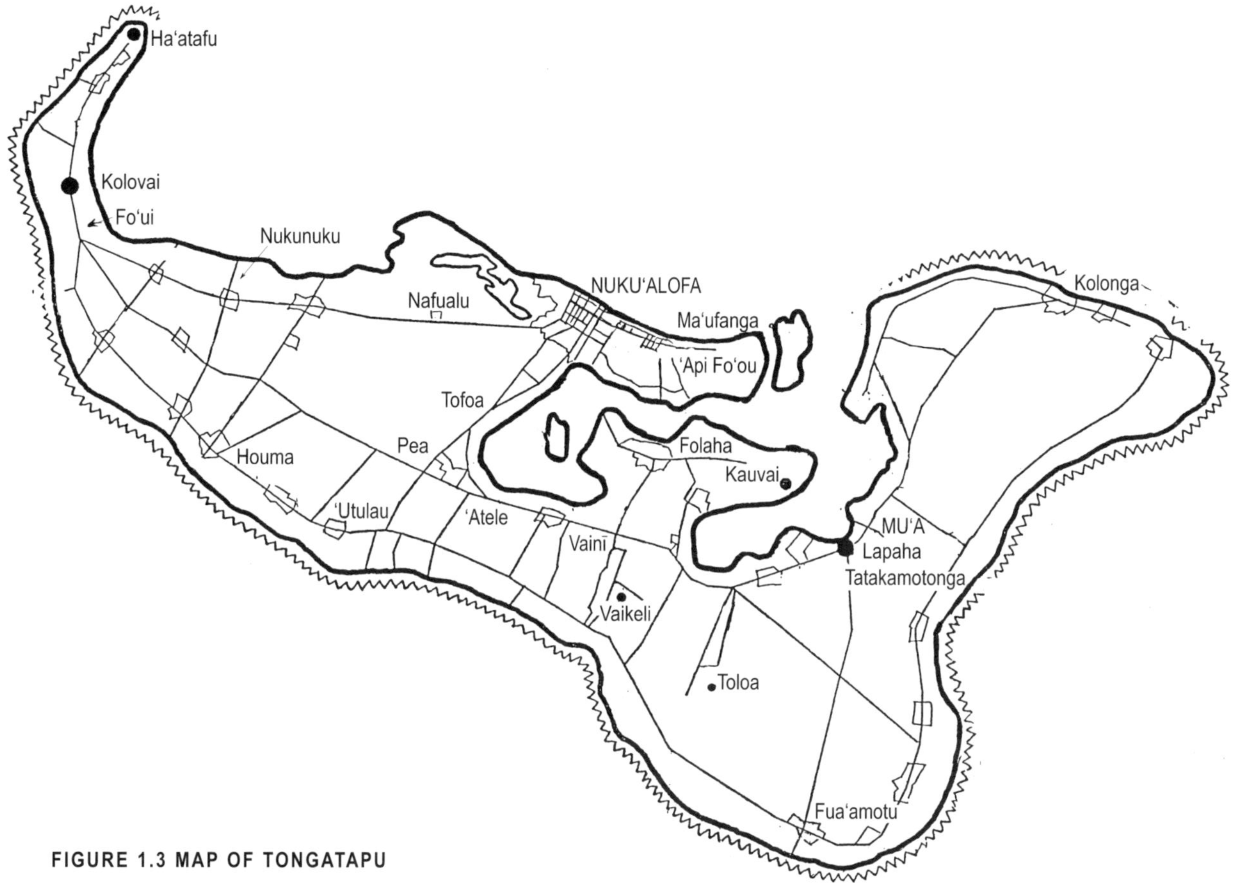

FIGURE 1.3 MAP OF TONGATAPU

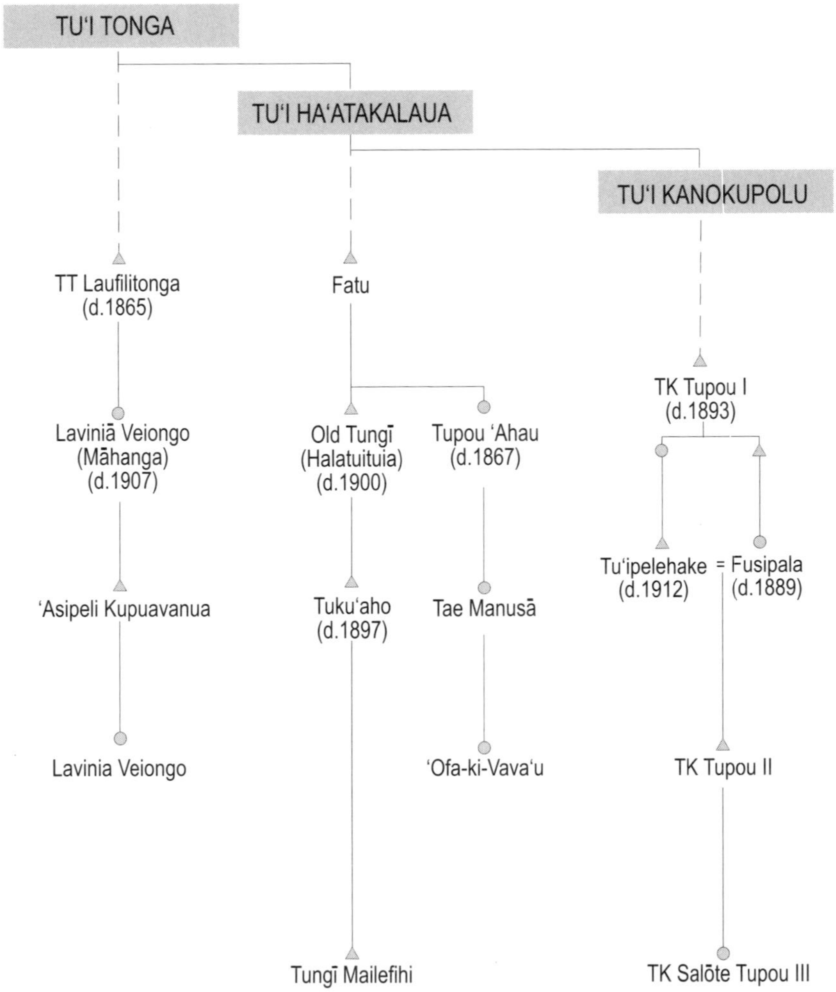

FIGURE 1.4 THE THREE ROYAL LINES

(The last Tu'i Ha'atakalaua died in 1799. The last Tu'i Tonga died in 1865.)

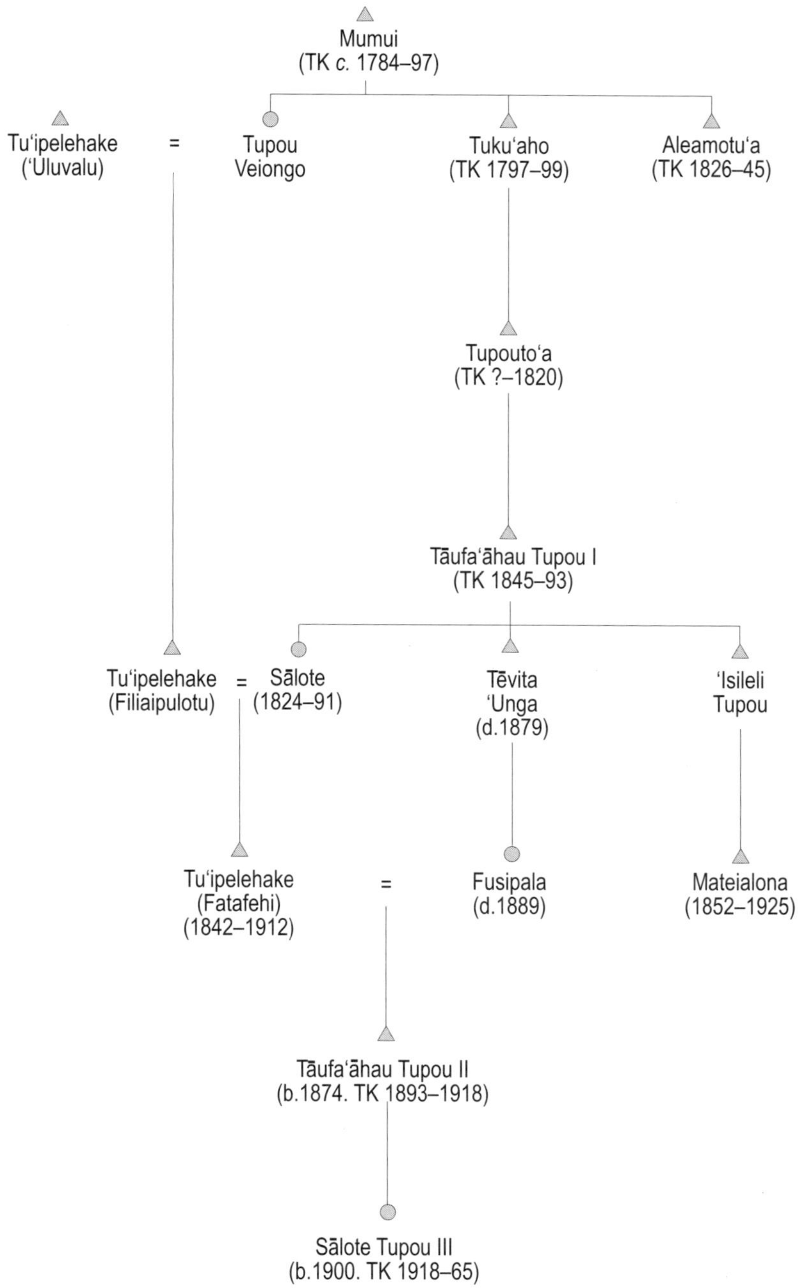

FIGURE 1.5 THE TUPOU DYNASTY

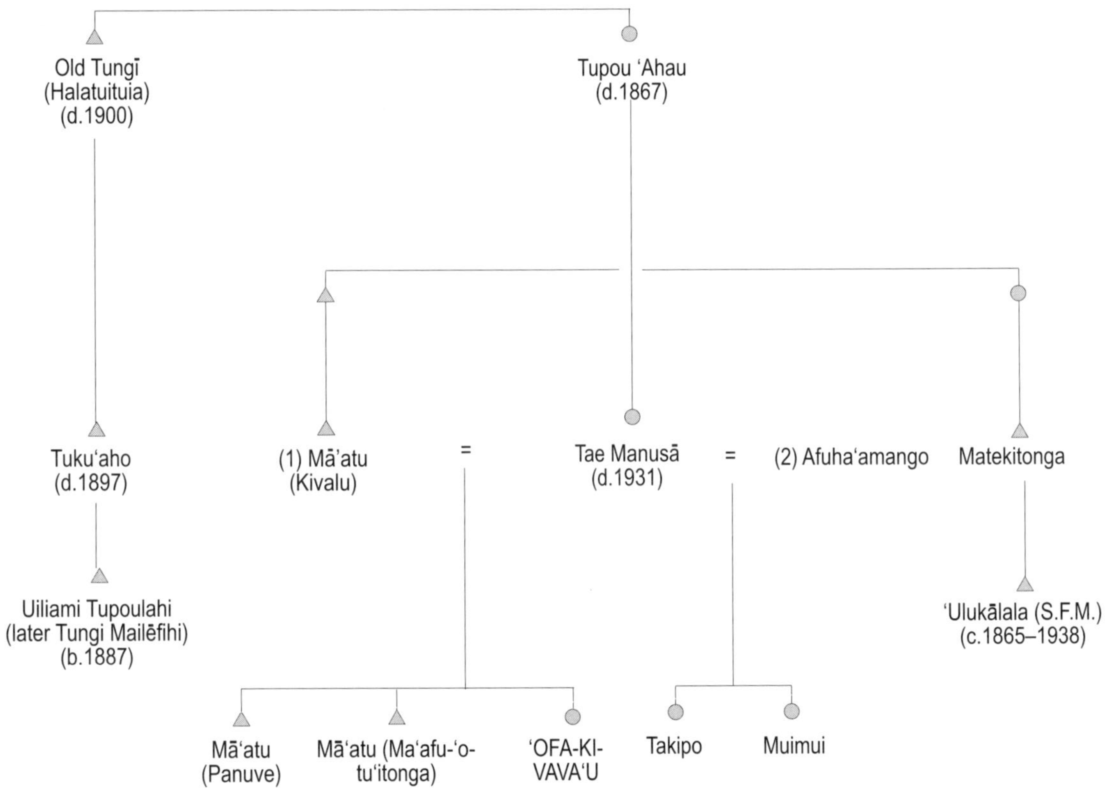

FIGURE 1.6 ‘OFA-KI-VAVA‘U AND HER MAJOR SUPPORTERS

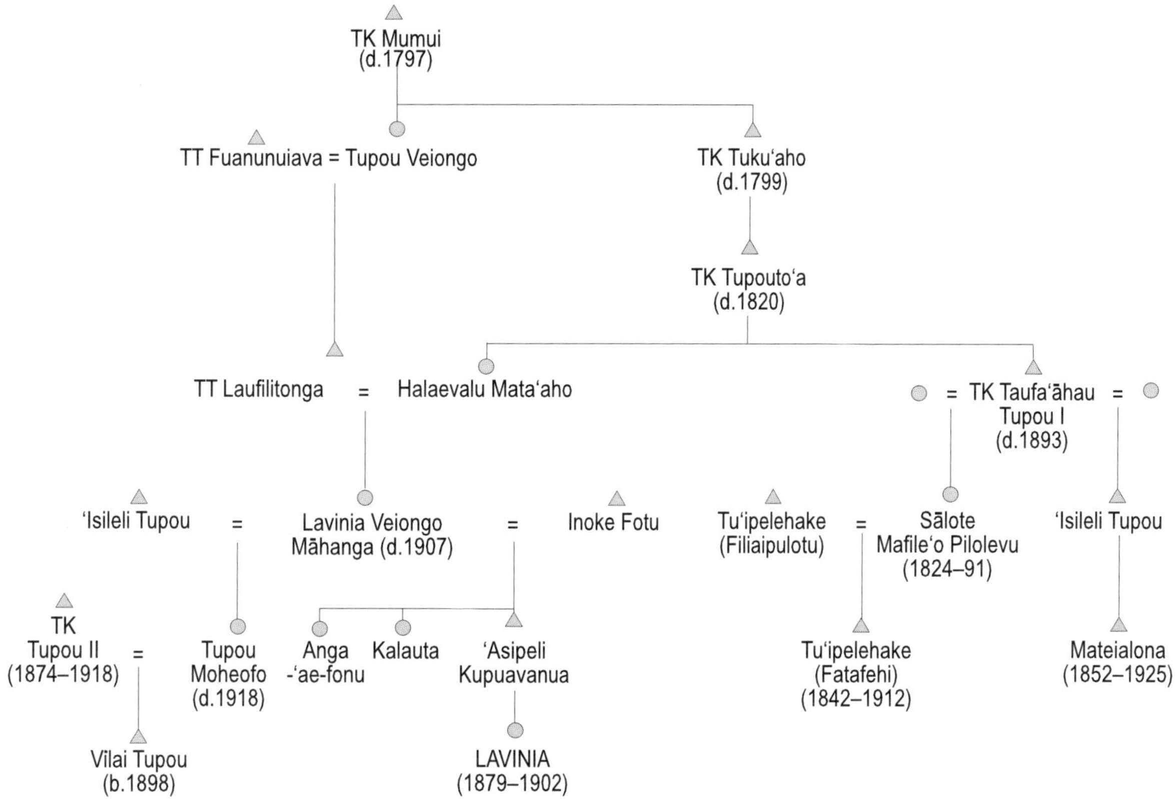

FIGURE 1.7 LAVINIA AND HER MAJOR SUPPORTERS

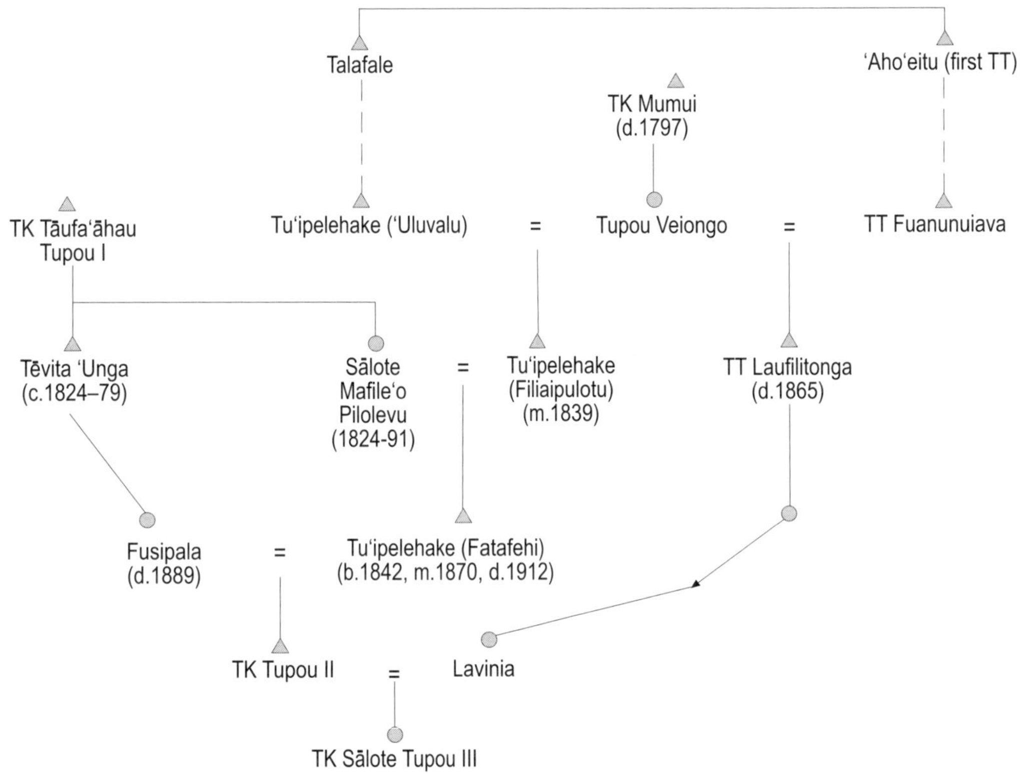

FIGURE 1.8 THE TU'IPELEHAKE LINE UNTIL 1912

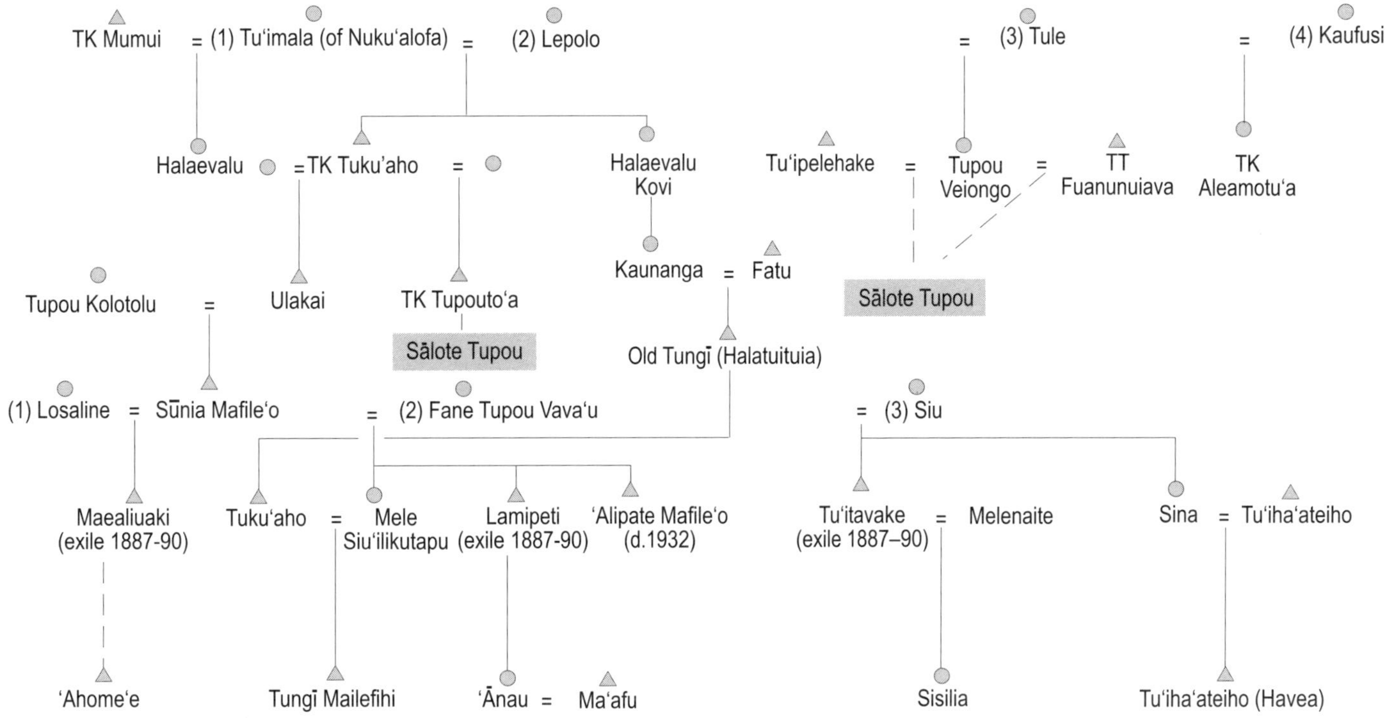

FIGURE 1.9 THE KĀINGA OF KOLOMOTU'A

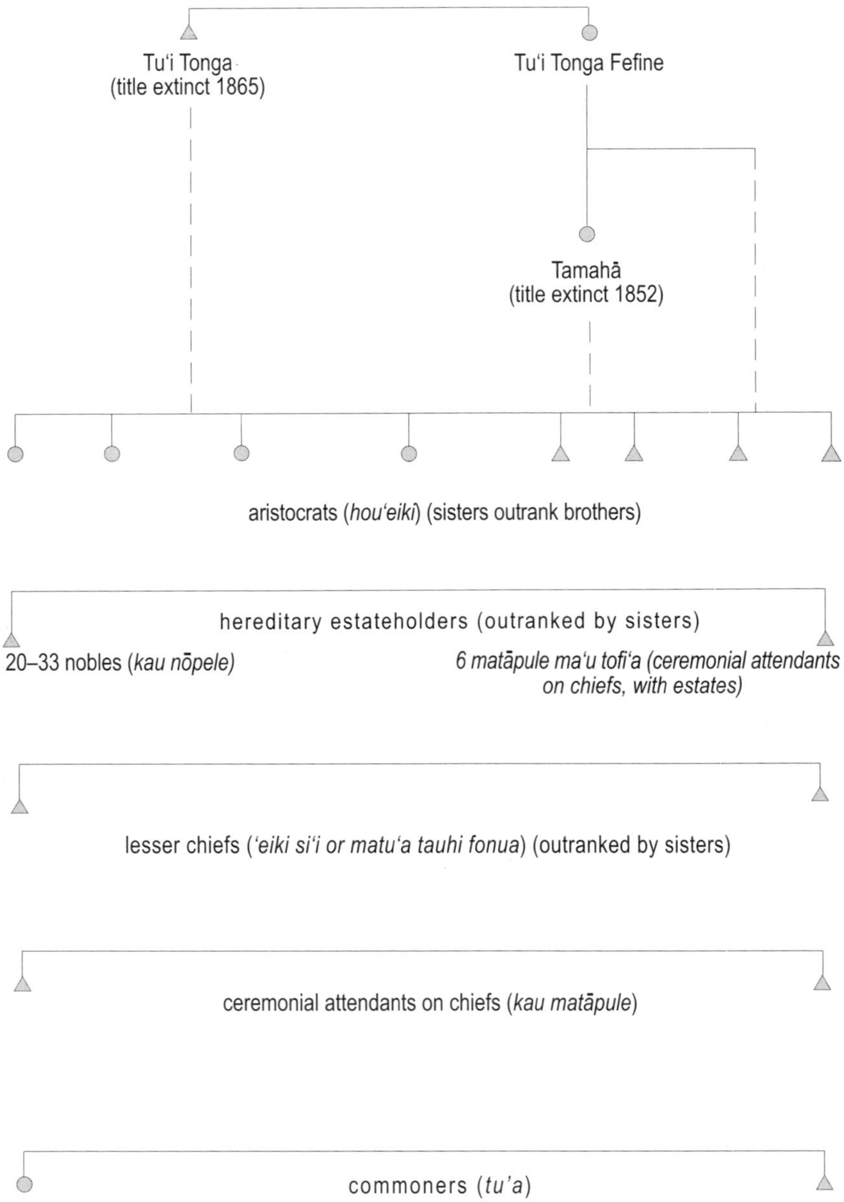

FIGURE 2.1 TONGAN SOCIETY AFTER 1875

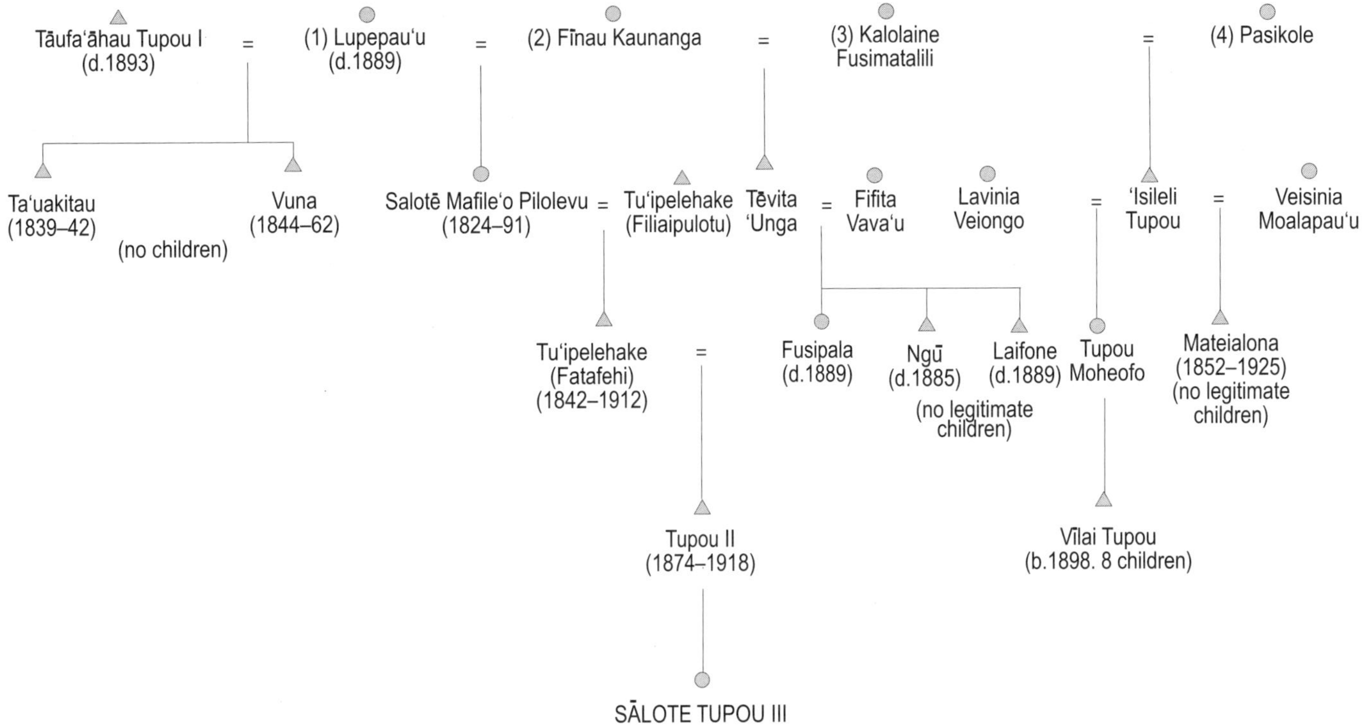

FIGURE 2.2 SOME OF THE DESCENDANTS OF TUPOU I

(Lupepauʻu was the highest ranking of Tupou I's wives, being the daughter of Makamalohi, son of the Tuʻi Tonga Fefine Fatafehi Lapaha.)

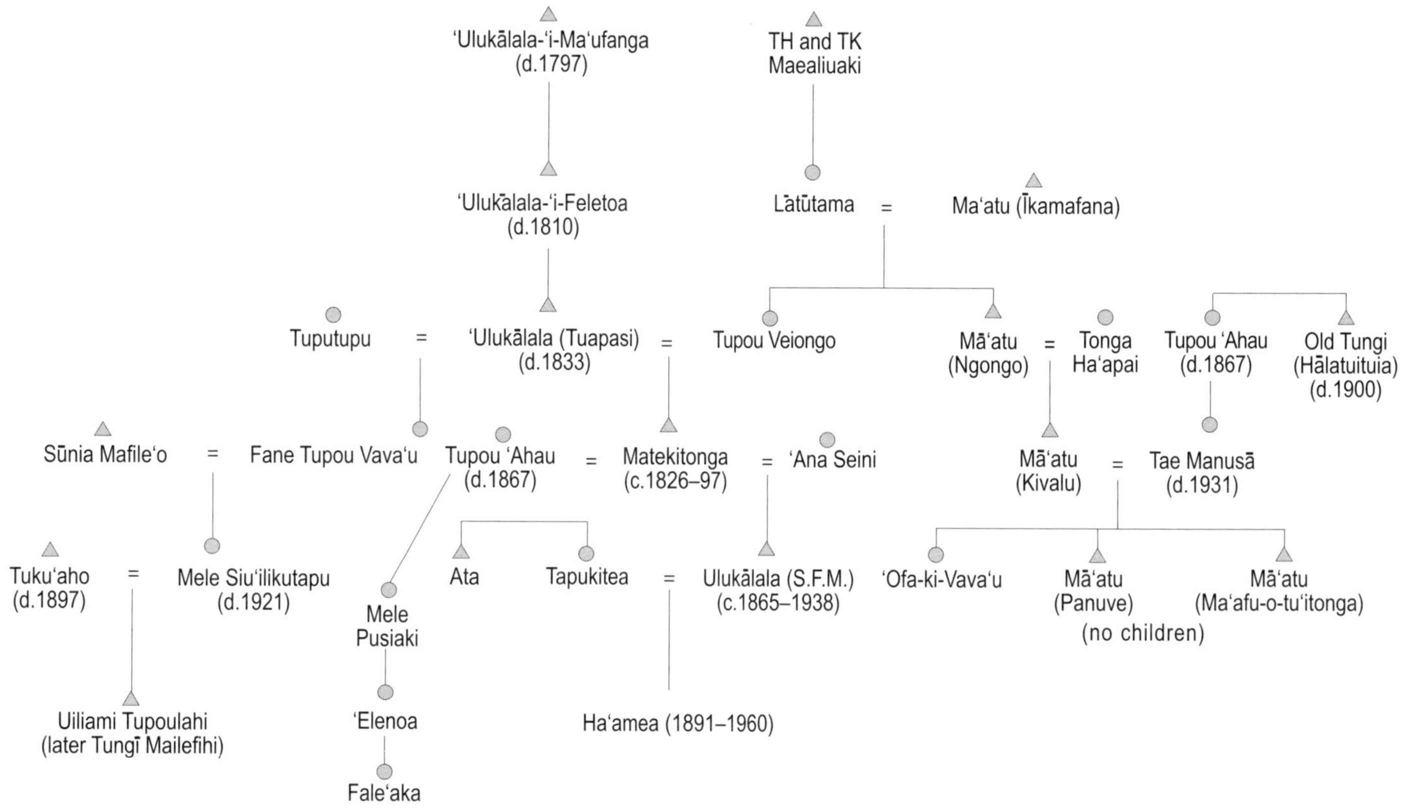

FIGURE 2.3 'ULUKĀLALA LINE, SHOWING CONNECTIONS WITH TUNGĪ AND MĀ'ATU LINES

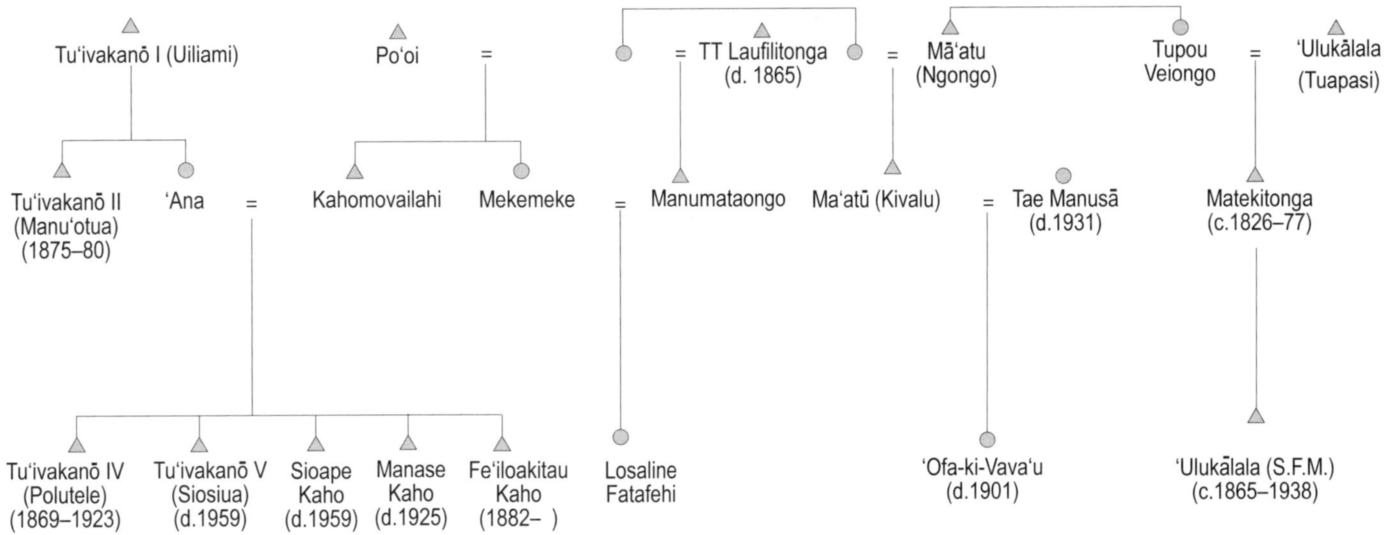

FIGURE 2.4 TUI‘VAKANŌ LINE, SHOWING CONNECTIONS WITH MĀ‘ATU AND ‘ULUKALALĀ
(Note that Tui‘vakanō III (Mānoa) was from an allied line.)

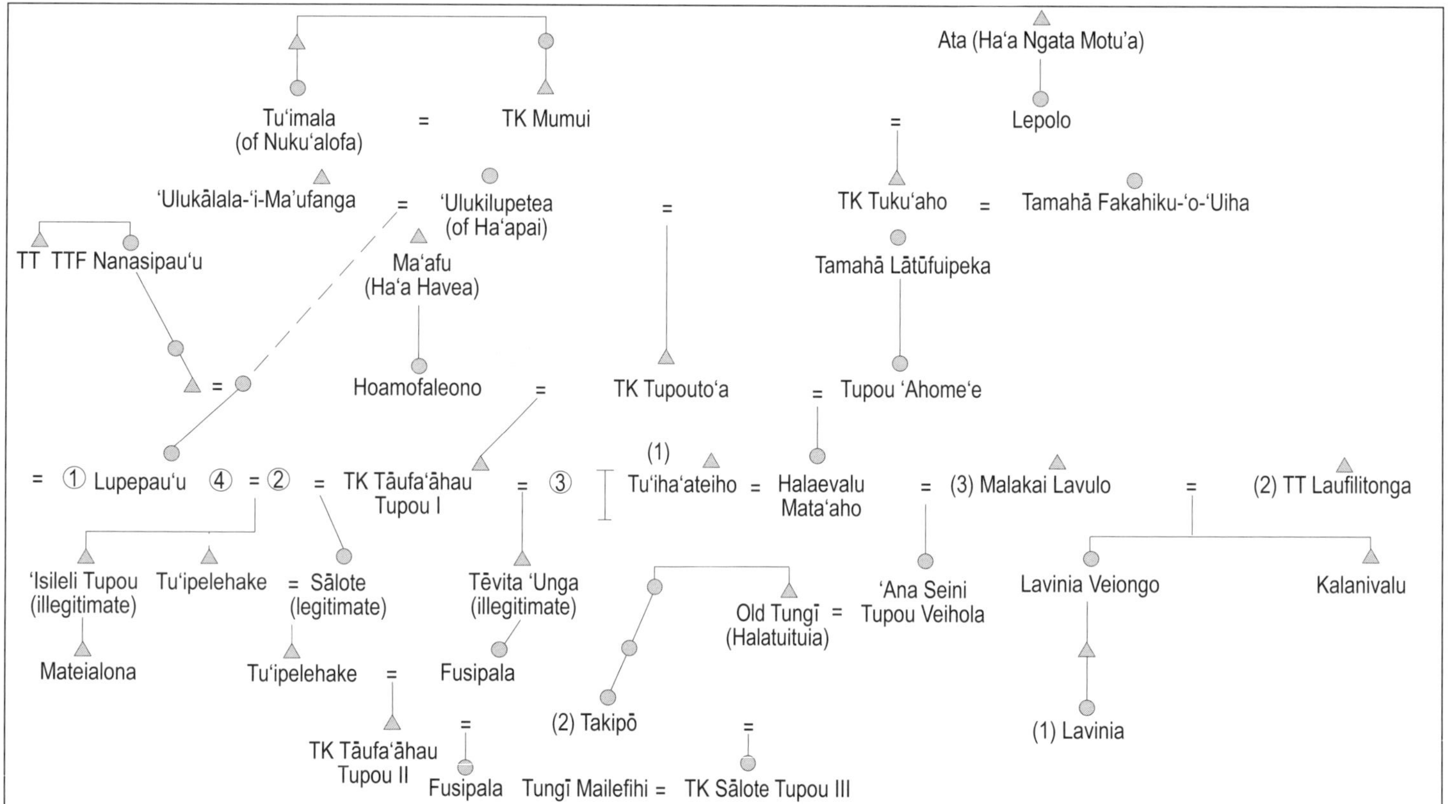

FIGURE 3.1 SIGNIFICANT MARRIAGES OF THE TUPOU DYNASTY
(Note how holders of the Tu'i Kanokupolu title intermarried with the Tu'i Tonga family.)

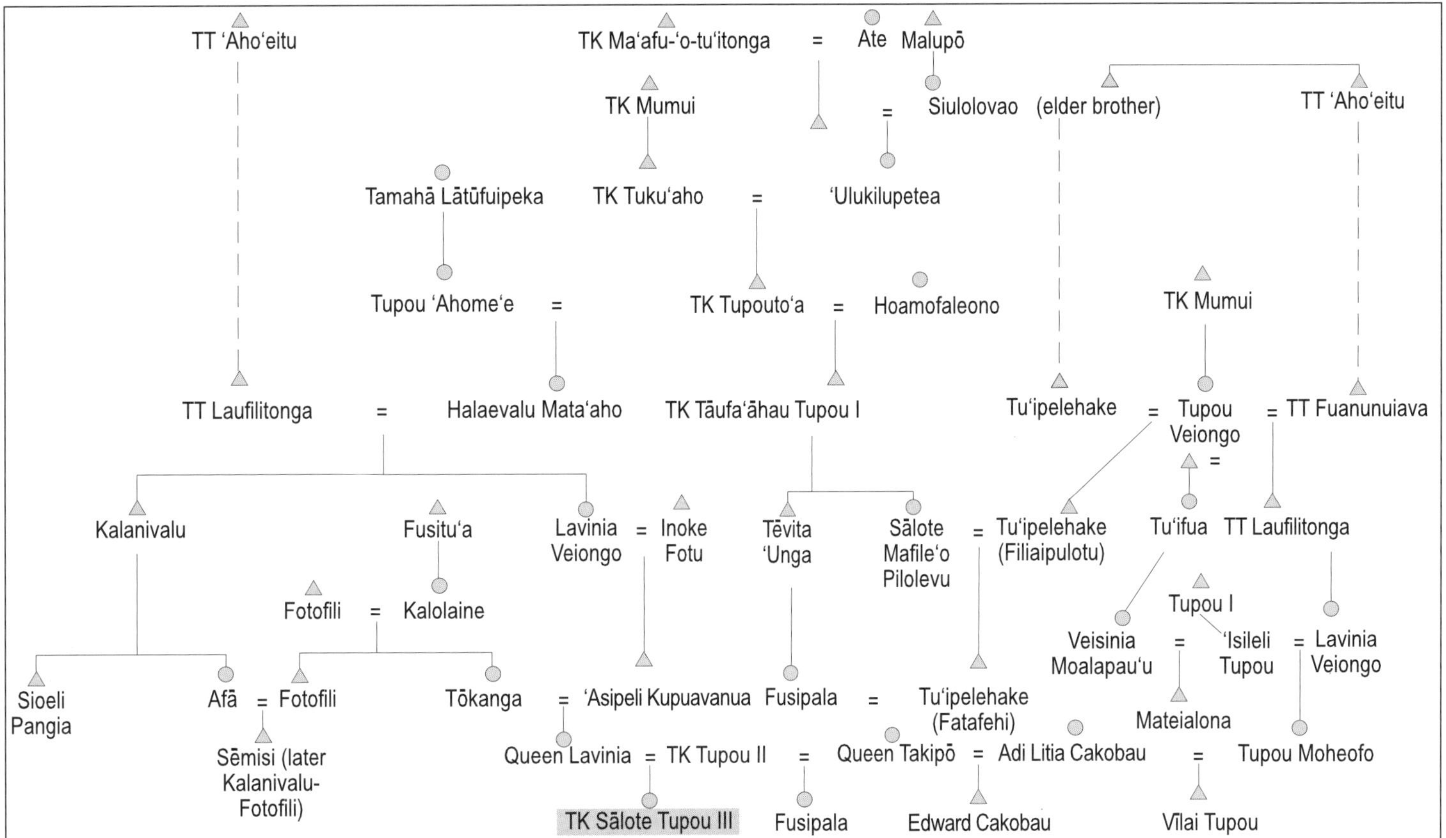

FIGURE 3.2 GENEALOGY OF SĀLOTE TUPOU III

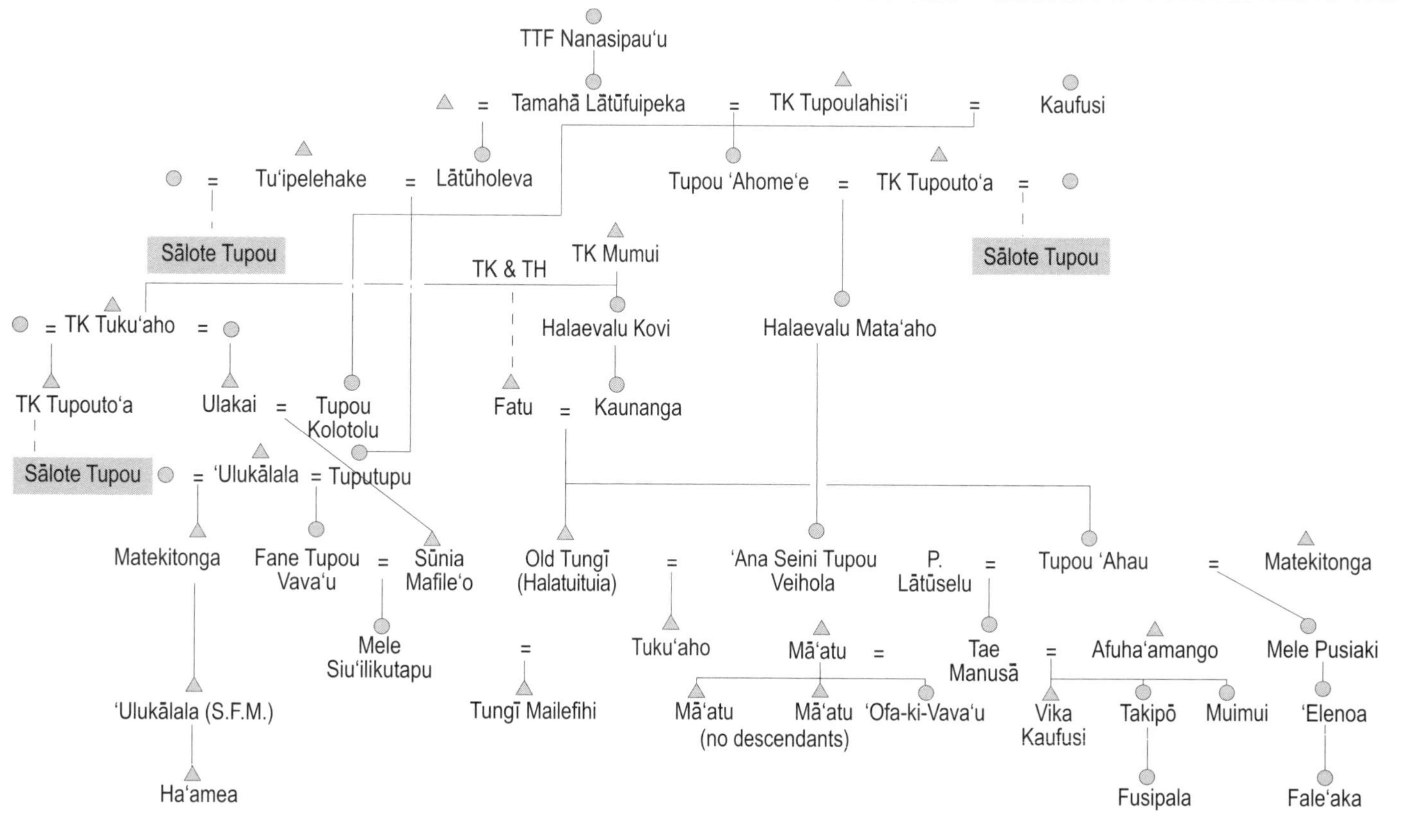

FIGURE 3.3 SIMPLIFIED GENEALOGY OF TUNGĪ MAILEFIHI

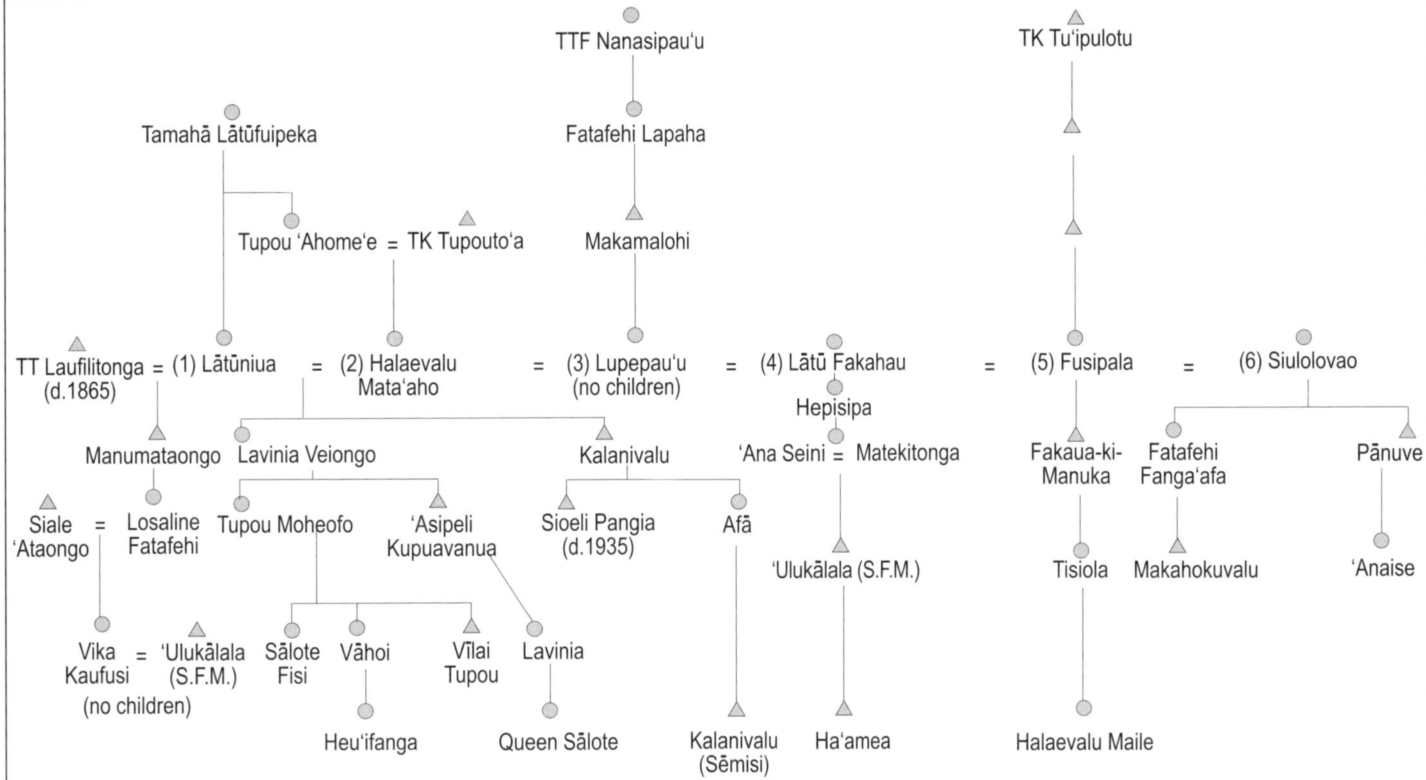

FIGURE 3.4 SOME DESCENDANTS OF THE TU'I TONGA LAUFILITONGA

(Laufilitonga had at least 18 wives, only six of whom appear in this genealogy.)

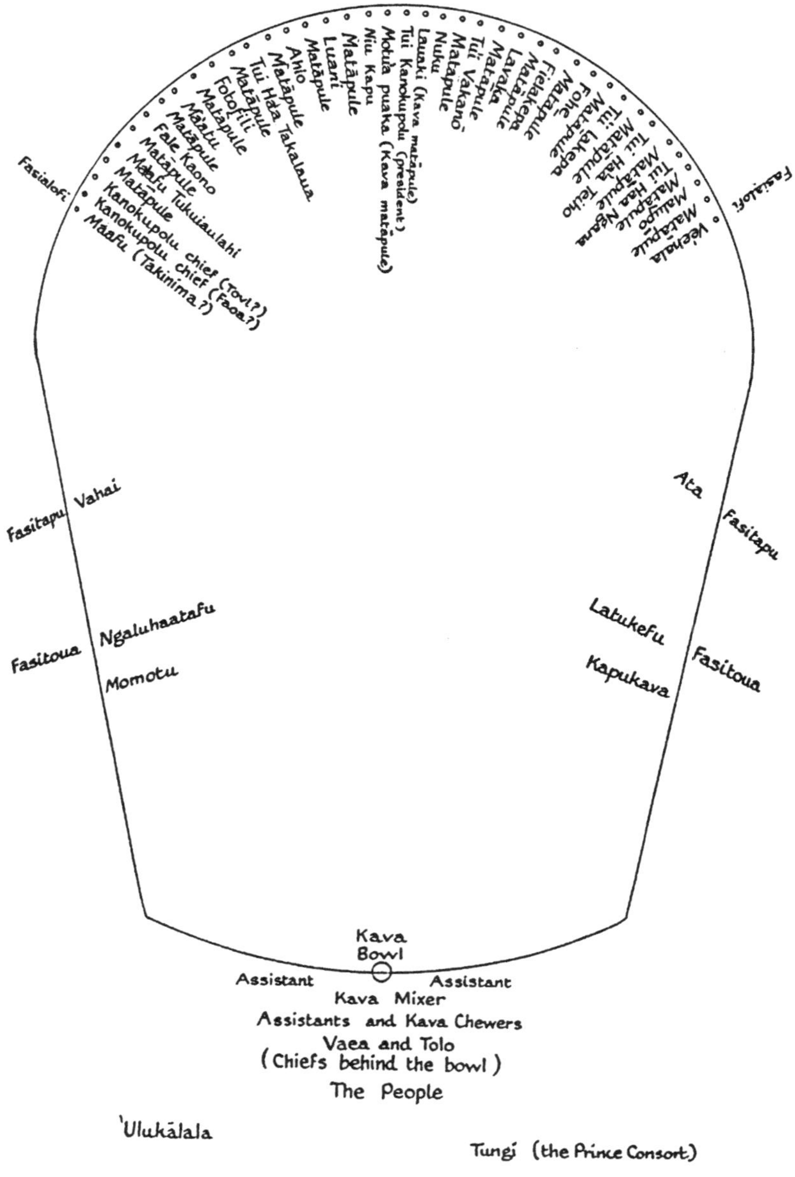

4.1 KAVA CIRCLE AT THE INSTALLATION OF QUEEN SĀLOTE AS TU'I KANOKUPOLU, 9 OCTOBER 1918. (from E.W. Gifford, *Tongan Society* (1929) p.96.)
Courtesy of the Bishop Museum, Honolulu.

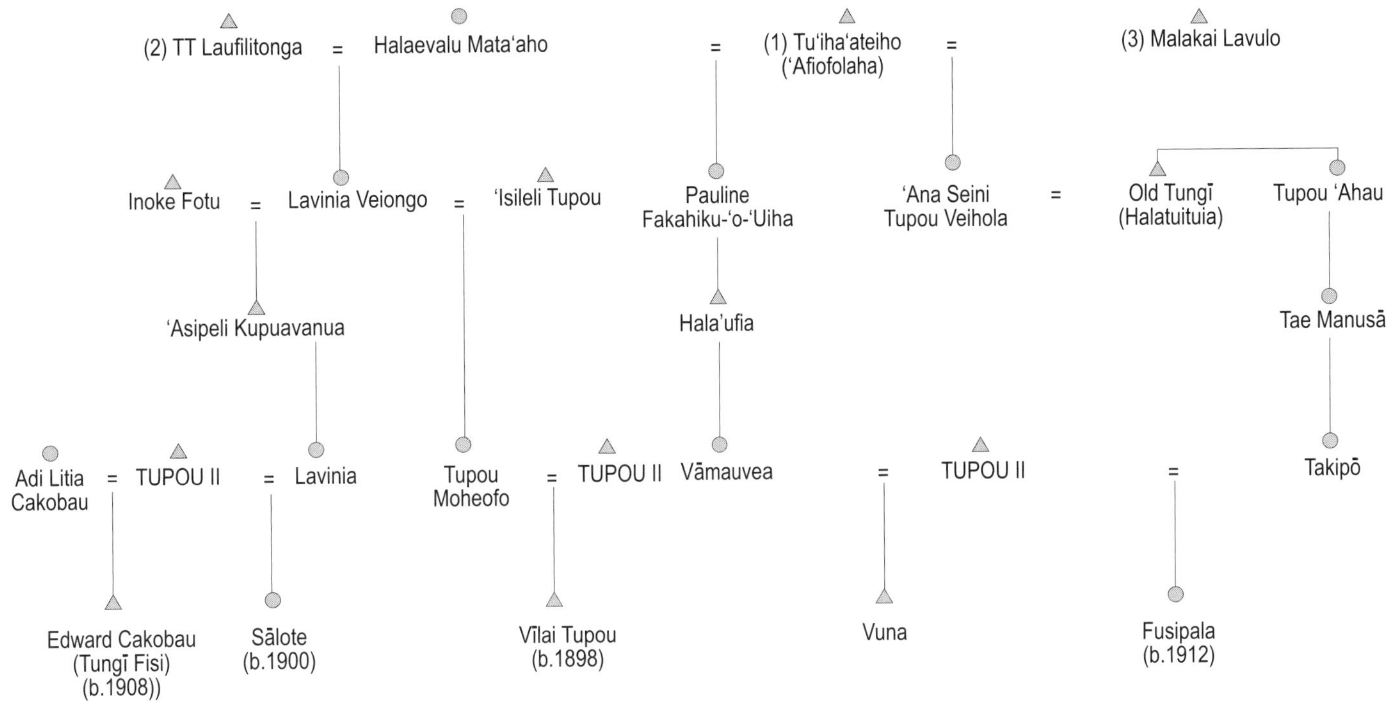

FIGURE 5.1 CHILDREN OF TUPOU II

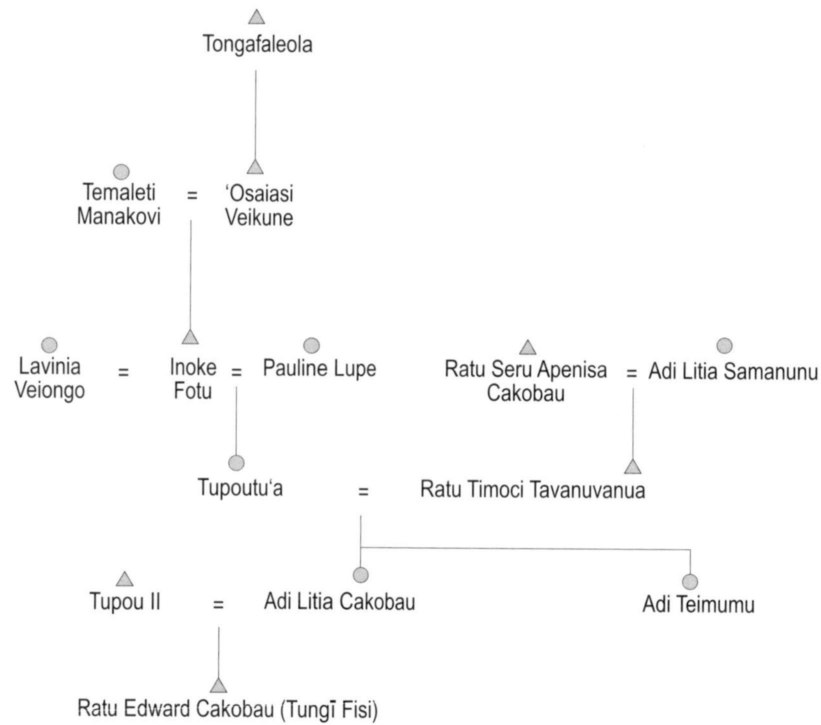

FIGURE 5.2 GENEALOGY OF RATU EDWARD CAKOBAU (TUNGĪ FISI)

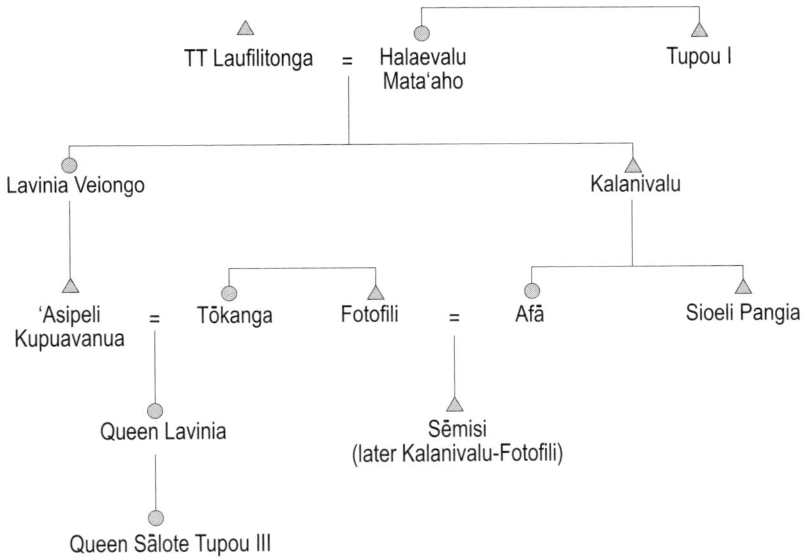

FIGURE 7.1 QUEEN SĀLOTE AS FAHU TO THE KALANIVALU AND FOTOFILI LINES

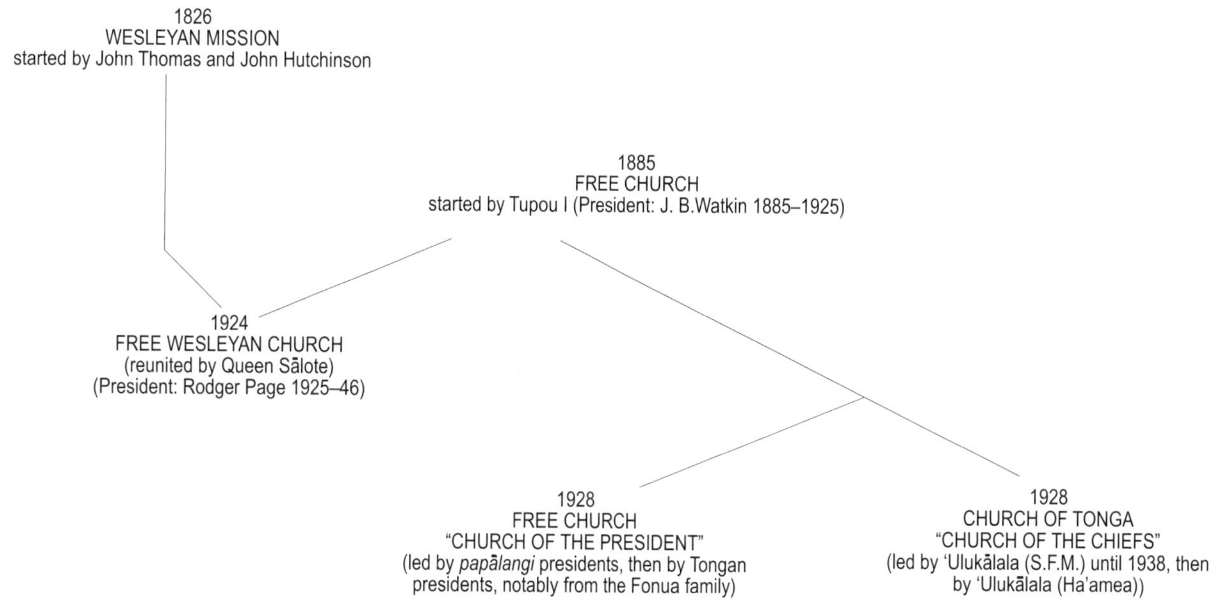

FIGURE 8.1 THE SPLITTING OF THE WESLEYAN CHURCHES (1885–1928)

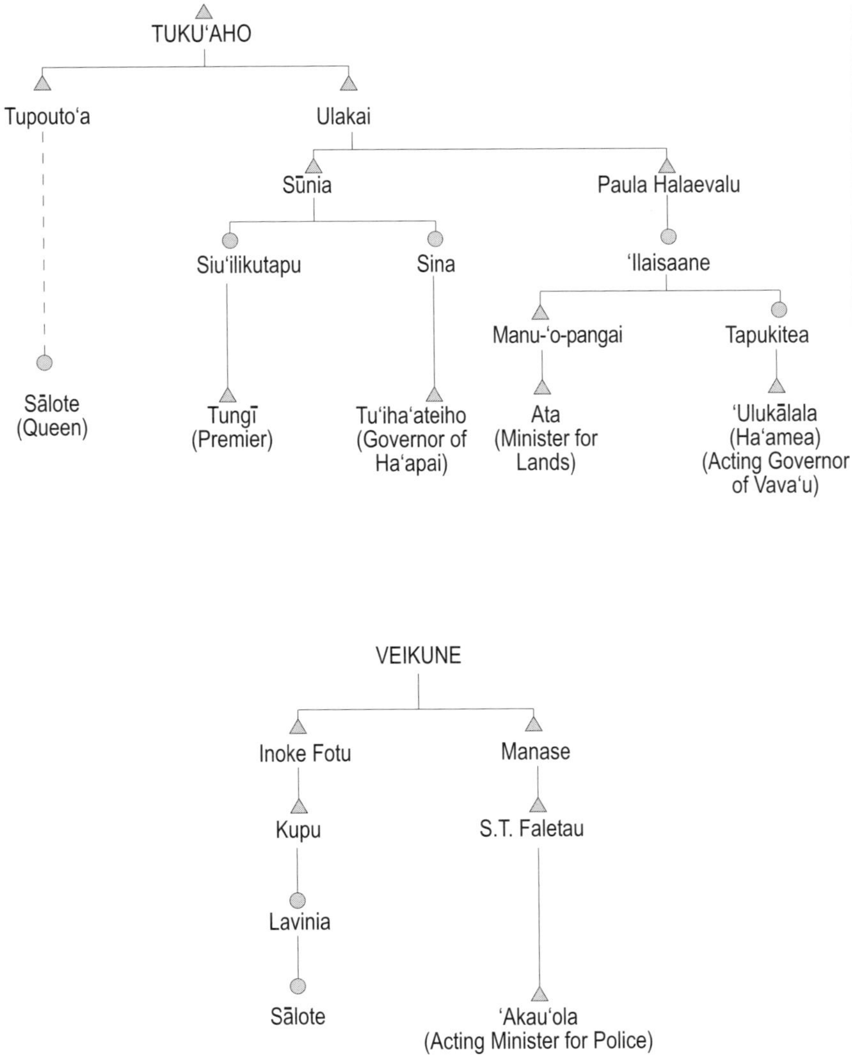

FIGURE 12.1 TWO GENEALOGICAL TABLES SHOWING RELATIONSHIPS BETWEEN MEMBERS OF THE GOVERNMENT 1939

(These tables were drawn by Sioape Kaho on 23 August 1939. Garvey Report, appendix xxiii.)

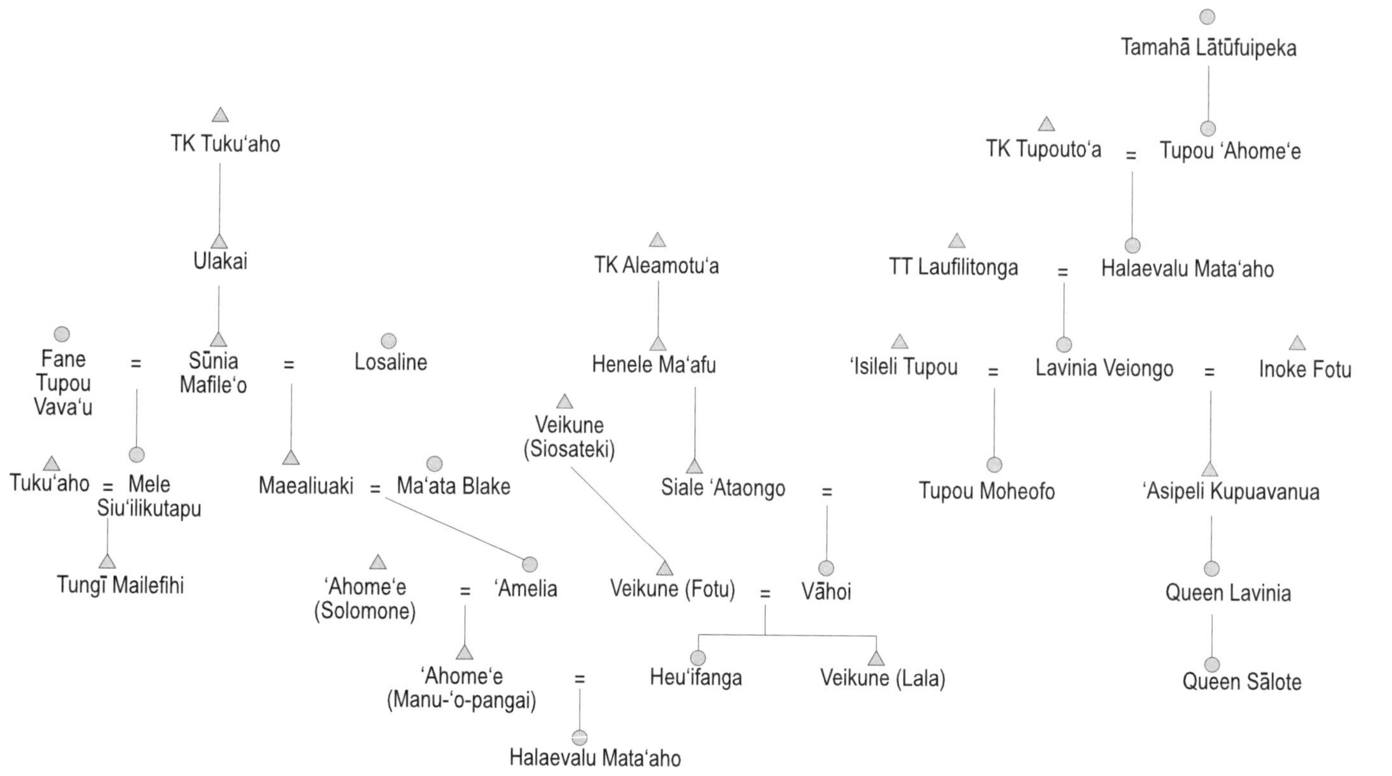

FIGURE 15.1 GENEALOGY OF HALAEVALU MATA‘AHO
(Note aristocratic female line.)

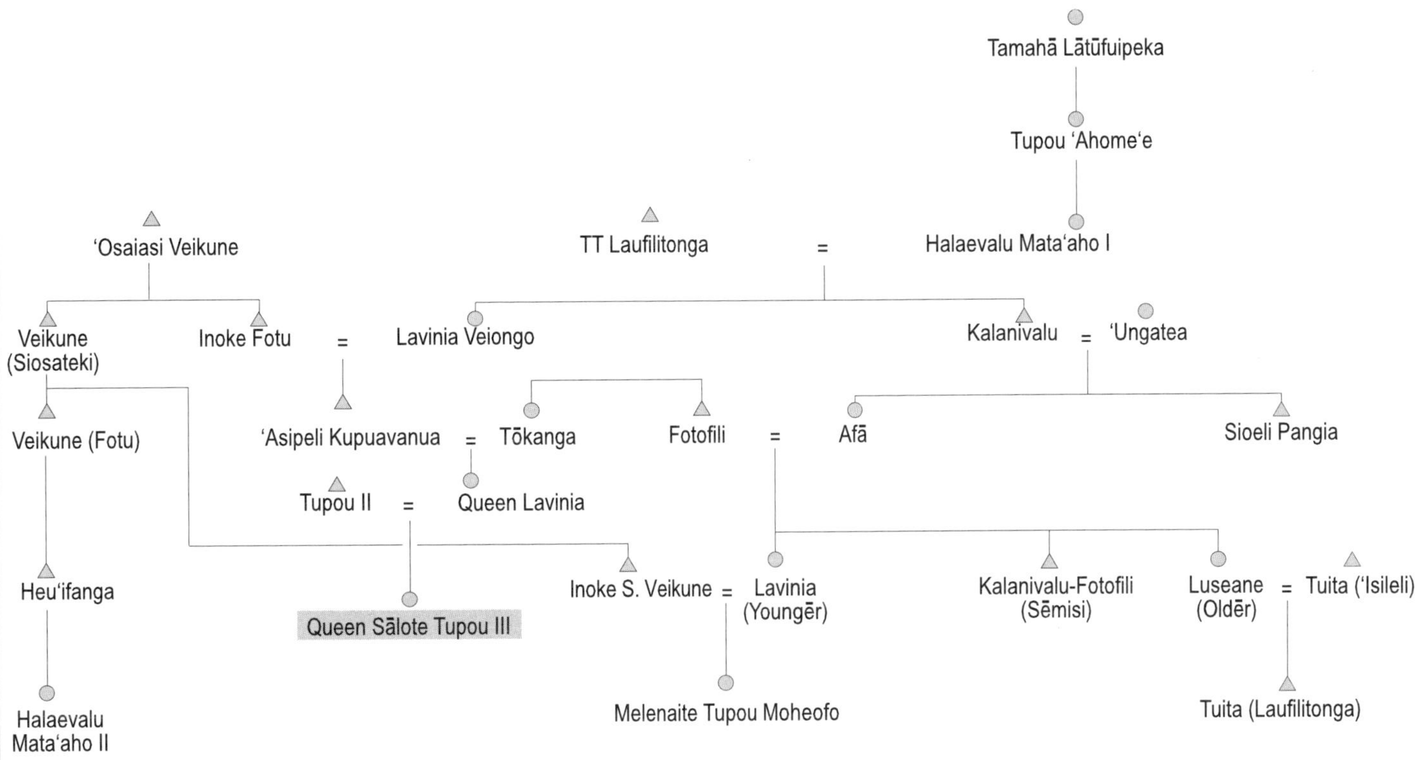

FIGURE 15.2 GENEALOGY OF MELENAITE TUPOU MOHEOFO
(Note relationship to Halaevalu Mata‘aho II through Halaevalu Mata‘aho I and Veikune family.)

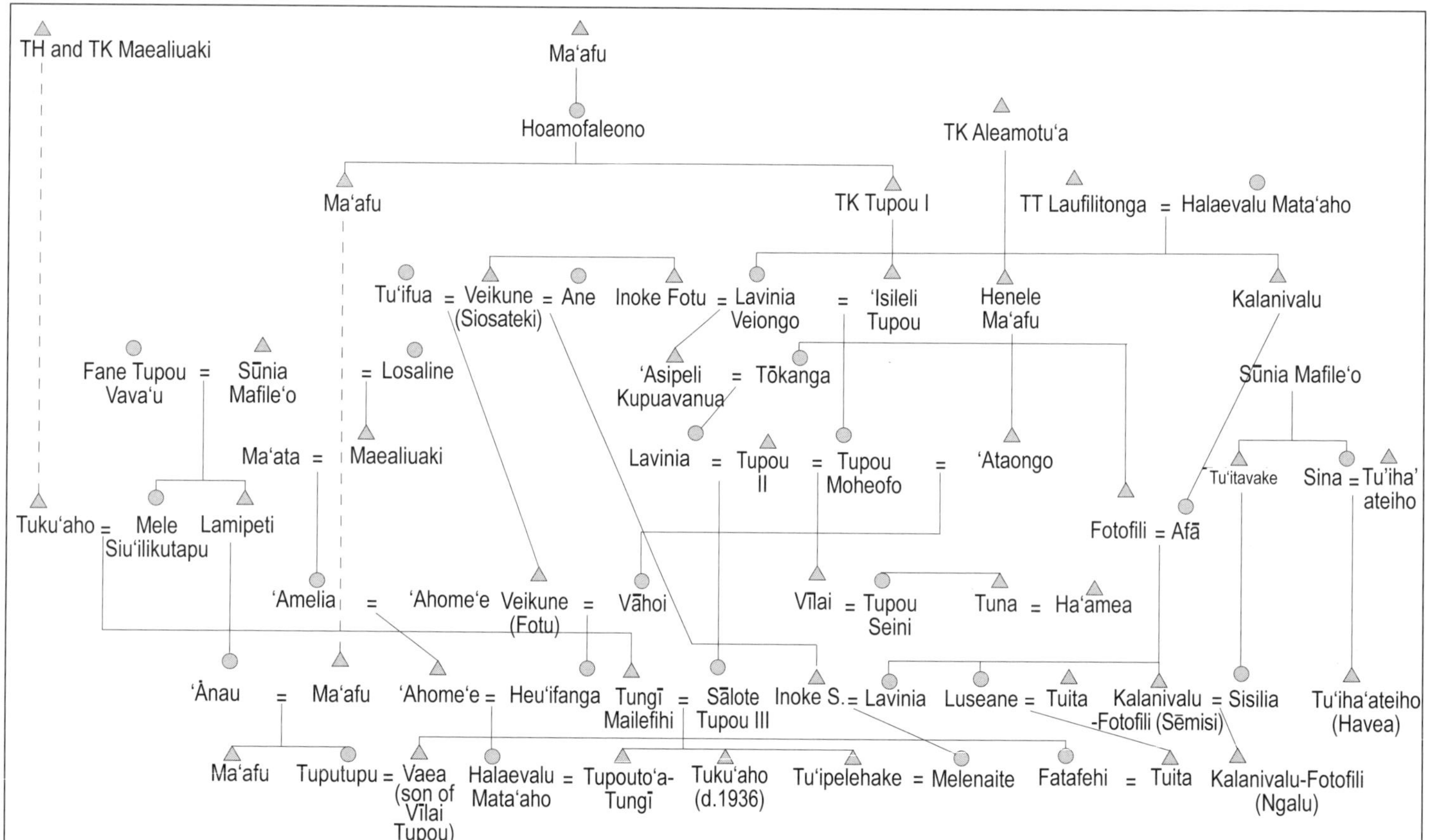

FIGURE 17.1 MARRIAGES OF CHIEFLY FAMILIES

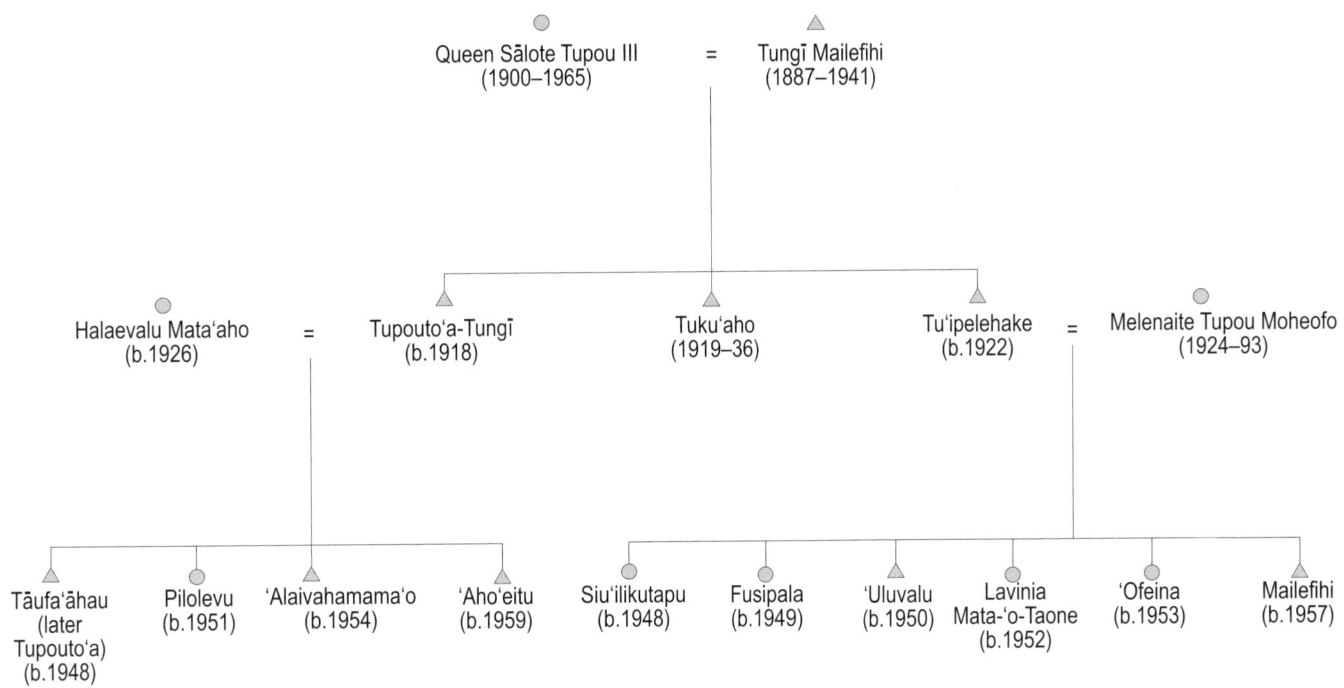

FIGURE 19.1 THE ROYAL HOUSE 1965

CHAPTER ONE

Her Mother's Daughter

"The Nobles . . . spoke out very plainly saying . . . no son of hers should ever reign over them" (R. Beckwith Leefe, 1899)[1]

SĀLOTE MAFILE'O PILOLEVU was born on 13 March 1900 in the white-painted, wooden, two-storey Palace by the sea in Nuku'alofa, the capital of Tonga (Figure 1.1). At this time (and indeed for all of her reign) the Palace was like a small village.[2] Nuku'alofa, about a mile square, was a larger village, divided into prestigious Kolomotu'a (Old Town) in which lived the great chiefs and the Kolofo'ou (New Town) section of traders and lesser chiefs (Figure 1.2). The Beach Road edged the harbour, and roads of crushed white coral led south and west to the countryside of the main island, Tongatapu (sacred Tonga), where lay the estates of the Tongatapu nobles and the farm allotments of lesser chiefs and commoners (Figure 1.3).[3] Village communities were scattered among the coconut palms that yielded copra, the main cash crop of Tonga, surrounded by acres of root crops and tropical fruit trees.

Some of the islands of Tonga are coral, and some volcanic. Tongatapu, the largest in the southernmost group, is divided into three districts: Western (Hihifo), Central (Vaheloto), and Eastern (Hahake), each dominated by their chiefs. To the east across a narrow but treacherous strait is mountainous 'Eua, known for its forests and parrots. To the north are scatterings of islands lying in shallow water, although close to the Tonga Trench, one of the deepest oceans of the world. Approximately 100 kilometres north of Tongatapu is the intensively settled central group of islands, named Ha'apai, and another 100 kilometres north the northern group Vava'u, renowned for its beautiful scenery and harbour. Both Ha'apai and Vava'u remembered periods of independence from Tongatapu. Much farther north again (about 200 kilometres north of Vava'u) are the aristocratic cousin, Niuatoputapu (Sacred Niua), and the poor cousin, Niuafo'ou (New Niua), outliers too remote to be often visited, speaking (in the case of Niuafo'ou) a Sāmoic language, and almost entirely independent of the central government.

The 150 or so islands of Tonga (about 30 inhabited) are part of Polynesia, lying in the south-west Pacific near where the International Dateline intersects the Tropic of Capricorn. Tonga's climate is semi-tropical, more temperate than the humid regions of its nearest neighbours, Fiji to the north-west and Sāmoa to the north-east, with whom it had traded, fought, and exchanged marriage partners for as long as all three could remember. From 1877, the British High Commissioner for the Western Pacific, whose headquarters were in Suva, Fiji, was a figure of dread in Tonga, for he had the power to deport indigenous as well as foreign residents and to annex the country. During the second half of the nineteenth century Tonga signed treaties with several European powers and with the USA, but from 1900 British interests dominated after Tonga had unwillingly signed the exclusive Treaty of Friendship with Great Britain.

Tongans are united in race and (except for the case of Niuafo'ou) by language, but riven by ancient rivalries. In 1900, when Sālote was born, Tonga was a world in microcosm, for the dramas that occurred in this small area and among this small population in the southern hemisphere were as revealing of the human condition as the politics of larger and more populous countries of the northern hemisphere. Before Europeans settled in Tonga, the population had been much larger than the 20,000 in the year of Sālote's birth, perhaps 50,000. Since the 1700s, when Tonga was first visited by Europeans, the population had been severely reduced by civil wars, famine, natural catastrophes, and introduced diseases. When one considers that only the aristocracy and lesser chiefs, not commoners, counted in public life, the number of participants in political affairs was very small. Sālote would be gratified by the steady increase in population during her reign, until it had almost quadrupled at the time of her death.

Tonga's smallness made politics and government very personal. Many of the events described in these pages were played out in the square mile of Nuku'alofa, although their origins often lay in the ambitions and rivalries of nobles and chiefs in the three districts and in the central and northern islands, once independent and still determined to resist the centralization of power and resources in Nuku'alofa. To a large degree the nobles (or the lesser chiefs representing them) ruled their estates as they had always done, their word being the law of their locality.

In 1900 Tonga was hardly known to the outside world, and during the lifetime of Sālote foreigners in Tonga numbered only a few hundreds. The complexities of Tonga's social structure are difficult to comprehend, prestige depending on personal/absolute rank (descent from the ancient sacred ruler), relative rank/rank within the *kāinga* (see Glossary), and title (control of land and resources). The key to understanding the hierarchy, as Sālote said, was a knowledge of genealogies. People of European descent (*papālangi*) are unaccustomed to learning genealogies, which (for them) consist of lists of difficult names. But Tongan chiefs learn them for the same reason as *papālangi* count their money: birth determines their status in their world. Just as *papālangi* inheritances of property will fluctuate from generation to generation, so marriages, births, and deaths affect the current genealogical status of chiefs.

For *papālangi*, recollection of at least three titles (lines of "kings") will make the subsequent pages of this book more accessible (Figure 1.4). Briefly, membership of the aristocracy was determined by descent from the highest and most ancient line, the sacred kings named Tu'i Tonga. Until the rise of the Tupou dynasty (of which Sālote would be the third), the second line of descent was that of Tu'i Ha'atakalaua, the last titleholder dying in 1799. In the eighteenth century the forerunners of the Tupou dynasty had elevated the Tu'i Kanokupolu title to third in the ladder of prestige (Figure 1.5). How this came about will be explained in chapter 2, where other titles of *mana* (superior status) will also be introduced. How Sālote, the twenty-first Tu'i Kanokupolu, elevated that title to primary rank is one of the topics of this volume.

Sālote, when she became Queen, commented on the continuing importance of ancestors to the Tongan people. Although the last acknowledged holder of the sacred title of Tu'i Tonga had died in 1865, descent from this line, from the eldest sister (Tu'i Tonga Fefine) of the Tu'i Tonga, and especially from the "eldest" daughter of the Tu'i Tonga Fefine (the Tamahā) determined the personal rank from which the great privileges of the aristocracy derived. Many of these aristocrats resented the elevation of the Tupou dynasty (Figure 1.5), indeed the elevation of the Tu'i Kanokupolu title itself. And chiefs who still controlled the people, land, and resources continued to resist centralization of power, which was the achievement of the nineteenth Tu'i Kanokupolu and first of the Tupou dynasty (Tāufa'āhau Tupou I) in the nineteenth century.

Sālote was born not only into her own personal/absolute and *kāinga* rank and as heir to a title, but also into a political situation that would affect her personal life and define her goals as Queen. In the year before her birth, factionalism endemic to the kingdom of Tonga was exacerbated by the dispute over the choice of a marriage partner for the young King, Tupou II. The question would not have arisen in traditional times, for the King would have married a woman from each of the *ngaahi kāinga* with whom he wished to ally himself, and the sons of the marriages would have contended in due course for the inheritance of the father. What made the choice of a marriage partner so critical in 1899 was that Christianity allowed only one wife, and the Constitution of 1875 stated that the eldest son by this wife would automatically be the heir to the father's title.

Increasing concentration of power and resources in the hands of the Tu'i Kanokupolu made marriage to that title highly desirable. So strong was the feeling that the supporters of the two candidates, Lavinia Veiongo and 'Ofa-ki-Vava'u ("love to Vava'u", commonly called 'Ofa), fought with axes, clubs, and bottles in the streets of Nuku'alofa, and burnt down each other's houses.

The noble Tungī (Old Tungī),[4] greatest of the chiefs in terms of lands and supporters, who would have been Tu'i Ha'atakalaua (Figure 1.4) if that title was still conferred, was by traditional criteria more qualified for the title of Tu'i Kanokupolu than Tupou I's 18-year-old great-grandson, Tupou II (Figure 1.5). Traditional appointments depended upon seniority, ability, warrior qualities, and recognition of other chiefs, in particular the recognition of older chiefly women and of those chiefs whose titles were "brothers" and "sons" to the title in question. Old Tungī's suitability for the Tu'i Kanokupolu title had been recognized by Tupou I in an amendment to the Constitution of 1885, which made him successor if Tupou II died without an heir. Old Tungī could have pushed his claim when Tupou I died in 1893 (on the grounds that the heir was too young), but he stood aside on the understanding that Tupou II would eventually marry 'Ofa, his great-niece. However, in 1899, when all the preparations for the wedding had been made, the King changed his mind and declared that, instead of 'Ofa, he would marry Lavinia. Both young women had the aristocratic blood of the Tu'i Tonga, but 'Ofa was also descended from the great female figures of Tongan genealogy (Figure 1.6), while Lavinia was descended from the Tu'i Tonga only through her father, Kupuavanua (Figure 1.7). Shockingly, Lavinia's maternal line could not be remembered beyond two generations, having its origins in Niuafo'ou, whose people were (literally and metaphorically) on the margins of Tongan society (Figure 1.1).

'Ofa was supported by many powerful chiefs, for she was *fahu* (privileged, by virtue of being sister's granddaughter) to Old Tungī.[5] However, Lavinia was supported by the King's father and uncle, Tu'ipelehake (Fatafehi) and Mateialona. Other supporters of Lavinia were her grandmother Lavinia Veiongo (Old Lavinia), "eldest" daughter of the last Tu'i Tonga, and Old Lavinia's daughters, Anga-'ae-fonu and Tupou Moheofo, the last being the mother of the King's illegitimate son Vīlai (Figure 1.7).[6] Anga-'ae-fonu and her brother Kalauta had "adopted" Lavinia (which automatically increased her chiefly status), but Old Lavinia and Tupou Moheofo were the most formidable members of that family.

Although the opposition of the chiefs to Lavinia was said to have been because of her weak maternal line, this was only part of the story. In later life, Queen Sālote would say that although 'Ofa was of higher rank, Lavinia "had more lines in her", meaning that there were many of the great names of Tongan genealogy in her ancestry.[7] For example, descent from Halaevalu Mata'aho

(Figure 1.7) would become an important indicator of chiefliness. Comparison of genealogies was, of course, the privilege of high-ranking chiefly women, and their judgement often favoured their own line.

Tupou II rejected marriage to ʻOfa in spite of her high rank because of the ambition of her and Old Tungī's supporters. And this was not a new thing. Soon after his accession, Tupou II showed his resentment of the claims of that family by dismissing Old Tungī's son (Tukuʻaho) from the premiership. When Tukuʻaho died suddenly in 1897, a knife of "foreign design" was found on his body (the implication being that he was about to make an attempt on the young King's life at the instigation of foreigners). After his son's death, Old Tungī was more determined than ever to restore his family's fortunes by a marriage between ʻOfa and the King.

A story frequently told in Tonga is that the King summoned the two girls to the Palace. ʻOfa came proudly into the King's presence, with a train of attendants, and took a seat beside him. When the King asked her what her response would be if he proposed marriage, she was noncommittal. Lavinia came next, wearing a simple Japanese cream silk dress and a *kiekie* (girdle), with her aunt Tupou Moheofo as her sole attendant. Lavinia entered the room with downcast eyes and sat silently on the floor just inside the door, as was appropriate for a person of lower rank in the presence of a higher-ranking person. When the King asked her the same question he had asked ʻOfa, Lavinia replied that she would do as the King wished. In this narrative Lavinia is portrayed as the ideal of Tongan womanhood (*molumalu*).

The arrogance and ambition attributed to ʻOfa in this story was really the arrogance and ambition of her supporters. But the humility and modesty attributed to Lavinia did not reflect any modesty on the part of her relations, for they were as ambitious and arrogant as their rivals. However, Lavinia's supporters were considerably less threatening to the King.

The *hau* or most powerful warrior chief traditionally marked the peak of his achievements by marrying a woman of the Tuʻi Tonga family, and this custom must have influenced the King in his choice. Another attractive feature of the alliance was the advocacy of Old Lavinia and her daughters, which would translate into transfer to the Tuʻi Kanokupolu of wealth of the Tuʻi Tonga in the form of historic fine-mats (*kie hingoa*) and other collectibles (*koloa*), this transfer validating the Tupou dynasty as supreme rulers of Tonga.[8] The Tupou dynasty aspired to be the acknowledged heir to the *mana* of the Tuʻi Tonga, and the symbolic value of possession of the Tuʻi Tonga *koloa* cannot be measured by European standards or easily explained to outsiders.

Marriages by Tuʻi Tonga women to lower-ranking chiefs for economic reasons were common in traditional Tonga, and such marriages did not diminish the women's personal rank. Thus, although Old Lavinia despised the King as an upstart and descendant of upstarts, she realized that the marriage to her "half-shell" (i.e. of high rank through only one parent) granddaughter would give her access to the great economic resources of the Tu'i Kanokupolu.

Traditionally, decisions about marriage were made by the elders of the families. Thus it was that 31 chiefs who had become nobles by the terms of Tupou I's Constitution believed themselves entitled to choose the King's bride, and they met in Nuku'alofa for that purpose. When the vote was taken on the second day of their deliberations, 17 voted in favour of 'Ofa and only seven for Lavinia. However, when a deputation of nobles came to see the King on 23 May, he thanked them and stated that he still wished to marry Lavinia. The British Vice-Consul, R. Beckwith Leefe, reported what followed:

> The Nobles were exceedingly irritated at this and spoke out very plainly saying that if the King insisted on marrying Lavinia he could do so but no son of hers should ever reign over them, others said they should leave at once and refuse to be at either the ceremony or the Feast which is the great insult according to Tongan ideas.[9]

The King's refusal to accept the choice of the nobles sparked more brawling between the supporters of the two candidates. Queen Victoria's birthday (24 May) was celebrated in reasonable calm, but Leefe reported that on the following day:

> The Nobles again met and went in a body to the King to remonstrate with him on his marriage with Lavinia and told him they could not assent that the Queen should be chosen out of the Royal line. His Majesty said he would send an answer and on the 26th the King sent to say he would not marry for ever – all but 3 of the Nobles took fright at this and on Saturday the 27 May wrote to say that the King knew their minds but "do as you like". The King announced that their meetings were over, and that they could return to their houses, as he did not intend to marry at all.
>
> On the 29 [May] the Nobles gave in . . . and went to the King and told Him He could please himself, upon which the King said very well if it is your wish for me to please myself I shall marry Lavinia . . . The whole town is in gloom . . .

Pleasing himself was what Tupou II did best, for he lacked the wisdom to see how politically divisive his actions were, and how long-lasting and potentially devastating the enmity of the *kāinga* of the rejected candidate would be.

E. E. V. Collocott, missionary and anthropologist, described Tupou II as "a big man, six feet two inches in height, well-built and handsome. Pleasant and dignified, he had little taste for the stately trimmings or tiring minutiae of kingship".[10] The King did have a taste for display, and he spared no expense in the European-style celebrations of his marriage with Lavinia, and ensured that the pews would be full by inviting all the *papālangi* who were resident in Nuku'alofa to the charming, wooden, neo-gothic Royal Chapel in the Palace grounds for the wedding ceremony and a reception on 1 June.[11] Large pieces of highly prized black bark cloth were laid along the approaches to the chapel, and the interior was decorated with hundreds of little Tongan flags, ornamental stars, and greenery. The King wore a uniform of blue, richly laced with gold, bearing medals of his own design, and a crimson mantle. Lavinia wore white satin, a veil, and orange blossoms, and was accompanied by six bridesmaids, also in white satin.

The report in the *Auckland Weekly News* shows that not all the nobles insulted the King and Lavinia by their absence. Being a *papālangi* newspaper, it listed only the male guests. Among these were supporters of the marriage, such as Tu'ipelehake and Mateialona, and Lavinia's father, and also some of the opponents, including 'Ofa's brother Mā'atu (Pānuve) and 'Ulukālala (Siaosi Fīnau Mīsini), who were leaders among the would-be independent chiefs, whom Sālote would later call the "Reactionary Party".[12] The grandson and heir of Old Tungī, Uiliami (William) Tupoulahi, was one of the pages, dressed in *papālangi* mediaeval costume and carrying an edge of the King's crimson mantle. After a choir sang the wedding anthem he had written for the occasion, Tupou II placed a diadem on Lavinia's head and stated in a clear voice: "I today appoint Lavinia to be Queen of Tonga." This was his gift to Lavinia's Tu'i Tonga relatives.

'Ofa's female supporters were less willing to be reconciled than the male supporters, and did not attend the royal wedding. In any case, they had other business. On the King's wedding day, in another part of Nuku'alofa, 'Ofa's mother's family dressed 'Ofa in bridal clothes and carried her through the streets, shouting "*Tuē, tuē*", the traditional cheer for a marriage party. Food, mats, and bark cloth prepared for her wedding were presented to her family, even though 'Ofa had no husband by her side. As a conciliatory gesture and in recognition of 'Ofa's rank, the King and Lavinia sent her a tier of their wedding cake.[13]

One or two days later, at the Tongan wedding ceremony (*tu'uvala*) of Tupou II and Queen Lavinia, there were great exchanges of property among the chiefly families who were parties to the alliance, and fine-mats and other *koloa* brought by the Tu'i Tonga women became the property of the Tu'i Kanokupolu. But a price had to be paid: for several years the young King and Queen hardly ventured from the Palace by the sea, even for a drive in the King's carriage, for fear of riot and assassination.[14]

Although 'Ofa was passed over, Old Tungī did not relinquish hopes that the Tu'i Kanokupolu title and power would one day come into the possession of his family, and three months before his death, when he heard the 13-gun salute (drumbeats, in another version of the story) that announced the birth of a daughter to Lavinia, he claimed her for his 12-year-old grandson, Uiliami

Tupoulahi ("A wife for Willy", he said). But the women of his family, in particular 'Ofa's mother (Tae Manusā), refused to be reconciled with the King, and expressed their anger by inviting Bishop Alfred Willis to set up a branch of the Church of England in Tonga in order to draw supporters away from the King's Free Church.[15]

The only daughter of His Majesty Tāufa'āhau Tupou II and Queen Lavinia was baptised in the Royal Chapel as Sālote Mafile'o Pilolevu, the name of her great-grandmother, the only daughter of Tupou I (Figure 1.7).[16] The infant princess, like all Tongans, belonged to both her mother's *kāinga* and her father's. She would need all of their support, for she was an object of hostility because of the circumstances of her parents' marriage. Although she ascribed to Queen Lavinia all the virtues, Sālote would admit that her mother was hated because of her relatives.[17]

There was no certainty that any Tongan chief would continue to rule Tonga, for while the King was choosing a bride, Britain, Germany, and the USA were reallocating their areas of influence in the Pacific, and they agreed that Tonga would be included in the area dominated by Britain. Thus, when Basil Thomson, envoy of the British government, visited the kingdom in April 1900, he took advantage of the turmoil in the "impulsive, faction-ridden little kingdom" to pressure the King into signing a new Treaty of Friendship between Great Britain and Tonga, a treaty that would make Tonga a British-protected state (see chapter 2).

Thomson kissed the three-weeks-old princess on her forehead, but when a deputation of New Zealand parliamentarians seeking a Pacific empire visited the kingdom later in the year, the King refused their request to photograph the infant princess. Only Queen Lavinia, wearing an elaborate dress in the European fashion of the time, was photographed with Prime Minister and Mrs Seddon on the verandah of the Palace.[18]

'Ofa and Lavinia had no part in the continuing enmity between their chiefly supporters, and 'Ofa danced at the celebrations of the King's twenty-seventh birthday on 18 June 1901. But when 'Ofa contracted tuberculosis and died in December 1901, her supporters claimed that her death was caused by grief and distress at the King's rejection, and they commemorated this by naming the place where she lived out her last days as Kaitangi ("to cry when eating"). The funeral on 14 December 1901 at the chiefly burial ground by the sea, Mala'e

'Aloa, aroused all the old passions, and a number of mourners were jailed for rioting.[19]

Animosity seems to have been confined to the supporters of the two young women. Not only did the King write a poetic "Lament for 'Ofa", but Lavinia had visited 'Ofa during her final illness, and attended her funeral, and may have caught the tubercular infection from 'Ofa, for it soon became apparent that the Queen was very ill. Despite daily reports of improvement, Queen Lavinia died at the Palace on 24 April 1902,[20] only a few weeks after Princess Sālote's second birthday. Tupou II deeply mourned his bride (only 23 years of age at the time of her death) and honoured her by an immense royal funeral, for she lay in state for four days and was buried at Mala'e Kula, the royal cemetery built in Nuku'alofa for the interment of his illustrious predecessor, Tupou I. Queen Lavinia's grave was in due course marked by a costly and ostentatious marble monument on which a weeping infant Sālote was depicted.[21]

As a young child Sālote tried to remember her mother. She was told that Lavinia had gone to the Royal Chapel each day at midday to pray. So at three or four years of age, Sālote often went to the Chapel, and reflected on her mother. Her mother's name had been shortened to Nia, and when the infant Sālote heard a hymn in which the syllables *nia* occurred, she thought the hymn must refer to her mother.[22]

Except for the grief of the King and the continuing enmity of 'Ofa's supporters, it was almost as though the King had never married, for young, motherless children often did not survive infancy. But Sālote was a healthy child, her attendants fed her the best food, and she flourished. Tongan custom requires that the father's family (particularly his sister) rules a child, and the mother's family nurtures the child. The King had no sister or woman in the appropriate relationship to undertake the upbringing of Sālote, and this allowed relatives on both sides to indulge her. Of her mother's family, Anga-'ae-fonu, her mother's aunt, supervised her upbringing for some years, but possibly died or went abroad when Sālote was young, for nothing more is heard of her.[23] Tupou Moheofo, the other aunt, lived in Fiji with her son, Sālote's illegitimate half-brother Vīlai. Queen Lavinia's Niuafo'ou relations were only too anxious to demonstrate their connection to the royal house by waiting on their kinswoman's daughter, but the attentions of inferior relatives were only too likely to remind people of the inferiority of her maternal line.

On the other hand, Sālote's great-grandmother, the "mountain of chiefly attributes", Old Lavinia, came to live in one of the houses (known as Pālesi or "Paris") in the Palace grounds, and Sālote observed the servility of all Tongans in their dealings with her. Old Lavinia's gender and Tu'i Tonga descent made her the highest-ranking person in the kingdom, and she insisted on constant acknowledgement of her rank. Sālote resented Old Lavinia's unconcealed contempt for the King, for when Old Lavinia referred to him, she used the language of abuse, usually reserved for the lowest people and for animals.[24] Sālote's recollections of her great-grandmother are supported by the observations of Sir Everard Im Thurn, High Commissioner for the Western Pacific, who met Old Lavinia in January 1905.

> . . . the highest lady in the land . . . is now very old and heavy . . . She has a splendidly powerful head and is, I am certain, intellectually a very powerful person in a massive savage sort of way . . . It was she who when the present King in accordance with precedent, and with the wishes of the Chiefs, was about to marry Offa [*sic*] who dynastically was the only suitable bride for him, insisted on his marrying her own granddaughter another Lavinia instead, and thus began the rift in the lute of things political in Tonga, which has split the King away from his people. She has the most supreme contempt for the King, and she expressed this freely to me, speaking of him as "that boy" and scornfully demanding "Who made him King?" . . . there is a splendid savage courtliness about her which smacks of old days . . .[25]

Old Lavinia died on 7 April 1907, soon after Sālote's seventh birthday. As "eldest" daughter of the last Tu'i Tonga, Old Lavinia was buried in the tomb of an earlier Tu'i Tonga (the tomb known as Paepae-'o-Tele'a), at Lapaha, the ancient Tu'i Tonga capital.[26] Sālote could not remember who came to fetch her, but it was clearly someone who had the princess's interests at heart, for she was called to attend the funeral as *fahu*. The *fahu* is the person of greatest honour at the funeral and recipient of the major share of the presentations brought by other mourners. The *fahu* should have been a descendant of Old Lavinia's father's sister, and the King protested that Sālote was not in the correct relationship. Sālote presided nevertheless.

This temporary elevation did not mean that Sālote was widely accepted as the King's heir, but she was of importance at the Palace, still waited upon by her mother's Niuafo'ou relations, and spoilt by her attendants. By her own account, until she was seven years old she was an arrogant child, encouraged to bully her playmates,[27] the daughters of the *matāpule*s (ceremonial attendants) brought by the King's instructions to the Palace. The more important Sālote was, the greater honour was reflected on her attendants, and playmates and attendants were referred to in derogatory language to emphasise Sālote's superiority to them.[28] Although Sālote claimed she had been treated as an adult when she was young, her attendants carried her about, even when she was seven and eight years of age, to reduce her contact with the earth that commoners trod.[29]

Sālote's situation as the King's daughter allowed her to be "very naughty and spoiled" as a child and to have a "temper", and she sometimes tested her father's leniency. She recollected one occasion when her father beat her very severely with a coconut-rib broom for lying about an arithmetic lesson, a chastisement more frequently used for commoners, but not unknown for chiefly children. Her response to this chastisement was surprise and anger, but in the end she "graciously forgave him".[30] This was the only time Sālote could recall being physically punished.

Although the King would prove to be an inadequate model for a future monarch, he was a loving and indulgent father, and included Sālote in his constant round of pleasures. Relationships – even *kāinga* relationships – have to be renewed to be kept alive, and for Tongan chiefs this meant travelling about. The highlight for Sālote was when the King took her with him to the island of Lifuka in Ha'apai (Figure 1.1), where he built a palace in 1905, and where he loved to fish and sail his favourite yacht, *'Onelua*, in the regattas he had initiated and invariably won. Whether in Nuku'alofa, Ha'apai, or Vava'u, the Princess was getting to know her future subjects. She also had the opportunity to learn the customs and rituals by sitting in the King's place when presentations were brought to any of the King's residences.

After the death of Old Lavinia, the Tu'i Tonga people neglected the young princess, and this is perhaps the reason why she remembered her father's father, Tu'ipelehake (Fatafehi), with particular affection. In Sālote's childhood, Tu'ipelehake lived first at Finefekai in the centre of town, and then in the two-storeyed wooden house Pikula, near the south-east edge of town. There was considerable affection between the three generations, and the "stories" that Tu'ipelehake and her father told Sālote were the beginnings of the storehouse of knowledge that would be significant when she became Queen and had to assert her authority over the Tongan nobles and chiefs. Although Tu'ipelehake had very high personal rank and his title had great *mana* through being descended from the elder, divine brother of the first Tu'i Tonga (Figure 1.8), he treated his people as relations not slaves, in contrast with the arrogance of Old Lavinia and other aristocrats.

Some time after the death of Old Lavinia the King decided that something more was required for Sālote than being looked after by "everybody and nobody" at the Palace. His uncle Mateialona, who had been Governor of Ha'apai 1897–1905, was appointed Premier in January 1905 (Figure 1.7) and took up residence in a ground-hugging wooden bungalow called Fai-'a-koka.[31] The house was on the Beach Road in the Kolomotu'a section of Nuku'alofa, west of the Palace, beyond the small, wooden home of 'Ulukālala (called Newcastle, or Niukāsā) with its decorative boards, beyond the elegant British Consulate and Residency, and beyond the at-once familiar and ghostly burial ground of the chiefs called Mala'e 'Aloa (Figure 1.2). Some time after her seventh birthday Sālote went to live with her great-uncle during the week, returning to the Palace at the weekends. At Fai-'a-koka Sālote came under the loving care and discipline not only of Mateialona, but also of his wife, Sela

(Sarah) Kata, and Sela's widowed sister, Lesieli Tongamohenoa (known as Rachel Tonga).

Mateialona, Sela, and Rachel had been educated at the prestigious Wesleyan secondary school, Tupou College. Im Thurn described Rachel and Sela as "Tongan ladies certainly the most intelligent and best-mannered I have seen".[32] Sālote was again the recipient of much love and attention, but with discipline. Rachel, in particular, became both teacher and foster mother to Sālote, and for the rest of her life Sālote recalled with love and gratitude Rachel's affectionate care. Sālote later claimed that a sense of duty had been "drilled into her" when she was young, for Rachel taught her that a chief has responsibilities as well as privileges. Even after she became Queen, Sālote would turn to Rachel for comfort in times of stress, and Rachel would provide a safe place to sleep and bowls of warm bread-and-milk.

Like the King and many of the nobles and chiefs, Mateialona, Sela, and Rachel were *fakapapālangi* (living a partly European lifestyle). They dressed in the height of Edwardian fashion, ate at a table, had a spotless kitchen, and kept a pug dog as a pet; Mateialona had a morning cap and a night cap. The household members were staunch Old Wesleyans, and attended worship in the Old Wesleyan chapel on the top of Sia-ko-Veiongo, the hill overlooking the Palace, Kolomotu'a, and the sea (Figure 1.2). Although Sālote had been baptised in the Free Church and attended church services on Sunday with her father and grandfather, during the week she took part in Mateialona's family prayers, listened to readings from the Wesleyan translation of the Bible, and sang Wesleyan hymns.[33] Living at Fai-'a-koka also gave Sālote the opportunity to get to know her Kolomotu'a *kāinga*. *Kāinga* in this case means the chiefs and people living on the land of their superior chief. Sālote would later refer to the *kāinga* of Kolomotu'a as her *fānau* (children), those relations with whom she had the closest emotional ties.[34] Their common descent was from Mumui (d. 1797), the thirteenth Tu'i Kanokupolu and the first to take up residence in Nuku'alofa (Figure 1.9). There was a rift between these Kolomotu'a chiefs and the house of Tupou, and the King himself may have been glad of the opportunity to heal the quarrel.[35]

Tupou II clearly needed allies, and the traditional way to gain them was by another marriage. Several candidates were considered. When Sālote was about seven years old, she heard Tu'ipelehake and Mateialona talking to the King at the Palace about his new marriage. The bride would be Takipō, half-sister of 'Ofa and daughter of Tae Manusā by a Vava'u *matāpule* called Afuha'amango (Figure 1.6).[36] The wedding took place on 11 November 1909, when Takipō was of legal age to marry (16 years). The bride's family, determined to outshine the 1899 wedding celebrations, provided a wedding dress costing £100 and a trousseau worth £500. The King spent £400 on the *fakapapālangi* wedding ceremony and breakfast.[37] These were huge sums at that time.

In traditional Tonga the offspring of an earlier marriage might be killed. Defeated chiefs went into exile with their followers, either permanently or to return with foreign warriors to claim their inheritance. Although the King claimed that he was sending Sālote away purely for her education, her new status was demonstrated by the fact that none of the companions customary for a princess accompanied her. Furthermore, she was sent on the earliest possible monthly steamer (December 1909) following the King's remarriage. Clearly, the reason for her exile was that she was Queen Lavinia's daughter, and the King and chiefs expected that Takipō would have a son, who would become the King's heir.

Rachel Tonga took Sālote to Auckland and left her with a family called Kronfeld, the mother being part-Sāmoan and the father a German-Jewish trader with whom the King did business.[38] The shock and suddenness of being transported from Nuku'alofa, where she was a focus of attention, to a place where she had no one to command would be a lifelong lesson for Sālote on the uncertainty of fortune. From this point on, Sālote considered her childhood "hard", although by objective criteria she continued to be very privileged.[39]

The Kronfeld house in Eden Crescent, on a hillside near the harbour and close to the business district, was called 'Oli Ula (garland of *'oli* flowers). Gustav Kronfeld was wealthy, and the family entertained a great deal, including the famous composer of marches for brass bands, John Philip Sousa, which interested the princess, whose compatriots had a passion for band music, and who was herself musical. The Kronfelds had children, 13-year-old Mina being the daughter closest in age to Sālote. During the next three years (1910–12) the King paid for a governess (Miss Mabel Wallers) and piano teacher (Mr Sam Jackson) to come to the Kronfield house to teach Sālote.[40] Sālote missed her customary churchgoing, and found her own way to St Paul's, a Church of England church in Symonds Street, near the University of Auckland. She was confirmed as a member of the Anglican Church during this time, but as her father neither knew of it nor gave his consent, it remains a puzzling event.[41]

Although the Kronfelds were kind to her, Sālote was very homesick, and on 11 August 1911 she wrote to her father: "I am very happy that you say I shall leave [Auckland] for Tonga on 5 December . . . I am quite dead with home-sickness, for every day I wish I was in Tonga, and I long for 5 December. I have really had enough of this land."[42]

In 1913 Sālote was sent as a boarder to the Anglican Diocesan School for Girls in Epsom, an affluent suburb of Auckland. Her two years at boarding school were to be the most carefree of her life. The students were from the privileged class, discipline was mild, and the cheerful companionship of school life must have reminded her of the busy life of the Palace. She was popular at the school, a school friend describing Sālote as a great asset in basketball games because she was already taller than her peers and played with good humour; she was also a light and graceful dancer of the hesitation-waltz and the tango.

Another school friend recalled that her title of Princess was not used, and she was required to tidy her room and do her own mending. She was not so acculturated that she forgot what was "proper" according to Tongan custom, and steadfastly refused to perform the (by Tongan standards indecent) "knees outward bend" exercise in the gym class. The "temper", which Sālote later said she found difficult to control, was not provoked in this cheerful and supportive environment.[43]

Not surprisingly, Sālote romanticized her early life, seeing herself as the centre of others' concerns. Although her teachers could not have been certain that Sālote would be Queen, she believed that they carefully planned her activities and promoted her friendships with well-connected pupils in order to prepare her for her future life. Sālote had a great capacity for enjoyment, and she long remembered the concerts, carefully selected plays, pantomimes, and homes of approved school friends whom she visited, describing these in her letters to Rachel. She also demonstrated her considerable powers of persuasion, for when she indicated to her teachers that she "liked history" but had no aptitude for figures, they encouraged her to concentrate on history and did not force her to do arithmetic. She was addicted to schoolgirl stories of the time, and acquired a habit of reading that would be lifelong.[44]

New Zealand was part of the British Empire, and the Diocesan School was as patriotic as any other privileged institution in Auckland. At an impressionable age Sālote observed the loyalty of New Zealanders during the coronation of King-Emperor George V in 1911 and in face of the approaching war. What British subjects believed was due to royalty reinforced her own experience of Tongan royalty, and the rhetoric of patriotism would find its way into the speeches she later made to her own people. Since Tonga was now a British-protected state, it was fortunate that Sālote believed that Britain had a maternal concern for the far-flung corners of Empire.

The outbreak of war in August 1914 interrupted Sālote's education. The warring European empires had "possessions" in the Pacific, which brought the war close to Tonga. On 6 October 1914 Tupou II wrote affectionately to his daughter:

> I am greatly apprehensive in case during your voyage here the German man-o'-war fleet should capture the steamer, or shoot it down, or take all as prisoners with you included. That is why I am very afraid for you to return now. So let us wait and see . . .
>
> This is the end of my little letter to you, but my love will never ever end . . . [45] [TF]

Later, the King agreed that Sālote should come to Tonga for the Christmas holidays, intending that she would return to Auckland early in 1915. But this did not happen. On the day after Sālote's fifteenth birthday, Tupou II wrote to the headmistress to explain that although he himself wished the Princess to continue her education, the chiefs had persuaded him to keep the Princess in Tonga.[46] After five years of marriage, Takipō still had no son (only two daughters, one of whom had not survived infancy), and according to Tupou I's Constitution of 1875 Sālote was now the heir-presumptive to the Tu'i Kanokupolu title and a great matrimonial prize. It was no wonder that "the chiefs" wanted her to remain in Tonga.

Photographs taken during her two years at the Diocesan School are a contrast. In one she wears the school uniform of shirt and skirt, and is tall and slight, not yet the nearly 190cm of her full adult height, and still lacking the plumpness appropriate for a woman of chiefly rank. In another school photograph (not in this book), she is outgrowing her pleated uniform, tied loosely around her waist. She had inherited the dark skin of her mother, darker than was approved by the honey-skinned aristocrats of Tongatapu, and her features are rounded and pleasant. Her black hair is thick and luxuriant. The photos, not being coloured, do not show her dark brown eyes. She looks serious.

Two other photographs reveal more of her *fakapapālangi* side. In one she seems plumper, and is dressed in the expensive fashion of the day in an elegant hat, furs, muff, and button-up boots. There is no suggestion of meekness or humility in her expression. On the contrary, she looks full of confidence, even arrogance, a child dressed as a stylish adult. The fourth photograph shows an attractive young woman, again expensively dressed, with a glint of humour in her face. One wonders which photograph the King sent her future consort (see chapter 3)!

Although longing to be in Tonga, Sālote had also come to love Auckland, and throughout her life would consider it to be her second home. In her two years in boarding school she had enjoyed relative freedom; but in Tonga, while she was unmarried and her father lived, Sālote had no independent life. She was obliged to live at the Palace with the King, Queen Takipō, and their infant daughter, and to obey her father in everything. During the three years that followed her return from school Sālote waited for her father to choose her husband, learnt her duties as a chiefly woman, but hardly began to appreciate what it would mean to be her father's heir.

Now aged 15, Sālote was a healthy adolescent, imperfectly educated in the formal sense (something she would always regret), and without much idea of the world beyond enjoying the privileges of royalty. She was happy to be reunited with her beloved father, although she had to share him with his second family. Although she loved her younger sister, Fusipala, she was estranged from Queen Takipō, partly (one feels) because of mischief-making by some people close to the Palace.

Sālote was intelligent and curious, and it could not have escaped her notice that there had been a change in the political life of Tonga while she was away. When she left Tonga in 1909 her own grandfather and great-uncle (Tu'ipelehake and Mateialona) had led the government and entered the Palace as part of the family; but two years before her return at the end of 1914 the King ceased to be the effective ruler of Tonga, rarely being consulted about major decisions concerning the welfare of the country. In short, the King had wasted his inheritance. Now that it looked as though Sālote would succeed her father, the question was how much of that inheritance mortgaged by Tupou II could be retrieved, and which of the chiefs would become her consort and possibly her political mentor.

Left: Tāufa'āhau, Tu'i Kanokupolu (known as Tupou I). He reunited Tonga after decades of civil wars. *From Thomas West* South-Central Polynesia. [1]

Below: Sālote Mafile'o Pilolevu (only daughter of Tupou I, after whom Queen Sālote was named); 'Ana Seini Tupou Veihola (daughter of Halaevalu Mata'aho, niece of Tupou I), who was one of the several wives of Old Tungī and mother of Tuku'aho (d. 1897); and Tu'ipelehake (Fatafehi), son of Sālote and father of Tupou II. *Courtesy of Te Papa Tongarewa, Wellington.* (Ref. C17496.) [2]

Above: Old Tungī (Halatuituia), father of Tuku'aho, great-uncle of 'Ofa-ki-Vava'u. He would have been Tu'i Ha'atakalaua (a senior title to the Tu'i Kanokupolu title of the Tupou dynasty) if the title had still been conferred. *Courtesy of the family of Rodger Page.* [3]

Right: Tuku'aho, only son of Old Tungī, and favoured by the British. He was Premier 1890-93 until dismissed by his rival, Tupou II. Tuku'aho married the high-ranking Mele Siu'ilikutapu and died in 1897, leaving one son. *Courtesy of the family of Rodger Page.* [4]

RIGHT: ‘Ofa-ki-Vava‘u, great-niece of Old Tungī. Most of the great chiefs expected her to marry Tupou II. [5]

BELOW: Wedding of Tupou II and Lavinia, 1 June 1899. [7]

ABOVE: Tu‘ipelehake (Fatafehi), father of Tupou II. His mother was Sālote, only daughter of Tāufa‘āhau Tupou I, and he married Fusipala, granddaughter of Tāufa‘āhau Tupou I by another line. *Courtesy of the family of Rodger Page.* [6]

Left: Queen Lavinia and Mrs Seddon, wife of the Prime Minister of New Zealand, Nuku'alofa 1900. Seddon and a group of parliamentarians did an island tour while contemplating a New Zealand Empire. *Courtesy of Alexander Turnbull Library. (Ref. F107010 1/2.)* [8]

Centre Left: A picnic arranged by Tae Manusā, mother of 'Ofa-ki-Vava'u, 1902. On the left are Bishop Willis, who was invited by Tae to set up the Church of England in Tonga, and Hamilton Hunter, first British Agent & Consul to Tonga (1901–09). On the right (with Helen Campbell on her lap) is Tae. *Courtesy of Clarence F. Michalis. (Ref. 9672.)* [9]

Below: The King's birthday dancers (front row). Tupou II lived a *papālangi* lifestyle, while enjoying all the prerogatives of being a high chief of Tonga. [10]

ABOVE: The wedding of Tupou II and Takipō, 22 November 1909. Takipō was the half-sister of ʻOfa-ki-Vavaʻu, the rival of Queen Lavinia. *Courtesy of Mark and Carolyn Blackburn.* [13]

RIGHT: After the death of Rachel Tonga's husband, she lived with her sister Sela Kata and her brother-in-law, Mateialona. Rachel Tonga is holding the pug dog. Mateialona was a grandson of Tāufaʻāhau Tupou I, and was Premier 1905–12. *Courtesy of the family of Rodger Page.* [12]

LEFT: Rachel Tonga (Lesieli Tongamohenoa) as a young woman. She was educated at Tupou College, married a Wesleyan minister, and remained a Wesleyan after Tupou I formed the breakaway Free Church in 1885. She became Princess Sālote's foster mother in 1907. [11]

LEFT: Princess Sālote, aged about 15 years. [17]

BELOW: Princess Sālote, aged about seven years, in Nuku'alofa.[14]

RIGHT: Princess Sālote in school uniform. [15]

FAR RIGHT: Princess Sālote, aged about 13 years. *Courtesy of 'Eva Ve'ehala.* [16]

Right: Prince Tāufa'āhau (later Tupou II) in Auckland, New Zealand, c.1889. Both of his parents were grandchildren of Tāufa'āhau Tupou I, but he inherited his title through his mother, Fusipala. *Courtesy of HRH Princess Taone Ma'afu.* [18]

Below: 'Ulukālala (Siaosi Fīnau Mīsini), great chief of Vava'u, twice Governor of Vava'u, Speaker of Parliament and Privy Councillor 1915–38. 'Ulukālala continued the rivalry begun by his male line in the 1790s. [19]

Below: The Kolofo'ou section of Nuku'alofa, 1910. *Courtesy of the family of Rodger Page.* [20]

Above: A postcard from the 1920s showing a street scene, the war memorial, the post office (which also housed the treasury), and Vuna wharf. In the centre is the Palace. [23]

Above: Veikune (Siosateki), Premier 1893–1904. His brother, Inoke Fotu, married Old Lavinia and was grandfather of Queen Lavinia, but Siosateki was considered to be of relatively low rank. [21]

Top Right: Parliament House was also used as the Supreme Court. Parliament was elected, but represented the interests of rival chiefly factions, and was frequently opposed to the Palace. *Courtesy of the family of Rodger Page.* [22]

Right: Cowley's Bakery was typical of Nuku'alofa shops in the early twentieth century. [24]

Top Right: The Royal Chapel and the Palace, Nuku'alofa. The Palace was built in the mid 1860s and the Chapel in 1883, both by Tāufa'āhau Tupou I. [25]

Centre Right: Pikula, one of the prestigious houses of Nuku'alofa. Tu'ipelehake (Fatafehi) lived here for some years prior to his death in 1912. [26]

Below: Nuku'alofa. The main street (later called Tāufa'āhau Road), looking from the south towards Vuna wharf. [27]

CHAPTER TWO

Ancestors and Antecedents

"The King himself is to blame for the late troubles."
(Sir Everard Im Thurn, Diary, 7 Jan. 1905)

PRINCESS SĀLOTE'S LEGITIMACY as heir to the King was derived from the Constitution of 1875, which named the eldest legitimate male descendant (or in the absence of male, the female) as the heir. Her credibility would depend on gaining recognition that she was indeed the ranking descendant of the sacred Tu'i Tonga as well as of the lesser-ranking Tu'i Kanokupolu title. Winning that recognition would depend very much on her strength of character. While Sālote emphasised her Tu'i Tonga descent, she strongly believed that God had destined the end of the rule of the Tu'i Tonga and the elevation of the Tu'i Kanokupolu title. She also believed that it was her manifest destiny to secure a pre-eminent and unchallengeable place for the Tupou dynasty not only as modern holders of the Tu'i Kanokupolu title, but as rulers of a reunited Tongan kingdom.

Three ancestral identities were important in Sālote's ideology: the Tu'i Tonga, because of his sacred *mana*; her great-great-grandfather, Tāufa'āhau Tupou I, because he reunited Tonga and introduced the modern state; and her father, who, though a negative model in many ways, instilled in her both the determination to maintain the "right" of the Tupou dynasty to rule and the importance of the preservation of Tongan identity.

Relative/*kāinga* rank determined the privileges of individuals in relation to each other. The personal/absolute rank of the aristocracy (*hou'eiki*) was derived from descent from the Tu'i Tonga; even higher rank from his eldest sister, the Tu'i Tonga Fefine (Female Ruler of Tonga); and highest of all from her eldest daughter (the Tamahā). Tongan society was like a pyramid, reflecting this pattern, each person being ranked in relation to all others, the sister outranking the brother, and her descendants outranking his, and so on. The *mana* of titles also depended on their closeness to the Tu'i Tonga. Another influence on the power structures was the belief that Tonga had once been peaceful and united under Tu'i Tonga leadership. Sālote would often call for a return to the peace and unity of past times as well as claiming the blessing of the Christian God.

The first Tu'i Tonga was said to have been the son of Tangaloa, a god in Tongan mythology, and a woman of Tonga. For many centuries, the legend says, the Tu'i Tonga and Tu'i Tonga Fefine ruled absolutely and unchallenged by the chiefs by means of the sacred *mana* of their line. They were *tapu* (sacred, prohibited), and any disrespectful action towards them invited the most severe penalties. The Tu'i Tonga was not only inferior in rank to his sister, but he gave precedence to her children, even before his own children. In spite of the sister's superior rank, it was said that the title of Tu'i Tonga descended from father to the eldest son of his highest-ranking wife, rather than to the sister's children. Captain James Cook is said to have seen the end of the peaceful and prosperous era of the Tu'i Tonga when he visited Tonga in the 1770s and described a densely populated, well-cultivated countryside and a peaceful people.

In spite of their supposedly unchallengeable status, several Tu'i Tonga were assassinated. Possibly in the fifteenth century,[1] one of the Tu'i Tonga "kings" relinquished his secular power, designating his brother (the Tu'i Ha'atakalaua) ruler of the kingdom, while he and the Tu'i Tonga Fefine retained the privileges of the sacred *mana*. Early in the seventeenth century,[2] the sixth Tu'i Ha'atakalaua created for his son, Ngata,[3] the title of Tu'i Kanokupolu and made him governor of the Western (Hihifo) District of Tongatapu, while holders of the two senior titles remained in the then capital, Lapaha, in the Eastern (Hahake) District of Tongatapu (Figures 1.3 and 1.4). Tribute continued to be brought to the Tu'i Tonga from Ha'apai and Vava'u, and possibly from as far off as Sāmoa. Shortly after Captain Cook's last visit (1777) civil wars broke out. The Tu'i Tonga fled to Vava'u, the last Tu'i Ha'atakalaua was killed in battle, and the Tu'i Kanokupolu title became the pre-eminent title of power.

Another ancestor who was important for Sālote was the thirteenth Tu'i Kanokupolu, Mumui (d.1797), who at some time before the 1780s took up residence at Nuku'alofa (Figure 1.5). It was through Mumui that Sālote traced her relationship to the *kāinga* of Kolomotu'a, who lived on Mumui's land. Mumui's great-grandson, Tāufa'āhau (now known as Tupou I), introduced Christianity, a series of codes of law, a Constitution, emancipation of the landless serfs, and land reform. Tāufaʻāhau also attempted to abolish features of Tongan society he believed to be oppressive, but with limited success.

Tāufaʻāhau was important to Sālote, not only because he was Tonga's first Christian king but because he reunited the kingdom. He won a pre-eminent position by defeating Laufilitonga (who would be the last Tuʻi Tonga) at the Battle of Velata in Haʻapai in 1826, by taking over Vavaʻu in 1833, and by fighting the chiefs of Tongatapu until 1852, thus putting an end to the civil wars that had occurred intermittently for about 70 years and reuniting the kingdom. Haʻapai was the only part of the kingdom that accepted Tāufaʻāhau wholeheartedly. Chiefs in other parts of the kingdom (Vavaʻu and the Central and Eastern districts of Tongatapu) continually looked for opportunities to reassert their independence.

At his baptism by Wesleyan missionaries in 1831, Tāufaʻāhau took the name George (Siaosi) and at his installation as Tuʻi Kanokupolu in 1845 he took the title Tupou, and was known as King George Tupou by his *papālangi* contemporaries. Tāufaʻāhau had children by a number of women, but in 1834 he was married in a Christian ceremony to Lupepauʻu, who had taken the name Sālote (Charlotte) at her baptism. George/Siaosi and Charlotte/Sālote would thereafter be recurring names in the genealogies of the Tupou dynasty.[4] The marriage of Tāufaʻāhau Tupou and Lupepauʻu Sālote lasted for 55 years (from 1834 until her death in 1889). Their two sons predeceased them, dying in 1842 and 1862.

Tupou made conversion to the Wesleyan denomination a benchmark of loyalty to himself, and supporters of the Tuʻi Tonga line consequently adhered to Roman Catholicism. One of the important effects of the coming of Christianity in 1826[5] was that legitimate marriage was more clearly defined. Where in the past only the liaisons of high chiefs were marked by ceremonies, now everyone could have their marriages and the births of their children recorded in the registers of their church. With legalized marriage eventually came the principle of inheritance by primogeniture, instead of by warfare or the choice of senior members of the *kāinga*.

Tāufaʻāhau was installed as Tuʻi Kanokupolu on 4 December 1845, but he did not take up residence in Tongatapu for several years. He then chose Nukuʻalofa as his capital because traders and missionaries had made it their chief port. So 1845 was the real beginning of the Tupou dynasty and also of the second period that profoundly affected the ideology of Queen Sālote Tupou III, for it was to Tāufaʻāhau Tupou I that the Queen often referred as a model of enlightened rule.

It is said that on a visit to Sydney, Australia, in 1853, Tupou was shocked to see the poverty of the least privileged of that town, and determined that such deprivation would never happen in Tonga. In truth, Tupou had advocated subdivision of land among the common people in Vavaʻu in the 1830s, when famine had followed warfare and drought.[6] His prime motive in land reform was to ensure the food supply by encouraging all of the population to plant and harvest. Tupou's land reform was linked with social reform, for he declared an end to three traditional practices: that of *tapu* (reserving certain foods and luxuries for the aristocrats); that of *fahu* (rights of a sister and her descendants over the property of her brother and his descendants); and that of *fatongia* (unpaid labour by commoners for chiefs). If Tupou's reforms had been effective, they would have destroyed the power of the aristocracy, who derived their privileges from their control over the goods and labour of their social inferiors. For very different reasons, Tupou II and Queen Sālote felt these reforms destabilized the kingdom, and although Tupou's 1862 Edict of Emancipation was celebrated, after his death the practices of *tapu*, *fahu*, and *fatongia* were merely moderated.

In the Constitution of 1875 Tupou elevated certain chiefs to be nobles and *matāpule ma'u tofi'a* (that is, hereditary estateholders or trustees of the land) and entrusted to them the responsibility of subdividing their estates into eight-and-a-quarter-acre farm allotments, each adult male (chief and commoner) being entitled to one allotment. Altogether, between 1875 and 1882, Tupou appointed 30 nobles and six *matāpule ma'u tofi'a* (Figure 2.1).[7] Succession to their titles and estates was by the law of primogeniture, which took away one powerful motive for warfare. But, as Sālote would discover, primogeniture meant estateholders who lacked qualities of leadership. Instead of being a working élite, as Tupou had intended (nobles also being members of Parliament), they were as determined to take advantage of their privileges as any of the Tu'i Tonga aristocracy.

Habit is hard to eradicate, and in spite of his legal codes and ostensible relinquishment of privileges, Tupou expected that people would continue to obey him. Although the Constitution guaranteed freedom of speech and freedom of religion, in 1885 the King demanded all the Wesleyans join *his* new church, the Free Church, which he founded in opposition to the Wesleyan Mission, which had been established in 1826. For many Tongans, loyalty to the Wesleyan Mission was a matter of conscience, and for other chiefs it was an opportunity to express their resentment of Tupou's reforms, particularly his exclusion of distinguished chiefs from the ranks of hereditary estateholders and hence from their former lands. When Tupou's northern warriors came with blackened faces and clubs and guns in their hands, many chiefs and people submitted to Tupou, but a remnant did not, and these were clubbed, beaten, shot, marooned on deserted islands, had their lands taken from them, or were sent into exile. Among the exiles of 1887–90 were members of Tupou's own family, including his only daughter, another Sālote, and his "illegitimate" grandson Mateialona. Queen Sālote would make an attempt to heal the wounds of this time a major priority.

Tupou had responded strongly to other, more subtle, challenges. The last Tu'i Tonga, Laufilitonga, died in 1865, bequeathing the Tu'i Tonga's special prerogatives and ceremonies (and perhaps his title) to Tu'ipelehake (Fatafehi), the son of his half-brother through their mother (Figure 1.8). Tu'ipelehake's personal rank and rank by title were very high, the title being descended from the *eldest* divine brother of the first Tu'i Tonga and recently improved by marriage.[8] Tu'ipelehake knew what happened to chiefs who set themselves up in opposition to Tupou, and he relinquished significant honours in Tupou's favour.[9] Tupou was installed as Tu'i Tonga in Vava'u in 1865,[10] then allowed the title to lapse, probably because the Tongatapu chiefs did not recognize his installation. From this time Tupou was referred to in the language formerly reserved for the Tu'i Tonga, sharing this distinction with Tu'ipelehake.[11] Other honours, such as the *tapu* on his person, and introduction of elements of the Tu'i Tonga's sacred *taumafa kava* (royal *kava* ceremony) into the *kava* ceremony of the Tu'i Kanokupolu also began at this time (see Glossary for *kava*).

Tu'ipelehake (Fatafehi), the son of Tupou's only daughter, Sālote, married his cousin Fusipala in 1870 (Figures 1.8 and 2.2). As grandson and because of his great *mana* Tu'ipelehake was an obvious and appropriate heir for Tupou; but Tupou instead named an "illegitimate" son, Tēvita 'Unga, as his heir, and 'Unga's legitimate descendants after him.[12] 'Unga died in 1879 and his sons in 1885 and 1889, and only daughter, Fusipala, also in 1889. The only legitimate grandson of 'Unga was Prince Tāufa'āhau, the son of Fusipala and Tu'ipelehake. In the event of Prince Tāufa'āhau predeceasing him, Tupou named neither Tu'ipelehake nor Mateialona (whose chiefly rank was reflected in their portly size), but Old Tungī (see chapter 1). Nevertheless many Tongan chiefs continued to believe that Tu'ipelehake was both the rightful Tu'i Tonga and rightful Tu'i Kanokupolu.

The young Prince Tāufa'āhau was of high rank through his father, Tu'ipelehake, although his place in the succession to the Tu'i Kanokupolu title came from his mother. He had none of the traditional qualifications for leadership (seniority, success as a warrior, and outstanding ability), but Tupou confirmed the succession in a will dated 24 November 1889.[13] The old King may well have believed that no matter what he did, the chiefs he had ennobled and the chiefs he had disinherited would combine after his death to overthrow the central government and to repossess themselves of their traditional lands and privileges.[14]

Prince Tāufa'āhau was born in Vava'u in 1874, and brought up in Ha'apai.[15] He was 15 years old when his mother, Fusipala, died. His father then married a woman from Sāmoa and filled his house (first Finefekai, then Pikula) in Nuku'alofa with Sāmoan relations and retainers, leaving no place for the only surviving son of his first marriage. Tāufa'āhau spent some time at the Government College in Nuku'alofa, then a few months with a tutor

(C. D. Whitcombe) in Auckland, then again attended the Government College. Whitcombe's son gives an attractive picture of an amiable and energetic young Tāufa'āhau while he was in Auckland, every evening racing the tram along Khyber Pass Road to Newmarket and coming home via Parnell.[16] When Tāufa'āhau returned to Tonga, he was said to be the ringleader of a group of boys who toured the islands of Tonga in 1890 with a magic lantern to raise money to pay the salary of his erstwhile tutor,[17] which suggests that he was enterprising. After he left school, Tupou appointed him town officer of Holopeka, a small village in Ha'apai, rather than let him pass his time idly in Nuku'alofa.[18] Although the Old King had confirmed that his great-grandson was his heir, he had grave reservations about his character. His doubts were expressed in a letter of 16 February 1892, in which he castigated the young prince for his traditional ideas about property, Tāufa'āhau having behaved like a *fahu* in regard to his future subjects' possessions:

> I am writing to tell you that you have broken a clause of the Constitution: "That everyone has absolute right to his own possessions." . . . I consider you to be a thief. You have been doing this for years, through your ignorance and stupidity. And I have been silent because it was you. But you must know that I am very angry . . . I am warning you that if this [behaviour] continues, we will have to prosecute you, in order that you will pay for your actions.[19]

The major reason for allowing such an obviously unsuitable youth to succeed him could have been the "disloyalty" of Tupou's other relations, who continued as Old Wesleyans instead of joining his Free Church.[20] Tupou may also have felt that to deny his great-grandson's inheritance would undermine the rights of hereditary estateholders and even commoners to succeed to the land of their fathers as set out in the Constitution, thus negating the land reform most dear to his heart.

When Tupou died on 18 February 1893, his grandsons – Tu'ipelehake and Mateialona – did not dispute the succession. As we learned in chapter 1, Old Tungī could have claimed the Tu'i Kanokupolu title on the grounds of his seniority, but he stood aside on the understanding that the 18-year-old Tāufa'āhau would marry his great-niece, 'Ofa-ki-Vava'u. The British hoped Tāufa'āhau would stand aside, not for Tu'ipelehake or Mateialona, but for his cousin Tuku'aho (son of Old Tungī), now in his thirties, whose appointment as Premier in 1890 had been at their instigation (Figure 1.6).[21] The British also respected the provisions of the Constitution that guaranteed inheritance by the eldest male of the designated line, so they did not interfere, even when the young King dismissed Tuku'aho from the premiership soon after his succession.

The traditional period of mourning for the Tu'i Tonga was 100 days, so the young King appears to have hurried through the mourning rituals for his venerable predecessor. Barely a month after Tupou's death, Tāufa'āhau was crowned as Tupou II on 17 March 1893, and soon showed his unfitness for high office. Tupou II's biographer ('Ēseta Fusitu'a) explains Tupou II's character by saying that "as a child his whims were obeyed, abilities exaggerated, and faults humoured".[22] When reminiscing about her father, Queen Sālote did not deny his faults, but excused him, saying that, as a youth, "No one was really looking after him", and she commented that in the crises of his reign he did "his best, but no example had been set for him".[23] In short, Tupou II behaved like the later Tu'i Tongas in that he claimed the privileges of high office without the responsibilities.

Tupou II's self-indulgent behaviour has also been "explained" by the fact that he had no *mehekitanga* (father's eldest sister) or sister to direct him, and therefore no *fahu* (sister's children or father's sister's children) to curb him by exercising superior rights. On the contrary, intermarriages among his ancestors made him *fahu* to many of his own relations (Figure 2.2),[24] and he acted as though he was *fahu* to all his subjects, making great demands upon them.

Added to the indulgences that a Tongan chief could command were those introduced by *papālangi*. Being *fakapapālangi* (doing things in the European style) had come to be synonymous with high birth and sophistication, and the young King's parents and uncles, his grandfather and grandmother, even his great-grandfather had been *fakapapālangi* to some extent. Once he became king, Tupou II spent extravagantly on *papālangi* clothes, jewellery, perfumes, and alcohol.[25] He exercised his chiefly prerogatives by having a series of mistresses. Given to enthusiasms and fond of gadgets (novelties, they were then called), he acquired a multitude of *papālangi* toys and luxuries. Whenever he needed money to pay for his indulgences, he sent a boy with a bag over to the Treasury, regardless of the salary voted him by Parliament.[26] This conspicuous expenditure was chiefly, and expected from one of his rank, but the hereditary estateholders were angered by his assumption that he could also deprive them of estates granted by the Constitution and laws.

The young King's faults appear to be ones of temperament, not intelligence. He had a considerable gift for music and he wrote songs (both words and music) for *lakalaka* (Tongan dance) and anthems for Tongan choirs. Since Tupou II's critics were mostly in Nuku'alofa, he spent many months of the year on his Ha'apai estates, where, according to Collocott, he was seen at his best.[27] When in Tongatapu he divided his time between his estates at Tufumāhina (near the lagoon) or on the island of Pangaimotu, where the fishing was good. At Mataki'eua, adjoining Tufumāhina, he built a course for horseracing for the entertainment of *papālangi* friends and *fakapapālangi* chiefs. By 1899, when he married Lavinia, the kingdom was virtually bankrupt.

When criticism mounted, Tupou II appeared incapable of recognizing it as such or that it was dangerous for him. By the end of the century the question was not whether the British would interfere in Tonga, but the extent of that interference. Tonga had few assets to attract foreigners, but strong links had been forged between resource-rich Fiji and Tonga through centuries of trade and intermarriage, and many Tongans lived permanently in the Lau group of Fiji, about 800 kilometres from the northern islands of Tonga. Fiji had become a British colony in 1874, and Tonga had signed a treaty with Great Britain in 1879, two years after the Western Pacific High Commission was set up in Suva. For the convenience of the Commission, Tonga took its date and time from Suva (thus forcing the International Dateline to take an easterly loop around the kingdom). In spite of Tonga's treaties with other powers (France 1855, Germany 1876, and the United States of America 1886), Britain decided that its interests in Fiji would best be served by asserting prime influence over Tonga and thus preventing civil disturbances that might have echoes in Fiji. In accordance with the policy of the Colonial Office in London, this control would be exercised with the least possible expense to Britain.

In 1899, when Great Britain, Germany, and the United States reallocated their territories in the Pacific, Britain relinquished all claim to Sāmoa in exchange for the recognition by Germany and the USA that Tonga came solely within the British sphere of influence. Thus Basil Thomson came as a special envoy in 1900 to persuade Tupou II to sign a new Treaty of Friendship with Great Britain.[28] The draft of the treaty gave Britain most-favoured-nation status and allowed Britain to control Tonga's relations with foreign countries, and also to exercise jurisdiction over all non-Tongan residents. Instead of the former British Vice-Consul, who reported events in Tonga but could not intervene, a British Agent & Consul would be appointed by the Colonial Office on the advice of the High Commissioner to represent the British government in Tonga. The new Agent & Consul would have the power to intervene in government.

Thomson's view was that the nobles and chiefs were still so angry with the King over his marriage to Lavinia that they would welcome British intervention.[29] The nobles and chiefs did indeed want to punish the King, but not at the expense of "losing Tonga's flag" (i.e. loss of independence). They flattered Thomson with their attentions, while hoping delay would provide a miracle – perhaps intervention from the French. But Thomson was as devious as the nobles and chiefs and, ignoring Tupou II's refusal to sign the clause of the Treaty dealing with foreign relations, declared to the assembly on Mala'e Pangai (the open space between the Palace and the wharf) that Tonga was forthwith a British-protected state. When Thomson read the words *pule'anga malu'i* (protected state), a "kind of sob" rose from the crowd. After the raising of British and Tongan flags, Thomson departed, feeling "rather cheap".[30] The treaty was ratified in 1901, the clause about foreign relations that the King had refused to sign being deemed to be a silent clause.

The King, still believing he was untouchable, ignored the warning implicit in Thomson's visit. In 1902 the Acting High Commissioner listed four causes of dissatisfaction within the kingdom that would justify greater control by the British: the corruption and inefficiency of the government; the exactions of personal and other services by the nobles and chiefs (*fatongia*) on common people; the selfishness of the King; and the government's failure to carry out Tupou I's land reforms.[31]

The King assumed that childhood indulgence would be his lot throughout his lifetime and that his privileges were of paramount importance to his subjects. Not all Tongans shared the King's belief in his sacred rights, but they at least understood his assumptions: the *papālangi* did not, expecting the ruler to guarantee good government. In 1896 Dr James Egan Moulton, Principal of Tupou College, who had lived for most of the previous 30 years in Tonga, had seen great promise in Tupou II, describing him as "exceedingly intelligent", but by 1904 Moulton expressed the opinion that few Tongans or *papālangi* would regret it if the King were deposed, for "he lived for himself alone".[32] In 1901, R. Beckwith Leefe, the outgoing British Vice-Consul to Tonga, described Tupou II as "an egregious young prevaricator". Hamilton Hunter, the first British Agent & Consul to Tonga (1901–09), described Tupou II as "a very selfish and vain man, and though proud of the outward pomp and show of his position, appears to be utterly regardless of the well-being of his people, and so long as his wishes are gratified he is happy". The remote Colonial Office in London, informed by Hunter, referred to Tupou II as a "sensuous and besotted monarch" and as "oppressive and despotic".[33]

Complaints by Tongans, mostly about land, were sent to the High Commissioner of the Western Pacific via Hunter. Always in need of money, Tupou II had reclaimed rents from Crown land Tupou I had given to the government and also demanded rents from those who had been living rent-free on royal estates. Many chiefs who were not hereditary estateholders (that is, not named as nobles or *kau matāpule ma'u tofi'a*) still retained significant holdings of land by custom, and resisted incorporation of these customary holdings into the King's or other hereditary estates. While these customary landholders agitated, and boundaries of estates remained uncertain, neither nobles, nor foreign leaseholders, nor Tongan smallholders felt secure. The nobles clearly wanted the situation stabilized, for Hunter reported that when he suggested to the nobles that "one of the first things to do would be to survey all the lands, and to give to each Noble a grant for his land . . . They were delighted with the idea. More than one said 'Then the King or Government will not be able to rob us of our hereditary lands'."[34] Hunter failed to see (or chose not to see) that the nobles were taking advantage of the weakness of Tupou II's government to reclaim their autonomy, quarrelling with the King and each other over the boundaries of their estates, always seeking more for themselves, so that an exasperated Dr Moulton said: "The Nobles are the curse of the country".[35]

The uncertainties over estates were compounded by the King's legal right to increase the number of nobles. In 1894 he had created without much comment the chief Lasike as the thirty-first noble, but when he rewarded his loyal Premier, Siosateki, a Vava'u chief, with a noble title, Veikune, in 1903, the nobles were outraged.[36] Hunter claimed that the nobles were aggrieved because of Veikune's inferior personal rank, but in truth they believed the King was elevating Veikune at the expense of other chiefs, in particular Veikune's rival, 'Ulukālala (Siaosi Fīnau Mīsini), the great chief of Vava'u, who had already complained that there were too many Veikunes in government.[37]

Hunter reported that if 'Ulukālala chose to lead the disaffected chiefs, "the present administration would not last a week".[38] In 1904, possibly at the instigation of Veikune, the King dismissed 'Ulukālala from his appointment as Governor of Vava'u (Figure 2.3).[39] This 'Ulukālala would be a leader of the "Reactionary Party" during the first two decades of Queen Sālote's reign.

Papālangi had a variety of complaints. Traders resented the Premier giving all the government contracts to one firm and were incensed when the King included basic *papālangi* foods in the list of dutiable goods. *Papālangi* leases had not been renewed, and "the Government keep no register of mortgages [i.e. leases], and make no provision for transfers of portions of property".[40] The *papālangi* traders demanded administration by a legislative council of foreigners, presided over by a British Resident; abolition of the office of noble, it "being an innovation and not a Tongan custom";[41] and reasonable terms and rents for land. Their complaints about land tenure were connected to the erratic supply of copra to the traders, but they echoed the concerns of Tupou I about the effect of uncertainty of tenure on the food supply of the country:

> Under the original Constitution granted (1875) by the late King George, each chief and his descendants was guaranteed possession of his land for ever. Since then the Constitution and the laws have been altered so often, that at the present time no one can tell when he will be dispossessed of his land by his superior. The present King has claimed and taken possession of lands formerly held by chiefs, and the chiefs have followed the evil example with regard to their inferiors.
>
> The effect of this is, that the natives in general, have for years past stopped planting cocoa nuts, thus effectually [*sic*] lessening the output of our staple commodity of export, and the great bulk of the land remains uncultivated. None will go to the trouble of planting land of which he may be dispossessed at any moment. Thus, laziness and indifference are encouraged and thrive, with the consequence that every year in the principal island of the group (Tongatabu) there is a scarcity of food; and the natives planting less than formerly, have less

> copra to sell for their support to their own detriment and that of the foreigners and the country in general.
>
> Under the late King [Tupou I] the condition of the country was not so.[42]

By 1903 complaints were so numerous that the Agent & Consul recommended deposing and deporting Tupou II and installing his father, Tu'ipelehake, in his place. Tu'ipelehake consented "in order to save the flag".[43] High Commissioner Jackson proposed a visit in 1903, but was refused permission to land on the reasonable grounds that there was an epidemic of measles in Fiji, whence he had come.[44] The King's triumph at preventing the visit was described by Dr Moulton, who also reflected on the King's indifference to the welfare of the people.

> In spite of heavy rain the King had a week-long Katoanga to celebrate the anniversary of his coronation. The people, women and girls, sat in the wet day after day with very little food inside them. Talavai [asking for medicine] now heavy in consequence. The King highly elated at his victory – defiance over the High Commissioner last year and still being on the throne . . . Some of the songs [that accompanied the dances] at the Katoanga referred to this [victory].[45]

The King's triumph was shortlived. In December 1904 the new High Commissioner, Sir Everard Im Thurn, came from Suva empowered to deport the King and to install Tu'ipelehake, but not to annex the kingdom without further consultation with the Secretary of State for Colonies.[46] An audit of government finances persuaded Im Thurn to deport Premier Veikune (Siosateki) and his son Fotu, the custodians of a now-empty Treasury.[47]

After listening to complaints by traders and chiefs alike, Im Thurn gave the King a choice between being deposed and deported, on the one hand, and signing a Supplementary Agreement to the 1900 Treaty of Friendship, on the other. The King protested, but again lacking the support of the nobles and chiefs, he could not avoid signing. The Supplementary Agreement, which was to guide British–Tongan relations during the next half-century, consisted of twelve points, some dealing with short-term reform and some with long-term policies. The most significant points were those that stated that the King would "rule with and through the Chiefs" (clause 1), the King must consult with the British Agent & Consul and take his advice (clause 2), laws were to be published in English and Tongan (clause 4), lands were to be distributed as promised by Tupou I (clause 5), rents of the lands that Tupou I had assigned to the government must be returned to the government and not be regarded as part of the King's income (clause 6), the leases of *papālangi* were to be renewed (clause 7), new appointments to the public service and changes among leading officials were to be made only after consultation with the British Agent &

Consul (clause 9 and 10), and rights of succession and inheritance were guaranteed (clause 12).[48]

Encouraged by Consul Hunter's predictions that Tupou II would be deported, an alliance of chiefs had been particularly outspoken. Rumour had it that Polutele Kaho, spokesman for the alliance, hoped the High Commissioner would make him president of a Tongan republic.[49] Polutele's influence depended upon the patronage of two chiefs of high rank, Mā'atu and 'Ulukālala, all three having opposed the King's marriage to Lavinia. The British considered Polutele to be the most able of the young chiefs, but Hunter was mistaken when he described the three as loyal to Britain, for they wanted Britain to remove the King and then leave Tonga alone.

The British appointed Polutele as Minister for Police, and 'Ulukālala was reinstated as Governor of Vava'u, a post he would soon lose again because of his intemperate behaviour.[50] Tu'ipelehake was appointed Minister for Lands and Finance, and his cousin, Mateialona, as Premier.

Although Hunter's powers were increased by the Supplementary Agreement, he was disappointed that Britain had not annexed Tonga or deported or deposed the King. British control was, however, reinforced by the appointment of a *papālangi* (R. L. Skeen) as Chief Justice, and other *papālangi* to lesser positions in government. Im Thurn arranged for a loan to tide the government over, and hoped that reform would be effected through Hunter's advisory powers. Left out of the Supplementary Agreement, for clause 5 was merely a pious hope, was any workable plan for survey of boundaries of estates and registration of allotments. The rights claimed by customary landholders were disregarded.

The King signed the Supplementary Agreement under duress, but "The King himself is to blame for the late troubles," said Im Thurn, and recorded that "we passed the King's garden, and there I caught a glimpse of the King, with absolutely nothing on but a black cloth *sulu*, rolling disconsolately on the floor of his summerhouse".[51] Im Thurn felt no sympathy, but Princess Sālote, not quite five years old, witnessed her father's distress, his "feeling of desperate loneliness", and his belief that he had "betrayed his heritage" by signing the Agreement. Sālote was able to comfort the King, and he told her, "You brought me back."[52] Thus Sālote asserted that she was important to and loved by her father.

Mateialona and Tu'ipelehake were now in charge, but only as long as they acted on the advice of the British Agent & Consul. They had hitherto been the King's staunchest allies, and among the supporters of Queen Lavinia. Now they were guided by their fear that Tonga would lose its independence if they did not ensure that the kingdom was competently ruled and kept solvent. When Tupou II went to New Zealand in 1905 to seek legal advice, Mateialona advertised in the Auckland and Sydney newspapers (doubtless on the advice of Consul Hunter) that the government of Tonga would not be responsible for debts the King incurred. The King took with him a petition signed by a number of chiefs; Mateialona sent a counter-petition (some chiefs signing both petitions), which supported the Tongan government as set up in 1905.[53] From this journey in 1905 and another in 1907, the King returned to Tonga empty-handed. Im Thurn issued another warning and the overseas visits ceased.[54]

Tupou II argued that the Supplementary Agreement breached article 3 of the Treaty of Friendship, in which Britain undertook not to interfere in Tonga's internal affairs.[55] He simply refused to listen to Hunter's advice. But Mateialona listened, and the government prospered, the finances of the kingdom were made sound, new public buildings and wharves were built, and measures taken to ensure the water supply. The King had no interest in wharves and water supplies, and a rift developed between him and Mateialona and Tu'ipelehake, which had not healed when Tu'ipelehake died in 1912.[56]

The King had learned a lesson of sorts: that he needed allies. He attempted to win this support by promising certain chiefs that he would make them nobles and thus confirm their rights to their customary lands.[57] The Parliaments of 1909 and 1912 (in which all 32 nobles had seats) refused to support the King's promised grants, and when the King appealed to the new High Commissioner, Sir Francis May, in 1911, to support his plan to ennoble more chiefs, his pleas were brushed aside.[58] These chiefs would ask Sālote to fulfil the King's promises.

Hamilton Hunter was transferred in 1909, and W. Telfer Campbell appointed Agent & Consul in his place. Campbell had less judgement and experience than Hunter, and he made a major error in relation to a trading co-operative to which nearly all the nobles and chiefs belonged. The co-operative bore the name Tonga Ma'a Tonga Kautaha (Tonga for the Tongans Co-operative), and it came to be associated in the Tongan mind with freedom from foreign intervention. The TMTK was widely popular, and British and German traders complained to Campbell of unfair competition. When Mateialona (on the advice of Campbell) closed the TMTK, the founder of the co-operative, A. D. Cameron, took legal action against the government and won his case on appeal, the government having to pay costs. The lawyers' fees were extraordinarily high, and Mateialona was forced to resign the premiership in order to escape impeachment.[59]

Campbell was replaced by Acting Agent & Consul Islay McOwan (1912–13), who now made a brief appearance in the country that he would greatly influence in the first decade of Sālote's reign.[60] McOwan paved the way for his later appointment by establishing a friendly relationship with the King, whom he treated with tact and respect. McOwan carried out the High Commissioner's instructions so successfully that the community petitioned that his appointment continue.

Events in the 1912 Parliament would have a great impact upon Queen Sālote's reign. Not only had Mateialona been forced to resign to avoid a threatened impeachment, but the governors of Ha'apai and Vava'u (S. Tu'itavake and S. T. Faletau) were impeached and dismissed for following Campbell's instructions in relation to the TMTK. Mateialona, Tu'itavake, and Faletau were all Old Wesleyans. Samisoni Siaki Lolohea and Motekiai Taukolo Langi, both Free Church and conspicuous supporters of what would become the "Reactionary Party" of 'Ulukālala, Mā'atu, and Polutele Kaho, had initiated the impeachments. These five men would be actors in major events in the early part of Sālote's reign, in which impeachment and threat of impeachment would be used in attempts to coerce Sālote's government. The rhetoric of the "Reactionary Party" was anti-British, but its policies arose from a desire for independence, not only from the British, but also from the Tupou dynasty.

The King had not been a member of the TMTK, but he took advantage of the wave of anti-British sentiment that followed its closure and the lawsuits to seek out much-needed allies. Cameron's Auckland lawyer, R. N. Moody, advised the King to appoint as his new Premier and Chief European Clerk two people who had earlier been the King's conspicuous enemies. Moody's reasoning was that it was better for the King to have these two on his side rather than to have them continue as enemies. So Polutele Kaho, reputed republican, replaced Mateialona as Premier. As Chief European Clerk the King appointed George Scott, a Tasmanian lawyer, who had once hoped that the "black bastard" of a King would soon be "dead".[61] Scott was not a favourite with the Western Pacific High Commission, whose officers had described him in 1906 as the "least unsuitable candidate" for the post of Collector of Customs in Tonga.[62] To cement the new alliance, Scott's Tongan wife, Kalo Lolohea, wrote the "Takipō Waltz" in honour of Tupou II's second Queen, the waltz becoming a favourite at the dances at the recently erected Victoria Memorial Hall.[63] Sālote would find it difficult to rid herself of Polutele and Scott.

Polutele, like Scott, was an unlikely ally of Tupou II. In 1905 a conspirator had implicated Polutele in a plot to assassinate the King. Further, the King had seduced Polutele's niece and become the father of her child. In 1912 Polutele abandoned hopes of further preferment by the British and allied himself with the King, accepting not only the appointment as Premier but also the noble title Tu'ivakanō (Figure 2.4).[64] The arrangement turned out to be one of mutual convenience: Polutele gained political power and estates, and he would ensure the continuance of the King's extravagant *fakapapālangi* lifestyle. The situation was a familiar one in Tongan polity, for in legend the ancient sacred ruler had voluntarily relinquished his secular power to a lesser chief to protect his privileges. Tu'ivakanō would now run the country as though he were a republican president, for the Privy Council (of which the King was President) failed to meet for months at a time, allowing the Cabinet (presided over by the Premier) to determine government policies.

Under Tu'ivakanō (Polutele), the membership of Parliament was drastically reduced.[65] Instead of all 32 nobles sitting in Parliament, seven of their number would be elected by the nobles to represent them. The number of "people's representatives" was likewise reduced from 32 to seven. The King had the power to appoint as many ministers as he liked, and at this time he appointed seven. Tu'ivakanō doubtless influenced the King's choice of ministers, but these appointments also depended on the consent of the British Agent & Consul. Even if membership of Parliament were not in Tu'ivakanō's gift, he must have found 21 members of Parliament significantly easier to manage than 64 plus ministers. Tu'ivakanō's patron, 'Ulukālala, was appointed Speaker and Privy Councillor in 1915, positions that gave him the status he craved. However, the Agent & Consul would not consent to the appointment of his ally Mā'atu as a magistrate, because of Mā'atu's abusive lifestyle.[66] Mā'atu was not only a drunkard, but was nicknamed "the Whip", because of his violence towards his own people.

Consul Campbell's interference with the TMTK, the consequent fall of Mateialona's government, and the approaching war in Europe between Britain and Germany moderated British interference, thus increasing Tu'ivakanō's power. An older, experienced, soon-to-retire Agent & Consul, H. E. W. Grant, was appointed (1913–16). Grant was not only noticeably less interventionist than either Hunter or Campbell, but he followed the pattern set up by McOwan in being tactful and friendly in his dealings with the King. When Grant retired in 1916, G. B. Smith-Rewse, an able, young and energetic administrator, was appointed Acting Agent & Consul. Smith-Rewse was appalled at the decline in government and its finances and reported to his superiors with considerable disquiet:

> The greatest evil appears to be at the present time that the country is ruled not for the benefit of the whole community but for a small clique, of which the Premier Tuivakano and Mr. G. Scott are the leaders. This party practically controls the Privy Council and the Legislative Assembly and any measures that do not have their support, are doomed to failure. His Majesty the King is, as has so often been reported before, an obstacle in the way of all progress and still only considers his own selfish needs . . .
>
> [I] can confidentially state that the combination of Tuivakano as Premier and Mr. Scott as Premier's Clerk is impossible, if any progress is to be made. Mr. Scott is virtually Premier and by some means or other has gained an ascendancy over Tuivakano . . . I am aware that Tuivakano has done excellent work in the past as Minister for Police and it is extremely regrettable that such an able man should have been led astray, but the fact remains. That the country is ruled for the benefit of the Premier and his friends is shown clearly by the case of J. B. Maatu, whose appointment as Extra Magistrate I refused to sanction on account of his character . . .[67]

Even the formerly neat capital was languishing, for Smith-Rewse complained that the grounds of the Palace were in a "disgraceful condition", and Nuku'alofa "dilapidated and neglected".[68] The High Commissioner took note and re-appointed Islay McOwan as the substantive Agent & Consul. McOwan took up his appointment in August 1917, just in time to attend the wedding of Princess Sālote. McOwan's task was to point out to Sālote – once she became Queen – the advantages of the British alliance spurned by her father, and to correct the ill-effects of Tupou II's reign.

Despite his considerable failings as a monarch, Tupou II did not deal harshly with his people, as did many nobles who governed their estates with considerable brutality. Within the family circle, where difficult decisions were rarely required, he exhibited much kindness. Princess Sālote loved him dearly. A second daughter, by Queen Takipō, 'Elisiva Fusipala Tauki'onelua (Princess 'Onelua), born on 20 March 1911, died on 11 August 1911. The third daughter, 'Elisiva Fusipala Tauki'onetuku (Princess Fusipala), was born 26 July 1912 and was second in line to the King's titles, after Princess Sālote.

The King had been very grieved by the death of Princess 'Onelua, and altogether the last years of his reign were sad ones. The companionship of Princess Sālote after her return from Auckland must have been a comfort for him, for marriage to Takipō had never been more than one of convenience. Declining health played its part in the King's semi-retirement, and in 1917 he was diagnosed as suffering from tuberculosis. There was no hope of recovery, despite periods of remission when the King enjoyed his usual entertainments. The King had not prepared Sālote for her duties as monarch, for he did not understand these duties himself, but he did understand that, failing a legitimate brother, Sālote would need a powerful male chief by her side to carry out the proper functions of a "brother" in looking after the land. Male ("brother") functions were complementary with female ("sister") functions. The saying was that "Men provide and women divide", meaning that men were responsible for practical matters such as looking after the land and its produce (men's wealth), while women were responsible for the relationships that were demonstrated by giving and receiving of both men's wealth and women's wealth (*koloa*), applied as much at the national level as it did in the villages.

The King's own experience when he married Queen Lavinia made him aware of the potential divisiveness of Sālote's marriage. Whomsoever he chose as a husband for Sālote, some chiefs would be delighted but others would certainly be alienated. So it was with reluctance that the King turned his attention to the question of the marriage of his heir.

The outcome of Tupou II's reign was a diminished inheritance for his daughter Sālote. Instead of the united kingdom bequeathed to him by Tupou I, the King had acted in ways that revived divisiveness within the kingdom and weakness at the centre. He discovered too late that his behaviour led only to loss of influence over chiefs, who would take advantage of his shortcomings. He failed to realize that *mana* is sustained by ability and authority, which depend upon real power. It was fortunate for Tonga that Sālote inherited the strength of character of earlier forebears, and re-examined the policies of her immediate predecessor. Her intelligence would serve her well; but she was also dependent upon the King's choice of a "brother" to support and assist her.

CHAPTER THREE

A Dynastic Marriage

"It is a rare thing for fibre to be joined with fibre . . ."
(Sione Havea, *Koe Havea*, 1941)

IT WAS SĀLOTE'S GOOD FORTUNE that the King chose as her husband someone who not only gave her personal happiness but would be "fibre" joined with her own "fibre". The Tu'i Kanokupolu chiefs had continually been elevated by advantageous marriages (Figure 3.1), and the King well understood that the weakness of Sālote's maternal line (Figure 3.2) would have to be compensated for by marriage to a chief of high rank to protect her status and to ensure the rank of her children. If Tupou II had had a sister, that sister (as Sālote's *mehekitanga*) would also have been involved in the choice of a husband. As it was, Tupou II was faced with a situation similar to the one that had surrounded his own marriage to Queen Lavinia (chapter 1): the choice of one chief would inevitably lead to the anger of the supporters of the rejected candidate. It is no wonder that the King hesitated long after Sālote's sixteenth birthday, when she could legally marry.

Sālote never questioned the King's right to choose her future partner; nor that sentiment would play no part in his selection. Her husband would be chosen for his personal rank, title, and the support he could bring to the house of Tupou.[1] To many observers, the obvious candidate was the former Uiliami Tupoulahi, now the holder of the noble title of Tungī, and known as Tungī Mailefihi (Figure 3.3): firstly because he represented the more senior (though extinct) title of Tu'i Ha'atakalaua; secondly because he was third in the line of succession to the Tu'i Kanokupolu title after the King's daughters; and thirdly because he had the largest estates in the kingdom and the support of many of the Tongatapu chiefs. Against him was the fact that Tungī Mailefihi was an Old Wesleyan, and this powerful minority was distrusted by the majority of the chiefs as possibly compromising Tonga's independence in favour of the British.[2] There was also the traditional hostility between the northern chiefs and Tongatapu chiefs, especially the chiefs of the Eastern District of Tongatapu whom Tungī represented. At this time the northern chiefs controlled the government through Ha'apai-connected Tu'ivakanō (Polutele) and his patrons 'Ulukālala and Mā'atu, and they would not readily agree to a Tongatapu chief coming to such a position of influence. This was in spite of the fact that Tungī had connections with the northern group of Vava'u through his mother's mother (Figure 3.3), had been Governor of Vava'u since 1912, and was then living in Neiafu, the main town of the Vava'u group (Figure 1.1).

The northern candidate for Sālote's hand in marriage was Ha'amea, son of 'Ulukālala (Figure 2.3). He was personable, nine years older than Sālote, educated in New Zealand, and, like Sālote and Tungī, was a descendant of a Tamahā (eldest daughter of the Tu'i Tonga Fefine), in his case Tu'imala. 'Ulukālala was the greatest chief in Vava'u. Ha'amea's mother was from the Ata line (chiefs very close to the Tu'i Kanokupolu). So he had the support of most of the northern chiefs and could hope for some Tongatapu Western District chiefs to support him.

Sālote was 14 when she returned from school in Auckland in December 1914. She would later regret that her Western education had been cut short, but the traditional knowledge she acquired during the three years between her return from school and her marriage was an essential accomplishment for women of rank, who were its custodians and had to put forward convincingly those versions that favoured their own *kāinga*. This knowledge of traditions would be crucial for Sālote's exercise of traditional power.

Sālote would make it known that her instruction was from impeccable Tu'i Tonga sources, for Losaline Fatafehi (granddaughter of the last Tu'i Tonga), and therefore a great-aunt to Sālote (Figure 3.4), passed on to her the detailed and complex knowledge of genealogies essential for determining the rank, privileges, and obligations of the chiefs.[3] Not only was Losaline of the highest descent, but she had learned the genealogies from the last Tamahā, 'Amelia Fakahiku-'o-'Uiha (d.1852). From Losaline and other high-ranking women Sālote learned the classification and uses of named fine-mats (*kie hingoa*) and other *koloa* in the treasure-house of the Tu'i Kanokupolu, the criteria that determined their distribution on ceremonial occasions, and the narrative associated with the most chiefly of the named fine-mats. This wealth of collectibles was visible proof of her own illustrious ancestry, for many of the named fine-mats had come from Sāmoa via Tu'i Tonga women to the Tu'i

Kanokupolu at the time of their marriages. The narrative explained not only the origin of each piece, but the prestigious occasions when each had passed from one chiefly line to another.

While Sālote claimed that "rank is everything", and Tupou I believed that land was everything, food was an obsession with people whose isolation from the world and vulnerability to natural disasters meant unpredictable alternations between abundance and scarcity. Food was a form of wealth, a political tool, and played an important part in ritual. When Sālote said that she was "naturally good" at dividing food, she meant that she understood the principles that determined the entitlement of each of the chiefs and their *kāinga* to a share of food (and *koloa*) after a ceremonial presentation. Personal rank was changed only by the births and deaths of the higher ranking, but rank within the *kāinga* varied according to the occasion, and bitter quarrels could ensue if the chiefs felt their share of food or *koloa* was an inadequate acknowledgement of their *kāinga* ranking.

In addition to traditional knowledge, an appearance of being cosmopolitan was an indication of status. Like Tupou II, Sālote was interested in *papālangi* fashions, and her contemporaries, the pretty young Halaevalu (great-granddaughter of the last Tu'i Tonga – Figure 3.4) and other girls of chiefly rank, would come, wearing fashionable Western-style clothes (even gloves!), for afternoon tea and to discuss the clothes they had seen in their fashion books or worn by passengers on the monthly steamer, which would then be copied by local dressmakers.

Sālote said that she had left Tonga a child and returned as a woman, but there were still personal lessons for Sālote to learn during these years of her adolescence. A letter of 6 December 1913 written during a visit home suggests that at that time Sālote was fond of Queen Takipō, but continuous residence at the Palace after her return (and probably mischievous gossip) led Sālote to dislike someone who was presented to her as Queen Lavinia's rival. Sālote claimed that the King and Takipō were not well suited to each other, and consequently she made Takipō's life "a torment".[4] She would never be reconciled to her father's second marriage, nor to the fact that she now shared her father's love with his second family. Part of Sālote's dislike must have arisen from the insistence of Takipō's family upon treating Princess Fusipala as the only truly royal princess and Sālote as irrelevant. Sālote would not concede that Takipō outranked Queen Lavinia (or that Fusipala outranked herself), recollecting that although Takipō's female line was high, Takipō's father (Tēvita Ula Afuha'amango) was merely a *matāpule*, not much better than a commoner. Much later, Sālote would make scathing comments about the women of that family (Figure 1.6), saying that they had bad blood, in the same way as (she said) there were character faults in many of the female descendants of the Tu'i Tonga.[5]

In spite of her "shameful" Niuafoʻou connection, Sālote was a descendant of the Tuʻi Tonga Laufilitonga and also of the Tamahā Lātūfuipeka and the heir to the title of Tuʻi Kanokupolu, so her marriage was of great interest to the chiefs. Sālote turned 16, and the King still made no announcement. A year later, when she was 17, various chiefs and local dignitaries asked the Acting British Agent & Consul, G. B. Smith-Rewse, if he would use his influence to bring about the marriage of Sālote to Tungī Mailefihi.[6] Strictly speaking, the Agent & Consul had no right to intervene in purely internal matters, and the request itself was unusual, suggesting a deep concern on the part of the petitioners that delay would allow a recurrence of the disturbances that marked the King's marriage to Queen Lavinia. Smith-Rewse was soon aware that there was more to the request than uneasiness, and that something underhand was being planned in connection with the princess's delayed marriage.[7]

A short time would elapse before Smith-Rewse understood that the chiefs of the "Reactionary Party" (as Sālote would later call them) were planning a *coup*. The first indications were expressed as concern for the King's health. On 4 May 1917 Premier Tuʻivakanō (Polutele) asked Smith-Rewse, as a matter of form, to approve a trip to Australia at very short notice for the King to seek medical treatment. When Smith-Rewse returned to the Consulate after the meeting with the cabinet and an audience with the King, he found "authentic and reliable information" awaiting him, which showed the very short notice was only for him and the King, and not for the Premier and his friends.

"There is something peculiar in the very anxious desire on the part of two or three to get His Majesty so hurriedly away," wrote Rev. Jabez Bunting Watkin, longtime President of the Free Church.[8] Smith-Rewse was still not sure what the "something peculiar" was, but he reported to his superiors in Fiji, "there is no doubt some political idea at the back of it". Soon the Agent & Consul was convinced that Tuʻivakanō, Scott, and the Chief Medical Officer (Dr Cowan) had conspired to frighten the King into going abroad at the shortest possible notice. When the King informed Smith-Rewse that he intended to appoint ʻUlukālala as Regent in his absence, the aims of the conspirators became clearer.

Haste and the proposed appointment of ʻUlukālala as Regent were crucial elements of the intrigue. Haste would prevent the King from announcing his choice of a consort for Sālote prior to his departure, and this power would devolve by tradition and the Constitution to the Regent.[9] As Regent, ʻUlukālala could betroth Sālote to his son, Haʻamea. The obedience Haʻamea owed to his father would ensure that ʻUlukālala would in effect be Regent for life. The plan depended upon the King dying overseas before Sālote reached her eighteenth birthday; that is, within the next nine months, as seemed very likely. It was a truly desperate plan, but the stakes for the "Reactionary Party" were exceedingly high.

Alternative explanations have been given for these events. One was that when the King died overseas, Tu'ivakanō planned to have himself installed as President of the Republic of Tonga.[10] The other explanation was that upon the King's death, 'Ulukālala would announce the betrothal of Ha'amea to Princess Fusipala (then five years old), then persuade Tungī to marry Domenika (with whom Tungī was reputed to be in love), thus isolating Sālote so no one would accept her as Queen.[11] This would clear the way for 'Ulukālala to continue as Regent for Fusipala. The flaw in this third explanation was that although Tungī had been dilatory in pressing the King to settle the matter of the marriage, he was unlikely to be so easily excluded from consideration. What is certain is that 'Ulukālala sought to become Regent before any of the other chiefs could prevent it, and to remain Regent for as long as he could.

Smith-Rewse was convinced that troubles would ensue if he did not take immediate action. His first duty was to inquire into the practicality of the King going overseas. Dr Cowan had diagnosed the King's illness as tuberculosis, but agreed that a month's delay would not seriously affect the King's health! (This suggests that Cowan believed the King would soon die, and that no treatment could benefit him.) The King himself caused a minor (but not insuperable) problem by insisting that the Queen and both princesses should accompany him. Smith-Rewse easily persuaded the Master of the *Talune* not to take the royal party on board until there was suitable accommodation for an infectious passenger and until their landing permits for Australia were in order.

Smith-Rewse then informed the King (as was Smith-Rewse's right under the Supplementary Agreement) that he would not consent to the appointment of 'Ulukālala as Regent. Without the powers of a Regent, 'Ulukālala would have no say in Princess Sālote's marriage. The conspiracy began to fall apart. It seemed that Sālote would not marry Ha'amea. 'Ulukālala salvaged what he could from the situation by (later) claiming that the King had promised his younger daughter, Princess Fusipala, would marry Ha'amea when she reached marriageable age.

Tungī, alerted by his friends to events in the capital, left Vava'u by the June steamer and confronted the King with his superior claim to Sālote's hand. Considering his personal rank, his connections, and his place in the line of succession, Tungī's claim could not be denied. Perhaps the King was angered at the discovery that his health had not, after all, been the primary concern of his advisers, for while Tungī was still on his way to Nuku'alofa, the King began the preparations for the wedding of his elder daughter.[12]

The marriage alliance of a royal princess to a chief of exceedingly high rank had to be marked by very special ceremonies. Not only was the quantity of food and *koloa* important, its quality, the variety, the rarity of a significant number of items, as well as general suitability had to be ensured. In short, the rank of the participants had to be demonstrated in the traditional way: with quality and abundance. Three months was scarcely long enough for the food to be grown and harvested, pigs and other animals fattened, flowers gathered for the making of perfumed oil, and for the chiefs to assemble *koloa*, both old and new, in the form of fine-mats, bark cloth, perfumed oil, rare basketry, combs, wooden pillows, and other traditional items that the two extended families would present to each other at the *tu'uvala*.

These three months were also needed for preparations for the Western-style wedding, for many items were purchased from New Zealand and Australia. The King's Private Secretary, Sione Filipe Tongilava, ordered a wedding cake from Buchanan's in Auckland.[13] The cake would be eight feet high, weigh 500 pounds, and cost £65. Buchanan's decorated it with Tonga's coat of arms, the motto *Koe 'Otua mo Toga* [sic] *ko hoku tofi'a* (God and Tonga are my inheritance), and added the initials SMP (Sālote Mafile'o Pilolevu) and WT (William Tungī) on the sides. The cake was dispatched from Auckland on 18 August complete with instructions for its reassembly in Tonga. New plates and cutlery were also ordered for the breakfast, and a local liquor licence obtained. The King borrowed £450 to pay for the reception.[14]

Sālote's wedding clothes came from Australia. "A tall, handsome girl" (Collocott), she appeared in bridal white on 19 September, the day of her Western-style wedding, which was two days after the *fakalēlea* (the guarding of the bride by the bridegroom's relatives, originally designed to prevent the bride running away). The wedding dress was white crêpe-de-chine, trimmed with pearls, worn with a long court train brocaded with silk lined with pink ninon, "richly worked with an appropriate and chaste design", and a veil hand-made in Sydney, and so on.[15] The bridesmaids were seven young women of rank.[16] The bridegroom wore well-cut trousers (with the required "droop" onto the shoes), a shirt with a bat-wing collar, and a frock coat. The Royal Chapel was decorated much as in 1899, with the addition of a huge floral bell: when a ribbon was pulled, confetti fell from the bell over the bridal couple. After the ceremony, a reception was held on the lawn in front of the Palace (Fangatapu or Sacred Foreshore). Formal photographs show the young, rounded face of the 17-year-old bride and the handsome seriousness of her 29-year-old groom. In the fashion of the time, he stands beside his wife, so the difference between her superior height (now more than 180 centimetres) and his average height is not noticeable.

The Tongan ceremony took place on 21 September. Sālote wore two of the Tu'i Tonga named fine-mats: the *Kie Vela* and possibly *Lālanga-'a-'Ulukilu-petea*.[17] Gifford recorded the dances that were performed, including a *kailao* ('Uvean dance), *mā'ulu'ulu* (Sāmoan dance), *tau fakaniua* (Niuatoputapu dance), and *meke* (Fijian dance). Chiefs had ordered their people to prepare *lakalaka* (Tongan dances), many especially choreographed for the occasion. The songs accompanying the several *lakalaka* extolled the advantages of the marriage alliance.[18] It was an extremely grand occasion.

There are several extant photographs of the Western-style wedding, but only one of Sālote leaving the Palace for the *tu'uvala*. Tungī Mailefihi doubtless was equally splendidly dressed in historic *kie hingoa* of his line. Although not as tall as Sālote, Tungī was a handsome man, solidly built, and the couple must have looked very splendid (if rather portly) in layer upon layer of fine-mats.

Two persons who are inferior in *kāinga* ranking to the bride and groom are chosen to have special roles (*fa'ēhuki*) at a chiefly Tongan wedding ceremony, and the bride and groom each symbolically "sit" on their laps while the *kava* is served. In the old days a defeated rival would have left Tonga before the marriage (and Ha'amea was reported to have gone to New Zealand), but 'Ulukālala remained to be best man at the Western-style ceremony and the *fa'ēhuki* for Tungī at the *tu'uvala*. It was said that the Ha'a Ngata (Tu'i Kanokupolu) people laughed when Tungī Mailefihi reached over his shoulder and dropped the ash of his cigar into 'Ulukālala's lap, a clear demonstration of his superiority by all the ranking systems[19] (Figure 3.3) – and perhaps a gesture of triumph because of the prize now won. 'Ulukālala could add this insult to the long list (beginning with the usurpation of his "kingdom" of Vava'u in 1833) that would contribute much to the political troubles of the next two decades.

The brief description of the Tongan wedding ceremony by Islay McOwan, who arrived in Tonga in August 1917 to take over as Agent & Consul from Smith-Rewse, gives only a small idea of the elaborate rituals of the *tu'uvala*, but shows his full awareness of the political significance of the alliance.

> The three following days [after the Western-style wedding] were devoted to native ceremonies, including the presentation and exchange of property between the royal house and the family of the Tugis [*sic*], native dances and feasting, all of which excited the greatest interest and enthusiasm. The kava ceremony at which the bride and bridegroom seated on the laps of their respective foster parents on a huge pile of mats and native cloth drank a bowl of kava together was an interesting feature, while the presentation and distribution of some hundreds of roasted pigs, large quantities of native cloth and numerous mats was an unusual sight, even in the Pacific, owing to the scale on which the presentations were made . . .
>
> From a political point of view the marriage is not without significance as the bride and bridegroom are both prospective heirs to the throne of Tonga, the former failing male issue and the latter failing direct male or female issue of the present King. The connection of these two families eliminates therefore the possibility of any controversy arising on the death of the present King as to the succession.[20]

This marriage did indeed end one ancient dynastic contest, but revived others. By marrying a Tongatapu chief of the especially hated Eastern District,

Sālote alienated the "Reactionary Party", many of whom were descendants of warriors who had fought beside her ancestor Tupou I. Many of the Ha'apai chiefs with whom she had become familiar during visits to the King's Ha'apai estates during her childhood now turned against her. The Vava'u chiefs rallied behind 'Ulukālala.

Sālote would have alienated some chiefs whoever she married, and remaining unmarried was an unthinkable option. The King's choice proved to be a wise one, for Tungī would give Sālote strong support. He was experienced in government, devoted to the *fonua* (land-and-people), and had the support of the Tongatapu chiefs. In time it became clear that his personal qualities complemented Sālote's own considerable attributes.

Tungī Mailefihi's whole life had prepared him to be a leader of Tonga. He was born Uiliami Tupoulahi on 1 November 1887 at Fatai, the house of his father, Tuku'aho, which lay a short distance from the Palace along the Beach Road in the Kolofo'ou section of Nuku'alofa (Figure 1.2). Even as an infant he was reputed to have extraordinary physical strength, which would stand him in good stead in adult life. His mother was the exceedingly high-ranking Mele Siu'ilikutapu, daughter of Sūnia Mafile'o, one of the great chiefs of Kolomotu'a (Figure 1.9). Uiliami's complex genealogy was a matter for comment from his childhood, as Queen Sālote related when recalling the origin of his nickname, Mailefihi.

> One day Losaline Fatafehi went to the home of [Old] Tungi and his wife 'Esetia . . . When Losa arrived, 'Esetia was not yet ready, and Tungi was sitting in his room. He called Losa to come to his room so they could talk about Fiji [presumably she had recently visited Fiji]. After talking for a while, the little son of Siu and Tuku'aho came in. His name was Viliami Tuku'aho. As the boy played around (he was about four), Losa said, "This boy has all the chiefly lineages tangled in him like myrtle [*mailefihi*]." Tungi was silent for a while before saying, "Losa, you are right about my grandchild, and those words appeal to me, so he will be called Mailefihi."[21] [MT]

As a child, Mailefihi became accustomed to command. His personal *matāpule*, Helu, carried the young Mailefihi around in his arms or on his back, even when Mailefihi was six or seven years of age, for such was the custom with high-born children.[22] In 1896, when Mailefihi was eight years old, Tupou II arranged for him and some other young chiefs, including Solomone Ula (heir to the Ata title), Molitoni Fisi'ihoi Fīnau, Saula Funaki, and Tonga Lātū to attend Newington College, Sydney.[23] Mailefihi was recalled to Tonga after the death of his father, Tuku'aho, in 1897. He then lived at his grandfather's house, called Latai (not to be confused with Fatai), in the Kolofo'ou section of Nuku'alofa. Old Tungī belonged to the Free Church, but after he died in 1900, his young widow, 'Esetia, sent Mailefihi to the Catholic school, 'Api Fo'ou, at Ma'ufanga, where the teachers were French priests. His mother's brothers, who were Old Wesleyans, then came and took him to Tupou College, the Wesleyan school where his father and uncles had been pupils.[24] At that time Tupou College was in Kolomotu'a, near the homes of his mother's *kāinga* (chapter 1).

Mailefihi was thereafter under the influence of his mother and her brothers, 'Alipate Mafile'o and Sione Lamipeti, and her half-brothers, Maealiuaki and Tu'itavake (Figure 1.9). Lamipeti, Maealiuaki, and Tu'itavake had been among the Old Wesleyans exiled by Tupou I in 1887–90 because of their refusal to join the King's Free Church. These uncles were determined that Mailefihi would be a loyal Old Wesleyan, hence his removal to Tupou College. After Mailefihi graduated in 1905, he became a tutor at the College. He had a nice bass voice and was fond of singing ballads, including duets with his lifelong friend Ata, at concerts at the Tupou College hall. From the time of the death of his grandfather Old Tungī in 1900, Mailefihi was the first male in the royal line of succession to the Tu'i Kanokupolu title, so the *papālangi* traders referred to him as "the Crown Prince".[25]

Mailefihi could not be installed in the Tungī title until he was 21 years of age. In the meantime he received nothing from his estates, these being administered by Sione Tovi, an illegitimate son of his grandfather.[26] As trustee, Tovi was the recipient of all the presentations and beneficiary of the *fatongia* of the people who lived on the Tungī estates. There was some feeling among the people about the heir being an Old Wesleyan, but when Mailefihi was installed as Tungī in 1909, he gave the highest priority to leadership of his people.[27] His passion was the land, his own estates in particular, and he put his considerable energies into looking after the people, the animals, and the produce of the land. He was intelligent and energetic in the things that interested him. One of his admirers (Sione Havea) described him thus:

> He is not like Pakava [in legend], who leaves the burden to the people while he puts his feet up and does not raise a finger . . .
>
> He distributed his land to the people to a greater extent than is required by the law; for it is clear that he who has much land is more prosperous than he whose land is poor. Some have opposed his giving of larger portions (15 acres) to those who will work the land. This is typical of him, for he will always do what he believes is right. He is zealous in working and farming . . .[28] [SAH]

In 1911 Tungī Mailefihi represented Tonga at the coronation of George V, being only the third Tongan to visit England. Mele Siu'ilikutapu wept inconsolably at his departure, believing she would never see her son again. "It was almost like saying farewell at the graveside," he said, for the risks of travel at any time were great, and he would be exposed to diseases common in England to which Polynesians had little resistance. It was typical of Tungī Mailefihi that he took advantage of the opportunity to make a tour of Britain after the coronation. A story told of a visit to a factory shows his extraordinary physical strength, for he took an iron rod from a workman and bent it easily with his bare hands. Basil Thomson wrote to Tupou II: "You would have rejoiced to see how profitably Tugi [*sic*] spent his time in studying the customs and industries of this country with a view to being of service to his country when the time comes. He made astonishing progress in learning English, which he now speaks very well indeed."[29]

Tungī returned to Tonga from England in 1912 in time to witness Mateialona's forced resignation from the premiership (chapter 2) and the funeral of the King's father, Tu'ipelehake, at which Mele Siu'ilikutapu was *fahu*.[30] Prior to his travels, Tungī had a minor government appointment, and some chiefs expected he would be appointed Premier to succeed Mateialona, but the King had already appointed Tu'ivakanō. When the King proposed appointing 'Ulukālala as Governor of Vava'u (although he had twice been dismissed from that office) in place of the impeached S. T. Faletau, Islay McOwan, who had just taken up his appointment as Acting Agent & Consul, would not give his consent, and instead advised Tupou II to appoint Tungī. McOwan reported to his superiors:

> Tugi is the person who, in my opinion, would be the most suitable successor to Mateialona [as Premier] . . . He is, however, wanting in experience. He is a young man of about 25 years of age, intelligent and active in mind and body and is a general favourite amongst both Europeans and natives but I fear that, unless his energies are directed into some useful channels, he may, by reason of his undoubted influence, become a disturbing factor in local politics. I may mention that before the opening of Parliament at its recent sessions, it came to my hearing that Tugi intended to propose a vote of no confidence in the Ministry as a whole. I therefore sent for him and quietly discussed with him the proposal. After pointing out to him that the laws and constitution of Tonga did not allow for such procedure and warning him of the trouble that might ensue, he agreed to abandon his proposal, and at the same time thanked me for my advice.[31]

Although his mother's mother was from Vava'u (Figure 3.3), and her family would give him good support, Tungī must have had some regret about leaving his own estates in Tongatapu in 1912 to take up his appointment as Governor of Vava'u. However, he would gain valuable experience in administration and be removed from politics of the central government while his rivals were ascendant. Bishop Blanc, who visited Tungī in Vava'u in 1912, commented that Tungī was a very agreeable person, but rather bored with his duties as Governor.[32] Tungī's abilities and energies required a larger arena.

The King could not ignore Tungī as a candidate for Sālote's hand in marriage. On 12 January 1914, while Sālote was still at school in Auckland, Tungī wrote to the King to thank him for a photograph of the princess. On 23 June 1916 (soon after Sālote's sixteenth birthday) Tu'ivakanō wrote confidentially to Tungī, saying that Takipō was unlikely to have more children, and the King had not yet determined when Princess Sālote would marry.[33] The letter was less friendly than it at first appears, for Tu'ivakanō did not want Tungī in Nuku'alofa, especially not as Sālote's consort. In March 1917 Tu'ivakanō attempted to undermine Tungī's political support by accusing him and his friends Ata and Fisi'ihoi of plotting against the government.[34] The plan of the "Reactionary Party" (already related) to prevent Sālote marrying Tungī followed soon after this accusation.

In her late-life reminiscences, Sālote said that she would have married anyone her father chose for her, but she was fortunate in that she loved her husband. There is no doubt that she loved Tungī passionately throughout their marriage, up to and beyond his death. On his side it was a political marriage to a young cousin, but his affection for her was nevertheless strong and enduring. He was already experienced in public life, and would teach Sālote many things she needed to know as ruler of Tonga.

While his enemies hated Tungī, his supporters, including Sālote, would hear no ill of him. The *kāinga* of Kolomotu'a through whom Sālote and Tungī were related (Figure 1.9) lived at the Palace door, and they would give the royal couple practical support. Members of persecuted minorities learn the value of constancy, and Tungī was loyal not only to his church, but to all with whom he formed alliances. Although he was suspected of factional preferences, he would put Sālote's interests and those of the kingdom before other concerns. Although Sālote was lower in *kāinga* ranking (she was descended from brothers of Tungī's female ancestors – Figure 3.3),[35] her gender and title ensured Tungī was fully aware of his duty to Sālote as an "elder sister" and as the Tu'i Kanokupolu. He would have no ambition separate from hers.

Collocott, who knew Tungī at this time, described him as "of rather short medium height, but powerfully built . . . He was a wise man of steady judgment, and no prince ever thought and laboured with more sincerity and affection to bring forth things for the happiness of the people."[36]

Two months after the wedding Tungī returned to Vava'u, leaving Sālote, already pregnant, with his family in Nuku'alofa; but she spent much of her time with her ailing father. The King had now been ill for many months and unable to undertake royal duties such as the Opening of Parliament. Towards the end of 1917 McOwan agreed that 'Ulukālala should represent the King in Privy Council.[37] After one failed attempt to see the King, Dr Lynch, the Chief Medical Officer of Fiji (sent by the High Commissioner for the Western Pacific), arrived in December 1917 on the warship *Fantome* to examine him, and confirmed Dr Cowan's diagnosis of tuberculosis.[38] The King had by now lost all interest in going abroad.

Everyone knew Tupou II was dying, but Tongan custom prohibited this being stated publicly. In spite of her pregnancy, during the long, humid summer of 1917/18, Sālote travelled from Nuku'alofa to visit her dearly loved father where he sought cooling breezes at his house at I (Fan) on the south-eastern side of the island. To get there, she had to travel by carriage to Ma'ufanga, then by boat across the lagoon to Mu'a, then by carriage to I.[39] This was a tiring journey, and Tungī's gentle affection and concern for his young wife during her ordeal is shown in a letter he wrote to her in February 1918 from Vava'u.

> I am glad you are there to look after the sick man [the King]. Even though you cannot do much for him, the important thing is the comfort you give him. I am very sorry that I cannot help him, but I am reassured that you are there. I hope the doctor from Fiji will be able to make a correct diagnosis and then we shall know what to do. Let us hope that he will soon be well, for it is a worry his being in that state . . .
>
> There may not be another boat before your birthday. May the Lord be kind to you and give you a blessing, and that day will come many times until you have achieved your purpose in life.[40] [TF]

Tungī's letter ended by asking her to make sure that his orders relating to his estates had been carried out. His requests suggest a confidence in his young wife that was promising in the early days of their relationship.

As the King's death steadily approached – the presage was that a spring of water in 'Uiha, Ha'apai, turned red – the young princess appeared too preoccupied with her grief to have any thought that the outcome of that death would be her own assumption of the royal titles of Tu'i Kanokupolu and Queen. With Tungī as her consort and her own strength of character, there would be no faltering when the day arrived.

CHAPTER FOUR

The First Year of a Reign

"The Queen is very young and inexperienced and is incapable, in my judgment, of discharging the duties devolving upon her . . ." (Islay McOwan, 1918)[1]

BEFORE HER ACCESSION, Sālote understood that being Queen would involve "hard work, heartbreak, as well as great honour",[2] but she began her reign, she said, knowing nothing of the duties of kingship. She would learn a great deal about political reality and about the requirements of leadership, particularly about responsibilities for the welfare of others, during a difficult – often traumatic – first year. After an uncertain start, Sālote began to show the personal qualities that would bring her renown. The rest came with experience.

At the end of the summer of 1917/18 Tupou II had returned from I to the Palace, and he died there early in the morning of 5 April 1918. Consul McOwan reported that the immediate cause of death was heart failure, although he had been diagnosed as having tuberculosis (chapter 3). The King was 43 years of age and had just completed a reign of 25 years.

Princess Sālote had her eighteenth birthday on 13 March 1918, only three weeks before the King's death, so by the terms of the Constitution she could succeed her father without the need for an intervening Regent. (If there had been need for a Regent, McOwan would undoubtedly have arranged for the appointment of Tungī.) In the event it was McOwan who arranged for a brief meeting of the Privy Council at 2 p.m. on the day of the King's death to confirm that Sālote was her father's successor and to discuss the funeral arrangements. The Privy Council met again at 10 a.m. on 6 April, so Sālote could take her oath of office and her ministers swear allegiance to her. Her succession was proclaimed at the Mala'e Pangai on the same day. On 8 and 9 April the nobles and chiefs from Ha'apai and Vava'u (including Tungī) arrived and swore allegiance to Sālote as Queen and Tu'i Kanokupolu.[3]

The King's death at the Palace made it unusable until water was sprinkled in all the rooms on 1 May to remove the *tapu*. Between 5 April and 1 May, therefore, the young Queen slept in the Royal Chapel in the Palace grounds, returning to Tungī's house (Fatai: Figure 1.2) to eat and bathe. From the time she became Queen, the only Tongan person she could eat meals with was Tungī, and after his death she always ate alone, as befitted the most elevated person in the kingdom.[4]

Nevertheless contradictions often occur on Tongan ceremonial occasions. Sālote was inferior (*liongi*) at her father's funeral because all children are ranked lower than their father. A *liongi* wears a very large, ragged mat, the size depending on the closeness of the relationship to the deceased (some mats being the full height of the person), and the hair of the *liongi* women is either worn untied and dishevelled or cut short. Sālote may have worn a *liongi* mat, but her hair was not cut.[5] In contrast with this lowly status, she was a person of consequence as the new Tu'i Kanokupolu, receiving all the presentations due to the Tu'i Kanokupolu, even those from the aristocrats, who were descended from the Tu'i Tonga.[6]

Even at this early stage of her reign, and even in the midst of genuine grief, Sālote took the opportunity – as she so frequently did in the years to come – to demonstrate the *mana* of the Tu'i Kanokupolu through ritual. In contrast to the funeral ceremonies of Tupou I, which had lasted only one month, and those of her grandfather Tu'ipelehake, which had lasted five months, Sālote decreed a six-month period of mourning, thus exceeding the customary 100 days of mourning formerly observed for the Tu'i Tonga. The ceremonies of Tupou II's funeral were the most elaborate ever witnessed by the participants, not just on the day of the burial, but during the whole period of mourning.[7]

Like the royal weddings already described, the funeral ceremonies for Tupou II were a mixture of foreign and traditional rites. The flag flew at half-mast, the Palace was draped in materials of purple and black, and the King lay in state in the throne room. Many of the population dressed in black garments and relatives in appropriate categories wore *liongi* mats. The Ha'a Tufunga (royal undertakers) occupied the Palace grounds, and because they could not touch food, male relatives also took up residence in order to feed them, adding 300 people to the normal number of inhabitants. The making of bark cloth, dancing, and singing (other than hymns), even the weeding of gardens, were prohibited. During all of the nights between the King's death and his burial, torches tended by small groups from different parts of Tonga burned around the Palace walls in the ceremony of *takipō*.

On the morning of 10 April the coffin containing the King's body was brought from the throne room in the Palace and placed on a massive catafalque (*kauala* or *fata*), five metres high and four metres square, constructed especially for the occasion, and draped in black with purple and white ribbons. The platform of the catafalque was covered with mats. After the coffin was placed on the platform, it was draped with a Tongan flag, and the crown placed on the flag. Poles extended from the platform so that hundreds of men (260 in rotation, according to one report) could carry the whole structure to Mala'e Kula, a kilometre distant, while a brass band played Handel's "Dead March" from *Saul* (rehearsed near the Palace prior to the King's death!). The royal family and other relations walked behind the band, Queen Sālote and Queen Takipō being "heavily veiled". Students from Tupou II's old school, Government College, lined the route and saluted the coffin as it was carried past. Behind the students were seated the remainder of the mourners, said to number 3000 of the King's 22,000 erstwhile subjects. After a burial service conducted by the royal chaplain, Rev. J. B. Watkin, the King was interred in a grave beside that of his great predecessor (Tupou I), his first wife (Queen Lavinia), his father (Tu'ipelehake), and his daughter (Princess 'Onelua).

The coronation would not take place until the six months of mourning were over, but Sālote immediately took over the functions of the sovereign ("I didn't know the first thing about government. Old Tongilava used to tell me what to do"[8]). In the early days of her reign Sālote was uncertain whom she should listen to: the Consul, her ministers, her Secretary, or her consort. Tungī's role in the new regime was neither obvious nor planned, and a few days after her father's death (possibly before Tungī came from Vava'u), Sālote told McOwan that she wished Tungī to be crowned King when she was crowned Queen. On 12 April McOwan wrote to the High Commissioner for the Western Pacific:

> I have . . . had an audience with the Queen at which Her Majesty intimated that she desired to share the responsibilities and the privileges of her high office with her husband and that with the consent of the Legislative Assembly and the approval of His Britannic Majesty's Government she desired that they should be crowned King and Queen of Tonga . . .
>
> The Queen is very young and inexperienced and is incapable, in my judgment, of discharging the duties devolving upon her and some difficulty may be experienced from Her Majesty's inability to distinguish between good and bad advice where the interests of the Kingdom are concerned.[9]

With the formal recommendation McOwan added the suggestion that Tungī should act as the Executive of government, rather than Sālote. The High Commissioner forwarded the Queen's request to London. The Secretary of State for Colonies gave his consent, but by an accident of wartime the consent of the Colonial Office did not reach Tonga until after Sālote's coronation – alone – on 11 October.[10] In the interval McOwan began to revise his opinion of Sālote. After several meetings with the Queen and Tungī during April and May he reported to the High Commissioner: "The consultations which I have had with Her Majesty and Uiliami Tungi have been marked by the good feeling and the good sense of both."[11]

The Premier, Tu'ivakanō, began six months' overseas leave on 12 April, and was not informed of a Privy Council meeting held on that day, although he was still in the country. So Tungī was present and Tu'ivakanō absent when the Chief Justice proposed that Tungī be appointed Acting Premier during Tu'ivakanō's leave. The Queen consented, failing to inform the Privy Council that the Consul had already approved the appointment of Ata. There was clearly some manoeuvring within the Privy Council, and at an audience on 17 April McOwan reminded the Queen that according to the Constitution only she could make senior appointments, but by the terms of the Supplementary Agreement of 1905 she was obliged to consult him (and only him) before doing so: she was not required to consult the Privy Council. McOwan then gave his willing consent to the appointment of Tungī as Acting Premier for the six months of Tu'ivakanō's leave, thus ensuring his place in government while waiting for the Colonial Office's response to the suggestion of a double coronation.[12]

Among the problems inherited by the Queen were the King's debts, some going back as far as her own schooldays in Auckland. In April 1918, by the first steamer to leave the country after her accession, Sālote wrote to the King's creditors telling them that it would take a little while for the late King's finances to be sorted out, but assuring them that they would be paid. For these debts and other expenses connected with the royal funeral, the Queen borrowed from the government £1000 repayable at £50 a month in addition to the loan she would repay at £25 a month for renovations to the Palace, which had fallen into disrepair in the King's last years. There would be another loan from the government of £1000 on 14 October.[13] As economy measures, the two-storey palace the King had built at Lifuka, Ha'apai, was sold to the trading company Burns Philp, and the royal barge was allowed to rot on the beach.

In spite of good intentions, the Queen did not find finances easy. She knew exactly what fine-mats and other *koloa* she had stored in Pālesi (the house "Paris" in the Palace grounds), but not what was in her safe. Early in her reign, Sione Filipe Tongilava, the Private Secretary whom she had inherited from her father, kept Sālote's personal accounts, but so many demands were made upon her purse by chiefs and her relations that it was soon arranged that Tungī would look after her salary.[14] This did not free her from debt. In 1921 she borrowed £600 from the Free Church, to be repaid at a rate of £50 a month, and borrowed again from the government in 1922 to pay for a holiday in New

Zealand.[15] Unlike her father, she would soon see the advantages of avoiding debt, and she generally lived within her means. What her means were is not clear, for in addition to her salary from the government of £2000 a year, there were rents and income from copra from the royal estates.

An extravagant gesture in 1918 was her decision to build an elaborate and costly memorial to her father. Parliament of that year voted £500 towards the memorial, and in the early years of her reign the Queen travelled throughout the kingdom to hold meetings (*fono*) and ask for the money required. The memorial would cost many thousands of pounds before it was unveiled in December 1924, but its symbolic value was that it stood beside the memorial to Tupou I.[16] Important to Sālote personally was that it matched the memorial the King had built for Queen Lavinia.

Sālote and Tungī returned to the renovated Palace just before the birth of their eldest son, Prince Siaosi (George) Tāufa'āhau Tupoulahi, on 4 July. Six days later, on 10 July, Tungī and the nobles Ata and Ma'afu represented the Queen at the Opening of the first Parliament of her reign. Since the country was in mourning and Premier Tu'ivakanō was overseas, the parliamentary session was a quiet one. The period of mourning ended with presentations at the Palace on 4–7 October and the washing of special black stones (*kaukau* or *lanu kilikili*) at the graveside on 8 October, followed by the placing of the stones on the grave (*hifo kilikili*).[17]

On the following day, 9 October, Sālote was installed in the title of Tu'i Kanokupolu during a royal *taumafa kava* on the Mala'e Pangai. Tongilava recorded that she wore a pair of fine-mats (one being *Lālanga-'a-'Ulukilupetea*) and a large, fine, soft mat, whitish in colour, which is folded so that it fans out when released (*fihu palavalu*).[18] The occasion was described by an unknown correspondent of a shortlived local newspaper, the *Recorder*:

> The day broke fine, and long before the time appointed for the ceremony the people assembled in great numbers and seated themselves, as is the Tongan custom, in orderly fashion under the shade of the *toa* trees . . . which marked the boundaries of the *malae* [Mala'e Pangai]. Near to the Palace walls there had been erected a structure some twenty feet square and about twelve feet high, and this was most effectively decorated with tropical palm growth and festooned with long lines of *sisi*, or garlands, made up of ribbon-like material from the bark of the *fau* [hibiscus] tree and interwoven with flowers . . . Under this canopy of greenery was a raised dais covered with fine mats, and upon it was placed the Royal Chair . . .
>
> As the hour of ten struck there emerged from the Palace a dark-faced but most picturesque personage, bearing aloft two long spears to which were attached several streamers of coloured material. He moved forward in a light prancing manner from side to side of the avenue of Norfolk pines which fronts

the Palace, and at times he would halt a moment and cautiously glance from right to left; he would then make a sudden lunge forward with the spears as if seeking out a foe hidden by the wayside; thence on again, to repeat the action a few moments later. His pace was rapid but quiet. A pleasing accompaniment to his progress along the avenue was the soft rustle of the spear-streamers as they fluttered gaily in the breeze, and the musical tinkle of many small nut-shells attached to his waist and ankles . . . His duties were evidently those of a herald announcing the approach of an important personage, for being content, apparently, that all ahead was well, he returned to meet the Royal Party which by this time had come from within the Palace.

The Queen, who was in full native costume, came forward in a dignified manner, and in close order following was a party of about 100 female attendants who carried at its full length a fine mat over sixty feet long. Preceded by the herald, the Royal Party made its way up the centre of the ground and approached the canopy of greenery, where seated on either side of the dais were the high chiefs of Tonga. In extended order they formed a big half-circle, and sat in their appointed places facing the open space in front of the canopy. And so they quietly awaited the approach of their young Queen.

Her Majesty having seated herself on the dais, the attendants fell in behind and spread the long mat in a fan-shaped manner at the back of the Royal Chair.

For a few minutes there was a stillness over all, but presently was heard a chanting of many voices, and a large party of mat-clad natives appeared at the entrance to the ground. In four sections, and chanting the while, they came slowly towards where the Queen sat in state. Close by stood the herald in statue-like fashion, and so he remained until the whole party had paid their respects and had retired.

Then came a party with an offering in the form of a large root of *kava*. This, together with other gifts of food, was placed on the ground not many yards from the canopy.

Meanwhile the body of singers had retired and become seated in the centre of the ground, and preparations were made for the making of *kava* – the beverage peculiar to Polynesia and without which no native ceremony is complete . . .

The command having gone forth to prepare the *kava*, there was much activity on the part of the persons selected for this important work . . .

There was a great deal of formality in the matter of the distribution of the *kava*, and much time was taken up in this direction, but after the ceremony had been fully observed, attention was given to the food offering. The herald, who up till this time had been a silent observer of these proceedings, now became a prominent figure, and with uplifted spear and with streamers flying he warily approached the line of foodstuffs and selecting a certain dainty morsel – a well-cooked young sucking pig – he made a good aim and let fly the spear which hit truly the intended mark, the pig's liver. Springing forward he gently lifted on

> the point of the spear the offering of the day and presented it to the Queen. From thence the food was distributed amongst the high chiefs.[19]
>
> Way was now made for the orators, and they came and delivered themselves of speeches, the keynote of which was their acknowledgment of the right of Tu'i Salote to rule over the Tongan people, and they expressed their loyalty to their ruler. Other addresses appropriate to the occasion were also delivered, and the proceedings terminated with the retirement of the Queen to the Palace.[20]

The missionary and anthropologist E. E. V. Collocott added explanatory notes to the above description, also a diagram of the seating in the circle, showing that not all the "high chiefs" were present (see Figure 4.1).[21] Ata and Ve'ehala, both high chiefs of the Ha'a Ngata (the Tu'i Kanokupolu's own *ha'a* (clan group)) and therefore essential performers in the installation, were the orators mentioned, and they instructed the new Tu'i Kanokupolu in her duties. The "dark-faced but most picturesque personage" was someone with Fiji connections; that is, he was a "stranger", not a Tongan. The singers were part of the procession dragging the *kava* root into the circle, and Collocott recorded the words they sang. Many people brought the water to make the *kava*, thus demonstrating the numbers of people the Tu'i Kanokupolu could command. The fibre strainers of *fau* used in the making of the *kava* were named for the *ha'a* of Tonga who were represented. On either side of the Tu'i Kanokupolu sat Motu'apuaka and Lauaki, two of her *matāpule*. Motu'apuaka directed the distribution of the *kava* (Lauaki having directed the distribution at Tupou II's funeral). A series of speeches urged the chiefs and people to support the Queen and to attend to food production. The Queen could not have summed up the kingdom's needs better if she had given the speeches herself.

There were some notable absences from the *taumafa kava* of the new Tu'i Kanokupolu. Sioeli Pangia, grandson of last Tu'i Tonga, was absent, although he attended the European-style coronation two days later. 'Ulukālala was assigned a place, but did not attend, and his *kava* was poured on the ground. Compared with later circles over which Queen Sālote would preside, the 1918 circle was quite small, suggesting that the primary allegiance of many chiefs still lay elsewhere. The most important task ahead of Sālote was the difficult one of persuading the chiefs that their first loyalty was to her as Tu'i Kanokupolu.

Tupou I had been installed as Tu'i Kanokupolu on 4 December 1845 while sitting with his back to a *koka* tree in the village of Kolovai. Part of that *koka* tree was incorporated into the throne on which Sālote sat in the Royal Chapel when crowned on 11 October by the Rev. J. B. Watkin, assisted by the Rev. Edwin Harkness, both ministers of the Free Church. The *Recorder* once again gave a full report of the event, including a detailed description of Sālote's gown of "rich ivory satin" decorated with seed pearls, and her royal cloak of cardinal velvet trimmed with a three-inch-wide ermine border, a cloak that would become familiar to watchers of the royal Opening and Closing of Parliament in the 1920s and 1930s. Harkness presented her with the Bible she holds in her coronation photograph.

On Sunday, 13 October, the three-months-old Prince Tāufa'āhau was baptised in the Royal Chapel by Watkin and Harkness. Presentations made at the beginning of the month had marked the end of the mourning period for the King. Then there were presentations to mark Sālote's installation as Tu'i Kanokupolu and coronation as Queen. The celebrations on Monday 14 October were to acknowledge that there was an heir.[22]

These events in the first six months of the Queen's reign had proceeded in proper order: no one challenged the daughter of Queen Lavinia.

November brought the worst crisis of her reign: the "Spanish" influenza, which was part of a worldwide epidemic that had spread throughout the Western world in the last months of World War One. The high death toll in Tonga (estimates vary but the figure of 2000 individuals or 8 per cent of the population was given at the time) was the outcome of a failure at foreign ports and by Tonga to enforce quarantine regulations on the steamer *Talune*.[23] This ship belonged to the Union Steam Ship Company, and it arrived in Nuku'alofa on its regular monthly voyage on 12 November 1918 from New Zealand via Fiji and Western Sāmoa (the death toll in the last would be approximately 25 per cent of the population). The *Talune* had stopped briefly at Neiafu (Vava'u), then Lifuka (Ha'apai), before Nuku'alofa (Tongatapu). The first cases of influenza occurred within a few days. As the disease spread from the three centres, travel ceased, and the 30 or so inhabited islands of Tonga were isolated from each other. On some of the islands, the loss of life was so severe that few were left to relate the course of the disease or record the incidence of death. The Palace in Nuku'alofa, which normally resembled a bustling village, was suddenly deserted as people returned to their homes either to look after their families or because they were too ill to do otherwise.

The Chief Medical Officer had gone to Fiji to get supplies, and the medical officer of Vava'u was the only doctor in the kingdom. On 25 November the Queen's yacht *'Onelua* sailed to Fiji to request help, but no help was forthcoming for several months, for the medical resources in Fiji were already overstretched by influenza in its own population.

In her late-life reminiscences, the Queen stated that mutual loyalty should exist between chief and people; but the Queen failed in this first serious test of her leadership. Her government broke down and took no action whatsoever to ameliorate the effects of the epidemic, either locally or nationally. Tongans looked after their own families as best they could, and on Tongatapu it was left to McOwan, missionaries of different denominations, and other *papālangi* to organize food supplies, to do whatever nursing was possible, and to bury the dead. As the number of dead mounted, the church bells in Nuku'alofa ceased to toll, and an extraordinary quiet fell over the town, as indeed it must have fallen over every village in the kingdom. The deaths were particularly high among young adults, for these arose too soon from their sickbeds to tend the children and elderly, and thus developed pneumonia, which was the ultimate cause of death.

Collocott, now living at Tupou College near the Nuku'alofa cemetery called Telekava (Figure 1.2), described his experiences:

> . . . the head Tongan dispenser in Nukualofa fell ill, and the hospital, with its stock of medicines, was closed. The disease spread everywhere. The people, accustomed to go several times a week to their gardens [farm allotments], lay sick and without food in their homes. Soon the sick were the dead and dying. A party of sailors from a British barque anchored in Nukualofa dug graves, and then a long trench for common burial. One or two Tongan ministers stayed in the cemetery to pray over the bodies brought in quick succession for burial. The dear familiar movement of everyday life was stilled. On a hot windless day I looked out on a stretch of white road shimmering in the midday sun, where men and women were wont to come and go, and children to play; but now no living thing stirred. Presently a cart, bearing a long bundle wrapped in native cloth, came into view at one end, moved slowly along and out of sight, towards the cemetery.
>
> Coo Baker, who was living in Lifuka [Ha'apai] with her two sisters, happened to be in Nukualofa. Day by day, and far into the night, she strove, almost past human strength, to win the sick back to life. Well-nigh overcome by weariness and sickness she discovered that occasional doses of steel drops [*sic*] gave her fresh energy and checked the disease, or at least seconded her own indomitable spirit in its determination not to yield . . . As she walked along the dark and empty roads swarms of hungry dogs, whom no one was able to care for, crowded after her . . .
>
> Rodger Page [Chairman of the Wesleyan Mission], although neither he nor his wife and child escaped the disease, lent me much aid, dispensed medicines to hundreds of people who came to him, and then, sick himself, he put his life in pawn and with horse and sulky, drove about the villages, distributing medicine, inspiring hope and courage. A young German, Carl Riechelmann, sick himself, rode daily to the help of others, till he fell from his bicycle and was taken home to die. A Tongan man, ill and haggard, came to the mission house for medicine. Rodger Page told him he should be home in bed, and the man, crying, "But it's for my child," fell unconscious on the verandah.
>
> In a Tongan home relief visitors found a tiny mite of a girl, who seemed no more than four or five years of age, nursing grandparents, parents, brothers and sisters . . .

> After some days of almost hopeless struggle the progress of the disease was stayed by concerted efforts led by the British Consul, Islay McOwen [*sic*]. Those who were well were organised to help the sick. The Englishman, Alfred Cowley, a lover of books whom nature intended to be a writer and teacher of economics, but whom destiny had made into a planter who ran bakery and butchering businesses, slew beasts and brewed cauldrons of soup. The hospital was opened . . . [24]

That was just Tongatapu. How much worse must it have been where there were no *papālangi* helpers at hand! Sālote had her own recollection of the epidemic, and of the isolation of the Palace. Forty years later, Elizabeth Bott Spillius recorded the Queen's account.

> Everything came to a standstill. There was no social life – people crept into their houses to die. Some died because they were too weak to get food. The Consul . . . organized a soup kitchen and handed out food to the people who were strong enough to come for it. A ship called, and the Consul got the crew to clean out the houses and make graves. People were buried like dogs – no ceremonies, just bundled into the graves. The sailors dug communal graves . . .
>
> In the Palace, where there were usually so many people, everything was very quiet. All the matapules and the women had crept home to be sick in their own houses. The only ones who stayed were old Va'eno, Tungi's matapule, and Fakafuli. Fakafuli was a lunatic who had been hanging round the Palace . . . By some miracle he didn't get the flu, and he was the only one who could go about the town and get food.
>
> Her Majesty was upstairs with Tungi and Taufa [the prince, just four months old]. Tungi was very ill. For three days he was unconscious, lying very still with his face very red, and all smooth and shiny. Her Majesty was ill too, but had no fever. If she tried to walk her knees bumped into each other, but she could feed Taufa and wash him and herself. Taufa wasn't sick at all, and fortunately he was very good and spent most of the time sleeping.
>
> Fakafuli never seemed to sleep. During the night he went the rounds of Kolomotu'a and Kolofo'ou [the western and eastern sections of Nuku'alofa], and in the morning Her Majesty would be wakened by a shout from below. "Kuini! So and so is dead in Kolomotu'a! So and so is dead in Kolofo'ou! Fifty have died in Ma'ufanga!" She would come to with a shudder and set about the day's work of feeding and bathing the baby and herself.
>
> For days and days on end they had chicken soup, which old Va'eno and Fakafuli made in the kitchen. There was only one hen with three chickens in the palace at the time, and each day when Her Majesty looked out she would see them running about the grounds. "Fakafuli, how is it we are having chicken soup all the time?" "It's those three chickens we have." So the neighbours were missing many chickens, but most of them were too sick to mind . . .

> After Tungi had been lying unconscious for three days, Ku Baker came. She was a nurse, and really she was the only medical person around . . . But Ku was doing her best – just what one would expect of her somehow, in spite of all her determination to use the family silver when there was nothing to eat with it. She washed Tungi down with cold water, and after that he began to sweat. The Queen took his clothes off and went on bathing him. She couldn't lift him because he was so heavy, so she rolled him from side to side, mopping as she went. The next day he came to, and said "What am I doing with no clothes on?" . . .
>
> Slowly people began to recover. The first meeting of the church everyone looked at each other, hunting for the faces of their relatives, wondering who was still alive . . .
>
> Tupoumoheofo died. She went out in a sulky with Vilai, and by the time they got to their destination she was desperately sick and died the next day. Tuita came to the Queen and asked if she had anything that Tupoumoheofo could be buried in . . . Years later when they moved Tupoumoheofo's body to Mu'a to bury her properly, they found a bit of the white material still clinging to the bones, and a bit of *fala paongo* [pandanus mat] too.[25]

The effects of the epidemic were felt for at least a generation, for not only had all families suffered grievous losses, but there was constant fear of a recurrence. Four of the 32 nobles died, also three Catholic priests, the Governor of Ha'apai (Maeakafa), and Mrs Watkin.[26] Tupou Moheofo (referred to in the extract above) died on 24 November, her son Vīlai Tupou being Sālote's half-brother.

Queen Takipō, aged 25, also died, on 26 November. She had been living with Princess Fusipala at Finefekai on Tāufa'āhau Road (the main road of Nuku'alofa) since the death of the King. Takipō was buried at Mala'e 'Aloa, the chiefly burial ground in Kolomotu'a, not in Mala'e Kula, the royal burial ground where the King and Princess 'Onelua (and Queen Lavinia) were buried. Tupou Moheofo was reburied at Mu'a (as befitted her rank) some years after the epidemic, but Queen Takipō remained at Mala'e 'Aloa. Queen Sālote explained that Takipō had returned to her own family after the death of Tupou II, so it was the responsibility of her birth family to attend to her burial. While this was in accordance with Tongan custom, one wonders whether Sālote had determined to exclude Takipō from Mala'e Kula so Queen Lavinia would be the only acknowledged progenitor of royal offspring of her generation.

McOwan described the course of the epidemic, with feeling, in his report to the High Commissioner for the Western Pacific, and added:

> The most discouraging feature of the outbreak was the apathy and indifference of the native chiefs to the suffering and distress of their people and I regret to

say that the Premier [Tu'ivakanō] was no exception. On the day that the relief work was started he was out driving in his motor car quite recovered. I appealed to him for assistance in obtaining labour for the work of burying the dead but the same afternoon he sent a message to me that he was unable to obtain any men. From that time until conditions had considerably improved I neither saw nor heard of him again until I called at his house and urged him to bestir himself and to call upon the other nobles to lend a helping hand to the people.

When conditions were at their worst, not a single Tongan was procurable for the most urgent work. [But] I saw two strong able-bodied men depositing roasted pigs which they had brought in from one of the country villages, in front of the Palace.

Such incidents cause one to revise one's estimates of the Tongan character and show them incapable of strong feeling and unfitted for the high responsibilities of self-government.[27]

For Tongans, Islay McOwan was an example of Christianity and British colonial officialdom at their very best. His practical assistance for people who were not his relations was a matter for comment at every social *kava* circle. The ministers of the Wesleyan Mission expressed their appreciation for his efforts by recording: "In our trouble and stress your devotion was our comfort and help. But we Tongans are not surprised at your goodness, for it is truly said that a father loves his son, and Tonga is the child of Britain, indebted to her for Christianity, Knowledge, and Civilisation . . ."[28]

McOwan did not mention Queen Sālote and Tungī in his first report, but he responded critically when they showed themselves unmindful of the suffering of the people by proposing, early in December, to go on a royal progress through villages of Tongatapu where the epidemic was still raging. McOwan advised the Queen and Tungī that more deaths would follow, for the chiefs would command sick villagers to prepare presentations on a scale appropriate for the visit of great chiefs. There was a note of strong reprimand in McOwan's letter advising the Queen and Tungī to abandon the proposed progress, and suggesting that the Queen should summon the Privy Council to determine what measures could be taken for relief work on a larger scale than was possible by the few dozen who had hitherto carried the burden. Up until that time, McOwan said, the relief workers had been "persons outside the government service, while some members of the government remain inert and volunteer no assistance whatsoever".[29]

Sālote took the reproach to heart, and was never again so neglectful of the welfare of her subjects. In 1919 she wholeheartedly supported the establishment of the Department of Health, free medical attention for all, and the appointment of the much-loved and devoted Chief Medical Officer, Dr C. M. Dawson. She would support the establishment in 1929 of the Central Medical

School in Suva, where Tongans and other Pacific Islanders would receive basic medical training.[30] And she would have a continuing interest in public health, in the training of nurses, and particularly in the health of mothers and babies.

The immediate, and politically important, outcome of the 1918 epidemic was the sealing of a close and sympathetic collaboration between Queen Sālote, Tungī, and McOwan. The Queen and her consort were impressed by the personal and practical assistance McOwan had given to Tongans during the epidemic: here was a striking model of leadership, one in which a chief cared for his people.

In learning these responsibilities the Queen was enormously helped not only by the experience and advice of McOwan, but also the support of Tungī. It would not be an easy road, and the "good feeling and good sense" of both Sālote and Tungī would be sorely tested. Even though the kingdom was small in area, of one race, and almost of one language, there were conflicting interests to consider and complex issues to take into account. The young Queen also had domestic matters to attend to, although the domestic issues were so intertwined with the politics and business of the realm that they could not be considered separately.

Looking back over her life, Sālote commented that leadership involved not only marriage to the right person, "but hard work had a lot to do with it, and strong character, also kindness".[31] Sālote never wavered from the belief that her high position was hers by right; but, unlike her father, she very soon came to believe that chiefly privilege could be maintained only through the exercise of political power, and that a strong central government was essential to the promotion of the interests of her dynasty. She would learn to take a broad view, not to confuse the personal with the political, and not to be deterred by setbacks. Once her goals were firmly in place, she did not waver from her goals: to secure her own future and that of her dynasty.

CHAPTER FIVE

At Home at the Palace

". . . hard work had a lot to do with it, and strong character, also kindness"
(Queen Sālote, 1959)[1]

QUEEN SĀLOTE AIMED TO make of the Tongan nation one *kāinga*, but in the early years of her reign she had to pay attention to her immediate family. At 2.15 a.m. on 4 July 1918 Prince Siaosi (George) Tāufa'āhau Tupoulahi, the eldest of her sons, was born, weighing 11 pounds. The Queen suffered painful tears during the birth, and she believed that they were the origin of later health problems.[2] Two more princes would be born to Sālote and Tungī: Prince Uiliami (William) Tuku'aho, born on 5 November 1919, and Prince Sione (John) Ngū Manumataongo, born on 7 January 1922.

When Tāufa'āhau was born, Sālote was still grief-stricken at the death of her father, and she found motherhood difficult to combine with her other new duties. Except when the Palace was deserted during the influenza epidemic, there were women to help look after the baby, but she missed Rachel Tonga, who went to Ha'apai with Sela and Mateialona in December 1918 when Mateialona replaced the Governor of Ha'apai who had died during the epidemic.

At that same time Sālote suddenly found herself responsible for two of her father's children who had been orphaned by the influenza epidemic. Her half-sister, the six-year-old Princess Fusipala, had lost father and mother in the same year (Figure 5.1). Sālote longed for a daughter, and her affectionate nature made her want to mother the child whose guardian she now became, but

Fusipala's mother's people undermined her intentions. In Tongan custom, the father's family disciplines the child, and the mother's family nurtures her, but Queen Takipō's family claimed exclusive rights over the child.

Since the Queen could not bring up Fusipala without interference from the mother's people, Sālote sent her half-sister, as she had been sent when young and motherless, to the household of Mateialona, in Ha'apai, where the young princess would be looked after lovingly by Sela and Rachel Tonga. Fusipala's mother's people followed her to Ha'apai, and complained that by giving Fusipala little household tasks to do Rachel was treating her as a servant. In 1920, again with her own experience as a precedent, the Queen sent the young princess alone to Auckland, to live with a *papālangi* family until she had learned enough English to attend the Diocesan School for Girls.

Like Fusipala, Sālote's half-brother Vīlai Tupou had lost father (Tupou II) and mother (Tupou Moheofo) in the same year (Figure 5.1). Vīlai was related to Sālote through both his parents, for they shared a father and Tupou Moheofo was the aunt who had accompanied the young Lavinia on her fateful visit to the Palace in 1899, and was thus a great-aunt of Sālote. Tupou Moheofo was a daughter of Old Lavinia, who had the rank of "eldest" daughter of the last Tu'i Tonga. Vīlai was thus of exceedingly high rank through his mother and was the only chief Sālote admitted to have personal rank comparable with that of Tungī. But Vīlai was not a noble, did not even possess a title, and thus had no lands or people to support him. As head of the family Sālote was bound to provide for him, but it was Tungī who arranged for him to marry, on 18 March 1919, Tupou Seini, the elder of the two daughters of Vaea, noble of Houma.[3] Vīlai was about 20 years of age at the time of his marriage.

Although Tupou Seini was rather older than Vīlai (she had been considered as a possible bride for the King before he married Takipō) the marriage pleased both families. Vīlai's exceedingly high personal rank added lustre to the Vaea title, and Vaea's people would provide for him and his children. And since Vaea had no sons, the title and estates would be the inheritance of the eldest son of Vīlai and Tupou Seini. The marriage satisfied the Palace because the comparatively low rank of Tupou Seini's maternal line meant that Vīlai and Tupou Seini's children would not outrank the royal children. Vīlai was always very loyal to the Queen, and Sālote rewarded this loyalty by being a benevolent *mehekitanga* to Vīlai's eight children, sending mats and bark cloth at the time of their births and to the all-important first birthdays.[4]

Vīlai and Tupou Seini took up residence at Kaitangi, the town allotment opposite the Mala'e Kula, where 'Ofa-ki-Vava'u had lived her last days (Figure 1.2). Vīlai's marriage ensured a supply of food from Vaea's estates, but Vīlai looked to the Queen for an income. On 28 April 1919 Vīlai wrote to reproach her for forgetting to pay his taxes, which resulted in him having to pay a fine, ending the letter with the words "my love to you and your blessed face".[5] This letter suggests an unexpected familiarity, for the sister is *tapu* to the brother, and both should practise sister–brother avoidance, but there was nothing unusual in a sister providing for a brother. Sālote may have been further well-disposed to her brother because he was, according to McOwan, "quiet and well-behaved".[6] Sālote arranged training with the Fiji police in Suva, and after his return in 1924 made him one of her Royal Guards as well as her Aide-de-Camp. In 1926 she appointed him to the prestigious post of captain of her Royal Guards. His appointments guaranteed constant, easy access to the Palace, and during the remainder of his life he would play the traditional role of a supportive brother who respects his sister in all things.

Vīlai appears in personality to have resembled his grandfather, Tu'ipelehake, who had carried his high rank with ease. Vīlai was generally popular because he was sociable with men regardless of their rank, but his easygoing manner annoyed arrogant chiefs, such as 'Ulukālala, who thought Vīlai should stand on his dignity.[7]

At one time (certainly before 1927) the people of Pelehake (a village in the Eastern District of Tongatapu) came to the Queen and asked her to appoint Vīlai as the new Tu'ipelehake, for the title had been vacant since the death of Sālote and Vīlai's grandfather in 1912. This would have been an appropriate appointment, for Vīlai qualified by being the grandson of the previous holder and also by very high personal rank. If the Queen had acceded to the request of the Pelehake people, Vīlai would have gained an independence and a following that she would have deemed inappropriate in spite of her brother's loyalty to her. Vīlai did not need a title, she may have argued, because his son was already heir to the Vaea title, and at this time the Queen did not envisage that two noble titles could be held by one person. In any case, she promised the people, she had someone else of high rank in mind as the future Tu'ipelehake. This was her youngest son, who would be appointed Tu'ipelehake in 1945.

Sālote, Fusipala, and Vīlai had two more acknowledged half-brothers. One was Edward Cakobau, born to Tupou II and Adi Litia Cakobau in 1908 (Figures 5.1 and 5.2). Adi Cakobau's father was a Fijian chief of rank, and her mother was part-Tongan, of the Veikune family, so Edward was a distant cousin to Sālote on her mother's side as well as half-brother through their father. When Sālote passed through Fiji on her way to New Zealand or Australia, she visited Adi Cakobau, but she may not have known Edward personally (because of brother–sister avoidance) until he visited Tonga for the first time in 1934.

Another brother, Vuna, did not receive the honours accorded to Vīlai and Edward, because his mother's personal rank was considerably lower than that of the mothers of his half-siblings. Sālote would have overlooked his lack of rank if he had shown ability and been willing to fulfil the traditional role of brother by supporting her. Vuna lived an ordinary life and married a woman of inferior rank, so his children were not chiefs.

Sālote said that in the difficult first year of her reign she was helped by her Private Secretary, Sione Filipe Tongilava. He had been her father's Secretary, and was treated as a distant relation, particularly as Tupou Seini's mother had been from the Tongilava family. Tongilava lived in the short road that led from the Palace to Kaitangi and the Mala'e Kula, and every weekday morning he walked up to his office in a room at the back of the Palace, overlooking the large back garden. He was an active member of the Free Church, and became a stalwart of the Free Wesleyan Church after the reunion of 1924. He dealt with the Queen's correspondence, including requests for a royal audience from the Agent & Consul or officers from visiting Royal Navy ships, kept accounts, and lists of presentations brought to the Palace.

Papālangi visitors with appointments entered by the main gate and by the front door. The only *papālangi* who had informal access to the Palace were the royal chaplain and a member of the Riechelmann family, Mrs Lilla Bagnall, who acted as a social secretary as well as a friend to the Queen and helped with preparations on those rare occasions when the Queen entertained in European style, checking the wording of the invitations and making sure that the table had been correctly set by Tongan servants. Just as the Tu'i Tonga had foreigners to attend him because his person was *tapu* to Tongans, Mrs Bagnall could measure the Queen for clothes to be ordered from Auckland or Sydney, and would be excused breaches of protocol, such as standing in the Queen's presence.

There was no privacy to speak of at the Palace. Peering over the edge of the windowsill of his office, Tongilava noted the comings and goings of the Tongans, who entered the grounds through one of the two sets of gates behind the Palace, which were protected by the Royal Guards. He recorded the fact of celebrations, and the numbers and kinds of presentations made to the Queen, but to the disappointment of historians and anthropologists did not record which dances were performed on which occasion. Nor did Tongilava describe what the dancers wore, for the costume particular to each village for each dance was familiar to everyone. All dances for public performance were brought first to the Palace, so the Queen could approve not only the quality of the performance but the position of dancers that signified their status in their village. Later in her reign, a group from each school would come and dance for her in the afternoons at the end of the school year.

Tongilava also noted whether the root of *kava* that always formed part of presentations was prepared for drinking by pounding and infusion of the roots with water or whether the root was simply left. It was an honour when the Queen drank *kava* with the presenters. More commonly, the root of *kava* was not prepared for drinking. Some of the Queen's *matāpule*, who were always present on the back verandah or in the *vangavanga* (the passageway between the Palace and kitchen), waiting to receive presentations and thank the people on the Queen's behalf, would prepare and drink social *kava* simply to while away the hours. *Kava* is a mild narcotic, but it was rarely drunk to excess.

There were constant presences in the royal household: the royal family itself, the Queen's and Tungī's *matāpules*, Tongilava, the Royal Guards on duty, the children sent to be companions to the princes, and the few servants paid for from the Queen's allowances. There were also frequent changes: relatives who came for short periods to serve the Queen and her children, people who came to cook in the kitchen or look after the garden, people summoned to the Palace to talk about church matters or to help with the logistics of the great celebrations that would absorb the Queen for months at a time. There was a constant stream of people bringing food to the Palace: raw food, which was prepared for the Queen and her family by the cooks, and cooked food, which was eaten by people who were staying at the Palace or living at Talakaepau, the royal compound across the road to the west. The remains of the food prepared for Sālote could not be eaten by others, because it was *tapu*. It was said that a foreigner who broke the *tapu* by smoking near where the Queen's food was being prepared collapsed and died soon after. *Papālangi* witnessing the huge quantities of food brought to the Palace rarely understood the dynamics of presentation and redistribution among the chiefs and people. In the acquisition and distribution of food and *koloa* the Queen visibly controlled the very means of life itself and proved herself to be a great chief.

Tongilava rarely recorded the ordinary comings and goings at the Palace. Chiefly women spent whole days at the Palace gossiping with each other or attending to indefinable duties. People of rank slept overnight either in the Palace itself or in one of the buildings in the Palace grounds or at Talakaepau – or Mapu-'a-fuiva (Watkin's house) after it reverted to the royal family (Figure 1.2). Lack of a bed was no problem, as the waist-mat (*ta'ovala*) was removed from the body and placed on the floor to make bedding, and a piece of bark cloth would serve as covering on a cool night. The Queen's cousin, Halaevalu (Figure 3.4), recalled staying at the Palace for several weeks at a time and sleeping in the Queen's room with others of the Queen's women.

Halaevalu related that the Queen liked old women to come and talk with her, to tell her "stories", for the Queen wanted to know everything that was happening or had happened in the kingdom. Pamela Bourne, who visited Tonga in the early years of the reign, commented that the Palace was full of the Queen's "destitute great-aunts".[8] Again there was a lack of understanding on the part of *papālangi*. These women were elderly relatives of the Queen, dependent upon her for food, and they could perform small tasks at the Palace without loss of dignity. In general, women of high rank did no physical work; they directed the making and care of fine-mats and bark cloth, ordered their brothers and their brothers' families about, and attended funerals. There were other relations at the Palace whom the Queen would put in their place by treating them as servants. They would say that they were proud to serve the Queen, because it demonstrated that they were "family". For example, Tiliti, an illegitimate half-brother of Queen Lavinia, was cook at the Palace for some years.[9] Being a servant of course ensured that one was fed.

The Queen did not personally organize the upkeep of the Palace, but those who had duties knew that she would notice anything left undone that should have been done, and who was responsible for work well done or for neglect. In 1917 Smith-Rewse had complained that the grounds of the Palace were in a "disgraceful condition", but in the Queen's reign the Palace was kept clean by groups of villagers who came periodically to clean up the Palace grounds or scrub the Palace.[10] Sione Havea commented in *Koe Havea* (1941): "Like Tungī, the Queen likes places to be kept clean and suitably furnished. She tells people to dress appropriately, and to act kindly and speak respectfully. To have a leader who lives in such harmony with the people is an education in itself"[SAH].

A Tongan approaching the Palace on horseback was expected to dismount from his horse and lead it until both were again some distance away. At the approach of the Queen's carriage (her car after 1922), Tongans immediately sat beside the road with heads bared and bowed until she had passed. In the presence of the Queen, people would sit without moving for hours in the sun or rain if that was required of them. All Tongans had access to the Palace grounds, and if the Queen agreed to see them (she would keep them waiting if she was displeased with them), they entered the Queen's presence on their knees, wearing a waist-mat appropriate for the occasion over their best clothes. Then they sat on the floor just inside the door, waiting for the Queen to speak. There was a certain tension in the fact that the Queen wished people to confide in her, but at the same time they sat at her feet and addressed her in the language formerly reserved for the divine person of the Tu'i Tonga. It was not unusual for people to embrace and kiss the Queen's feet.

The Tongan language rarely indicates gender, but it clearly indicates the relative rank of the person speaking and the person spoken to, no two persons being of equal rank.[11] Using the appropriate language for a superior indicates *faka'apa'apa* or respect. The three orders of language are: the royal language, language used for persons of superior rank, and language used for people of inferior rank. The royal language was used exclusively for the Queen and God. 'Ene 'Afio (Her Majesty) and Kuini (Queen) were reserved for Queen Sālote, as modern equivalents of ancient honorifics; and *Ta'ahine*, literally meaning "young woman", but used also as a term of respect.[12] The language used for the Queen indicated not only her paramount status, but also her qualities as a person. Her size (which was chiefly) was another indicator of her rank, and her movements were slow and dignified; thus she gave "shade" to her people.[13] In the Queen's presence, even a very high-ranking chief would refer to himself derogatively, as her "male slave" or "a miserable floating coconut shell", for example.[14]

The second order of language (superior or chiefly language) was used to refer to or in addressing Tungī, the royal princes, Princess Fusipala, and other aristocrats. Respect that was due to the Queen was also the entitlement (but to a lesser degree) of all the members of the royal family and persons of very high rank. The third order of language was used by and about commoners. A higher-ranking person would use the third order when referring to any lower-ranking person or might use the language of abuse; that is, certain expressions that were considered to be very insulting, as when Old Lavinia referred to Tupou II in terms usually used for animals (chapter 1).

Those who knew the Queen well (such as members of her own family and Rodger and Hannah Page) called her Sālote. This did not indicate unwonted familiarity, for the personal name of a chief (other than those known only by their titles) was special for that person, which accounts for the stories of the Queen renaming certain women who had been christened Sālote. Some of these stories are examples of the Queen's bad "temper", which she struggled to control. While the Queen renamed young girls Hina or some other innocuous name, an older woman was told to take the insulting name Mahae-ua-'i-Ha'apai, which means "Torn in Two at Ha'apai" (an example of abusive language, for it can mean to lose one's virginity). Another was renamed Luseni (Lucerne), horse's food, which is very insulting; and yet another man's name was changed to Afi Kakaha (Blazing Fire), which is somewhat shocking.

The Queen also gave new names to compliment individuals. The heir of the noble Sioeli Pangia had been christened Sēmisi (James), which the Queen considered too undignified for a noble titleholder. So when Sēmisi succeeded his uncle, she created the title Kalanivalu for him, Kalanivalu being the personal name of his grandfather. The Queen was often asked to give a name to a newborn, and she took trouble over these names, explaining the historical connections to the parents. The children of favoured *papālangi* (such as the children of missionaries) were given complimentary chiefly names. For example, Queen Sālote named Rodger and Hannah Page's son Siale – a flowering bush; and Harold and Olive Wood's eldest daughter, Janet, Ongo'alupe – Response of the Dove (of the Ark).

Tungī's driver and personal attendant was given the name Helu (Comb), recalling the *matāpule* Helu who had carried him about as a child. This second Helu was "adopted" by Tungī, and Tungī arranged his marriage to Nānisi Kavapalu from an Old Wesleyan family. Later in the Queen's reign, Nānisi became one of the Queen's female confidantes. Nānisi Helu and Hena Tāpuaka and other women were referred to as the Queen's "eyes and ears", and in the evenings the Queen often sent for them so they could tell her the gossip of the town. From them she often learned about problems before they became public knowledge and could decide whether intervention would be useful or not. In her later years Hena worked at the telephone exchange, and people were reluctant to exercise their right of free speech in case Hena was listening in and would relate their private concerns at the Palace.

The Queen said that in traditional times people were proud of a chief who treated them badly, because this was an indication of the chief's strength, but she herself took great pride in being loved and respected by her people because she treated them well, as family. The virtues that she ascribed to her mother, Queen Lavinia, of being a devout Christian, and of being loved by the people because of her concern for their welfare, were the very qualities that the Queen wished people to recognize in herself: this was the "kindness" she referred to as a necessary quality for a leader. It had nothing to do with softness or sentiment, neither of which qualities could be used to describe Sālote. Indeed, the respect chiefs and people had for the Queen was tinged with fear, for she could be a formidable person when the occasion required strength. But, although her anger could be quickly aroused, she was never vindictive, and was quick to forgive. She reproved people, especially if they failed to behave as was appropriate for their rank, either high or low. She would make excuses for high-ranking chiefs, but it was only in her later years that she learned to appreciate the abilities of commoners. For example, when Ata and Ve'ehala (Feleti Vī) were accused of crimes, she felt the punishment meted out by the courts was harsh, but she tolerated very harsh penalties meted out to commoners for noticeably trivial offences. People might be "equal in the sight of God", but not in the sight of the Queen – not in the early decades of her reign.

After the birth of Sione Ngū, the third of the royal princes, Sālote felt in need of a holiday, and went to New Zealand for several months. (She possibly also took the opportunity to seek legal advice on problems of the Free Church – see chapter 8.) When she had first left Tonga for Auckland in December 1909, as a princess with an uncertain future, Sālote had been accompanied only by Rachel Tonga. By contrast, when she left Tonga on 31 October 1922, having been Queen for four and a half years, she set out royally with the three princes, three chiefly women (Halaevalu, Simoa, and Tuna Vaea) as her companions, women to look after her and the children, the newly appointed noble Ve'ehala (Feleti Vī) to act as secretary, and 'Anaise Tongilava to place in school, a party possibly of about 12 people. Ten-year-old Princess Fusipala, now at school in Auckland, joined them for part of their holiday. Halaevalu recalled that although the visit was a private one, the Queen was invited to attend official functions, they were given free tickets to the cinema and opera, and the Queen was photographed wearing a very elegant gown with her hair done in the height of fashion. Very important to the Queen was that during a four-day stay at the Grand Hotel at Rotorua, high-born Māori came to see her, as they had come to visit Tupou II on an earlier visit, recognizing her as Polynesian royalty. The Governor of New Zealand, Lord Jellicoe, also came, and a photograph was taken at the marae of a group, with Queen Sālote dressed as a Māori chief.

The Queen had taken out a loan of £340 from the government to pay for this holiday (chapter 4), but after her return to Tonga there were letters about unpaid accounts for taxis, hospital and funeral expenses (for the eldest son of Veikune), and repairs to the house she and her entourage had occupied in Auckland. As the landlord pointed out, the understanding was that the house would be occupied by five or six people, but had been inhabited by up to 23 people, for those few Tongans who were resident in New Zealand took the opportunity to serve the Queen, which implied becoming part of the household. The Privy Council agreed that £450 should be advanced to the Queen to settle the accounts, and that she would repay the government at the rate of £66 13s. 4d. a month.[15] Although it was clear that her income was inadequate to maintain the Palace and all its inhabitants and to support her entourage whenever she left Nuku'alofa, her annual salary remained at £2000 per annum for many years. She would not be relieved of the expense of maintaining the Palace until 1927, and did not leave the country again until 1935. A Civil List was still several decades away.

An example of the expenses that the Queen might incur, but could not foresee, were the hospital and funeral expenses of Siosateki Vuna, son and heir of her kinsman, the noble Veikune (Fotu), who took ill and died while she was in Auckland. It was part of the duty of a high chief such as Sālote to pay expenses that occurred when she was near by, and certainly not to expect reimbursement.

After the Queen returned to Tonga from New Zealand, the family circle increased. In 1921 (in accordance with a promise made by her father in 1912) she had appointed Mateialona a noble with the new title, Tupouto'a. In 1923 she appointed him as Minister for Lands to succeed Tungī when Tungī became Premier.[16] Mateialona's wife, Sela, had died of cancer in 1921, and Rachel had continued to keep house for Tupouto'a in Ha'apai. Now she accompanied him to Nuku'alofa and they lived in a house the Queen provided at Talakaepau. Church matters were very stressful at that time, and the Queen had her third miscarriage on 6 April 1924. She would need the quiet space provided by Rachel. Tungī also would visit the two old people informally to take a cup of tea and talk.

Sālote sent her sons in turn to Rachel for early instruction and discipline, and Rachel recorded in her diary that on one occasion Tungī sent Prince Tāufa'āhau to her because "he beat dear little Johnny [Sione Ngū]". In her old age Rachel found teaching the young princes very demanding, and of the eldest she concluded, despairingly, that he "don't like to learn".[17] Rachel also made clothes for the little princes, including a velvet suit for Prince Tāufa'āhau on his sixth birthday, 4 July 1924.

Sālote and Tungī endeavoured to train the princes for their roles as future leaders, especially the eldest, on whom all their ambitions were concentrated.

The princes were expected to obey their father and to observe the *tapu* that surrounded his person and possessions. But Tongan children are never the property of their parents alone, and although Tungī was a strict disciplinarian, the princes learned that they were special in the eyes of others. Discipline by the parents was almost impossible when everyone else praised their most commonplace actions as being miraculous and brought them extravagant gifts.

It is said that when the Queen was angry, her voice could be heard on the other side of the road. One such occasion was on 1 December 1926, when Tongilava noted that "Queen beats Tāufa'āhau for being habitually disobedient". On another occasion Prince Tāufa'āhau emptied the contents of a precious bottle of lavender water on the garden. Halaevalu related that Sālote beat him so forcefully that his welts had to be bathed afterwards. Beatings were, of course, the usual way of disciplining children at that time, by *papālangi* and Tongans alike.

Halaevalu recalled that the young Tāufa'āhau never cried, unlike his brothers, Tuku'aho and Sione Ngū, who habitually cried for trivial reasons. Tuku'aho was more indulged than the other two princes, for he had rheumatic fever as a young child, and was frequently ill during his childhood. Because Tuku'aho was so much in her company, and in the absence of a daughter, the Queen entrusted to him the chiefly knowledge she had acquired when she was a young woman.

After some time with Rachel, the princes were sent to the Wesleyan "European School".[18] Dorothy Ferguson, who taught the two younger princes, records that they had a retinue, even at the school, eager to do their bidding, to give them gifts, and to endure their spoilt behaviour: "*19 July 1927*. I had to reprimand Prince John [Sione Ngū] . . . for punching another boy in the eye. Smacked his hand (far too softly) and stood him in corner. He did not worry about it."[19] Dorothy Ferguson also recorded the time when the eldest prince dressed himself in gardening clothes in order to supervise the schoolboys working in the school gardens, but did not work himself. So Prince Tāufa'āhau did not resemble his father, for Tungī was a prodigious worker who enjoyed labouring alongside his people.

On 5 July 1927, the day after his ninth birthday, Prince Tāufa'āhau was sent to Tupou College at Nafualu. He ate his meals with the family of the Principal, A. Harold Wood, in order to prepare him for the overseas schooling that had already been determined upon. He would then go to Toumui, the home of the head tutor, Sione Havea, for a generous helping of Tongan food. By now, the Crown Prince had decided that, after all, he *did* like to learn, and took his schooling seriously. Tuku'aho and Sione Ngū later joined him at Tupou College, but Tuku'aho continued to miss many of his classes because of illness. An example of the problem of disciplining the princes was that when people from the Western District saw Prince Sione Ngū doing his "punishment duty", they went to the Principal and offered to do the prince's punishment for him. The offer was declined, as agreed with the princes' royal parents.

Sālote could have chosen to remain within the Palace environment, simply receiving the material support and honour that had compensated Tupou II for his powerlessness. If Sālote had chosen such a life, the chiefs of the "Reactionary Party" would have continued to rule in her name over an essentially fractured kingdom. But early in her reign and partly due to the influence of Tungī, she decided that she would claim real power in her kingdom. And since she intended to unite her kingdom under her effective rule, she must leave the Palace from time to time and persuade the chiefs to acknowledge her leadership. But first she needed allies, and these were present in the form of her consort and his *kāinga* and also in her British advisers, who wanted, above all, that she be an ally and an effective "native ruler".

CHAPTER SIX

The British Connection

"The Friendship of Great Britain is Tonga's dearest possession."
(Queen Sālote, 1922)[1]

SOON AFTER HER ACCESSION to the throne Sālote willingly promised the British that she would observe the provisions of the Treaty of Friendship and the Supplementary Agreement.[2] She also promised that she would rule according to the Constitution and laws of Tonga, as a "constitutional monarch". Given the ambiguities of the Constitution and the contradictions between the Constitution and the laws, to say nothing of the conflict between the Constitution and the Supplementary Agreement, her promises lacked precision. But she had made a significant commitment to an alliance with the British, as well as to "law and order".

The Queen's promises were not a formality. She took them seriously, knowing that it was no small matter to reverse the policies of her father. Reversal not only suggested a lack of filial respect, but also invited the resentment of the "Reactionary Party", which attributed the reversal of royal policy to Tungī's influence, for he, like other Old Wesleyans, was pro-British. But although she undoubtedly listened to her consort's advice, there were other reasons for Sālote's choice. Firstly, she gained a favourable impression of Great Britain during her schooldays in Auckland. Secondly, she did not intend to be dominated by the "Reactionary Party" as her father had been in the last years of his life. It will be recalled that the chiefs who were now members of the "Reactionary Party" had been the supporters of 'Ofa and Takipō. The Queen had good reason to believe that they would show no loyalty to Queen Lavinia's daughter. Thirdly, the "Reactionary Party" was opposed to the strong, central government set up by Tupou I, but the British would support such a government. By ensuring strong, central government, she would ensure the survival of her own dynasty.

When the "Reactionary Party" made opposition to the Supplementary Agreement its rallying point, they were seeking to embarrass the Queen with a reminder of her deviation from the policy of her predecessor, for Tupou II had not only unwillingly signed the Supplementary Agreement to the Treaty of Friendship in 1905, but also resented it throughout his reign.

Queen Sālote countered suggestions that she was less patriotic than her opponents by always describing the British alliance as one of unmixed blessing for Tonga, claiming that far from compromising Tonga's independence, it protected her realm from appropriation by less desirable European and colonial powers. In so far as Tonga was "independent", it was by virtue of being a British-protected state, instead of being a protectorate, although both terms were used by the British at different times.[3] Both states had "native rulers", but, generally speaking, a protectorate was governed by a British administrator, while in a protected state the British representative was an adviser. In Tonga's case there was a fine line between the two, for reinterpretations of the Supplementary Agreement made the Agent & Consul at times look more like an administrator than an adviser.

Concurrently with these reinterpretations was a change in British policy. Unbeknownst to the Queen (but quickly understood by her), the 1920s saw the emergence of the dual mandate policy, which put an end to the coercive gunboat diplomacy practised in the time of Tupou I and Tupou II. The basic assumption of dual mandate was that the European power was preparing the subordinate partner for self-government. Thus reports on Tonga in the 1920s constantly evaluated Sālote's abilities as a ruler, and estimated how far the British could entrust areas of government to her. While annexation was discussed several times in the early years of her reign, it was not an option after 1924 (chapter 8). When this happy condition was reached, Sālote shrewdly did not confide in her nobles and chiefs that they no longer needed to fear being made a colony, for it suited her that they remain slightly anxious.

Sālote's understanding of the dual mandate policy, what the British required of her, and the likely rewards of the alliance was shown in a speech at the Opening of Parliament in 1925, when she said:

> If we are wise and work faithfully and well what can restrict our freedom or our increasing happiness? I speak freely and confidently, for the obvious desire of Great Britain in these days is to deal kindly with those countries over which she exercises protection if they continue to administer their affairs justly and well

and exercise wisdom in maintaining peace and increasing the national well-being. In such circumstances she will respect and protect their freedom.[4]

Appearances as well as comprehension were important. Queen Sālote and Tungī were *fakapapālangi* in that they spoke excellent English, wore *papālangi* clothes (even hats and shoes on special occasions), followed international news, and introduced conveniences to the Palace as they became available. But *papālangi* additions to their lifestyle did not affect their Tongan values, such as a sense of community, hierarchy, and mutual obligation. A mistaken assumption made by some *papālangi* was that Tongans wanted to embrace Western civilization in its totality, and that only imperfect understanding, lack of technique, and lack of education prevented the transformation of Tongan society into a mirror-image of contemporary British society. Like her compatriots, Sālote selected only what she wanted from the West, and embraced a mixture of Tongan and Christian values. She managed to persuade most of the more influential members of the *papālangi* community that this was the best way for Tonga, but it caused friction with those *papālangi* who could not – or would not – comprehend that Tonga was deliberately making its own choices.

One who did comprehend was the Agent & Consul. Since Tonga was one of the more remote and isolated territories of the British Empire, the skills and personality of the Agent & Consul were of utmost importance. Islay McOwan had been well trained as an officer of the Western Pacific High Commission. He was a large (therefore chiefly), slightly awkward-looking man, who had strong ideas of right and wrong, but did not (except at the time of the influenza epidemic) condemn those with other customs. Like the Queen, McOwan genuinely believed that British protection advantaged Tonga. He was clearly an intelligent and perceptive man, firm in his views, and once convinced that Sālote had real ability as a ruler and her goals were consistent with British interests he gave her wholehearted support. E. E. V. Collocott described him as an athletic man keen on sport. "His mind was keen and incisive, quickly grasping the essentials of problems presented to him. His temper was firm and patient, his interest in the welfare of Tongans and foreigners genuine and deep."[5]

Sālote came to believe that there were certain areas for which her British adviser should accept responsibility: the behaviour of *papālangi*, in particular, and the bureaucracy that had evolved since the Constitution of 1875 (and had less to do with governance than the traditional ways of influencing the people). The alliance between Sālote and McOwan was cemented by the fact that the British wanted precisely what Queen Sālote also most desired: first, peace and unity, and then the security of the Tupou dynasty as effective "native rulers".

Reinterpretations of the Supplementary Agreement in this friendlier climate effectively restored to the Agent & Consul powers lost over the debacle of the

Tonga Ma'a Tonga Kautaha (chapter 2). Soon after his arrival in 1917 McOwan noted that the government's estimates of revenue and expenditure had not been submitted to the Agent & Consul since 1911 and that recently expenditure had exceeded revenue. He suggested to his superiors that his powers should include advice on the finances of Tonga. This resulted in an agreement in 1918 between the British and Tongan governments that the Agent & Consul would approve the annual estimates of revenue and expenditure, and that any proposed extraordinary expenditure (special warrants) would also have to be approved by him.[6] This led to much greater financial stability for the kingdom, but it became a point of contention in Parliament, especially when a substantial surplus was built up but not expended in times of need (chapter 11).

Sālote had far less to fear from her British advisers than from the "Reactionary Party", and she did not conceal from the latter how much she valued the British alliance: in her speeches at the annual Opening of Parliament she always welcomed and thanked the Agent & Consul and made frequent references to the benefits to Tonga of his advice. McOwan was the guest of honour (second only to herself) at any function he attended. Among the important annual events were the speech nights of Tupou College and the Government College, and both the Queen and the Consul addressed the assembly, she in Tongan and he in English. Such dual appearances had a dual meaning: for while the Consul appeared as protector of the Queen, the Queen appeared as protector of Tonga against annexation by the British.

McOwan set a pattern for the future relationship between the Consul and the Queen in which courtesy and chivalry were required as well as sound advice. For example, where in 1921 the High Commissioner deemed "tact and firmness" were the most desirable qualities of an Acting Agent & Consul to Tonga, in 1933 the High Commissioner passed over more senior men in order to appoint an Acting Agent & Consul with "social qualifications".[7]

McOwan noted in the early days of Sālote's reign that many of the nobles and chiefs did not support the Queen; but he was able to assure his superiors that she was steadily winning them over to her cause. The more confidence the British had in her, the more the Tongan nobles and chiefs were impressed by her political skills, by her knowledge of *papālangi* ways, and by the ease with which she moved in two worlds. And as the Tongan élite was won over, the British were even more impressed with her abilities. And so on.

Winning the support of the chiefs proved to be a slower and more difficult process. In the interim McOwan saw that the Queen was at a disadvantage because of her inexperience and because the "Reactionary Party" was entrenched in Parliament and the bureaucracy. Palace supporters were in the minority, partly because graduates of the Wesleyan Tupou College (and the Catholic 'Api Fo'ou College) had been excluded from government by Tupou I, who reserved places for Government College "Old Boys". Although Tupou II had not enforced this exclusion – several well-known Old Wesleyans serving in his government – the privileges of the Government College "Old Boys" were jealously guarded, most notably by the removal of Old Wesleyans from government by the "Reactionary Party" in 1912 (chapter 2).

Three potential Palace supporters were removed in 1917–18. One was the noble Vaea (Siosaia Pau'uvale Loloa'atonga), future father-in-law of Vīlai Tupou, who had been forced to resign as Minister for Police in October 1917 after a drunken brawl with Premier Tu'ivakanō and Molitoni Fisi'ihoi Fīnau.[8] The second was Siosaia Sipu, father of Sālote's cousin and friend Halaevalu. Sipu was Minister for Lands, but was accused of accepting bribes for leases, suspended in July 1917, resigned in March 1918, and died in Sāmoa before the year was out.[9] The third was Ata (Solomone Ula), longtime friend of Tungī, who had been appointed Minister for Police in Vaea's place, and confessed to embezzling money from the Lord Kitchener Memorial Fund. In December 1918 McOwan prevailed upon the Queen to dismiss Ata, as required by the Constitution.[10]

At the time of the Queen's accession, there were two *papālangi* ministers: the Auditor-General, James Darrell Wall, who was appointed in 1915; and the Chief Justice, Herbert Cecil Stronge, selected by the Colonial Office in London and appointed by Tupou II in 1917. McOwan advised the Queen to appoint William Garfield Bagnall as Minister for Finance and Alexander Brooke Wallace as Minister for Public Works. Bagnall had come to Tonga as a salesman in 1904 and married a local girl, Lilla Riechelmann (chapter 5). He was employed by the government as a clerk in 1905 at the instigation of Sir Everard Im Thurn (chapter 2). Wallace had been Chief Surveyor and Director of Public Works since 1911. Bagnall and Wallace took their places in the Privy Council in January 1919. McOwan also advised the appointment of Tu'ivakanō's younger brother, Sioape Kaho, as Minister for Police, presumably to make the two *papālangi* appointments more palatable to the "Reactionary Party".[11] The strategy would signally fail.

McOwan's hopes that four *papālangi* ministers would strengthen the Queen's party and his own influence were also disappointed. Bagnall was loyal to the Queen because of his wife's connections, but issues soon arose that concerned the status and influence of these ministers *vis-à-vis* the Consul. As Privy Councillors, Stronge, Wallace, and Wall felt diminished when Queen Sālote listened to McOwan's advice rather than to theirs.[12] The willingness of the three to make common cause with the "Reactionary Party" made the Queen reluctant to trust them, as did their tendency to discuss Privy Council matters at the Nuku'alofa Club.[13]

Because of his powers over finance and senior appointments, and because he had the Queen's ear, many *papālangi* saw Islay McOwan as the true ruler of Tonga. He was referred to as a "philanthropic adviser" or a "silent dictator", according to the side of the fence the speaker was situated on.[14] During 1918 McOwan did indeed frequently attend meetings of Privy Council, of which the Queen was President, but he soon decided to appear only when specifically invited.[15] Sālote ignored the comments about the Palace's relationship with the Consul, and treated each piece of consular advice as though it were totally disinterested. In turn, McOwan not only praised the Queen in his official reports, and treated her with courtesy as a sovereign and sensitivity as an individual, he also increasingly took her part when she was challenged by the chiefs and their *papālangi* supporters. However, when McOwan suggested that the Queen appoint sufficient ministers to ensure a loyal majority in Privy Council and Parliament, Sālote did not accept this advice, an indication that she would follow her own judgement when this conflicted with the Consul's advice.

McOwan was disinclined to give any credence to *papālangi* critics, whose motives he believed to be ignoble, and suggested to his superiors that his own "shadowy powers" be strengthened in order to overcome the difficulties faced by the Queen from the ministers he had advised her to appoint. In a letter to the High Commissioner early in 1925, he said:

> It would be a comparatively easy matter to administer the affairs of the Protectorate [*sic*] with the plenary powers of an administrator but to guide and direct a native administration and to maintain an effective control of the finances with such shadowy powers as are given under the Treaty and Supplementary Agreement is a difficult and at times unsatisfactory task. It can be accomplished only by the co-operation and good will of both parties to the agreements and while I have experienced no difficulty in maintaining harmonious and cordial relations with the Queen and native members of the Government, curiously enough it has not always been an easy matter to maintain similar official relations with some of the European members of the Government. This is due, I think, to the fact that neither the Queen nor the native Premier [Tungī from 1923] exercise a controlling influence on the European members one or two of whom appear to resent the Agent and Consul taking any greater part in the administration than that of approving formally appointments made by the Cabinet and of expenditure proposed by the Government . . . the Queen and the Premier . . . are strongly of opinion that a controlling influence should be exercised by the Agent and Consul in the interests of Tongan and European alike.[16]

In spite of McOwan's plea, the High Commissioner was unwilling to increase the Agent & Consul's powers in order to ensure the good behaviour of the *papālangi* ministers. In another letter of 1925, McOwan described the advisory role the Agent & Consul *vis-à-vis* the government of Tonga. The letter is notable because it expresses McOwan's confidence in Sālote's good intentions.

> [T]he Agent and Consul's dealings are confined to those with the Queen and with the Premier [Tungī] as head of the Government. He [the Consul] does not interfere in any way with departmental administration, that is to say no executive or other orders are issued by him to Ministers or the Heads of Departments . . . No case has yet arisen during my term of office in which a real grievance was not adjusted upon the attention of the Government being drawn to it, either by the complainant himself or later by the Agent and Consul. The reason for this is that the Government is *wholly desirous of doing justice to all, Europeans and Tongans alike.*[17] [my italics]

The degree of *papālangi* influence in Tongan affairs was out of proportion to their numbers. The census of 1921 shows that there were 571 *papālangi* residents in Tonga: 37 were employees of the government, 30 of whom lived in Nuku'alofa; 126 were businessmen, 60 of whom lived in Nuku'alofa; and 18 were missionaries, 10 of whom lived in Nuku'alofa or near by.[18] Difficulties were caused when *papālangi* took whichever side served their own interests in a quarrel among Tongans. Generally speaking, in the 1920s and 1930s missionaries of all the churches (the Catholics with some reservations) and some traders supported Sālote and McOwan, because she represented peace and authority. Other traders and employees of the government (collectively known as "the Beach" because they lived near the wharves) allied themselves with the "Reactionary Party" with whom they shared commercial interests.

The Beach *papālangi* of Tonga did not resemble the happy beachcombers of paradise fiction. They were as difficult as the *papālangi* ministers to deal with because their discontent expressed itself in rumours and (according to McOwan) mischief-making. McOwan could have dealt with overt rebellion in the courtroom in the Consulate, but rumour-mongering was not against the law. There was a long history of *papālangi* disaffection, beginning with the complaints that led to the visit of High Commissioner Sir Everard Im Thurn in 1905. Im Thurn complained that a deputation of members of the Beach had little but grievances to talk about, and they were "another case of the white or semi white residents of a Pacific Island kingdom failing to conceive that the natives can have any rights or just claims against them".[19] And 12 years later, Acting Agent & Consul Smith-Rewse had written that "the island trader is inclined to be too immoderate in his demands and to consider his rights superior to the natives of the country, while my desire is to see an efficient Government and the rights of the Tongan commoner safeguarded and the spirit of British justice inculcated into the minds of all".[20]

The complaints of the Beach about Sālote should be interpreted in the light of this record of self-interest. And it should be remembered that she had *papālangi* supporters, and partisanship reflected economic factors. Dorothy Ferguson (teacher in Tonga 1927–30) gives quite a picture of the more privileged sector of *papālangi* society, divided among themselves according to their economic circumstances, and concerned with maintaining their respectability and social position. The weddings of the young *papālangi* women of that stratum that Ferguson describes were as much an indicator of the social position of their families as the weddings of the Tongan chiefly women. The annual dance of the Nuku'alofa Club was a much talked-about social event and the only occasion when the Nuku'alofa Club opened its doors to women. At the other end of the economic spectrum were those who barely made a living, had arrived in Tonga more by chance than by choice, and could see little hope for betterment of their condition.

Some of the more economically advantaged of the *papālangi* traders were faithful members of the Wesleyan Mission; for example, Mr Davidson, whose car was so often lent to the Wesleyans that Tongans referred to it as the "Mission car". At the top of Tongan *papālangi* society was the Cocker family, Wesleyans from Yorkshire, who were also very loyal members of the Wesleyan Mission. Some members of the Beach attended the Church of England,[21] but others allied themselves (at least politically) with the Free Church, which they saw as resisting the control of the Agent & Consul, who limited their freedom as traders. The Catholic Bishop Blanc believed that these *papālangi* supported the "Reactionary Party" out of fear of colonization, which would mean taxation. Blanc may, however, have given too simple an explanation for these allegiances.

Division in the *papālangi* community, like the split in the Tongan community, was clearly seen in their support for one or other of the secondary schools. The Palace party (Tongan and *papālangi* alike) made known their loyalty to Tupou College (owned by the Wesleyan Mission), while most of the Beach and the "Reactionary Party" came out on the side of the Government College (which was properly a Free Church school generously subsidized by the government). The Beach went to the school sports and barracked noisily for Government College, thus sending a barely disguised message to the Palace. How many of the *papālangi* actually understood that battle on the sports field were re-enactments of ancient battles among Tongans is hard to discern. Students and "Old Boys" of 'Api Fo'ou Catholic college, originally Tu'i Tonga followers, stayed out of the fray, and were rewarded by the Queen impressing on them that she was descended from the last Tu'i Tonga, and thus a transfer of loyalty to her was in order.

The battle between Tupou and Government colleges (that is, between two political factions) extended beyond the sports field. When the two schools were both in Nuku'alofa, the students fought across the Mala'e Kula. There were permanent guards at the schools and on the Mission House, even after most of the Tupou College students moved to Nafualu in 1922. "Old Boys" kept the battles alive. For example, the police were drawn mainly from Government College (because of Tupou I's preference for the school), and used their power to harass Tupou College boys. How aware the *papālangi* were of the dangers of the historical rivalry in which they became involved is a moot point, but they were very partisan.

Sālote discouraged *papālangi* from taking sides in Tongan quarrels. Her strategy was to elevate *papālangi* to a chiefly status, but outside the Tongan structures of society. Whereas in 1890 Basil Thomson had commented, "The manners of the average Tongan to a white man whom he dislikes and does not fear leave much to be desired. I found myself jostled off the road by men on horseback, and subjected to many other petty annoyances",[22] Sālote would not permit such behaviour. *Papālangi* frequently broke *tapu* out of ignorance, but Sālote instructed her people to overlook their nonconformity. Their privileges – such as comfortable seats in the shade at official functions (instead of sitting on the ground in the sun with the Tongans) – emphasized that they were different – and separate.

Even without the Queen's intervention, most Tongans had very little contact with *papālangi* outside the secondary schools. Traders and the few plantation-owners tended to employ their own relations to help in the store and when harvesting coconuts. The Queen encouraged government departments to employ Tongans instead of *papālangi* where this was reasonable, but realized that *papālangi* with technical skills were required until sufficient Tongans were trained to fill their places.

Missionaries, though small in number, were influential in the Tongan community because they were schoolteachers as well as preachers. Missionaries tended to be isolated from their compatriots, geographically as well as socially, partly because they were generally better educated, and partly because the missionaries disapproved of the Beach as suppliers of alcohol and exploiters of Tongans (traders said that the missionaries were also exploiters), for traders kept copra prices artificially low and the price of imports artificially high.[23] The Queen chose to turn a blind eye to trading practices, but missionaries openly criticized their compatriots.

From the outset of her reign the Queen was anxious to improve the educational system and medical services, and since most missionaries were engaged in education and some provided medical attention, she valued them for what they did for the people, whether they belonged to her church or not. Unlike the *papālangi* employees of government, the small salaries of missionaries were usually paid from overseas, so to all intents and purposes they were working for Tonga out of love.[24] The Queen made her protection of missionaries known by frequent gifts of food and mats and bark cloth. The response of the Catholic Father Tremblay on his first meeting with her is typical of the reaction of all *papālangi* missionaries regardless of denomination: "As I shook hands with her for the first time, I immediately felt her deep sincerity and maternal solicitude, qualities I admired more and more in her as my years in her Kingdom rolled by. I knew she was interested in our Mission and was glad to be there with us."[25]

Differences between Catholics and Protestants, and between the Old Wesleyans and Free Church, not only reflected ancient divisions among the Tongan community and prejudices brought from the homelands of the missionaries, but current politics. The Catholic Bishop Blanc believed Sālote was wholly under the influence of her consort, whose loyalties as an Old Wesleyan implied anti-Catholic bias. Blanc was not alone in his views. Rev. J. B. Watkin, President of the Free Church, also complained that Sālote was completely dominated by Tungī. "Watkin has a pronounced dislike for Tungī, and did not fail to show his alleged faults to the Native ministers assembled in his study," wrote Rev. Edwin Harkness to Rev. M. A. Rugby Pratt.[26] Pratt visited Tonga in 1922 and reported: "Mr Watkin holds that the Queen is handicapped by the extreme unpopularity of her Consort, who is hated throughout the group. Mr Watkin says that he is not overcoming that unpopularity. Mr Page says he [Tungī] is growing in popularity and that if he were a Free Church man instead of a Wesleyan would be a whitehaired boy with Mr Watkin."[27]

Although he had officiated at Sālote's wedding, had placed the crown on her head at her coronation, and had baptised her three sons, Watkin was easily persuaded by the Beach that Tungī planned to demote him. To protect his position Watkin refused to acknowledge that Queen Sālote, like her predecessors Tupou I and Tupou II, was temporal head of the Free Church. This issue would come to a head in 1923–24 (chapter 8).

Rodger Page, head of the Wesleyan Mission, quickly impressed the Queen through his attempts to heal the divisions between the churches. Missionaries and their wives of all denominations frequently helped each other out, making common cause on social issues and baking for each other's church bazaars. No visitor was more welcome than Rodger Page at the home of the Watkins, and Hannah Page was baking a cake for the Church of England bazaar when she took ill and died in 1939. Dorothy Ferguson reported visiting the daughter of the President of the Free Church, Robert Gordon-Kirgan, and attending a farewell party for a Mormon missionary. Page, Watkin, and Blanc had together petitioned Parliament during Tupou II's reign,[28] and Page and Blanc were among those who had approached Smith-Rewse in 1917 asking him to put an end to the delay over the marriage of Sālote (chapter 3). But Watkin watched with alarm the close friendship which was developing between the Queen and Rodger and Hannah Page at the instigation of Tungī Mailefihi.

There were changes in the *papālangi* community in the early years. In 1919 Dr C. M. Dawson, "a born and trained healer" (Collocott), arrived to take over the medical department. A. R. Brown (later known as the anthropologist A. Radcliffe-Brown) resigned his brief tenure as Director of Education (January

1918–October 1919),[29] and was replaced in 1921 by Ragnar Hyne. Herbert Selwood, Headmaster of the Government College, arrived in the same year. Rev. Edwin Harkness, a moderating influence in the Free Church, returned to New Zealand in 1922, and Watkin did not replace him. Also in 1922 Rev. E. E. V. Collocott, minister and scholar, opened the school year at the new site of Tupou College at Nafualu, and left Tonga at the end of 1923.

Queen Sālote agreed with McOwan in 1920 that there was a "certain class of white man [who] can no longer find legitimate cause for complaint against the Government" and were allying themselves with the "Reactionary Party" for their own purposes.[30] Two *papālangi* of the Beach were considered to be ringleaders in causing trouble for the Queen and Tungī, and would play a significant role in the politics of the 1920s: John McLean Masterton and George Scott.

Masterton had come to Tonga some time before 1904–5, when he defended the government ousted by Im Thurn.[31] He married J. B. Watkin's daughter and lived with his in-laws at Mapu-'a-fuiva, the house next to the Palace that the royal family made available to Watkin as President of the Free Church and royal chaplain. In 1911, when the fall of Mateialona seemed certain, Masterton was thought to be scheming to become Premier. The High Commissioner dashed his hopes, agreeing only that Masterton be appointed Chief Postmaster and Chief Collector of Customs, positions he held until 1926.[32] These were senior appointments, and when Agent & Consul H. E. W. Grant left Tonga suddenly in 1916 because of ill-health, Masterton was appointed Vice-Consul until G. B. Smith-Rewse arrived to take over as Acting Agent & Consul. This appointment set a precedent, for between 1916 and 1924 Masterton was Vice-Consul whenever the Agent & Consul was absent and no Acting Agent & Consul was available. The powers of a Vice-Consul were limited, for (unlike an Acting Agent & Consul) he had no access to confidential papers, and was instructed to refer matters of a political nature to Suva; but if Masterton as Vice-Consul exercised more powers than were proper, there was no one in Tonga to stop him.

In 1921, when McOwan was recalled to Fiji for a time to act as Colonial Secretary, the Queen requested that an Acting Agent & Consul to be appointed, for the alternative – dividing the position between Masterton as Vice-Consul and George Scott as Deputy Judicial Commissioner – was unacceptable to her.[33] Her apprehensions would prove to be justified in 1923–24 when it became evident these officials, with their entrenched local interests, could cause great difficulty for the government they were meant to serve (chapter 8).

George Scott was a Tasmanian lawyer who had come to Tonga in 1900 and married a Tongan woman in 1906. Scott's early hostility to Tupou II, alliance with Tu'ivakanō in 1912, and appointment as Chief European Clerk in the Premier's Department have already been related (see chapter 2). He was Acting

LEFT: Fe'iloakitau Kaho (brother of Polutele and Sioape), Ha'amea (son of 'Ulukālala), and Namomo, 1920s. Although he was not a member of Parliament, Fe'iloakitau was identified as being a member of the "Reactionary Party". *Courtesy of 'Eva Ve'ehala.* [28]

RIGHT: Wedding portrait of Princess Sālote and Tungī Mailefihi, 19 September 1917. This, the first of the two wedding ceremonies, was wholly *papālangi* in style. [29]

RIGHT: Princess Sālote leaves the Palace for her *tu'uvala* (Tongan wedding), 21 September 1917. [30]

BELOW: *Koloa* (i.e. mats, bark cloth, baskets, bottles of perfumed oil) of Princess Sālote's *tu'uvala*, 21 September 1917. *Courtesy of Auckland Institute and Museum. Ref. C 21645.)* [31]

Above: The funeral of Tupou II, 10 April 1918. The men in suits and hats standing on the *kauala* (platform carrying the coffin), the other people standing, and the umbrellas all suggest that the custom of being seated and bareheaded in the presence of a great chief was not observed. Compare the photographs of the funeral of Tungī Mailefihi and that of Queen Sālote. [32]

Left: The coronation of Queen Sālote in the Royal Chapel, 11 October 1918. From left: Sioeli Pangia, ʻUlukālala (S. F. M.), Tungī Mailefihi, Queen Sālote, and one of the Queen's two pages. Two days previously (9 October) Queen Sālote had been installed in the title of Tuʻi Kanokupolu. [33]

RIGHT: Mele Siu'ilikutapu, mother of Uiliami Tupoulahi (later Tungī Mailefihi). *Courtesy of the family of Rodger Page.* [34]

BELOW: A Tongan Village [36]

ABOVE: Uiliami Tupoulahi (later Tungī Mailefihi), son of Mele Siu'ilikutapu and Tuku'aho, and grandson of Old Tungī. He briefly attended Newington College in Sydney, later attended and was a tutor at Tupou College on its Nuku'alofa site. [35]

RIGHT: Tupou College tutors, 1909. *Standing:* 'Ikani Taliai, Tēvita Kata, Suliasi Tolu, Lesinali Tovi. *Seated:* Uiliami Tupoulahi (later Tungī Mailefihi), Sione Havea (Head Tutor), and Lotima Palu. *Courtesy of Siupeli Taliai.* [37]

LEFT: The Royal Guards, with flag of Tonga and saluting battery. *Courtesy of Kurt Düring.* [38]

RIGHT: Mapu-'a-fuiva. Rev. J. B. Watkin (President of the Free Church 1885–1925) lived in this house until his death in January 1925, when it reverted to the royal family, who used it for the overflow of royal guests, e.g. at the centenary celebrations of December 1945. [39]

BELOW: Visit to Rotorua, New Zealand, 1923. *Standing:* Lord Jellicoe (Governor-General of New Zealand), the Maori king, Queen Sālote (wearing Maori cloak and headband), Lilla Bagnall. *Seated:* Ve'ehala (Feleti Vī) holding Prince Tāufa'āhau, Halaevalu holding Prince Tuku'aho, Tuna Vaea, Simoa holding Prince Sione Ngū. Ve'ehala married Simoa in 1924. *Courtesy of Adrienne Kaeppler.* [40]

Above: Sir Cecil Rodwell (High Commissioner of the Western Pacific) visited Tonga in November 1920 to inquire into the rebellion of the chiefs in Parliament. *From left:* Sir Cecil Rodwell, Captain Clive Brewster, Queen Sālote, Tu'ivakanō (Polutele), Mrs McOwan, Islay McOwan (British Agent & Consul). [42]

Right: Prince Tāufa'āhau, aged 10, as one of the members of the Tupou College choir touring Australia, 1928. [41]

Below: Wedding of Rev. George Harris and Ruth Fabrin, 1926. *Back row*: Tungī Mailefihi, A. H. Wood holding daughter Janet, Doris Smith, unknown lady, Beryl Greig, Matron Armstrong, Rodger Page, Mrs Rankin, Mrs Denny, Mr Rankin, Rachel Tonga. *Front row*: Herbert Selwood, George Harris, Ruth Fabrin, Hannah Page, Queen Sālote, Gwen Blamires, Tu'iha'ateiho (Havea), Miss Cordy, Dr Olive Wood, Charles Dalton, Ata (Solomone). [43]

LEFT: R. N. Moody, barrister in Tonga Ma'a Tonga Kautaha cases 1910–11, represented the Free Church 1924. *Courtesy of Dr R. F. and L. Moody.* [46]

BELOW: Group, possibly at the 1926 centenary celebrations. *Back row:* George Harris, Rodger Page, Mr Rabone, Tungī Mailefihi, A. H. Wood holding daughter Janet, Miss Rabone, Charles Moore, A. M. Sanders. *Front row:* Mrs Rabone, Hannah Page, Queen Sālote, Mrs McOwan, Lilla Bagnall, Dr Olive Wood, with one of the princes (Tuku'aho?) seated at the front. [44]

BELOW: Privy Council c. 1926. *Left to right:* W. G. Bagnall, Tungī Mailefihi, 'Ulukālala (S. F. M.), A. B. Wallace, Queen Sālote (President), J. D. Wall, Kenneth Horne, Ha'amea, Veikune (Fotu), Sioape Kaho, S. F. Tongilava (Clerk to Privy Council), Ata (Solomone). [45]

Above: George Scott, barrister, Chief European Clerk in the Premier's Department 1913–23, Judge of the Land Court 1923–32, and occasional Acting Chief Justice. *Courtesy of Lily Goodwin.* [47]

Right: Rachel Tonga, not long before her death on 4 August 1928. [48]

Below: Tungī Mailefihi with Rodger and Hannah Page. [49]

Chief Justice from 1915 until 1917, but the High Commissioner would not agree to his being given the substantive appointment. Tu'ivakanō then suggested that Scott be appointed Attorney-General and sit in the Privy Council, Cabinet, and Parliament instead of Chief Justice Stronge. A separation of the judiciary from the legislative functions of government was a reasonable suggestion, but Tu'ivakanō's motives were clearly to get his own man into a powerful position, and again the High Commissioner withheld his consent.[34]

Scott and his wife and daughters lived on the Beach Road in the Kolofo'ou section of Nuku'alofa, in the house later known as the Beach House. Scott had the right of private practice, and Dorothy Ferguson considered him to be very rich, with his own launch and lease of an island. Scott's wealth, his long residence in Tonga, and his official positions inevitably made him influential among the traders of the Beach.

Between 1915 and 1932, Scott was appointed Acting Chief Justice whenever the Chief Justice was absent. This put him in the position of advising and influencing each newly arrived Chief Justice. Since Scott was an open supporter of the "Reactionary Party", his advice was frequently contrary to the interests of the Palace. McOwan commented that Scott's hostility towards Queen Sālote and Tungī was "more personal than public", but he did not elaborate on the comment.[35]

Like Blanc, Watkin, Masterton, and members of the "Reactionary Party", Scott viewed Tungī with considerable hostility. Thus Sālote was determined to remove Scott from the Premier's Office before she appointed Tungī as Premier.[36] In the light of Scott's popularity with the "Reactionary Party", outright dismissal was not an option. The Land Court Act of 1921 offered a way out, and Scott was appointed Judge of the Land Court in 1923. To the Queen's dismay, once Scott was installed in this position he claimed the power to determine inheritance of the hereditary estates of nobles and *kau matāpule ma'u tofi'a*, power that had not been envisaged by the government in the drafting of the Act (chapter 9).[37] Scott also saw himself as a champion of the chiefs who held land by customary right only, but not according to written law (chapters 8 and 9),[38] the most conspicuous being the chiefs embittered by the Queen's inability to fulfil her father's promises to make them nobles.

The High Commissioner had the power to remove a *papālangi* whose behaviour was unacceptable; for example, Premier Shirley Baker in 1890. But the High Commission was unwilling to take such drastic action while the *papālangi* simply talked sedition. Sālote had to tolerate Masterton and Scott, and even Watkin, who preached treasonable sermons (chapter 8).

The Queen relied on McOwan to deal with unacceptable behaviour among *papālangi*, and a case in point was the *papālangi* ministers. From Sālote's point of view the Agent & Consul had advised the appointment of *papālangi* senior officials, so it was logical that he should curb them when necessary. In 1923 matters came to a head over whether a bonus should be paid to ministers on half-pay leave. McOwan said no, even though the Privy Council was prepared to allow it. The *papālangi* ministers immediately affected were Stronge and Wall, who expected to go on extended leave in 1923. McOwan did not improve their tempers when he reproached them for a lack of integrity and for lack of courtesy in their dealings with the Queen and her consort.[39] Stronge attacked Tungī for not standing up to the Agent & Consul, saying in a Privy Council meeting that Tungī was like a butcher's boy taking weekly orders, a reference to Tungī's regular weekly meeting with the Agent & Consul.[40]

McOwan reported that Stronge and Wall had persuaded the Tongan members of Parliament that the Supplementary Agreement deprived the government of its power to administer its own affairs,[41] although in fact the "Reactionary Party" needed no persuasion. Believing that Stronge and Wall should be loyal to him (as representative of the British government) and to the Queen (who had appointed them and to whom they had sworn loyalty), McOwan complained of their outrageous behaviour:

> It must always be a difficult matter for an official acting in an advisory capacity to a Government to conduct himself in such a manner as to maintain an effective control of the situation without exciting suspicion that he is trying to usurp authority. With a proud, sensitive people like the Tongans, who are suspicious of interference and jealous of their authority and independence, one must always be on one's guard. One hardly expects, however, that the European officials . . . will set themselves deliberately to disturb official relations and render one's position still more difficult and delicate . . .
>
> Since their return from leave last year these two officers [Stronge and Wall] have lost no opportunity of urging the Cabinet and the Privy Council to reject my advice with the result that much unnecessary friction has been caused with consequent delay in the transaction of public business.
>
> The latest manifestation of their attitude occurred at a recent meeting of the Privy Council . . . Mr. Stronge, in addressing the Council on the subject of the relations between the Government of Tonga and the Agent and Consul gave utterance to remarks which were calculated to cause a breach of these relations and which gave the gravest offence to the Queen and her Tongan ministers. The Auditor-General, Mr. J. D. Wall, who has supported and encouraged the Chief Justice in his opposition, aggravated offence by laughing at the remarks and only desisted upon seeing the scandalized look on the faces of the Queen and the other members of the Council.[42]

If the *papālangi* ministers felt that such behaviour would weaken the alliance between the Queen, Tungī, and McOwan, they were mistaken. The alliance was firm, for the Queen counted on McOwan's support. In a personal letter to the

High Commissioner just prior to McOwan's departure in 1926 the Queen described the change in the relations between the Tongan Crown and the British Agent & Consul to Tonga that had occurred during the period of McOwan's appointment. Having by this time been Queen for eight years, Sālote could write with full confidence as sovereign to a friendly government.

> You doubtless recall that, in the years previous to Mr. McOwan's occupancy of the post, there existed suspicion, misunderstanding, and friction that was, to say the least, irritating to both your Government and mine. Tonga is under lasting debt to Mr. McOwan for the way in which he has created a good understanding and complete confidence.
>
> You are well aware that my Kingdom is very small, and that if my people are to retain a national existence it can only be secured by the continued friendship and help of Great Britain. The sound condition of our finances owes much to his wise counsel and steady progress in national works are indebted to his practical advice.[43]

To the casual observer, particularly those who set great store on the bureaucracy of Western-style institutions, the Queen appeared to leave affairs of the government wholly in the hands of McOwan and Tungī. This illusion was deliberately created, for a sacred ruler does not need to intervene in the daily business of government. A sacred ruler governs while appearing not to govern; but she formulated policies herself after consultation with Tungī and McOwan.

Sālote won the total confidence of the British, disarming them by trusting them. Whether on a formal occasion, or when they talked in the afternoon on the Palace verandah, or when she called in at the Residency during her evening walks, she won over one Consul after another to her cause. They would appreciate that they depended on her personally for the effective governance of Tonga, just as she depended on them.

Winning over *papālangi* was only one part of the story. Although Sālote would always play down the extent of the opposition to her rule in the early years of her reign, her second great achievement was gaining the confidence of the chiefs and nobles, and persuading them that their interests would be best served by supporting her as unquestioned holder of the supreme title.

Queen Sālote was fully aware that she needed help with governance of her people. Her genuine humility arose in part from Christian conviction, but also from a wise assessment of the political realities of Tonga's situation. But this humility was accompanied by confidence that arose from her sense of a high destiny and of responsibility for the welfare of Tonga.

CHAPTER SEVEN

Aristocrats, Nobles, and Lesser Chiefs

"The chiefly blood counts more than any line." (Queen Sālote, 1959)[1]

IN THE LATTER PART OF QUEEN Sālote's reign, when political friction was almost non-existent, it was assumed that harmony had always been the case, that the Queen had always been universally accepted as Tonga's legitimate ruler. The truth was that she herself created the image of the much-loved monarch of the latter part of her life. By contrast, in the early years of her reign many of her chiefs opposed her, and would have been glad to see her go. Lacking sufficient support from her own people, she (like many threatened rulers throughout history) sought it from outside the kingdom, but converted that weakness into a strength by winning not only the wholehearted support of her British allies, but also the respect of the chiefs and people. In the early years, however, Queen Sālote's constant references to the desirability of peace and unity were because there was no peace or unity.

The challenges to Queen Sālote were not because she was a woman: for she was "sister" to many of the highest-ranking male chiefs. There were other reasons for the reluctance of chiefs to accept her as their ruler. The first was that in spite of her Tu'i Tonga descent, her *personal* rank was lower than some of the other members of the aristocracy, due to the inferiority of her maternal line. The second was that the elevation of the Tupou dynasty was comparatively recent, and some chiefs privately denied its legitimacy. Although in conversation with Elizabeth Bott Spillius Queen Sālote admitted that her personal rank was "low" (in the aristocratic hierarchy), she strongly asserted the legitimacy of her dynasty and the importance of her title. It would be the Queen who reshaped history so that relationship to the Tupou dynasty was the route to power instead of descent from the Tu'i Tonga.

Queen Sālote became a master strategist in attaining what the British called her "influence" over her people. In a sense she had only a few political strategies, which she perfected over the years, aimed at elevating her own reputation and the status of her title and dynasty. These strategies dealt with the past and the future as much as the present, suggesting new emphases in genealogies, and assigning new rankings to future generations through the marriages of her contemporaries. After all, truth is what the chief says, and history is what the highest chief says.

In some ways, one could say the Queen played a game of bluff, for she was concerned with people's perceptions of their places in the hierarchy. As time went on, the ranks of certain chiefs would be "improved" merely because she gave them her seal of approval, and the reputations of other chiefs declined because of her disapproval. And marriages being the most important means of elevation, her promotion of certain marriages as rewards and blocking of others as punishment would be a powerful means of bringing the chiefs into line. Such manoeuvrings depended upon the authority derived from a forceful personality with consistent aims.

In the early years of her reign, Sālote had to deal with ranking women and men who challenged her authority. All of these were included in the general term "chiefs", but are more specifically identified as aristocrats (*hou'eiki*), nobles (*nōpele*), and lesser chiefs (*'eiki si'i*). The aristocrats were those chiefs whose descent from the sacred Tu'i Tonga gave them (especially the women) special privileges. The nobles were hereditary estateholders, whose power arose from their control of the land-and-people. The term "nobles" usually (though inaccurately) includes the *kau matāpule ma'u tofi'a*, who also were hereditary estateholders, but were not entitled to separate representation in Parliament, as the nobles were. The third powerful group were the lesser chiefs, whose power depended upon their local influence. Hereditary estateholders were often represented in the villages by lesser, resident chiefs (*matu'a tauhi fonua* or caretakers), who might be fortunate enough also to be appointed town officers or district officers, another reward in the Queen's gift.

Queen Sālote's youth, marriage, and the status of her maternal line were the major causes of difficulty. Her youth was corrected by time. Although her marriage alienated most of the Ha'apai chiefs and some of the Vava'u chiefs, it ensured the support of most of the Tongatapu chiefs. The deaths of higher-ranking aristocrats, the manipulation of the marriages, the increasing recognition that the Queen was the repository of traditional lore, her authority as the expert on genealogies, and the sheer force of her personality combined to improve her rank. In the end, Sālote's achievements as sovereign elevated the rank of her maternal line in the same way as Tupou I's victories elevated the *mana* of the Tu'i Kanokupolu title.

Sālote was so successful in "forgetting" the slights that she suffered during this early period that they did not long survive in the memories of her subjects, and we usually have to rely on the written record of foreigners to measure the extent of opposition that is hinted at in oral sources. Another written source is the record of Parliament. Although Parliament was a minor instrument of government, it provided a place in which members of the "Reactionary Party" could air their opinions and grievances. Parliament was an élite body, being composed of nobles, ministers who often were nobles, and "representatives of the people" who were chiefly relatives of nobles. Parliament could amend but not initiate legislation; it could impeach; it could block the vote on finances; and it could attempt to intimidate the monarch, a tactic that worked with Tupou II and would be tried with Queen Sālote.

In the early years three nobles dominated Parliament through their leadership of the "Reactionary Party": Tu'ivakanō (Polutele), the Premier; 'Ulukālala (Siaosi Fīnau Mīsini), Speaker of Parliament; and Mā'atu (Pānuve), a nobles' representative and brother of the rejected 'Ofa (chapter 1).[2] Although Tu'ivakanō's estates were in the Western District of Tongatapu, his family came from Ha'apai, which had forgotten its former allegiance to the line of Tupou. Tu'ivakanō had a strong character, and was intelligent and industrious in advancing the cause of his aristocratic superiors. 'Ulukālala's ancestors had a claim to the Tu'i Kanokupolu title, and were longtime opponents of the Tupou dynasty (Figure 2.3). 'Ulukālala's particular grievances were that in the course of the civil wars Tupou I had "stolen" the Tu'i Vava'u title from the 'Ulukālalas and, having twice been Governor of Vava'u, this 'Ulukālala had twice been deprived of that appointment by the King upon the insistence of the British. Mā'atu was the noble of the remote Niuatoputapu, indulged in Tongatapu because of his high rank. Islay McOwan reported that: "The representatives [in Parliament] are indeed very largely in the hands of one Maatu, a noble of high rank but a man of low moral character, who has for this reason been excluded [by the British] from Government service."[3] It is no wonder, then, that abolition of the Supplementary Agreement to the Treaty of Friendship with the British became the rallying cry of the "Reactionary Party".

Sālote did not fear Mā'atu or 'Ulukālala, but she longed to dismiss Tu'ivakanō and replace him with Tungī Mailefihi. She hesitated, however, for Tungī's unpopularity among the Ha'apai and Vava'u chiefs had affected her own popularity in those island groups, and his promotion could be politically difficult. Tu'ivakanō had the support of Parliament and, in spite of Smith-Rewse's adverse reports in 1917, McOwan appreciated Tu'ivakanō's abilities. On 8 August 1918 McOwan wrote that "[Tu'ivakanō is] the most influential man in

Tonga at the present time and has certainly the courage of his convictions . . . He has a broader outlook, is endowed with a clear vision and with his rank as a Noble is entitled to be considered the most conspicuous figure in Tongan politics."[4] Tu'ivakanō's inertia during the influenza epidemic in November 1918 disillusioned McOwan, but, surprisingly, he still did not advise Sālote to press for the Premier's resignation.

Tu'ivakanō stacked the 1918–20 Parliament well. Three of his brothers (Siosiua, Sioape, and Manase Kaho) were members, Sioape being appointed Minister for Police in January 1919. Tu'ivakanō's cousin Molitoni Fisi'ihoi Fīnau was the leader of the "representatives of the people". Samisoni Siaki Lolohea (a representative for Ha'apai) and Motekiai Taukolo Langi (Tongatapu) had moved the impeachments of 1912 (chapter 2). Motekiai and Lolohea had grievances, for Motekiai had been disbarred from appearing as a pleader in the courts, while Lolohea was the son of one of the chiefs whom Tupou II had promised to ennoble, and Queen Sālote had failed to keep that promise.

Queen Sālote clearly had to control Parliament before she could make Tungī her Premier. It was her duty each year to attend the Opening of Parliament (in full coronation regalia until 1942) and to make a speech that would serve as a guide for the work of the session. She also attended the Closing of Parliament and commented, sometimes caustically, on what had happened during the session. Not surprisingly, many paragraphs of her speeches, referring to major events and projecting business still to be legislated for, were written for her, usually by Tungī and Tongilava, but the Queen's own voice is often clearly heard, telling the members not to discuss matters that were no concern of theirs; extolling the advantages of a society where everyone knew their place; exhorting the members to complete their business and go back to their villages where their real work lay; urging the nobles to distribute their lands and the people to register their allotments; thanking Great Britain for protecting Tonga; comparing its good fortune with the fortunes of other countries; and expounding the virtues of peace and unity.

Because of the recent birth of the Crown Prince, the Queen did not attend the Opening or Closing of Parliament in 1918. Tu'ivakanō was still on leave and the country still in mourning for the King, so the session was a quiet one. The 1919 session of Parliament was exceptionally brief, lasting only 16 days, but during that time the members presented a petition to the Queen, protesting against her recent appointments of two additional *papālangi* ministers, W. G. Bagnall and A. B. Wallace (chapter 6).

The members received no answer to their petition of 1919, and at the beginning of the 1920 session Fisi'ihoi proposed that Parliament should refuse to discuss any business until the Queen responded to their request that Bagnall and Wallace be removed from Parliament. When there was again no response from the Palace, Fisi'ihoi moved that Chief Justice Stronge and Wallace be impeached. That the members targeted Stronge and Wallace (and not the more recently appointed Bagnall) suggests that these were the most unpopular of the four *papālangi* ministers.

No sustainable charges were brought against Stronge. The motive for attacking Wallace seems to have been his arrogant behaviour towards Tongans, but the members claimed that Wallace had used his previous position as Director of Public Works to his own advantage, a charge that was investigated but could not be sustained.[5] McOwan reported to the High Commissioner that:

> The Queen has not the influence over these men [members of Parliament] that her late father possessed and I am glad to say that neither Her Majesty nor her consort seek to obtain that influence by resorting to methods which would be derogatory to their rank, to their dignity and to the respect in which they are held by all classes of the community.[6]

The 1920 Parliament also proposed two amendments to the Constitution. First, that the Queen could not appoint more than seven ministers (for the additional *papālangi* ministers made eight, not counting the governors of Ha'apai and Vava'u, who attended Parliament and also Privy Council when they were in Nuku'alofa); second, that the Chief Justice relinquish his seat in Privy Council, Cabinet, and Parliament. It was proposed (yet again) that George Scott, Tu'ivakanō's Chief European Clerk, should be appointed Attorney-General and Crown Solicitor and replace Stronge in Privy Council, Cabinet, and Parliament. Neither the Queen nor the Consul would countenance Scott being promoted.

The official record of each day's proceedings in the Parliament was presented to Queen Sālote and McOwan. On the day that the members refused to transact business and the day after (24 and 25 June 1920), the members came three times to see the Queen, and McOwan and the Premier came once.[7] On 2 July the Privy Council considered the members' petition that Scott should be appointed Attorney-General and Crown Solicitor, and decided against the proposal. After the meeting the Queen wrote to the Speaker, pointing out the difficulties if the members persisted in impeaching the Chief Justice, for who would hear the charges against him? On 20 July Fisi'ihoi withdrew the Bill of Impeachment because it was "causing the Queen trouble".[8]

The Queen had won that round, but she knew that the "Reactionary Party" was not defeated. Sālote sent three nobles – Tungī, Sioeli Pangia (the aristocratic noble of Lapaha), and Ma'afu of Vaini – to represent her at the Closing of Parliament. The speech that was delivered to Parliament on her behalf (and these paragraphs were surely her own) show the forthrightness of an aristocrat and the confidence of a legitimate ruler. She summed up her view of correct relationships within Tongan society, asserting that Parliament's role was negligible compared with her own. Sālote's monarchistic views would not vary over the years.

> I think it right that . . . I should make clear to the members of this House that the Legislative Assembly has its own proper functions which are defined in the Law and the Constitution, and that it will be both advantageous and render everybody's duties less burdensome if each person will be careful to refrain from interfering with the concerns of others. If, on the other hand, persons are free to intermeddle with concerns that are the prerogative of others, then, beyond all doubt, the failure of each person carefully to abide by and observe the particular powers vested in him will result in conflict and the shattering of the charm that the individual possession of those powers affords . . .
>
> What is the real meaning of Love of Country? It means to work, to cling to our own peculiar customs that are good and ought not to be abandoned. The things to be prized by us are love, respect, and mutual helpfulness . . .
>
> Some of the Nobles have little affection for their people, and some of the people have been raised above their proper station in life, and have attempted to put themselves on a level with the Nobles . . .
>
> I ask of you to fill your lives with love of your homeland, and let it not be lip love only but real living love. I urge you to preserve jealously the great good fortune which we at present enjoy in Tonga, and to banish from your country those opinions and modes of thought which in other countries are eating up, wasting, and destroying their greatest treasure – Peace.[9]

The "love, respect, and mutual helpfulness" the Queen referred to were *'ofa* (love tinged with fear), which she sought from her subjects, *faka'apa'apa* (respect) that the inferior owes the superior, and mutual helpfulness was ideally the interdependence of chiefs and people. The comment on "other countries" was certainly a reference to the Russian Revolution, which was very much in the thoughts of politicians at this time.[10] Devoted as she was to the idea of God-appointed monarchs, the Queen was filled with horror at the reports of the killing of the Czar and his family in 1917 and the takeover of the government of Russia by revolutionaries.

McOwan also was appalled at the behaviour of the members of the Parliament, and he wrote to the Queen:

> Though the last session was the longest since the House was re-constituted [in 1915], most of the time was occupied in mischievous obstruction and idle opposition to the policy of the Government. I cannot recall a single instance of useful suggestions emanating from the representatives for the progress of the country or for the benefit of the people, yet throughout the discussions and debates, their love for the people and for their country is said to be the motive

> for their actions, whereas it is apparent that they are prompted by persons, probably Europeans, who are ill-disposed towards the Government.
>
> I hope the good advice which Your Majesty has given to the elected members will be accepted by them in the spirit in which it is offered and that they will be more careful in future to confine their attention to the legitimate work of the legislature and leave matters which do not concern them to those who are responsible under the laws and Constitution of the Kingdom.[11]

The consensus of the views of Queen and Consul should be noted.

The High Commissioner for the Western Pacific, Sir Cecil Rodwell, made an official visit to Tonga in November 1920 to confer with the Queen and McOwan. Mā'atu led a deputation of members of Parliament (seven nobles and five of the "representatives of the people") to wait on Rodwell. The issues raised by the deputation were: the financial control exercised by the Agent & Consul; the appointments of two additional *papālangi* as ministers; Wallace's fitness for office; the Privy Council's disregard for parliamentary resolutions; the undesirability of the Supplementary Agreement as inconsistent with the Constitution.

The members were proposing that Parliament play a greater role in government, and that the Agent & Consul and Privy Council (that is, the Queen-in-Council) should play less. Rodwell gave them a flat denial, making it clear that the Supplementary Agreement and the powers of the Agent & Consul were non-negotiable areas. He told the members they should take advantage of the experience of the four *papālangi* ministers, reproached them for their failure to co-operate with the Queen, and informed them that if they could not find common ground with the Queen and Privy Council the whole matter would be referred to the Secretary of State for the Colonies with the recommendation that the existing status of Tonga be reconsidered.[12] As Rodwell's correspondence with the Colonial Office in London shows, what Rodwell had in mind was the annexation of Tonga.

Rodwell agreed with McOwan that Parliament was an "irresponsible body of mischief-makers" who were "in favour of the continuance of a corrupt and inefficient administration" of the last years of Tupou II.[13] Rodwell and McOwan also blamed those *papālangi*, who "foment ill-feeling amongst the members of the Government". The Queen must have been alarmed at the threat implied in the visit, but wisely informed Rodwell that she did not wish to increase the number of ministers in order to ensure a majority of supporters in Parliament. Such a blatant measure would have caused outrage in Parliament, and might have extended to the kingdom and caused comment overseas.[14] Her request to Rodwell that no more Mormon missionaries be allowed to enter Tonga because they were a disturbing element in the kingdom was not clearly explained, but she may have suspected the American Mormons encouraged the "democratic" tendencies of the "Reactionary Party".[15] It was not only that the Queen's aristocratic inclinations made her distrust democratic processes – as she then understood them – but she knew that the "Reactionary Party" truly aimed at absolute power for itself.

Rodwell had reservations about the Queen, but he was prepared to give her a chance to control the Parliament. On 21 January 1921, he wrote to the Secretary of State for the Colonies: "Whether the existing constitution can last will depend largely upon the ability of the Queen to hold her own with the Nobles and representatives, who together have a majority in the Legislative Assembly. Sooner or later I fear that a crisis is bound to arise, with the result that annexation will become inevitable or that recourse will be necessary to further deportations."[16] What deportations did Rodwell have in mind? It is unlikely that he meant either the Queen or her consort. Did he mean parliamentarians? The mischief-making *papālangi*? Premier Tu'ivakanō? While the Queen was willing enough to use the threat of annexation to control the members of Parliament, she would have resisted suggestions for the removal of even the most troublesome of her own subjects. On balance, it seems most likely that the "deportations" Rodwell had in mind were those of mischief-making *papālangi*.

At the Closing of the 1922 session of Parliament Queen Sālote reminded the representatives that Tonga must *prove* that it could govern itself, for "other countries which are manifestly unfit for self-government have been annexed to the British Empire, as has been done with various groups in the Pacific".[17] Indeed the Queen needed all of her persuasive powers, and Sione Havea (*Koe Havea*, 1941) had confidence in the power of her oratory.

> The thing that amazes everyone is the Queen's gift for oratory. She touches the hearts of the people when she speaks to them. I consider her to be Tupou I's equal in oratory. Tupou I was a powerful speaker in time of war, when his warriors were going into battle . . . But Sālote's speeches pertain to peace and worship. She has the gift of getting to the heart of things . . . When she speaks at a meeting or to the people, or in Parliament, she makes her points hit home . . . I believe she may be compared to Caesar and Cicero, and to the famous orators of Greece or Rome. [SAH]

The Queen wanted Tu'ivakanō to go, but only to his own estates, and she renewed her attempts to replace him as Premier. In 1918 she had recognized a claim Tu'ivakanō made to the land-and-people of Matafonua in the Western District of Tongatapu as part of his estates, although tampered records suggest that his claim was a dubious one. Shortly after Rodwell's visit, she promised him the land-and-people of Matahau (also in the Western District) provided he resigned from the premiership. Tu'ivakanō took both Matafonua and Matahau, but did not resign until 20 June 1923, just before his death, on 4 August 1923.[18] The Queen appointed Tungī Premier from 21 June 1923.

Although the Queen valued Tungī primarily as an exemplary leader in the traditional mould, his appointment as Premier was an essential step in her becoming an effective ruler of Tonga. Although Tungī already exercised great influence as an aristocrat of exceedingly high rank and as Minister for Lands, his appointment as Premier would confirm him as the Queen's right hand. As Premier he would also have rewards such as government appointments (and salaries!) at his disposal, and would control the Parliament and the Western-style administration on which British advisers set such store. The Premier was responsible for steering through Parliament the laws that originated in Privy Council, and which organized Tongan society along lines desired by the Queen and Tungī. Further, the Queen needed money to implement their joint policies in regards to health and education, and Tungī was keen to provide these funds by an increase in the export of copra and other crops, through the Premier's control of the Department of Agriculture.

Tu'ivakanō's demise and Tungī's appointment were far from being the end of the "Reactionary Party". Tu'ivakanō's brother Sioape Kaho, Minister for Police, was even more hostile to the partnership of Sālote and Tungī. Sioape's antagonism was bolstered by his marriage to Muimui, sister of Queen Takipō and the rejected 'Ofa (Figure 3.3). Muimui and Sioape made their disaffection clear by behaving as though Princess Fusipala, the daughter of Queen Takipō, outranked the daughter of Queen Lavinia. "[Personal] Rank overrules everything", Queen Sālote said, but she denied that she was outranked by her younger sister.

The Queen might equally have said that "land overrules everything". While rank was a matter for constant contention, access to land meant prestige and power as well as survival. The Queen could win over nobles by assurance that the hereditary estates they held by virtue of the Constitution were secure against the claims of lesser chiefs who held their lands by custom only. The Queen could appoint – even create – titles whenever she wished, but a title without land-and-people was worth very little. Hereditary estateholders could claim that all the land was already divided between the nobles, the six *matāpule ma'u tofi'a*, the Queen, and the government, and they strongly opposed the creation of more hereditary titles.

The most outspoken of the chiefs who claimed land by customary right were those from Ha'apai and Vava'u, who also resented the dominance of Tongatapu. Customary landholders wanted the same security of tenure that Tupou I had given to the hereditary estateholders, which meant they must be appointed either nobles or *matāpule ma'u tofi'a* or lose their land. A few were very persistent, and among the chiefs who approached Sālote within months of her accession to remind her of past promises were the Kaho brothers (especially

Siosiua, the second of the brothers) and Siaki Lolohea, all Ha'apai chiefs.[19] The self-derogatory phrases in Siaki Lolohea's begging letter were a matter of protocol, for Lolohea was not humble, and there was an implied threat if the Queen did not grant his request.

> I am encouraged to approach you when I remember how Queen Esther petitioned the King [in the Bible] . . . It was the intention of His Majesty Tubou II to make Iki Lolohea [Lolohea's father] a Noble, and also to give him a piece of land of his own . . . Please fulfil Tubou's promise to Iki, a lowly subject, by giving me a handful of dust to be my own . . . I said in my letter to His Majesty Tubou II, if he would be merciful, to give me Pangai in Lifuka, from the boundary with Hihifo (including towns and bush) to the end of Koulo (up to the beginning of the shallow water leading to Foa), except Holopeka, which is part of the estate of Tu'i'afitu. Also a section of land called Pangai in Foa, in which I at present own a tax allotment . . . When they were distributing Foa, Iki asked Tubou I "What about Pangai?", and Tubou I said to Iki that he and his descendants will possess it because it belonged to their forefathers . . .
>
> Yours is the kingdom. Yours is the land. Yours is the people, which bring wealth to Your Majesty and family.
>
> But this poor lowly subject, if you will not remember my dear face I shall be out in the street, homeless like an aborted coconut, and become a laughing stock of the people . . . [20] [TF]

The Queen could not make either Lolohea or Siosiua a noble without alienating the existing hereditary estateholders. Although Tu'ivakanō assigned to his brothers some of the land-and-people of his estates for their support, the refusal rankled as much with the Kahos as with Lolohea.

The difficulty in increasing the number of nobles was demonstrated when Queen Sālote proposed to appoint her great-uncle Mateialona a noble. Mateialona was a grandson of Tupou I, had been Governor of Ha'apai 1897–1905, Premier 1905–12, and (at the age of 66 and during the influenza epidemic) again appointed by her as Governor of Ha'apai 1918–24. Collocott had no doubt of Mateialona's aristocratic antecedents, describing him as "a large, stout man whose forthright bluntness was enlivened by a pawky humour, and graced by a dignified courtesy of indefinable charm, somehow born, as I suppose, of ten centuries of royal breeding".[21] The British supported the appointment, for they had been privy to the promise made by Tupou II to Mateialona in 1912 to make him a noble. The Queen created a new title for Mateialona, that of Tupouto'a, which had been the personal name of the father of Tupou I (Figure 1.5).

The Queen wrote the letter of appointment for the new Tupouto'a in January 1921, but it took longer to determine which lands would be attached to the title. In the case of Veikune, whom Tupou II had made a noble in 1903, his estates had been made up of land-and-people previously belonging to his relations, but such a solution was not available for Tupouto'a. Some of the land that would be gazetted as Tupouto'a's estates had formerly been given to the government by Tupou I, and some had formerly belonged to the chief Valu (of the village of 'Utulau on Tongatapu) and the chief Fanua Lofanga (chief of the island of Lofanga in Ha'apai). Valu and Fanua Lofanga (like Tungī and Tupouto'a) were Old Wesleyans, and Tungī persuaded them to relinquish the lands they held by customary right to provide estates for Tupouto'a. Rachel Tonga, Mateialona's sister-in-law, recorded in her diary how, after Tupouto'a received his title, 'Utulau people brought food to their new chief, and danced for him, and the new Tupouto'a sent food to 'Utulau.[22] Custom required that Tupouto'a continue to recognize Valu and Fanua Lofanga as chiefs of their lands, although subordinate to himself.

The cobbled-together estates of Tupouto'a were satisfactory for a chief who had no legitimate heirs, and the name Tupouto'a had considerable *mana*, as is shown by an incident soon after Tupouto'a was installed in his title, which was related to Elizabeth Bott Spillius by the Queen in 1959. The story shows not only the *mana* of the name Tupouto'a, but also how the Queen was already the arbiter on matters of protocol that were indicators of chiefly status. The Queen also subtly complimented 'Ulukālala before ruling that Tupouto'a's title was superior, but the decision favoured the Queen too, for Tu'i Kanokupolu Tupouto'a was father of the first Tupou.

> *The new title Tupouto'a.* When they were having their first faikava (this was in 1921) 'Ulukalala asked to sit in the circle instead of at the head, but Mateialona (Tupouto'a) thought 'Ulukalala should sit at the head. Tupouto'a said that 'Ulukalala was older, meaning that the title was more ancient, and 'Ulukalala said that Tupouto'a was king, meaning that the original Tupouto'a had been Tu'i Kanokupolu, so he should sit at the head. One of the matapules after listening to the argument for some hours, came to the Queen and said "'Ulukalala and Tupouto'a are arguing about who should sit at the head of the circle. 'Ulukalala says Tupouto'a should, and Tupouto'a says 'Ulukalala should, and we can't have our kava because they are arguing." The Queen said this was an unusual sort of argument, usually they would each claim the right to sit at the head. The Queen told the matapule that 'Ulukalala's wishes should prevail in this matter for the Ha'a Ngata were the keepers of the kava and were the ones who would settle such disputes about kava. So the matapule went back with this message and told the disputants and the other matapules. Tupouto'a consented, and went muttering and grumbling to the head of the ring.[23]

The high personal rank of the new Tupouto'a was again demonstrated at his funeral, for he died on 15 September 1925 and was buried in the chiefly burial ground of Mala'e 'Aloa, the presentations continuing until 30 September.[24] A story related by the Queen about this funeral records also the interconnectedness of chiefs, the Queen's relations with the Tu'i Tonga people, and again her role as an arbiter of custom at an early time in her reign. The details of the argument may be hard to follow, but what is important about the story is that the Queen had the last word.

> When Mateialona [Tupouto'a] died, a group of women came from Sioeli Pangia [grandson of the last Tu'i Tonga] with koloa. I asked whose hala [connection or route] this was. Malia said it was "Sioeli's and ours". Malia was a descendant of Halaevalu Mata'aho [half-sister of Tupou I and one of the wives of the last Tu'i Tonga]. Ele, one of the other women there, was also a descendant of Halaevalu Mata'aho. Malia said this hala was fakatu'itonga [in the manner of the Tu'i Tonga people], and it was the Tu'i Tonga's hala to his sister Tu'ifua. I told Malia and Ele that they should be bringing Halaevalu Mata'aho's hala to her brother Tu'i Kanokupolu Taufa'ahau. They should not be coming in with the Tu'i Tonga's hala to his sister. I knew there would be quarrelling when they came to divide the koloa [collectibles] that I gave back to them. Ele said to me that all my generation was fie poto [trying to be clever], and I said "That's all right. Yours are all vale [foolish]."
>
> Actually Sioeli Pangia is a descendant of *both* Tu'i Tonga *and* Halaevalu Mata'aho, so I suppose he could go by either hala – either the Tu'i Tonga to his sister Tu'ifua, or Halaevalu Mata'aho's to her brother Taufa'ahau. But what isn't good is for people who are descended *only* from Halaevalu Mata'aho to go mixing themselves up with people who are also descended from the Tu'i Tonga.[25]

Although the Queen appointed the successors to the titles of hereditary estateholders and increasingly was the arbiter of chiefly quarrels, neither the aristocracy nor the nobles could be relied upon to be loyal to her. One of her challengers was the aristocratic noble of Lapaha, Sioeli Pangia (Figure 3.4). Sioeli usually remained aloof from the Palace, but on one occasion in 1924 he was to be installed in a minor title, and his people should have brought to the Palace the presentations due from a new titleholder. A man from Kolovai reported to Sālote that pigs were being cut up at Sioeli's place. On 30 October, when the Queen heard of it, she sent the nobles Ata and Fohe to Lapaha to remind Sioeli that his action was tantamount to a declaration of war, and to inform him that she was ready to answer his challenge. Sioeli came to the Palace in tears and wearing a big, ragged waist-mat to show his humility and to beg the Queen's forgiveness for what he claimed was a misunderstanding.[26]

Sioeli's grandfather the Tu'i Tonga Laufilitonga is said to have given his *kava* (that is, place in the *kava* ceremony) to a Catholic priest. Sioeli was reputed to have been equally provocative, for the royal *taumafa kava* now belonged to the Tu'i Kanokupolu, and Sioeli had no business giving it to anyone else. On one occasion only did Sālote invite a *papālangi* to sit in the *taumafa kava*, and perhaps the two events were connected. In 1925 the Queen invited High Commissioner Sir Eyre Hutson to sit as a *member* of the circle over which she presided, an indication to all Tongans that he recognized her as the legitimate Tu'i Kanokupolu and the rightness of her presiding over the royal *kava*.

In 1924 Sālote tested Sioeli Pangia's loyalty by inviting him to join the reunited Free Wesleyan Church of which she had recently become the temporal head. He did so and became a lay preacher.[27] But when Sioeli claimed as part of his estates the lands where the Tu'i Tonga graves lay, Sālote was adamant that they were not his. Tongilava recorded in his diary on 10 March 1926 that "Sioeli Pangia came in the morning and again in the afternoon and brought a letter for Her Majesty, in which he agrees to that land in Mu'a being disposed of as the Queen wishes, to lease or in any way that will enable her to look after that land for the government and the land-and-people". The relinquishing of the Tu'i Tonga graves (*langi*) and the Ha'amonga-'a-Maui (prehistoric trilithon) by Sioeli to the Crown was again recorded in 1935, in accordance with the Land (Amendment) Act of 1934.[28]

The place where Sioeli lived in Lapaha was known as Malila. A tortoise who lived in the Palace grounds, supposedly brought to Tonga by Captain Cook, was named Tu'i Malila (the King of Malila). One can assume that this was a Tongan joke.

Behind these "challenges" by Sioeli and responses by Sālote was her determination to quash any claims that Sioeli was the heir to the *mana* of the Tu'i Tonga. Sālote herself claimed that *mana*, because the Tu'i Kanokupolu was now the *only* "king" in Tonga, and because she was the descendant of the sister of Sioeli's father (Figure 3.4). Futa Helu has pointed out that the imagery in Sālote's poetry relates to the Tu'i Tonga, which would remind listeners of her own Tu'i Tonga descent. And although the Queen wrote laments after the deaths of some other high-born Tongans, Sioeli did not earn such a compliment. On the contrary, Sālote thought he was a very bad example to other nobles.[29]

Sioeli was the son of Kalanivalu, twin brother of Old Lavinia. Sioeli had no legitimate children, and his heir was the son of his sister, Afā. Sālote gave the sister's son the title Kalanivalu, which would remind him that he was descended from the brother while she was descended from the sister; that is, she was *fahu* to him. The heir, Sēmisi, also inherited the Fotofili title, and again Sālote was descended from the sister while Sēmisi was descended from the brother (Figure 7.1). Sālote thus doubly outranked the new Kalanivalu by *kāinga* ranking, which put an end to any Tu'i Tonga pretensions he might have. Nevertheless, the Fotofili line had come up in the world thanks to its connections with Queen

Sālote and the Tu'i Tonga, and when Tōkanga (the sister of Fotofili and the Queen's mother's mother) died in April 1929, the high chiefs brought to the Palace presentations appropriate for a very great chief. Tōkanga was buried in Mala'e 'Aloa, the funeral ceremonies continuing for two weeks.[30] The elaborate ritual and length of the ceremonies were a public declaration that Tōkanga was of high rank *because* she was the grandmother of the Queen.

The nobles and chiefs who had fought most strongly in support of the Tu'i Tonga against Sālote's ancestors were the Ha'a Havea of the Central District of Tongatapu. One of the Ha'a Havea chiefs was Lavaka, noble of Pea. His ancestors had been subdued by Tupou I after a three-month siege that ended the civil wars. When Lavaka omitted a traditional courtesy due to the Queen, she called for her car and set out for Pea. Someone hurried to warn Lavaka, so that when Sālote arrived he was already seated beside the road, wearing the large, ragged waist-mat that showed his humility and acknowledged her superior rank. The Queen forgave him, but left him trembling.[31]

Kāinga rank is relative. Thus it was important to Sālote and Tungī that other aristocrats should marry in such a way that their children would not outrank the princes. Both Sālote and Tungī were credited with arranging – and blocking – marriages of aristocrats. In his biographical writings in *Koe Havea* (1941), Sione Havea said: "If a noble is in need of a wife to give him high-ranking descendants, [the Queen] gives him a woman of her own house to marry" [SAH]. What Sione Havea does not make clear is that aristocrats were encouraged to marry middle-ranking chiefs, not other aristocrats. Not all marriages were arranged, it is true; for aristocrats, like anyone else, married for personal preference rather than political reasons, and not infrequently eloped rather than risk intervention from the Palace.[32] The Queen let it be known how much she disapproved of elopements of aristocrats, deeming them to be an act of disrespect to herself as well as to the couple's parents and *mehekitanga*.

By "her own house" Sione Havea may have meant the prestigious *kāinga* of Kolomotu'a, through whom Sālote and Tungī were related, for women of this *kāinga* were married to nobles and their heirs (Figure 17.1) with remarkable consistency. By contrast, the Queen promoted marriages of Tu'i Tonga women to untitled men of relatively low rank, which made their children "half-shells" (aristocratic on only one side) and less likely to marry well. A surprising number of the aristocrats and nobles had no children, which the Queen attributed to their opposition to Christianity.

In spite of the Constitution, which required that the eldest son inherit the title of a noble father, Tupou I and II had continued to appoint the uncle, brother, or adopted son of the previous titleholder in the old way; that is, the one who was deemed by virtue of seniority and experience to be a proven leader. The Queen was determined to respect the Constitution and laws, but was unhappy about the fact that elders were passed over in favour of young men who often did not care about their *kāinga*. People blamed her (she said) for not overriding the Constitution and appointing the most suitable person.[33]

As the aristocratic blood was diluted by marriage, hereditary estateholders became the most privileged in the community, for their control of land-and-people gave them economic dominance. Their relations were often tempted to challenge the appointed titleholder on the grounds that at some time since the Constitution (or even before it) the title had *not* gone to the eldest son or his heirs. In Queen Sālote's lifetime, contested titles of nobles were Tu'ivakanō 1923, Fulivai 1926, 1960, Vaha'i 1927, Tu'i'afitu 1931, Kalanivalu 1937, 1945, Niukapu 1940, Nuku 1949. The decline in the number of claims after the 1940s could have been due to a more settled succession, but also because the Queen discouraged would-be claimants, many of whom, she said, that been encouraged by Sioape Kaho. Up to the point when a claimant lodged his claim in the court, the Queen could use her own knowledge of genealogies to discourage claimants (for example, for Vaea and Ma'afu titles). Once a claim was lodged in the court, she did not interfere, whatever her opinion, because she recognized that respect for the law was a prime principle in an ordered society.

The Queen was able to appoint senior members of the *kāinga* as trustees for minors; for example, Luani (1918–31), Ve'ehala (1927–47), Ma'afu (1936–55), Vaea (1939–42), Fakafanua (1949–55), Veikune (1949–65), Malupō (1952–56, though not a minor), Tupouto'a (1925–36), Tu'ipelehake (1912–43, Tungī was trustee after her accession), Mā'atu (which became vacant in 1934 and remained vacant in her lifetime). 'Ulukālala and Ata (vacant from 1960) and Lavaka (vacant from 1964) also had trustees. In former times the trustee had all the privileges of a titleholder, and indeed often became the titleholder, but in Sālote's time the trustee was charged with using the income from the estates for the benefit of the heir (for his education, for example), and the Queen dismissed the trustee if he did not carry out his duties as instructed.

There were dissensions about titles and about the relative rank of the aristocrats, but control of land-and-people was the most emotive of issues. Gifford records that during the early 1920s, when a noble or a *matāpule ma'u tofi'a* died, his neighbours moved boundary markers to increase their own estate at the heir's expense. The hereditary estateholders obstructed attempts to survey boundaries of estates, as this would make further encroachment more difficult.[34] Failure by the government to survey boundaries was used as an excuse by hereditary estateholders for their failure to distribute land among their people.

It was Tupou I's intention when he appointed hereditary estateholders that each should hold a small portion of the estate for his personal use (usually 8–10 per cent of the whole) and distribute the remainder among his people; that is, the greater proportion of any estate was held *in trust* until it could be distributed. The Law of 1907 specifically stated that "[hereditary estateholders] shall have no power to refuse a tax allotment to any person lawfully residing upon his land nor to dispossess any person to whom the Minister of lands may have granted a tax allotment . . . His interest in the land is limited to receiving the rents" (561, *Laws 1903*). But in 1915 Parliament passed legislation that required the written permission of the hereditary estateholder before a tax (farm) allotment could be registered, instead of registration being authorized by the Minister for Lands.[35] The hereditary estateholders were able to exact *fatongia* from people living on their estates with the promise that written permission for registration would be forthcoming.

Legally speaking, if an allotment was not registered, the hereditary estateholder could resume the land at any time, or grant it to another person. One example of customary rights versus the rights of hereditary estateholders was in relation to land occupied by churches. When Tupou I set up his new Free Church in 1885, he asked nobles to allow churches to be built on their lands, and most agreed. Since the Free Church rarely took out leases and almost never paid rent, the hereditary estateholders considered these lands to be still part of their estates. In accordance with the law, but doubtless motivated by his own Old Wesleyan allegiance, Tungī attempted in 1922 to resume land that the Free Church occupied on his estate at Fua'amotu. The President of the Free Church, J. B. Watkin, appealed to the Privy Council, which ordered Tungī to return the land.[36] This was a recognition of a customary right to land and would be referred to as such in the Church Affair of 1923–24 (chapter 8).

Tungī, like other hereditary estateholders, believed that he was the absolute ruler of his land-and-people, but he agreed with Tupou I's dictum that land would not be productive unless it was distributed among commoners to plant and harvest. Accordingly Tungī distributed land among the people on his own estates and on the estates for which he was the trustee. If a man was industrious, Tungī would allocate to him more that the eight-and-a-quarter acres required by law.[37] The Queen added her voice, constantly urging people to register their allotments.

The Queen believed that stability depended on modified forms of traditional institutions such as *fatongia*, *tapu*, and *fahu*, which Tupou I had attempted to abolish. But *fatongia* was now called *kavenga* (the labour that commoners do for their chiefs out of love, not because they are forced as was the case with *fatongia*). The worst aspects of *tapu* (categories of food being reserved for chiefs, for example) were effectively prohibited, and social sanctions were applied to a *fahu* who took too much advantage of her/his superior *kāinga* relationship. Nevertheless, physical abuse and exploitation of commoners by their chief continued.

The Queen respected the law and Constitution, but her authority over the people depended on neither of these. She attributed her achievements to strong character and hard work. Her knowledge of people and attention to the everyday concerns of her people were also important factors. People came to the Palace to seek her assistance long before they considered taking these concerns to a government department or one of the courts. Again, Sione Havea has something to say about her everyday priorities:

> She has set up an association to support education for women. She has begun a group for women . . . When food is sent to her by the chiefs and the people, she shares it with Tupou College and the Girls' College. She encourages the high chiefs to see that their children are educated here in Tonga and abroad. If the children of the nobles are neglected, the Queen sends them to school at her own expense . . . She is like Maui the fisherman, who pulled up the islands of Tonga from the bottom of the sea . . . To have a leader who lives in such harmony with the people is an education in itself. (*Koe Havea*, 1941) [SAH]

Even Tungī's enemies said Sālote could not have learnt so much and so quickly without the constant support of Tungī. For her, Tungī was a prime example of a chief who looked after his people. Like the Queen, he was besieged by petitioners, who came to him more because he was a great aristocrat than because he was Premier. As Sione Havea said:

> I believe there is scarcely a person living in Tonga who has not at some time asked for something from him – a house, a horse, seed yams, money. Even when they do not ask, Tungī gives them things . . . When a village finds it difficult to make its annual contribution to the work of the Church, they look to Tungī to give them jobs. When their taxes are due, they come in hordes to ask Tungī for money. We should be more considerate, for no one has endless supplies of money. It is acceptable to ask for favours, but the asking should be done with consideration. Tungī carries heavy responsibilities on behalf of the sovereign. I consider that the Queen is very fortunate to have a husband with such varied talents, capable of doing things indoors and outdoors. Wherever there is a need, Tungī is ready to respond . . . (*Koe Havea*, 1941) [SAH]

Sālote gave full credit to Tungī as consort and Premier, but it is clear that she had a natural talent for relationships, and her concern for people, once awakened, was assured and consistent. Short-term losses did not persuade her to abandon her long-term objectives. This last attribute would stand her in good stead in the matter of the reunion of the churches that would take up much of her time in 1923 and 1924.

Before that great trial of her reign, the qualities for which Sālote would later be renowned had emerged: authority, intelligence, and a conviction that Tongans must cling to the customs that gave them a distinct identity. But the Queen still needed allies, and some compromises had to be made in order to win over not only aristocrats and hereditary estateholders to her cause, but also satisfy the aspirations of the lesser chiefs. The opportunity came with the Church Affair.

CHAPTER EIGHT

God and Tonga Are My Inheritance[I]

"I am one who has already pledged to shoulder all the responsibilities, great or small, politically, nationally, or of religion." (Queen Sālote, 1923)[2]

IT IS COMMON FOR TONGAN and *papālangi* alike to talk of Queen Sālote's attempt to reunite two churches in 1923–24 as a religious cause. The Queen herself explained that behind her endeavour was the more important issue of reuniting the kingdom. In 1923 the Free Church, founded by Tupou I in 1885, was the most numerous and powerful body in the kingdom. The Free Church had virtually belonged to Tupou I, but – ironically, given its history – it had become a bastion for those who opposed not only the Tupou dynasty but also the hereditary estateholders appointed by Tupou I.

In 1885 Tupou I had chosen Rev. Jabez Bunting Watkin, a Wesleyan missionary, to be President of his new church, but Tupou remained the undoubted temporal head until his death in 1893.[3] Watkin had baptised Sālote, was the celebrant at Sālote's marriage with Tungī, had crowned her, and had baptised her three sons. At her accession in 1918, Watkin was 81 years of age to Sālote's 18 years.

The Free Church had financed Tupou II's visits to New Zealand when he sought to have the Supplementary Agreement declared unconstitutional. In 1921 the Free Church had lent Sālote money, which she repaid. But in the last years of Tupou II and the early years of Sālote's reign this Church refused to "lend" any more money to the aristocracy and nobles. The Free Church was now run for the benefit of a corrupt clergy and dominated by lesser chiefs who were members of the "Reactionary Party". Watkin and his Tongan clergy already had a reputation for meddling in politics,[4] and it was their politics as much as their debased religion that caused Sālote considerable concern.

The Queen believed that church and state should be the "twin pillars" of the kingdom and indivisible. Tupou I and Tupou II had been recognized as the temporal heads of the Free Church; so when Watkin and his clergy refused to recognize Sālote as temporal head of the church they were denying the legitimacy of her accession to the titles of Tu'i Kanokupolu and sovereign. The Queen could not allow such a large organization – one founded by her own ancestor – to be independent of her authority under the pretence of religious freedom. What began as her attempt to reclaim her rightful position in the church developed into a determination to reform a corrupt church, and then into a movement to ensure national unity by means of religious unity – at least of those churches that shared the Wesleyan heritage.

In 1923–24 as in the 1880s, the overriding question was that of loyalty. Tupou I had risen to eminence with the help of Wesleyan missionaries, but when secure he felt irked by their attempts to exercise spiritual authority over him. He commanded his subjects to show their "love" for him by leaving the Wesleyan Mission and joining his Free Church (Figure 8.1). Those who did not join were deemed by him not to be martyrs for conscience' sake, but in civil rebellion against the King – and were punished accordingly (chapter 2). Tupou II continued as the temporal head, the Free Church being proclaimed to be the state church in 1898. But by 1911 Tupou II was protesting that "the Chiefs and myself, not possessing the laws of the church, seem to be outside and take no part in it".[5] Tupou II was as ineffective as a leader of the Free Church as he was as leader of the nation, and by the time Sālote became Queen, the church was a totally independent and powerful organization within the kingdom.

At the time of Queen Sālote's accession the Free Church reflected Tongan society in its organization (hierarchical), ethics (Tongan not European), and loyalties (to their local chiefs). The power of these lesser chiefs within the "Reactionary Party" would be shown in the troubles of 1923–24. Tupou I had asked the hereditary estateholders to allow Free Church buildings to be built on their lands, and by 1918 there was a Free Church church in almost every village in the kingdom. Unlike the other churches, the Free Church did not have formal leases (and usually paid no rent) for land occupied by church buildings, clergy houses and allotments, and church schools on the estates of the hereditary estateholders. The hereditary estateholders took the initiative by querying the legal and financial condition of the church. In 1917 the noble Mā'atu (Pānuve) wrote to the Conference of the Free Church (the church's governing body) on behalf of the hereditary estateholders to ask for formal leases.[6] Rev. Edwin Harkness, the only *papālangi* minister other than Watkin in the Free Church, replied favourably, but nothing was done.[7] Bishop Blanc, of the Catholic Church in Tonga, believed that the moves for reform began when the noble Vaea asked Watkin for a loan of money and was refused.[8]

In May 1920 the Queen, spurred on by the hereditary estateholders, asked Watkin to publish the Constitution and Law of the church.[9] The reply was a curt refusal, denying Sālote any greater role in the church than that of any other lay member. Watkin wrote to Sālote:

> We are astounded at the request – from the time of Tubou I from 1885–93, and then Tubou II 1893–1918, there was never the slightest desire on their part to touch the matters, but in any case you should first have spoken to the President, and some of the Representatives, and some of the Ministers, with reference to this matter, for it is clear that the procedure of the Free Church is the same as the Wesleyan Church which from its establishment to the year 1885 did not print the Constitution and Laws you have requested . . . [10]

A petition to Sālote from some nobles and chiefs in August–September 1922 summed up their opinions:

> The subject of this petition: It is with regard to the Free Church of Tonga . . . most people . . . maintain that the said church is owned and ruled solely by the European minister now holding the office of President and those native ministers and other people who first established it. They reckon that as Tubou I and some chiefs were merely ordinary church members the same footing applies to latter days. In our humble findings this church should be under the protectorship of Your Majesty and Your Majesty's Government . . . Owing to the shifty methods of those ministers now in authority and seemingly wary of avoiding the subject of the church's history they are most unreliable to depend on and we have tolerated their ways quite far enough . . . [11]

Sālote took until May 1923 to consider her response to this petition. She then asserted that since Tupou I appointed Watkin as President of the Free Church in 1885, it followed that she (as Tupou's heir) had the same power and that "this Church still stands and it should be correctly called the Government-controlled Church of the Ruling Sovereign and chiefs and people of Tonga".[12]

Armed with Sālote's reply, the nobles challenged Watkin, and were rebuffed as Sālote had been. On 31 July 1923 they submitted a formal appeal to the Privy Council, asking that action be taken over the "unjust and unsatisfactory leadership of those ministers in charge".[13] They accused Watkin of usurping "full reign and authority". They also accused him and the clergy of extorting money from the people, and with disbursing that money without proper authority, for their own benefit. The nobles were protesting that the natural order had been reversed, and the clergy had taken over the status and perquisites that were normally those of the great chiefs and hereditary estateholders.

This reversal of roles was occurring at the highest level, for when Sālote attended the annual Conference of the church in Ha'apai in 1922, Watkin was treated as though he were the Tu'i Tonga (being carried ashore in his boat, for example) and the presentations made to him far exceeded the presentations made to the Queen.[14] Ha'apai, once the stronghold of the Tupou dynasty, was pointedly defying her. Sālote gave no publicity to the insult, but strengthened her determination to challenge directly the organization that attributed to someone else the *mana* of the sacred ruler.[15]

In this matter the Queen showed that in the few years since her accession, she had acquired wisdom in her handling of situations. Although there were long intervals in the correspondence in the early years (when she presumably sought advice), she would act swiftly and decisively when such action was required. In a situation where so many diverse interests were involved, the discretion and restraint she showed were notable in one so young.

The Queen now acted strongly, by summoning the clergy of the Free Church to meet Free Church nobles and chiefs under her auspices in the Royal Chapel on 10 and 14 September 1923.[16] She had chosen the venue for the encounter well: no chief or minister entering the Palace grounds could fail to remember what was due to her as Tu'i Kanokupolu, and the Royal Chapel reminded them of Tupou I (its builder). In her formal speech at the commencement of the proceedings, the Queen reminded the gathering of her authority as head of church and state to call them together ("today the two olive trees bow down to me"), and that when Tongans did not settle disputes among themselves, intervention from outside the kingdom could ensue. The Queen told the meeting that the Privy Council wanted the matter settled by the court, but she herself wished for differences to be settled peacefully within the church, for "the decision of the court satisfies one party, but not the other". The Queen thus showed her preference for mediation and reconciliation.

The Queen continued by relating the events that had led to the meeting, beginning with complaints in 1905 about the corruption in the church, and ending with the fact that (after many requests) she had obtained the original Constitution of the Free Church from Watkin that very morning. (She did not inform the members that she had sent her brother, Vīlai, to Watkin's house to coax the Constitution from him. Vīlai had a "sweet mouth".[17])

Sālote then urged those gathered in the Royal Chapel to speak out so that "under the command and guidance of the Lord, we may this day correct the affairs of the church by ourselves". The nobles and chiefs then spoke, reprimanding the clergy for usurping the Queen's authority, for financial corruption, for their lack of spirituality, and for their inadequate teaching. As

Vili Lausi'i said to the clergy, "As for your saintliness? Who would believe it? I don't think a cockroach would be saved by your preaching."

Inspired by Sālote, the nobles and chiefs demanded the following reforms: the publication of the Constitution (of August 1885) and Law of the Free Church; the appointment of lay trustees; the return to the original name (Free Wesleyan Church, instead of the familiarly used Free Church); an audit of the church's books; and an invitation to *papālangi* missionaries to come to Tonga. When the clergy demurred and asked for immunity, the Queen and the nobles and chiefs declared that they would give no further financial support to the church until reforms were under way. When called upon to vote for reform, Watkin and three other ministers refrained from voting at all.

Following the September meetings, audits of the church were carried out. It was discovered that no financial statements had been presented to the annual Conference since 1885.[18] Watkin's salary was £800 (plus another £100 as royal chaplain), larger than any salary in Tonga except the Queen's.[19] Watkin held keys for safes all over the kingdom, and would empty these when he was on tour (if they were not already empty). Some money had been misappropriated by clergy, some had been "lent" to nobles, chiefs, and *papālangi* traders, usually without any firm arrangement for repayment. Some of the account books recorded purchases by Jehovah and loans to God. The superintendent minister of Ha'apai had used church money for his teeth, beds, household goods, and two boats. The superintendent minister of Vava'u had used church money to buy a timber house for a relative, and a piano and a motor lorry for himself. Jehovah had, apparently, purchased barbed wire. In Vava'u only £289 of the £3736 supposedly in the church safes could be found. There was no record of the money collected at the 1920 and 1921 annual collection (*misinale*) in Tongatapu. The audits showed that at least £30,000 of the church funds were unaccounted for, and the church heavily in debt.[20]

During the 40 years he had been President, Watkin had given his ministers no theological training. McOwan reported that "the native clergy are inherently lacking in those moral qualities that are vital in a religious organization". Bishop Blanc reported that the clergy were so ill-educated that in Conference they disputed whether the Bible was written by John Wesley or the Catholic Church! Watkin had ordained 92 ministers, although there were only 42 parishes, and eight or 10 ministers resided in some villages, most having no duties. Some clergy had no salaries, but others received £80–100 per annum, far in excess of those paid to the clergy of the Wesleyan Mission.[21]

Sālote was sensitive to overseas criticism that would inevitably follow revelations of the corruption within the Free Church. Even before the audit was complete, Sālote let it be known that if reforms were not undertaken, she and the nobles would leave the Free Church and establish another church. Soon after this declaration, some "progressive chiefs" of the Free Church approached

Sālote and asked her to begin negotiations for reunion with the Old Wesleyans.[22] The chiefs must, of course, have known that such a request would be favourably received. A powerful reason for the Queen acceding to their request to promote reunion was that Tungī was a loyal Old Wesleyan, while she and her sons had been baptised in the Free Church. A family that did not worship in the same church was not a good example for the kingdom. Indeed some people claimed that the Queen's attempt to reunite the churches was to please her consort. But since the Old Wesleyans were required to make many concessions, it seems that the Queen had other reasons, not the least of which was to bring Ha'apai and Vava'u chiefs into line.

On 23 October 1923 the Queen formally approached Rev. Rodger Page, with a proposal for reunion of the Free Church with its parent church, the Wesleyan Mission.[23] Reunion of the two Wesleyan churches had been discussed frequently over the previous 40 years, and the District Meeting of the Wesleyan Mission had voted each year in favour of reunion.[24] But now that reunion looked possible, those Old Wesleyans who had suffered – or whose families had suffered – from persecution in the 1880s had second thoughts. Many felt that reunion would be disloyal to the memory of Dr James Egan Moulton, founder and first principal of Tupou College, where they had received their education. Further, they would be swamped by the much larger church, for the Old Wesleyans were said to number 4296 compared with 17,180 Free Church adherents. It was a measure of Tungī's rank and influence that the Old Wesleyans agreed, albeit reluctantly, to reunion.

For 40 years the Free Church had stoutly maintained that it was "Methodist" (i.e. Wesleyan) in dogma and practice, so there appeared to be no obstacle. Indeed members of the two churches had commonly assisted in the preparations and participated in each other's church festivals. In the last months of 1923 and early months of 1924 Sālote tested her personal influence and used her oratorical skills when travelling through the island groups, asking the chiefs and people of both churches to support her. She wrote personal letters to the Quarterly Meetings of the Free Church, which were to meet in November and December, asking them to vote on two questions: first, the return to the original name of Free Wesleyan Church, and, second, whether they would agree to reunion with the Old Wesleyans.[25]

When McOwan left Tonga on 20 December 1923 on five months' leave, he believed there would be no major difficulties in the reunion of the churches, and he commended the Queen's attitude as being "outwardly neutral, quietly observant".[26] Throughout the whole affair, except for a notable burst of anger in April, the Queen would show her leadership skills, acting in a restrained manner in spite of repeated provocation.

In McOwan's absence, J. M. Masterton, son-in-law of Watkin, was British Vice-Consul, and George Scott, who had been Acting Chief Justice since

Stronge went on leave in August 1923, was Acting Judicial Commissioner. The two appointments would prove unfortunate, for while closely connected with Watkin, Masterton and Scott were still Sālote's official advisers in the early months of 1924, when she encountered difficulties. Far from advising and supporting her, as their appointments required, the two *papālangi* increased Sālote's difficulties by their open support for the anti-unionists. Scott, who had right of private practice, gave legal advice to Watkin and the anti-unionists.

Watkin appeared unmoved by the financial corruption revealed by the audits. "We hope there will be no further difficulty now that this correction has been accomplished," he wrote to Sālote and the nobles on 8 January 1924. He was extremely offended when he heard in February that Sālote had referred to him as a "source of trouble" and a "burden". He offered his resignation, which would take effect a year later, for he wished to be the first President of the reunited church. This would vindicate his actions in 1885, when he had left his ministry in one church to become the President of another church.[27] Sālote did not take up the offer of resignation at this time, and Watkin was persuaded by his friends not to persist.

The first formal move towards reunion was a summons by the Queen to representatives of the two churches to meet with her in the Royal Chapel on 20 and 21 February 1924 to discuss amendments to the Constitution of the Free Church that would, she hoped, make it acceptable to both parties.[28] It was agreed that ministers would preach in each other's churches, that the Wesleyan Mission would cease to exist in the following May, and that the Old Wesleyans would join the Free Church under its original name of Free Wesleyan Church. The reunited church would be governed by an annual Conference, which would give it financial and organizational independence, and would send representatives to the policymaking General Conference of the Methodist Church of Australasia. It was this last provision that made the anti-unionists claim that whatever name the reunited church bore, the reality was that the members of the Free Church were joining the Old Wesleyans.

Watkin was now only a few days short of his eighty-seventh birthday, and he excused himself from taking part in combined services on the grounds of age and infirmity. When his Tongan and *papālangi* advisers asked him to reconsider reunion, he wavered. On 14 March he assured one of the anti-unionists that "I stand firm in the Free Church".[29] But the very next day he signed the joint Constitution that would reunite the two churches. When he realized finally that the Queen did not intend him to be the first President of the reunited church, he resiled from the proposal.[30]

Land and other property now became an issue. To all appearances, the Free Church had a great deal more property than the Old Wesleyans, but the Free Church held their land only by customary right. The Free Church had a bigger income, but it also had greater expenditure, more debts, and more outstanding loans than the Wesleyan Mission.

Sālote counted on the nobles to influence their people in favour of reunion; but lesser chiefs, who represented the nobles in the villages, had more influence over the daily lives of the people than the nobles did, and these lesser chiefs threw their lot in with "the Watkinites", who now claimed to stand for customary rights and independence from the central government. The petitions against reunion, which began circulating in March 1924, were organized by some of these lesser chiefs: Samisoni Siaki Lolohea in Ha'apai, Tēvita Tapueluelu and the Afuha'amango family in Vava'u, and Motekiai Taukolo Langi in Tongatapu. Sioape Kaho and Tonga Faleola of Vava'u helped to spread rumours.[31] All of these had grievances against the royal house that had nothing to do with religion. Indeed it was the secular political agendas of such leaders and their influence over their own people that was at the root of the difficulties of 1924.

There were rumours that these events would put a stop to Sālote's rule, and that Tonga would become a republic. McOwan described Siaki Lolohea as a "Bolshevist" who would "proclaim a republic in Tonga tomorrow".[32] Samisoni Puli'uvea Afuha'amango was charged in March 1924 with defamation for referring to Sālote as a "foolish Queen" and a "cheating and lying Queen", and making derogatory remarks about her Niuafo'ou ancestry.[33]

Tonga Faleola and Sioape Kaho attempted to draw the Catholics into the quarrel by insinuating that the Queen would turn her attention to that church if she succeeded in reuniting the two Wesleyan churches. Faleola offered to bring the Vava'u people into the Catholic Church if Bishop Blanc would take sides, confirming that loyalty to the Free Church was not the motive for Faleola's opposition to the Queen. Blanc believed that Sālote was acting in a tyrannical manner, but he refused to be involved, instructing his followers to remain neutral. Blanc attributed the support of some *papālangi* traders for the anti-unionists to their fear of annexation and subsequent taxation, and believed that McOwan (still on leave) was at that very moment discussing annexation with his superiors in Suva.[34]

The Queen's wish for more *papālangi* missionaries to come to Tonga to encourage the spiritual life of the reunited church also incurred opposition. The anti-unionists did not want "white control", and Watkin attracted support when he declared that he intended a Tongan would succeed him as President of the Free Church.[35] The intensity of feeling among the *papālangi* anti-unionists was recorded by a traveller, Elinor Mordaunt. She was the guest in Ha'apai of the daughters of Shirley Baker, who had helped Tupou I to set up the Free Church. The Misses Baker convinced Miss Mordaunt that Sālote was attempting to force the Tongan people to abandon the Free Church they loved. Proceeding to Tongatapu, Elinor Mordaunt sought out the Queen in her garden in Mu'a, and unceremoniously introduced herself as an expert on Tongan affairs:

> I was out of temper and would not drink [*kava*], telling the queen very plainly what I thought of her, expressing it as my opinion that if she persisted in her course in regard to the people's religion she would end by losing her kingdom. With the placidity of all very fat people, however, she kept perfectly calm under my onslaught, reiterating the words "You must ask my husband that" – "You must tell my husband that" – "I leave that to my husband", until, out of patience with her I got up and flung back to the motor, without so much as the semblance of an obeisance or good-bye.[36]

Once again the Queen showed great self-control in the face of provocation, and her references to her husband were rather a refusal to engage in conversation and a deflection of Miss Mordaunt's intrusion than an abrogation of responsibility.

The Free Church had been generous with loans to traders, a situation unlikely to continue in a reformed church, and this "material gain",[37] together with the influence of Masterton and Scott were sufficient to rally some of the *papālangi* traders against the proposed reunion.[38] McOwan blamed longtime *papālangi* residents – Scott and Masterton, in particular – for "mischievous interference" and "mischievous suggestions" that were leading the churches to litigation. Masterton was two-faced, McOwan said, for he had reported to Suva that all was quiet and he hoped Watkin would retire, while accusing Tungī of stealing Free Church property that the signatories to the February agreement had agreed to share. The Acting High Commissioner concluded that Masterton was acrimonious and regrettably partisan.[39] McOwan reported:

> When it is remembered that land ownership and religion are the subjects of the dispute, one would be filled with astonishment and even admiration at the control Tongan people, individually and collectively, have exercised over their feelings, were it not quite patent that the dispute is not really of their making but had been engineered and kept alive by interfering and mischief-making Europeans.[40]

There were *papālangi* supporters of the Queen who opposed reunion for other reasons. Some of the families – notably the Cocker family, Yorkshire Methodists – had witnessed the persecutions of the 1880s and believed the Old Wesleyans should be allowed to retain their separate identity as a close-knit community.

Blanc attributed the miscarriage that Sālote suffered early in April 1924 to her anger when she heard that 'Ulukālala (who had been a signatory in

February and March to the amended Constitution) had openly declared on 2 April that he would join the anti-unionists.[41] McOwan commented that 'Ulukālala's "greatest weakness is that he would rather be the leader of a small faction than take a subordinate place in a larger movement".[42] 'Ulukālala was a symbol of independent chieftainship, and his defection lent respectability to what had been up until that time a movement by lesser chiefs.

In the midst of the difficult church/political negotiations the Queen lamented the death of her miscarried son, whom she named 'Alaivahamama'o, in a moving lament she entitled "Tu'ifua's tears for 'Alaivahamama'o":

> Tell the 'esi of Pānuve
> That my child is lost from me.

In spite of the audits and the absence of leases, the anti-unionists persisted in believing that the Free Church assets were enormous, and were persuaded by their *papālangi* allies that they would win if they took legal action. The anti-unionists now claimed all former Free Church properties on the grounds that it was the true church of Tupou I. They produced a draft Constitution of January 1885, which had been in the possession of the Baker family, in which Tupou I's church was referred to as the Free Church, instead of the name Free Wesleyan Church used in the August 1885 Constitution. Scott advised the anti-unionists to retain the services of R. N. Moody, an Auckland barrister who had impressed the locals with his victory in the matter of the Tonga Ma'a Tonga Kautaha in 1910–11. Moody accepted the brief, and sent a solicitor, Mr Goodwin, to Tonga on the April steamer to prepare for litigation.[43] Unfortunately for the anti-union camp, Moody's experience in World War One had turned him into an alcoholic.[44]

Elinor Mordaunt was not the only one persuaded that Tonga was on the brink of civil war and Sālote would soon be forced to abdicate. Blanc recorded that the Privy Council had passed an ordinance to control the use and distribution of firearms, and that 25 cases of dynamite had been stolen from the government stores.[45] Nothing more was heard of the dynamite, but talk of civil war continued.

As feelings rose, Rodger Page regretted having entered negotiations for reunion. If he could have withdrawn, he would have done so, but he realized that such a withdrawal would put the Queen in an intolerable position.[46] Page instructed his members not to engage in disputes with the anti-unionists, who now used the term "Wesleyan" pejoratively to apply to the pro-union faction within the old Free Church. Overseas newspapers were informed by "An Old Resident" that the pro-unionist and anti-unionist factions were fighting all over the kingdom, that men were killed, and that peace-loving anti-unionists were driven from their churches by axe-wielding pro-unionists.[47] Apart from an incident in Vava'u, none of these rumours of violence was substantiated, but they served to increase tension in the community.

Watkin now made no secret of the fact that he wanted the deposition of the Queen. In April he preached sermons on the abdication of the Kaiser of Germany, the murder of the Czar of Russia, and the advantages of democracy.[48] An incensed deputation of nobles borrowed a car and drove out to Mu'a, where Sālote was still recovering from her miscarriage, and asked that Watkin be deported for his treason.[49] Sālote was not at all averse to the notion, indeed exile was a traditional way of dealing with difficult people, but she would not be provoked into taking precipitate action. She informed the nobles that she would wait for the return of McOwan and Chief Justice Stronge in May, and seek their advice.

The immediate spark for Watkin's treasonable sermons may have been Sālote's offer (on 9 April) of a pension of £600 a year and continued occupation of his house, Mapu-'a-fuiva, if he would resign from the presidency of the Free Church.[50] On 16 April she withdrew her offer and *demanded* that he resign. This was the first day of the Conference of the Free Church, and Watkin had taken the opportunity to interview ministers individually, asking them to repudiate their earlier consent to reunion. He was now fully persuaded that reunion was "a trick" to bring the Free Church back into the fold from which it had seceded in 1885.[51]

Watkin was now openly defiant and hostile to the Queen. Acting on the premise that if Tupou I could appoint Watkin, she could dismiss him, Sālote wrote a letter of dismissal on 17 April. After laying on his shoulders all the blame for the maladministration and corruption in the church, Sālote reproached him for his personal betrayal of her:

> . . . you promised me "that you would support to the utmost of your ability my attempt to bring about the union of the two churches, &c". Each promise you made was like a solemn oath in the presence of Jehovah. But the things you have done recently, supporting the letters, petitions, and threats of litigation of some of the ministers, makes it appear that you have turned away, and set your heart on killing and crushing to pieces and overturning my work that you already promised to support, and render it useless, and to shame me by trampling it in the dust under your feet.[52] [TF]

Watkin simply ignored the Queen's letter and continued to interview the ministers. On 22 April the Queen decided on confrontation and went to Conference to address the members.[53] To them she related the history of the schism in 1885, and assured them that what Tupou I had sought was recognition (by the General Conference of the Methodist Church of Australasia) that his

favour of Watkin and his supporters. Crompton accordingly preserved his reputation for never losing a case by returning to Suva on 26 May, promising to return for the appeal. McOwan, who returned to Tonga on the steamer that took Crompton away, concurred with Crompton's assessment of Scott, saying that "[Scott is] not only an alarmist but he is strongly opposed to the union on grounds which are more personal than public. It would be better if he were less ready to interfere with and oppose the Queen and her Consort in this as in other matters".[61]

Crompton's departure left the "Nobles and Chiefs of Tonga" without representation and Sālote without a legal adviser, for since his return from leave Chief Justice Stronge had declined to advise her on the grounds that he would have to hear the appeal from the Land Court.[62] In summing up Stronge's career in Tonga, McOwan described him as having "the reputation of being a conscientious and hard-working official where the work of his own Department was concerned, but as a member of the Cabinet and Privy Council he was regarded as being plain and blunt of speech and manners to the verge of rudeness, unsympathetic and tactless in his dealings with the natives, without administrative ability and with little knowledge of men and affairs".[63]

The Queen had been without a consular or legal adviser for many months, and McOwan was determined to compensate for what he considered to be bias shown by the *papālangi* of the Beach, and to use his influence for "peace and justice".[64] He believed that Watkin had not acted in an ethical manner, and indeed was guilty of dereliction of duty in relation to his flock, but he avoided direct confrontation. When 17 nobles requested that Watkin be deported, he undertook to forward the request to Suva if the nobles could provide more solid evidence of treason than a sermon. He advised the nobles that they "could more loyally serve their Queen by following Her Majesty's example of tactfulness, patience and moderation in their dealing with those who did not see eye-to-eye with them in this Church controversy".[65] It was advice that the nobles were unlikely to heed.

On 22 May the Wesleyan Mission in Tonga ceased to exist, and its members joined the reunited Free Wesleyan Church, which claimed to be the continuing "Church of Tubou" under its original name. This claim would be tested in the courts, and since Crompton's departure, the newly arrived minister, Harold Wood, found himself acting as barrister for the nobles and pro-unionists in the Land Court.[66] Caught up in the fervour of the occasion, it was not until much later that Wood realized that the nobles used him, the reunited church, and the court cases for their own purposes: to strengthen their hold on the land. The nobles also expected to use the reunited church as a private bank in the way they had once used the Free Church.

Before his departure for Fiji, Crompton advised Wood to make a strong, aggressive attack upon the maladministration of Watkin and the corruption of his ministers, but Wood was prevented from following this strategy by the Queen's and Page's hopes of ultimate reconciliation with the anti-unionists.[67]

The plaintiffs in the Land Court case of 10–13 and 21 June 1924 were Watkin and his ministers, also Tapueluelu of Vava'u, Siaki Lolohea of Ha'apai, and Motekiai Taukolo Langi of Tongatapu, and they were represented by Moody. 'Ulukālala, as was his wont, used his influence behind the scenes. The defendants were the new President of the Free Wesleyan Church (Setaleki Manu), members of the Free Wesleyan Church, and the nobles, including Fakafanua, whose land was being used as a test case, and they were represented by Wood. Since his return from leave McOwan had looked through the consular files and had located documents relevant to the case, and he sat in the court every day to observe the proceedings.

Moody began with an "unjustifiable attack" on the Queen.[68] He did not argue his case on either Tongan enacted or customary law, but instead relied solely on English and Scottish law, taking as a precedent the case of the Wee Fraes, the remnant of a Scottish church who had won ownership of the property against a much larger seceding group because they were judged to be fulfilling the wishes of the founder of their church. Moody also argued that the nobles had, at the instigation of Tupou I, made outright verbal gifts of land to the Free Church during and after 1885, and that the anti-unionists were now the rightful "owners" of these lands because they had followed the wishes of Tupou I by remaining separate from the Old Wesleyans.

Wood argued that Tongan law did not provide for either gifts or sale of land, so without leases the plaintiffs had no right to occupy the land in question. Whatever rights they might have were vested in the pro-unionists, for Tupou I's expressed wish that his church re-establish connection with the parent church in Australia was now fulfilled. Wood was able to quote from a Blue Book of 1888, provided by McOwan, in which printed correspondence proved that Tupou I had wished his church to be a Conference associated with the General Conference of the Methodist Church of Australasia.[69]

As Crompton had predicted, Scott gave his judgment on 21 June in favour of the anti-unionists on the basis of Moody's arguments, without reference to the documents in the Blue Book. The nobles went to wait on the Queen, and Wood reported that they were "wild at the opposition, which affects all their land".[70] Blanc applauded the decision and commented that the nobles had misled the Queen with their "foolish, shallow, and self-interested flattery".[71] Some ministers and members who had agreed to reunion now changed their minds and rejoined the Free Church, the estimates varying between 3000 and 8000.

There was no doubt in McOwan's mind (as there was none in the Queen's) that the issue was not religion, but a challenge to Sālote's rights and prerogatives as sovereign. McOwan commended her calmness in the face of continued provocation, for July and August yielded further examples of disrespect and defiance, this time by Moody and Stronge. Stronge had declared soon after the Land Court case that if the anti-unionists filed a writ in the Supreme Court (over which he presided) relating to property other than land, he would be prevented from sitting on the Privy Council when the appeal from the Land Court was heard. The anti-unionists accordingly issued a writ in the Supreme Court.[72] Stronge's declaration raised the possibility of the appeal being heard by the Chief Justice of Sāmoa or Fiji or in a British court, the last course being favoured by Stronge and Moody.

In his opening address to the Land Court, Moody had attacked the Queen, accusing her of cant and of ill-using the aged Watkin. No one, he said, could respect her after reading her letter dismissing Watkin. On 25 June and 14 August, Moody wrote to the Queen stating that the Privy Council would not be impartial if she insisted (as was her constitutional right) upon presiding when the appeal was heard. "My plain duty to my clients compels me to object to any tribunal in which Your Majesty has had any voice, or in which Your Majesty has anything to do with the selection of its members . . . "[73]

Moody counted upon the litigation ultimately being settled by a British court, where English law would apply. Copies of his letters were sent to the *Fiji Times* and *New Zealand Herald*, the latter commenting that

> Her Majesty, the Queen of Tonga, has acted in a very despotic manner and that selected tribunal is not a body comprised of disinterested individuals . . . It was unfortunate that a certain exalted lady had delegated to herself an office which she did not possess. She had endeavoured to become what the King of England would not dare to become, a minister of the word as well as sovereign of the realm.[74]

This overseas coverage would have been more damaging to the Queen had not the Australian newspapers taken her side, publishing articles written by Wood that put the case for the Queen and the pro-unionists.

McOwan suspected that Moody was prolonging litigation in order to obtain more fees, for he was charging the anti-unionists 1500 guineas (£1575) a month, compared with Crompton's total fee of £1250 for ten weeks' work. McOwan reported to the Acting High Commissioner that Stronge's partiality in the matter had strengthened the Queen's determination to take her rightful place as President of the Privy Council when it heard the appeal:

> For some reason unknown to me the Chief Justice had conceived a strong antipathy to the Queen and Prince Consort and had not concealed it in public. The Queen had not failed to observe this attitude and believed that the dislike for herself amounted to a prejudice in favour of the respondents in the case. Her

Majesty was determined for this and for other reasons principally of policy, the case should be heard in accordance with law by the Privy Council and by no other tribunal. In justice to the Queen, I must say that I think there was justification for her attitude.[75]

McOwan sent telegrams almost daily to Suva, assuring the officials of the High Commission that the only way to settle the dispute once and for all was for the appeal to be heard by the Privy Council. The High Commission officials feared that if the Privy Council heard the appeal without the Chief Justice its decision would not be accepted and the Queen's government thus brought into disrepute. Sālote's suggestion that McOwan be co-opted as a member of the Privy Council was unacceptable to the Acting High Commissioner, but he offered instead to send a barrister from the Fiji Service, James Scott Neill, to assist the Privy Council.[76] Neill's reputation was such that his appointment would ensure the legal respectability of the proceedings.

Crompton had now returned to Tonga to represent the pro-unionists in the Supreme Court case over property other than land. Records and exhibits from the Land Court case had been sent to the Queen pending the appeal, and Stronge asked for them to be sent to the Supreme Court.[77] Sālote feared that the exhibits might never be returned if she relinquished them, so she informed Stronge that as the exhibits had been sent to her as President of the Privy Council, she could not release them without the consent of that Council, and promised that she would bring the matter before the next meeting. She added: "you will, no doubt, appreciate my difficulty in this matter, especially as I am deprived at present, for reasons which will be obvious to you, of the privilege of consulting the legal adviser to the Crown [Stronge himself]".[78]

On the first day of the Supreme Court case, 5 August, the Queen put the exhibits into her private safe and took the key with her to I, her holiday home on the south-east coast, leaving Crompton and Tongilava to face Stronge's wrath. After threatening to jail Tongilava for contempt of court, Stronge adjourned the case, then had a mild heart attack, brought on by his extreme anger.[79] McOwan again urged Stronge to take his place on the Privy Council, and Stronge agreed, provided that the appeal settled both cases, and provided that he presided over the appeal. McOwan cabled his answer to the Acting High Commissioner, who replied that if Stronge had no objection to presiding over the Privy Council in the appeal, he could have no objection to sitting as a member. In the face of so direct an instruction, Stronge agreed to take his customary place.[80]

The Queen, the Acting High Commissioner, McOwan, and Stronge agreed that this appeal would settle all litigation. This decision, taken to resolve one legal problem, had far-reaching consequences. There would be no resiling from this pronouncement by the British government. The recognition of the independence of Tonga's judiciary system was an important outcome, ensuring the continuing independence of Tonga, and a consequence of the Queen's determination not to relinquish any of the rights guaranteed by the Constitution.

Moody would not accept the decision that the Privy Council would be the ultimate Court of Appeal for Tonga. He blamed Stronge for capitulating and took a leaf out of Crompton's book by leaving Tonga before the appeal could be heard. He assured his clients that no matter what happened, the British courts would hear an appeal and would find in their favour.[81]

The Privy Council met in Parliament House on 1–6, 11, and 12 September.[82] Crowds of Tongans filled the building and packed the open ground around it. After the preliminaries, Tungī, Tupouto'a, and 'Ulukālala withdrew, pleading special interests, and Sioape Kaho pleaded illness and did not attend.[83] This left the Queen as President, Stronge, Bagnall, Wallace, and Neill (the last co-opted for the duration of the appeal). The Queen had resolved not to speak, but she took notes on the whole proceedings. Moody's deputy, Ellis, appeared long enough to predict civil disorder if the decision favoured the pro-unionists, and to repeat that the Free Church would appeal to the British courts. Then Ellis withdrew, leaving the anti-unionists unrepresented.

Crompton presented the arguments on behalf of the nobles and pro-unionists, basing their case on Tongan law and the legitimacy of the pro-unionists of the Free Wesleyan Church as the true heirs of Tupou I's church, citing the Blue Book of 1888. Neill and Stronge gave separate judgments, both in favour of the pro-unionists, and Bagnall and Wallace concurred. On hearing the judgment, the crowd spontaneously sang the Tongan national anthem; the Queen's supporters thronged the Palace to demonstrate their loyalty to her; and Rachel Tonga (then living at Talakaepau, near the Palace) summed up their feelings when she wrote in her diary that the case established that everything truly belonged to the Queen.[84]

This was the end of the court cases, but it was not the end of bitterness. When Sālote attended Watkin's funeral in January 1925, the Free Church mourners turned their backs to her. This was an extreme insult, but Sālote ignored it rather than feed the dissenters' claims of persecution.[85]

Setaleki Manu, first President of the reunited Free Wesleyan Church, soon disgraced himself by using his new status to marry a girl aged 19, although he was in his dotage. Page was elected President by the 1925 Conference, and was re-elected President each year until he retired in 1946. The Queen appointed Page as her royal chaplain, and he was thereafter her spiritual director and secular adviser, interpreter, translator, and *papālangi* secretary when confidential official letters had to be written in English.

Page's discretion and patience were rewarded, for he became Sālote's most trusted confidant and friend. It was well known that Page suffered severely from seasickness. When the Queen's yacht approached Nuku'alofa harbour at the same time as the boat in which Page was returning from his inter-island visits, she instructed that Page's boat should be allowed to enter harbour before her own. This was the "kindness" that went with hard work and a strong character to make her such an effective leader. Rodger Page would be a true and loyal friend, taking to his grave the many secrets the Queen entrusted to him.

The High Commissioner, Sir Eyre Hutson, made an official visit on 5–9 August 1925. Hutson was approached by 'Ulukālala and a crowd of petitioners, asking that the matter of church property be taken to a British court. The High Commissioner refused their request, urging them instead to support the Queen in her attempts to secure national unity.[86] Sālote assured Hutson that without "outside" (that is, *papālangi*) support this group of "diehards" would lose their identity. On 17 August she issued a call for national unity.

> You are all aware that two years ago, at the urgent request of Chiefs, Ministers and people, meetings were held to find some way of correcting abuses that had crept into our Church, and that, as a result of these conferences, union was brought about between the two severed Churches. I gave the movement my support not because of any particular leaning to one Church or the other, but because I felt that this church union was a big step towards the national unity that was always so dear to the heart of Tubou I and so necessary to the well-being of our Kingdom and people. I feel it a great privilege that in the Providence of God I have been able to help in this great work . . . I ask you at this time . . . not to magnify the little things that make divisions but to exalt the big things that make for national peace, and in a spirit of generosity and patriotism look beyond ourselves and let us give our best to unite Tonga into one happy and contented people. It is my earnest wish. I ask your sympathy and co-operation not only out of love and veneration for Tubou I but on behalf of Tonga and its people.[87]

This speech is an outstanding example of the many stirring speeches that the Queen was to make throughout her reign. Even in translation (possibly done by Page), her ability to get to the heart of the matter using simple language is clearly demonstrated.

Hutson was very impressed by the Queen's personality and her desire for reconciliation with her erstwhile foes. But national unity was not for 'Ulukālala, Siaki Lolohea, Tapueluelu, and nine others who signed a petition on 15 September 1924, sent by Ellis to the Secretary of State for the Colonies in the hopes that the Privy Council of Great Britain would hear an appeal from the decision of the Privy Council of Tonga.[88] Although the British government informed them it would not interfere in the matter, the anti-unionists continued to collect money for the hoped-for appeal.[89]

Matters took another turn in 1928. Between 1924 and 1928 'Ulukālala, as befitted a great aristocratic noble, had regarded the Free Church as his personal property. He used Free Church money to build a house for his son Ha'amea in expectation of Ha'amea's marriage with Princess Fusipala. After litigation in 1928 over property and finance the Free Church split in two: the Free Church would thereafter be familiarly known as the "Church of the President", for it had a *papālangi* (later a Tongan) President; and the Church of Tonga would be familiarly known as the "Church of the Chiefs", for it was owned by 'Ulukālala and his chiefly supporters. Very few Vava'u people joined 'Ulukālala's church: he had been away from Vava'u for too long, and the people remained loyal to the Free Church as instructed by Tapueluelu. 'Ulukālala's church members mostly lived in Ha'apai, many being supporters of Siaki Lolohea. In accordance with chiefly custom, 'Ulukalala would be succeeded as the President of the "Church of the Chiefs" by Ha'amea.[90]

Rodger Page found that few of the nobles honoured the promises made prior to litigation that they would grant formal leases to the reunited church. Even the land formerly leased by the Wesleyan Mission was in doubt, for Stronge refused to transfer those leases to the reunited Free Wesleyan Church. Page begged the Privy Council to intervene, on the grounds of a partially fulfilled contract, but Sālote and Tungī were unwilling to antagonize the nobles by forcing them to fulfil their promises.[91] Over the years Page acquired a reputation for being very canny in his negotiations with individual nobles for leases for the Free Wesleyan Church.

Finances were another problem for Page. Having established that they were true heirs of the Free Church, the Free Wesleyan Church was liable for the debts of that church. These debts were not repaid in full until 1944.[92] To make matters worse, Page was besieged by nobles and chiefs asking for "loans" as rewards for the support they had given to the Queen by becoming pro-unionists. Unwilling to offend, Page granted more "loans" than he personally thought advisable. Finances were further stretched because all Tongan ministers were now paid the generous stipends formerly paid by Watkin.[93] An additional 20 ministers had been ordained at the 1924 Conference of the Free Church in order to secure a majority in the reunited church, and this prevented the ordination for new candidates for some years. The newly acquired debts of the Free Wesleyan Church made the recruitment of overseas missionaries as spiritual directors impossible, for although salaries were paid by the Australian church, missionaries required schools and other infrastructure for their work.

The Free Wesleyan Church was effectively the possession of the Queen, in the same way as the Free Church had been the possession of Tupou I, and the "Church of the Chiefs" was the possession of 'Ulukālala. The Queen hoped to revitalize the spiritual life of the church, but was reluctant to introduce structural changes, thus keeping the church in a time warp from which, even after her death, it would be difficult to escape. The Free Wesleyan Church conspicuously deferred to the Queen's authority as leader of the church, and openly expressed its support in prayers and sermons. Each year she advised Page on the appointments of ministers to different parishes, and on promotions to positions of greater responsibility. She took over the women's organization known as the Ako Tapu or Ako Angelo (Holy School or School for Angels). In 1935 she introduced Ako Lotu (Christian Endeavour) for women and men and in 1955 the Kaluseti (Crusaders) for women only. It was a great honour to be a member of a group of which the Queen was the patron. Being a lay preacher, trustee, choir master, or steward were all considered to be positions of honour, and women and men flocked to join the church choirs.

Sālote was a regular attender at worship; she contributed generously to the annual collection and encouraged others to follow her example by presiding at the annual *misinale*. She was a class leader, she prepared Bible studies, she prayed at prayer meetings, and stood up to join in the *talaloto* (religious testimony). She might be too tired to go downstairs to attend Privy Council, but she would call out her driver to take her to a Pō Tokoni (literally, "help night") or to observe an evening of Bible Cricket in a village where she had a particular interest.[94]

When the annual Conference was held in Nuku'alofa, the Queen received representatives from other islands at the Palace. She travelled to Ha'apai or Vava'u when the Conference was held in those island groups. She always opened Conference with a stirring speech, the recurring theme being unity, and was available during the week-long meeting to discuss church business with church leaders.

After reunion the Free Wesleyan Church was numerically the strongest church in Tonga, its buildings visible in every village. The church upheld the traditional hierarchy of Tongan society. The ministers respected and supported the nobles and chiefs, just as the President of the church respected and supported the Queen. Indeed, the noble or chief of the village was always more honoured than the minister: the chief had a prominent seat during the church service, the place of honour at feasts, the major share of presentations. Nobles and chiefs were encouraged by Sālote to become lay preachers and trustees of the village church, and to represent their congregations at the Quarterly Meetings and the annual Conference. Ministers often came from the cadet branches of chiefly lines.

The church was responsible for another significant change in Tongan society, for it elevated the status of "wife" above that of the "sister", who traditionally had been the most highly respected member of any *kāinga*. Although the sister was still respected in secular society, in the *kāinga lotu* (church fellowship) it was the wife of the chief of the village and the wife of the minister who were leaders of women's groups.

There was some compensation for the chiefs whose customary right to land would now never be recognized by law, except for the eight-and-a-quarter acres to which every commoner was entitled. The Queen saw to it that district officers and town officers were appointed from this group. When the noble did not live in the village (he had a house in only one of his villages and increasingly lived in Nuku'alofa), the local chief acted on his behalf, allocating land and ensuring that commoners did their *fatongia* for the noble, and benefiting himself in a comparable though lesser manner. Although the hereditary estateholders had the most benefit from the system, true power at the local level seemed to lie in the hands of these chiefs. One such chief was the dissenting Siaki Lolohea. When the Queen visited Ha'apai in 1925, Lolohea came and apologized for his opposition to her over church reunion, "His howls could be heard for miles", it was reported. She rewarded him with some land, and recognized (and increased) his influence by appointing him a District Officer.[95]

Reconciliation was the major concern of Sālote and Tungī, and they were fully supported in this endeavour by Rodger Page. But Sālote and Tungī went further, offering generous friendship to their opponents. When Sālote leased land to Tupou College (the Free Wesleyan secondary college) for farming, Tungī did the same for Government College, the bastion of the Free Church. Sālote (and, in turn, her sons) opened new churches for all denominations, launched church boats, presided over the annual collection to defray church expenses, were honoured guests at church and school functions. Although Bishop Blanc remained suspicious, the Queen rewarded the Catholic hierarchy for not taking advantage of the 1924 crisis by offering friendship and by showering gifts upon the nuns, including those living in remote areas, for she truly appreciated the work they were doing for the Tongan people. Since she could not bring the Catholic Church into union with other churches, she would ensure that Catholicism would not offer a refuge to the disloyal. The Catholic Church had been the church of the Tu'i Tonga, and she intended to supplant the Tu'i Tonga.

Sālote understood the symbolic value of anniversaries in bringing people together to celebrate her leadership (even if they were ostensibly celebrating something else). The year 1926 was the centenary of the arrival of John Thomas and John Hutchinson as Wesleyan missionaries,[96] and all Tongans were encouraged to join in the week-long thanksgiving celebrations. Fortuitously, Thomas and Hutchinson had set up their first mission at Ha'atafu at the westernmost point of Tongatapu, so the first day's celebrations were held in the Western District, where the nobles and chiefs were "younger brothers" and "sons" of the Tu'i Kanokupolu title. As the Queen's car approached the village of Fo'ui, the people demonstrated their love and loyalty by carrying her car, in which she was still seated, through the village, in the same way as people had carried the Tu'i Tonga about on a platform or boat.[97]

On the following days the centenary celebrations moved to Nuku'alofa, a place associated with the rise of the Tupou dynasty as well as the early days of the Wesleyan Mission. Spectacular presentations of food and *koloa* were made to Sālote as head of church and state. There were feasts, dancing, concerts, services, all-night prayer vigils, during which the fervour of the people reached extraordinary heights of emotion. Later in the year the Queen and Rodger Page went north to Ha'apai and Vava'u to continue the celebrations. Villagers in Vava'u, who had been practising their dances for nine months, could barely contain their enthusiasm during the Sabbath, and began dancing for the Queen at 3 a.m. on Monday morning.[98]

Sālote had taken an enormous risk in undertaking the reunion of the two Wesleyan churches, not so much for the churches as for her own prestige. As far as the churches were concerned, reunion was only partial; and as far as the Queen was concerned, she was successful in that a significant number of her people declared their loyalty to her; but others had openly opposed her. She showed herself skilled in the art of political manoeuvring, had won the wholehearted admiration of significant Britons, and had put an end to all talk of annexation. She would never again put her reputation on the line by advocating a particular cause so publicly.

Although it was only a partial victory, reunion proved to be a major milestone in her assumption of supremacy. Sālote was only 24 years of age and had been Queen for only six years when the two churches legally took the name Free Wesleyan Church of Tonga. Its leadership and members were openly committed to the royal house and to the continuance of the Tupou dynasty. The Free Church leadership, on the other hand, although effective at the local level, was not particularly visible at the national level and was soon preoccupied with internal disputes.

The Queen had also won over the nobles. They would thereafter see their interests to be bound up with those of the royal house. The Queen may have felt "stuck" with the nobles, only few of whom had any real ability, but she kept to the unspoken bargain made in the law courts in 1924 that the Tupou dynasty and the hereditary estateholders had a common cause, the preservation of the status quo, particularly in relation to land.

The Queen must have regretted that opposition to the royal house had been so public, and she would be especially careful that less publicity was given to later problems. Altogether the experience of dealing with *papālangi* and Tongans in the affair of church reunion would stand her in good stead in the issue that next confronted her: the implications of the Constitution and Law as set before her by her chief justices. When her authority was again challenged, her responses were those of one confident of her place as ruler of Tonga. During the difficulties of the later years she would use all of the skills that had been so visible and valuable in the church reunion affair.

CHAPTER NINE

Problems with Judges

"My desire is to faithfully abide by my Coronation oath in upholding the Constitution of Tonga and governing according to its laws." (Queen Sālote, 1926)[1]

IN A REPORT TO THE HIGH Commissioner of the Western Pacific in September 1924, Consul McOwan stated that an outcome of church reunion was that Queen Sālote occupied a higher place in the estimation of the chiefs and people than at any previous time during her six-year reign.[2] Certainly the strength of her response to challenges, the consistency of her course, and the authority she exercised had impressed her own people. But not all *papālangi* were as admiring of Sālote as McOwan, and they still sought to undermine Sālote's authority. She did not, however, assume that all *papālangi* were hostile, and indeed she clearly distinguished between those who supported her and those who did not.

For Sālote, the most troublesome and publicly visible of the difficult *papālangi* were several chief justices. The Chief Justice of Tonga was "selected" by the Colonial Office, the name being sent to the Queen for approval. Tonga was so small and isolated and the salary offered by the government so small (compared with colonial postings) that the applicants for the post were unlikely to be of high calibre. Unfortunately, while the paper qualifications were checked by the Colonial Office, no one considered whether a candidate's personality was suited to such a posting. The character of most who held that office in the 1920s and 1930s were inappropriate for the isolation and responsibilities they would undertake.

The Queen really had no choice in the appointment, for she did not meet the person nominated prior to his arrival in Tonga. Most of these legal men regarded the posting as a stepping-stone to something better, and only one (Stronge, who failed in his first application for another posting) stayed for more than one term. The chief justices had no understanding of (and little interest in) the customary law of Tonga. Most had an exaggerated sense of their own importance. This was in sharp contrast to the consuls, who were generally of high calibre. The High Commissioner knew personally the men he selected to be Agent & Consul or Acting Consul, and he took into account the special circumstances of the posting to Tonga. While the Agent & Consul treated the Queen with courtesy, the chief justices did not, in part due (as already stated) to the influence of George Scott (chapters 6 and 8).

Chief Justice Stronge, who had taken up his appointment in 1917, showed contempt for the Queen's prerogatives and for the Constitution of Tonga in 1924 when he attempted to deny her her place as President of the Privy Council (chapter 8). In the same year, he sent laws to be published in the *Tonga Government Gazette* without her signature.[3] In the months prior to his departure in May 1925 Stronge's behaviour towards the Queen was so outrageous that Privy Council meetings were cancelled in order to avoid a confrontation that would scandalize even the most determined of Tongan royal opponents.[4]

As an outcome of the events of 1924, the Queen was in command of a large support group among her own people. That she had also won over the support of her British advisers was publicly declared during August 1925, when the new High Commissioner of the Western Pacific, Sir Eyre Hutson, made an official visit to Tonga. Hutson's visit was a marked contrast to that of Sir Cecil Rodwell in 1920. Even though the Free Church people still aired their grievances and some of them, led by 'Ulukālala, presented a petition to Hutson (chapter 8), there was no talk of deportations or annexation. The Queen must have been gratified when Hutson assured her in a private interview that she had the wholehearted confidence of the British government.

> I desire to assure Your Majesty in person . . . that His [Britannic] Majesty's Government desire no departure from the understandings reached with regard to the relations between Your Majesty's Government and the British Agent and Consul and the High Commissioner. Further, I have to assure Your Majesty that the aim of His Majesty the King, and of His Government is one of goodwill towards Tonga; and an earnest desire to see your Kingdom continue to prosper under your wise and good Government, and by the continuance of advice to assist in promoting the contentment and happiness of your people.[5]

It was during this visit that Sālote took the highly unusual step of inviting the High Commissioner to take a place in the circle of her *taumafa kava*. It was a delicate compliment to him, but also an action that signified to all Tongans that Hutson recognized her legitimacy as Tu'i Kanokupolu. Both publicly and privately, Hutson was thanked for the benefits Britain's advice and protection had brought to Tonga.[6] In the private interview

> [the Queen] expressed to me her deep appreciation of the assistance and advice rendered to her by His Majesty's Government. I was deeply impressed with her personality, she is only twenty-five years of age: but she displays great dignity in her position, has acquired an intimate knowledge of native customs and traditions, and she undoubtedly commands the respect of the people.[7]

This acknowledgement of Sālote's "intimate knowledge of native customs and traditions" was to set the tone for future British–Tongan relations, just as much as her sincere expressions of gratitude for the "great benefits" Tonga had derived from the advice and protection of the British government. From this time on the Queen embodied tradition in the eyes of Tongan and *papālangi* alike. She provided "shade" for all Tongans, whether they had supported or opposed her in the recent matter of the churches.

The 1925 visit was not all mutual congratulation. The Queen took the opportunity to ask Hutson to transfer one of her troublesome *papālangi* ministers, J. D. Wall, Auditor-General since 1915, who had expressed discontent in a petition to the Secretary of State for the Colonies about McOwan's interference and high-handedness in the affairs of the Tonga government.[8] Wall and the now-departed Stronge had been particularly aggrieved when McOwan blocked the payment of a bonus to officers on half-pay leave (chapter 6). The Queen gave as a reason for dismissing Wall that since Bagnall's appointment as Minister for Finance (in 1919) she did not need an Auditor-General, at least not in Privy Council. The request for the removal of Wall was a reasonable one, but Hutson assumed that if he persuaded Wall to withdraw his complaint, the Queen would no longer object to his presence in government.[9] The Queen graciously accepted Hutson's decision – and patiently waited for another opportunity to decrease the number of *papālangi* in the Privy Council.[10]

Another request from Sālote to Hutson would lead to a confrontation with her new Chief Justice, William Kenneth Horne, who arrived shortly after Hutson's departure. The Queen's great-uncle, the noble Tupouto'a (Mateialona), was now 73 years of age, his health was failing, and he wished to retire from his post as Minister for Lands. The Queen had undoubtedly discussed the new appointment with McOwan, but seeking the explicit approval of Hutson was a wise course. Simply to maintain the existing balance of opinion in Privy Council, Tupouto'a's successor had to be as loyal to Sālote as Tupouto'a had been. Further, Sālote and Tungī were committed to distribution of land as required by the Constitution and Law, and they needed a Minister for Lands sympathetic to this course. The new Minister had to have judgement and tact, and be respected by the majority of nobles and chiefs in the exercise of a difficult portfolio.

In the Queen's view, the chief who best fitted these requirements was Ata (Solomone Ula), boyhood companion of Tungī and a leading chief in the Ha'a Ngata (the group of titleholders who were deemed to be "younger brothers" and "sons" of the Tu'i Kanokupolu). Sālote told Hutson frankly that Ata had been dismissed by her as Minister for Police in 1918 because of misappropriation of funds, but (she assured Hutson) the nobles and chiefs would welcome the clemency shown by Ata's reinstatement as a minister. After consultation with McOwan, Hutson assured the Queen that he had no objection to the appointment.

Horne arrived on the September steamer, and George Scott (as Acting Chief Justice), Wall, and Sioape Kaho rushed to inform him about the impediments to the appointment of Ata.[11] The three convinced Horne that the Queen had acted unconstitutionally and, without taking time to consult with McOwan, Horne challenged Ata's appointment on two grounds: that the Queen could not appoint a minister without the consent of Privy Council, and Ata's unfitness for the appointment. Horne threatened to challenge the validity of the appointment at Ata's swearing-in, adding that any actions by Ata as Minister for Lands would be invalid and (in the absence of a statute of limitations) anyone could lay charges against him for the offence that had led to his 1918 dismissal. Convinced that she had acted correctly, Sālote proceeded to confirm Ata's appointment.

The Queen pointed out to Horne that the Constitution (cl. 55) allowed her to appoint and dismiss her ministers without reference to the Privy Council, and that this prerogative was limited only by the Treaty of Friendship and Supplementary Agreement, which required her to consult with the Agent & Consul in the appointment of senior officials.[12] Horne argued that s. 9 of the Law of 1903 automatically amended the Constitution. Advised by Robert Crompton by letter, and then in person, the Queen asserted that s. 9 had been a dead letter from the time of its enactment.

Neither the Queen nor Horne would budge, so Horne suggested that their correspondence should be submitted to the High Commissioner. The Queen agreed, but declared that she would not be bound by opinion from outside the kingdom, as the courts and Parliament of Tonga were the sole interpreters of the Constitution and the Law.[13] Since the British government had only recently affirmed the complete independence of Tonga in judicial matters, the High Commissioner decided not to waste his officials' time by providing an opinion that would not be binding.

The issue for Sālote was her prerogatives as set out in the Constitution and Law. On this occasion Parliament agreed with her, and when asked in 1926 to clarify s. 9, it amended the law to make it consistent with the Constitution.[14]

She could continue to appoint and dismiss ministers without consulting the Privy Council. By this time, Ata had already held his appointment for seven months without any other person challenging him.

Sālote considered Horne to be provocative and hostile, and she was determined to force him to admit that she was the reigning sovereign of the kingdom, not a nominee of the British. She expressed her opinions forthrightly in a letter of February 1926.

> I would remind you that though Tonga is a British Protectorate, it is not a British possession . . .
>
> The use of the words "purport to act" is an instance of the discourtesy and offensive tone of your letters. The Minister of Lands has been appointed under my hand and seal and in accordance with the terms of clause 55 of the Constitution. This fact should be sufficient to justify the expectation that the Chief Justice of the Kingdom would not question the validity of the appointment in a letter to me bearing no mark of the confidential nature of the contents . . .
>
> In conclusion, I take this opportunity of saying that your attitude throughout has appeared to me to be obstructive and antagonistic, and the tone of your previous letters on the subject have been dictatorial and discourteous. If your endeavour has been to treat me with every possible courtesy, I can only say that it has not been made apparent and that you have signally failed.[15]

Another issue relating to the Queen's prerogatives was not so easily settled. Again the Constitution and the Law were at odds. The Constitution stated that the heir of an hereditary estateholder was his eldest son or, failing a son, the nearest male relative; but there had been occasions when a title had been given to a brother or representative of a cadet branch of the family, either because he showed leadership qualities, or because the natural heir was youthful or absent. Indeed, Tupou I and Tupou II had continued to appoint the person they deemed best qualified to be leader of the *kāinga*. Thus by the 1920s there were different branches within the various *kāinga* whose ancestors had held the title at some time or other.

When George Scott was appointed Judge of the Land Court in 1923, he claimed that the Land Court Act 1921 had given him the power to determine not only the boundaries to estates but also disputes over succession to the titles of hereditary estateholders. Queen Sālote denied that this interpretation had been intended in the drafting, and that such a reading conflicted with cl. 48 and 90 of the Constitution, which stated quite explicitly that the Queen had the right to grant both "titles of honour" and land. Certainly no one challenged her right as Tu'i Kanokupolu to appoint men to chiefly titles where hereditary estates were not involved,[16] and she could also appoint as many *matāpule* as she liked to serve her as ceremonial attendants.

Chief Justice Stronge had recognized the Queen's rights in 1918 when he asked to determine the heir to a title and estates of 'Akau'ola.[17] Her prerogatives had been exercised when she appointed Mateialona to the title Tupouto'a in 1921 and granted him estates. She had also recognized Tu'ivakanō's claim to the villages of Matafonua and Matahau in 1918 and 1921. And she had given a piece of land to Siaki Lolohea in 1925.

Stronge may have intended Scott's reading when he drafted the law, but it is difficult to believe that the nobles sitting in Parliament that year would have passed such an Act without comment if they had a similar understanding,[18] for it simply invited others to challenge the current holder of any title where hereditary estates were concerned.

George Scott chose the case of the noble title Fulivai to challenge the Queen's prerogatives. In March 1919 the Queen had written a letter of appointment (*tohi fakanofo*) for 'Iki Tupou as the new Fulivai. His ancestors had held the title *before* the Constitution was proclaimed and the title had reverted to that branch of the *kāinga* of Fulivai some years before. 'Iki Tupou had been called by his new title and received a cup of *kava* in the *taumafa kava*. Then Tēvita 'Uluilakepa claimed the title as a descendant of Kaianuanu, the chief whom Tupou I had appointed Fulivai in 1880. After a hearing in the Land Court, Scott gave his judgment in favour of the 'Uluilakepa on 15 October 1924, and used this as an opportunity to make an explicit attack upon the Queen.

> Although a noble's title has been conferred and the defendant was given a letter of appointment from Her Majesty and it will be assumed that there is no need for Her Majesty to appoint another noble while the present holder is alive and is a legitimate heir of the former holder of the title nevertheless it is not right for Her Majesty to confer titles on nobles without a thorough research being made to ascertain the lawful heirs to such titles. That is why cases of this nature are brought before the court and it is the duty of this court to decide. With all due respect to Her Majesty, I am satisfied that no letter of appointment of the nature of the matter in question will hinder this court from acting in accordance with the constitution and the Law of Tonga.[19]

Scott's assumption of the right to determine the heir to the title and estates of a hereditary estateholder may have been a genuine reading of the Act, and he may have been convinced that injustices had been done to rightful heirs, but one can't help feeling that Scott was influenced by Queen Sālote's opponents of the "Reactionary Party" and was determined to undermine her prerogatives. As McOwan said, in another context, Scott's motives were sometimes more personal than public, and he certainly appeared to loathe both the Queen and her consort. As we have already seen in the course of this book, it was very difficult for people to be impersonal in such a small official world, and Scott may well have resented being outwitted by a "native (woman) ruler", and been determined to increase his own status by taking over some of the regal powers.

When Horne arrived in Tonga in September 1925, the Fulivai Appeal to Privy Council was still pending. A second claim had been lodged in the Land Court, to the noble title of Tuʻivakanō, by Molitoni Fisiʻihoi Fīnau on behalf of his son, Lupeti, great-grandson of Tuʻivakanō (Mānoa), who had held the title prior to 1912. In 1912 Tupou II had appointed Polutele Kaho as Tuʻivakanō, and that Tuʻivakanō became Scott's patron and ally. He was the sister's son of an earlier holder of the Tuʻivakanō title (Manuʻotua), who had held the title at the time of the Constitution (Figure 2.4). When Tuʻivakanō (Polutele) died in 1923, there were no sons to inherit, so the title passed to his brother Siosiua. Lupeti's claim was heard in 1924 and 1925, and Scott's judgment in favour of Siosiua was made on 21 October 1925, four weeks after Horne arrived in Tonga.

When Sālote signed the Land Court Act of 1921, she envisaged that the Land Court (like its predecessor, the Lands Commission) would hear disputes over the boundaries of estates and allotments, and over inheritance of farm and town allotments by commoners, but she would not have signed the Act if she had thought that it would deprive her of the prerogative to determine the rights of inheritance to the titles of hereditary estateholders. To her mind, such titleholders were first and foremost leaders of their people, and their trusteeship of the land was a subsidiary function to that of leadership.[20]

Furthermore, in Tonga, women were the guardians of genealogies, and it was important for Sālote that she, above all chiefly women, be recognized as the ultimate authority on the genealogies of the chiefs. For a *papālangi* – and a *male* at that – to take away a title once it was bestowed by herself was to undermine both her authority and the chiefly system of leadership. Neither Scott nor any other *papālangi* was qualified to discern the qualities of leadership or to disentangle the genealogies of the chiefs. In view of Scott's sympathy with customary landholding,[21] it was ironic that he was so unsympathetic to the Queen's assertion of her customary right.

Horne agreed with Scott's interpretation of the Act. Like other chief justices he assumed that the modern Law was supreme, and that Tonga had entered an era in which custom would have no place. He summed up his views on the place of the Constitution and Law in Tongan life in a letter to McOwan.

> I realize that the great changes made by the Constitution could not be carried out without mistakes, and that allowances must be made. The imposition of an alien and modern system upon a pre-existing primitive system, though carried out, in its inception at least with evangelical fervour, would not destroy with one clean cut customs which are engrained in Tongan life. These have lingered on; while, at the same time, the new legal conceptions have not been fully

> understood. But current practice, partly drawn from the past and partly from misunderstanding of the present are nevertheless a dwindling element, and are not entitled, in the face of so much legislation on the matter to rank as custom or usage, in the sense that these classifications are understood in law.[22]

This statement sums up perfectly the assumption of Horne that Tonga intended to become a Westernized state so custom must be eradicated. To the Queen it appeared that her customary rights *were* supported by the Constitution, and that Scott and Horne were misreading the Land Court Act 1921. McOwan agreed with her reading of the Act, but could not challenge the Chief Justice on legal matters. Sālote was dependent on the (too remote – and expensive) advice of Robert Crompton when faced with the combined legal opinions of Horne and Scott.

Horne and Scott interpreted Tongan law according to English principles and applied English law when there was no Tongan law.[23] They also interpreted custom and the Constitution with European assumptions. They acted as though the status of hereditary estateholders in Tonga was analogous to those of the British peerage: that is, that the hereditary estateholders were landowners in an absolute sense. Sālote argued that the land reforms of Tupou I had not basically changed the three customary types of landholding: the Constitution confirmed that the Tu'i Kanokupolu (as heir to the Tu'i Tonga) *owned* all the land; the hereditary estateholders held the land *in trust* in order to distribute it among their *kāinga*; and all adult members of the *kāinga* had the right of *use*. (The only real change was that commoners who were formerly slaves were now recognized as *kāinga*.)

Sālote pointed out that in the Tongan version of the Land Court Act 1921 the distinction was quite clear, two Tongan words (*kelekele* and *fonua*) being used where one word (land) appeared in the English version. *Kelekele* meant the soil and the produce of the soil, and she was willing for the Land Court to decide matters related to the distribution of the *kelekele* among commoners. *Fonua* meant land-and-people, implying leadership of the *kāinga*, and the Land Court could not, she said, decide about leadership. What Horne and Scott were doing was splitting the *fonua*, and making land all-important and leadership of people irrelevant.

Sālote would not accept this division, and claimed precedent, saying that Tupou I had not intended the principle of primogeniture to be rigidly adhered to. Since both Tupou I and Tupou II had named in the traditional way successors to titles of nobles after consultation with the *ha'a* and *kāinga* concerned (sometimes an adopted or illegitimate son had been appointed, sometimes a brother of the former titleholder), she could do the same. She could see the unfortunate possibilities of appointing someone to a position of responsibility on the grounds of birth alone: "a young boy of 21 comes into the title before he has the knowledge which he should have to be the *'ulumotua* or leader. This is a great loss to Tongan society (literally: This is a great loss of power of goodness for the nation)".[24]

The Queen could not sustain an argument against the law of primogeniture (her own inheritance had depended on being the elder of two legitimate children), so the discussion focused on who should determine the branch from which the "eldest son" should come. The Queen suggested a compromise: that a Committee of Privileges – consisting of the Premier (Tungī), the Chief Justice, and the Speaker of Parliament ('Ulukālala) – should be set up, and when there was a dispute about succession to the title of a noble this committee could assist her to determine the rightful heir.[25] The exclusion of Scott from the committee must have been deliberate.

However, Horne and Scott would not compromise. McOwan advised Sālote to refer the whole matter to Parliament.[26] But Privy Council had to agree, first with the Queen's proposal, and then about referring the matter to Parliament. As a last-minute attempt to influence the Privy Council, Sālote informed the members that the Land Court Act 1921 was unconstitutional, since members of Parliament who were not nobles had voted upon it.[27] In spite of this argument, the Privy Council voted at their meeting on 11 June 1926 not to refer the matter to Parliament, but to allow the Land Court to determine claims to titles of the hereditary estateholders.[28]

Without a record of proceedings of Privy Council on that day, it is not possible to say why the members of Privy Council voted against the Queen's expressed wishes. Sālote (who had had a minor operation on 11 May) and 'Ulukālala were both absent, and Tungī was in the chair. Four *papālangi* members (Horne, Wallace, Wall, and Bagnall) were present, and also four Tongan members (Ata, Veikune, Ha'amea, and Sioape Kaho). If all the *papālangi* voted with Horne, it needed the support of only one Tongan to swing the vote in against the Queen. The most likely Tongan member was Sioape, for (according to the Queen) he loved to stir things up by suggesting people should go to court and claim titles and land.[29]

The sudden death of an official in Suva in 1926 necessitated McOwan's departure just after the vital Privy Council meeting, and there was six months' delay before the arrival of his successor.[30] By the time the new Agent & Consul arrived, it was too late for the Queen to reclaim her traditional prerogative. Until the end of her life Sālote regretted this defeat, saying that people blamed her for appointing as nobles young men who had no leadership qualities and who enjoyed the privileges of rents and presentations without carrying out their obligations to the people living on their estates.[31] Incumbent titleholders asked her to do something about the aggravation of having to defend their right to their titles against several claimants. The Queen would quietly make the best of the situation, using her knowledge of genealogies to discourage possible claimants (for example, for the titles of Ma'afu and Vaea). But once the claims had been lodged, she could do little, even when the Privy Council sat as a Court of Appeal, because of the presence of the Chief Justice and other *papālangi*.

When Sālote and Tungī were informed that McOwan would be transferred by the High Commissioner to another appointment, they asked him to choose as McOwan's successor a man with a legal background and experience of the Pacific.[32] They believed that this was the only way to counter legal challenges from the Chief Justice and Judge of the Land Court without resort to expensive legal advice from overseas. They were delighted when they were informed that McOwan's successor was James Scott Neill, a barrister with 14 years service in Fiji, who had been the co-opted member of the Privy Council in September 1924.

During the six months between McOwan's departure in mid 1926 and the arrival of Neill in January 1927, a disadvantage of constitutional monarchy was brought home to the Queen in a particularly painful way. One of Sālote's most trusted friends and contemporaries was Feleti Vī, whom the Queen had appointed as successor to his father's noble title of Ve'ehala in 1922.[33] Ve'ehala had supported Sālote in the matter of church reunion. In January 1924 Sālote had approved his marriage to Simoa, sister of the noble Tuita, a woman of exceedingly high rank, who had (like Ve'ehala) accompanied her on her holiday to New Zealand in 1922–23. Simoa had been "adopted" by Mele Siu'ilikutapu, mother of Tungī, which made the marriage even more prestigious.

In September 1926 Ve'ehala was convicted of stealing £20 from the steamer *Tofua*, and sentenced by Horne to two years' imprisonment. The sentence was severe, but worse was to come. Clause 48 of the Constitution stated that a noble could be deprived of his title only for treason. However, Sālote had given her assent to the Nobles Titles Succession Act (Law 11 of 1923), which provided that "any noble convicted of a felony" should lose his title.[34] Sālote obviously had not envisaged such an outcome, and she felt for Ve'ehala because, as she wrote to Sioape Kaho, "he is a well-known man of Tonga and a chief of rank".[35] In Tongan custom a chief cannot commit a theft, for he has absolute rights to the property of his inferiors, and Sālote considered that restitution would be sufficient. But once Ve'ehala was convicted by the courts, she had no choice other than to deprive him of his title. For some months she did nothing, perhaps hoping that Neill would suggest a way out. But Neill's coming was delayed, and in a letter of 17 December 1926 Horne pressed her to act according to the law.[36] Ve'ehala became Feleti Vī again.

Sālote took this opportunity to show the chiefs and people that whatever power the law had over them, she was still able to confer conspicuous benefits upon those who served her well. Feleti Vī was no longer entitled to the annual allowance that was paid to all of the nobles, nor to rents from his former estates, nor could he represent the nobles in Parliament, which would have given him another salary. To compensate him for his losses, Sālote made him her driver, a position with few duties but with status and a salary. The Queen also gave him a house on the royal compound Talakaepau, across the road from the Palace. She chose the trustee for his son (Leilua) with care, so he would succeed to an undiminished inheritance. Leilua was awarded one of the overseas scholarships set up by her to educate the heirs to noble titles.[37]

While Feleti Vī was the subject of much gossip, and was compensated for his loss of title and income, a young commoner from the island of Ofu in the Vava'u group was hanged in 1926 for the rape and murder of a young girl, the evidence being circumstantial. This event was mentioned only in passing in Horne's annual report as the Chief Justice.[38]

These disputes of 1925 and 1926 – added to those of 1924 – made several things abundantly clear to Sālote. The first was that open government led to challenges to her authority by *papālangi* and Tongans alike. The second was that *papālangi* ministers did not feel any obligation to be loyal to her. During her reign there was never a "loyal Opposition" in Tonga in the Westminster sense of that term. The third was that she could not rely upon the Agent & Consul always to be there when she needed him to control the *papālangi* ministers.

Neill's coming was followed by an amendment to the Treaty of Friendship that changed the legal status of *papālangi* in Tonga and set out very clearly that he was a legal adviser. Until 1927 *papālangi* and other non-Tongans had not been subject to Tongan Law. In the 1927 amendment the British and Tongan governments agreed that *papālangi*, part-*papālangi*, and other foreigners would be subject to Tongan law and courts in the case of misdemeanours and crimes punishable by less than two years in prison. More serious crimes would continue to be tried in the consular court. An outcome of the amendment was that all draft legislation that affected non-Tongans, effectively all legislation, would now be submitted to the Agent & Consul for his advice.[39] Considering the contradictions and confusions in Tongan law and Neill's abilities, this could only benefit Tonga.

It was clear to Neill that there was a need for a consolidated Land Act, drawing together all the land acts of previous parliaments and redefining the powers of the Executive, Legislature, and Judiciary. The consolidated Land Act 1927, drafted by Horne and extensively revised on Neill's advice, diminished the power and prestige of the Land Court by increasing the power of the Minister for Lands.[40] Scott's powers were further diminished (on paper) by his being required to send to the Privy Council all copies of evidence, findings, and recommendations, "in lieu of deciding the question". Scott ignored this rule by always giving his judgment before sending the papers to the Privy Council.[41] He could not, however, prevent appeals from his judgments.

The Land Act 1927 benefited the hereditary estateholders more than any other section of the community. Their former encroachments on each other's lands, on the customary holdings of other chiefs, and on government lands were now legalized, although they continued to dispute boundaries. The hopes of the customary landholders that their claims would be acknowledged were ended by Part IV of the Land Act, which recognized only two types of landholding: first, the hereditary estateholders' estates, and, second, the tax and town allotments of commoners (which was everyone who was not a noble or *matāpule ma'u tofi'a*, even if they had chiefly blood).[42]

Some customary landholders continued to control many acres of land by dividing and registering them under the names of family members, and the former status of customary landholders were sometimes remembered by their *kāinga* long after these lands had been subdivided. But without estates, such chiefs no longer had the means of rewarding their people, and (until higher education became a marker of status and basis of income) no high-ranking woman would marry a chief without land. It was the lesser chiefs (the former customary landholders) who took advantage of education, government employment, and the church to win status in the community, and they would over several decades become a modern élite with economic power in the community. The Queen herself was not reluctant that this should be so. But she was less enthusiastic about members of this educated élite becoming attractive marriage partners for members of the aristocracy.

The passing of the consolidated Land Act 1927 was assured: Sālote gave it full consideration and approval; Tungī's suggestions had been incorporated; Horne had taken due note of Neill's amendments; the ministers had approved it in Privy Council; the representatives of the nobles in Parliament would welcome it. Nevertheless the Land Act took seven days to pass through Parliament, confirming that land was above all things the central concern of all Tongans.[43]

The year 1927 saw the solution of another problem relating to land and titles. According to Constitution and Law, Prince Tāufa'āhau, the eldest of the three princes, was the heir to four titles (Tu'i Kanokupolu, Tungī, Tu'ipelehake, and Tupouto'a), while Prince Tuku'aho and Prince Sione Ngū had no legal right to any titles. The Queen could have created titles for the younger princes, but such titles would have no estates. The Royal Estates Act 1927 determined that the Crown Prince would inherit the title Tupouto'a when he turned 18, as well as being heir to the Tu'i Kanokupolu title, and that Prince Sione Ngū would inherit the title and estates of Tu'ipelehake when he reached 21 years of age. The Tungī title would be in the Queen's gift, and it was assumed that Prince Tuku'aho would succeed his father in that title.

The Queen consented to a complete revision of the Law, undertaken by Horne under Neill's supervision. The Law had not been revised since 1903 and amendments had created so many contradictions that Neill was sure that no magistrate could make any sense of them.[44] When the revised law book came to Parliament for approval in 1929, there appeared rephrasings in the

Constitution that made it consistent with the Law, rather than the other way round.[45] Neill must have drawn Sālote's attention to these amendments to the Constitution, and obtained her consent, but these rewordings were not put separately to Parliament.

In the early part of Sālote's reign there had been only two – sometimes only one – legally qualified persons in Tonga (the Chief Justice and George Scott). Between 1928 and 1932 there were five. Neill was the best qualified, and he advised the government on legislation, drafted by the Chief Justice, who was second in rank, and who presided over the Supreme Court.[46] Neill persuaded Horne that he could fulfil his duty better by working with the Queen than against her, and a more harmonious atmosphere now prevailed in Privy Council.[47] Horne was succeeded by C. M. Murray-Aynsley, who was mostly remembered for the splendid singing voice of his Russian wife. The third legal official was the *papālangi* Chief Magistrate, Captain C. B. Pearson, who arrived in November 1928, and remained until 1932.[48] The fourth legal official was George Scott, Judge of the Land Court.

In addition to Neill, the Chief Justice, Scott, and Pearson, there was Ragnar Hyne, Director of Education since 1919. Hyne was called to the Queensland Bar in 1924. In 1932 he was also appointed Secretary to the Premier, and on 8 June 1936 succeeded Murray-Aynsley as Chief Justice. He left Tonga in 1938 to take up an appointment in the British Solomon Islands Protectorate.[49]

With the coming of Neill in 1927 harmony appeared to be assured, except that the Queen still had to tolerate four *papālangi* in the Privy Council. Like McOwan, Neill urged the Tongan ministers to stand up to the *papālangi* members, but the Privy Council continued to rely on him to ensure the co-operation of the *papālangi* members. Neill reported thus:

> A difficulty with which the Agent [& Consul] is not infrequently faced is the fact that the Tongan Ministers will not accept responsibility. Decisions are taken by the Executive which, on occasions, the Tongan Ministers hope will not be accepted by the Agent and a responsibility which properly belongs to the Ministers is transferred to the Agent. Again, cases are not infrequent when action should in the first instance be taken by the Executive but the matter in issue is referred to the Agent for decision and a responsibility is thus shelved.[50]

The Queen's view was that since she was bound by her coronation oath, the ministers should equally observe the oaths of loyalty they had sworn to her when taking office. She believed that harmony within the Privy Council (as within the larger society) more important than forcing a decision.[51] The result was that Privy Council decisions were sometimes postponed for long periods of time, a procedure well understood in the traditional context, but exasperating for Neill and others who felt government should constantly be doing something.[52] An event in 1928 eased the situation somewhat by the removal of one *papālangi* minister.

In 1927 Parliament had approved the appointment of the Chief Magistrate and a Chief Inspector of Police (both *papālangi*), but their salaries appeared for the first time in the estimates in 1928.[53] The members of Parliament were outraged because they were simultaneously asked to approve the amalgamation of the posts of Governor and Magistrate of Ha'apai and of Governor and Magistrate of Vava'u and the retirement of 12 constables (all Tongans). It appeared that the two new *papālangi* appointments were funded by the retirement of 14 Tongans. Parliament responded thus: it refused to approve the salary of the new *papālangi* Chief Inspector of Police or to consent to the amalgamation of the posts of Governor and Magistrate in Ha'apai and Vava'u; it reinstated the 12 constables; it deleted the salary of a copra inspector (always an unpopular official); and it voted in favour of an extra scholarship for a Tongan to study overseas.

Sālote asked the members to reinstate the salary of the new Chief Inspector of Police, and they did as she requested. Then they voted to delete the salary of the Minister for Public Works, A. B. Wallace.[54] Wallace was unpopular and he was absent, which meant that criticisms did not have to be made to his face. Sālote was more than willing for Wallace to depart, for it had recently come to her notice that Wallace had a discreditable past.[55] She did not, however, wish to appear to be acting under pressure from Parliament, whose members were her inferiors, so she delayed making any decision.

Neill and Horne also were absent from the kingdom, and the Acting Consul, W. E. Russell, was required by the High Commissioner to refer major political matters to Suva. Thus it was near the end of Wallace's leave when the Queen asked the High Commissioner, Sir Eyre Hutson, to arrange for a letter of dismissal to be handed to Wallace when he arrived in Suva on his way back to Tonga. The reasons she gave Hutson for dismissing Wallace were his lack of competence and her wish to reorganize the Department of Works under the Chief Surveyor, who would not have ministerial status.[56] Sālote reminded Hutson of one of Parliament's few powers; that is, to refuse supply to the government. She believed that the members would refuse supply if their wishes in relation to Wallace were disregarded.

Hutson was not pleased at the manner of Wallace's dismissal, but it was only two years since Sālote's constitutional right to appoint and dismiss her ministers had been affirmed by Parliament. Hutson agreed that Wallace should go, but suggested that he should be allowed to resign and be given the pension to which he was entitled. Hutson added that if Sālote was contemplating dismissing other ministers, she should seek the approval of the Agent & Consul in plenty of time.[57] Sālote was careful to do this before dismissing Ha'amea, son and heir of 'Ulukālala, from his post as Governor of Vava'u a few months later (chapter 10).

In 1929 Parliament again deleted appointments provided for in the estimates, and Sālote again wrote to ask for the items to be reinstated. The members did as she asked, but with some reluctance.[58] Neill saw the events of 1928 and 1929 not as dissension from the Queen, but as a "natural and healthy desire on the part of the Tongans to be allowed to manage their own affairs as much as possible".[59] In 1931, he reported to the High Commissioner that

> The Government is in a minority in the Assembly and it is dependent upon a reasoned exposition of [its] view to secure the passage of any legislation. I have observed a tendency on the part of the Executive not to treat Parliament openly. The elected members know this and suspicion is bred. I have constantly advised the Premier to pursue a course he can defend in Parliament and to avail himself of the services of elected members for committee purposes. The elected side, on the whole, is weak in debate and unversed in procedure; some of the members, however, show an aptitude for parliamentary work. Difficulties are overcome on many occasions through the personal influence of the Premier in conversations after parliamentary hours and adverse votes then withdrawn. Some of the difficulties I fear are created by the Government.[60]

Such advice fell on deaf ears. To Sālote, as to all Tongans, all criticism was hostile, and to keep the members of Parliament informed of the deliberations of the Privy Council and to allow them to form committees would have been inviting members to take an interest in matters that (to the royal mind) were no concern of theirs. In Sālote's view, Parliament was an aberration of history, rather than an arm of government.

The Depression of the 1930s hit Tonga's economy very hard, for the price of copra plummeted. But the Queen may have felt the decline in government revenue was a small price to pay for the opportunity of dispensing with the services of *papālangi* in the name of economy. With the blessing of the Agent & Consul, J. D. Wall, aged 60, was retired at the end of 1931 in spite of his protests. His successor was not given the status of minister and Privy Councillor, so there were now only two *papālangi* ministers: the Chief Justice and the Minister for Finance. The Land Court had sat for only eight days in 1932, and Scott, now aged 55, was retired at the end of that year. Although his Tongan wife and children lived in Auckland, Scott remained in Tonga until he died of cancer in 1938.

Neill reported in 1931 that "Loyalty to the Throne is deep seated and Her Majesty exercises a wise and powerful influence among her people".[61] This was only one of several favourable reports on Sālote sent by the Agent & Consul to Suva and by the High Commissioner of the Western Pacific to the Secretary of State for the Colonies in London. In 1932 Sālote received an award that gave her great pleasure: she was appointed Dame Commander of the Order of the

British Empire (DBE). Sir Murchison Fletcher, then High Commissioner of the Western Pacific, came to invest Sālote with the order. Sālote used Fletcher's visit in September 1932 as she had used Hutson's visit in August 1925, to demonstrate to the Tongan chiefs and people and to the foreigners resident within the kingdom and outside it that she was recognized as the supreme chief of Tonga by the most prestigious ruler in the world.

Possibly no event in the previous 14 years of Sālote's reign had been as carefully prepared for as this event. The investiture took place in the throne room in the Palace, with all the dignity of such a ceremony in Great Britain. In honour of the occasion Sālote wore the finest of the fine-mats that were the treasures of her dynasty. Afterwards, she emerged from the Palace wearing the order and accompanied by the High Commissioner, Neill, her ministers, and the High Commissioner's aides for the playing of the British and Tongan national anthems and the taking of photographs on the Palace steps.

On the day following the investiture, 2000 people gathered outside a new summer "palace" built in the form of a large Tongan house near the shore at Lotoleveleva, some four kilometres west of Sālote's permanent residence. The Queen, the High Commissioner, the Neills, and other important *papālangi* guests sat inside the house, while the remainder of the guests sat outside (the Tongans thus being sufficiently removed from the Queen's presence to allow them to eat). This feast honoured both Fletcher as representative of the British King-Emperor and Sālote herself as a new DBE. The best food was brought from all over Tonga. The dances and songs that formed the entertainment had been rehearsed for months beforehand to ensure that the Queen's discriminating eye would observe only the best performances. Large-scale presentations were made to both the High Commissioner and to Sālote.[62]

On this occasion, as on every public occasion, the *papālangi* residents were treated as honoured guests, conveying an impression of a harmonious relationship between the *papālangi* and Tongan communities. Since the majority of the foreign residents were of British origin, the investiture of the DBE was pleasing to them and commanded a new respect for Sālote.

It was Fletcher's pleasant duty to report to the Secretary of State for Colonies his impressions of Sālote:

> I was very much impressed by the personality of the Queen. She combines a dignified presence and carriage with a quiet charm which is most attractive, and there is no mistaking the fact that she is supreme in Tonga. It is a pleasure to see the instinctive deference, free from all restraint or affectation, which is accorded to this gracious lady by her subjects.[63]

If Sālote had been able to read this report she would have been gratified, not only by the praise, but by the acknowledgement that she was treated with "instinctive deference" by her people. The early doubts that had existed among the British advisers that she would be able to rule had been transformed into an assumption that she did not *need* to act politically, that she was more than a political ruler. It was what she most wished for: the assumption that there was no need for achievement, that, like the sacred rulers of ancient Tonga, her eminence was universally recognized. The overseas press criticisms that Sālote had endured in 1924 were now a thing of the past. From this time Sālote was treated by *papālangi* royal watchers with a mixture of respect and romanticism.[64]

Sione Havea reflected upon the impression the award made on the minds of Tongans:

> It [the DBE] is given only to a person who is greatly respected, and whose life is fully dedicated to the ideals of British royalty . . .
>
> The British have recognized that same quality in our Queen, the quality of dedication to her country and to religion . . . The British recognize that here is someone who loves her people. We Tongans look up to her, whether it is in Conference [of the Free Wesleyan Church] or any other activity, or when we see her at the agricultural show. We do our part knowing that sooner or later she will see and know about the work we are doing. (*Koe Havea*, 1941) [SAH]

The last sentence sums up a great deal about Sālote, for she did see and know about "everything" that happened in the kingdom, and her approval was valued and her disapproval feared. People worked together better for the knowledge that their work would be noticed and praised or blamed.

The Queen was not as dependent upon Neill as she had been upon McOwan. Although Neill was a valued adviser, he was often absent from the kingdom during his 10-year appointment. Further, the Queen's *mana*, which was now obvious to all Tongans, had become visible even to *papālangi*. The Queen's much commented upon "influence" was shorthand for saying that many matters were no longer the concern of her British advisers, although she doubtless was glad to talk about politics to the Consul, who would maintain confidentiality.

Personal matters were, as always, confided to Rodger Page. The personal matters that concerned Sālote most as the first decade of her reign ended and the second began was the Queen's relationship with her half-sister Fusipala and the question of Fusipala's marriage. Where G. B. Smith-Rewse had played a significant part in bringing about the marriage of Sālote with Tungī, Neill would have no say about – indeed never officially commented upon – Fusipala. Sālote did not make it public that her relationship with her half-sister, particularly between 1928 and 1933, became political as well as personal.

CHAPTER TEN

The Queen's Sister: Princess Fusipala

"That's why we are so strong to-day, because we are willing to sacrifice anything for our chiefs, for our ruler; for the head of the family . . . With us, love of our country and love of our custom must come first." (Queen Sālote, 1959)[1]

REFLECTING ON HER OWN MARRIAGE, Queen Sālote said that she would have married anyone her father told her to marry, but she was fortunate he chose Tungī, whom she loved. High-ranking women were not expected to follow their own desires in marriage, but to marry for the benefit of their *kāinga*. A woman's *kāinga* was advantaged if the father of her child had high personal rank and substantial economic resources, and took the alliance implied in the marriage seriously.[2] The "gift" she gave to her husband's family were their children, her rank being deemed more important than that of the father in determining the rank of the children.

Sālote and Tungī were both advantaged by their marriage. Their sons not only had high personal rank, but were descended from the three titles that had been ascendant in living memory: the Tu'i Tonga (through both parents), the Tu'i Ha'atakalaua (through their father), and the Tu'i Kanokupolu (through their mother). Their place in the hierarchy was assured, provided other chiefs with equally illustrious genealogies did not marry other high-ranking persons and have children. We have already seen how some marriages were promoted by Sālote and Tungī, and others were blocked in order to prevent the births of very high-ranking children.

Division in Tongan life was often referred to as originating in the quarrel over whether Tupou II would marry 'Ofa-ki-Vava'u or Lavinia. It is hardly surprising that this image was perpetuated, for Princess Fusipala was held up by the family of her mother (Queen Takipō, sister of ʻOfa-ki-Vavaʻu: Figure 1.6) as superior in rank to Sālote, the daughter of Queen Lavinia (Figure 1.7). The potency of that rivalry could be extinguished if Fusipala married a chief who was loyal to the Queen instead of one intent on carrying on that (or any other) feud. But Fusipala's mother's family wanted her to marry not only to advantage their *kāinga*, but in a way that diminished the personal rank of the Queen's children. Torn as she was between her half-sister and her mother's relations, the story of Fusipala has elements of high tragedy.[3]

Fusipala's mother's family were descendants of Old Tungī's sister (Tupou ʻAhau), and therefore were *fahu* to Tungī Mailefihi, and thus to Sālote (as Tungī's wife) and to the royal princes. The Queen fully acknowledged their status as *fahu*, but countered by making comments about people who exploited such a relationship. While recognizing the claims of Tupou ʻAhau's descendants upon him, Tungī made no secret of the fact that his first loyalty was to Sālote.

Sālote became her half-sister's guardian in 1918 after the death of Queen Takipō. Fusipala owed obedience to Sālote as Tuʻi Kanokupolu and the head of her *kāinga*; but in traditional terms Fusipala was *uho tau* (rival, sibling of the same father but different mother), and she could divide the kingdom by encouraging the disloyalty of dissident chiefs. The mother's family "nourishes" the child, while the father's family "governs" the child, that is *ʻOku tauhi e he niʻihi kae pule e niʻihi* (Some do the caring and others do the governing). However, Queen Takipō's relations demanded full control of the young Princess. Queen Sālote removed the child from their care to prevent her from being thoroughly spoilt, not only by over-indulgence but by listening to her mother's relatives.

The most formidable of Fusipala's relations were Tae Manusā and Muimui (mother and sister of Queen Takipō), the latter a large, overbearing woman, about 24 years of age in 1918 (Figure 3.3). Muimui was the second wife of Sioape Kaho, Minister for Police and a leader of the "Reactionary Party". Sioape shared the responsibilities of godparent to Fusipala with his brother Tuʻivakanō (Polutele).[4] Fusipala's mother's relatives claimed that Tupou II had promised his younger daughter would marry Haʻamea, son of Sioape's patron ʻUlukālala, when she was old enough (Figure 2.3).

If the King had made such a promise, it would have been binding on both his daughters, but Sālote denied that such a promise had been made. Contrary to popular opinion, the Queen did not oppose the proposal of marriage to Haʻamea, but she was unwilling to force her sister into an unwanted marriage.

The difference in personal rank of the sisters was not great, but there were differences in personality. Although of a passionate nature, Sālote was guided by a keen political sense and an understanding of the power of public opinion. Fusipala was self-indulgent and not very aware of her power to harm others.

There was little difference in the experience of the two sisters, for Fusipala's early life followed the lines that had been determined for Sālote by their father. When Sālote was seven years old, she had been sent to live with her "grandfather", Mateialona; when Fusipala was six, she also was sent to live with Mateialona, then Governor of Ha'apai. Rachel Tonga, Mateialona's sister-in-law, gave Fusipala the same lessons that she had given Sālote as a child.

Fusipala returned to the Palace some time before July 1920, and on her eighth birthday, 26 July 1920, received enormous presentations at the Palace, at about the same time as Takipō's half-brother Mā'atu (Panuve) was leading a rebellion in Parliament. These presentations at least matched those made to Prince Tāufa'āhau earlier that month on his second birthday. If the Queen needed a warning sign that Fusipala would be a focus for dissident chiefs, this was one. The solution was to send Fusipala overseas for schooling, just as Sālote had been sent after the King's second marriage.

Sālote had been nine years of age when she went to New Zealand, Fusipala was eight. Like Sālote, Fusipala was without companions when she left Tonga on 11 December 1920. Again like Sālote, Fusipala lived in Auckland with a *papālangi* family, a Mrs Nankervis of the Tindall family, before being enrolled at the Anglican Diocesan School for Girls.[5] Remembering her own happy time at this school, Sālote was disappointed that Fusipala was not happy, believing that Fusipala should take advantage of the opportunity to learn. Fusipala was allowed to return to Tonga at the end of 1925, when she was 13 years of age.

Even though Fusipala was not yet of marriageable age, her mother's people urged the betrothal of Fusipala to Ha'amea. But Ha'amea's father, 'Ulukālala, had just betrayed the Queen in the enterprise most dear to her heart (the reunion of the two Wesleyan churches) and had set himself up as the temporal head of the seceding Free Church.

Sālote and Tungī decided to remove Fusipala once again from the influence of her mother's family. They took advantage in mid-1926 of the attendance of Australian church people at the centenary celebrations of the coming of Christianity to send her to the Methodist Ladies' College in Melbourne, Australia. Sālote and Tungī hoped that Fusipala would become a loyal member of the Methodist Church in Australia, and subsequently a loyal member of the Free Wesleyan Church of Tonga, rather than following her grandmother Tae Manusā into the Anglican Church or ricocheting like her uncle Sioape between the Roman Catholic and Free Church. The reports that Sālote received from Dr W. H. Fitchett, principal of the Methodist Ladies' College, were hopeful.

> She is proving herself a good student, with a quick mind and willingness to work, and she wins the respect and affection both of her fellow students and her teachers. Her general conduct is admirable, and I think she finds a real enjoyment in the life of the MLC. In music, she really has a touch of genius . . .

> A week ago, Fusipala was on the programme for a pianoforte solo by one of the great masters, and she played it magnificently. If it had been the Town Hall she would have been encored. The girls cheered her till she had to go back to the piano.[6]

A school friend, Elsie Scholes, confirmed that Fusipala was friendly and popular, and developed her gifts for music, for she played not only the piano, but also the organ, violin, and ukulele, and had a good singing voice. She was in demand to perform Tongan dances, but otherwise lived the life of a *papālangi* teenager of that time.[7] Her feelings about the proposed marriage to Ha'amea were disclosed (probably not for the first time) in a letter to the Queen of 25 May 1927, while she was still a student at the College:

> . . . you don't seem even to believe that I am not going to get married at all. You must realise by now that I have got more sense and that I am getting desperate over it. "Fefine tabu" be hanged and let it go to blazes. Every hour brings me nearer to that awful man who is nearly three times my age, and you are not going to marry him so you cannot possibly understand what my feelings are. I am leaving everything in your hands. Please, please, tell everybody in Tonga that you don't want me to marry at all, for I would rather be dead than be a step-mother to about half a dozen kids.[8]

Sālote heard her plea, and put no pressure on her sister. Soon afterwards (19 August 1927), Fusipala wrote contritely to her sister, saying that the Queen "carried all her punishments". She had been disobedient to her sister, and people were now saying "nasty things" about the Queen, but she (Fusipala) was to blame. The Queen, she wrote, was the person she loved best, and she wanted to serve the Queen. Fusipala had read a story in the Melbourne *Sun* that alleged that Tongans had ignored the Queen's birthday the previous March. Fusipala, assuming the story was true, wanted to know the cause.

When a Tupou College choir toured Australia in the early months of 1928, Fusipala joined in some of their Melbourne concerts, dancing the *tau'olunga* (solo dance for a young woman), playing the piano, and singing "Drink to me only with thine eyes" while the choir hummed the accompaniment.[9] Crown Prince Tāufa'āhau was a privileged member of the choir, but Fusipala showed no aloofness with the other members in spite of her royal rank, giving the Tupou College boys advice about *papālangi* ways, helping to prepare food for them, and taking them to visit *papālangi* families.[10] Among the boys of the choir was a commoner, Tēvita Tu'ipulotu Toutaiolepo, and he and the princess formed a romantic attachment. He was two years older than Fusipala and the first Tongan to win the government-sponsored overseas scholarship to Newington College, Sydney, the Queen personally contributing to his school

Left: Ve'ehala (Feleti Vī), wearing dance costume and holding a choir conductor's baton. *Courtesy of 'Eva Ve'ehala.* [50]

Below: Investiture of Queen Sālote as Dame Commander of the Order of the British Empire (DBE), 8 September 1932. *Standing at back:* Chief Justice C. M. Murray-Aynsley, naval officer, aide-de-camp, Rodger Page, British Agent & Consul J. S. Neill, W. G. Bagnall, Ata (Solomone), Tungī Mailefihi, Sioape Kaho, Vīlai Tupou, S. F. Tongilava. *Standing at front:* High Commissioner for the Western Pacific Sir Murchison Fletcher, Queen Sālote. *Seated:* Nuku (Pulu), 'Ulukālala (S. F. M.), Mā'atu (Ma'afu-'o-tu'itonga), Fakafanua, Tu'ivakanō (Siosiua), Fielakepa (Niumeitola), not identified. *Courtesy of the family of Rodger Page.* [51]

Above: Muimui Kaho, sister of Queen Takipō and aunt of Princess Fusipala. Muimui was the second wife of Sioape Kaho, Minister for Police, 1919–39. *Courtesy of Tulua Studios. (Ref. T8988–11.)* [54]

Left: Princess Fusipala in dance costume, at the home of a school friend in Ararat, Australia, 1927. *Courtesy of Elsie Scholes.* [53]

Right: The royal family. *Standing:* Prince Tāufa'āhau and Princess Fusipala. *Seated:* Tungī Mailefihi and Queen Sālote. *At front:* Prince Tuku'aho and Prince Sione Ngū. *Courtesy of the family of Rodger Page.* [52]

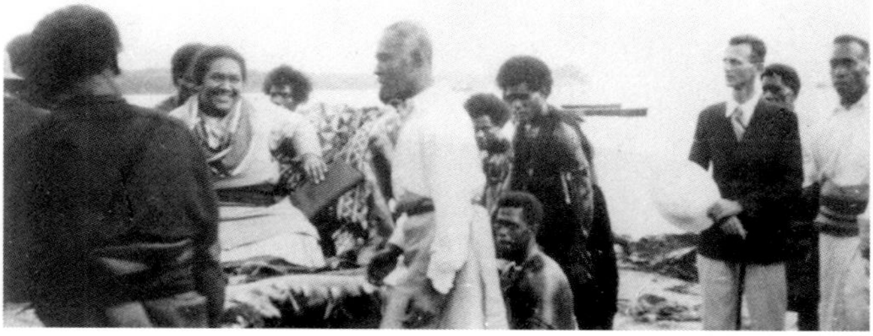

Above: Queen Sālote arrives at Lakeba, Fiji, for the celebration of the centenary of Christianity. She is greeted by Ratu Lala Sukuna, 12 October 1935. [56]

Left: Tuna Vaea, sister of Tupou Seini (wife of Vīlai Tupou). Tuna married Ha'amea (son of 'Ulukālala) in 1934. [55]

Below: Rehearsal of Tongan combined choirs in Palace grounds, probably 1935. [57]

Above: Kauvai, one of the country houses of Queen Sālote. At either end are oval-shaped Tongan houses, which are joined by a long room. Note the thatched roof, later replaced with an iron roof. *Courtesy of HRH Nanansipau'u Tuku'aho.* [58]

Above: Ha'a Tufunga (royal undertakers) sitting at the grave of Prince Tuku'aho. *Courtesy of Doris Smith.* [60]

Right: Sione Havea, Head Tutor, Tupou College, and author of frequently quoted biographies of Tongan notables in *Koe Havea* (1941). [59]

Above: Investiture of Tungī Mailefihi as Commander of the Order of the British Empire (CBE), 28 July 1937. (Note that most of the Tongans are in mourning.) *Back row:* W. G. Bagnall, unidentified, Sioape Kaho, Rodger Page. *Next row:* Vīlai Tupou, J. S. Neill, Queen Sālote, Tungī Mailefihi, Ata (Solomone). *Side:* S. F. Tongilava, ʻUlukālala (S. F. M.). *Seated:* the nobles Tuʻiʻafitu, Vahaʻi (Vilisoni Namoa), Tuʻivakanō (Siosiua), Nuku (Pulu), Fielakepa (S. Niumeitolu), Kalanivalu (Sēmisi), ʻAhomeʻe (Tēvita Manu-ʻo-pangai), Fakafanua (Kisione). *Courtesy of Baron Vaea.* [62]

Above Right: Queen Sālote wearing a Maori cloak during visit to New Zealand in 1936. [63]

Right: Queen Sālote, c. 1936. This photograph should be compared with that taken on her wedding day. The rounded face of innocence has matured into a face of one who has experienced many of life's sorrows. [61]

ABOVE: Tungī Mailefihi, probably during visit to New Zealand in 1936. [64]

TOP RIGHT: Nuku'alofa. Parliament House is on the far left (fenced in), the Police Headquarters has a verandah, the two-storey Stone Building housed the Premier's and other government departments, the Fale Kai (later the Lands Office), is in the middle, and in the distance are pine trees of the Hala Paini (Pine Road), which is pictured on many pieces of bark cloth. On the right is the Treasury and Post Office building, and in the foreground right is the wireless station. [66]

RIGHT: Queen Sālote and Vīlai Tupou. [65]

Above: Fai-‘a-koka. Queen Sālote lived here as a child with Mateialona, Sela, and Rachel Tonga. The Stuarts complained of its inadequacies in 1938. [70]

Right: Nuku‘alofa. The house known as “the Chief Justice’s house”, but occupied by the Bagnalls in 1938. [69]

Above: British Agent & Consul A. L. Armstrong, Chief Justice W. H. Stuart, Minister for Lands Ata (Solomone), Minister for Finance W. G. Bagnall, Minister for Police Sioape Kaho. A rare moment of harmony at the flagpole, 1938. *Courtesy of Auckland Institute and Museum. (Ref. C30762.)* [67]

Left: Chief Justice W. H. Stuart and Tēvita Tu‘ipulotu Toutaiolepo. Tēvita’s name was associated with that of Princess Fusipala, but at this time (1938) he was an interpreter in the law courts. *Courtesy of Kurt Düring.* [68]

ABOVE: Queen Sālote returning from either the Opening or Closing of Parliament, 1938. The Queen is wearing her coronation robes. In the background is the building known as the Stone Building, which housed the Premier's and other government departments. The band of Government College precedes the Queen's car and the Royal Guards follow. The school boys lining the route are waving Tongan flags. *Courtesy of the Auckland Institute and Museum. (Ref. 30760.)* [71]

CENTRE LEFT: The British Residency, 1938. Until 1939 only gentlemen called to mark His Britannic Majesty's birthday. *Courtesy of the Auckland Institute and Museum. (Ref C30761.)* [73]

LEFT: *Kupesi* (pattern made from coconut bark and ribs and used for designs on *ngatu*) showing schoolhouse of Tupou College, Nafualu. Now at museum, Tupou College, Toloa. *Courtesy of Phyllis Herda.* [72]

fees. Fusipala left Melbourne in December 1928, and the young people kept up a romantic correspondence between Tonga and Sydney.[11]

At the time of her return to Tonga Fusipala had spent nearly half of her 16 years overseas and had absorbed many *papālangi* values, including ideas of romantic love and individual choice in marriage, which were contrary to the Tongan custom of chiefly marriage for economic and dynastic reasons. The Queen could not consent to the Princess's romance with Tēvita, but she wisely decided not to prohibit the correspondence. Tungī, on the other hand, grumbled that Fusipala was distracting Tēvita from his studies. Fusipala responded by giving Tungī the nickname "Jack Dempsey", the name of a well-known boxer of the day, presumably because of Tungī's solid, stocky build.

For the four years following Fusipala's return, the matter of the Princess's marriage was the most pressing political question before Sālote. Fusipala was fourth in the line of succession, after the three princes, who by 1928 were 10, nine, and six years of age. In Tongan experience, children did not necessarily live to adult life, so the fourth in the line of succession could not be disregarded by either Sālote or Muimui, who now emerged as the prime antagonists in the matter of the Princess's marriage. Sālote had the upper hand, for custom and the Constitution (cl. 36) stated that Fusipala could not marry without the Queen's consent unless she was willing to be removed from the line of succession and to be considered dead by her father's *kāinga*. Although Sālote chose not to threaten her sister, Muimui was aware of the Queen's power to disinherit her sister, and could not encourage her niece to disregard her sister's wishes. Instead she continually harassed the Queen with proposed marriages, hoping the Queen would agree to one that Muimui supported.

Physically, the sisters were a contrast. Sālote was handsome, close to 190cm tall and of chiefly proportions, dark-skinned, and with a husky, almost mannish, voice. Fusipala was considered to be beautiful, with pale skin and graceful movements, slender and only 170cm tall, somewhat less than the admired chiefly proportions.[12] Fusipala had a train of girl friends of her own age whom she could command, some from the Kolisi Fefine (Women's College, later called Queen Sālote College) and some from among her aunt Muimui and uncle Sioape's relations, such as Sioape's niece, Tupou Kaho (later Tupou Posesi Fanua). Except for the threat of marriage hanging over her head, Fusipala led the leisurely life of a chiefly woman, of gossip and social events. She was in demand for concerts, playing piano solos and singing "Drink to me only with thine eyes" at the Tupou College speech night.[13] She trained a girls' basketball team, and helped the girls at the Kolisi Fefine with their handicrafts and singing. She went to the funeral of her mother's mother, Tae Manusā, who died on 5 July 1931 and was buried at the chiefly village of the Tungī family. She attended the Free Wesleyan Church on Sundays and the fiftieth anniversary celebrations of Government College in 1932. When Fusipala visited Siaine, the home of her aunt Muimui and uncle

Sioape, the presentations made to her were more elaborate and the dances more frequent than those for the Queen at the Palace.[14]

Two events of 1928 reinforced Sālote's reluctance to promote a marriage between Fusipala and Ha'amea. The first event was the split in the Free Church of Tonga, which ended in the separation of the new Church of Tonga (known as the "Church of the Chiefs") headed by 'Ulukālala (Ha'amea's father) from the Free Church (known as the "Church of the President") (chapter 8). Religious division reflected secular divisions, as Consul Neill explained when commenting upon this new breakaway of the churches.

> It is impossible to divorce the religious question from any political review of modern Tonga. The great majority of the chiefs and people belong to the Wesleyan Free Church [*sic*]. The dissentients in the last dispute are now divided between the Free Church and the Church of Tonga. The latter church was founded in 1928 by Finau Ulukalala, the Minister of the Crown. The founder is a chief of the highest rank and a man of great power. He has his church, as the old chief had his resident missionary: the congregation are his personal followers. Finau Ulukalala has played a prominent part in modern Tongan politics. His character, although it may not bear the strictest investigation, is powerful and attractive . . . [15]

'Ulukālala founding a new church instead of returning to the Queen's church was a major statement of political independence from the Crown. The Queen could not be seen to reward such disloyalty with the hand of the Princess.

The second event was a revelation at the end of 1928 that Ha'amea had embezzled funds while Governor of Ha'apai. As we have seen in the cases of Ata and Ve'ehala, Sālote was disinclined to regard misappropriation of funds by chiefs of high rank as a serious crime, but she had learned that the law, which underpinned an orderly if imperfect society, disbarred chiefs guilty of misappropriation from holding government appointments. Ata and Ve'ehala had suffered from the law, and there could be no reason to protect Ha'amea. The theft could not in any case be concealed, and with the consent of the Acting Agent & Consul (W. E. Russell) Sālote dismissed Ha'amea from his position as Governor (by this time of Vava'u) and from the public service.

In the eyes of Tongans generally, Ha'amea's actions were no barrier to his marriage with the Princess. Eventually Fusipala, 17 years old in 1929, bent to the pressure from Muimui and Sioape, and agreed, albeit with reluctance, to marry the 38-year-old Ha'amea. In 1929 or 1930 the Queen took Fusipala to Vava'u for a celebration of the betrothal. At the last moment, while the sisters were still in Vava'u, Fusipala again changed her mind, and told the Queen that she would not marry Ha'amea after all. The Vava'u people ('Ulukālala's people) were angry and blamed the Queen for not forcing Fusipala. The Queen deemed it wise to leave Vava'u rather hurriedly.[16]

Tungī suggested the great chief Tu'iha'ateiho (Havea). Tu'iha'ateiho outranked Ha'amea, for he was descended from the Tamahā, daughter of the Tu'i Tonga Fefine.[17] In August 1931 Fusipala agreed to marry Tu'iha'ateiho, but withdrew her promise soon afterwards, saying that he was too boring and too old (33 years old to the Princess's 19 years).

Fusipala then became engaged to a chief only six years older than herself: Lala, the son and heir of the noble Veikune, who was also Queen Sālote's second cousin, through Queen Lavinia (Figure 15.1). There were rumours that Fusipala had made too much of a personal commitment to Lala. Then throughout Tonga the story was told that Muimui had walked to the Palace, gone upstairs, and "dragged" Fusipala away in front of Sālote's eyes.[18] Such was Muimui's reputation as a domineering woman and her rank as *fahu* to Tungī's family that this story was credible. But Tongilava recorded in his diary on 13 February 1932 that Fusipala had "run away" (*hola*) from the Palace and gone to Siaine, the home of Muimui and Sioape Kaho. The departure of Fusipala from the Palace (leaving her sister's protection) was considered to be such a scandal that Tongilava recorded it in red ink in his diary, the only other event recorded in red ink being the day of Fusipala's return.[19]

Lala was of exceedingly high rank. Muimui's objections to him were probably that the Veikunes were related to the Queen and rivals of the 'Ulukālala chiefs in Vava'u. Another reason for the end of the engagement to Lala was that there was now an even more eligible suitor on the scene.[20] Fusipala justified ending her engagement to Lala by saying that Lala was a "bitter" man. She had now offended the Veikune family as well as the families of Ha'amea and Tu'iha'ateiho, and the Queen had to deal with the anger of the relatives of the rejected suitors, being the one who was blamed. Muimui revelled in the disruption, and accused Sālote of being jealous of Fusipala having so many suitors.[21]

It soon became clear that Fusipala had run away from the Palace to avoid telling the Queen of her latest engagement. It was Muimui who came to tell the Queen that Fusipala and Sālote's cousin Sēmisi had sworn an oath before God to marry. Sēmisi's mother was granddaughter of the last Tu'i Tonga, and Sēmisi was heir to his uncle Sioeli Pangia, the great chief of Lapaha, who had inherited some of the lands (though not the title) of the Tu'i Tonga (Figure 7.1). Sēmisi was also heir to his father's title, Fotofili, and would have extensive estates from the two titles. Sālote was not impressed by Fusipala and Sēmisi's oath, but could not be indifferent to the marriage plans of any descendant of the Tu'i Tonga, let alone Sēmisi.

Sēmisi was attractive to Fusipala not only because of his high rank but also because he was near to her own age, being 20 years old to Fusipala's 19. If Fusipala married Sēmisi, their children could outrank the princes in the eyes of many of the aristocracy. So Muimui and her *kāinga* forgot about Ha'amea, and tried to force Sālote to consent so Fusipala would not lose her place in the succession. Muimui again accused Sālote of being jealous of Fusipala, and uttered veiled threats about the consequences of opposing the match. Sālote was not so easily confounded, and pointed out to Muimui that if she gave her consent to Fusipala's marriage to Sēmisi, she would offend the *kāinga* of Ha'amea, Tu'iha'ateiho, and Lala. After some reflection, the Queen told Muimui that Fusipala could marry any of the other three chiefs with her consent, but definitely not Sēmisi.

Sālote had the means to impress her views upon Sēmisi. Firstly, Sālote doubly outranked Sēmisi by *kāinga* ranking, for she was descended from Old Lavinia, the sister of Sēmisi's grandfather, Kalanivalu; and her mother's mother was sister to Sēmisi's father, Fotofili (Figure 7.1). She was his *fahu*, and he had to obey her. Secondly, there was a rival claimant to the title and estates of Sioeli Pangia, and considering Sālote's influence on such matters it would be unwise to defy her when such a claim was pending.

When it became clear that Sālote would never consent to them marrying each other, Sēmisi and Fusipala asked Rodger Page, as President of the Free Wesleyan Church, to absolve them of their solemn vow to marry. On 8 March 1932 Fusipala, Sēmisi, and Page came together to the Palace to see Sālote. Soon after this, Sēmisi was told that he should marry Sisilia, first cousin of Tungī on his mother's side (Figure 1.9). Although Sisilia's rank was high through her Kolomotu'a father, her mother was the sister of the lesser-ranking Siaki Lolohea of Ha'apai. Sisilia was staying with her maternal uncle in Ha'apai in order (she said) to avoid Lala's attentions. So Tungī advised Sioeli Pangia to take Sēmisi to Ha'apai to meet Sisilia. Sēmisi and Sisilia were married in Nuku'alofa on 8 June. The Queen attended the Tongan ceremony on 10 June, where – being Sēmisi's *fahu* – she distributed the *koloa*.[22]

Sālote claimed that she had nothing to do personally with arranging Sēmisi and Sisilia's marriage; but the match advantaged her. As Tungī 's first cousin, Sisilia was high enough to marry Sēmisi, but not too high, and their children could not outrank Sālote and Tungī's sons. It is likely that Tungī arranged the marriage, since he was *fahu* (father's sister's son) to Sisilia. It would not have been the first time Tungī had arranged advantageous marriages for his Kolomotu'a relatives. And since Tungī's mother had been sister to a number of brothers, Tungī and the princes were now *fahu* to an increasing number of nobles (Figure 17.1).

On the day that Rodger Page absolved Sēmisi and Fusipala of their vow to marry, Fusipala wrote to Sālote's Secretary, Sione Filipe Tongilava, begging him to intercede with Sālote on her behalf.[23] Fusipala acknowledged that the Queen had cause to be angry with her, because of her disobedience, and admitted that she had humiliated the Queen by her behaviour, but she felt unable to return to the Palace. Nor did she wish to remain dependent upon

Muimui and Sioape, who were angry with her for disappointing their hopes. Fusipala begged the Queen, through Tongilava, to allow her to set up a household at Finefekai, the house on Tāufaʻāhau Road in Nukuʻalofa in which her grandfather Tuʻipelehake and her mother had lived at different times. However, Fusipala could not be trusted to set up her own household, so, unhappy and indecisive, she remained with Muimui. Sālote recorded that Muimui thrashed Fusipala while the girl was with her, in order to punish her for her vacillations; other people claimed that Muimui hit Fusipala and pulled her hair to show Sālote that she had the "right" to do so. Sālote endured this provocation. Fusipala now engaged in self-destructive behaviour, eating little and smoking a great deal.[24]

The Queen had ambivalent feelings about Fusipala at this time, although she attributed the negative emotions to members of the royal household, such as Tungī , not to herself. The Queen commented that "the one who disliked Fusipala most of all was [Prince] Tukuʻaho", suggesting that Fusipala had made other enemies among the nobles and chiefs. Certainly Fusipala had angered the *kāinga* of the four chiefs whom she had briefly consented to marry. Now Sēmisi was safely married; the great chief Tuʻihaʻateiho had gone to Sāmoa to arrange for his marriage to Leafā, a Sāmoan woman of rank; and Lala Veikune showed no further interest in marrying the Princess. This left the way open for a renewal of the proposal of Haʻamea.

Haʻamea himself did not want to marry Fusipala, for he was in love with Tuna Vaea, sister-in-law of Sālote's half-brother Vīlai. Without actually advocating the match, Sālote showed her approval by asking Tuna to come and stay at the Palace. In a sense she was "adopting" Tuna as one of her own family, suggesting that she was a suitable bride for Haʻamea without putting her opinion in words. ʻUlukālala had promised Haʻamea that if Fusipala would not marry him, he could marry Tuna, but ʻUlukālala would not relinquish hope of Fusipala until she was well and truly out of reach.

Thus it was that on 2 August 1932, six months after Fusipala had left the Palace and five months after her engagement to Sēmisi had come to an end, ʻUlukālala came to the Palace with Fusipala's uncle, the high-ranking noble Māʻatu (Maʻafu-ʻo-tuʻitonga), to ask Sālote to give her consent to the marriage of Fusipala with Haʻamea. Being assured of Fusipala's consent, Sālote agreed, and showed her good faith by ordering wedding clothes and a wedding cake from Auckland for her sister's wedding. The wedding cake arrived on 20 September, but Fusipala remained at Siaine with Muimui.

On 20 October, soon after the announcement of Fusipala's engagement, Sālote and Fusipala met at the funeral of ʻAlipate Mafileʻo, uncle of Tungī and great chief of Kolomotuʻa. On 22 October Fusipala asked the Queen if she could return to the Palace. The Queen gave her willing consent, and on 24 October sent their uncle, Matekitonga, to bring Fusipala home.[25]

Once she was back in the Palace, Fusipala told Sālote that she had been coerced by her aunt Muimui into agreeing to marry Ha'amea, and wished to withdraw her consent. Sālote perceived that her sister was on the edge of a nervous breakdown, for the Princess ate very little, had lost weight, could not sleep, drank alcohol, and smoked cigarettes constantly. Alarmed, the Queen called in Dr Dawson, and he advised that the Princess go overseas for a holiday in order to recover her health. The Queen agreed.

There was now the possibility of a very eligible suitor, one likely to please everyone (except possibly Muimui and her *kāinga*), for it would take Fusipala away from Tonga. This proposed suitor was George Cakobau, second cousin of Edward Cakobau, Sālote and Fusipala's half-brother. George Cakobau was now 20 years of age, the same age as Fusipala, he had been educated at Newington College, and the two young people had met at least once, in December 1928, when Fusipala visited her Fijian relations in Bau.[26] As well as being descended in the male line from Cakobau the Vunivalu, George's mother was Adi Torika of the chiefly house of Cakaudrove, which made him *fahu* to much of Viti Levu. Marriages between Tongan women of high rank and Fijian chiefs had occurred over the centuries, so the match was in accordance with tradition. George Cakobau's high rank meant he would be acceptable to the chiefs of Tonga, and his youth and *papālangi* education made him acceptable to Fusipala. The advantages of the match for the royal family were that Fusipala would marry someone of rank high enough for the King's daughter, but would live outside Tonga. This proposed marriage could not have been a new idea for Sālote, but as George was now old enough to marry, the time for the proposal was appropriate. Fusipala agreed to the match and to live outside Tonga.

It was not only Fusipala's health that made an overseas trip advisable. It would allow time to pass before another marriage plan was made public. Rev. Harold Wood and Dr Olive Wood would leave Tonga on 21 November to take the second Tupou College choir to Australia for a tour, and Sālote took advantage of their consent to chaperone Fusipala to send her away with very little notice. Many Tongans believed that Fusipala was being sent away to prevent the marriage to Ha'amea; and Saiatua Lavulo recalled that as the steamer pulled away from the wharf, Fusipala said, "Nofo ā, Tonga. Nofo ā" (Goodbye, Tonga. Goodbye), as though she did not expect to return.[27]

Fusipala appeared to enjoy herself once the ship had left Tonga. The High Commissioner put a car at her disposal while she was in Suva, and she went on a shopping spree in Auckland, spending £100 on dresses, the equivalent of thousands of dollars in modern currency.[28] In Sydney Fusipala stayed with a Methodist family, the Hewitts. A letter from Fusipala to the Queen shows her full of affection and high spirits. It also shows that she was still writing to Tēvita, who had returned to Tonga the previous October and entered the Tongan civil service.[29]

I feel very sorry for poor Nusi Havea, because she is in a very bad way with homesickness.[30] I have written to her and have rang her up and have quite a long confab in Tongan while everybody stick round [*sic*] to hear what the Tongan language is like. I want to go and see her but Mrs Hewitt will not allow me to go by myself – so I must be satisfied with the telephone conversations . . .

The three little snaps which I enclose were taken last week in one of the largest drapery shops in Sydney. There is a new photographic machine by which one can be photographed 6 times for the large sum of one shilling and one has only to wait 6 minutes for their development. I know they are dreadful, but just the same I would like to see the silly expressions on the face – and what more can you expect. Before you can say "Jack Robinson" the six are taken. I shall also send two snaps taken this month and you will be able to see by them how well I am looking and what a size I am.

Did I tell you that I have had my hair cut? I simply had to because it was so untidy and also found to my consternation that my hair was coming out. Forgive me, but I assure you it has improved my personal appearance – I don't think.

Mrs Hewitt sends her love and she would like me to mention that she helped me to choose a frock yesterday. We went into about seven shops looking for a plain wine-coloured morocain frock and at last we found one in the seventh shop and we got it for a bargain – £2.2.0. It is a lovely little dress.

Please give everybody my love. My very best love to John [Sione Ngū] and Tuku'aho and I hope the latter enjoys Nafualu.

With lots and lots of love –

Your loving sister Elisiva [Fusipala]

PS. I have not mentioned Tevita's name very much because I am offended with him. Something has put me out a little, but it will pass.[31]

A week before Fusipala had left Tonga it was announced that Crown Prince Tāufa'āhau had come second in the scholarship examinations in open competition with other secondary school boys.[32] So, after ten years as Premier, Tungī took his first overseas leave, leaving Nuku'alofa with Tāufa'āhau on 3 December 1932 for a holiday in New Zealand, and then to Sydney to enrol the Prince at Newington College.[33] Tungī was thus in Sydney when Fusipala took ill in February. In March she appeared to be improving, and her passage back to Tonga was booked for 27 April, on the same ship as the Wood family and the Tupou College choir. But Fusipala's condition deteriorated, and after a few weeks in hospital she died of tubercular peritonitis on 21 April 1933.[34]

On 27 April, Fusipala's body left Australia on the *Niagara*, accompanied by Tungī, the Wood family, and the Tupou College choir. The Queen sent the government steamer *Hifofua* and the Ha'a Tufunga (royal undertakers) to Suva to bring her sister's body home. A thousand Tongans came to the Suva wharf with mats and bark cloth and watched the transfer of the coffin to the *Hifofua*, singing their farewell, "Till we meet at Jesu's feet".[35] The body of the Princess arrived in Tonga on 10 May, and was taken to the throne room at the Palace for two days of lying-in-state and the *takipō* (ceremony of lights).

From the time Fusipala left Siaine, Muimui had refused to have anything to do with her "daughter". She refused to open the letters Fusipala sent her or even to speak about her. She acted as though Fusipala were dead. Now Fusipala was really dead. The Queen asked Muimui to come to the Palace, and left her alone with Fusipala's body. It was only then that Muimui's tears flowed.[36]

The Queen could have decided to bury Fusipala with Takipō in the Mala'e 'Aloa, but instead she gave her a royal funeral. Her body was carried to Mala'e Kula on a catafalque used only for royal personages, and accompanied by the royal undertakers. Fusipala was buried on 12 May with all the ceremony appropriate for a Queen's sister in the vault of their grandfather Tu'ipelehake. Tungī and Vīlai were *liongi* at Fusipala's funeral, for Fusipala was *fahu* to both.

During the two days in which Fusipala's body lay in state in the Palace, the Queen was heard to weep for her sister, and out of her grief came two laments. In the second of these laments, "*Koe tutulu 'a 'Ene 'Afio*" ("The weeping of the Queen [for Fusipala]"), she wrote:

> 'Elisiva [Fusipala's first name] pe'i ke tu'u hake
> Ke ke 'eva 'i hota lotofale
> Na'e kasa 'aki pe ho vā'e.
>
> Awake, 'Elisiva, and walk
> that I may see your beautiful feet,
> which were like a torch of lights
> as you walked around our house. [MT]

On the day that Fusipala's body arrived in Tonga, Tu'iha'ateiho returned to Tonga with his Sāmoan bride, Leafā. They would have no children. Lala Veikune married 'Ofa, illegitimate daughter of Sioape Kaho, in 1942 and was appointed as the noble Veikune in 1951. In 1934, the year after Fusipala's death, Edward Cakobau, half-brother of Sālote and Fusipala, came to Tonga for the first time, with a Fijian football team. It was during this visit that Edward was honoured as a Tongan chief, being nicknamed Tungī Fisi (Fijian Tungī),[37] and Tungī Mailefihi offered him land if he would come to live in Tonga. Edward's relationship to the Queen was not stated in so many words, but was implicitly acknowledged by the welcome he was given.

During the visit Edward was best man at the wedding of Ha'amea and Tuna Vaea. This was the most splendid traditional marriage in Tonga since Sālote's own. The presence of Sālote, Tungī, Edward, and Vīlai at the two wedding ceremonies minimized the fact that Ha'amea was marrying a woman of rank inferior to his own. The Queen's approval was made amply clear by the *papālangi* wedding being celebrated in the Royal Chapel, with the royal chaplain officiating. The Tongan wedding ceremony followed the next day, in the Palace grounds, and Sālote distributed the *koloa*. Ha'amea and Tuna had no children and this contributed to the continuing harmony between the Palace and the household of Ha'amea.

Ha'amea's mother was from the family of the noble Ata, Tungī's close friend.[38] Ha'amea was loyal to 'Ulukālala during his father's lifetime, but his connection with the Ata family predisposed him towards the royal house. Although the Queen had dismissed Ha'amea in 1928 for embezzlement when he was Governor of Ha'apai, she pardoned him in 1932. In 1938, after the death of his father, Sālote appointed Ha'amea a noble, giving him the title 'Ulukālala, which had been the personal name of his father and of his famous ancestors whose struggle against the Tupou dynasty had now ended. In 1939 Sālote appointed him Governor of Vava'u, indicating that she trusted him to rule on her behalf the land his ancestors had long claimed as their independent fiefdom. In 1950, after the death of Ata (Solomone Ula) she appointed him to the title that was most closely associated with the Tu'i Kanokupolu, and he was known as 'Ulukālala-Ata (Ha'amea) until his death on 12 September 1960.

The loyalty that Ha'amea exhibited to both his father and to his sovereign was a quality much valued by the Queen, and was in sharp contrast to Fusipala's seeming lack of awareness of what was due to her sister and sovereign. When Muimui encouraged Fusipala's several engagements, she was inviting the Queen to declare her preference for one chiefly faction over another. The Queen refused to be trapped in this way, instead giving her sister an opportunity to show her loyalty to the head of her family by making a considered choice. When Sālote recounted the story to Elizabeth Bott Spillius 25 years after Fusipala's death, it was clear from her narration that it was the superficiality of Fusipala's affections that had hurt Sālote most. Fusipala's failure to do her duty had put an enormous strain on the royal family and on relations between the interrelated chiefly houses. Sālote's own affection for her sister had been sorely tested.

Fusipala (rather like her father, Tupou II) wished to enjoy the privileges of rank without the obligations. Her folly lay in her unwillingness to acknowledge the possible outcome of her actions, and in her failure to act in the interests of the kingdom, rather than in her personal interests. The Queen grieved over the loss of her sister, but that very death removed a divisive factor from Tongan life.

Sālote was consistent in her ideal of devotion to duty. When Edward VIII, King of England and head of the British Empire, abdicated in 1936 in order to marry Mrs Simpson, she wholly disapproved of his actions, for his duty lay in marrying appropriately to his station in life and carrying out the rôle for which he had been trained. Nor did Sālote ask others to do what she was not prepared to do herself. Indeed one of her outstanding qualities was her ability to put aside personal considerations and to act, as she put it, "in the interests of unity and peace".

On several occasions in the 1930s, she would be called upon to put aside her own feelings in order to work for the greater good of the kingdom. She would act loyally towards those who served her loyally. The outstanding example was the mutuality of her relationship with her consort, Tungī Mailefihi.

CHAPTER ELEVEN

The Queen's Consort: Tungī Mailefihi

"They are like the posts of a house, one on this side and one on the other, holding the house secure and fastened." (Sione Havea, *Koe Havea*, 1941)

AGENT & CONSUL NEILL RECORDED that Tungī Mailefihi was always in attendance when he waited upon the Queen at the Palace.[1] The relationship of Sālote and Tungī was defined by Tongan custom: as her political "brother", Tungī was her main support, one who respected and deferred to his "sister". But his position also resembled that of the *hau*, whose duty it was to protect the sacred ruler.

No two events indicate the differences between the status of Sālote and Tungī more than the circumstances of their separate investitures. As already described in chapter 9, the High Commissioner himself came in 1932 to invest Sālote with the DBE, and 2000 guests attended the feast and entertainments that followed. In 1937, five years after Sālote's investiture, Tungī was invested with the order of a Commander of the Order of the British Empire (CBE). Appropriately, in British and Tongan terms, it was not as distinguished an honour as Sālote's, nor did the High Commissioner come to bestow it in person, it being Neill's last official duty before the end of his term in Tonga. The nobles, the ministers, and the Queen's Guards attended at the Palace on 28 July 1937, photographs were taken, but the dinner party the Queen gave the following evening was as much a farewell to Neill as a compliment to Tungī. On 6 August, after Neill's departure, representatives of the Free Wesleyan Church and of Tupou College made a magnificent feast for Tungī, with presentations. It was significant that these festivities were organized by a section of the community only.

To make their partnership effective, Sālote acquired the *mana* of the sacred ruler who could do no wrong, while Tungī was the *hau* or secular ruler, who fought the battles on behalf of the sacred ruler, and carried the criticism for unpopular policies. In the eyes of some, such as Sione Havea, Tungī could do no wrong, but other Tongans hated him, seeing him as a factional leader while the Queen succeeded in becoming the national leader. In effect, Tungī paid the price for her success. To the chiefs and people, Sālote seemed to be the one who mitigated the harshness of life, while Tungī (despite his legendary generosity) appeared to be insisting on the letter of the law, both traditional and modern. By the 1930s the criticism of Tungī had become very personal, and (to *papālangi* eyes at least) there appeared to be a rift in the royal marriage, for Tungī spent many of his lunchtimes and evenings drinking at the bar of the Nuku'alofa Club. On Friday afternoons he left for his estates, often taking the princes with him, and returned on Sunday evening. Sālote could not disapprove of these weekend visits, as her ideal chief spent time getting to know his people and working with them, as Tungī did.

When Sālote visited his chiefly village of Tatakamotonga, Tungī made presentations appropriate to her rank, but some said this was to discourage her visits, for she knew that presentations were a burden to his people. It was said that Tungī discouraged Sālote's visits because he had weekend affairs with women on his estates. The Queen was hurt by the stories of Tungī's sexual infidelity. (A story is told that when the Crown Prince referred to a resemblance of Tungī's illegitimate daughter to their father, the Queen threw down the tray on which her tea was being served.[2]) However, sexual infidelity was almost expected of a great chief and it was not only beneath the Queen's dignity to reproach her consort, but important to her not to allow her enemies to see that she was hurt.

As Premier from 1923, Tungī was invaluable to the Queen. He would invite members of Parliament to a *faikava* (social *kava* drinking) at night to discuss contentious matters out of the public eye. The protocol of the *faikava* relaxed the rule that required a lesser-ranking person merely to agree with a person of higher rank. Nobles and chiefs who knew their opinions would not prevail in Parliament had the opportunity to be heard at length in the *faikava*, and this opportunity was greatly valued. And Tungī could be very persuasive in the informality of the *faikava* circle.

To the foreign mind, the *faikava* meant long delays in decision-making; but for the Tongan members it had the satisfaction of Tongans working out matters themselves. Another advantage was that no *papālangi* attended. The *papālangi* ministers may well have been discussing the same issues at the Nuku'alofa Club (from which all Tongans except the ministers were excluded), but the *papālangi* cared for victory, not consensus, which was foremost in Tungī's mind.

The success of Tungī's *faikava* did not necessarily mean an end to discussions in Parliament. But it was discouraged by the fact that Privy Council initiated legislation but did not supply background information to Parliament unless the Law and Constitution required it. Nor was Cabinet more helpful, and no parliamentary committees were formed. Lack of information did not prevent discussion, but when, at the end of the session, "representatives of the people" brought before the House petitions from their constituents, they must have known that little notice would be taken of these motions. The ensuing discussion gave opportunities for grandstanding, but the motions were usually defeated, and neither Cabinet nor the Privy Council was obliged to give motions approved by the House serious consideration. Parliament could amend bills sent to them by the Privy Council, but if the Queen did not wish to sign amended bills, she referred them to the Agent & Consul for advice.

The Queen was an inspiring and skilful orator, who spoke to the nation on public occasions. Sālote could hold *fono* in any village or district in the kingdom. In the *fono*, unlike the *faikava*, the Queen simply expressed her wishes, and had to be obeyed. Nobles and chiefs could hold *fono* only in their own villages, and it was only on his own estates that Tungī could speak in the "uncompromising imperative"[3] to tell the people of the new laws and regulations affecting village life.

Few personal letters of Tungī's have survived; nor did he keep a diary. Indeed, in the 1930s communication by the written word was still rare in Tonga. Even conversation was often indirect and allusive, *heliaki* (metaphor) being commonly used in private as well as public discourse. The most dramatic forms of communication were the great celebrations of the Queen's reign. These were royal command performances that demonstrated the Queen's reputation and her growing authority over the nobles and chiefs. Such ceremonies were not spontaneous, but highly orchestrated events, in which chiefs were informed that presentations of food and *koloa* were expected. Each chief commanded his people to provide the food and *koloa* and to practise a dance for the occasion. When all was ready, the chief led his people to the Palace.

Tungī's heart was in the land and land reform. In 1918 he made a private agreement with his own people at Kauvai (then called Toi) regarding the distribution of land, but Premier Tu'ivakanō had intervened to prevent the scheme. A similar plan for subdivision among Tungī's people at Havelu Liku in 1931 was more successful.[4] Tungī also set an example of productive farming. At Kauvai he experimented with crops, kept a dairy herd, and fattened pigs; he planted all the known varieties of yams; he recorded the types of fish found in Tongan waters; he supported the government's experimental farm at Vaikeli; he inaugurated the annual agricultural shows, at which he won many prizes; he set up a market for sale of produce in Nuku'alofa; and he looked for alternative exports for Tonga when the price of copra plummeted in the 1930s. Tungī's own, high-quality copra fetched the top price when the inferior copra sold through government auspices fetched low prices.[5] Tungī's commercial policies were no more popular than his land reforms, and the carts bringing food crops to the market he had established in the capital were attacked by irate villagers who depended on exchanges of food within the village and had no money to buy it in Nuku'alofa.[6]

Tungī, like most politicians, was blamed for situations created by forces beyond his control. In years when there was no hurricane or drought, and the price for copra was steady, a Tongan male had no difficulty in cutting sufficient copra for his annual 36 shillings tax. If there were three bad years in succession, as in 1931–33, he might beg enough for his taxes from a better-off member of his *kāinga*. But as the prices continued to drop during the Depression (in 1926 the price of copra had been £18 3s a ton, and by 1937 it was £8 15s a ton), many Tongans fell into arrears with their taxes. Tungī attempted to get a banana industry going as an alternative to copra, but Tonga was in competition with island groups that had a much better shipping service.

To the Tongan way of thinking it was totally unreasonable for the government to demand more money in a time of hardship when it already had a surplus of £140,495 (in 1931) invested abroad. When hundreds of distress warrants continued to be issued every year, the blame fell on Tungī. Feeling ran especially high in Ha'apai and Vava'u, where less of the tax revenue was spent on public works than in Tongatapu. In October 1933 Vava'u people refused to pay their taxes, blaming Tungī for their distress. In 1937 there were 7721 summonses and commitment warrants in Tongatapu alone, of which 6000 were for non-payment of taxes. For the whole group 15,000 warrants were on issue, but not executed, of which 12,000 were for non-payment of tax. Since only 6000 Tongans were liable for payment of tax, and not all of them were in jail, some taxpayers had clearly not paid for several years. Prison labour was paid at threepence (one quarter of one shilling) a day, so those in jail had little hope of paying either their arrears or tax due in the current year.

More and more people came to Tungī, asking for money for their taxes. Always generous, Tungī paid the taxes of many, whether they were people from his estates or not, himself running into debt to do so.[7] Tungī employed others at Kauvai so they would earn money to pay their taxes. Realizing the importance of education to that generation of young people, both the Queen and Tungī paid school fees for many students, girls as well as boys, whose families were distressed. Left to his own devices, Tungī would have expended the government surplus rather than demand taxes of people who could not pay them. But Neill was adamant.

Some *papālangi* traders blamed Tungī for declining prices for copra, saying that he was ineffectual, particularly as his heavy consumption of alcohol became more and more obvious.[8] Then the number of *papālangi* in government was reduced in an effort to compensate for decreasing government revenues. A number of *papālangi* traders left Tonga because they could no longer make a living. Wesleyan missionaries, paid by their home church in Australia, agreed to cuts in their already small salaries.

After Tungī became Premier in 1923, he met with the Agent & Consul every Tuesday morning to discuss government business. Although the Treaty of Friendship and the Supplementary Agreement obliged Tungī to act on the Agent & Consul's advice on matters relating to finance, law, and senior appointments, it was clear that he also sought Neill's advice on economic and political policy and the day-to-day running of the administration. Tungī's "dependence" upon Neill was seen as Tungī's weakness. In the *Fiji Times* of 15 June 1937, "Anon." put into words what many *papālangi* were thinking: that the government of Tonga would collapse without the guiding hand of Neill. "Where the Tonga Government ends and the British Agent & Consul begins or vice versa, nobody is given the slightest inkling, an insidious secrecy prevails. The voice may be the voice of Jacob but the hands are the hands of Esau [a biblical reference]."

Ironically, while he was ruling the government with a rod of iron, Neill deplored the dependence of the government of Tonga upon the advice of the Agent & Consul, and suggested in his report for 1935 that

> . . . in the development of modern Tongan Administration the position of the Agent [& Consul] has become more clearly defined. He is consulted in the every day affairs of the Government . . .
>
> Reference has been made in previous reports to the repugnance of the Tongan ministers to accept responsibility. Decisions are taken in Executive which it is known will not prove acceptable to the Agent and disapproval of the latter is frequently welcomed. It is a strange attribute of Tongan polity; its recognition is essential to proper understanding.
>
> Experience of the Tongan forces the conclusion that, although many of the attributes of Western civilisation appear on the surface, the foundation is not deeply laid. It would be unreasonable to expect that it would be otherwise and it would be a misinterpretation of Tongan polity to read the Constitution too literally. Western ideas and its phraseology have been freely used without a true understanding of their import.[9]

Twenty years later, in his reminiscences on his life in Tonga, Neill gave a more detailed and kinder view of Tungī.

> During my term of office I saw much of Tugi [*sic*] . . . and we became close friends. He was a leading figure in the Western Pacific, a statesman wise in counsel, generous and charitable in his views. The people loved him as much as they respected him . . . He used to call at the Consulate in the Residency grounds every Tuesday morning and there, over an informal bowl of kava, we discussed affairs of state and matters of general interest. They were delightful mornings and I am sure my late friend enjoyed them as much as I did. All my official correspondence with the Government of Tonga was conducted through his office, though we did much preliminary work in our weekly conversations.
>
> Tugi was a short, powerfully built man. He was always calm and unperturbed and his sense of humour was infectious. Our conversations had their lighter sides too. . . .
>
> At week-ends he went off to his private estate. There he would discard the European clothes which he wore in Nukualofa and stroll round his coconut plantation in Tongan dress, inspecting the work done and talking to his own people. He was a good agriculturist, loved the land and was happiest when close to it.[10]

Neill did not note that it was an unusual and welcome experience for Tungī to be able to discuss matters freely, for the Queen was probably the only other person with whom he could discuss policy. An incident in 1933 demonstrated how determined the opposition to the government could be. At the instigation of the Agent & Consul, the Privy Council sent down a bill designed to secure a preferential tariff for the British Empire (12.5 per cent, compared with 25 per cent for non-British imports).[11] The members of Parliament refused to pass it. It was widely believed that Japanese shopkeepers had bribed the members, and even long nights of *faikava* with Tungī could not persuade them to change their votes.[12] Neill's solution (that the Queen appoint seven more ministers to outnumber the elected members) was rejected by the Queen both because of the expense of more ministerial salaries and because Privy Council would thereby be doubled in size. Since neither Tungī nor Neill could resolve the difficulty, Sālote summoned the members to the Palace, explained the situation, and requested them to change their vote. This forceful form of persuasion resulted in the passing of an amended Bill, reducing the discrepancy between the two tariffs.

Addressing the members at the Closing of the parliamentary session, Sālote castigated them, contrasting her own role as a national leader, always considering the wider and long-term interests of the people as a whole, with their narrow and short-term objectives: "The Government aimed at securing the advantages for Tonga which not only had present values, but which would continue to increase as time went on. Your objective was to make things easier for the people just for this present difficult period. The one had a national outlook, the other was for individual advantage."[13]

Tungī shared in the traditional duties that occupied the Queen. She gave the births, marriages, and deaths of the high chiefs a great deal of her time and attention, sending the appropriate gifts of mats and bark cloth and, if the deceased person was of high rank and closely related to the royal house, attending the funeral. Attendance provided opportunities for affirming the interconnectedness and hierarchy of the chiefs, matters of importance in the search for unity and stability.

Tungī was in the north when his cousin Mā'atu (Ma'afu-'o-tu'itonga), son of Tae Manusā, died on 12 October 1934 (see Figure 3.3). This Mā'atu and his brother, who had held the title before him, were brothers of 'Ofa-ki-Vava'u and half-brothers of Queen Takipō (Figure 1.6). Both brothers had lived a self-indulgent life, and had oppressed the people who were in their care; but they were of very high rank and *fahu* to Tungī and the princes. Mā'atu's body was brought to lie in state in Pālesi (Paris), the round building in the Palace grounds. Then the Queen accompanied the body to Uoleva, Tungī's house in his village of Tatakamotonga on the Tungī estates. The Queen, Prince Tuku'aho, and Prince Sione Ngū, the Agent & Consul, ministers of the crown, and chiefly women and men accompanied the body to the burial alongside Tae Manusā at Lo'amanu, the burial site of Mulikiha'amea, Tungī's ancestor who had been killed in 1799, during the civil wars. Upon his return to Tongatapu on the 18th, Tungī joined the Queen and princes at Tatakamotonga, where the funeral ceremonies continued. The Queen and Tungī returned to Nuku'alofa briefly on the 19th to attend a Privy Council meeting, then returned to the funeral until the 23rd.

The Queen was *fahu* to Sioeli Pangia (Figure 7.1). When Sioeli died on 29 May 1935, the Queen left for Sioeli's place at Lapaha in the middle of the night, with Tungī and the two princes following the next morning. Sioeli was buried in Paepae-'o-Tele'a, one of the *langi* of the Tu'i Tonga, where Old Lavinia had been buried in 1907. Tungī and the two princes came and went, but the Queen remained at Lapaha until 4 June, when she returned to Nuku'alofa to prepare for the Opening of Parliament on 6 June, and to attend another chiefly funeral at the Mala'e 'Aloa.

At funerals of the great chiefs the Queen was able not only to restate her own place in the genealogies of the high chiefs, but also to instruct the mourners on their duties, and to ensure that the person was buried in the right place and that the proper ceremonies were carried out. If she was in the correct relationship she would order the division of the food and *koloa* so that everyone received their appropriate share.

In 1935 the Queen went to Australia to attend the celebration of the centenary of Methodism in the state of Victoria (whose capital is Melbourne). A second reason for the journey was to spend time with the Crown Prince, who had been a student at Newington College, Sydney, since the beginning of 1933.

As the time for the journey approached, the Queen's health caused some anxiety. The Queen believed her health problems had caused three miscarriages in the 1920s, but she now felt generally unwell.[14] Dr Olive Wood examined the Queen at the Palace, told her that there was a possibility of cancer, and advised her to seek medical advice while in Australia.

Tungī was obliged to observe regulations, and as he had already used his triennial overseas leave to go to Sydney with Prince Tāufa'āhau in 1933, he did not accompany the Queen. Rodger Page escorted her and acted as her adviser, and two young Tongan women went to attend upon the Queen.[15] Although the visit was a private one, Page found it difficult to protect the Queen from journalists and photographers, who responded very positively to Sālote. They reported that she was a shy and reserved person who "shunned all display of ostentation", who "bore the ordeal [of being stared at] with quiet dignity". Her "charm and poise made a good impression upon the fickle Sydney crowds".[16]

In the first three weeks of her stay in Sydney the Queen consented to a few official receptions as well as attending Methodist Church functions. Otherwise she stayed quietly with Rev. John and Mrs Burton at the George Brown College in Haberfield.[17] The Queen was glad of the opportunity to talk with Prince Tāufa'āhau and Lupeti Fīnau, at Newington College, and she encouraged them not only to pursue their studies diligently but also to live temperate lives.[18] Her son had already reassured her in a letter written during his first year in Sydney:

> It is all true what you said in your letter concerning conduct, but since I arrived in this country I have been cautious and realize that I must be careful in all the things I do, which helps me a lot.
>
> The age-group to which I belong is known as the years of foolishness and interference, but I am still sticking to my own way and the ways of my country. I am not attracted by the doings of the boys here. Queen, don't doubt my conduct. I am alert all the time, and if I make a mistake I will try my best to correct it immediately. I have pledged to myself that one of my mottos will be to retain a clear conscience and be perfect before the heavenly Father.[19]

Sydney specialists concurred with Dr Olive Wood's diagnosis of cancer, and Dr Wood's sister, Dr Susie O'Reilly, performed a hysterectomy in the War Memorial Hospital on 22 August 1935. The Queen was grateful for the care she received, and declared that "my empty cup is full to overflowing".[20] Because of a prolonged stay in hospital, the visit to the centenary celebrations in Victoria had to be cancelled, the Crown Prince attending in her place.

Prior to leaving Tonga the Queen had arranged for many mats, bales of bark cloth, and 1000 bottles of perfumed oil to be sent to Fiji, for she would attend the celebrations of the centenary of the coming of Christianity to Fiji on her way home. When she arrived at the Lakeba in the Lau group (where Tongans had brought the Gospel in 1835), she was given a welcome appropriate for the greatest of chiefs: she was the last to leave the *Katoomba*, being carried ashore in a decorated canoe; she was received by the high chief Ratu Lala Sukuna; she walked along a mat that no one else's feet had touched; she was given a chiefly welcome in the council house; and suitable presentations (including 10 *tabua* – whale's teeth) were made to her.[21] Recognition by Fijian chiefs was her due, but it must have been gratifying nevertheless. Upon her return to Tonga from Fiji there was a celebration lasting for two weeks, for it commemorated this memorable visit as well as being a thanksgiving for her return in good health.[22]

The Crown Prince was happy and industrious at Newington College, but soon after her return to Tonga the Queen and Tungī had cause to be concerned about the health of the second prince, Tuku'aho. In traditional society, brothers with the same father but different mothers were expected to be rivals (*uho tau*), while brothers with the same mother but different fathers were expected to support each other (*uho taha*), especially the "eldest", the one chosen to be the champion of his generation. Since the royal princes had the same mother and father, there were forces pushing them together and forces pushing them apart. Tonga had had enough of factionalism and civil wars, and the Queen and Tungī were earnest in their endeavours to promote affection rather than rivalry between the princes.

The model for the princes was the Ha'a Ngata, made up of the descendants of Ngata, the first Tu'i Kanokupolu. Ngata had arrived in his future domains in the Western District of Tongatapu wrapped in a mat with his two brothers so that the three appeared to be one person with three heads ('Ulutolu). Just so must the two younger princes support the eldest son of the royal house: Crown Prince Tāufa'āhau, who was heir to his mother's title of Tu'i Kanokupolu.

Although Tungī played his part in disciplining his sons, it was left to the Queen to "drill" (her expression) the imperative for loyalty into her younger sons. Prince Sione Ngū, not a deep thinker but with an amiable temperament, wanted only to enjoy himself, and would be influenced by the wishes of his parents. Prince Tuku'aho was neither as easygoing as his younger brother nor as studious as his elder brother. He had rheumatic fever as a child, and had always been sickly, which drew his mother close to him. Thus Tuku'aho acquired the traditional knowledge that Sālote would have passed on to a daughter if there had been one. He learned the genealogies of the chiefly families, the ordering of ceremonies, the principles guiding the division of food and the distribution of *koloa*, the order of precedence in the three ranking systems, the languages that indicated differences in rank, and the respects (*fakatapu*) that had to be made in the preliminaries to formal speeches.

When Fusipala died in 1933, Tungī and Tāufa'āhau were in Sydney, so it fell to Tuku'aho to order the ceremonies appropriate for the Queen's half-sister and their *fahu* until Tungī returned with the body. During the Queen's absence in

1935, Tuku'aho frequently represented her in receiving Tongan people at the Palace. Although it was not explicitly stated in the Royal Estates Act 1927, it was clear that the Tungī title would be his if he outlived Tungī, and his brothers would thus pay him the respect due to a father. And Tuku'aho's influence throughout Tonga would be great, for he was better known by the people than his brothers.[23]

But this was not to be. The Queen returned to Tonga on 16 October 1935, and by November Tongilava reported that Tuku'aho was seriously ill. Sālote cared for Tuku'aho in his last illness, in constant attendance at his bedside, delegating most of her public duties to Tungī and her ministers. During the hot summer, Sālote took Tuku'aho to the house at Lotoleveleva and also to Tungī's house on the lagoon at Kauvai. All her efforts were fruitless. Harold Wood recorded in his diary on 12 April that Tuku'aho was dying, a fact known to everyone, but which could not be openly stated.[24] Although the Chief Medical Officer, Dr Bull, was in charge of the case, the Queen asked Dr Olive Wood to see Tuku'aho. Dr Wood diagnosed dropsy, and 30 pints of fluid were drained from him on 23 April. All of Nuku'alofa was quiet: no music or other noise was permitted, and the annual Anzac Day service by the government flagpole on 25 April was limited to a brief prayer by Page.

While the whole kingdom was praying for him at the Queen's request, Tuku'aho died at the Palace at 11.30 p.m. on Tuesday 28 April 1936. After a lying-in-state in the throne room on 29 and 30 April, he was buried on Friday 1 May at Mala'e Kula in the vault of Queen Lavinia.[25] Sālote and Tungī personally supervised the ceremonies during the first period of mourning,[26] and the Queen wrote a lament, full of her personal grief and referring to the disappointed hopes of Tungī:

1. 'E Tungī, ke fakamolemole
'I he fakatu'a e fa'ele
Kuo 'ikai nofo 'a Taufale
Ke talifekau kiate koe.

2. Tuku'aho e tau 'i Folaha
Neu nongo pe 'o fiefia
'O lau 'eau te ke 'aonga
Kia Tungī mo hono kāinga.

3. Hoku 'ofa 'oku, hoku 'ofa fau
He tehina 'o Tāufa'āhau
Na'e lau pe tokua 'eau
'E mo'ui ko hono to'omata'u . . . [27]

* * *

1. Forgive me, Tungī,
for this uncivil birth,
Taufale has not stayed
to carry out your commands.

2. Tuku'aho-e-tau-'i-Folaha,
I lived in glad anticipation
of the day you would be of service
to Tungī and his people.

3. Oh, how great is my love
for the younger brother of Tāufa'āhau.
I always thought he would one day be
his main support . . . [MT]

After the months of caring for Tuku'aho and the trauma of his death, the Queen suffered a complete breakdown.[28] It was decided that she should again visit Sydney for a rest and medical checkup, and that Tungī (now due for leave) would accompany her.[29] They sailed on the *Fetu'u'aho* on 30 May, only a month after Tuku'aho's death, and were met in Suva by the Acting High Commissioner (C.J.J.T. Barton) in full uniform, although it was recognized that both the Queen's health and her mourning precluded an official reception.[30] Barton reported that the Queen "was nervous, but this wore off", and she went immediately to Adi Cakobau's house at Draiba in the car provided for her. Tungī talked with Barton and High Commission officials, one subject for conversation being Tungī's concern about the Tongan students at the Central Medical School who acquired bad habits, such as a taste for alcohol. Barton commented that Tungī himself had appeared to have "lunched too well".

The medical report on the Queen was reassuring, and the holiday in Sydney helped to restore her health. She and Tungī stayed at Hampton Court, King's Cross, and she was soon reporting on the academic progress of Prince Tāufa'āhau and Lupeti, her meetings with people, her visits to churches throughout the Sydney area, and her plans for the future, especially for the Christian Endeavour, which she had founded the previous year. The following letter was written to Sau Faupula, a minister of the Free Wesleyan Church, whose character and intelligence was recognized by the Queen in spite of his commoner birth.

Our stay here is all right; the cold days have gone and the warm weather has come and this year has not been as cold as last year. On the contrary, Sydney has come to the beauty of spring. Lupeti and Taufa are staying here with us in their holidays. They have finished their tests and seem to have got on all right, but they are working hard for their big exam, and we all wish them luck.

I still go about on Sundays. In the week Tungi was ill with flu, I didn't go to church, but stayed here and listened to the service on the wireless. Otherwise, I have been to church at Gordon, Ashfield, Mosman, Linfield, Parramatta, Bondi, Botany . . . and there remains Manly next Sunday and Hartville on my last Sunday. I always attend the [evening?] service in Wesley Chapel in the city on the Sundays that I am here.

I went to La Perouse and met the Aborigines. They were happy when we talked together and let the children and women come and shake hands, and they smoked leaves and threw boomerangs. Then we went to Canberra where the Government took us about. Next week I shall go with Tungi to Newcastle to open their bazaar on 14 September. We shall sail from Sydney on 25 September 1936 in the biggest vessel of the company, the *Awatea*. We shall probably spend about two and a half weeks in New Zealand and then sail in the *Matua* in October.

Thank you for the work you are doing with our Christian Endeavour Society. I have hopes for our Society in Nuku'alofa, for Mataele, who will pay great attention to it, is there; and it will be easy to discuss ways in which it can be improved. It has been in the church since my return last year, and there has also been that huge committee which was set up. As my health was going back I have watched from outside. I still feel weaker than ever, but I hope to go into the Christian Endeavour again when I go home. I don't know whether it will be of any use or not – if not, there could easily be a little slipping back; but the main thing is for the Society to be useful to the young men and women we are trying to help.[31] [DR]

The Queen was fond of reading, and while recuperating in Sydney read books about the Aborigines of Australia (whom she found "mysterious") and another about Japan, promising to bring these books back to Tonga for others to read. She referred to an invitation to be patron of the Polynesian Club in Sydney, a responsibility she passed on to the Crown Prince.

In New Zealand in October the Queen and Tungī visited Te Puea Hērangi and her cousin, King Korokī, at Tūrangawaewae.[32] The *New Zealand Herald* reported: "The [Tongan royal] party was received with the ceremonious Maori welcome, and many traditional *poi* dances, songs and *haka*s were performed for their benefit. The Queen's ladies-in-waiting sang Tongan songs to guitar accompaniments, these greatly interesting the Maori performers."[33] In Auckland the Queen met again with Te Puea, and with members of the small Tongan community, the Kronfeld family, and *papālangi* who had once resided in Tonga. Members of the Methodist Church in Auckland were proud of the only Methodist monarch and were delighted to welcome and assist Sālote and Tungī.

When the Crown Prince returned to Tonga for the Christmas holidays in December 1936 he was able to take his part in the final ceremonies of Tuku'aho's funeral. During that visit the Queen wrote a letter appointing Tāufa'āhau as the noble Tupouto'a (retrospectively from his eighteenth birthday the previous July), but his brother's recent death delayed the *pongipongi* (presentations made to the Queen by his people on behalf of their new chief) until 21 January 1938 when he was again holidaying in Tonga.[34]

The Crown Prince (now known as Tupouto'a), Prince Sione Ngū, and 'Alipate Tupou (son of Vīlai and the Queen's nephew) left Tonga together on the *Matua* on 9 February 1938. Distinctions of rank were still observed, for although 'Alipate was first cousin to the princes, he travelled as a deck passenger, while the princes had cabin accommodation.[35] Tupouto'a had enrolled to commence an Arts–Law degree at the University of Sydney that year. Sione Ngū would spend three years in Auckland with a private tutor (Rev. H. A. Sharp) preparatory to attending Newington (1941–42); and 'Alipate would be the first of the nobles' heirs to attend Wesley College near Auckland (1938–41).

With Tuku'aho dead and the other two princes overseas, Sālote found herself in 1938 more on her own than previously, if anyone could be said to be alone when there were so many people living at and coming in and out of the Palace and its grounds. Tongilava's diary shows that from this time Sālote attended more church meetings in Nuku'alofa and the villages of Tongatapu than previously, and her letters show an increasing interest in evangelical church organizations and more time spent on the preparation for Bible classes. She also put on weight about this time, and did not lose the extra pounds until the middle 1940s.

Sālote's Christian belief was not seen to be incompatible with her position as the sacred ruler of Tonga. In August–September 1937 Kalanivalu (Sēmisi) claimed land that had formerly belonged to the Tu'i Tonga, on the grounds that he was the Tu'i Tonga's heir. An aristocratic witness gave evidence that Kalanivalu had no claim, for the Tu'i Kanokupolu had "succeeded to all the powers of the Tu'i Tonga and dispossessed him". Ragnar Hyne, now Chief Justice and Judge of the Land Court, gave his judgment against Kalanivalu, stating what was universally recognized: "the descendant of the Tu'i Tonga had, at the time of the granting of the Constitution lost all claim to the title of Tu'i Tonga. This latter [title] had been granted to King George Tupou I, while as to the land, the Tu'i Tonga had . . . been dispossessed by the Tu'i Kanokupolu, i.e. King George Tupou I."[36]

This recognition that Sālote, Tupou I's heir as Tu'i Kanokupolu, was the inheritor of the rights and privileges of the Tu'i Tonga was timely, for it preceded the celebrations in October 1938 of the twentieth anniversary of her coronation. The activities resembled the silver jubilee celebrations of George V in 1935, except that Sālote's festivities exceeded the King-Emperor's by two days, lasting six days (11–16 October) instead of his four. There were ceremonies of every kind: flag-raising and gun salutes, formal addresses from all sections of the community made to Sālote on the Mala'e Pangai; a small service in the Royal Chapel and a large thanksgiving service in the Free Wesleyan Church in Nuku'alofa as well as in every village. There was a reception at the Palace, dancing, feasting, games, a regatta, and an agricultural show. There was a special issue of stamps, and a *taumafa kava* over which Sālote presided, and at which every titled chief was expected to take his place. There had possibly been no such celebration since the presentation of the first-fruits (*'inasi*) to the Tu'i Tonga in the eighteenth century.

There could be no more suitable occasion for making explicit what was already implicit in the nature and scale of the celebrations. Sālote was more than a political leader, more than a great chief, more than a constitutional monarch. These celebrations were for the ruler who had inherited the mantle and *mana* of the legendary sacred ruler of Tonga, the Tu'i Tonga. Appropriately it was Tungī who, in the presence of the chiefs and people, made the speech that proclaimed not only Sālote's personal achievements and the achievements of her dynasty, but her legitimate claim by descent (the chiefly blood) to be heir of this ancient line of sacred rulers of Tonga.

> From the history of our land we learn that the kingship did not come to us by craft, nor was it set up by the will of the people, nor was it acquired by force, but from time immemorial there has always been a sovereign ruler. Though at times the office has passed from one branch of the royal family to another, nevertheless there has been *an unbroken succession of that one royal line from the first ruler even to Your Majesty*. We greatly rejoice in the knowledge that such is the case. There is no likelihood of our forgetting the illustrious family of which Your Majesty is the third in succession.
>
> A review of the past strengthens our determination to follow your leadership, for we feel that by so doing, Tonga will continue to retain its position as a kingdom among the kingdoms of the world.[37] [my italics]

The Queen responded more modestly, but equally powerfully:

> I desire to express my love to the Nobles, the Ministers of State, His Britannic Majesty's Agent and Consul, and to all, especially the children. I glorify God for His unspeakable love which is manifested towards us to-day. I deeply appreciate the good wishes which have been uttered, the affection which has been shown to me and the joyfulness which is everywhere apparent. For the twenty years during which I have had the charge of ruling this land, I have been ever conscious of my high privilege in being called of God to rule over a people like you, a people peace-loving, a people affectionate and of ready response.

> Although I feel that I had no special gift to bring to this charge and that I have not been able to accomplish very much, nevertheless I have always endeavoured to make my service to my people my first duty. May the blessing of God ever rest upon this little land of ours so that, whatever changes the future may bring, Tonga may ever be a land of which we can be proud.[38]

To mark the Queen's twentieth anniversary, Neill's successor as Agent & Consul, A. L. Armstrong, recommended to Tungī that there should (at last) be a tax amnesty, so that many prisoners jailed for non-payment of the poll tax were released. A tenfold increase in the rate of pay for a day's labour in jail was introduced (from threepence to 30 pence), giving prisoners some chance of clearing outstanding debts.[39]

An incident at the Government College in 1938 indicated that there were some who continued to dissent from the Tupou dynasty. Since its foundation by Tupou I in 1882, Government College (to all intents and purposes a Free Church secondary school subsidized by the government) had special privileges, some of which had eventually been extended to Tupou College (the Free Wesleyan Church secondary school) and later to 'Api Fo'ou (the Catholic school at Ma'ufanga). Government College was also well known to be the bastion of the "Reactionary Party".

It was proposed that Government College be moved out of Nuku'alofa and become an agricultural college. The suggestion appeared more than sensible, for most Tongan males became farmers; but Government College students and "Old Boys" believed the intention was to exclude them from academic study and thus from salaried employment. As a graduate of the rival Tupou College, Tungī was blamed. In 1938, when the removal was finally determined upon, feeling ran so high that 48 students of Government College renounced their allegiance to Queen Sālote and pledged loyal service to King George VI of Great Britain.[40] This "rebellion" was shortlived, and was more a protest against what were perceived to be Tungī's machinations than against the Queen herself.

A "brother" supports and is always loyal to his "sister", but the relationship truly is one of mutual support in the interests of the *kāinga*. When a severe crisis occurred in the government in 1938–40, the Queen showed that she was as loyal to Tungī as he had always been to her. The loyalty arose from deep personal love for him as well as an awareness of the national interest.

CHAPTER TWELVE

The Chief Justice Plays the Champion

" . . . every Tongan Minister . . . was impeached for maladministration"
(Armstrong to Sir Harry Luke, 1940)[1]

THE YEARS 1938–40 in Tonga are unusually well documented, with a large body of correspondence and a Report written by Ronald Garvey for the Western Pacific High Commission.[2] The Report not only shows that the Queen was in control of her kingdom but also gives a portrait of a small but complex society in which one dissident person could spark a major crisis. The continuing dissatisfactions of some Tongan chiefs would be the tinder for the events of these years while the coming of three new *papālangi* to Tonga would be the fuel.

The deaths of former leaders of the "Reactionary Party" – Mā'atu, 'Ulukālala, and George Scott – had left Sioape Kaho, Minister for Police, as the undisputed leader of the "Reactionary Party". Sioape was popular because he refused to execute thousands of distress warrants issued for non-payment of the poll tax and did not implement prison reforms agreed to by a government committee.[3] Further, although Sioape had no title, his lifestyle was that of a great chief: he gave lavish feasts and ran up debts with the storekeepers; he had a substantial piece of land on the estates of his brother Tu'ivakanō in the Western District of Tongatapu; and the people living on this land supplied unpaid labour, food, *koloa*, and cash whenever Sioape and his wife, Muimui, wanted them.[4]

However, Sioape was an unsatisfactory minister, as far as carrying out his duties was concerned, and an investigation into the Police and Prisons departments in 1937 revealed that Sioape had used the police force and prisoners as free labour on his land.[5] The death of Sioape's protector, 'Ulukālala, on 10 November 1938 made it easier for Sālote to invite Sioape to retire on the grounds of age.[6] Sioape realized that he would have to do something dramatic to prevent the invitation becoming a command.

The reduction in the number of government employees during the Depression had put the government in a vulnerable situation, especially as far as legal work was concerned. In the early 1930s, as an economy measure, three legal positions (Chief Justice, Judge of the Land Court, and Chief Magistrate) had been combined with that of Secretary to the Premier, in the person of Ragnar Hyne, who was also Director of Education. While Neill was Agent & Consul, the concentration of legal appointments caused no problems, but his successor, Arthur L. Armstrong, had no legal qualifications, nor did he have the administrative experience or strength of character of McOwan and Neill.

Ragnar Hyne, Director of Education 1920–38, Secretary to the Premier 1932–38, Chief Magistrate 1933–38, Chief Justice and Judge of the Land Court 1936–38, left Tonga in March 1938 to take up an appointment in the British Solomon Islands Protectorate. Albert George Lowe replaced Hyne as Secretary to the Premier and Legal Adviser to the government from March 1938, and as Acting Chief Justice from March until the arrival of the new Chief Justice, William Hemming Stuart, on 8 June 1938. Stuart would also be Judge of the Land Court, Chief Magistrate, Privy Councillor, and a member of the government in Parliament. By June 1938 the government's three main *papālangi* advisers – Armstrong, Stuart, and Lowe – were newcomers unfamiliar with the nature of Tongan leadership, the structure of Tongan society, and Tongan custom. All three had fatal flaws in their characters.

Stuart, 54 years of age when he came to Tonga, was a South African who had been admitted to the bar at the Middle Temple, London, in 1909. He had been adviser to the native rulers of Basutoland (1917–20) and Pondoland (1925–26) and a member of the Legislative Assembly of South Africa (1915–24).[7] He persisted in claiming that he was a British Imperial Government Officer, "one of the loneliest sentries of the Empire", in spite of swearing an oath of loyalty to Queen Sālote and being paid by the government of Tonga.[8] Stuart was new and he was garrulous. He failed to uphold the dignity of his own office, horrifying Tongans and *papālangi* alike by attending the Supreme Court in dirty shorts and even dirtier tennis shoes.[9]

Stuart made no secret of the fact that he despised the colonials who were well represented in the *papālangi* community. One colonial who irritated Stuart was Lowe, a New Zealander, about 40 years of age when he came to Tonga. Lowe had qualified as a solicitor in 1924 and was admitted to the bar in 1933. In Tonga he was granted limited right of private practice to supplement his small salary as Secretary to the Premier. This, and his appointment as Legal Adviser to the government, brought Stuart and Lowe into frequent contact. Further, the house assigned to Lowe by the government was Pikula, where Sālote's grandfather Tuʻipelehake had once lived, and this immediately gave him prestige in the community, a factor that would soon become very clear to Stuart.

Mrs Starr Stuart was related to (possibly a daughter of) Dr Jim Jameson, supporter of Cecil Rhodes, notorious for the Jameson Raid in South Africa. Mr and Mrs Stuart thought of themselves as "English" and therefore superior to both the Tongan and *papālangi* communities, and expected that their social status would be on a par with that of the Agent & Consul and that they would have easy access to the Palace. Although the Queen was constantly visited by her Tongan subjects, the only *papālangi* with easy access to the Palace were Rodger Page and her social secretary, Mrs Lilla Bagnall, the wife of the Minister for Finance. The Queen invited Mrs Stuart and Mrs Bagnall to afternoon tea a few weeks after the arrival of the Stuarts, and Mr and Mrs Stuart the following month.[10] The Stuarts soon realized that far from becoming Palace *habitués* and having the private ear of the Queen, Sālote expected to see Mr Stuart only at the Privy Council meetings on Thursday mornings and Mrs Stuart only at the public functions the Queen had consented to attend and to which *papālangi* of status were invited.

The Stuarts soon came to believe that the social position they thought was rightfully theirs was occupied by William Garfield Bagnall and Lilla Bagnall. Mrs Bagnall's father was a Riechelmann and her mother a Cocker, both families long resident in Tonga and well-to-do leaders of social life in the *papālangi* community.[11] Mrs Bagnall was proud of her connection with the royal family, going back to the time of Queen Takipō.[12] Mr Bagnall's position, his salary, his wife's family connections and long association with the Palace meant that the Bagnalls had considerable status. The Stuarts believed – or found it convenient to believe – that the Bagnalls deliberately conspired to diminish their status in the eyes of the *papālangi* community and the chiefs, and that Bagnall exerted a tyrannical influence over the government and the Agent & Consul.

The spark for what later became a conflagration arose from Bagnall's refusal to allow the Tongan government to pay for the Stuarts' excess baggage or for travel expenses exceeding those of a direct passage from London. The payment was determined by regulations and the conditions had been agreed with the Colonial Office, but Bagnall's refusal was interpreted by the Stuarts as motivated by determination to show them, from the outset, the Bagnalls' superiority.[13]

The next grievance related to the houses occupied by the two couples.[14] Housing was the prime status symbol in the *papālangi* community. The senior employees of the Tongan government were provided with "quarters" by the government, and these government houses were ranked, just as their occupiers were ranked. The Stuarts soon discovered that the house occupied by the

Bagnalls in the centre of town was known locally as the Chief Justice's house. The Stuarts were assigned the bungalow that the Bagnalls had vacated four years earlier. This was Fai-'a-koka, a sprawling weatherboard house very pleasantly situated facing the sea on the Beach Road in Kolomotu'a. Shirley Baker (erstwhile Premier) had built it for himself in the 1880s, and Queen Sālote had lived there as a child when it was Mateialona's house. So the house was prestigious, but the Stuarts complained that it was in a state of disrepair, that it was too small (that is, smaller than the house occupied by the Bagnalls), and that it was too far from the court-house (that is, farther than the house occupied by the Bagnalls), necessitating their buying a car, an expense that might not have been necessary if Stuart had lived closer to his office.

Armstrong would not admit that the Stuarts had a genuine grievance. Fai-'a-koka was close to the Residency, and more pleasantly situated than the other house. The Stuarts had arrived without prior notice, before repairs could be carried out, and the government had repaired and greatly improved Fai-'a-koka soon after their arrival. But the continued occupancy by the Bagnalls of "their" house symbolized for the Stuarts the usurpation of the Stuarts' rightful place in the *papālangi* community and in the eyes of the Tongan people.

Stuart claimed that Bagnall had engineered the situation where he and the Chief Justice were the only *papālangi* members of the Privy Council in order to exercise greater powers himself. Bagnall aggravated the situation by choosing to address the Privy Council in Tongan, so that Stuart heard Bagnall's opinions only through an interpreter.[15]

Stuart was further outraged when Bagnall presided over the Privy Council when it was considering an appeal against a judgment Stuart had given in the Supreme Court. A half-caste had been convicted of intoxicating and attempting to rape a woman who was the mistress of one of the traders. Tongan custom prevented the Queen from hearing evidence of a sexual nature in the presence of chiefs who were her kinsmen. 'Ulukālala, who normally presided in Sālote's absence, had died 11 days earlier. Stuart was disqualified because he had already given his judgment in the case. Sioape Kaho, as Minister for Police, was the Prosecutor, and already involved in giving evidence.[16] Tungī chose not to preside, perhaps feeling that a *papālangi* should hear the appeal of a part-European.

Stuart chose to assume that Bagnall, who had no legal qualifications, frequently presided over the Privy Council, although he could easily have discovered that this was not the case. Stuart then proposed that cl. 90 of the Constitution should be suspended so that he could sit on the Privy Council when it was hearing appeals against his own judgments, but neither Sālote nor Armstrong favoured this as a permanent solution to an out-of-the-ordinary situation. Stuart then attempted to force the Privy Council to follow his advice, rather than the established procedures or the advice of the Agent & Consul, by threatening that the British government would intervene if the Privy Council did not act as he demanded.[17]

Bagnall did not in fact have the political influence Stuart attributed to him. He was a rather ineffectual person, owing his professional and social position more to his wife's connections than to his own abilities. Although he was Minister for Finance, the Agent & Consul advised the government on financial matters such as the annual estimates of revenue and expenditure, taxation, and foreign investment of the government surplus.

Armstrong found that Stuart would not acknowledge his superior position as Agent & Consul in relation to the government of Tonga. Sālote and Tungī were disappointed that the Agent & Consul could not persuade the Chief Justice to act with propriety,[18] for, having failed to dominate the Privy Council, Stuart now held it up to ridicule, predicting its decisions and threatening to dismiss government employees, although he did not have the power to do so. Stuart also informed the Privy Council of his decisions on legal cases before he had heard the evidence.[19]

The Chief Justice was, for professional reasons, somewhat isolated from other residents of Nuku'alofa, and Tungī's preference for an inferior official, Lowe, must have humiliated a status-conscious man such as Stuart. Lowe not only saw Tungī every day in his office, but the two spent many hours drinking and discussing farming – and possibly legal matters – in full view of the other members of the Nuku'alofa Club.[20]

H. E. Maude (Acting Agent & Consul in 1941) commented harshly on the *papālangi* in government employment at this time.

> . . . few [*papālangi*] officers can speak more than a word or two of Tongan . . . The stultifying effects on Europeans of long service in a small and isolated country such as Tonga cannot be over-estimated. To persons who have not experienced such conditions I doubt if they can be really explained: the mind vegetates, the trivial everyday problems of official routine appear of almost insuperable difficulty and, as a consequence, everything is postponed until the last moment; the importance to the world of one's decisions, and local affairs in general, becomes progressively magnified as the sense of humour degenerates; while private life is made unhappy by the incessant gossip and feuds of the various social cliques caused, once again, by the too limited horizons of the country.[21]

On some matters the Beach not only agreed, but showed admirable discretion. Ronald Garvey reported that: "I formed the opinion that members of the [*papālangi*] public had for many years been dissatisfied with Mr. Bagnall's conduct of business affairs which were placed before him, as Treasurer, for decision. He was bitterly hated by certain sections of the community and certainly feared by the majority of the junior officials."[22]

In spite of their chronic dissatisfaction with and hostility to Bagnall, the *papālangi* would not take Stuart's side against Bagnall because (as they explained to Garvey), Stuart had "done the right thing in the wrong way". They were desperate not to become involved, even though (or perhaps because) they were subjected to a barrage of complaints from the Stuarts.[23] When Mrs Stuart publicly humiliated Mrs Bagnall by removing her chair at the Anzac Day service in April 1939, leaving her standing at an inappropriate moment, and when Mrs Stuart began to attend private social functions even though she was not invited, the Beach excluded the Stuarts from the social life of the community.[24] Armstrong declined to invite them to the Residency, even for official functions, on the grounds that neither of the Stuarts could be relied upon to behave themselves.[25] Even the Queen considered declining an invitation to a formal dinner for the Governor-General of New Zealand to which Armstrong had invited the Stuarts, but was persuaded that her absence would create a public scandal.[26] The Bagnalls, by contrast, were welcome at all social functions, thus aggravating the whole situation.[27]

Stuart attacked Armstrong, and Mrs Stuart attacked both the Armstrongs, intemperately and in public.[28] Armstrong suffered a great deal of misrepresentation from Stuart, who wrote letters to the High Commissioner and to the Colonial Office complaining that Armstrong was under Bagnall's influence. Armstrong was unable to respond to persons whose actions were so contrary to his own ideas of proper behaviour, and internalized his feelings in recurrent episodes of bad health.

Stuart turned next to the Tongan community, in particular the remnants of the "Reactionary Party". The outcome was a petition to Privy Council in March 1939 complaining about Bagnall's inadequacies as Minister for Finance. Stuart (without prior consultation with the Queen) called on the Privy Council to inquire into Bagnall's conduct as Treasurer. The Queen, presiding over the Privy Council, very firmly reminded Stuart of her considerable powers and of her impartiality in government matters.

> I do not intend to take a vote of the Privy Council. You [the Ministers] are here to assist in my office and in the use of my prerogatives I must act within the Constitution. I wish to thank you for giving me your advice. I do not wish to say anything at the present time as we have not yet the whole facts, and I have also received a petition signed by 150 people with reference to the Treasurer. I do not desire to delay this matter for any personal reasons but I have only learned today of what has happened.
>
> I will not use my prerogative in any partisan spirit. I have dismissed [on earlier occasions] relatives and personal friends from their offices because their conduct demanded it. I do not wish to act because some folk have petitioned but what I do wish is to do my duty in a way that I feel to be right.[29]

The Queen's assurance that she would institute an inquiry into the Treasury did not prevent Stuart from continuing his attacks on Bagnall. Stuart's supporters hoped that an inquiry into government would so discredit Tungī that he would have to resign, in the same way as Mateialona had been forced to resign in 1912. The Queen, on Armstrong's advice, delayed the inquiry because of a forthcoming trial of a Treasury employee. But when months went by with no sign of an inquiry, the Queen appeared to be protecting Bagnall.

The person who was most willing to listen to Stuart was Sioape Kaho, who had not yet taken up the Queen's suggestion that he resign. Sioape ingratiated himself with Stuart, persuading him that the government was corrupt and nepotistic (Figure 12.1), that until Stuart's arrival Sioape alone of the ministers was truly disinterested, that the "Reactionary Party" was serving the will of the people and was supported by the majority of the members of Parliament. Stuart was impressed by Sioape, so much so that in the Parliament of 1939 he described Sioape as an upright and much-wronged man and attempted to insert into a Bill of Indemnity a clause cancelling all of Sioape's debts to the government.[30] Stuart was only too willing to believe the assertions of Sioape and his friends that there was a conspiracy by a "camarilla", consisting of Tungī, Armstrong, Bagnall, and Lowe, to keep the Queen in ignorance of the true state of affairs in her government. Stuart informed the High Commissioner that the Queen was grateful to him for his efforts to bring down the "camarilla", reporting that "Her Majesty personally thanked me for my vigilance, taking Her only opportunity when away from the 'Camarilla'".[31]

Stuart thus presented himself to the Colonial Office as the champion not only of those who claimed to be an oppressed minority, but also of the Queen herself. Contrary to Stuart's perception, Sālote knew exactly what her ministers were doing – including Stuart – and about Stuart's association with the "Reactionary Party".

Totally lacking in discretion, Stuart and his garrulous wife recounted, to anyone who would listen, confidential government business. It was difficult for the people involved to respond to the charges made by the Stuarts because these were so wide-ranging and couched in such personal terms. The Queen sought the advice of the High Commissioner, who in turn sought the advice of the Colonial Office, who (on the eve of World War Two) had other matters on its mind. The Queen discontinued Privy Council meetings to avoid further confrontations between Stuart and Bagnall, and Tungī discontinued Cabinet meetings for the same reason.[32]

Stuart accused Tungī not only of being part of a "camarilla" undermining the Queen's authority, but also of having a "gang" of disreputable friends whom he protected when they broke the law. Tungī denied the existence of a gang, or any knowledge of its supposed membership. One person identified by Stuart as being a "gang" member was 'Uliti Palu, who, although only a commoner, had

Above: Queen Sālote and Honor Maude at a Red Cross bazaar 1941. Behind them are ʻAhomeʻe (Tēvita Manu-ʻo-pangai) and Kalanivalu (Sēmisi). *Courtesy of Harry and Honor Maude.* [75]

Above: A garden party at the British Residency, 8 June 1939, to celebrate George VI's birthday. *Left to right:* ʻAhomeʻe (Tēvita Manu-ʻo-pangai), Miss I. Pulu, Mrs Tupou Posesi Fanua, Mrs J. Skudder, Miss Fetutuki ʻOneʻone (who went to Sydney with Queen Sālote in 1935), Mr J. Skudder, Kalanivalu (Sēmisi). *Courtesy of the Auckland Institute and Museum. (Ref C30763.)* [74]

Right: Tuʻihaʻateiho (Havea), ʻUlukālala (Haʻamea), Tungī Mailefihi, and Ata (Solomone) 1941. *Courtesy of Harry and Honor Maude.* [76]

Above: The funeral of Tungī Mailefihi, at Mala'e Kula, 22 July 1941, showing the procession, *kauala* (platform carrying the coffin), and seated mourners. *Courtesy of Harry and Honor Maude.* [77]

Right: Sir Harry Luke (High Commissioner for the Western Pacific) visits the barracks of the Tonga Defence Force, 1941. *Courtesy of the Auckland Institute and Museum. (C30764.)* [78]

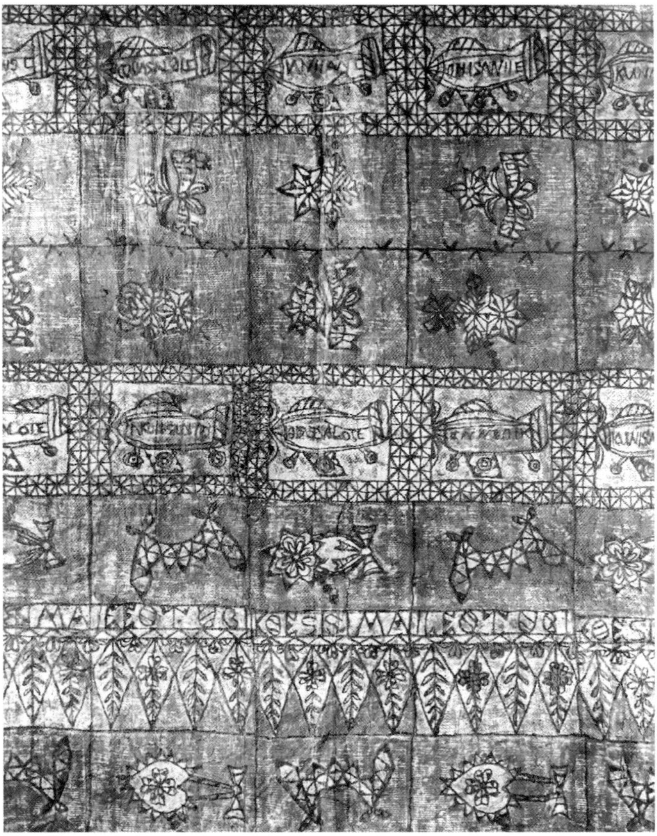

ABOVE: The Spitfire *Queen Sālote*. In addition to supporting other wartime funds, Tongans raised enough money to buy four Spitfires. The *Queen Sālote* and the *Prince Tungī* were in combat in the European war. The third Spitfire, *Tupou I*, was prevented from participating in the Pacific theatre by the end of the war. The fourth was not built. *Courtesy of the Auckland Institute and Museum. (Ref C 28238.)* [79]

LEFT: *Ngatu* (decorated bark cloth) records historical events as well as including stylized designs. The Spitfire *Queen Sālote* is depicted on this piece of *ngatu*, which is called "The Sisi Maile of Tungī". *Courtesy of British Museum. (Ref MM 031854/A.)* [80]

RIGHT: The Governor-General of New Zealand, Sir Bernard Freyberg, meets two Tongan ex-commandos, who are wearing their medals. On the left is Simote Vea Mahe, and on the right is Sione Inukiha'angana. *National Archives: National Publicity Studios Photographic Collection.* [82]

LEFT: Lieutenant Henry Taliai, who was killed in the fighting in the Solomons, 1943. *Courtesy of Siupeli Taliai.* [81]

BELOW: Tonga Defence Force. *Left to right:* Vīlai Tupou, 'Akau'ola, Feleti Vī, 'Alipate Tu'ifua, Samiu Fonua. *Courtesy of Kurt Düring.* [84]

RIGHT: Rev. Sau Faupula was a trusted confidant of Queen Sālote. [83]

LEFT: Postcard commemorating the centenary of the installation of Tupou I as Tu'i Kanokupolu 4 December 1845/1945. At the top are Tupou I, Queen Sālote Tupou III, and Tupou II. In the middle is the coat-of-arms and flag of Tonga, then Crown Prince Tupouto'a-Tungī in his graduation robes and Prince Tu'ipelehake. At the bottom are the Palace, the throne, and the Mala'e Kula. *Courtesy of Auckland Institute and Museum. (Ref C30759.)* [85]

BELOW: The *papālangi*-style double wedding of (*from left to right*) Crown Prince Tupouto'a-Tungī and Halaevalu Mata'aho, and Melenaite Tupou Moheofo and Prince Tu'ipelehake, 10 June 1947. They were married in the Royal Chapel. With them are Queen Sālote and Vīlai Tupou. [86]

ABOVE: The *tu'uvala* (Tongan royal wedding) on 12 June 1947. *Left to right*: Crown Prince Tupouto'a-Tungī and Halaevalu Mata'aho, and Melenaite Tupou Moheofo and Prince Tu'ipelehake. The couples are seated on piles of mats and bark cloth under a canopy made of bark cloth, with some of the presentations in the foreground of the picture. Behind each of the four is a *fa'ēhuki* (relative of the mother). *Courtesy of the family of Rodger Page.* [88]

ABOVE: The *tu'uvala* (Tongan royal wedding) on 12 June 1947. *Left to right:* Prince Tu'ipelehake and Melenaite Tupou Moheofo, and Crown Prince Tupouto'a-Tungī and Halaevalu Mata'aho. The couples walk on bark cloth towards the shelter on the Mala'e Pangai. [87]

Left: Queen Sālote in London, June 1953. *Photo by Lotte Meitner-Graf.* [90]

Below: Queen Sālote waves to the crowds from an open carriage returning from Westminster Abbey after the coronation of Queen Elizabeth II, 2 June 1953. Sitting opposite the Queen is the Sultan of Kelantan. *Courtesy of Popperfoto.* [89]

ABOVE: Queen Sālote at Methodist Ladies' College, Melbourne, Australia, 8 August 1953, where she laid the foundation stone of a new building. *Left to right:* Queen Sālote, Dr Olive Wood, unidentified, Princess Mata'aho, Mrs Windrum (?), Rev. Dr A. Harold Wood, unidentified, Miss Lindsay, Miss Dahle. The college now has memorial windows to Queen Sālote and Princess Fusipala (the latter attended MLC 1926–28). [91]

LEFT: Princess Siu'ilikutapu, eldest daughter of Prince Tu'ipelehake, presents flowers to Queen Elizabeth II at the beginning of the royal visit to Tonga, 19 December 1953. *Courtesy of Alan Sayers* [92]

been educated at Tupou College and taken up a scholarship to Newington College, Sydney, and belonged to an Old Wesleyan family. After his return to Tonga from Sydney, Palu had become a clerk in the savings bank, for which Bagnall was responsible, and in 1939 he appeared before Stuart on a charge of embezzlement. In the course of the case it was revealed that Palu had acted as a messenger between Bagnall and his mistress, a young half-caste woman, Fanny, related to Palu's wife. Stuart concluded that Bagnall had condoned Palu's thefts from the savings bank and profited by them, using the funds to keep his mistress. Stuart commented that Fanny had recently left the country with a quantity of heavy luggage.[33]

On 5 May 1939, in the 51-page judgment on the case, Stuart condemned Palu, and asserted that Bagnall (who had appeared in the case only as a witness) was guilty of theft, perjury, adultery, and collusion. Stuart outlined for the benefit of the jury the means by which a minister could be impeached by Parliament and predicted that Bagnall would not be a minister much longer. Stuart also stated that "a fool and a knave" had condoned Palu's thefts. At least some of those who heard the judgment understood Stuart to mean that Tungī was a fool and Bagnall was a knave. People were not very convinced when Stuart explained that he had meant that Bagnall was both fool and knave.

On the evening of the judgment, Tungī and Lowe (according to Stuart) got exceedingly drunk together and were stranded somewhere in the countryside in Lowe's car. In his role as local newspaper, Stuart reported his views to *papālangi* residents, Tongans, and visitors to the kingdom alike, implying that there was a connection between his judgment in the Supreme Court and Tungī and Lowe's drinking bout.[34]

The Queen was concerned at the distress Stuart's accusations caused Mrs Bagnall, but much more by the attack on Tungī. Stuart's assumption that the Queen would consent to her consort being demoted from his position as Premier was probably fostered by Sioape, who longed to occupy that position himself. Unknown to Stuart, on the day that Stuart gave his judgment, the Queen wrote to the High Commissioner, Sir Harry Luke, and requested the removal of Stuart.[35]

It is clear from this letter that Sālote stood firmly by her consort. It was also clear that what she most disliked about Stuart's conduct was that he would "strengthen the element ever ready to create faction and destructively criticize the government". The Queen did not want it to appear that Stuart was being recalled because of his criticism of the government, so she asked Luke to arrange Stuart's recall in such a manner that it would provoke no comment in Tonga. Given Stuart's determination to air his opinion to all and sundry, a discreet removal was, of course, impossible.

Stuart claimed that he was "the hero of the hour", had "great prestige", and was speaking for "the people", who were unhappily dominated by Bagnall.[36]

Unable to distinguish between the malicious gossip, ambition, vested interests of the "Reactionary Party", on the one hand, and genuine grievances, on the other, Stuart chose to assume that Sioape and the "Reactionary Party" were genuinely working for the good of "the people" and that he (Stuart) could benefit Tonga by introducing reforms to the parliamentary system to make it more like the Westminster system. Having failed to control the Privy Council, Stuart now sought power by control of Parliament.

Two of Stuart's actions persuaded those members of Parliament who also longed for power and influence that they had a true champion in the new Chief Justice. The first was Stuart's reversal of a decision by Ragnar Hyne, relating to the noble title of Niukapu. Stuart had found on appeal in favour of the claimant of the title and lands against a man whose claim had been recognized for more than 20 years (and who was represented by Lowe). The judgment revived the hopes of others whose claims to estates had not been recognized by the Constitution and the Law, for they believed that Stuart showed his partiality to *them* by disallowing evidence brought by Tungī and Lowe.[37] The second event was Stuart's proposal that Bagnall should be impeached. The possibility of impeachment reminded the opposition of the heady days of 1912, when another Premier had been forced to resign under threat of impeachment, and the governors of Ha'apai and Vava'u impeached and dismissed (chapter 2). They also recalled the way pressure from Parliament had led to the resignation of Wallace in 1928. Would history repeat itself?

In Tongan eyes, Bagnall's indiscretions were insignificant compared with the centuries-long struggle between chiefly lines in which *papālangi* allies were now commonplace. Sioape hoped Stuart would spearhead a *coup d'état* that would catapult him (Sioape) into the premiership once held by his eldest brother, Tu'ivakanō (Polutele). The Queen was again pressing for Sioape's resignation, so Sioape had nothing to lose and everything to gain by supporting Stuart.

What the "Reactionary Party" wanted was the impeachment of Tungī and his chief supporters in the Cabinet. The support of the Chief Justice of Tonga made this impeachment and a subsequent dismissal seem possible. The Queen remained outwardly calm. She did not enlighten Stuart as to her true feelings or her determination to use all of her considerable political skills in defending Tungī.

Sir Harry Luke was sympathetic to Sālote's plight, for he had "formed an unfavourable opinion" of both Stuarts during his visit to Tonga in December 1938.[38] Armstrong believed Stuart had forfeited his position through his disloyalty to the government that employed him, his threats, and his stirring up of disaffection. Since the good behaviour upon which the continuance of Stuart's appointment depended was noticeably absent, there was every reason to remove him. But whatever her constitutional prerogatives, Sālote knew that she could not be rid of Stuart without the consent of the Colonial Office, which had selected him for the position. She could only hope that the good relations she had done so much to create between Tonga and Great Britain would ensure this consent.

The whole situation was a test of Sālote's ability to control an awkward situation. She gave Stuart no cause for complaint against her, or any reason for him to complain that she treated him differently from her other ministers. When he asked for an audience, she saw him, and listened quietly to his barely concealed threats about what would happen to Tonga if she did not act upon his advice.

There are three explanations – not necessarily exclusive – for Stuart's behaviour in Tonga. The most obvious is that he had great expectations of his appointment and had been hurt and humiliated by what he deemed was unjust treatment at the hands of the *papālangi* officials in Tonga. The second was that he was trying to impress the Colonial Office with his fearless exposures in order to be given a more prestigious appointment. The third was hopes for conspicuous promotion within Tonga, that his connections in the Colonial Office would lead to the appointment as either Premier or Administrator during the impending war. My own reading of the situation is that Stuart, seeing that war was coming, hoped to be appointed as Administrator of the kingdom, with Sālote as nominal head of an acquiescent government. Stuart's former appointments as adviser to "native rulers" in South Africa makes his actions more comprehensible. Stuart seems not to have understood the difference between Tonga's status as a protected state and that of a protectorate. In the former, the Consul advised; in the latter the British administrator ruled. Or perhaps he understood and looked for a change in Tonga's status in the event of war.

Stuart's behaviour was increasingly unbalanced. Still unaware that Sālote had requested his removal from the country, Stuart attempted to force her hand. Since the Privy Council still had not met, and his interviews with her had not been productive of the outcomes he wished for, he sent her a message by Feleti Vī, the Queen's driver, accusing Tungī of misconduct, and saying that if Bagnall was not dismissed or forced to resign Stuart would send a report to the Colonial Office, a "deadly weapon" that would "uncover Tungī". By urging Sālote to consider her son, and to act before it was too late, he appeared to be threatening an end to her dynasty if she did not comply with his demands.[39]

When there was no reaction from the Palace to his message, Stuart again looked to Parliament as a means of forcing a response. The Queen had delayed calling Parliament, while looking for a reply from the Secretary of State for the Colonies. Stuart told Tungī that the clause in the Constitution requiring that "the Legislative Assembly shall meet at least once every twelve months" meant that it had to be summoned within 12 months of the Opening of Parliament of the previous year, and not (as had been the practice hitherto) to summon it within twelve months of the Closing of the previous year. Tungī was not prepared to accept Stuart's interpretation, but Stuart did not need to press it, for the summoning of Parliament was so much delayed that it did not conform to either interpretation. Sālote sought the consent of the High Commissioner to further delay the summoning of Parliament to avoid a confrontation: "My Premier has explained to me the practically insurmountable difficulties with which he is continuously faced because of the Chief Justice's attitude."[40]

At last a letter came from the Colonial Office, advising against the removal of Stuart and in favour of an official inquiry into his accusations of maladministration, in particular his accusations against Bagnall. An outside investigator was suggested, since Stuart had accused almost everyone in Tonga of dereliction of duty. The Colonial Office was concerned lest the Tongan government appear to be covering up a bad situation by simply removing the critic, Stuart, a senior official whose allegations had to be taken seriously.[41] Further, it was important to avoid a technical mistake in the inquiry. Suggesting that an outsider preside over an inquiry put the matter into the hands of Sir Harry Luke, the High Commissioner, but no suitable official was immediately available, causing further delay.

Since Stuart was to remain, the Queen could no longer delay Parliament, but on 22 July 1939, a week before Parliament was due to meet, she formally requested the resignations of both Bagnall and Sioape, the former on the grounds of ill-health and the latter on the grounds of age. Stuart criticized the Queen directly for the first time, saying that she had asked for Sioape's resignation upon hearing that Sioape was preparing a Bill of Impeachment against Bagnall.

Sālote's decision to retire Bagnall had been made in consultation with Armstrong on 17 July. Armstrong gave his consent in the belief that Bagnall was innocent of Stuart's charges. Telegrams instructing Armstrong to advise the Queen not to accept Bagnall's resignation came too late, for Sālote had already chosen his and Sioape's successors: H. E. Nicolson, already employed by the Treasury, as Minister for Finance, and ʻAkauʻola, a *matāpule maʻu tofiʻa*, who had been Governor of Vavaʻu since 1932, as Minister for Police. All the Tongan Privy Councillors were now supporters of the government, as Sālote and Tungī believed was right and proper, and Nicolson knew what was expected of him. Although Sioape accused Sālote and Tungī of nepotism (Figure 12.1), no Tongan (even Sioape) thought there was anything wrong with appointing one's supporters (it would be foolish to appoint enemies! and no one was neutral), and Armstrong did not object. Privy Council and Cabinet meetings were resumed.

Sālote's own position was difficult. Armstrong should have advised the suspension of Bagnall when he was accused in Stuart's judgment of 5 May, pending the inquiry into the administration of the Treasury. Bagnall's sudden resignation just before Parliament met made it appear that Sālote was shielding Bagnall, which in a sense she was, because both she and Armstrong believed Bagnall had been unjustly accused.

There was bound to be an explosion in Parliament. After the Queen made her speech at the official Opening of Parliament, the first business of the members was to elect a committee to prepare an Address-in-Reply, usually brief and formal, acknowledging the main points of the royal speech. Stuart was elected to the 1939 committee, which took the opportunity to deplore the Queen's acceptance of Bagnall's resignation after a Bill for Impeachment had been lodged; to express regret at Sioape's enforced retirement; and to threaten that Parliament would use legislation to punish Bagnall and to reward Sioape. The Reply (clearly written by Stuart) also predicted that Parliament's powers should and would be strengthened.

> . . . we understand and sympathize fully with the difficult position in which Your Majesty and the Premier have been placed, and we trust and believe that the responsibility for such difficulties, the creation of which we resent, will be adequately apportioned by us . . .
>
> With regard to the changes in personnel in the high Officials of Your Majesty's Government we join in Your Majesty's regret at the loss of the services of the Minister of Police and trust that he will receive completely adequate recognition for a long life well spent in the Service both of Your Majesty and Your Majesty's Honoured father . . .
>
> On the 21st July, Your Majesty accepted the resignation of the impeached official. Your Majesty by such action enabled the impeached person to escape from the jurisdiction of the Law of Your Majesty's Kingdom, and has thereby indicated a point at which *the Prerogative of Your Majesty's Legislative Assembly requires strengthening*. We may feel it our duty to concur most respectfully with what may have been Your Majesty's view and with the hard logic of facts in ultimately accepting the proposition that it was better for the Kingdom that the Honourable Mr W. G. Bagnall should be permitted to avoid Impeachment, but in such case he should in the interests of Justice be well advised to leave Tonga. As to the civil results of a resignation which we must treat as purely evasive we will submit a suitable amendment to the Indemnity Bill when introduced, in the interests of the conservation of the finances of Your Majesty's Kingdom.[42] [my italics]

An Indemnity Bill, approved by Privy Council, had been designed to legalize the late calling of Parliament. Stuart proposed that a sub-committee of Parliament should reconsider it. The sub-committee reintroduced clauses that the Privy Council had rejected, namely clauses cancelling Sioape's debts to the government; depriving Bagnall of his pension; insisting upon the dismissal of

Tungī's Secretary, Lowe; allowing for the impeachment of an ex-minister (Bagnall); and protecting everyone (except Lowe and Treasury officials) from litigation as a consequence of their actions during the four months prior to the parliamentary session. The amended Bill, like the Address-in-Reply, was clearly the work of Stuart.

A petition (dated 17 August 1939) to Parliament signed by 1100 persons asked for the dismissal of all the ministers except Sioape and Stuart. Eight of the 14 elected members of Parliament were from Ha'apai and Vava'u, and they not only resented the hegemony of Nuku'alofa but blamed Tungī for their being unequal sufferers during the Depression. Some members made fulsome speeches in praise of Stuart, and five members seconded a motion to increase Stuart's salary "so he would never leave Tonga".[43] Siosaia Mataele, a Tongatapu member, wrote to the High Commissioner, praising Stuart for "expending all his energies trying to teach the people and leading them in the right path".[44] A Vava'u representative, 'Unga Afuha'amango, first cousin of Queen Takipō and Muimui Kaho and elder brother of Samisoni Puli'uvea Afuha'amango (who was tried for defamation of the Queen in 1924), wrote to the *Pacific Islands Monthly* to say that:

> We rejoice that at last we have a man who acts quickly and firmly . . . Hitherto, we were getting so tired of the intolerable inconsistency, extravagance, indecision, and postponing "method" of Government heads. Now all that sort of nonsense is being gradually but surely cleared away, and the culprits made to "toe the line" by order of His Honour [Stuart].[45]

In a letter to the Colonial Office, Stuart claimed to be the "hero of the hour" because of his stand against the "hated Treasurer", and expressed his confidence that he would prevail because he was supported by a wave of popular approval.[46]

Stuart must have been aware of the Queen's prerogatives, that the Queen was not a constitutional monarch in the English sense, and that the Parliament of Tonga lacked the powers of the Parliament of Westminster. He intended to change all that, urging the members to ignore the Queen's known wishes:

> This Parliament is the Free Parliament of Tonga, and it is only right that you should be informed of the correct and true position of things . . . there was a report going about during the last week . . . "The Queen has made known her decision about this law." But the report is false and I do not believe it. If the report were true it would appear that the Queen wished to rule autocratically, ignoring the will of the people . . . [47]

Stuart was endeavouring to secure for himself the powers he denied the Queen. He won support by advocating the sort of land reform long desired by the lesser chiefs, such as a proposal that succession to titles and estates by primogeniture be abandoned and the traditional method of succession by choice be reinstated. His concerns about access to education and a proposal that only "true-blue Englishmen" (instead of colonials) should be appointed to government positions also had an airing. Some proposals from his supporters were withdrawn without being voted upon, and others were strongly opposed, showing that the rebels had no agreed platform of reforms.

On the day after the Opening of the parliamentary session (2 August 1939) Ronald Garvey, representing the Western Pacific High Commission, arrived to hold an "informal inquiry" into Stuart's allegations.[48] He reported that Stuart's "intemperate attack" upon the government through the "reactionary element" in Parliament ruled out any possibility that the Queen would agree to the continuance of Stuart's appointment.[49]

When the Indemnity Bill came before the Queen for her royal assent, she returned it to Parliament with a request that the offending clauses be removed and the original Bill referred to the High Commissioner for his opinion. On the one hand it was difficult for the Tongans to refuse a direct request made by the Queen, on the other they would lose face if they acceded to her request without at least a show of independence. Siosaia Mataele, people's representative for Tongatapu, moved that the whole Bill be repealed, but Stuart's face-saving motion that the whole Bill be referred to the High Commissioner was passed by 10 votes to seven.

Stuart's new career as leader of a "loyal Opposition" came to an abrupt halt because of the imminence of war. The Queen had assured Sir Harry Luke during his first visit to Tonga (in December 1938) as High Commissioner that Tonga would fully support Britain in the event of war. Garvey's visit was also related to the impending war.[50] On 25 August Sālote asked Parliament to approve the placing of "all Tonga's resources" at Britain's disposal when war was declared. Garvey appealed to Stuart to act as a loyal Britisher and to "place himself unreservedly in the Consul's hands". Such a request could not be refused by "one of the loneliest sentries of the Empire".

Sālote's confident assurance of Tonga's support in the coming war convinced Garvey that her great "influence" over the people and even over Parliament was undiminished. Parliament passed the required war legislation without demur, and when war was declared on 3 September, they consented (in response to the Queen's request) to curtail the session so they could return to their people to explain how the war would affect Tonga.[51] The members had enjoyed the grandstanding, but it had now come to an end – for that year, at least.

It quickly became clear to Garvey that correction of administrative irregularities, especially in the Treasury, was required, but the greater problem was the personality clashes between *papālangi* in Tonga. Garvey concluded that Stuart was overbearing and Armstrong not sufficiently judicious in his actions. Only Sālote escaped Garvey's criticism, for he recognized that she had acted correctly in very difficult circumstances. As she said, when her two advisers – the Consul and the Chief Justice – differed, it was very difficult for her to resolve their differences. Sālote once again blamed *papālangi* for stirring up trouble in Tonga,[52] saying that she felt it was "improper" for the Chief Justice to be stirring up the opponents of her government and encouraging the "Reactionary Party" to attack her ministers. Garvey commented on their conversation:

> . . . Her Majesty stated that although a number of Mr Stuart's official actions were open to criticism that to which she chiefly took exception was the manner in which the Chief Justice discussed official matters with all and sundry, including the Tongans themselves; such discussions frequently including his personal suspicions and probable actions.
>
> Her Majesty explained to me that Tongans have always held the position of Chief Justice in high regard, so much so that a Chief Justice's words and actions are above criticism and his statements implicitly believed. Her Majesty informed me that as a result of this attitude the common people were now convinced, in view of the Chief Justice's indiscreet conversations, that Mr Bagnall, the late Minister of Finance, had stolen money from the Treasury and that he was being shielded by his friends in the Tongan Government from his just deserts . . . Her Majesty also stated that although, in her estimation, the affair was now a small matter confined mostly to official circles, the Tongans were quick to take sides in a quarrel and she feared the old religious differences, which had caused so much unrest in Tonga in the past, might again become evident as, during the course of the present Parliament it was clear that Mr Stuart was educating the Representatives of the People to attack Government . . . Her Majesty stated that she considered there was no simple solution of the present situation other than the removal of Mr Stuart from the Kingdom as he was obviously a politician at heart and she considered that on that score he would always be a troublemaker in Tonga.[53]

Queen Sālote explained the rivalries in terms that Garvey could comprehend. She did not tell him that the "old religious differences" were the modern way of expressing centuries-old, traditional rivalries. She was acute in recognizing that Stuart was a "politician at heart", not simply a bearer of grudges. Garvey's Report shows that he felt the Queen was reasonable in her comments on the situation.

As for Tungī, his views were "an echo of the Queen's". Tungī told Garvey that running a bureaucracy did not come easily to him, and that he needed expert advice and assistance from a friendly source; that is, the Agent & Consul. Tungī believed that Armstrong's abilities were inferior to those of McOwan and Neill, as Armstrong had been unable to deal with the situation created by Stuart.

> The Premier informed me that in his opinion the Agent and Consul could not handle the Chief Justice and that was the root cause of all the trouble. Together with Her Majesty, he stated that if Mr Neill had still been in Tonga there would have been no trouble as Mr Neill, with his legal qualifications, would have had the knowledge to deal with the legal side of the dispute. I inquired whether he considered that the Agent and Consul should be a man with legal qualifications and he replied emphatically in the affirmative.[54]

Garvey's opinion of Tungī was that he was an "easy-going individual, of rather weak character, who can be easily led", and that the appointment of Lowe as his Secretary had been an unfortunate one.

> Mr A. G. Lowe, a New Zealand barrister, selected through the Government Agents in Auckland, was appointed to the position of Secretary 18 months ago. He has no previous experience of administration and he has definitely been a bad influence on Tungi. The two are close friends and have a community of interest in farming. They do not keep strict office hours and spend too much time in the Nuku'alofa Club, which is close to the Premier's Office, where they consume rather more beer than is wise in a small community which listens to every item of gossip and elaborates every molehill into a mountain.[55]

Garvey concluded that Stuart had pinpointed real weaknesses in the government, especially in the Premier's Department and the Treasury, even though he had gone about his reforming attempts in the wrong way.[56]

> As a result of many conversations with the Chief Justice I formed the impression that his attacks on individuals in the Tonga Government, either in Court or in Parliament, had their origin in a conviction that the affairs of Government were not being properly or efficiently conducted by those individuals. My enquiries proved to me that except in the case of the Director of Education, there were good grounds for Mr Stuart's attitude, particularly as regards the Treasury and the Premier's Department. Unfortunately in the cases of Mr Bagnall and Mr Lowe (the Premier's Secretary) the Chief Justice has talked so freely to almost anyone who was prepared to listen to him that it is difficult to convince oneself that personal animosity was not also a contributory cause of his attack.[57]

Garvey concluded that because there were grounds for Stuart's accusations it would be unwise to remove Stuart: "although I am of the opinion that by temperament he is unsuited to hold a position in a small community such as Tonga . . . his methods of dealing with local situations are open to criticism".[58] Garvey believed that Stuart had not so much created tensions in Tongan society as drawn them out, and he commented:

> Feeling was sharply divided among the Tongans. Those loyal to the Government felt that the Chief Justice was stirring up trouble which would quickly get out of his control and lead to widespread disaffection throughout the islands, while the other section of opinion, held by the reactionary party, supported chiefly by the Representatives of the People, claimed that they had at last found a man who would give them redress from their grievances.[59]

Stuart had clearly gone too far, and the Secretary of State for Colonies reminded him of his duties. Luke added a sharp reproof.

Sālote responded very coolly to Luke's recommendations about inquiries into government departments.[60] She and Tungī had often thought that there should be changes in the present system of administration, she said, and an inquiry into the financial systems was desirable. And she responded positively to a suggested review of the appropriateness of *papālangi* sitting in the Privy Council, Cabinet, and Parliament. However, she could not agree that a general inquiry into the administration of government was necessary, saying that what was required was the appointment of a legally qualified Agent & Consul who would strongly support Tungī and keep the *papālangi* in line.[61]

Armstrong and Stuart were outwardly reconciled; the Privy Council agreed to release Lowe from his contract so he could return to New Zealand and join the armed forces; and Bagnall retired to the countryside to await the inquiry and then returned to New Zealand.

Sālote assured Garvey that the members of the "Reactionary Party" in Parliament were motivated by their opposition to the Supplementary Agreement and a wish to stir up old quarrels and destroy the unity of the kingdom. She hoped that the departure of Sioape Kaho from government would leave them without a leader. In her official speech at the Opening of Parliament on 27 June 1940, Sālote urged the members to forget their differences and to support the worldwide struggle against oppression. She reminded them of the debt Tonga owed to the British government.[62] The members assured Her Majesty of their "complete devotion to the cause of humanity now being sustained by the British Empire".

A week later 'Unga Afuha'amango brought before Parliament bills of impeachment against Tungī and the other four Tongan ministers of the Crown: Tu'iha'ateiho (Havea), Governor of Ha'apai; 'Ulukālala (Ha'amea), Governor of Vava'u; Ata (Solomone Ula), Minister for Lands; and 'Akau'ola, Minister for Police. Sālote saw the hand of Sioape Kaho in the impeachments. Members of Parliament had to vote on whether they would hear the charges or dismiss them out of hand. Nicolson seconded Stuart's motion to hear the charges and the majority agreed, presumably so members could air their grievances. Sālote was angered by this attack on chiefs whom she had personally appointed to her government, but she did not try to prevent the charges being heard.

Stuart denied involvement in the impeachments of 1940, but Afuha'amango counted on him to draw out the larger issues behind seemingly trivial charges. Parliament formed itself into a court under Stuart's presidency to hear the charges. The one against Tungī related to a prisoner, Peni Lātūselu, who while in prison for fraudulent conversion had been convicted of plotting to assassinate all Tongan members of the Cabinet. Tungī and Bagnall had approved a request from Sioape to punish Lātūselu when there was no quorum in cabinet. Tungī admitted the charge, saying that other members of Cabinet had been absent in different parts of the kingdom. The members of Parliament voted 17 to 2 to acquit Tungī. The two members who voted for conviction of Tungī were Afuha'amango and Taniela Tonga, the latter aggrieved at losing the Tu'i'afitu title in a court case prior to Stuart's arrival.

Afuha'amango's other six charges were all related to land. Tu'iha'ateiho, Ata, 'Ulukālala, and 'Akau'ola, all hereditary estateholders, were charged with illegally assigning or illegally depriving individuals of allotments. There were two votes for the impeachment of Ata on the first charge, the second being withdrawn. There was one vote for impeachment of 'Akau'ola. Tu'iha'ateiho was acquitted unanimously. The hearing of the charges against 'Ulukālala (Ha'amea) and the second charge against 'Akau'ola were postponed – and never heard. If Afuha'amango and other members hoped that these charges would open up a discussion about customary land rights, as foreshadowed in Stuart's judgment in the Niukapu case, they were to be disappointed.

Stuart's detachment during the hearing of the impeachments was certainly disappointing for those who had previously seen him as a spokesperson for the "Reactionary Party", for he had now lost interest in introducing parliamentary democracy to Tonga. Without prior consultation with the Privy Council or Armstrong (as required by Law and the Treaty amendment of 1927), Stuart introduced into Parliament a Wartime Contingencies Bill, providing that "absolute power is hereby placed in the hands of Her Majesty in Council", and that the "Queen in Council is given special and absolute powers to deal with all aliens in any matter whatsoever".[63] If this Bill had become law, it would have deprived the Agent & Consul of his right to advise the Queen and her government as set out in the Supplementary Agreement and amendments to the Treaty. It would also have deprived Tungī of his constitutional powers as Premier. And non-Tongans would have lost all rights. Whether the members fully understood that the Chief Justice intended that he himself would rule through the Privy Council is a moot point. Sālote wisely referred the Bill to Armstrong, who referred it to the High Commissioner, as one more example of Stuart's overbearing behaviour.

On the last day of the parliamentary session, Sālote wrote to Luke to ask again, but more urgently, that Stuart be recalled. She quoted from a letter from Tungī to herself, which stated that

> His Honour shows no disposition to work in concert with Your Majesty's Cabinet or Privy Council and his attitude of domination has, in my opinion, been extremely prejudicial to the good working of Your Majesty's Government. In Parliament, His Honour had taken it upon himself to produce measures for consideration without first conferring with the Government or, in fact, to any of those who should have had an opportunity of giving the measures earlier consideration. On numerous occasions I myself, as Your Majesty's Premier, and also the Government have received definite assurance of His Honour that certain measures, drafted by him, were legally in order and carried out the intention of the Government; later it has been proved that the assurance was wholly incorrect.[64]

Stuart had now been in the country for two years of his three-year term. Sālote was so determined that he go that she offered to pay the whole of his salary for the third year and the expenses of his removal from Tonga. Considering the financial situation of Tonga after the Depression, this offer indicates her resolve to be rid of Stuart. The letter stated that Stuart's actions not only undermined the unity she had worked consistently for but threatened Tonga's alliance with Great Britain:

> I myself feel that the influence of Mr Stuart is far from beneficial to the welfare of good Government. It seems to me that he gets very much more satisfaction from developing some petty intrigue which he thinks will increase his influence, rather than working for the unity of the people.
>
> Then there is his inability to realise the position of the Consul according to the Treaty and Agreement . . . Unfortunately he does not seem to realise that he is playing with fire; his careless words are readily taken up by those of the reactionary party . . . who are still resenting the terms of the [Supplementary] agreement.[65]

Stuart endeavoured to prove his loyalty to Great Britain by appointing himself director of counter-espionage against the Japanese.[66] Since Tonga was not ready unilaterally to declare war against the Japanese, his activities had alarming aspects. Despite Armstrong's assurances that the Japanese government had not issued an ultimatum to the British government, Stuart mobilized the Tonga Defence Force one midnight when a Japanese cargo vessel was in port, and issued the soldiers with live ammunition.[67]

It was now clear that Stuart had intended to usurp the powers of the Queen, the Agent & Consul, and the government of Tonga. Luke strongly supported Sālote's request for Stuart's removal, writing to the Secretary of State for the Colonies that:

> strong protests have been received from the Queen and Agent and Consul against actions of Stuart which are without doubt a menace to good Government

> and productive of deplorable discord and disunity in Tonga and difficulties for the Government. The Queen again presses urgently for his withdrawal from Tonga . . .
>
> In the interests of good relations, especially in view of the extremely helpful and loyal attitude of that Kingdom in connexion with the war, I urge his immediate withdrawal. If another post cannot be found for him I ask that his appointment in Tonga should be terminated on grounds of general policy by whatever power to that end may he open to His Majesty's Government.[68]

Luke's strong recommendation had its effect. On 23 October 1940 Stuart at last departed from Tonga, assuming that his transfer to British Guiana was a promotion because of his good work in Tonga.[69] A footnote to the story of the Stuarts was that the *Rangitane* was torpedoed after leaving Auckland and the passengers deposited by the Germans on Emirau, an island off the coast of Papua New Guinea. The passengers reckoned that the company of the Stuarts was the most traumatic aspect of the experience. Stuart was last heard of punching a man in a cinema queue in Georgetown, British Guiana.[70]

Why did Stuart attract support in Tonga? The Queen and all those close to her were strongly opposed to him. Many of the *papālangi* residents believed he had exposed problems in the administration of the kingdom, even though he had gone about it in the wrong way, and they were annoyed by him and his wife as individuals. The traditional enemies of the Tupou dynasty – and Tungī's traditional enemies – were enthusiastic about what Stuart was doing, and this gave him the impression that he was a popular reformer. The "Reactionary Party" wanted Tungī to be deposed by Stuart, and one of themselves succeed as Premier, and the Parliament's powers to be increased. Garvey concluded that some reforms were required, but he was clearly an admirer of Queen Sālote, and he was full of praise for her impeccable behaviour in a difficult situation.

Stuart and Mrs Stuart were clearly hurt by what they saw as the failure of the local hierarchy to accord them the status to which they were entitled. His background as the all-important adviser to "native rulers" in southern Africa led him to expect an important role in the affairs of the kingdom; and he found it convenient to take the complaints of the "Reactionary Party" at face value. While Stuart began by deploring the dissimilarities between the government of Tonga and the Westminster system, he ended by seeking the role of dictator for himself in the event of war. While not directly criticizing the Queen, he was ready to ride roughshod over her constitutional powers in order to grasp power for himself.

The charges of maladministration and perjury against Bagnall were never heard. Many Tongans believed him to be guilty, and there were frequent references in the Parliament in the 1940s and 1950s to the fact that he had been shielded and retired with a government pension more generous than that available to the locals.

Armstrong's health was badly affected by the task of trying to keep the peace in Tonga. His hands had been tied by the impending inquiry and the continuance of Stuart's appointment being confidentially referred to London. When Stuart claimed compensation from the government of Tonga for uninsured property lost on the *Rangitane*, Armstrong could no longer control himself, and he informed the High Commissioner that Stuart's behaviour in Tonga had "earned for him the loathing and contempt of every person who values the ordinary decencies of life".[71]

The departure of Stuart meant the virtual end of the "Reactionary Party" as a force in Tongan politics. H. E. Maude, who was appointed Acting Agent & Consul in 1941 while Armstrong was on much-needed leave, carried out an inquiry into the administration of the government of Tonga. Maude recommended that instead of a resident Chief Justice who was also adviser to the government, the Chief Justice of Fiji should come to Tonga to hear cases in the Supreme Court and appeals to the Privy Council; and instead of Secretary to the Premier, there should be a Secretary to Government, with legal qualifications, seconded from the Colonial Service, who would act as Legal Adviser to the government, but not have a seat in Privy Council, Cabinet, or Parliament. The Minister for Finance, Nicolson, would then be the only *papālangi* on Privy Council. Nicolson's successor, George Goodacre, would be the last *papālangi* member of the Privy Council, and when he retired in 1961, Mahe 'Uli'uli Tupouniua was appointed his successor.

The Queen had been put in a very difficult position. The Treaty of Friendship and the Constitution required her to take the advice of the British Agent & Consul and the Chief Justice. For all his good will, Armstrong failed to advise her to listen to Stuart's legitimate grievances (about his house, for instance) and to distance herself from Bagnall by suspending him pending the inquiry. Getting advice from Suva and London delayed matters inordinately. Nevertheless the Stuart affair proved that Queen Sālote had learned the craft of ruling. She showed those qualities so desirable in a leader and an ally: she was patient, discreet, trustworthy, consistent. She refrained from impulsive action, in spite of extreme provocation. She rewarded the loyalty of her ministers with loyalty, in particular Tungī, making it quite clear to the British authorities, as she had made it clear to her subjects, that Tungī was indispensable to her. It was Stuart's inability to understand this loyalty – and the essential disloyalty of the "Reactionary Party" – that was his undoing.

Stuart's departure promised better things in spite of the war. But the Queen, who had suffered from considerable personal and political stress during the first 22 years of her reign, soon found that she would suffer a greater loss and have to face a challenge from *papālangi* unlike those she had encountered before.

CHAPTER THIRTEEN

The Greatest Loss of All

"The honours I have received were through my husband's goodness . . ."
(Queen Sālote, 1941)[1]

As World War Two approached, the British government sought the support of all countries, even the smallest, within the British Empire. Thus in December 1938, when Sir Harry Luke made his first visit to Tonga as the British High Commissioner for the Western Pacific, he asked Queen Sālote what she intended to do if Great Britain and Germany went to war. Without hesitation, the Queen responded that she would place all of Tonga's resources at the disposal of Great Britain. Her reason for co-operation was (she said) that Tonga owed a debt of gratitude to Great Britain for protection against other foreign interests, and especially for its advice on the internal government of the country. Thus on 25 August 1939 Parliament passed the required war legislation at the Queen's request, and on 3 September 1939, Tonga (population 33,000) declared war on Germany (population 75 million) along with other countries who would be known collectively as "the allies".

Tonga's Treaty of Friendship of 1900 with Great Britain required the latter to defend the southern kingdom; but at the outbreak of war Britain handed over this responsibility to New Zealand, along with responsibility for the other territories of the Western Pacific High Commission.[2] The British Agent & Consul, A. L. Armstrong, continued as Tonga's adviser on civil matters. He would be intermediary between the Queen and the government of Tonga, on the one hand, and the allied forces, on the other.

Tonga did not wait for New Zealand. At the outbreak of war, the government, on behalf of Queen Sālote, called for volunteers to join the Tonga Defence Force, and virtually every adult male in the kingdom volunteered, including 26 *papālangi*. The first group of 100 men was selected within a week of the declaration of war. Tungī Mailefihi, royal consort, great chief, and Premier, became colonel-in-chief; and the Minister for Police, 'Akau'ola (Siosateki Faletau), who had served with the New Zealand forces during World War One, was commissioned by the Queen as lieutenant-colonel and commandant.[3] The Chief Medical Officer, Dr Brown, became Major Brown, and A. W. Servante (teacher at the Government College), A. G. Lowe (Secretary to the Premier), and H. W. Stoner were commissioned as captains. Feleti Vī (the former Ve'ehala) was commissioned a second lieutenant, and A. Tu'ifua as a lieutenant.[4]

At later dates additional officers were seconded to the Tonga Defence Force from Fiji and New Zealand.[5] All Tonga Defence Force officers – local or otherwise – received their commissions from Queen Sālote, and swore allegiance to her. The first 100 men of the Tonga Defence Force did not wait for overseas officers or weapons, but began drilling with sticks at a firing range built by hand at Sopu.[6] The numbers of the Tonga Defence Force soon increased to 250, then in 1941 to 800.[7]

Tupou Posesi Fanua remembers the day in September 1939 when the Queen called on Tongan men to enlist in the Tonga Defence Force.

> There was a big platform put up at the old Stone Building [where the Premier's and several other government departments had their offices] opposite the Lands Office, and there she stayed . . . Her Majesty seemed to know exactly what to do, what to wear for the occasion, things like that, and her command of language and words was really very amazing. I just remember her sitting there, everyone was on the Mala'e, and she came, she walked there [from the Palace]. Her husband wasn't there. It gave you the impression she was alone or something like that. She stood there and she spoke to the people. All the people were standing there. She walked down from the Palace and she said: "My people, I want to tell you today [that] I have made a decision that no woman has a right to do, but I have made it as Queen. We will support England in the war today, until the end of the war. . . . those who want to take on the responsibility of training to be soldiers to defend Tonga will march down, and there will be a medical officer there who will check you up. Sign your name there. England is in trouble, and we owe a lot to England because England has been protecting us for years now." And she reeled off a lot of advantages that we had got from England. . . .
>
> And the next time I saw her, she was on the platform with her husband beside her. And the people! They were almost mad, trying to get into the room through the little entrance. They had to tell them to form lines. Old people –

even women – wanted to go and enlist. And you know, I could see, watching from the other side, under the tree, she was almost in tears, she was laughing at all those women.

"We can do it! We can do it!" And all those women were pushing men, and they were trying to get into this room. It was really a wonderful sight that day. If it moved you – what about her? . . . the thing that was so amazing was how she could rally her people together.[8]

In spite of the enthusiasm of the women, the Tonga Defence Force was an all-male organization. The Queen recruited women to go to the British Residency to collect cut-out pieces of khaki cloth to sew into Tonga Defence Force uniforms (shorts and shirts), mostly by hand. She also organized groups of women to roll up bandages and to assemble field-dressing kits. She reviewed the troops and went to inspect the barracks, built by voluntary labour, and to make sure the workers had enough food. As was customary when working groups gathered, the Tonga Defence Force and labourers were fed by different villages in turn. The privileges of chiefs were still observed, and a particularly delicious beef stew made under the direction of Margaret Armstrong, wife of the British Agent & Consul, as the contribution of the Kolomotu'a section of Nuku'alofa, found its way to the Palace hangers-on (not to the royal family, of course!) because it was considered too good for commoners.[9]

The headquarters of the Tonga Defence Force were initially on the Mala'e Pangai (between the Palace and the wharf) in Nuku'alofa. In November 1939 (the end of the school year), they were moved to the Government College site near Maile Taha (One Mile – from the Flagstaff), just south of the Mala'e Kula. In January 1940, they were moved a few hundred metres to the former grounds of Tupou College to the west of the Mala'e Kula.

Judith Hornabrook described the Tonga Defence Force as having an "informal, domestic character".[10] In the early days two companies guarded the airfield at Fua'amotu in the Eastern District (one being later sent to Kolovai in the Western District) and another two companies were in Nuku'alofa (one later being sent to Mataki'eua in the Central District). Coastwatching was undertaken throughout the Tongan group of islands, using runners in the absence of a wireless system. In the second year of its existence, Tonga Defence Force men were paid (five pence per day for privates, two shillings per day for lieutenants), and more volunteers were accepted. Eventually there would be two battalions (2000 Tongans). These two battalions made up 12 per cent of the male population of Tonga.[11]

Each month Queen Sālote set aside approximately 10 per cent of her salary as her contribution to the war effort. At her instigation, the government of Tonga allocated £20,000 for defence for each of the first two years of the war, £25,000 in the third year, £12,500 in the fourth, and £20,000 in later years.

Tongans were self-sufficient as far as their own food supply was concerned; but the Depression of the 1930s meant that by 1939 there was little in the way of imported, storable food and general merchandise in the country. Since shipping was now irregular and supplies uncertain, caches of food were hidden all over the island in case of an emergency, such as a hurricane. The Tongan government took control of imports and exports and became the sole purchaser and exporter of copra at steadily increasing prices. On the advice of the British Agent & Consul the government rationed petrol and fixed the prices of imported goods.[12]

A censorship board was set up, and 'Amanaki Havea recalls receiving in Australia letters from home full of holes cut by the censors.[13] A daily newssheet relayed in English the equally censored war news. The Queen was an avid follower of the war news, and when she heard of the Battle for Britain and the bombing of London in 1940 she wrote to the Agent & Consul: "I desire to take this opportunity of once again assuring you of the deep and heartfelt sympathy and admiration of the Tongan people for the people of Britain in their hour of trial and to express my unshakeable belief that it is not God's will that so noble a people should be defeated by so barbaric a foe."[14]

It seemed that none of the voluntary organizations (except the Home Guard, which was all male and included *papālangi* residents) could function without the Queen's help. Vividly visualizing bombs dropping on defenceless Tongans, the Queen asked Margaret Armstrong, a trained and experienced nurse, to give First Aid classes to a group of women. As Margaret Armstrong said, "The Queen's knowledge of her subjects would ensure that the women chosen for the classes would be the right type."

The women selected by the Queen for the first class gathered nervously at the gate of the Residency, dressed in their best clothes and *sisi*s (a long skirt made of hibiscus fibres, and with a decorated waistband), because the Queen was to attend the class. Protocol was further observed as the students sat on the floor of the wide verandah at the Residency. The skeleton Siale Falanisē (Charlie Frenchman) was borrowed from Tupou College for the occasion. Margaret Armstrong could not help reflecting on the anatomical extremes that faced the class: the Queen, overflowing her armchair; herself a slender *papālangi* behind a table; and the skeleton Siale Falanisē dangling beside them. The Queen personally gave out certificates to those who completed the course.

The Queen had founded a dramatic company called Hengihengi 'a Tonga (Dawn of Tonga), which performed plays. Before the war it acted out legends, but during the war, in order to raise funds for the Red Cross, the Queen wrote and produced a play about an air raid, in which her First Aid group played out the roles for which they had been trained. The part for a boy required him to call out, "It's a raid", but he kept saying, "It's a rape", until Queen Sālote explained the difference.[15]

The Queen was patron of the Red Cross, the St John Ambulance, and the Spitfire Fund. In 1940 and 1941, instead of the annual *levée* (*papālangi* gentlemen only) on the official birthday of the King-Emperor of the British Empire, there were bazaars in the grounds of the British Residency for which Tongan women provided handicrafts and *papālangi* women provided cakes for sale. *Papālangi*-style dances (*hulohula*) were held under her sponsorship to raise funds. When (in 1943) two platoons of Tonga Defence Force soldiers went overseas, Sālote organized a Comforts Fund to provide cigarettes, razors, and sweets for them.[16]

Queen Sālote offered to the British government 546 acres (partly Tungī's estates and partly those of Tu'ipelehake) for an airfield for the Royal New Zealand Air Force (RNZAF) for the peppercorn rent of one shilling a year. Material for the airfield was donated by the nobles and labour donated by the commoners, including the construction of five miles of approach road. All the early work on the airfield was done by hand, and when a bulldozer arrived from New Zealand to level out the field, the whole population of Tongatapu (Tongan and *papālangi* alike) flocked to the field to view this amazing piece of technology.

The first aircraft landed at Fua'amotu on 15 March 1940. Margaret Armstrong recorded that when the Queen was first offered a flight on an aeroplane, the chiefs would not allow her to accept. When the offer was repeated some time later, the Queen accepted with alacrity, on the condition that the flight take place at once, before any of the chiefs got to hear of it.

The war occupied a great deal of Sālote's time, and increased the responsibilities of her consort. After spending his days in the Premier's office in Nuku'alofa, Tungī Mailefihi spent his nights at the Fua'amotu airfield, for to him fell the task of organizing the materials donated by the nobles and labour donated by the people. When not at Fua'amotu, Tungi was often conferring with the New Zealand officers stationed at Mu'a and Nuku'alofa. Personal supervision, personal contact with the people, and sharing of tasks were the aspects of traditional leadership that appealed to Tungī, and at which he excelled. To be active among his people allowed Tungī to be seen at his best. It was in the midst of these duties that Tungī died of a heart attack, on Sunday, 20 July 1941, aged 54, at Uoleva, his house at Tatakamotonga, the chief village of his estate.

The diaries of Sione Filipe Tongilava show that on several occasions earlier that year Tungī had not been well. On the Saturday evening, 19 July, Tungī had dinner with Harry and Honor Maude, the Acting Agent & Consul and his wife, at the British Residency.[17] After dinner he returned briefly to the Palace and spoke with the Queen before leaving for Uoleva to organize food for the wedding of Vīlai's daughter Palu Vava'u to Tēvita Tu'ipulotu Toutaiolepo.[18] After church and lunch on Sunday, Tungī lay down for a nap. The heart attack occurred soon after.[19] The nearest telephone was at the airfield at Fua'amotu, and someone was sent to telephone the Palace and tell the Queen that Tungī was ill. The Queen sent for the Chief Medical Officer, then set out in her car for Tatakamotonga, with pillows to ease Tungī's journey back to town. It was only when she arrived at Tatakamotonga that she discovered that Tungī was already dead.

Instead of a lying-in-state in the throne room or Royal Chapel, Sālote had Tungī's body taken upstairs to her own room in the Palace.[20] There he lay until 22 July, when he was brought downstairs just before the funeral so the chiefs and *papālangi* leaders of the community could pay their last respects. Although Sālote was too stricken with grief to follow Tungī's body in the funeral procession, she decided every detail of the funeral, so that the ceremonies would in every respect be appropriate for the royal consort, highest-ranking male chief of the kingdom, descendant of the royal line of the Tu'i Ha'atakalaua, father of princes. In one matter she did not follow custom, for instead of being interred with his father and grandfather at Tatakamotonga, Tungī was put to rest with the members of the Tupou dynasty at the Mala'e Kula, in a vault destined to be Sālote's own resting place.

All of the passionate love that Sālote had felt for Tungī during the years of their marriage was concentrated in an outpouring of grief. This high chief had been her *hau* – her most loyal supporter and also a political ally who had carried much of the responsibility for realizing their joint policies. Their sons, Tupouto'a and Sione Ngū, were in Sydney, so Sālote felt there was no one with whom she could share her sorrow, and she kept to her room upstairs in the Palace. During this time of mourning no fires were lit at the Palace, and no food cooked. Food was prepared for the Queen at Talakaepau, but she could neither eat or sleep, spending her days and nights in weeping, "*'Eiki, tokoni mai*" (Lord, help me). The *tapu* that prevented the chiefs or people from approaching her in her grief did not apply to foreigners, so one of the Queen's women (Nānisi Helu) went to the Mission House and confided their concern for the Queen to Rodger Page.[21]

Two years earlier, Hannah Page, Rodger Page's wife, had died after a brief illness, and Sālote and Tungī had made all the arrangements, providing mats and bark cloth appropriate for a chiefly funeral and a burial place at Mala'e 'Aloa, the burial ground of the chiefs.[22] So it was as a recently bereaved husband as well as royal chaplain that Rodger Page came to comfort Sālote as she had so recently comforted him. The *tapu* that prevented Tongans from eating in her presence did not apply to him, so each day he brought a basket of food to the Palace and stood at the foot of the stairs, calling up to her for permission to ascend. When this permission was granted, Page would climb the stairs and persuade the Queen to eat a little of the food he had brought.

Gradually the Queen began to take up her duties again. In those early days of her widowhood, she later recalled, she was sustained only by her Christian faith. However, as she wrote to her close friend Sau Faupula (whose young wife had died earlier that year), her faith was strained in the struggle to keep going.

> *27 July*. I pray and read the Bible – but by habit, not with thought. One should prepare in good days so one can bear trouble – so one does not panic when meeting a loss like this. I am preparing for the days to come, when our relatives have gone away.
>
> *28 July*. Page was overcome with emotion [at the memorial service for Tungī]. Page was one of Tungi's best friends, and he tried to bring out everything he knew about him. All that he said were truths I felt inwardly and outwardly, and he told so much that people could not take it in . . .
>
> *29 Sept*. The problems of loneliness, as you said, are really overwhelming. [TFB]

Sālote's love for Tungī had been expressed in joyous love songs (such as *Tòli Fisi*) during his lifetime. Now her grief for his death was expressed in love songs and laments.[23] There is haunting poetry in these songs, which were set to plaintive music. For example, *'Oketi*, for which Queen Sālote wrote both words and music.

1. Si'i hengihengi e kuo 'alu
Kapakau ai si'ete manatu
Ki he 'oketi fisi e hahau
Tauleva ki he pa'anga ngalu.

2. 'Anga'anga ni kuo me'a noa
Ka falala he funga hau'alofa
Ki ho 'imisi maka koloa
Tui fakaholo ko hoto kahoa.

3. Ta'alo e malu 'i he efiafi
Pea te hahanu launoa ki ai
Ke 'iloa mai 'ene tupulaki
'A e 'ofa he poukei langakali.

Tau: Sino ni 'a pe ka melie lau
Pea kona ai ki ha'o fekau
Ka neongo ia 'e Kalatiola
Na'a kuo ta'engata ha'ata ni 'ofa.

* * *

1. Gone is that dear dawn
To which, as wings, clung my remembrances
Of the orchid, the bloom of the dew,
(Which I) Adorn till the end of time.

2. This body has become a thing of no worth
Overcome by all-conquering love
For your image of precious stones
I will string them for my garland.

3. The shade of evening beckons
To which I direct my lamentations.
If the magnitude were only known
Of the love (I bear) for the bouquet of langakali.

Chorus: Alas that this body, sweet enticement to gossip,
Is only poison to your mission.
Yet do you not see, Gladiola,[24]
This love of mine may never end. [MT]

The qualities of Tungī's personality and leadership were appreciated by many people only after his death. Harry Maude, like his predecessors as Consul, had a great affection for Tungī, and in a personal letter to Luke he showed a perceptive appreciation of Tungī's role in the government of Tonga.

> This terrible blow which has struck Tonga has caused us all to realize, what one was apt to take for granted at that time, that everything in the Kingdom revolved round Tungi and that it was his engaging personality and ability to "put things over" with the Tongans which caused the local administration to work so easily . . . Tungi was equally at home in European and Tongan circles, and discussions with him were a real pleasure. I don't believe that I have ever felt the death of anyone so keenly – for Tonga it is a sheer tragedy . . . The Queen was quite prostrate with grief and could not attend the ceremony . . .
>
> Up to the present the Queen has kept strictly to her bedroom at the top of the Palace and has only come down twice since Tungi's death. Once to attend a memorial service [the one referred to in the letter of 28 July quoted above] . . . and once to listen to the broadcast tributes to Tungi from Suva radio.[25]

So erratic were communications in wartime that Tupouto'a and Sione Ngū read of Tungī's death in the Sydney newspapers before the Queen's telegrams reached them. The princes asked the Queen to delay the final ceremonies of the funeral until their return, but when the princes could not come home that Christmas holiday, the Queen decided not to delay any further. Deferral would have meant that members of the Ha'a Tufunga (the attendants for a royal funeral) and Tungī's *kau matāpule* would remain at the graveside instead of joining the rest of the population, which was evacuated to the countryside after the bombing of Pearl Harbor.

There was another departure from custom, for Uoleva, the house where Tungī had died, was now *tapu* and should have been burned to the ground. But, because of a shortage of timber, the Queen agreed to a proposal by Rodger Page that the house be taken to Toloa, where Tupou College had its farm, and where the College was destined to move after the war. Tungī's house, joined to Page's old house from I on the south-east coast of Tongatapu, has been the residence of the Principal of Tupou College for the past 50 years.

During the months of mourning following Tungī's death, Sālote walked after dark along the beach front of Kolomotu'a with one or more of her women in order to get exercise. She sometimes called at the British Residency during these walks to talk to Armstrong about matters relating to the war, and to plan with Margaret Armstrong the various activities that had come to a halt because of public mourning and which would not resume without the Queen's leadership. Also, Sālote sometimes called at the Mission House in the evening, as she had done with Tungī before the war, to discuss church and other matters with Rodger Page, who was not only her counsellor in her grief, her chaplain, a censor, and a member of the Home Guard, but also her unofficial adviser on almost everything.

To succeed Tungī as Premier the Queen appointed Ata (Solomone Ula), a longtime friend of Tungī, described by Collocott as "a gay and friendly man, an excellent athlete, whose perfect balance of body and grace of movement were a joy to the eye".[26] Ata was about 58 years old when he became Premier, had been Minister for Lands since 1925, and was renowned for his fine tenor voice and skill as a tennis player. Tungī and Ata had often sung duets at evening parties at the Mission House, and Ata had graced the local tennis courts.

Ata already had a unique position among the chiefs, his Western District title entitling him to speak openly to the Queen. As a noble and a Privy Councillor, Ata had already sworn to serve the Queen, and wartime agreements meant he would now be obliged to listen and act upon the advice of the Consul even more than Tungī had done. Sālote sometimes felt that she could not go on, but the demands of the time and the needs of the people roused her from her sorrow. Standing alone, she would show her capacity to deal with a situation that once again threatened her authority. Unlike the British, the American forces who would come in 1942 assumed that they were in total charge of the kingdom of Tonga, and acted accordingly.

CHAPTER FOURTEEN

America Invades Tonga

"a good many have lost their sense of values . . ." (Queen Sālote, 1942)[1]

ON 7 DECEMBER 1941 THE JAPANESE bombed the American Pacific Naval Fleet at Pearl Harbor and 240 planes on the ground at Hickham Field in Hawai'i. Within a few hours, at noon on 8 December (local time), Tonga declared war on Japan, along with "the allies" and the United States of America.[2] The difference between the war with Germany and the war with Japan was that although Germany had warships and submarines in the Pacific, they had not directly threatened Tonga. Now the possibility facing Tonga was invasion.

Since the Japanese had been everywhere in the Pacific in the 1930s, they were very well informed about harbours and installations. Vava'u, the northern group of the Tongan islands, had an excellent harbour, and the capital, Nuku'alofa, had a wireless station with a wide range. It was feared that the Japanese would bomb the wireless station before swooping across the Pacific to cut off the USA from Australia, the logical base for an attempt to halt the frighteningly swift Japanese advance. Further, the USA needed a string of airfields across the Pacific, and the one so painstakingly built at Fua'amotu by the Tongans and New Zealanders was highly desirable.

When the news of the bombing of Pearl Harbor reached Tonga, the girls and boys who had been at boarding schools on the main island of Tongatapu were immediately sent to their homes, the *Hifofua* (government steamer) appearing, seemingly miraculously, to take those who lived in the central and northern island groups of Ha'apai and Vava'u. Fear of invasion by the Japanese was such that *papālangi* and part-*papālangi* women and children were compulsorily evacuated on the *Matua*, which left Nuku'alofa on 20 December 1941. The *Matua* normally accommodated 40 passengers, but 250 were crammed aboard. The evacuees landed at Fiji or New Zealand, some making their way to Australia. The expected south-east thrust by Japan did not eventuate, as the Japanese instead moved rapidly southwards. Many of the *Matua* passengers returned to Tonga as soon as the authorities permitted them to do so.

One of the unwilling evacuees was Margaret Armstrong, wife of the British Agent & Consul. Another was Mrs Mary Thompson, the principal of Queen Sālote College, as the Kolisi Fefine was now called.[3] During Mrs Thompson's year-long absence and the requisitioning of the college by the military in 1942, the Queen offered land on her estate at Tufumāhina, beside the lagoon, for classes taught by the Tongan staff. Government College (to be renamed Tonga College in 1943) moved inland to 'Atele at the beginning of 1942, and its old site was requisitioned; as was Vaiola Hospital near by and the Catholic boys' school, 'Api Fo'ou, at Ma'ufanga, about three kilometres eastward along the coast from Nuku'alofa.

At the outbreak of war with Japan the inhabitants of Nuku'alofa were ordered to remove themselves from the capital and the vicinity of the wireless station and stay with their relatives in the villages for fear of bombing. The Queen set a good example by retiring first to Fua'amotu and then to 'Ahononou, on the southern coast. Tongan houses are easily erected, and a large house was built at 'Ahononou for the Queen under the shelter of trees that provided camouflage. The Queen's house was about 30 feet by 15 feet, with a raised wooden floor, woven coconut-leaf walls and a coconut-leaf thatched roof. The Queen was accompanied by a retinue of her ADC, Guards, and women attendants, and visitors came and went as at the Palace. Smaller Tongan houses were built around the main house to serve as the Queen's bath-house, the kitchen, and to house the Royal Guards, retinue, and visitors. Margaret Armstrong noted that the Queen's bath-tub was made of a solid piece of wood, four feet across, hollowed out and placed in her private bath-house. Near the house was a sheltered beach, where her attendants and the Royal Guards could bathe, and a large cave in which the entire royal household could shelter in the event of an air raid. The Queen described the house at 'Ahononou as her "little coconut-leaf house", but she was more comfortable than many commoners who were evacuated and who found life difficult because both shelter and drinking water were in short supply in the villages.[4]

The skeleton Siale Falanisē was again in demand, for the Queen foresaw casualties if the airfield at Fua'amotu was bombed by the Japanese. A letter she wrote on 23 December 1941 from Halaliku to Sau Faupula, then a tutor at

Tupou College, shows not only her expectation that Tonga would be bombed but also attention to detail and thoroughness, and her willingness to assist the war effort in practical ways.

> I am writing this letter as a request. If you can send Siale Falanisē here to Fua'amotu for some First Aid classes, I shall call together some of the women. Uiliami Tufui [a graduate of the Central Medical School] can teach them and I can help. Then we shall be ready to help injured soldiers at the airfield. I have told the First Aid group in town to consult the doctor in charge if any emergency occurs: they should also help nurses at the hospital. No preparations have been made here, so I told the Fua'amotu people to form their own First Aid group. Uiliami has agreed to give classes and to give instructions to the women on how to treat injured people. Siale can be looked after at the minister's place during the time of the classes, which will go on for two or three weeks. Once the teaching about the bones is over, we shall return Siale. If you leave Siale at Mr Page's home [in Nuku'alofa], I shall fetch Siale and bring him here. [TFB]

On 2 March 1942, she wrote again to Sau Faupula, a letter that showed her warmth and concern for people, and treating her own discomforts with humour. Indeed the Queen's sense of humour is often apparent in her letters to Sau.

> I am making a request for some of your sugar cane from Toloa [where the Tupou College farm was]. If this is all right, some men will go from here and get it. I need it to finish my house, for it is all done now except the verandah. If you are coming to Toloa again, bring some of the others over to have a Games Night (there are some games here that we are using) and to see my house. I am grateful for the love of the people in providing a house for me to live and hide in. Surely there is a crumb of your memorial service for Sione Havea [formerly Head Tutor of Tupou College, who had just died] that we may share, for in such an abundant life we must be able to have a share and there be some over.
>
> We were talking about Sione Havea yesterday with Moeaki and Peseti, who spent Sunday with us. Talakai preached the sermon. It was of spiritual value, but unfortunately it rained very heavily and the church was flooded. Talakai was all right because he stood up to preach, but we sat down and were almost swimming in the middle of the building, and some things came to pieces as I tried to stop shivering. [DR]

In 1942 New Zealand handed over the defence of Tonga to the United States of America. The Queen agreed that the USA could use Tonga as a base for the duration of the Pacific War, but neither the Queen nor her advisers knew exactly when American forces would come or how many. An American warship and seaplane arrived on 3 March 1942, and on 31 March two reconnaissance officers. During April more ships came, including a hospital ship, which soon departed for the Battle of the Coral Sea. On 29 April another 10 or 11 warships arrived and soon departed. On 9 and 15 May troopships arrived with 7000 soldiers and 1000 Navy personnel and a squadron of the US Army Air Corps to set up the American bases on Tongatapu. Armstrong estimated that the initial force of BLEACHER (as it was codenamed), which effectively took over the island on 9 May, equalled about half the total population of Tongatapu (that is, about 10,000). At one time there were nearly 40 ships in Nuku'alofa harbour.[5] When Army, Navy, and Air Corps put in to harbour en route to the battlefields, the number of strangers could exceed the total population of Tongatapu. It seems that something like 30,000 Americans visited Tonga for short or long periods during the war years.

Everything from the BLEACHER ships had to be offloaded at Vuna wharf, with the exception of barges that went ashore at Ma'ufanga. The lists of material that went ashore, as recorded in the official US "History of Tongatabu", are awesome: equipment and tools of all kinds, weaponry, vehicles, tents and Quonset huts, refrigerators, machinery to drill for water, fuel, and vast quantities of food and beverages. The US forces requisitioned 767 acres of land, some for the extension of the runway at the airfield, to be covered with steel Marston matting. Tongans under the direction of New Zealanders had already carried out 80 per cent of the work on the airfield for US$56,000, and the remaining 20 per cent was completed by the Americans for just under US$500,000. "This type of wild spending both overawed and amused the New Zealanders", commented the US official historian.[6] Between April and October 1942 the airfield was a base for Kittyhawks, and later for fighter planes and transit aircraft.

A farm at Vaikeli provided fresh vegetables for the US forces and also for the New Zealanders. Anti-aircraft units of the 77th US Coastal Artillery set up on the north coast and at the airfield; the Navy Advanced Base was at Ma'ufanga; the Construction Battalion at Havelu, just south of Nuku'alofa; the US Air Corps at Fua'amotu. At the height of the "invasion" (as the Americans called it) there were 13 camps scattered over Tongatapu, and 5000 soldiers lived in requisitioned or especially built Tongan houses. The remainder lived in Quonset huts, which replaced tents in coconut groves, under the trees for camouflage, coconuts being removed from the trees and thrown away, as it did not occur to the Americans that these were Tonga's primary cash crop. However, copra soon took second place as an income-earner, because providing services for the American troops proved to be very lucrative for the local people.

Siupeli Taliai tells how as a schoolboy at Tupou College, Nafualu, situated on the main road to the Western District, the first he knew of the arrival of the Americans was the sound and sight of many ten-wheeled trucks being driven past the school in clouds of dust one Sunday afternoon. In the following months, students closely observed the goings-on in the US Army camp next to the school. On Saturday nights, Siupeli and a friend rode their bicycles from Kolovai (where Siupeli's father was the Free Wesleyan minister) out to Ha'atafu on the westernmost tip of Tongatapu to watch American movies.[7]

Sir Harry Luke came for a visit a few days before the arrival of the troopships. The visit was a surprise, and the Queen described the occasion to Sau Faupula in a letter dated 8 May 1942.

> This is a funny thing. The Governor of Fiji [Luke] arrived here suddenly on Monday without anyone letting us know. We [i.e. her attendants] rushed about putting in order the little coconut leaf house, for no preparation had been made. However, we went in and sat down on the floor together and talked for a long time, and then we visited the singing practice of the Primary School that was being held in the church. Liongi said that the dresses of the singers were worse than my coconut leaf house, but they were hidden by the beauty of the children's singing, and it was the same with my house – the dirty coconut leaf walls were concealed by our interesting conversation. It turned out that the Premier's Office had been notified, but the Secretary [to Government] forgot to tell us.[8] [DR]

The Queen did not record her thoughts on the arrival of the Americans, but wrote on 14 May that the Minister for Lands had been to ask her about land for the Americans to build their hospital and cemetery. People who live on small islands are always preoccupied with food supplies and preparations for ritual. The Queen was no exception, and recorded where food crops and *hiapo* (the mulberry bushes whose inner bark [*tutu*] was used for bark cloth) were planted.

> I miss Tungi more than ever these days. His knowledge and reliable strength were always a stand-by . . . We have started our *'ufi* [yam] planting with the Guards, and begun clearing our left side. If it had not been for the annual collection, for which the people had to prepare the copra, the people of 'Ahononou would also have begun planting, but they will do that after the bazaar. Taka-'i-Houma from 'Eua [the island east of Tongatapu] is here, and we have decided that he will cultivate our little crop. 'Eua is possibly better for planting *tutu*, but I am not sure about that. [TFB]

The Queen also directed the preserving of bananas, which was done by peeling the bananas and storing the fruit in pits in the ground, where it fermented (17 May 1942, DR). In a the letter of 24 May, she showed that her personal grief was still overwhelming:

> One feels the heaviness of the burden only when one stops and starts, stops and

starts. The way to do it is to do it continuously, and one gets used to it . . . I don't really mind the burden because I am looking forward to the return of Tupouto'a and Ngū to share it. What I care about is to do things in the right way, so that when the time comes for someone else to carry on the work, there are no problems of mine for them, only those of their own making. If there are problems, it is because of my limited knowledge. . . . We widows and widowers with children are fortunate, for we have hopes. Yet even those without hopes should trust in the Lord, who will guide us. Time seems to pass slowly, but in fact time goes very quickly, for it will be only a little while [until death]. I sometimes try to find consolation by thinking, but that only brings more worries. Let God have His own way in His own time, for that is true peace. [TFB]

The Americans had assumed that Tongans would be "savages", and were surprised to find schools, medical services, clean villages, and polite and intelligent inhabitants who were regular church attenders and practising Christians.[9] They also found a land fertile for food crops and a sea full of fish, with pigs and chickens to add occasional interest to the menu. Only a few Tongans were businessmen or professionals, the majority being full-time farmers and fishermen. Small stores in the villages were adjuncts of businesses in Nuku'alofa, acting as collection points for copra and doing only casual selling. At that time most Tongans lived in houses made out of poles covered with branches of the coconut palm, the poles being more or less permanent, and the coconut branches being renewed every year or so. Except for the occasional hurricane or tropical downpours of rain, the climate was pleasant and sufficiently warm for light clothing year-round. There were telephones and electricity only at the Palace and a few other homes, but that did not bother the Americans, who brought their own. There were a few dozen motor-cars in Tonga, most (but not all) belonging to *papālangi*. Better-off Tongans owned a cart, implying ownership of a malnourished and often ill-treated horse, and for most Tongans walking from one side of the island to the other presented no difficulty. Tonga was the best place in the world for people who wanted a quiet, uneventful, healthy existence; but all that changed when the Americans came.

The Americans took over coastwatching from the Tonga Defence Force and built a series of huge observation towers across Tongatapu, including one 75 feet high at the end of Vuna wharf. On board the hospital ships were 47 doctors and 52 nurses, who set up the 900-bed 7th Evacuation Hospital at Houma, on the south coast, ready for the wounded from other parts of the Pacific.[10] An American military cemetery was established at Mataki'eua, on the slope of the hill above the lagoon, and on 31 July 1942 the first 10 American naval and marine personnel were buried there. Before long, 20 more US servicemen were buried there, and six New Zealanders.[11]

It was intended that the US Navy Advanced Base around Ma'ufanga would set up sufficient storage space for provisions for one-third of the US fleet. Thus the Navy not only took over the large Burns Philp warehouse but also assembled 17 large Quonset huts for stores, and built two tank farms for fuel.

Black American troops of the 77th US Coastal Artillery were segregated from *papālangi* American troops. The *papālangi* officers took over the house formerly belonging to the businessman Arthur Cocker on the main street in Nuku'alofa as a club, and the Queen sent a gift of mats. Officers could also join the local *papālangi* at the Nuku'alofa Club. The *papālangi* US troops had their recreation area at the old Government College site, while the Black troops had theirs at the village of Kolonga, on the north-east coast about 20 kilometres from Nuku'alofa by road, and separated from it by the lagoon.

The Americans claimed that the Tongans welcomed their friendliness after the standoffishness of the British and "colonials". The Armstrongs, on the other hand, deplored the racial segregation in the American armed forces and reported that they and their Tongan staff and neighbours had very friendly relations with the members of the all-Black unit in charge of anti-aircraft defence on Sia-ko-Veiongo, the hill behind the British Residency.[12]

The Queen granted the US Island Commander, Brigadier-General B. C. Lockwood, and Commander C. E. Olsen (in charge of the US Naval contingent), an audience, but by agreement with the British, the Agent & Consul (Armstrong until mid-1943, then C. W. T. Johnson) represented the government of Tonga in consultations with the Americans, keeping the Queen and the Premier, Ata, informed. A very time-consuming argument between the British and the Americans occurred over whether the whole of Tonga (as the British wished) or only Tongatapu (as the Americans wished) would be defended in the case of an attack. This was a strange argument since Vava'u harbour, widely considered to be one of the best in the Pacific, would be left unprotected if the American view prevailed – as it did.

New Zealand officers in the Tonga Defence Force had been given their commissions by Queen Sālote and had sworn loyalty to her, but the US forces acted independently of the government of Tonga, and felt that "The goddam British were always poking their noses in it".[13] Until the New Zealander Brigadier-General F. L. Hunt took over from Lockwood as Island Commander on 2 March 1943 there were in effect two governments in Tonga: the US ruled the US military, while the Queen ruled the Tongan population and the Tonga Defence Force, with the British Agent & Consul as her adviser and channel of communication with the US officers. The arrangement worked well enough, but only because the Queen and Consul rarely challenged US actions. The US choice of the word "invasion" to describe their presence in Tonga suggests they felt licensed to act as conquerors, and the US Navy often ignored the authority of Hunt and his successor, Major Hardy, as Island Commander.

In comparison, life at ʻAhononou was quite relaxed. When Margaret Armstrong went to spend a few days with the Queen, she was surprised to find Sālote sitting cross-legged on a deck chair. Of course the Queen was never alone: there were always women to attend her at all times of the day or night, to sleep on the floor near her bed to guard her, and to carry out her instructions. There were also servants to prepare her food, clean the house, and do the laundry. There were male and female "relatives" who came to visit for shorter or longer periods. The Queen would not withhold permission for their coming. Sometimes a group of musicians came in the evening so the Queen could work on the settings for her latest poems. The Queen also chose women to whom she could impart her knowledge, so they could carry on her knowledge of genealogies and traditions. It was a relaxation to write poetry and to reflect on matters that were of continuing interest to her, instead of thinking too much about the occupation of her country by foreigners. Her reflections were sometimes conveyed to Sau Faupula.

> Liongi and I were talking about your inquiry about the word *fakalekesi* ("with special care"), and ʻAhio's saying that it was a Samoan word, and I said, "ʻAhio only is Samoan; the word is a true Tongan word." It refers to something that one does for oneself and does not do as a family as we do many things, because *fakaleke* means to provide one's own little separate room, which is one's *leke*. I believe it comes from the looking after the bundle of mats belonging to chiefly women, whose valuable treasure was put into a bundle. Not many people had to do with making it up – only oneself and one's own touched it. It was a wonderful thing to see how carefully it was made up and the care taken that the little creases were made to lie flat, and the looking out for moths – work to be done only by the steadfast and the very patient. If it was a very large bundle, it was often left for old women to do. There was a particular type of tying – it was not tied up anyhow. And so I believe that the word was derived from this work, for it was the work that was done *fakalekeleke'aki*.[14] [DR]

In the same letter the Queen proposed visiting Nafualu on Wesley Day (held on 20 May instead of the usual 24 May in 1942). She was concerned with the practical arrangements, and not imposing on the Tupou College community. The visit was made to keep in touch with her people, not to show her own importance.

> If it is held there [at Nafualu], perhaps you will consent to our going and staying in your house, for it is too far to go from here just to the service [and back in one day]. If you do entertain us, please just do it in the same way as when we went to the annual collection. This is a much smaller affair, for it is only a church society thing. I shall discuss with Liongi how the members of our Fuaʻamotu Christian

> Endeavour will get to you, as we do not wish to be a trouble to anyone; we can provide people to prepare our meals. The thing that matters is that we don't have a lot of eating on this visit. Otherwise the little thing I have prepared [her talk] will be swamped by other events, valuable as these may be at the right time. A Tongan house will be quite sufficient for Fua'amotu [people], and one room and a verandah will be quite enough for me . . . [DR]

The Queen maintained the dignity of her position, as far as the military were concerned, by remaining aloof. This was consistent with her pre-war relationship with *papālangi* (which was distant), but little of any significance happened among the Tongan population without her knowledge, either before or after the event. Thus, while appearing to be in retirement at 'Ahononou, Queen Sālote had constant personal contact with her own people through established networks and did what she could to control their behaviour in an uncontrollable situation. She encouraged young women of chiefly rank to go to other islands,[15] but the majority of the population of Tongatapu stayed put, fraternized seven days a week, and found life full of new and exciting events.

Armstrong and his successor, Johnson, had difficulty persuading the Americans that it was not necessary to shoot Tongans who came too near to the US stores, and trying to get small compensations for damage to property or injuries suffered at the hands of over-the-top troops. Indeed, one can only conclude after reading the accounts of their stay that the US troops were generally out of control during the whole of their time in Tonga. Behind the 1942 excesses were the high spirits of young men going to war, and behind those of 1943–45 the boredom of standing guard over inert matter.

The Tongans were extremely curious about the Americans and overwhelmed at the sight of their material possessions. The Americans needed local labour to assist with the unloading of their supplies and setting up camps, and to do laundry and the like. It was estimated that about 100 members of the Tonga Defence Force worked on unloading ships, 160 in camp construction, 70 on maintenance of roads, 60 on the airfield, and 88 employed by the US Army and another 350 by the Navy in miscellaneous duties.[16] Other Tongans worked in the camps, waited on tables, and did manual work. Some worked on the Army farm growing *papālangi* vegetables, sold their own Tongan vegetables and fruit, and loaded up carts with mats, baskets, and what the Americans called "hula skirts" (*sisis*) to sell at the camps. Tupou College boys were offered £2 a month to wait on tables at the airfield during their holidays, which was very welcome to those students over 16 years of age who had to pay taxes. Women who were molested or raped were well paid by their attackers to keep quiet.[17] Although some Americans took advantage of Tongan gullibility (one soldier "sold" a jeep to a Tongan), many others were generous, and many genuine – if shortlived – friendships were formed.

Left: Nose-flute players Ahiohio, Veʻehala, and unidentified. Early in the morning of 20 December 1953, they played outside the Palace where Queen Elizabeth II and the Duke of Edinburgh were staying. *Courtesy of David Attenborough.* [93]

Below: Feast during the royal visit to Tonga, 19–20 December 1953. *Left to right:* Queen Elizabeth II, Lavinia Kalanivalu, Queen Sālote, the Duke of Edinburgh. *Courtesy of Alan Sayers.* [94]

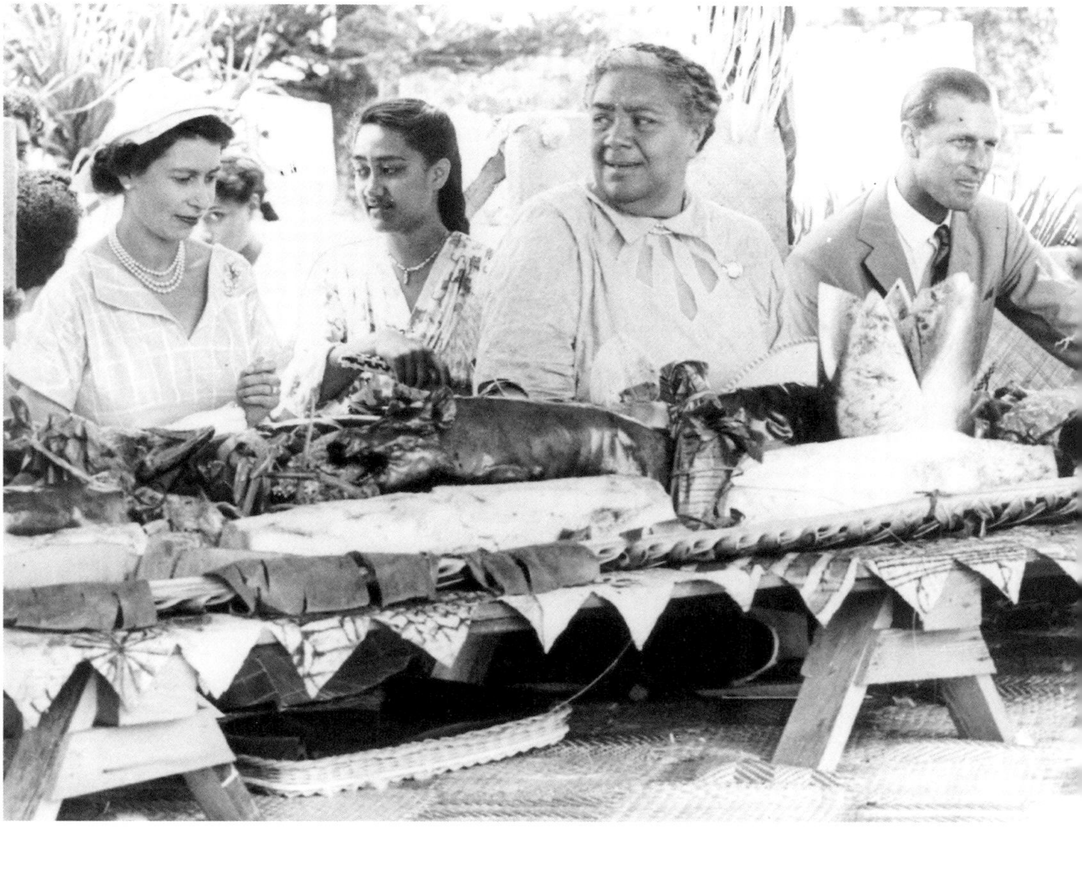

RIGHT: Nuku'alofa, 1950s, the Stone Building refurbished. The building still housed the Premier's and other government departments. *Courtesy of Ray Harrison.* [96]

BELOW: British Commissioner and Consul to Tonga, A. C. Reid, 1957–59, 1965–70. [95]

BELOW: Crown Prince and Premier Tupouto'a-Tungī, 1950s. *Courtesy of Ray Harrison.* [97]

ABOVE: The Centenary Church, Nuku'alofa. The project was mooted in 1926 to mark the centenary of the coming of Christianity to Tonga. Rodger Page returned to Tonga to supervise the moving of the old church in 1950. Volunteers did much of the construction work between 1950 and 1952. The official opening was on 25–27 September 1952. There are glass doors on both sides, which can be opened to include an outdoors congregation. *Courtesy of Kurt Düring.* [98]

Left: David Attenborough and Ve'ehala (Leilua) plan the filming of the *taumafa kava* of the Tu'i Kanokupolu at the Lo'au of 1959. *Courtesy of David Attenborough.* [101]

Below: Queen Sālote arrives to open Parliament. She is wearing the modern official Tongan costume, including one of the royal fine-mats. [99]

Right: Queen Sālote and Dilys Rowlands present prizes (turtle shells) at the Langa Fonua annual show. For some years this show replaced the annual agricultural show that was started by Tungī Mailefihi in the 1920s. *Courtesy of Kurt Düring.* [100]

RIGHT: Rehearsal for the *taumafa kava* of the Tu'i Kanokupolu, 1959. *Left to right:* Tupou Posesi Fanua (seated and taking notes), Ve'ehala (Leilua), Elizabeth Bott Spillius, Queen Sālote. *Courtesy of David Attenborough.* [102]

BELOW: Feast at Houma, 1959. David Attenborough is guest of honour on the right of the host, Vaea ('Alipate Tupou). *Courtesy of David Attenborough.* [103]

Left: The process of making bark cloth. *Top to bottom:* The bark is beaten into strips using a mallet on a tree trunk; *Kupesi* (patterns) are placed on a rounded board, and the white bark cloth is placed over the *kupesi*, so the pattern may be rubbed through; the definitive pattern is painted on by hand. The painters are Popua Akaveka (*née* Hokafonu), Mafile'o and Kapea Hokafonu, and the child is Fipe (now Sio). *Courtesy of David Attenborough.* [104]

Above: Baskets are made for carrying food, 1959. In the middle is Mele Mataele. *Courtesy of David Attenborough.* [105]

Left: Men bring food for the re-enactment of the *pongipongi* of Vaea ('Alipate Tupou), 1959. *Courtesy of David Attenborough.* [106]

LEFT: Queen Sālote, accompanied by Lutui, one of her *matāpule* from Ha'apai, arrives at the re-enactment of the *pongipongi* of Vaea, 1959. She is wearing one of the *kie hingoa* (named royal fine-mats). *Courtesy of David Attenborough.* [107]

BELOW: Bringing the *kava* root at the *taumafa kava* of the re-enactment of the *pongipongi* of Vaea, 1959. *Courtesy of David Attenborough.* [108]

Right: The making of the *kava* by Sefesi at the *taumafa kava*, 1959. *Top to bottom*: A stone is used on another stone to pound a piece of the root; the pieces of pounded root are placed in the *kava* bowl and water is added; Sefesi uses movements similar to those of dancers in the process of straining the root from the *kava*. *Courtesy of David Attenborough*. [109]

Security was erratic. When, on a Saturday, villagers swept up their leaves and burned them (their custom in preparation for the Sabbath), the Americans claimed that they were signalling to the enemy. When people carried lights along the roads at night to see their way home or when making their way to the backyard dunnies, they were accused of deliberately infringing the blackout regulations. On the other hand, the Americans did not think to advise the Queen's Private Secretary, Sione Filipe Tongilava, of the need for discretion, and he carefully recorded the number and type of ships coming into and leaving the harbour – a useful record if the Japanese had invaded!

The Americans believed there was no need to consult the locals about defence. As a consequence, early in 1942 the US survey ship *Sumner* ignored signals from the Tonga Defence Force shore battery commanding it to stop. A shot was fired over the *Sumner*'s bows, and when the shot was ignored, a second shot was fired. Only then did the *Sumner* stop and allow a pilot to board. Armstrong pointed out to the angry captain that Tonga had already been at war for two and a half years, and that the survey ship could have been a Japanese ship flying an American flag for all the shore battery knew.[18]

On 26 May 1942 a Royal New Zealand Air Force (RNZAF) Vincent scout bomber, whose top speed was 140 kilometres an hour, was taking photographs over Tongatapu when it was fired on by 10 American warships, and the air-raid warning sounded, sending people plunging into the ditches dug for just such a contingency. The plane came lower in order to show its insignia (under the misapprehension that the Americans would recognize the insignia of their allies), which resulted in more firing, but no hits.[19] The name of the New Zealand pilot, McKay, is still remembered in Tonga.

Such misunderstandings were soon cleared up. Although fraternization was officially prohibited, none of the villages was actually out of bounds to the American troops, so they were welcomed into Tongan homes. The Tongans gave them fresh food, and received cigarettes, beer, and tinned food in return. Cigarettes were widely available for the first time and smoking became commonplace in Tonga. And Tongans learned the elementary skills required to make home-brew to sell to the American soldiers.

Movies had been seen in Tonga before the war, but nothing like the new films, which were shown in banana sheds for the American troops and any Tongans who cared to attend. Marching and brass bands and ceremonies, including the raising and lowering of the flag, were also familiar, but these were now seen on a hitherto-unknown scale. Bugles and drums that had been the backbone of brass bands were eclipsed by new instruments and new music. There had been horseraces before, but there was now such a demand for this form of entertainment that the few horses capable of running at any speed appeared in different races under different names.

The Queen realized that the foreigners had plenty of money to spend and were looking for amusements. She encouraged regular bazaars and entertainments, such as *papālangi*-style dances, at which Americans could spend their money to the benefit of the various wartime funds. She also encouraged the making of handicrafts to sell to the soldiers, who were wild for things to send home before they went to the war zone. In addition to supporting the Red Cross and Tongan Comforts Fund, Tonga collected enough money during the war to buy four Spitfires for Great Britain's Royal Air Force. The three planes that were commissioned were named the *Queen Sālote*, *Prince Tungī*, and *Tupou I*, and the first two were flown in combat in Europe.[20] Tonga's overall contribution was outstanding for a country of its size and population, and its financial contribution considerably more than that of any other Pacific nation. This was, of course, at the instigation of Queen Sālote, who was proud of Tonga's role as part of the British Empire.

Before the war, Tongans had been reluctant to relinquish their preferred way of life in order to earn money. But that was at a time when a great deal of effort was required to obtain very little money. Now there was money in abundance, and very little effort required to obtain it. Every adult and many children on Tongatapu had the chance to earn, and were thus the envy of Tongans of the central and northern islands, who did not have those opportunities. Some of this excess money eventually reached the churches via the *misinale* (annual collection), a boon to the church schools, which had suffered considerably from the shortage of cash during the Depression and the disruption of the "invasion".[21] The Catholic Father Rodgers noted that "Father Boussit had more money than ever before! He made me preach and he took a collection at Ma'ufanga every Sunday."[22] The government benefited from the increased price of copra. Revenue for 1938/39 had been only £60,441; in 1941/42 it was £73,877, in 1942/43 it was £116,181, and in 1945/46 it was £136,014.[23]

Schoolboys who had not had pencils when the American troops arrived soon found themselves the possessors of fountain pens, boots, and new shirts. Other students ran away from school to hang around the camps, looking for opportunities to earn money. With money so easy to obtain, planting declined. At the Closing of Parliament in 1942, the Queen urged the people not to be overwhelmed by their change of circumstances: "Let us keep in mind the importance of our farms and urge our people to attend to them . . . we should warn our people about the pursuit of money because a good many have lost their sense of values . . . money is a good servant . . . but it is not a good master."[24] For once, her words were not heeded. The people realized that this was a once-in-a-lifetime opportunity and could not be persuaded to return exclusively to farming.

Men such as Tu'ilatai Mataele and women such as Tupou Posesi Fanua and Saiatua Lavulo were very much in demand because they spoke good English.[25] Tu'ilatai's grandfather, Siosaia Mataele, was a businessman and a member of

Parliament who had supported Chief Justice Stuart. Tu'ilatai's mother was Halaevalu, Sālote's cousin of very high chiefly rank (Figure 3.4). Tu'ilatai had learned English from American Mormon missionaries. When the Americans came, Tu'ilatai ran away from school and went to the wharf and asked for a job. The sailors gave him the nickname Joe, by which he is still known. After the war Joe was offered training in New Zealand, but he stayed in Tonga, used his wartime experience to start a stevedoring business, made a lot of money, married three times, and had many children.

Tupou was the only daughter of a minor chief, Fe'iloakitau Kaho. She had been "adopted" for a time by the Director of Education, Ragnar Hyne, and thus learned to speak English. In 1942 Tupou acted as an interpreter, and she enjoyed the contact with the Americans so much that she divorced her husband, Posesi, who was a medical officer with the Tonga Defence Force (where he learned to ride a motor bike), in order to be free to make friends with the Americans. Tupou really enjoyed the war, but when she took up residence with a naval officer, she was ostracized by the chiefly class and cut off the list of women invited to formal *papālangi*-style events. Only the determination of her uncle Sioape's wife, Muimui Kaho, rescued her from permanent social oblivion.

Saiatua Lavulo's mother's father was Benjamin Cocker, eldest son of Joshua Cocker. Saiatua was 25 years old in 1942, newly married to a policeman, when she was told that she had been appointed as the first Tongan policewoman. Tongan women infected with venereal diseases were put in jail, and Saiatua took them to the hospital to be treated by American Army doctors, and acted as interpreter between the doctors and their female patients.[26] Obedience to authority was so deeply inculcated in the Tongan mind that neither the government nor the women objected to this illegal detention. Because Tonga became a favoured place for leave from the battlefields, the incidence of venereal disease did not decline when the main body of troops moved on.

It seemed that the Queen was the only person in the kingdom who valued her privacy, and this inaccessibility led to comment and rumours. A scurrilous article appeared in the 30 August 1942 issue of *American Weekly*, and copies were circulated among the troops. The article claimed that the Queen was "ashamed of her heroic size and as she grew old and fat she developed an inferiority complex . . . [and was] unwilling to appear publicly", that she shunned *papālangi* society, and had outlived four husbands. It is true that in recent years the Queen's weight had grown out of proportion to her height (a temporary situation); but she was only 42 years of age, and very handsome. The Queen was devoted to the memory of her husband, and never considered remarrying. The article also ridiculed her arrival in robes, ermine-edged mantle, and crown to open Parliament in 1942, and said she would soon "turn over the government" to her two sons. The article came to the attention of Tongans, who were highly offended, and Ata wrote to Lockwood to protest about the "gratuitous insults" and to ask him to collect and destroy all copies in the kingdom.[27] Lockwood obliged as best he could.

As in pre-war Tonga, the Queen spent little time with *papālangi*, and her reclusiveness may have caused resentment among her wartime visitors. She remained at ʻAhononou except when reviewing the Tonga Defence Force, presiding over meetings in Nukuʻalofa, and making longer visits to Tupou College, at Nafualu. The Queen attended both the Annual Conference of the Free Wesleyan Church at Saione Motuʻa Chapel at Nafualu, and the Opening of Parliament in the Nafualu schoolhouse, both in June 1942. The formal Opening and Closing of Parliament had always been public occasions, and Americans watched the Queen's progress to the schoolhouse with fascination. Ever since her coronation in 1918 the Queen had followed the example of Tupou II by attending the Opening and Closing of Parliament dressed in her coronation robes and wearing a crown, accompanied by page boys dressed in white velvet and sporting feathered hats. There was covert and not-so-covert amusement among the Americans at this mimicking of British royalty, and their comments came to the Queen's attention, persuading her that it was time for a change. But she did not want it to appear that she was influenced by the American reaction, and during the remaining years of the war she sent noble representatives to Open and Close Parliament on her behalf. When, after the war, she again attended Parliament in person, she wore what would thereafter be her official costume: a long dress and one of her *kie hingoa*.

In her own way, Queen Sālote treated the Americans as the nation's guests. She realized that many of the Americans were extremely homesick, and she saw to it that parties were arranged for them, sent them food and other gifts according to Tongan custom, and met them at church, gratified when some soldiers showed a genuine interest in Christianity. On 24 May 1942 she wrote that some "white American soldiers" had sung an anthem at Fuaʻamotu: "We are very good friends, and they were very happy when the people showed their love, and they do care about the Church and its functions" [TFB].[28] But she thought it strange when some Americans invited themselves to sing for her or insisted on buying sweet potato she did not wish to sell.[29] Not surprisingly, the Americans did not understand Tongan royal protocol, and the Queen found their interest intrusive. In December 1942 the Consul asked American photographers to respect her privacy.

The war took its toll in lives in Tonga: an accidental drowning, a serviceman shot, a Tongan soldier who shot himself out of shame over the immorality of his sister, a woman killed by an Army truck, two children dead and five injured after they hit with sticks some shells they found on the sand flats near Nukunuku. Tongans died after drinking *hopi* (home-brew). A New Zealander drowned in spite of the efforts of two Tongan men to save him. Two Folaha men were killed in fighting between members of the Tonga Defence Force.[30]

Black American soldiers were blamed for the murder of two Tongans late in the evening of Sunday, 21 March 1943. Private battles between Tongans and American soldiers were not uncommon, and there had been a dispute at a dance the previous Friday, in which home-brew and the procuring of prostitutes played a part.[31] The shooting had occurred at Fua'amotu, and the Queen comforted the family. On 23 March 1943 she wrote:

> Three Americans shot two Tongans, brothers, at Fua'amotu. The Americans were Negroes. The two Tongans died and their mother was injured. The shooting was in anger, the result of a fight during a dance. The two men who were shot did not usually cause trouble at dances. Only one Negro has been caught and he is stubborn and reveals nothing about the others. Tupouto'a [the Crown Prince] decided to have the two men buried at once, and I stayed at Fua'amotu to help the parents. The woman may recover, but if she dies it will be because of her love for the two sons who have died already . . . Although the trouble was started by the Negroes, it was really caused by the dance, the home-brew, and the *pusipusi* [prostitutes]. [TFB][32]

Some Americans paid Tongans in advance for home-brew and prostitutes, and the Tongans did not always deliver, so both US soldiers and Tongan civilians were reluctant to co-operate in the subsequent investigation in case their illegal activities came to light. It seemed that several groups of soldiers were roaming the countryside that night, and no one was charged over the killings. No wonder that the Queen wished that there was less dancing during the war![33]

If Japan had won the long-drawn-out battle for Guadalcanal in 1942, Tonga would have become a major base for the US fleet; but Tonga's importance sharply declined with allied victories in the Pacific. In October 1942, 700 troops of the 34th Battalion (NZTS) took the place of the Americans who departed for the battle zones, making a garrison of 1697 New Zealand troops alongside 2118 Tongans, with 350 RNZAF. The New Zealanders, like their predecessors, were incorporated into the Tonga Defence Force. The 6th Canterbury Battalion replaced the 34th Battalion in March 1943, when Brigadier-General Hunt became Island Commander. In December 1943, 121 officers, 1066 other ranks, and two WAACS returned to New Zealand.[34] In February 1944, when Major Hardy took over from Hunt, the Tonga Defence Force was reduced to 38 New Zealand officers and 150 RNZAF, along with a small number of Tongan troops.

The New Zealanders had a lesser impact than the Americans on the Tongans.[35] Instead of bringing Quonset huts, hundreds of vehicles, and water-drilling and other equipment, as the Americans had done, the New Zealanders often had to make do with inferior equipment.[36] American generosity had fitted in very well with Tongan ideas of chiefly behaviour; by contrast, the New

Zealanders discriminated against the Tongans by paying their own men in the Tonga Defence Force more than they paid the Tongan equivalents.[37] The New Zealanders did not enjoy themselves as the Americans had done, but complained of lack of co-operation, of suffering "hardships and annoyances", and of enduring "improvisations and makeshifts which no European troops would have submitted to".[38] Nor would the New Zealanders permit Tongans to watch their movie shows.

During 1943 the Tongans who had been evacuated from Nuku'alofa were allowed to return to their homes. The Americans who remained in Tongatapu had too much time at their disposal, and lawlessness was the outcome of lax discipline. Drunkenness and brawling followed, and New Zealand soldiers were attacked and one killed by American soldiers.[39] Halaevalu recalled that it was "not all nice" to be in Nuku'alofa during the war, because Americans were constantly coming to the house to ask for home-brew.[40]

At about the same time as Hardy succeeded Hunt (February 1944) as Island Commander, Lieutenant-Commander Richard P. Hodsdon USNR assumed command of the US naval forces (which by then consisted of only five officers and 74 enlisted men) and also of other US forces still on the island. Hodsdon ignored the fact that Hardy was the senior officer. Officers who took unofficial leave in Tonga in 1943 and 1944 talked about but did not challenge Hodsdon, who "went native", living with one of Tonga's most notorious prostitutes, whom he had set up in her own house. Ribaldry resulted when the girl shared her favours – and indiscretions – with enlisted men.[41]

By that time most of the American officers lived openly with Tongan women.[42] Officers and other ranks made generous gifts to girlfriends and their families, including generators, carburettors, radios, food, cigarettes, alcohol, and petrol taken from American stores. At least one officer built an entire house for his girlfriend, using American materials and labour. One estimate quoted in the "History of Tongatabu" is that US$1 million worth of goods was given away to Tongans. Although that must be an exaggeration, it is clear that a great deal of Army and Navy property was given away to special friends. Hardly surprisingly, those Tongans who missed out on the largesse sometimes took matters into their own hands, helping themselves to the property that was (in many cases) either surplus to requirements or being given away to other villagers.

Other factors worked to exacerbate the situation. Whereas the Army drew most of its troops from the northern states, many of the Navy personnel (now effectively in charge) were from the racist southern states of America and therefore had little regard for the legal rights of the Tongans. And Hodsdon in effect relinquished command to the Navy doctor, Lieutenant-Commander Guyer, whose idea of a good evening out was to take a band of servicemen with loaded guns into the countryside, shoot at random, and beat up any Tongans they encountered.

In August 1944, thieves broke the padlock on a Navy warehouse (formerly belonging to Burns Philp) at Maʻufanga and (it was claimed) carried off 600 gallons of gasoline, 72 cases of cigarettes, 32 cases of beer, tools, and other equipment. Instead of referring the matter to the local police, the proper course of action, Guyer authorized roadblocks to stop suspected vehicles, and for two days he and Navy personnel, armed with revolvers and rifles, roamed the countryside and then Nukuʻalofa, arresting 40 Tongan suspects, who were thoroughly beaten up in Navy brigs at Maʻufanga.[43] Only eight of the 40 were convicted by the civil court, the sentences varying from ten lashes and eight months in jail to four years' imprisonment. Other charges were dismissed by Acting Chief Justice John Brownlees on the grounds that confessions had been obtained under excessive duress. Much of the property recovered by Guyer's raiders had been "freely and openly given away" by Americans at some time prior to the raid, some of it by servicemen participating in the raid.

On the second day of the raid, 15 August, US Navy personnel broke into the Kolomotuʻa home of the Premier, Ata, at 3 a.m. and lined him and his wife and family up against the wall while the house was searched. Then they proceeded to neighbouring houses, kicking down doors, firing revolvers, and interrogating anyone they came across.

Hodsdon himself was invisible for the whole two days of the raid. The more polite among the *papālangi* locals referred to him as a "pathetic old man", a "damned old fool", and a "silly ass". Not all US men approved of the raid, and some "vindictive enlisted men wanted to search the house of their Commanding Officer's girl friend. She, however, wisely disappeared with all her belongings and the search revealed nothing."

There had doubtless been thefts of US property by Tongans, but naming the events of those two days the "Cigarette Raid" trivialized what was a very serious breach of the rights of Tongan individuals. The stated intent, to round up the "bad boys", suggests troops tired of having no "enemy" on hand had decided to liven up their lives by taking on the local population. If the "invaders" had confined their activities to the countryside and not raided the homes of influential citizens in the most prestigious section of the capital of the kingdom, the incident might be less well known.

On the evidence available, neither the British Agent & Consul, Johnson, nor the High Commissioner for the Western Pacific, Sir Philip Mitchell, come out well from the affair. Both had a duty of care towards Tongan citizens of whatever rank. Johnson advised Mitchell, who was on friendly terms with high-ranking US officers, to hush the matter up. Nor was compensation seriously considered. For example, a man who was thoroughly beaten up simply because he owned a truck similar to that used in the raid, even though New Zealanders testified that he had spent the evening with them at Fuaʻamotu, was compensated with a few pieces of timber and US$1.

Ata protested about the breaking into his house and the subsequent treatment of his family during the raid, but Navy officers who attended a meeting with him came fully armed and recalcitrant. Indeed Hodsdon threatened to introduce martial law, and was prevented only by the fact that the ranking officer in Tonga, Hardy, believed that petty theft was insufficient reason for taking such an extreme measure. Hodsdon was replaced on 16 December 1944, after which a token garrison removed or sold off the few remaining assets.

The Queen's response is harder to explain. Margaret Armstrong, who left Tonga mid-1943 (that is, more than a year before the raid) reported that when Tongans came to the Queen to complain about the US forces, she would say, "Well, I can speak to the General and he will see that it is put right. But these *papālangi*s – these Americans – are here for only a short time. When they go, all will be forgotten; and they are here to help us and Britain in fighting the war against the Japanese and the Germans. It would be better just to be quiet and let it go."[44] The complainant could not refuse to heed royal advice. When some members of the Tonga Defence Force marched to the Palace and presented a list of grievances to the Queen, she sent them back to their camp, although at least one of their requests – a Tongan flag over the camp instead of the Union Jack – was acceded to.[45]

So, when Hodsdon claimed that the Queen approved the Navy action during the "Cigarette Raid", and that she acknowledged that Tongans had often stolen from the Americans and were now being taught an appropriate lesson, he may have been doing more than just pleading his own case. Since everyone else in the kingdom was talking about the "Cigarette Raid", the Queen must have discussed the matter with Johnson and agreed not to lay an official complaint that might lead to an international incident. Although not all the horrors of World War Two were known at that time, the Queen was aware of the carnage in Europe and the Pacific and of the many privations of the fighting men, and must have believed that the sufferings of the Tongans were small by comparison, only one injustice among many.

Towards the end of the war, the US government sent an account to the Tongan government for equipment that was to be left in Tonga. Both Armstrong and Johnson felt that in the calculation of the worth of the US roadbuilding and extension of the airfield (for example) the Americans had not taken into account the work carried out between September 1939 and the arrival of the Americans in May 1942. The Tongan government asked for the account to be reduced. When the US government offered goods for sale to the government of Tonga, it was said that the government refused, the Crown Prince believing that much would be abandoned when the US forces left. He was mistaken, for, as in other places in the Pacific, major pieces of equipment that were no longer required and could not be sold were simply pushed over the edge of the wharf, and abandoned buildings burned. The Americans not only assumed that the lives of the Tongans would be completely blank once they had gone, they placed little value on Tongan goodwill once the US forces had departed.

Some Tongans served overseas. The Queen's nephew Vaea ('Alipate Tupou) enlisted in the RNZAF and flew Catalinas (ferrying supplies to the Solomons). In 1943 the first of two Tonga Defence Force commando platoons were sent with the Fiji First Guerrillas to the Solomons, where two Tongan missionaries, Paula Havea and Sione Afu (like Tēvita Mone and 'Isikeli Hau'ofa in Papua New Guinea), continued to care for their people throughout the war. Both of the officers (Ben Masefield and Henry Taliai) of this first platoon were killed in action in 1943, and the Queen attended the memorial service for Taliai (a commoner) at the airfield.[46] A second platoon fought in Bougainville. Many of the Tongan troops who fought overseas were infected with malaria and dengue fever, and it was decided on 30 October 1944 that because of illness the members of the first contingent, then on leave in Tonga, would be demobilized without recall.

Henry Taliai was mentioned in despatches. Sione Inukiha'angana (brother of Saiatua Lavulo) and Simote Vea Mahe were awarded the British Military Medal and the American Silver Star for courage during the fighting in the Solomons, and Corporal Fusi of the second platoon a Military Medal. Sione Ma'asi, Siope Tafa, and Tēvita Ta'anga were mentioned in despatches.[47] The names of Taliai and Masefield are memorialized by being attached to Tonga Defence Force and Tongan Navy establishments.

To sum up the experience of war (at least of the early years), an anonymous Tongan penned the following poem about the experiences of Tonga during the war. It was entitled *Bomu* (Bomb).

1. 'Oku ou tumu he letiō
Na'e ha'u mei ai e ongoongo
Kae tala 'e he tēvolo
Kuo ofi e vaka Tokio
Kuo Pomu 'a Pago Pago.
Ka tau fetuku ki he Vao
Tapui e loto kolo
Veteki moe ngaahi ako.

Tau: 'Ae Tonga tu'u 'o laka pea to'o ho'o pā
Ko hota tu'unga kuo 'osi tuku ki 'olunga
Hota fatongia koe lotu pea moe tautapa
Koia pe 'e tokoni 'i he faingata'a.

2. Kae tu'utu'uni matu'aki fu'u lelei
Malu'i 'ae mo'ui
Koe me'a fai 'e māmāni,
Fetuku e vaivai moe fanga ki'i tamaiki
Na'a ha'u 'ae fili pea fakatu'utāmaki.

3. 'Ae Tonga keke tokanga
Koia e moto 'o e fonua,
'Oua 'e falala
Ki he ngāue 'a Natula,
Me'afana fonua, pe koe tau Malu'i Fonua.
Manuao pe Vakapuna, moe Sapamalini moe Heletā.

4. Ke tau nofo mo lotu.
Koia me'a 'oku totonu
Tōkanga'i hota kaha'u
Na'a hoko koe koto palakū.
He kuo hulu fau 'ae loi moe lapu
Ka 'oku mau tuku atu ki he 'Otua 'ae totonu.

* * *

1. I was surprised by the radio
from which came the news.
But the devil said
the Tokyo boat was approaching,
Pago Pago had been bombed.[48]
We were to move to the bush.
The town was closed,
The schools dismissed.

Refrain:
Tongans, get up and march and carry forth your shields.
Our position has been ceded from above.
Our duties are to pray and to worship.
That alone will help in times of hardship.

2. The command was good indeed.
Protect lives,
a thing done by every country,
remove the old people and young children
in case the enemy came and there would be trouble.

3. Tongans, be careful!
That is the motto of the land.
Do not put your trust in the work of Nature,
big guns, or the army,
man-o'-wars or planes, and submarines and swords.

4. Let us keep on praying. That alone is right.
Take care of our future
in case it is full of ugliness,
for lies and deceit are abundant,
but we leave the judgement to God. [MT]

The European war ended on 7 May 1945 and the war against Japan on 8 August 1945. Tonga had the satisfaction of being on the winning side. The numbers of the Tonga Defence Force had been greatly reduced during 1944 and the remainder were stood down in October 1945. The Force was not reconstituted until 1954.[49]

Few outward signs of the occupation remained in Tonga: Marston matting from the airfield was used for multiple purposes (the most visible being fences); Quonset huts became classrooms and hospital wards; a water tower loomed over Queen Sālote College. According to Collocott, the numbers of illegitimate births rose from 17 per cent to 24 per cent.[50] Few mixed-race children knew the names of their fathers, and none (it seems) of the fathers supported their children after they left Tonga: all were absorbed into Tongan families. Few of the Tongans had saved money from the years of plenty, although some (such as Joe Mataele) established profitable businesses based on the skills they learned during the war.

Among the very real benefits of the occupation was that the US Army doctors set up clinics and treated the people for injury and illness, using the most up-to-date equipment and medicines. They also gave practical demonstrations on public health measures. Most moving was a concerted attempt to reduce the incidence of tuberculosis, which had a tragic toll before the war.[51]

The official British report stated that the "evil effects of the occupation were not lasting". But Cecil Gribble (Director of Education) commented: "Superficially Tonga looks like its pre-war self, but for those who have eyes to see, deep and disquieting changes have taken place".[52] Among the unfortunate changes were widespread use of cigarettes and alcohol, which began in wartime because of the easy availability of both commodities. The system that had before the war limited legal consumption of alcohol to a 100 permit-holders gave way to equal access to alcoholic beverages. Tongan custom encouraged vast consumption of food when it was available, and this custom extended to alcohol and, to some extent, to cigarettes. Helen Taliai recalls that in the 1950s she saw Tongans lying unconscious at the roadside after drinking home-brew, and that the sale of methylated spirit was restricted because it was an ingredient of home-brew.[53] Lawlessness was a fact of life in 1942–44 – hardly surprising when tens of thousands of young men were having a last fling before the battlefield. American example was added to Tongan cupidity, and the Justice Department reported a steady postwar increase in crime.[54] James Spillius, for one, attributed the increase in violent crime to the availability of home-brew.[55]

Close observers of wartime and postwar Tonga could see the beginnings of a quiet revolution. For the first time in their lives, commoners had handled money over and above that needed to pay taxes or to give to the annual collection. There would be nothing like the cargo cult of other parts of the Pacific, but neither chiefs nor commoners forgot the desirable Western goods they had briefly known. High prices for copra during and after the war meant that cash continued to be available for all.[56]

An outstanding outcome of the occupation of Tongatapu was the increased emancipation of the commoner. While this had theoretically been granted by Tupou I in 1862, the year 1942 was when *tau'atāina* (freedom) received its greatest impetus. In a time of extraordinary plenty, the most common of the commoners, the "youngest" in the Tongatapu *kāinga*, for the first time in their lives were able to acquire and dispose of an income and goods. This knowledge could not leave them. It was no coincidence that commoner businesses flourished in the 1950s and 1960s much more than before the war.

At a time of change the Queen's reputation was enhanced. The Queen had never allowed herself to be seen as diminished by the invading forces. On the contrary, she was a gracious host, ignoring bad manners, though privately longing for her guests to depart. The British were grateful for her support – gratitude that would result in Tonga acting more independently than before.

A major political change after the war was in the relationship between Tonga and the British. Cecil Gribble commented that Tongans respected but did not love the British, and that they loved but did not respect the Americans, although that love wore off as relationships soured. Both love and respect for *papālangi* were in short supply after the war. The numbers of *papālangi* in government employment and business in Tonga had been greatly reduced during the 1930s Depression. Other *papālangi* who left during the war did not return, so there were greater employment opportunities for Tongans. After the war Britain did not have the resources to re-establish the British Empire as a major power, and postwar consuls did not have the influence McOwan and Neill had exercised before the war.

Doubtless Tonga would have changed even if there had been no war, but during the war Tongans had seen the material advantages of the Western lifestyle, and this knowledge could not be taken from them. Older Tongans would look back to what they believed was a kindlier time, when young people were obedient and everyone knew their obligations to each other; but the die was cast and the rate of change accelerated.

CHAPTER FIFTEEN

Mother and Sons

"that . . . family should do their utmost in trying to educate and lead and also give good advice to the young man they know will come to the title according to Law"
(Queen Sālote, "Showing Respect")[1]

BEFORE WORLD WAR TWO THERE had been dual leadership in Tonga, with Queen Sālote and Tungī Mailefihi taking different, but complementary roles. The postwar period would be marked by another style of dual leadership, where Queen Sālote and Crown Prince Tupouto'a again were leaders, but in different spheres and working independently of each other. The Queen kept alive traditions and the ideals of the *kāinga* and respect, and dealt with people's problems on a personal level, while the Crown Prince introduced impersonal policies of modernization that depended on ideas and organizations. The postwar partnership was of two people working side by side with very different ideals of society and government.

Tupouto'a was unlike his parents, not being as politically astute or farsighted, nor gifted with the ability of persuasion, nor able to relate to people on a personal level as they were. In some ways he resembled his grandfather Tupou II with his dreams and schemes, and his love of gadgets. Tupouto'a knew what he wanted, but he lacked the patience required to build firm foundations for his projects. Nevertheless, he had a powerful intellect, and impressed those who knew him with the breadth of his ideas and with his dedication to the welfare of the kingdom.

Tupouto'a returned to Tonga on 12 December 1942 with Bachelor's degrees in Arts and Law, the first Tongan to graduate from a university. He had left

Tonga for school 10 years earlier, and (because of the war) had not visited Tonga in the previous four years. The Queen was impressed as well as delighted with his achievements, and she appreciated what his education would mean for Tonga. She hoped that he would now spend some time in getting to know the people and in learning their traditions and customs, just as she had done when she had returned from school in Auckland in 1914. She reflected: "The pity of it is that he feels and thinks like a European . . . there has to be another complete change to make everything Tongan again, in order for him to carry out his true responsibilities."[2]

Tupouto'a, however, had been profoundly affected by his experience of Western values and material possessions, and was anxious to get on with the business of modernizing Tonga as rapidly as possible. He had no interest in the slow business of learning genealogies and ritual. His impatience was a concern for the Queen, who commented, "I personally consider that we would do very well to take things too slowly rather than too quickly."[3]

Tupouto'a was not only a high achiever in the *papālangi* world, he was the descendant of three royal bloodlines, and outranked all other Tongans, even the Queen. Although concerned lest the adulation of the people go to his head,[4] and despite his youth (he was now 24) and inexperience, Sālote decided that she would make use of his talents and qualifications by appointing him immediately to government. The Queen and Tungī Mailefihi had planned to make him Chief Justice of Tonga,[5] but the problems of the Justice Department (chapter 12) had recently been resolved by two appointments: a Visiting Chief Justice from Fiji, who (in theory) came to Tonga twice a year to hear Supreme Court cases and appeals to the Privy Council; and a legally qualified Secretary to Government.[6]

So, instead of appointing Tupouto'a to the Justice Department, the Queen chose him to lead two ministries to which she had always given high priority. He became Minister for Education on 1 February 1943 and Minister for Health on 6 November 1944.[7] To assist her son in his Education portfolio, the Queen persuaded Cecil Gribble, an Australian Methodist missionary who had been Principal of Tupou College 1939–43, to accept the position of Director of Education in May 1943, a position he held until 1946. There was a great deal to be done, for although primary education had been compulsory in Tonga since 1862, the law had been unenforceable because of the scarcity of trained teachers and the lack of school buildings and equipment.

If education was deemed to be Western education and medicine deemed to be Western medicine, then Tupouto'a was better equipped than anyone in the kingdom to reform both departments. The Queen and Tupouto'a agreed that it was highly desirable that Tongans be educated to take the place of *papālangi* in government service, and that *papālangi* medicine was needed in Tonga, not only to combat foreign diseases, but to improve the general health of the people.

Tupouto'a's first act as Minister for Education was to approve the reform of Tongan spelling, so that the b was replaced by p, j by s, and g by ng. The long vowel would be indicated by a macron, and the *fakau'a* (glottal stop) would be used consistently (see Notes on Tongan Spelling and Chiefly Titles).[8] In 1946 Tupouto'a appointed the linguist Rev. Dr C. M. Churchward to prepare a Tongan grammar and a Tongan–English dictionary, which were published in 1953 and 1959, both by Oxford University Press. Churchward's chief assistant was Feleti Vī (formerly Ve'ehala), renowned for his gifts as a musician and later as one of the mainstays of the Tonga Traditions Committee.

In order to accelerate Westernization, Tupouto'a decided Tonga should be a bilingual country. He brought in *papālangi* teachers and sent Tongans overseas for further education. Tupouto'a could influence the mission schools only through the Board of Education, so his efforts were focused on the government schools, over which he had total control. The Queen was not sorry when he took a special interest in Tonga College (the former Government College),[9] which had been the bastion of recalcitrant Free Church people. It had been intended that when Tonga College moved to the country it would be a vocational school, but Tupouto'a-Tungī reintroduced the academic stream, which pleased the "Old Boys" of the school.

On 8 February 1944, on the former site of Tonga College, south of the Mala'e Kula, Tupouto'a opened the Teachers' Training College, with Gribble as the first Principal, and a primary school (called the Side School), where students could do their practice teaching. Tupouto'a founded a magazine called *Tokoni Faiako* (Help for the Teacher) for the teachers in the village schools as well as at the students at the Teachers' Training College, and he made regular visits to the primary schools throughout Tonga in order to instruct and encourage the village teachers.

The Queen and Tungī Mailefihi had put great emphasis on the education of girls, paying the school fees of girls as well as boys; but Tupouto'a had ingested male chauvinistic ideology from Australians and did not give girls the same opportunities as boys. For example, only 10 of the 45 places in the Teachers' Training College were reserved for women in its first year, and overseas scholarships were awarded only to men, at least initially.

Tupouto'a took over the old "European School" from the Free Wesleyan Church, and used it as a nucleus for his Matriculation School (later renamed Tonga High School). It opened in 1947 on the old Tonga College site (shared with the Teachers' Training College) with 12 Tongan students and 26 *papālangi* students; eight more Tongan students were admitted in 1948; 10 more in 1949. Here students were taught mainly in English, and were prepared for the New Zealand University Entrance Examination. To emphasize its link with the private secondary schools overseas, the pupils had a school uniform: shorts, shirt, and a cap for the boys, and a dress and straw hat for the girls.

Tonga College, the Teachers' Training College, and Tonga High School would be Tupouto'a's pride and joy. He arranged for teachers from New Zealand to be seconded to the three schools. Although only a few foreign teachers stayed for more than their initial three-year appointment, the presence of up to five *papālangi* teachers in one school greatly improved the level of education.[10] By contrast, the Protestant mission schools, with no government subsidy, and unable to pay salaries equal to those offered by the government or paid to seconded teachers, mostly managed with one *papālangi* missionary and several Tongan tutors, and found it increasingly difficult to offer an education comparable to that in the government schools. Although the Catholic schools had several priests as teachers, they also envied the financial assistance being given to the government schools. Not everyone was pleased when Tupouto'a encouraged the Mormons, who were willing to pour money into providing modern education in the American style.

As the highest-ranking chief of Tonga, Tupouto'a was able to demand the government make funds available for overseas scholarships that (like the pre-war scholarships) were open to students of the secondary schools. In 1944/45 the government estimates allowed only £350 for overseas scholarships, but this increased steadily until it reached £5546 in 1961/62. In his Annual Report for 1956 the Crown Prince recorded that 30 Tongans were studying on overseas scholarships. Among those who benefited from the scholarships were Kaveinga Havea, Sione Na'a Fiefia, Mahe 'Uli'uli Tupouniua, Sione Siosiomalohi (better known as Sione Tapa). The Central Medical School in Suva continued to take Tongan scholarship winners such as Tilitili Puloka, Leopino Foliaki, and 'Opeti Lutui, who became Tongan Medical Practitioners. 'Amanaki Havea, the second Tongan university graduate, was educated by means of church scholarships, as were Siupeli Taliai and Sione Lātūkefu. Almost all Tongans educated abroad during Queen Sālote's reign returned to Tonga to work for the country.

Tupouto'a put a personal stamp on Tongan education policy. For example, he was a keen musician, importing brass instruments and ensuring salaries for bandmasters. He wrote a handbook on Tongan musical notation, *Koe Tohi Tu'ungafasi 'ae Kolisi Tonga* (The Book of Musical Scores Showing Various Parts [written for] Tonga College).[11] He introduced marching teams as part of the entertainment at celebrations. Competitive sports between Tupou College and Tonga College, which had been such emotive occasions before the war, were extended to include other schools.

The Queen was in two minds about Tupouto'a's modernization policy. She acknowledged the value of *papālangi* education, but her heart was in Tongan traditions, customs, and values. She explained her ambivalence:

> Some people believe that the true knowledge is to be educated and wise (i.e. by going to school), and this is true enough. But *a great part of the knowledge*

> *necessary to maintain Tongan society must be acquired locally, in Tonga*. It is not right to throw such wisdom away. I believe that after three or four generations of education it would be appropriate to use the knowledge gained through education only. Then we can put aside Tongan knowledge. But even so, there will be times when Tongan experience is needed for certain things in the country. I believe myself that, by rights, *Tongan custom should not be entirely wiped out, but should be improved to fit in with the times, and improved a bit more; for that is warmly accepted in the core of the life of the Tongans*. If there is a good substitute, then change something that seems to be useless, but do it gradually, not hurriedly, for haste will lead to too many things being abandoned. The people will feel confused and will not know what is right. Our work and our feelings will be confused too. It is the duty of the aristocrats to interpret these things to the people of the country so that they will take a keen interest in them and give their best for the benefit of all. The aristocrats must practise what they preach and support the valuable work that has been done by the kings ('Ha'a Tu'i) and go forward hand in hand in leadership of the country.[12] [translator not known, my italics]

In short, Queen Sālote understood that a country could and should benefit from the experiences of other countries, but not to the extent that it lost its own identity or simply succumbed to pressures for change without good reason.

In her caution about change, the Queen would have a partial ally in Prince Sione Ngū, who returned to Tonga in January 1944 after only one year at Gatton Agricultural College in Queensland. Although the Director of Agriculture had recently retired, the Queen did not appoint Ngū to that post: she wanted him to spend time learning about tradition and custom. The title of Tu'ipelehake (which would be his) was second only to her own in its sacred *mana*, and she wanted Ngū to set an example for other hereditary estateholders to follow. He was a good-natured and obedient son, and agreed to do as the Queen wished. He also had a gift for public speaking. In mid-1944 the Queen appointed him to the not very demanding position of visiting copra inspector, which would give him plenty of time to exercise his chiefly functions. He did not have a major appointment until the Queen appointed him Governor of Vava'u in 1949.[13]

It was not all traditions, however. The younger prince was much less serious than the elder, and liked to have a good time. Saiatua Lavulo recalls the pleasure of dressing up and going to balls patronized by the two princes. The Queen had not danced *papālangi* dances since she had left school in 1914, but she could sometimes be prevailed upon to watch others doing the tango or the foxtrot, and even more modern dances. Both princes were keen on the movies, and films were shown at the Palace, as well as at the larger villages of Tongatapu. The Crown Prince imported educational and religious films, hoping to become the sole distributor within the kingdom, and even toyed with the idea of setting up his own film company.[14]

Sione Ngū supported his elder brother in his different enterprises. For example, Tupouto'a formed a Law Society of Tonga, which held debates, one on the evening of 18 July 1945 at the Teachers' College being attended by both princes. Tupouto'a also founded a Society of Nobles, which met on 17 July 1948 for a feast. The business discussed was not recorded, but again the meeting was attended by both princes. Tupouto'a also experimented with products for export, such as handicrafts. By contrast, the younger prince took little interest in business or the bureaucracy, but appropriately for his chiefly status led a group of chiefly young men known as the *Kautaha Tau'atāina Talavou* (Bachelors' Club) and composed songs for them to sing when they met in the evenings to drink *kava*.

Both princes enjoyed a Westernized lifestyle. They owned evening dress suits as well as daytime Western-style wear. The Palace imported fresh meat (steaks and lamb) and preserved meat (luncheon sausage) to add variety to its usual fare, and asparagus, oysters, and mussels for special occasions. Cigarettes and alcohol were imported for the princes until both renounced alcohol and tobacco in the late 1940s. Having learned the *papālangi* way of securing possessions, Tupouto'a had his own little safe and kept his own key to it.

The Royal Estates Act of 1927 required that Prince Sione Ngū succeed to the title of Tu'ipelehake on his twenty-first birthday, which occurred in January 1943, while he was still in Australia. But Tu'ipelehake was a higher title than Tupouto'a, and the Queen felt it was inappropriate to appoint the younger son to a high-ranking title while the elder held a lesser title. The same Act had placed her consort's title of Tungī in the Queen's gift, but stated it was not to be given to the eldest son. In 1943 the Queen asked Parliament to amend this part of the Act, and when this was done, she wrote a letter appointing Sione Ngū as Tu'ipelehake (in September 1944), backdating it to January 1943, and another letter appointing Tupouto'a as Tungī on 27 March 1945. The Crown Prince was called by the Tungī title for the first time in the *taumafa kava* on that day, but it was agreed that the appropriate time for Tungī's people to bring his presentations would be in December, at the celebrations to mark the centenary of the installation of Tupou I in the title of Tu'i Kanokupolu when overseas dignitaries would be present.[15] The Crown Prince's official title was now Tupouto'a-Tungī, but he was known more familiarly as Tungī, and so signed his official correspondence. Tu'ipelehake would no longer be called Sione Ngū but familiarly by the name reserved for sacred chiefs, Fatafehi, and formally as Tu'ipelehake. On 14 July 1945 the people of the estates of Tu'ipelehake brought to the Queen the presentations of their new chief.

That year, 1945, proved to be a great one for celebrations. No sooner was the two-day (16–17 August) thanksgiving for peace over than all the chiefs and people began to prepare for the centenary celebrations of Tupou I's installation as Tu'i Kanokupolu. The celebrations would in fact honour the Tupou dynasty, for it encompassed the Queen's Silver Jubilee (delayed from 1943 because of the war) and the investiture of the Dame Grand Cross of the Order of the British Empire (GBE), which acknowledged the Queen's support for Great Britain during the war. Sālote would also present her high-achieving heir to those chiefs of the south-west Pacific who would be her guests.

Tongilava's diary shows how closely the Queen supervised the details of this event. On 28 August the Queen sent a *lakalaka* she had written to honour Tupou I to Makelesi Lokotui in Ha'apai, so that the dance could to be choreographed, the words memorized, and the music and dance rehearsed. On 10 October she sent another *lakalaka* ("Ko e ta'anga 'o e taunga peka 'i he senituli 'o Tupou I, 1945") to Ata for Kolovai, the village in the Western District of Tongatapu where Tupou I had been installed as Tu'i Kanokupolu. Altogether, the Queen wrote at least seven *lakalaka* for seven different villages to mark this occasion.

On 18 October Tongilava recorded that the Queen asked women to make mats and bark cloth for presentation to distinguished visitors. On 22 October the Queen called a meeting of the hereditary estateholders, the chiefs who looked after the land, the district officers, and town officers in order to tell them what would be required of them and their people, especially in the provision of food and *koloa*. From early November, the different villages came to the Palace to present their dances for her inspection. This was not a mere matter of form, for the Queen would change the position of dancers (determined by their rank in the village), as well as assessing whether the dances were of a sufficiently high standard for performance before her guests. On 15 November the Queen wrote to the governors (Tu'iha'ateiho and 'Ulukālala) to give them detailed instructions about the events that would be held in Ha'apai and Vava'u after the main celebrations on Tongatapu.

Everyone who was anyone in the south-west Pacific was invited to attend. Sāmoan and Fijian chiefs began arriving in mid-November. The Sāmoan chiefs who did not stay with relatives were the Queen's guests at Mapu-'a-fuiva (J. B. Watkin's former home, which had reverted to the royal family), while Fijian chiefs were accommodated at 'Otualea, opposite the main Free Wesleyan church.[16] Forty-three Sāmoan chiefs arrived on the *Matua* on 23 November, bringing presentations of 20 *pola* (food on long stretchers made of plaited coconut leaves). On 29 November the Sāmoan high chiefs Mālietoa and Tamasese and their wives arrived by plane. More Sāmoan chiefs arrived by the plane that brought the High Commissioner of the Western Pacific, Sir A. W. G. H. Grantham, and Lady Grantham on 1 December. On the following day the Fijian high chiefs Ratu Sukuna, Tui Nekesi, Tui Cadavu, and Tui Lakeba arrived, also by plane. The Queen ordered a number of prisoners to be set free on 3 December to mark the occasion.

The centenary day of Tupou I was 4 December. This was marked by ceremonies on the Mala'e Pangai, during which flags were raised and lowered and bands played. The High Commissioner read the letter from King George VI that accompanied the award of the GBE for the Queen (the actual investiture took place in the Palace). Speeches were made by the highest dignitaries (British, Tongan, Fijian, and Sāmoan); then a service led by Rodger Page, singing by the choirs, a 21-gun salute, and photographs. Entertainments followed in the afternoon and evening, at which the 'Api Fo'ou School band played. The garden party planned for Wednesday the 5th had to be cancelled because of rain, but dancing and band playing continued through the day and the next day. The programme shows that 24 *lakalaka*s were to be performed during the morning, and 12 *lakalaka*s, six *mā'ulu'ulu*s, and one *'otuhaka* in the afternoon of the 5th, while the Lapaha band played in the evening. There were sports on the 6th, followed by a performance by the Kolomotu'a band, and a regatta on the 7th, followed by a *papālangi*-style dance in the evening. The *pongipongi* of Tungī was on the 8th, and we can imagine that, with the all the resources of the Tungī estates at his disposal, the new Tungī's presentations to the Queen were spectacular.

On 9 December the Queen and the two princes sailed on the *Hifofua* with some of their Fijian and Sāmoan guests to continue the celebrations at Ha'apai and Vava'u. Other visitors remained in Tongatapu and continued to be fed and entertained for the remainder of the year. A lorry distributed among the Tongatapu chiefs some of the mats and bark cloth that had been given to the Queen by her guests, and in January and February of 1946 the Queen sent more mats and bark cloth to Ha'apai and Vava'u for distribution.

Such celebrations were superbly well organized, and indeed there were so many in the Queen's reign that the participants had plenty of practice. But the Queen and people were not so well prepared for a natural catastrophe. It was Tongan custom that, in times of drought and hurricane, affected islands were sustained by the other islands until they could rebuild their houses and plant more crops on their own land. But in 1946 there was an emergency that had long-lasting consequences.[17] On Monday, 9 September, and following days, a volcanic eruption on the northern outlier Niuafo'ou buried the village of Angahā, including the government offices, wireless station, copra stores, the house of the noble Fotofili, and the hospital. Crops were almost untouched by the eruption, so although cigarettes and medical supplies dropped by a US Catalina flying boat on 18 September were welcomed, offers of food were declined.

If Tungī Mailefihi had been alive, he would have been the chief decision-maker. Now it seemed that no one was in charge. There is no record of the Queen being involved in discussions in those early days, although she must have been kept informed. On 20 September the *Hifofua* arrived in Niuafo'ou with the new Minister for Lands, Tu'iha'ateiho, the noble Kalanivalu (who was trustee for the Fotofili title, the main landlord of the island), the Chief Medical Officer (Dr Brown), and a radio technician.[18]

This was not the first or worst volcanic eruption in Niuafo'ou, but it was unusual in that most of the government buildings had been destroyed, and considerable expense would be involved if these facilities were rebuilt. In its haste to avoid the expense of setting up a new infrastructure for the island, the government created greater problems for itself. The heads of households in Niuafo'ou were asked to vote on whether they would be evacuated or stay put; then the government made promises that influenced the vote: if the people agreed to leave, they would be able to take all their belongings and would be given land in Tongatapu or 'Eua. No promises were made about rebuilding of Angahā if they voted to stay. The majority of heads of households voted to go: 1078 in favour and 228 against. The government decided to evacuate the entire population of Niuafo'ou: none would be permitted to remain.

The population prepared for evacuation by dismantling their houses, piling up the house poles on the beach ready for loading, killing and salting animals, packing their mats and bark cloth, tools and household goods. The *Hifofua* removed some people and some of their belongings late in October. However, when the *Matua* arrived on 20 December to take the last group off the island, the people were informed that none of the possessions so carefully prepared would be taken on board. This was a fatal mistake. When this last group of 1200 people arrived at Nuku'alofa on Sunday, 22 December 1946, they had nothing. Most were taken to a hastily prepared camp site at Vaikeli or to Mataliku or Mataki'eua, the last two on the Queen's estates, south of Nuku'alofa.

The Niuafo'ou Evacuation Committee (made up of Tongatapu people) was unprepared for people without basic possessions: there was little shelter, and food was in scant supply. Taken from an island where food was plentiful and where their family possessions remained, the evacuees were dependent upon the good will of the people of Tongatapu for everything necessary to keep them alive.

The Queen had personal responsibility for many of the people. She was not only a descendant of a former Fotofili of Niuafo'ou, but she owned the estate of Mata'aho on the island. Her Niuafo'ou people took up residence in Tongan houses erected for the purpose on Fangatapu (the land in front of the Palace) and food was prepared for them in the Palace kitchen.[19] On the day after their arrival in Tongatapu they begged enough mats and pigs to make a formal presentation to the Queen. On 5 June of the following year they performed a *lakalaka* for the Queen prior to the wedding of her sons. On 7 August 1947 Tongilava recorded mats and bark cloth being taken from the Palace to the camps as blankets for sick Niuafo'ou women and children. The Niuafo'ou people found Tongatapu very cold after the year-round heat of their own island, and in the cold months in the middle of the following year some of the people became ill and died. The record shows that the Queen paid for bread for Niuafo'ou people.

Many Niuafo'ou people wished to return to their island, but the government would not admit it had made a mistake. In her speech at the Opening of Parliament in 1947, the Queen showed her awareness of the difficulties.

> You are all aware that since the last session of the Legislative Assembly misfortune endangered the District of Niuafo'ou; although there was no loss of life . . . the chief town was greatly damaged. Government buildings were nearly all destroyed. The Government at once realised its duty, and made arrangements for the evacuation of the inhabitants from the island. . . . Their personal belongings have not all been brought from Niuafo'ou, and the arrangements for their resettlement by Government have not been completed, although I trust that they will be in the near future. Hardships are unavoidable in their present position, and we share with the suffering they may have to experience.[20]

A major cause of suffering was the hostility of the Tongatapu people. The Niuafo'ou people were darker skinned, had different customs, and spoke their own (Sāmoic) language. Some Niuafo'ou people who were settled on Tungī's estates were given work at the farm at Kauvai. When Tungī's people attacked them, the Queen was enraged. Those who had transgressed came in a group to the Palace, abjectly, to beg her forgiveness, and the Queen showed her displeasure by keeping them waiting for a long time before allowing them to come before her. This was not the end of animosity. It seemed that no one wanted the Niuafo'ou people, and even Kalanivalu complained of them.[21]

The Queen enlisted the help of Free Wesleyan Church ministers in trying to resolve the animosity between Tongatapu and 'Eua people,[22] but it was the estateholder or his representative who was responsible for making farm and town allotments available for their own people. Without land the Niuafo'ou people could not provide for themselves or carry out their social obligations. Fusitu'a, one of the nobles of Niuafo'ou, had no land in the south, so the people looked to the Queen, Kalanivalu, and the government to provide allotments. In 1958 James Spillius was told that Kalanivalu had taken 1500 Niuafo'ou people from Tongatapu to 'Eua, in a total of 65 trips in one year, and that only 400 remained on his estates on Tongatapu. Spillius also recorded that pressure was put on some Niuafo'ou people to move from one site on 'Eua to another, suggesting that their allotments had not been registered.[23] The Niua people in 'Eua were even colder and more isolated from help than the people who remained on Tongatapu, but at least they had the allotments of land essential for survival.

Some Niuafo'ou people were content to remain in the south, partly because of the better opportunities for the education of their children. Others fretted to return to their northern island, and resettlement began in 1958 (12 years after the evacuation) with the return of 39 families. Government services were not re-established until the 1960s. The continuance of the Niuafoʻou Evacuation Committee into the next reign suggests that there were ongoing problems for the people who remained on Tongatapu and ʻEua.[24]

On 17 May 1949, at the same time as the Niuafoʻou people were still suffering considerable privation, the Queen, Tupoutoʻa-Tungī, and Tuʻipelehake summoned the chiefs, ministers of the churches, and people from the villages to meet at the Teachers' Training College to discuss a request from the United Nations for assistance for the poor and displaced persons "of Europe and the world" who were suffering as a result of the war. The Queen believed that the ordeal of displaced people in Europe was greater than that of local people, so there were fundraising events in July, August, and September for the displaced Europeans. The Queen's appeal raised £5000.

Speculation that had been rife among the Tongan aristocrats for more than 20 years ended in 1947 when the two princes announced their betrothals. Among the names of women who had been mentioned as prospective brides were Lavinia, daughter of Kalanivalu (Sēmisi) and Sisilia; Fatafehi, daughter of Vīlai Tupou and Tupou Seini; and Melenaite Tupou Moheofo, daughter of Inoke S. Veikune and Lavinia (sister of Kalanivalu (Sēmisi)).[25] As a Westernized Tongan, Tupoutoʻa-Tungī made his own choice; as a Tongan chief he chose a woman of rank. The noble ʻAhomeʻe (Manu-ʻo-pangai) and his high-ranking wife, Heuʻifanga (a great-great-granddaughter of the last Tuʻi Tonga), had a daughter, Halaevalu Mataʻaho, who had been educated at a convent school in New Zealand (Figure 15.1). Tupoutoʻa-Tungī saw her when she was helping with serving food during the centenary celebrations of December 1945 and determined that she would be his wife.[26] When ʻAhome'e was appointed Governor of Haʻapai in 1946, people guessed what was to come. Tuʻilatai (Joe) Mataele remembers being one of a band of musicians who went with Tupoutoʻa-Tungī to court Halaevalu Mataʻaho.[27]

Prince Tuʻipelehake, the traditionally obedient son, followed the Queen's wishes by choosing the high-ranking Melenaite Tupou Moheofo, another great-great-granddaughter of the last Tuʻi Tonga (Figure 15.2), who had been educated at Ravenswood Methodist School for Girls in Sydney. Tongilava noted that on the evenings of 31 December 1946 and 31 January 1947 Tuʻipelehake went with his *kau matāpule* and a band of singers and had *kava* with Melenaite. As was the custom with serious wooing, the *kava*-drinking and singing continued until daybreak. The taking of food by Halaevalu (the Queen's cousin) and her people to the home of Melenaite announced that Tu'ipelehake would marry Melenaite. On 7 January 1947, his 25th birthday, Tu'ipelehake sent cooked food to Melenaite's house in Kolofo'ou. This was in accordance with the custom that once the marriage was agreed upon, the bridegroom supported the bride by sending her food.

The Queen arranged a double wedding for the princes so there would be less burden upon the people than two separate weddings. At the time of the double wedding, 10–12 June 1947, Tupouto'a-Tungī was a few weeks short of his twenty-ninth birthday, Tu'ipelehake was 25, Mata'aho 21, and Melenaite 22. Once again, Sālote exhibited her talent for organization and her delight in ensuring that traditional ceremonies were carried out in every detail. There were presentations prior to the two weddings: the European ceremony on 10 June and the Tongan ceremony on 12 June. The Queen used the European wedding to make a statement about the contemporary Tongan way. Instead of "white weddings" in full European dress (as her own had been), Sālote chose for the bridegrooms *vala tupenu* (a cloth tied at the waist and falling to below the knee) and simple high-collared shirts without ties, with historic named fine-mats around the waist: *Laumata-'o-Fainga'a* for Tupouto'a-Tungī and *Hau-'o-Momo* for Tu'ipelehake. For Mata'aho and Melenaite, the Queen chose simple, white, long dresses and fine-mats (Melenaite's being the *Tokotoko*, and Mata'aho's not remembered) with no head-covering.[28] A. E. McKay, President of the Free Wesleyan Church, married the couples in the Royal Chapel, and the Queen asked her old friend Rodger Page (who had retired the previous year, but was on a brief visit) and John Burton, President-General of the Methodist Church of Australasia, to bless the wedding party.

On the day of their Tongan wedding ceremony Tupouto'a-Tungī, Tu'ipelehake, Mata'aho, and Melenaite wore clothes made of traditional materials. No expense was spared and no ritual dispensed with, which meant that celebrations continued for many days, with ample opportunity for all the chiefs and people to contribute in some part. The Queen sent a description to Sau Faupula, for publication in the Free Wesleyan Church newspaper, now called *Ko e Tohi Fanongonongo*.

Pikula, about two kilometres from the Palace and once the home of the Queen's grandfather Tu'ipelehake, was renovated for Tupouto'a-Tungī and Mata'aho. Tu'ipelehake and Melenaite lived at the Palace with the Queen. Sālote was delighted to have two daughters at last, and especially took Melenaite about with her, even on protracted visits to Kauvai. Her new daughters, she noted, had different talents. Melenaite was very good at dividing food and *koloa*, implying that she had a knowledge of the customary rights of individual chiefs, while Princess Mata'aho was more skilled in dealing with *papālangi* events, which would help her as the wife of a prince who was very fond of travel.[29]

Overseas travel was usually for business combined with pleasure, but Tupouto'a-Tungī's health caused some concern, and he visited New Zealand for a check-up in 1944 and again in 1948.[30] Late in 1947 the Queen herself went to Auckland to seek medical advice. All her teeth were removed, a common remedy at the time for toxic infections and non-specific complaints. She returned in plenty of time for the births of her first grandchildren and to give them their names: Prince Tāufa'āhau Manumataongo, born to Mata'aho on 4 May, and Princess Mele Siu'ilikutapu, born to Melenaite on 12 May 1948. The Queen also gave her grandchildren the family name Tuku'aho in memory of her son who had died young. The Queen wrote lullabies for Tāufa'āhau and Siu'ilikutapu as well as for most of the other grandchildren: three more born to Tupouto'a-Tungī and Mata'aho, and five more born to Tu'ipelehake and Melenaite.

In 1949 Ata informed the Queen that he wished to retire as Premier because of ill-health. The obvious choice as his successor was Tupouto'a-Tungī. The Crown Prince had dominated the government ever since his first appointment as a minister in 1943, and although he did not always get his own way (and indeed many found him difficult to understand), he swayed Parliament as no other member could; and he had an earnest doggedness that served him well. The Queen's decision to appoint him was made partly because she needed someone who understood the outside world, but also because she could not deny him the responsibility that he so eagerly sought. Tupouto'a-Tungī was only 31 years of age when the Queen appointed him Premier on 1 December 1949.

Tonga in the 1950s was different from what it had been when Sālote became Queen. The health measures of the 1920s and 1930s had lowered the incidence of infant mortality, so that families of fourteen or more children survived to adulthood and had many children in their turn. Thus the population had increased from 23,759 in 1921 to 43,388 in 1950, and would increase to 77,439 by 1966. After the war the price of copra rose, so Tongans had more money to spend on Western commodities and on the education of their children.[31] However, there was little improvement in communications: repeated attempts in the 1950s to establish an air service failed, and Tonga continued to be dependent upon the monthly steamer (the *Matua* or *Tofua*), and copra was still the only export crop earning a good income.

Because of his rank, education, and temperament, Tupouto'a-Tungī was a somewhat isolated person, but he was tireless in his endeavours to improve the wealth of Tonga, and he travelled widely to investigate enterprises in other nations, to seek markets for Tongan copra and bananas, and to improve communications with the outside world. He read technical magazines and wrote to overseas businesses to request brochures, details of products, and samples, especially of agricultural products and those that might be useful in small businesses.

The Queen took long periods of rest from her royal duties. In 1952 the government of Tonga purchased for the royal family a property, thereafter known as ʻAtalanga, in Epsom, a suburb of Auckland, New Zealand. From 1954 the Queen spent most of the summer months at ʻAtalanga, returning to Tonga early in the year, refreshed by her time abroad. Even when in the kingdom, the Queen took a less public part in government. Her formal speeches at the Opening and Closing of Parliament were often read by one of the nobles on her behalf. When she appeared in person, the members expressed their joy. This does not mean that she lost touch with what was happening in the kingdom, for she was constantly besieged by people bringing their problems and concerns to her, asking that she use her personal influence for their benefit.

The Queen hoped that the Crown Prince would heed her advice on priorities in leadership. But to her dismay the young prince was inclined to make his own decisions, without consultation with anyone, so that the policies put into effect as Premier were very much his own. He believed that he was so completely in charge in Tonga that he commented to the Sāmoan chief "His Highness" Mālietoa Tanumofili in a letter of 28 May 1962 on the advantage to Sāmoa of having two heads of state (one who could travel, while the other stayed at home), without seeming to appreciate that that was also the situation in Tonga.[32] From the 1950s Tupoutoʻa-Tungī travelled overseas in his capacity as Premier, as chairman of the Copra Board and Produce Board, and on behalf of other government enterprises, sometimes being away for six months of the year.[33]

Although Tupoutoʻa-Tungī was determined about the economic reform of Tonga, he was adamant in his opposition to political reform. The "Reactionary Party" was a spent force, and Sioape Kaho, now an old man in retirement, was increasingly isolated, but there were still some voices demanding change or raised in criticism. A Democratic Party was founded in 1953, and Loloma Mataele and Sēmisi Koloamatangi stood unsuccessfully as Democratic Party candidates in the 1954 elections.[34] Samisoni Puliʻuvea Afuhaʻamango, representative of Vavaʻu, carried on the tradition of his family members who had used Parliament as a platform to express their discontent, beginning with the rejection of ʻOfa in 1899, revived with the marriage plans of Princess Fusipala, and reappearing with the advent of Chief Justice Stuart. Vavaʻu had lost its former independence, and little of the taxes the Vavaʻu people paid were spent on that northern group. Puliʻuvea had quite a lot of support, for he expressed what many other people were thinking, especially when he said that government should concentrate on improving schools and hospitals (especially outside the capital) instead of attempting to establish expensive frills, such as an air service to the outside world.

Puli'uvea was charged with defamation of the Queen in 1924, with defamation of the Premier (Ata) in 1946, and with sedition in 1957, and was suspended from time to time for assault or contempt. In 1957 an over-zealous Minister for Police arrested him not only for saying that the Queen appointed her close relations to government, which no one denied, but also for sending a petition to representatives of European countries in various territories of the South Pacific. While he was in jail in Tongatapu, Vava'u re-elected him to Parliament. Brought to court, Puli'uvea scandalized everyone by referring to the Queen and her sons in chiefly language (royal language should be reserved for God, he said).

There is no such thing as neutrality in Tonga, and most people were (or found it expedient to be) blindly loyal to the royal house. Puli'uvea seemed to be the nearest to a "loyal Opposition" Tonga had at that time.[35] When Puli'uvea was acquitted after a four-day trial, the onlookers cheered and applauded, suggesting that a significant number were pleased he had spoken out. The Queen blamed her old adversary, Sioape Kaho, for preparing the bullets fired by Puli'uvea, implying that he was not responsible, and she sent Puli'uvea food when he was in jail to show that she bore him no ill-will. This gesture of the Queen's was very much commented upon, as she well knew it would be, and was remembered long after Puli'uvea's speeches were forgotten.

After a long career in Parliament, Puli'uvea retired in 1959. James and Elizabeth Spillius, who arrived in Tonga in the year before Puli'uvea retired, did not report anything about the Democratic Party or Puli'uvea's exploits. James Spillius did comment that in the Parliament of 1959 the people's representatives and ministers usually opposed to each other, so the nobles' representatives held the balance of power and almost always supported the ministers. Tongan ministers were still appointed virtually for life by the Queen.[36]

No one remembers if the Queen sent food to two young Tongan men who were sentenced to death (one for a particularly brutal murder and the other for abetting the murder). This was the first death sentence since 1926, when a man was hanged in Vava'u for the murder of a young girl. Dilys Rowlands believed that the Queen was distressed at having to sign the death warrants, and some Tongans believed that the Queen would not sign; but she did so, and on 4 August 1955 Kelekolio Kaihea Funaki and Uikilifi Nau were hanged for murder of Sosefo Monu Pahulu.[37]

Did the British Agent & Consul advise her to sign? He still had the Queen's ear, but not that of the Premier. The Consul's prestige had suffered during the war, when it appeared that his position as adviser to the government of Tonga was largely ignored by the US commanding officers. And C. W. T. Johnson, Agent & Consul from June 1943 until March 1949, felt that Tupouto'a-Tungī was rejecting the British alliance, and looking to the USA. Tupouto'a-Tungī's sought a variance of the agreement between Tonga and the British Ministry for

Food about copra, even though there was no surety that the USA would pay as much as the British. One Consul complained that the Premier deliberately withheld from him information about major schemes, and that he heard only from "outside sources" matters on which his advice should have been sought according to the terms of the Treaty of Friendship.[38] Another Consul reported that whenever he had a conversation with the Premier, even in the presence of the Queen, their conversation was drowned out by two transistor radios that Tupouto'a-Tungī wore around his neck and played at full volume.[39]

J. E. Windrum succeeded Johnson in March 1949, and during his term the post of High Commissioner of the Western Pacific was separated from that of Governor of Fiji (in 1952) and Mrs Windrum accompanied Queen Sālote to the coronation of Queen Elizabeth II (in 1953). C. R. H. Nott succeeded Windrum in 1954, and was succeeded in March 1957 by A. C. (Archie) Reid, who negotiated the revision of the Treaty of Friendship of 1958, and would return (following Q. L. V. Weston and E. J. Coode) in the last year of Queen Sālote's life. The 1920s dictum that the British Agent & Consul should be a gentleman had been followed to the letter, and Reid in particular did a great deal to retrieve the prestige of the British. The Queen continued the habit formed during the war of taking walks along the beach front at night, and of occasionally calling at the Residency to discuss policy matters away from the observant eyes and ears at the Palace.

The Queen's sacred *mana* made it appropriate that she had a less public role in the government of Tonga. This *mana* extended to the royal family, and James Spillius reported that the Queen and her sons were accorded the greatest respect by everyone in the nation. "When the Queen or one of the princes leaves on a ship, the customary noise and bustle of the wharf is stilled. One can almost hear a pin drop, for respect to a great chief is shown by silence. No one's head must be higher than the Queen's. People do not speak to the Queen and princes unless spoken to, and do not eat in their presence."[40]

If there was some dissatisfaction with government, it did not affect the respect the people had for the Queen. She did not need to command, for everyone knew what was required in the Queen's presence. One could truly say that the less the Queen commanded, the more her wishes became an imperative for those around her. It was part of Queen Sālote's skill as a ruler that both intimacy and respect could be maintained at one at the same time. She had learned very early in her reign that *mana* and respect came with knowledge, love, and some fear. This respect for the Queen had been enhanced by the recognition of *papālangi*, which was nowhere so clearly demonstrated as when the Queen ventured, for the first time, to the kingdom of another Queen, Elizabeth II, on the occasion of the latter's coronation. It was also an opportunity for her to affirm that her personal loyalty to Britain had not wavered.

CHAPTER SIXTEEN

At the Coronation of Queen Elizabeth II

"I . . . considered myself fortunate to be able to meet and greet with the happiness of that day." (Queen Sālote, writing in her diary about Queen Elizabeth II's coronation day, 1953)

IN THE SECOND HALF OF QUEEN Sālote's reign, it was clear that she had won wide respect, not only that of her own people, but also of the representatives of Great Britain in the Pacific and people in those other parts of the south-west Pacific she had visited. In 1953 she won wider popularity, in an event attended by the great and famous of the world. This was the coronation of Queen Elizabeth II of Great Britain, at which Queen Sālote was an official guest. She would become an example of popular monarchy at a time when there were not only fewer and fewer crowned heads in the world, but royalty was not always respected.

Queen Sālote had always been a fervent admirer of Great Britain, believing that that country lived by a high moral code. She was genuinely grateful for the protection Great Britain had given Tonga, for the guidance she had received from the different British Consuls, for the support of High Commissioners of the Western Pacific, and for the interest the Colonial Office had taken in Tongan affairs. She also valued highly the British honours with which she had been invested in 1932 and 1945.

By attending the coronation of Queen Elizabeth II in London in June 1953 the Queen entered a wider stage, and proved that she had that elusive quality, charisma. She attracted attention from the time she set foot on English soil: the newspapers were delighted with her co-operation and newsworthiness as the only female reigning monarch other than Queen Elizabeth herself and for her physical *presence*, and the British crowds loved her for her natural dignity and friendliness.

The diary Queen Sālote kept of the journey and coronation shows her enormous capacity for enjoyment. The whole journey was a great delight for her, and she was full of admiration for everything she saw and experienced. She was often at a loss for words, and on occasion baffled by cultural differences. When she attended the ballet, for example, she was surprised that there was no singing, because in Tonga dance begins with poetry that becomes a song that is choreographed. According to Tongan standards, the leg movements in ballet were not "decent", but she was sufficiently familiar with *papālangi* ways to know that what was unacceptable in Tonga was sometimes praised elsewhere.[1]

Sālote was fascinated by the arrangements made for the coronation guests, not only on the coronation day itself (and that was worthy of much comment), but also by the attention given to the individual programmes for the hundreds of official guests. J. S. Neill, who had been Agent & Consul in Tonga 1927–37, was appointed her *attaché* and stayed at the residence provided for her, a house in Weymouth Street in the West End of London. A cook and housemaid looked after her and her entourage: Princess Mata'aho (wife of the Crown Prince), Mrs Lois Windrum (wife of the current Agent & Consul), and her maid, Susana Helu. The Queen returned home full of gratitude to God for providing Tonga with such a protector.

Crowds on the wharf sang and wept as the Queen left Tonga on 23 March 1953 on the *Tofua*, fearing that she might not return from such a long journey. Many people had earlier come to the Palace to bid farewell, and she found the hardest part of the journey was saying goodbye to the old people who might not be alive when she returned. "Now promise. No going before I return," she would say, and the old people would promise.[2]

The *Tofua* travelled via Vava'u, Niue, Pago Pago (American Sāmoa), Apia (Western Sāmoa) and Suva to Auckland, where the Queen spent 10 days at 'Atalanga, her new Auckland home, purchased by the Tonga government in the previous year for the royal family. Representatives of the New Zealand government farewelled her on 18 April when the *Rangitoto* sailed from Wellington, as did Dr Kronfeld, son of the guardian of her childhood days in Auckland.

The trip itself was full of novelty, not only for the Queen but also for the other coronation passengers travelling with her. A visit to Pitcairn Island took place on a Sunday, and the Queen did not disembark, so her first port was Panama, on 4 May. She was welcomed by the British Consul, who entertained her for the day the ship was in port. As the ship sailed through the Panama Canal, the Queen commented:

> There are no words adequate for praising or describing the Canal, or the wonder and the beauty of the work. I stood there without moving, marvelling at the energy that lay behind the great improvements in technology and communication among the peoples of the world. My heart warmed at the sight I beheld, and I gave thanks for the privilege of seeing this famous scene of this modern age. [all translations of diary by MT]

The British Consul at Curaçao also met the Queen and entertained her. The Queen had afternoon tea at the British Women's Club, and she commented, as she was to comment many times in the weeks ahead: "It was a happy welcome that the British women gave us. The tea was good and everything went well. Best of all were the hospitality and friendliness of these dear people."

Coronation guests took it in turn to give small parties for their fellow travellers, and language difficulties were a source of interest: "The fun was that we did not know each other's language well." The Queen longed for them to be her guests in Tonga, so she could repay the many kindnesses of strangers.

England was sighted on 17 May. The Queen was again overwhelmed, this time by seeing, at last, the heart of the British Empire.

> Ah! how the emotions welled up in my heart, confusion mixed with excitement, nervousness, and feelings of anticipation. But these feelings were checked by the thought of my unworthiness, and my nervousness made me feel somewhat cold. Fortunately I did not once lose faith in the justice of the purpose for which I was sent by my government and my people, which was to carry out this duty. So I was determined to do everything to the best of my ability at all times, and if I was not perfectly successful, then at least I had done my best.

The *Rangitoto* docked in Southampton on the afternoon of 18 May. Mr Neill was on the wharf to greet the Queen and her party; so was Sir Arthur Bromley, who greeted the coronation guests on behalf of the government, and took them to a VIP lounge for afternoon tea while their luggage was brought ashore. The guests would travel to London by train. Mr Neill performed his first duty as the Queen's *attaché* by protecting her from the "newspaper reporters and photographers who stormed us, like a whirlwind".

The Queen was delighted with her London house. Although it was not large, she felt that it was a historical British house. She was pleased that it was central, and that she could observe the people passing in the street. At first she was alarmed about the number of events planned for her before and after the coronation and had to remind herself that she was now in the "great world", which is controlled by time, not in Tonga, where people pleased themselves about time. She was impressed by the thought that had gone into preparing each person's programme, and reflected that "It is no wonder, for it is, after all, Britain, in which abound justice, skilful organization, and wisdom".

On 19 May the Queen attended the third day of a cricket match at Lord's Cricket Ground between the Marylebone Cricket Club and an Australian team. Cricket is, of course, a game much enjoyed in Tonga, but this was possibly the first time she had observed an international match. The Duke and Duchess of Beaufort gave lunch in the Queen's honour in the President's dining-room. The Queen observed that although they had high chiefly rank, they were a "truly amiable and kind couple".

On the following day, the Queen went to the Chelsea Flower Show.

> There are no new words to describe this event other than to say it was wonderful and heavenly. This show is an annual event in Britain, and I can't guess at the feelings of those who have come often to see it, but for me it was a totally new experience. It was as if the show was in a different world. Quite apart from the really exceptional beauty [of the flowers], the work of creating and developing the plants was something to marvel at. Clearly a lot of effort and skill had gone into attaining such beauty. I wanted to return often while the show was on, for the two or three hours of my visit were hardly enough to take everything in.

Concerts, theatres, lunches, visits to hospitals, to Greenwich Naval College and Museum, to Covent Garden (where she saw Margot Fonteyn dance), to the British and Foreign Bible Society, Westminster Central Hall to hear Dr Sangster preach, to Canterbury Cathedral, to the British Council, to the Queen Charlotte Maternity Hospital, to a Royal Garden Party at Buckingham Palace, where the Queen and Princess Mata'aho were introduced to Queen Elizabeth and other members of the royal family ("We returned home full of joy"), Windsor Castle, and Hatfield House, and so on. Everywhere she went she attracted attention, not only because of her height, which made her conspicuous, but also by her personality and her obvious enjoyment of her experiences.

During her London stay the Queen received visitors at her temporary home, and constantly met British people who had lived and worked in the Pacific, as well as Pacific Islands chiefs such as Ratu Sukuna, Malaea, and Siaosi Kadavulevu. She recorded in her diary not only the great occasions and the meetings with famous people, but also the afternoon teas she gave for old friends, including a daughter of Sam Kronfeld and former students of the Anglican Diocesan School for Girls, Auckland.

One newspaper reported that even before the coronation Queen Sālote attracted attention: "During her short stay here Queen Sālote, whose genial dignity matches her proportions, has won an extraordinary quantity of affection from the British people."[3] On the evening before the coronation, Sālote made a broadcast on the BBC, while Tu'ifua Carrick (Princess Mata'aho's mother's sister, a chief of high rank who had married a *papālangi*) helped to prepare Princess Mata'aho's *ta'ovala* for the big day. Queen Sālote reported that "It had started to rain while it was still daylight, just light showers, but the streets were packed with people [camped in the streets, waiting for the coronation procession]. Later in the night, it rained more heavily."

For the coronation, the Queen wore a long dress and a named fine-mat (possibly *Lālanga-'a-'Ulukilupetea*), a mantle, and her British honours, and in her hair a comb with *lave'i tavake* (tropic-bird feathers indicating high chiefly rank).[4] Queen Sālote gave a full description of the events of 2 June:

> The instructions book was sent to me seven days before the coronation day. Mata'aho and Mrs Windrum were to leave the house at 7 a.m. in the car provided for us (by the British Council). Mr Neill and Susana were to leave at 7.30 a.m. (they had seats in one of the stands). I was to leave at 8 a.m. Everything was done according to the instructions. I was the only person in the car sent by the British government (royal service), and I was driven directly to the Palace, which I entered. Some of our group were already there. When we were all there (no one was late), the first carriage arrived and I got into it with the Sultan of Kelantan. No time was lost, for as soon as we entered the carriage it left immediately, so that the next one could pick up its passengers. It was admirable the way the drivers of the carriages knew their duties and times, and there was no hesitation or confusion.
>
> While we were waiting at the Palace, we had heard cheering, and knew that the cheers were for the contingent of mayors. Then it was our turn: the rulers of different countries. The cheering continued all the way to our destination [Westminster Abbey]. Not a moment was lost, for as soon as we descended from the carriage, we were ready to enter. Our carriage was the first to leave the Palace, and it would be the last to leave the Abbey after the coronation. It was the same at the Abbey: the pair who entered first would be the last to leave. I don't know the reason for this, but it was clear that it was easier to keep things in order by doing it that way.
>
> It was amazing how orderly everything was in such a large procession, among such loud cheering, band music, gun salutes, etc. Even the horses seemed to join in the effort to keep everything orderly that day.
>
> A band inside the Abbey played very softly in the intervals between the arrival of the different groups. A fanfare of trumpets indicated the entrance of each group, and there was a longer one when the Queen [Elizabeth II] and the Duke [of Edinburgh] arrived. I was the first of our group, with the Sultan of Zanzibar and his wife following, as required by the instructions. On the return journey, I was just behind them.

When we entered the transept of the Abbey, we separated, and I went to the right while the Sultan of Zanzibar and his wife went to the left, and the pairs that followed did the same. Rulers without spouses came last.

A diagram in the coronation edition of the *Daily Express* shows that Queen Sālote's seat was in one of the especially constructed galleries, looking directly down to the coronation chair, so she had a clear view of the whole coronation.

Five or ten minutes after our arrival there was a fanfare to announce the arrival of the prime ministers, led by Churchill and his wife. Then came Queen Elizabeth's family, led by the Queen Mother. Then Queen Elizabeth arrived with her entourage. The flagbearers and others with various duties led the way, followed by the bishops, then the Queen and the Duke entered together. That is all that I saw: I do not know what happened before our arrival.

My heart was deeply touched by being a witness of such a great occasion, with its dignity and rituals. It was a religious ceremony, with all its stateliness. Quite apart from the more obvious things, there were the uniforms, the jewels, the sword and sceptre, and the presentation of the Bible. The things that warmed me most were the moment when the Archbishop announced that she was the rightful sovereign and the sound of the voice of dear young Queen making her vows.

When the Queen and her husband moved forward to receive the Sacrament, her crown was removed. No one who took part in that stately ceremony will ever forget the expression on the Queen's face. An inner glow emanated from her features, and although she was tired, a new strength radiated from her. And no wonder, for she was blessed by millions, and warmth came from the people to support her as she accepted the responsibilities that were laid upon her. The solemnity of the occasion touched everyone, quite apart from its glory and beauty. The coming together of nation, land, and church in supporting the Crown was clear.

My heart marvelled most of all and was most glad at perceiving the great peace that reigned among the different peoples who were present at the ceremony. There were different nationalities, languages, religions, goals, and skills and levels of knowledge, but it was a wonder to see how people mingled together in peace and happiness. I am certain that this mixing of peoples could not be effected anywhere except in Britain. I was thankful that I was able to be part of such an event.

After the coronation we were led to an annexe of the Abbey and offered a light meal. It consisted of tea or a cold drink, with sandwiches and cake.

It was now beginning to rain. When we had finished eating, the rain seemed to be heavier. By the time we reached the carriages, it was drizzling. After about 15 minutes, rain fell for perhaps 20 minutes. It drizzled once more, then there were bouts of heavy rain until the procession reached the Palace. The kind policemen who were looking after the procession asked the occupants of each carriage if they would like the hood of the carriage put up, and they all said they would. But when we were asked about our carriage – and fortunately I was the one who was asked – I was so caught up in the warmth of the people and the feelings of grace flooding my heart from the recent ceremony that I could not bear to be excluded from any part of that day, good or bad. Everything on that day was a treasure. So I told the policeman to leave the hood of our carriage down. I did not think to ask the chief [the Sultan of Kelantan], and he maintained silence with good grace. I apologized to him a few days later, and he accepted my apology gladly. That day we were both saturated with rain, but we were happy.

It was not that the other chiefly guests did not wish to be wet, but they did not think to do as we did, and they were probably wiser. Even I did not plan it that way. I just suddenly got the feeling that I wanted to join the people in the happiness of the day, and my Tongan heart was excited and foolish. But I am still thankful that I was soaked with rain on that significant day.

All the rulers and prime ministers returned to the Palace to wait for the Queen. Our carriage reached the Palace at 4 p.m., then, after the Queen and Duke departed, I hurried home, arriving at 5.25 p.m. Mata'aho and Mrs Windrum had arrived home first, then Mr Neill and Susana. Mrs Windrum immediately led me to my room, for she feared that I might be ill because of my wet clothes; but there were no ill-effects.

I did not at all expect that people would make such a fuss over the fact that I was wet, for I did not know that my carriage was the only one that had driven in the procession with the hood down. I did not notice what others were doing: I was too busy doing what I thought I should do. I was grateful to the people and the newspapers for praising me for riding in the rain, and I am honoured by their attention, but it is the same to me whether I was noticed or not. I was only happy because of the happenings of the day and the warmth that the people felt for their sovereign.

One wonders if, sitting in Westminster Abbey, Queen Sālote reflected on her own coronation, when she was even younger than Queen Elizabeth, and the vows she had taken on her own coronation day. Certainly she believed with all her heart that God had appointed the young Queen to rule, just as God had appointed Sālote herself to rule a much smaller kingdom. She was confident that the young queen had a sacred trust and was possessed of a sacred *mana* that would help Elizabeth to carry out her responsibilities.

Neill described Queen Sālote's return to the house in Weymouth Street:

I shall never forget her appearance when she arrived back from the ceremony. The mantle of the Dame Grand Cross of the British Empire, which she wore

> over her Tongan national dress, was saturated and water poured off it as she went to her room. In spite of this drenching she was in her gayest mood and it was most moving to listen to her as she described the events of the day and her thoughts on the spiritual significance and solemnity of the Coronation itself.[5]

Neill also reported that he was wakened at midnight that night by two journalists with flowers, inquiring whether the Queen had caught a chill. That was just the beginning. By the time the Queen arose in the morning, her house was mobbed by journalists and others wanting to see her, photograph her, and interview her. Neill, she reported, "struggled" with the telephone all day.

On the evening of 3 June the Queen attended a coronation dinner for 500 guests. She was escorted by the Archbishop of Canterbury, and sat at a table with Sir Winston and Lady Churchill. She "returned home very happy" at this first meeting with Churchill, whom she had greatly admired since World War Two, when he had been Great Britain's wartime leader and a focus for patriotism throughout the British Empire. It was during this evening that Queen Sālote had the opportunity during a conversation with Queen Elizabeth to request that the royal visit to Tonga in December be extended beyond the proposed few hours.

On the following days, Queen Sālote laid a wreath at the cenotaph (the only woman, she noticed, to do so on that day), was photographed by Lotte Meitner-Graf, attended the Coronation Thanksgiving Service at St Paul's, the Lord Mayor's coronation luncheon at Guildhall, Trooping the Colour, the Royal Military Tournament, and garden parties at Lambeth Palace and Blenheim Palace. She was a guest on the *Pretoria Castle* for the Review of the Royal Navy and ships from foreign nations. At a party at Number 10 Downing Street (the British Prime Minister's official residence), she reported standing in the same place for two hours so she could observe Sir Winston Churchill. "I returned home with great happiness", she reported. Indeed, she often commented on her joy and on "overflowing with contentment" during the various official events in which she participated. Wherever she went, she was cheered by crowds who instantly recognized her from the photographs published in the newspapers.

From the 17 June until 2 July the Queen, Princess Mata'aho, Mr Neill, Mrs Windrum, and Susana Helu toured Scotland, the Isle of Man, and Ireland in two cars. Everywhere she went, the Queen was received by dignitaries of the place and warmly welcomed by the people. She was enormously impressed by the way the British had preserved their traditions and looked after historic buildings and places of historical interest, as well as by the towns and countryside. On her return to London, she commented that she was fatigued from the journey, and recorded: "I am so tired from the journey that I can hardly move. But even though my body is tired, my mind and heart are filled to the brim with happiness and thankfulness at everything I have experienced."

Her fatigue led to Princess Mata'aho representing her at the planting of a commemoration oak tree in Windsor Great Park. Just as the Tongan party was about to leave London, supplies of food the Queen had ordered in New Zealand arrived, and were distributed in Tongan fashion among their friends. (Food was still rationed in England.)

The Queen often said how much she would like to stay longer in some of the peculiarly British, picturesque, or historic places. When the day came for her to fly to Paris, she was overcome by emotion: "Ah! I am saddened to leave this land. Different emotions fill my heart. I never want to be parted from Britain. I fear it may be said that I am being silly or just flattering, but it is true. . . . We flew to a height of 95,000 [*sic*] feet, and I beheld beautiful Britain. I could hardly stop the tears as I looked down at the Cliffs of Dover."

In Paris as elsewhere the Queen was met and entertained by representatives of the British government. After sightseeing in Paris and its environs, the Queen and her party took a train to Geneva, where she visited the headquarters of the Red Cross and the World Council of Churches. She commented on the importance of the latter: "This is such a beautiful place. I am grateful for this support for human life. This is ammunition that will conquer the world. It is not noticed or well-known, but it will stand."

The royal party continued by car through Italy, and eventually arrived in Rome. The Queen had an audience with Pope Pius XII on 20 July, another highlight of her travels. Although she was impressed with the pomp of the Vatican, she was more aware of the fact that she was to meet with an important person. The description shows the Queen's eye for the detail of the physical surroundings, as well as her awareness of the protocol that surrounded her visit:

> We went today to visit His Holiness the Pope at 10 a.m. I count as one of the most important events of the trip the fact that I met the religious leader of millions of Christians in the world. At the Vatican (full court) I was given the complete reception for a sovereign. My heart was touched at this gesture of respect.
>
> As my car entered the gate, the guards were spaced out at each side of the road right to the Palace door. Someone descended the steps in front of the Palace to greet us as we arrived. The head of the guards was also there. He greeted me, then Mata'aho, Mrs Windrum, and Mr Neill. Behind him stood the bishop who welcomed visitors. We then entered the building. The head of the guards went first, then two guards, then I was next, with the bishop who greeted visitors and a priest on each side. (The priest seemed to be the one who ushered visitors to the Pope, for he opened all the doors for us to go through.) The rest of the party followed.
>
> We proceeded straight ahead, then we climbed up a very wide flight of marble stairs of 25 steps. We turned left, then climbed another flight of marble

stairs of about 25 steps. We then reached the first hall. Each side was lined by six guards, who were spaced out from each other. They stood at attention when we walked past. The door was opened and we entered a room in which 12 guards stood in pairs facing each other just as the guards in the hall did. This second set of guards had different uniforms from the first set of guards. We walked past these guards and at the end of the room a door was opened and we entered another room, which was just like the room we had just left. Again 12 guards were there facing each other just as the other guards did, and these had different uniforms. There were now three different sets of uniforms. After walking past the guards and reaching the end of the room, another door was opened and we entered a very long room. About halfway down the room (directly facing the door through which we entered) was a big, ornately decorated door, which was the entrance to the throne room of the Pope. The door was closed, and we turned to the right where the head priests of the Vatican were standing.

It was a long corridor, probably the waiting room for those who were going into the throne room, for it was carpeted and had several seats and expensive-looking curtains. At the end of the room, I was taken to a little table beside which was a door. My gloves were taken off there, and my handbag was placed there. The priest opened the door (after knocking three times) and I was ushered in. As I entered, I looked towards the right. The Pope was sitting at his writing desk. So this was his writing room. He stood up as I walked towards the desk; it took me one step only. He stretched out his hand and shook mine, and greeted me happily, then showed me to a chair opposite his. When I was seated, he sat down and said that he was glad I had come to see him for he knew I had attended the coronation of Queen Elizabeth. I thanked him for letting me visit him, for I did not wish to come to Rome and not see him, as I wished to convey to him the respect and love of the thousands of my people who were in the Catholic Church. He looked kindly and peaceful as we talked.

I was given 15 minutes to talk to him. When I saw the little gold clock on his table indicate that 15 minutes had gone, I did not feel at ease about getting up to say goodbye, for it was he who controlled the visit. He continued talking about the ways of the world, and then told me that he had appointed a Bishop for Tonga. That was the first I knew of the appointment of Sipita [John Rodgers]. After 20 minutes of conversation, he stood up and raised his hand and made the sign of the cross over my head, then he rang a little golden bell and I stood up. The door opened and Mata'aho, Mrs Windrum, and Mr Neill entered, and I introduced them. The Pope presented me with a gold medal, and gave a brass medal to each of the others in memory of our visit. My heart felt a warmth when I conversed with the Pope and heard his advice and blessings. They were a treasure to me. He was an aristocrat whose compassion and wisdom showed upon his face. I was surprised when we turned to go after bidding the Pope

> farewell, for he walked with us to the door. As I stepped outside, my heart was full of gladness and gratitude because of this great honour and the great humility shown to me by this aristocrat. After I left the room, all the heads of departments of the Vatican greeted me.
>
> We returned by a different route. After we descended only one flight of marble stairs, we went through halls whose floors seemed to slope downhill, then entered the waiting room of the cardinals. One Cardinal was there with three or four priests. Our party talked with the Cardinal, while a priest took me to a beautifully decorated room in which there were three golden chairs. The Secretary for Foreign Affairs, the Pope's Private Secretary, and I each took a chair. After we talked for a short while, we returned to the other room, then proceeded to the main hall. The Cardinal and the Pope's Secretary remained there, while the rest escorted us to our cars. We bade farewell to the dear priests and the heads of departments, then we left.
>
> Fifteen minutes after our return, the Secretary for Foreign Affairs and a priest arrived to reciprocate my visit to the Pope. We talked for 10 minutes, then they departed. I felt greatly blessed on this day, and I thanked God for letting me take part in this rare honour.

It was typical of the Queen that she recognized the high rank and the quality of leadership in the head of the Roman Catholic Church, and that she wished to communicate with someone who was important to thousands of her own subjects.

The Queen was impressed with the grandeur of Rome, and after a day of sightseeing and a dinner at the British Embassy, the royal party left for Naples. After another round of sightseeing, the Queen said goodbye to Mr Neill and boarded the *Orontes* on 23 July, accompanied by Princess Mata'aho, Mrs Windrum, and Susana. This was, for her, the end of the journey, and she reflected in her diary on all that had happened in the previous weeks:

> Ah! What can ever compare with my feeling that the trip was now over. Although there were still thousands of miles before we would reach Tonga, yet the journey had turned homeward. As the steamer left the Bay of Naples, I stood in my cabin and looked out to sea, and reflected on the mission completed, its goal, and the things that had occurred, and how the love of God and of the people had enveloped me wherever I went. Yes, and here I was on board the boat to return happily. My thoughts sank to unbearable depths, and I fell to my knees and praised God.

After all the happiness of travel, the Queen now did not feel well and kept to her cabin for the first week. Until Perth, she attended only a few functions on board, and waited until the decks were deserted before she took her evening walk. Although she was met by the Governor of each state of Australia and by other dignitaries, there was a special mention in her diary of those who had been missionaries to Tonga: Walter Shepherd and Mrs Shepherd and Kathleen Grimmett in Adelaide; Dr Harold Wood and Dr Olive Wood at the Methodist Ladies' College in Melbourne, where on 8 August she laid the foundation stone of a new building and had lunch. The visit to the Methodist Ladies' College had a special poignancy, for her half-sister, Fusipala, had been a pupil at the school in 1926–28. A chapel built at that school in the 1950s commemorates both Queen Sālote and Princess Fusipala in stained-glass windows.

At Sydney, unaware of the welcome that awaited her on a flotilla of boats on the harbour, Queen Sālote remained in her cabin until the *Orontes* berthed. Thousands welcomed her on the wharf, clapping and cheering her. Again she met with former missionaries: Rodger Page, Cecil and Isabel Gribble, Vivienne Norman, also Ronald Pearson (the builder of the Centenary Church, Nuku'alofa). There were also Tongan students and Mrs Hewitt, who had hosted Princess Fusipala in Sydney in the months before the Princess's death.

At last the time came to fly to New Zealand, and on arrival on 27 August at her Auckland home, 'Atalanga, Sālote reflected that she was at last in Tonga: "What happiness stormed my heart. Thanks be for the protection, and the guidance given me, that I had reached the final stage of the journey and the mission has been accomplished."

Queen Sālote was "fatigued from travelling the world", but after a medical check-up she immediately set about preparing for the royal visit of Queen Elizabeth and the Duke and Edinburgh to Tonga in December. With the assistance of Mrs Bagnall, she ordered:

> crockery, curtains, sheets, towels, etc. etc. Then there was the meat, such as chicken and turkey, and just little things to do with eating and drinking. It took the whole of that week and a part of the next week . . . After that, we had to arrange for a motor car to transport our royal visitors. Then we looked for silver cutlery for the dinner table. I had to attend to this personally, for the government responsibility was separate from my personal concerns.
>
> I met Kitione Lave in New Zealand, and I attended one of his boxing matches – he won.[6] I received a lot of gifts and invitations in New Zealand, but there was little time, and my strength was waning. However, my happiness was never little, and I was thankful for everything.

On 5 October the Queen arrived back in Tonga. She had been farewelled with tears in March, now she was welcomed with joyful celebrations that extended over a fortnight, and included dances and presentations. The Queen's popularity in Britain was by now known to everyone in Tonga, as was the great welcome she had received everywhere on her travels. Although her celebrity caused no surprise in the country where her *mana* was exceedingly high, joy and thankfulness for her successful tour and safe return were fully expressed in those two weeks. Queen Sālote wrote the following song about her visit to the coronation:

1. Mata me'a fo'oua
Siofia he masani
Matanga e fonua
Moe hala he Kanali
Vai to he mo'unga
Moe 'akau he tele'a
Fakalelu ne hounga
Ki he loto kavea

2. Ko e matangi kehekehe
Angi he 'otu tahina
Ko e talanoa 'eke
'O ha'ate fiefia
Tala hono fakaofo
Si'i le'o 'o natula
'Oku ongo he lololo
Ko hoto pale tu'a

3. A'usia 'ete 'alu
Kolomu'a e maama
Ko e fakatalutalu
Ne ngangatu hono tala
Seti'anga siueli
Tapa 'aho mo e po
Kalauni 'o e 'ofa
Ko si'oto manako

4. Kolo 'o e faka uo
Uta'anga fiefia
Si'i taloni e melino
'I he 'ano 'i Siniva
Tuku e tapuaki
Lau ai 'ete malo
Foki 'i he 'alavini
Ki he vaha mama'o.

Tau: Fie lau si'a ipu
Ne fonu mahuohua
'O tatau aipe
He la'a mo e 'uha
Kaekehe ne takua
He 'Otu Felenite
'I he langi 'oku nunu
Ai e palanite.

* * *

1. Seeing new things
relishing the splendour
scenery of the land
route through the Canal
waterfalls on the mountains
flora of the valleys
timely comfort
to the love-lorn heart.

2. Varied winds
fluttering the seas
voices asking
about my joy
tell the wonders
of the dear voice of nature
echoing in the deep
my shield and support.

3. My journey reached
the row of lights
from ancient days
its scented tales
where jewels are set
day and night sparkling
crown of love
my treasure

4. festive city
source of gaiety
throne of peace
Geneva's lakes

leave blessings
my gratitude abounds
before returning
to the deep sea.

Chorus: Speak of a cup
overflowing with goodness
the same
in sun and rain
as long as
the Friendly Isles are spoken of
in a sky studded
with planets. [MT]

The visit to Britain had been the fulfilment of a long-held dream. The British Press and public had first noticed Queen Sālote because (like Queen Elizabeth) she was a queen in her own right, then because she was conspicuous in any company ("the largest queen of the smallest kingdom"), and some at least would have known that the contribution by Tonga to the war effort had been outstanding considering the small size of the kingdom. Sālote's popularity reached fever pitch as the coronation drew near, and was overwhelming when hers was the only carriage to drive in the royal procession with the hood down. It was this sharing of enthusiasm with those who had camped out overnight in the streets that was so typical of her, and had won so many hearts. Far from abandoning royal dignity, she extended her royal "shade" to all of those with whom she came in contact.

Further, her expectations of the heart of the British Empire were more than fulfilled. In spite of the slow recovery from the destruction and deprivations of World War Two, Britain had put on a marvellous show that reflected months of organization and long experience of great events. Whether meeting officials from the Colonial Office, visiting an institution such as the British Council, or viewing a historic building, the Queen was greatly impressed by all she saw, and wished to share that pleasure with those around her. Thus enthusiasm met enthusiasm; her appreciation for the efforts of others was strongly expressed.

Queen Sālote had reached the zenith of her reputation. The qualities recognized in her by strangers were the same as those that had made her a loved and respected leader of her own people. Sheer force of personality had increased her rank and added to the lustre of her title. The Tupou dynasty was now, without doubt, supreme in Tonga.

It was only after the celebrations in Tonga for her successful tour and safe return were over that Queen Sālote was able to give her full attention to all the details of the coming royal visit. Sālote was not apprehensive of the task that lay before the Tongan people; rather, she was delighted that she could offer hospitality to Queen Elizabeth and the Duke of Edinburgh in truly regal Tongan style.

The royal visit to Tonga had originally been allocated only three hours on a Sunday. Not only was this time too short but it was restrictive, since dancing, large-scale presentations, and other rituals could not occur on the Sabbath. The Press also demanded more time for photographs of the meeting of the two royal personages. The news that the visit was extended to two days, Saturday and Sunday, 19 and 20 December 1953, came only 50 days before the event. The preparations and event are described by Kenneth Bain, Secretary to Government, in *The Official Record of the Royal Visit to Tonga*, and this is the main source for the following account.

From the time of Queen Sālote's return to Tonga, all other duties of the chiefs and employees of the government were put aside so they could concentrate on the visit. The Palace would be at the disposal of Queen Elizabeth and her husband, so Queen Sālote moved to Fatai, in Kolofo'ou, now the home of her son Tu'ipelehake, during the renovations and for the duration of the royal visit.

Tongans living in Nuku'alofa were requested to accommodate 70 journalists and photographers, which required beautification of their homes. Tu'ipelehake accepted responsibility for the feast on the Saturday to which a thousand guests would be invited, including all *papālangi* residents.

On the order of chiefs, pigs were fattened and food crops reserved in order to provide not just what would be adequate to eat, but a superabundance, which would indicate the heartfelt welcome of the Tongan chiefs and people. Quality gifts were prepared. Mats and bark cloth (some designs commemorating Sālote's visit to London[7]) decorated private and public places, many to be given to those accompanying the royal visitors. Songs were written to mark the occasion and dances rehearsed in the villages. There were instructions from the Queen about the dress required for the occasion: neatness, colour co-ordination, and *ta'ovala* would be required from everyone. Queen Sālote went to meet Queen Elizabeth and the Duke of Edinburgh at the wharf wearing the named fine-mat *Lālanga-'o-'Ulukilupetea*, reputed to be more than 600 years old. As the flying-boat landed on the waters of the harbour, the final touches in the form of flowers and greenery were added to a series of arches that welcomed the royal couple so all would be at their peak of freshness.

At the feast on the Saturday, 19 December, Crown Prince Tupouto'a-Tungī welcomed Queen Elizabeth and the Duke on behalf of Queen Sālote and the chiefs and people of Tonga.[8] Following the feast the royal party adjourned to the Mala'e to watch the dances, of which there were a variety: *me'etu'upaki*, *eke*, *kailao*, *tau'olunga*, *lakalaka*, and *mā'ulu'ulu*. Queen Sālote wrote the words of one *mā'ulu'ulu* especially for the occasion. Typically of Queen Sālote's poetry, there were allusions to her guests and the occasion, and also to Tonga's historic and mythic past.

1. Nepituno fai ha'o malelenga
Kuo u fanongo ha tala mahe'a
Tā ne kolosi 'ae 'Ekueta
'E he Hau tu'u fakaleveleva
Ko e siu fakahāko noa
'A e taulau tavake-oma
'O fekumi ki he 'api moana
'O e Matakali Polinisia.

Tau: He tuetuē kae fēfē
Ko e hakailangitau'anga ē
'Ofa ke tolonga 'o tuputupu'a
'A e Hau 'oku malu'i fonua.

2. Mafola e Pasifiki Saute
Hono 'otu motu ne lau afe
Ka ne fakakū pea 'anefē
Kalauni Sovaleni ne afe
'Eva he matangi fakatētē
Pea mo e 'ea e vaha mohe
He ko e afenga fakame'ite
Lata'anga 'oe manu ta'ane.

3. 'E Hina mo Sinilau ke hake
'I he fanga e 'otu Felenite
Tama ko Tangita koe pā ā
'Oku kei tu'u moe lau pē
Kuo lahi 'ae folau mole
He tautefua 'a niumotu'u e
'O fakamo'oni he 'aho koe
'A e tepi fakangali fefine.

* * *

1. Neptune, rejoice.
I have heard tell
that the equator has been traversed
by the imperial ruler.
Flying leisurely above,
two frigate birds
seek the ocean home
of the Polynesian race.

Refrain:
Shout out in joy!
Here is the reason for rejoicing.
May the dynasty that defends our land
for ever hold sway.

2. The South Pacific spreads widely
with its thousands of isles.
But when, oh when,
has a crowned sovereign turned hence
to savour the sea breezes
and the air between the islands.
For here is a pleasing sojourn
favoured by the wandering birds.

3. Hina and Sinilau, alight
on the shores of the Friendly Isles.
Here the shield stands,
symbol of our unity.
Many a voyage has been lost,
but Tonga alone has survived,
and this day may witness still
the dignified walk of free women. [MT]

Before dinner at the British Residency, Queen Elizabeth invested Queen Sālote with the order of Dame Grand Cross of the Royal Victorian Order (GCVO), the third British honour to be bestowed on the Queen of Tonga. After a private dance, Queen Elizabeth and the Duke of Edinburgh retired for the night, while 400 people kept torches alight all night around the Palace. Queen Sālote was driven around the Palace during the night so she was personally assured that all was well.

A group of nose-flute players awakened the royal guests on the second day of their visit, which began with a service at the recently completed Centenary

Church, during which a Tongan choir sang the "Sanctus" (in Latin) from Bach's *Mass in B Minor*. A private lunch at the Queen's country residence at Kauvai followed, while the companies of the *Gothic* and the *Black Prince* (which had arrived to take the royal guests away) were feasted at the Mala'e Pangai, between the Palace and the wharf. Before leaving the Palace, Queen Elizabeth recognized different people who had waited on the royal visitors. Nānisi Helu, one of Queen Sālote's women, told me that according to Tongan custom she entered the throne room on her knees, and when Queen Elizabeth thanked her and gave her a medal, Nānisi remembered what her mother had told her was the proper Tongan way to receive a gift, so taking the box containing the medal she raised her arms to place the gift briefly on her head. Also following Tongan custom, Nānisi gave the medal to Queen Sālote, but the Queen would not accept it.

A launch from the *Gothic* carried Queen Elizabeth and the Duke to the ship, and another carried Queen Sālote and members of the Tongan royal family in order to extend the farewells to the last moment. In her Christmas broadcast on the BBC shortly afterwards, the Queen referred to the visitors' experience of the "simple life of the Pacific Islander", but the truth was that no effort had been spared to make the visit a royal one that celebrated the alliance between two monarchs who shared a sacred duty to rule. Not the least was that Queen Sālote wanted the world – and particular her own subjects – to know that the word "Friendship" was what was now important in the Treaty of Friendship between Tonga and Great Britain.

There were outcomes of the two royal visits. One was that people throughout the English-speaking world heard of Tonga and its Queen. Assistance at times of disaster had always come from the Methodist Church of Australasia, but after 1953 assistance came from other sources also. After a major hurricane that caused great damage to Ha'apai and Vava'u on 16 March 1961 notable help was given not only by the churches but by the governments of Australia, New Zealand, Fiji, the United Kingdom, and the USA.[9]

Another outcome was that Tongans learned more about the outside world. Queen Sālote had won a great deal of good will for Tonga. Although Tupouto'a-Tungī was keen on an informal alliance with the USA, the two royal visits ensured that Tonga remained within the British Empire.

When Parliament suggested a revision of the Treaty of Friendship, Sālote confided in the Agent & Consul that she preferred the initiative to come from Britain, not from her own Parliament – and this was the way it was done.[10] Nevertheless, Tupouto'a-Tungī, as Premier, was the moving force behind the revision. He had not been happy about following the example of his predecessors in making weekly visits to the Consulate to seek the Agent & Consul's advice on matters of government, nor did he like the British Agent & Consul having so much say in Tonga's finances, for the latter not only had to approve the annual estimates of revenue and expenditure of the government, but his signature had to appear on special warrants for expenditure. Britain was in the process of divesting itself of many of its colonies and other responsibilities of empire, so the two governments agreed amicably to the revision of the Treaty. In future the Agent & Consul would give advice only when it was sought, and financial control came to an end. Britain still had to be consulted about foreign relations and it continued to be responsible for the defence of Tonga (through New Zealand). The Tonga Defence Force, which had ceased to exist in October 1945, and had been revived in 1954, would be substantially increased.[11]

Just as Tungī Mailefihi had always attended the Queen when granted audiences to the British Agent & Consul, Tupouto'a-Tungī was always with her when details of the revised Treaty were discussed with the Agent & Consul (now to be designated the British Commissioner and Consul), A. C. Reid. The Premier signed the revised Treaty on the Queen's behalf, and was made a Knight Commander of the Order of the British Empire (KBE).[12] But the Queen was the focus of the celebrations that followed.

The Queen felt nostalgia for the days when she and Tungī Mailefihi had depended upon the British Agent & Consul for advice and support. In her speech at the Closing of the 1958 session of Parliament, which followed the signing of the revised Treaty, she said: "Our hearts are full of gratitude when we consider how Tonga has been protected through turbulent periods of the past by the Treaty of Friendship. This should create in us a greater desire to give thanks to Almighty God for making the Treaty of Friendship an instrument whereby His mercy and loving kindness are vouchsafed to us."[13]

The Queen reminded Parliament of its new responsibilities at the Opening of a Special Session of Parliament in February 1959: "this will be the first occasion [Parliament] will act independently without seeking the advice on financial matters from our Friend and Protector".[14]

Although Tupouto'a-Tungī sometimes spent half of each year overseas, searching for new alliances and new markets, the Queen kept the British alliance before the eyes of her people. The advantages were stability. Largely due to Tupouto'a-Tungī's efforts, but with the Queen's willing consent, English became the second language of Tongans, and this in turn directed the policy of Tonga. In 1970 (when the Treaty was again revised) Tonga stayed within the British Commonwealth of Nations.

CHAPTER SEVENTEEN

Changing Roles

"it is a stretch of sea that I am accustomed to sail – the keeping and watching of good relationships among the people". (Queen Sālote to Sau Faupula, 25 Sept. 1942)

IN THE 1950S IT SEEMED THAT Queen Sālote had gone into semi-retirement, leaving government to the Crown Prince. Indeed, as early as 1953 the Queen talked of abdicating in his favour and going to live in Ha'apai.[1] Those to whom the Queen spoke about her possible abdication – Rodger Page, Father Tremblay, A. C. Reid, and Elizabeth Bott Spillius – all assured her that she was very much needed, first by the kingdom and second to guide the Crown Prince. So the Queen did not abdicate, instead spending more time away from the capital, visiting other islands in the Tongan group and passing the summer months in Auckland, with occasional visits to Australia. Perhaps travelling within the kingdom made her realize her enormous influence, and the impossibility of abdication, for whether she kept her Tu'i Kanokupolu title or not, and regardless of where she lived, the chiefs and people would still form a court around her.

The new dual leadership was different in style from the old. The major difference between the Queen and Tungī Mailefihi on the one hand and the Queen and Tupouto'a-Tungī on the other was that the first was a partnership, while the second was a contrast. Another difference between the old and new styles of dual leadership was that where Tungī Mailefihi had been primarily devoted to the development of farm produce for the benefit of Tongans and only secondarily for export, Tupouto'a-Tungī looked to the wider world for ideas for the development of different kinds of business to benefit the economy. If the Queen did not altogether approve of what the Crown Prince was doing, she did not interfere, knowing that public differences within the royal family would be harmful to its reputation. While she had strong opinions about what the country should be doing and how chiefs and people should behave, she left decisions relating to finance, trade, and shipping to the Premier and Cabinet. She concentrated on matters that had always been very close to her heart: trying to ensure that Tongans felt confidence in their own identity no matter what changes occurred.

Queen Sālote continued to encourage hereditary estateholders to distribute land among the people, but she seemed to give up hope that they would take their leadership duties seriously. Instead she focused more on ordinary people, influencing them to use their abilities for the good of the kingdom. As has already been mentioned, during Queen Sālote's reign almost all of those who went overseas for education returned to Tonga. She certainly had the gift of perceiving potential in others and knew how to foster those innate skills. Examples of encouragement was her support for Sau Faupula and his second wife, Manu, the former becoming Head Tutor of Tupou College and editor of *Ko e Tohi Fanongonongo* and the latter becoming the Head Tutor of Queen Sālote College for girls. Another was the brilliant and handsome Mānoa, son of Sione Havea, who eventually became Minister for Police. Among others were Temaleti Vakasiuola, of Fua'amotu, who became the Queen's dressmaker and was sent by the Queen to study dressmaking in Sydney, and Konai Helu Thaman, now Tonga's foremost poet and Head of the School of Humanities at the University of the South Pacific. Yet another was Sione Lātūkefu (chapter 18).

Queen Sālote set up networks in the Free Wesleyan Church throughout the kingdom as a way of keeping in touch with the people. She continued to lead a class-meeting of women of the Kolomotu'a congregation, who came together every week at the Palace. She prepared Bible studies and prayers for the Ako Lotu (Christian Endeavour) and other groups. These studies and prayers were not only thoughtful, but were based upon wide reading. She carried out the task with humour.

> It is not only Christian Endeavour but return to hard endeavour for some. There are some who cannot manage to learn by heart the outlines I write out, and we try two or three times. Then I give them the reasons and they try to learn them and make up their talks. It is tedious too, but sometimes it is funny. Kuea here cannot make up the talks, cannot learn by heart, cannot remember a thing he is told, pleases himself what he says when he gives a talk, and entirely disregards the little thing I have given him. However, that's the way of it and that's how their Christian Endeavour meetings are carried out here.[2]

A project dear to Queen Sālote's heart came to fruition in the 1950s. During the celebration in 1926 of the centenary of the coming of the missionaries John Thomas and John Hutchinson to Tonga, it was decided to build a Centenary Church in Nuku'alofa. The new church would commemorate the common origin of the Free Church and Free Wesleyan Church and symbolize the reunion of the two churches. The debts of the reunited Free Wesleyan Church, the Depression of the 1930s, and the war had all delayed the enterprise. When the project was revived, support was given because the church seemed also to be a memorial to Rodger Page, who retired due to ill health in 1946, after 40 years of devoted ministry in Tonga. On a visit in 1950 Page was the inspiration for 1000 people who came together with two lorries and a number of carts in the presence of the Queen and a brass band to move the large old wooden oval-shaped church of Kolomotu'a two hundred or so metres southwards, around the Maamaloa (later taken to Toloa) to allow space for the new building.[3] At the instigation of the Queen, young men left their allotments during the following months to mix concrete for the new church. The Centenary Church was opened on 25–27 September 1952 with much celebration.

This "cathedral" was then the largest church in Tonga, but even with seating for 2000, it could not contain the numbers that came to the major celebratory services or for the choir festivals. On such occasions the doors on both sides were opened to allow participation by those who crowded into the church grounds or sat upon the encircling stone wall. As was customary in Tongan churches, there were places set aside for special categories of people. The seats for the royal family were at the front, on the left hand side facing the pulpit. The Queen sat in the front row of this section, where she could not only keep an eye on the ministers, but also on the congregation, the choirs, and the children sitting on the floor at the front. Like the Lord watching over Israel, Queen Sālote was watching over her people!

The Queen made a very personal statement in this church building, for she arranged for two stained-glass windows to be made and installed. One was in memory of Mele Siu'ilikutapu and one in memory of Queen Lavinia. Every Sunday as the congregation looked above the minister's head they were reminded not only of the descent of the royal house from the highly ranked Mele Siu'ilikutapu, but that she was (daringly) matched by the very Queen Lavinia whom the chiefs had once scorned. No one would deny that the mother of Queen Sālote deserved that place of religious and secular eminence. Once divisive, Queen Lavinia's position as royal mother now made her a symbol of reconciliation.

Queen Sālote took great pride in the church, and was involved in its many happenings. On a Saturday evening she would often walk down to the church with one or two of her women to make sure that the building had been cleaned and decorated in preparation for the Sabbath. Woe betide any helpers who had not carried out their duty of preparation to the Queen's satisfaction!

The Queen used a visit in 1947 by Page to reconcile the "Old Boys" of Tupou College to the removal of the college from Nafualu to Toloa in the Eastern District, which occurred in the following year. On the Nafualu site the Queen was the moving spirit behind the setting up in June 1948 of a Bible College. To this new institution she gave the name Sia'atoutai ("Preparation of the Nets of Fishermen", a reference to Jesus' description of his disciples as "Fishers of Men").

After Rodger Page's retirement, the Queen relied more than ever on Sau Faupula, with whom she kept up a correspondence over 25 years. The recurring theme of the letters was that she did not wish to interfere, but only to pass on suggestions to people in the church. She continued to pay close attention to the stationing of all the ministers undertaken by the *papālangi* presidents of the Free Wesleyan Church. One might say that the Queen had a talent for the ordinary as well as the extraordinary, for she seemed to be ready with a solution to every problem. For example, in 1951, she personally decided that Rev. Ron and Ruth Woodgate should move from Tupou College to Sia'atoutai and that Rev. Howard and Janet Secomb should move from Vava'u to Tupou College.

In 1955 the Queen founded the Kaluseti (Crusaders). It resembled the Christian Endeavour except that it was an organization for women only. Leaders among the women of the villages attended a monthly meeting where the Queen (later Dilys Rowlands, Janet Secomb, and Ruth Woodgate) gave them guidance on the Bible studies for that month. The leaders then passed on what they had learned to the women in the villages. The Queen's Bible study notes were published by Sau Faupula in the church newspaper *Ko e Tohi Fanongonongo* so they could be used by the men also. The Queen also founded a fellowship for ministers' wives, so they could learn the roles expected of them in the church.

All these church activities took up a lot of the Queen's time, but in her view the importance of the church was not only to sustain a community but also to nourish the spiritual life of the people. She herself spent hours in reading and quiet reflection, and was comfortable in talking about her Christian faith. She had strong feelings about the struggle between good and evil, believing (as many did in the 1950s) that communism was the face of evil in the world. She did not, however, deny the existence of evil within her own kingdom and within individuals.

As a Tongan, Queen Sālote retained the ideal of the high status of women within any society or institution. She had always supported the education of girls at the Kolisi Fefine, the school renamed Queen Sālote College in 1941.[4] Ostensibly the school was named in honour of Sālote Lupepau'u, the wife of Tupou I, but the special day of the school was 13 March, Queen Sālote Tupou III's birthday. When Mary Thompson moved to Vava'u in 1945, Dilys Rowlands took over as Principal of the college until 1968. Dilys was devoted to the church and school in a way that struck a chord with the Queen. Together they planned church and secular events, especially those that involved women.

However, although nobles contributed to a fund set up by the Queen in 1938 to educate their eldest sons, there was no fund for chiefly – or commoner – girls. If they wanted more education than Tonga could provide they had to be financially supported by their own families. Halaevalu Mata'aho, later to marry Tupouto'a-Tungī, was a pupil at St Mary's convent school in Auckland; Melenaite Tupou Moheofo of the Veikune family, later to become the wife of Prince Tu'ipelehake, attended Ravenswood Methodist School for Girls in Sydney; Fatafehi (eldest daughter of Vīlai Tupou), later to marry Laufilitonga, heir to the Tuita title, and Tuputupu (daughter of the noble Ma'afu), who would marry the noble Vaea ('Alipate Tupou), were pupils at the Anglican Diocesan School for Girls in Auckland (Figure 17.1). In the 1950s some commoner girls trained as nurses. Fatafehi Mataele and Lesieli Soakai trained in Auckland; Moala Simiki, later Matron of Vaiola Hospital, and her sister 'Amelia trained in Sydney, their meagre allowances going to support their brother at Gatton Agricultural College in Queensland – an example of sister–brother support.

Queen Sālote's continuing emphasis on health, education, and land was demonstrated when, in 1953, she appointed Tu'ipelehake as Minister for Health and Lands, while Tupouto'a-Tungī continued as Minister for Education and Agriculture as well as Premier. The Queen counted the setting up of the Central Medical School in Suva in 1929 as the second important *personal* achievement of her reign (the first being the reunion of the churches in 1924). Now Tongans returning from the Central Medical School staffed rural dispensaries as well as the hospitals. In spite of the availability of doctors with CMS training the Queen's authority was such that when she told people to "starve a fever", they became skeletal rather than ignore her advice![5]

The Queen was well known for her rapport with children: "Come and sit by me" she would say. She was also pleased that the population steadily increased. But the Queen came to believe that the health of mothers could be improved by spacing children, and medical advice would help to reduce the number of abortions and prevent pregnancies for women in poor health. (Women who were admitted to Vaiola Hospital with mismanaged abortions numbered 21 in 1955, 19 in 1956, and 37 in 1957.) So a family planning service was set up in the 1950s with the Queen's support.

In 1953 the Queen set up the Queen Sālote School of Nursing to train girls locally in Western-style care. She always took a great personal interest in the school, speaking at end-of-year events and awarding the certificates. The appointment of the first university-qualified Tongan doctor (Dr Sione Tapa) as medical officer then Chief Medical Officer and the appointment of the first fully qualified Tongan nurse (Fatafehi Mataele) served to raise awareness of

Tonga's health problems, and to remind people that they were largely responsible for their own health.

Tuberculosis was a continuing concern for the Queen and the health workers. Although American doctors had focused on tuberculosis during the war it was still the most devastating public health problem. The total population of Tonga in 1956 was 55,000. In 1958 there were 155 new cases of tuberculosis registered at Vaiola Central Registry, and 25 deaths that year. In 1958 there was also a polio epidemic, in which there were 172 paralytic cases and 15 deaths.

The Queen was keen to improve the hospitals. By 1957 there were three hospitals (Vaiola in Nuku'alofa, Ngū in Neiafu, and Niu'ui in Lifuka). There were also six rural dispensaries (in Mu'a, Kolovai, 'Eua, Nomuka, Ha'afeva, and Niuatoputapu). Vaiola Hospital, built in 1923 behind the Kolisi Fefine, consisted of wooden buildings and Quonset huts left behind by the Americans. There was a tuberculosis ward, a typhoid ward, a general ward, a children's ward, a maternity ward, and a *papālangi* ward. Each ward was in a separate building. There was also an administration block, an outpatients' block (containing an eye clinic), a public health office (including outpatients for maternity cases), an X-ray and laboratory building, a pharmacy, medical stores, a kitchen for the tuberculosis ward and nurses; also the Chief Medical Officer's office, the matron's residence, the nurses' quarters, and a World Health Organisation (WHO) office.

Temporary huts were built in the grounds by relatives of patients and used by them for living and cooking while they were attending to their sick relatives. The attendant system was the custom, except for the tuberculosis ward. Medical treatment was free, but the relatives provided food, mattresses, bed covering, and did the chores, such as cleaning the wards. Although having one's relations around was generally considered good for the psychological welfare of the patients, the relatives did not always follow medical instructions, and applied inappropriate Tongan remedies when medical staff were not looking. While there was supposed to be only two attendants per patient, there were often more, leading to overcrowding in the wards.

A prime need in Tonga was for a clean and reliable water supply. Tonga had no rivers, and relied on rainwater catchment for its drinking water, while wells were dug for bathing and agricultural purposes. Although the US forces had removed their water-drilling equipment, some water tanks had been left behind. The better-off families had private tanks, with water collected from corrugated-iron roofs. The Public Works Department erected tanks in the villages, and it was the responsibility of the Town Officer to ensure that the tanks were cleaned and kept in good repair, a duty not carried out often enough. During the 1950s there were several epidemics of enteric fever, and skin diseases due to lack of clean water for bathing were common.

Rainwater was, of course, the preferred water for drinking and cooking, but even with roof, spouting, and tanks in good repair a household could run short of water in two months in dry weather. In 1956, 47.58 per cent of dwellings in Tonga still had thatched roofs, which did not allow for water catchment. Well water had to be carried in buckets, often a considerable distance, and was often brackish. Some householders boiled water before drinking it, others did not. When there was a shortage of water, people bathed in the sea and drank the juice of coconuts.

This was the background to WHO's Environmental Sanitation project, which in 1958 brought James Spillius, a social anthropologist, to Tonga, together with his anthropologist wife, Elizabeth Bott Spillius, to prepare for a piped water programme. The project was enthusiastically welcomed by the government and the people, and there was much rivalry among the villages as to which would be the first to get a piped water supply.

The Queen was also concerned about the changing roles of women in Tongan society. She heard about the Pan Pacific and South-East Asian Women's Association (PPSEAWA), which was designed to educate women so they could improve the living conditions of their families. The Queen felt that Tongan women were not yet ready to join an international organization, but she agreed to a group of women attending a PPSEAWA meeting in Christchurch in 1952 as observers. The women chosen were Dilys Rowlands, Manu Puloka (later Manu Faupula), Nānisi Helu, and Mafi Fīnau. The women reported very positively about the organization, but the Queen still felt that Tongan women were not ready. Instead, in mid-1954 the Queen set up the Langa Fonua 'a e Fefine Tonga (Nation Building by Women) with the help of Dilys Rowlands and women who were active in the organizations of different churches.[6]

Women had always had their own associations, notably the *kautaha* or work groups formed under the direction of the chief's sister (later the chief's wife) to make bark cloth. Women sometimes sat together while they wove mats. There were also women who harvested the reefs together. (In fact women were never alone!) The Langa Fonua was different in that it aimed to bring together women nationally. Dr 'Ana Taufe'ulungaki described the Langa Fonua thus:

> The Queen had three important aims: to maintain and develop the traditional ways of the Tongan people; to develop the home improvement skills and knowledge of women and thereby their working conditions; to improve the quality of life of all her people. With these skills and knowledge, a woman would gain confidence in her abilities and become less dependent and more self-sufficient; and would take pride in her traditions and heritages.[7]

It was recognized that public health measures designed to improve hygiene and sanitation would reduce the incidence of yaws, dysentery, typhoid, and skin infections, so the Queen encouraged the Langa Fonua to be active in public health. Later she was the inspiration behind the setting up of a Women's Public Health Committee in every village.[8] This happened after Langa Fonua was begun, and the committees took over local health functions from the Langa Fonua.

By the early 1960s there was a three-tiered structure of women's organizations, and the Queen was president and patron of all three. PPSEAWA was the body with international connections;[9] Langa Fonua was the national association; and the Women's Public Health Committees were the organizations at the village level. Memberships of PPSEAWA and Langa Fonua were made exclusive by the requirement of a small annual subscription. The Women's Public Health Committees were open to all, and were controlled at village level, under the actual or nominal leadership of the highest-ranking woman in the village.[10] The chief's wife had increasingly replaced the chief's sister as the natural leader of the village, and James Spillius described the role of the wife and how much depended upon her skills and willingness.

> The wife of the village's most important leader is usually automatically elected to be the head of the women's organizations in the village, especially the Women's Health Committee and the Langa Fonua. If she is an active leader, the activities of the committee are usually highly successful. But in addition, it is supposed to be the wife's job to "look after the people", which means to listen to their troubles, lend them food or money when they need it, and generally smooth over any differences and difficulties that may arise. It is usually a woman who decides how food should be divided among the people after a ceremony. In general, it is easier for the people to approach a woman than her husband.[11]

Women's Public Health Committees took over from Langa Fonua the responsibility for inspecting the homes of members, and these inspections became a feature of village life, a time when women would springclean their houses and proudly bring out for inspection the household items they had acquired by their own efforts, such as embroidered pillow slips and items of furniture. "Home improvements", such as kitchens, toilets, and bathrooms, were encouraged, and the Health Department taught women to recognize common diseases and how to give First Aid in cases of accidents.

One reason for the founding of the Langa Fonua was that the Queen did not want the women to fall behind the men who were being educated overseas. When the men returned to Tonga, they would be thinking about getting married. Instead of looking for high-ranking wives, as they were wont to do, the Queen felt they should be looking for women with good characters, and she prepared such women for a modern style of marriage. English language was taught, and some of the Langa Fonua women attended classes in Law given by the Judge of the Supreme Court. The Queen also used the Langa Fonua to encourage women's traditional skills in weaving and making bark cloth. She felt it was not enough for the women to make baskets and tablemats to earn an income from the occasional tourists from tourist ships, she wanted them to take pride in the quality of their work.

The Queen had supported Tungī Mailefihi's attempts to improve agriculture, but the inspiration had died with him, along with the demise of the annual agricultural show. The Queen encouraged women to use *papālangi* as well as the older kinds of vegetables, and to have their own chickens and piglets, in order to give their families a more varied and balanced diet. *Papālangi* skills such as sewing and the making of sponge cakes were also taught.

Elizabeth Bott Spillius reported that the Langa Fonua was criticized (presumably by *papālangi*) because it was perceived to be teaching a *papālangi* lifestyle at a time when cooking in Tonga was still being done over an open fire or in an earth oven. Certainly it took a long time for a cake to be baked in the traditional earth oven! Nevertheless different ways of cooking were much valued by the women. The women were eager to extend their skills, and no sooner was a new competence introduced than all the women took it up with enthusiasm. Sewing, crocheting, and needlework were already known, but new patterns and styles were encouraged, and these and patchwork quilts were judged at the annual Langa Fonua show day (which in many ways replaced the agricultural show), with prizes also for vegetables, animal husbandry, bark cloth, mats, and other handicrafts. Tortoise shells were presented by the Queen for the best-kept village and best-kept district.

In 1964 the Queen supervised all the arrangements for the tenth meeting of PPSEAWA, which would be held in Tonga. She moved from the Palace to the house Fai-'a-koka along the Beach Road in order that the organizers could come to see her without the protocol required at the Palace. She was assisted by the women who had been chosen by her to be the leaders of women's associations in all the churches, those who had been on her wartime committees, and who were conspicuous in the Langa Fonua 'a e Fefine Tonga. There was only one guest house in Nuku'alofa, so accommodation had to be provided in women's homes, and the Queen ensured that the guests were properly fed and looked after. The theme of the conference was "The role of women in preserving cultural heritage", which allowed a maximum of dancing and the exhibition of cultural artefacts. The PPSEAWA meeting was rated a great success.

Adrienne Kaeppler gave a paper for the Hawai'i delegation and was one of the two *hula* dancers for Hawai'i's cultural presentation. The *hula* dances greatly interested the Queen, and when Adrienne expressed a wish to learn Tongan dance, the Queen arranged for her to be taught by Vaisima Hopoate at Lapaha. Vaisima was a famous dancer and Lapaha was the pre-eminent place for Tongan dance.

The fact that women did not exercise the vote until 1960 may be due to Sālote's feeling that the *papālangi* form of government was irrelevant to women's lives. The law did affect women's lives, however. For example, women could not inherit land (though widows could have a life interest), and while this was deemed not to matter while women were provided for by their brothers, the time was coming when male kin would find it harder to provide a safe haven and material support for the women of their *kāinga* because of a shortage of land.[12]

Queen Sālote and Tungī Mailefihi had encouraged hereditary estateholders to distribute land as required by law and commoners to register their land once it was distributed, but both groups were slow to respond. Since her accession in 1918 the population of Tonga had more than doubled, and was continuing to rise, so the Queen realized that allocation of land would become increasingly difficult. One problem was the reluctance of hereditary estateholders to have their land surveyed. Land committees and land commissions early in the reign had looked at this problem, and surveys with local resources had been attempted on several occasions, but to little effect. In 1956 the government appointed a foreign company to conduct a cadastral survey of land prior to new efforts at distribution. In her speech at the Opening of Parliament in 1956 the Queen called on the hereditary estateholders to co-operate with the government "to achieve our obligation of providing land for the people", and at the Closing of Parliament in that same year, she stated:

> The task of subdividing the land into individual plots for distribution to those who are still landless is about to be undertaken, and I urge the co-operation of all for the attainment of this worthy end, in order to implement the provisions of the Constitution and the Land Law. We trust that this will solve the problems which have existed between chiefs and their peoples, as well as between individual families.[13]

The survey ended in September 1961. Even though many adult males subsequently gained legal title to allotments, the problems were far from solved. Tongans and *papālangi* observers alike commented that there was a sharp increase in illegal payment for land that the hereditary estateholders should by law have distributed without payment.[14] In her last speech to Parliament, in 1965, the Queen again expressed her concern about the landless: "I ask you to look to the land which was one of the freedoms granted by the Emancipation to provide for your families and to ease your burdens. This land was given to you that you may not have to work as slaves for others, for to do this would be contradictory to the spirit of the Constitution."[15]

Queen Sālote's interest in her people's welfare was genuine. No one could live in Tonga for more than a short time without realizing that her role was much more than that of a ceremonial head of government. It was true that she was the major recipient of formal presentations, but it was her chiefly function to receive in order to redistribute. She not only knew the names and identity of many of her subjects, and how they were related to each other, but she was available for those of her subjects who came seeking advice and assistance in personal and local matters.

Although theoretically the Queen had handed on many responsibilities to her sons, her life was still very demanding. In December 1959 Elizabeth Bott Spillius wrote to Tu'ifua Carrick (in London) and described the busyness of the Queen in carrying out all her duties:

> We see the Queen quite often because of our work [for the Tonga Traditions Committee]. I am helping the Committee to organize their records for the writing of a history of Tonga, and so I do a lot of my work with the Queen. But for the past five or six months she has been so frightfully busy that we haven't been able to do as much work as I would have liked. I think she does too much – Government, church, Langa Fonua, entertaining important visitors, organizing feasts and *kātoanga* [celebrations], looking after the family affairs, seeing her people about their land troubles – it's too much. However, she is going off for a holiday to New Zealand in March right after her birthday, and I hope she will have a good rest then.[16]

Behind what appear to be movements for change described in this chapter was the Queen's over-riding purposes: sufficient adaptation so Tonga could absorb the intrusions of the modern world. More important for her was the validation of Tongan values in the face of change, the preservation of Tongan identity, and perpetuation of cohesiveness in Tongan society. And behind what might appear to be the Queen propping up a society in which the benefits were unequally distributed (in contradiction to her avowed Christian beliefs) was a strong streak of realism. For the Queen it was more important that people have the *possible enough* (food and land, etc.) than to strive for the *impossible equality*. She was intelligent enough to realize that life is ambiguous and justice elusive, and like other political leaders she had to make realistic and tough decisions, which could look like accommodation. "Progress" was always an ambiguous word in her mouth, for (unlike her son who was anxious for technological advances) the Queen meant the retention of sufficient mutuality in kinship to ensure survival – and then something more, which would make life more comfortable and meaningful. Thus, concurrently with encouraging *papālangi*-style education and Christian values, the Queen sought also to preserve the best of Tongan customs in a new context. So, at the time when the Centenary Church was opened, the Queen Sālote School of Nursing was founded, and the Langa Fonua established, the Queen was also setting out to preserve traditions, not for their own sake but as an anchor for her people in the face of those changes that were chosen as well as those that were not. She would do this most notably through the Tonga Traditions Committee.

CHAPTER EIGHTEEN

Reconstructing Tradition

"Then Lo'au finished, and he corrected everything, and said that some things were wrong and some things were right" (E. W. Gifford, 1929)[1]

QUEEN SĀLOTE APPRECIATED the many advantages of modernization for herself and for Tonga, but she felt that postwar change was too rapid, and that traditions and customs were being too hastily discarded. The Queen recorded in the 1950s her feelings about innovation:

> we throw away the things that were known and used by our *kui ua* (great-grandfathers). The problem is that we are throwing away [our tradition] too quickly but have nothing to replace it, and we become gatherers of bits here and there. We have become pickers of crumbs, a generation of *kailu* (people who pick up things thrown away by others). It is very unfortunate because we still stand as Tonga, as a country, as a government, and yet we neglect the things that prove that we still have an identity of our own (literally are still a complete country, *fonua kakato*). That is the result of half-baked education (*ako tuku konga loto*) and shows the weakness of the leaders in holding on to their duties without knowing what they should be, and that is why they threw it away. We have looked at this throwing away of tradition with great sorrow, for our traditions are a good foundation for Tonga.[2] [translator unknown]

Queen Sālote's concern about the preservation of Tongan culture was not new or sudden. In 1936 the *Sydney Morning Herald* had reported:

> what spare time she has is being devoted to writing the legends and folklore, and for this she is obtaining material from many of the older natives under her rule.
>
> Her Majesty is also doing a great deal to revive native arts and crafts – the weaving of baskets and the making of tapa cloth. Some of the designs are almost forgotten, and Queen Salote hopes to stimulate the women and children to greater interest in their own crafts.[3]

Queen Sālote was *fakapapālangi*; that is, she had a good understanding of *papālangi* ways and enjoyed *papālangi* conveniences. Her Palace had *papālangi* furnishings and she ate *papālangi* as well as Tongan food. During her protracted holidays abroad she was able not only to rest from arduous duties back home but also to enjoy a *papālangi* lifestyle, including concerts and plays. It would be going much too far, however, to say that she had a *fakapapālangi* personality, for at heart she was a real Tongan.

There were outward signs of the Queen still being Tongan. The key to Tongan proper behaviour was *faka'apa'apa*, which is the respect a person of inferior status pays to anyone of superior status, within the family or within society at large. This respect consolidated the group, and the Queen emphasized that to play one's part within the group was an acknowledgement that one has a place. A more superficial but nevertheless very real indicator of belonging was uniformity of dress. In earlier days, as the Queen explained in her writings, the wearing of certain clothes and the way of wearing hair were an indication of one's rank.[4] The chiefs had known which waist-mat to wear on which special occasion. Certain garments could be worn only by the higher-ranking, and certainly not by commoners.[5]

Before World War Two men of high chiefly rank might on formal occasions wear a suit, waistcoat, with a stiff or soft shirt and tie, often with a hat, while high-ranking women had a wardrobe of frocks and hats and gloves. Perhaps during her visit to Great Britain the Queen noticed that there was general approval for the many guests who wore the clothes peculiar to their own countries. As already noted, before the royal visit to Tonga in December 1953, the Queen gave instructions that Tongan dress was to be worn. That is, the *vala tupenu* and over-dress with waist-mat for women and a *vala* with a shirt and tie, and waist-mat for men. Neatness was important, and women and men were asked to wear matching colours. Both women and men could have bare feet or wear sandals, but not shoes.[6]

The Queen had no influence on the ministers of the Free Church, who at all times wore black suits and boots when taking services. After a struggle Free Wesleyan Church ministers were allowed to wear the *vala* when preaching. Even the Judge of the Supreme Court, David Hunter, was affected by this emphasis on clothing, claiming in his annual report of 1961 that crimes were committed by Tongans wearing *papālangi* clothes.

Preservation of culture was more complex than a Tongan way of dressing. As early as 1936 the Queen wrote to Sau Faupula that she was thinking of setting up a "Lo'au group" (Lo'au being a wisdom figure of the Tongan past), for the preservation of custom and culture in Tonga. She told Sau that she had asked Havili Hafoka, a *matāpule*, to set up a group. "It would be a pity to see our culture lost", added the Queen.[7] Little came of this initiative until 1949, when, in a speech at the Closing of Parliament, the Queen referred to one of the motions (surely inspired by herself) before the House recommending the codification of Tongan customs and traditions.

> Such customs and traditions have always been practised and preserved by certain loyal families and individuals, but it is particularly pleasing to me that the matter of their permanent recording and publication in a form which would lead to a more widespread knowledge thereof and a more general observance of them should have been brought before the House for a more serious discussion, and I appreciate such a gesture and regard it as a further step forward towards the preservation of Tonga's national identity.[8]

In that session Parliament had proposed to mark her fiftieth birthday by setting up a committee to record Tongan customs. The outcome was the Kōmiti Tala Fakafonua (Tonga Traditions Committee), established in 1954, with the Queen as the chairperson and the noble Ve'ehala (son of her longtime friend Feleti Vī) as the Secretary and Keeper of the Public Record (sometimes referred to as Keeper of the Palace Records, a revealing confusion, for the Palace determined what would be the public record). The membership of the committee changed frequently, but notable members were Feleti Vī, Havili Hafoka, and Rev. Dr S. 'Amanaki Havea. The Queen paid the expenses of the committee herself until the government agreed to pay salaries in 1959.

The Queen gave three reasons for setting up the Tonga Traditions Committee. The first was that there were a number of cases in the Land Court that could be settled only if genealogies were available. The second was to collect materials for a history of Tonga, which would include her own reign. The third was to set up a museum and a library for the collection and preservation of artefacts and records.[9]

In 1957 the Queen was made one of three honorary members of the Polynesian Society (which had its headquarters in New Zealand) in recognition of her commitment to the study of traditions, so that it was not surprising that she appealed to the new Anthropology Department of The University of Auckland to recommend a trained person to assist the committee. The anthropologist Dorothy Crozier, who had visited Tonga in 1951, was approached, but she was engaged in cataloguing papers of the Western Pacific Archives, and regretfully declined.

Top Left: Queen Sālote drinks the first cup of *kava* from half of a polished coconut shell. *Courtesy of David Attenborough.* [110]

Centre Left: A server gives a cup of *kava* to one of the members of the circle, 1959. To the left is the Queen's shelter, and in the background are the Royal Chapel and Palace. *Courtesy of David Attenborough.* [111]

Bottom Left: People from Houma dance their *lakalaka* for Queen Sālote after the *taumafa kava*, 1959. *Courtesy of David Attenborough.* [112]

The funeral of Veikune (Lala), 1959. *Right: (left to right)* Heu'ifanga, Halaevalu Maile, 'Ofa, Seselo, unidentified, at the grave. *Below:* Fale'aka wearing *liongi* mat. She was Veikune's mother's brother's daughter, and therefore of inferior *kāinga* rank to Veikune. At the left are Luseane (daughter of Veikune) and Tanginitopa. *Courtesy of David Attenborough.* [113]

Top Left: 'Atalanga, Epsom, Auckland, soon after it was built in 1910. It was purchased for the royal family by the government of Tonga in 1952. Two hostels for Tongan students were later built in the grounds. The house is now surrounded by trees. *Courtesy of Mrs R. J. A. Temple.* [114]

Centre Left: Queen Sālote with nuns during a visit to 'Eua, 1961. Halaevalu Maile is seated behind the Queen. *Courtesy of Tulua Studios.* [115]

Below: The royal family, c.1962. *Back row:* Crown Prince Tupouto'a-Tungī and Prince Tu'ipelehake. *Middle row:* Prince 'Uluvalu, Prince 'Alaivahamama'o, Princess Siu'ilikutapu, Queen Sālote, Princess Pilolevu, Prince Mailefihi, Prince Tāufa'āhau. *Front row:* Princess Mata'aho with Prince 'Aho'eitu, Princesses 'Ofeina, Fusipala, and Taone, and Princess Melenaite. *Courtesy of Tulua Studios. (Ref. 574-11.)* [116]

RIGHT: Rodger Page and Queen Sālote during one of her visits to Sydney in the early 1960s. *Courtesy of family of Rodger Page.* [117]

ABOVE: Queen Sālote leaves Tonga for the last time. She is in a wheelchair and her hair is cut. *Courtesy of Tulua Studios.* [118]

ABOVE: After a lying-in-state at Government House, Auckland, Queen Sālote was taken to Whenuapai airport on 20 December 1965 for the flight to Tonga. Members of the royal family (*right*) follow the coffin. *Courtesy of Auckland Institute and Museum. (Ref NZ Herald).* [119]

LEFT: Ratu Sir Edward Cakobau, half-brother of Queen Sālote, wears a *liongi* mat, and is greeted by Tu'ipelehake when Edward arrives for the funeral of the Queen, December 1965. [120]

RIGHT: Order of the procession of the funeral of Queen Sālote, 23 December 1965. [121]

FUNERAL NOTICE.

ORDER OF PROCESSION.

(Thursday, 23rd Dec. 1965 at 10 a.m.)

1. Guard of Honour (Royal Guards, TDF detachment, 100 strong)
2. Police Band.
3. Officiating Clergy.
4. The Royal Bier.
5. Insignia bearers (Royal Children)
6. Their Majesties, the King and Queen.
7. Their Royal Highnesses, Prince Tu'ipelehake and Princess Melenaite.
8. The remainder of the Royal Children.
9. Their Excellencies (Heads of State) —
   Governor General of N.Z. and Lady Fergusson, A.D.C. and Lady-in-Waiting
   His Highness Malietoa and Miss S. Malietoa
   Governor of Fiji and Lady Jakeway
   Governor of American Samoa and Mrs. Lee
10. Other Representatives of Foreign Governments —
    The Rt. Hon. K. Holyoake and daughters, Mr. P. Barnes, Private Secretary
    The Hon. Mata'afa, Fetaui Mata'afa and Private Secretary
    H.B.M.'s Commissioner and Consul and Mrs. Reid
    R. N. Hamilton, Esq., Australian Commissioner, Fiji
    L. J. Link, Esq., U.S. Consul, Fiji
    The Rt. Hon. W. J. Scott, Minister for Marine, N.Z.
    P. D. Macdonald, C.M.G., Esquire, Colonial Secretary, Fiji
11. Representatives of Foreign Armed Services —
    Lt. General L. W. Thornton (Chief of Staff, N.Z.)
    Rear Admiral J. O. C. Ross (Chief Naval Staff, N.Z.)
    Colonel J. Morrison, Officer Commanding, Fiji Military Forces.
12. Ministers of the Crown (H.M.G.)
13. Heads of Churches —
    (a) Overseas : Rev. Witheford, President of the Methodist Church, N.Z.
    Rev. S. Tuilovoni, President of the Methodist Church, Fiji
    Rt. Rev. Vockler, Bishop in Polynesia.
    (b) Local : His Lordship J. L. Rodgers, S. M.
    Rev. Canon Fine Halapua, C. of E. and Mrs. Halapua.
    Rhondo S. Harmon, L.D.S. and Mrs. Harmon.
    Tuna 'Ulukalala, Church of Tonga.
    Paula Fonua, Free Church of Tonga.
    Manase Niuafe, S.D.A. Church.
14. Parliamentary Representatives —
    (a) N.Z. : The Hon. N. E. Kirk, M.P. – Leader of the Opposition N.Z.
    (b) Fiji : Ratu George Cakobau (Vunivalu) and Seruwaia Lelea.
    Ratu Mara and Adi Lala
    Ratu Penaia and Adi Laise
    Tui Nayau
    Ratu Dovi
    (c) Samoa.
    (d) Tonga
15. Chiefs of Fiji and Samoa
16. Nobles of Tonga.
17. Heads of Government Departments — Led by Hon. Judge and Mrs. Roberts.
18. European and Other Expatriate Community.
19. Relatives of the Royal Family.
20. Others.

The Premier's Office,
Nuku'alofa, Tonga.
22 Dec., 1965.

By Command,
M. J. CHALLONS.
Secretary to Government.

LEFT: The *kauala* (platform carrying the coffin) of Queen Sālote, which was carried by 200 Nuku'alofa men, enters Mala'e Kula, 23 December 1965. In the foreground are the ministers who will officiate at the funeral service. *Left to right:* Rev. Dr A. Harold Wood, Rev. S. Tonga Simiki, Rev. George Harris, Rev. Dr S. 'Amanaki Havea. *Courtesy of Department of Information, Suva.* [122]

ABOVE: The Ha'a Tufunga (royal undertakers) and helpers gather at the foot of the statue of Queen Lavinia (mother of Queen Sālote), Mala'e Kula, 23 December 1965 for the burial. *Courtesy of Auckland Institute and Museum. (Ref* NZ Herald.*) [123]*

Left: Women form a circle of mats and a circle of bark cloth around the entire gravesite in order to shield the burial from public view, Mala'e Kula, 23 December 1965. The statue of Tupou II (father of Queen Sālote) is on the right. *Courtesy of Department of Information, Suva.* [124]

Below: Senior girls of Queen Sālote College wait with floral tributes to cover the grave of Queen Sālote at the Mala'e Kula, 23 December 1965. *Courtesy of Auckland Institute and Museum. (Ref* NZ Herald.*)* [125]

In 1958 the World Health Organization sent an anthropologist, James Spillius, to report on the social factors that would have to be taken into consideration in establishing an adequate water supply to the villages. James Spillius was accompanied by his wife, Elizabeth Bott Spillius, also an anthropologist, whose recently published book on family networks was receiving critical and popular acclaim. For her first six months in Tonga, Elizabeth undertook a study of mother-and-child health, a topic dear to the Queen's heart, but still she did not meet the Queen. Just as Elizabeth was wondering, rather disconsolately, what she would do next, she was invited by the Queen to join the Tonga Traditions Committee as a paid co-ordinator. The salary was a "local salary" (i.e. small), but the opportunity was an anthropologist's dream: with the Queen as her patron, Elizabeth had access to everyone in the kingdom. The Queen gave her the name Nua, that of a beautiful woman who was much loved by the sacred ruler Tu'i Tonga Momo, and was the daughter of a chief named Lo'au. The significance of the name Nua was revealed when people started talking about the Queen as their new Lo'au, for the Queen treated Elizabeth as a daughter.

For two years, Elizabeth and James (as part of his own research) took notes, planned and carried out surveys, collected genealogy books and arranged for them to be typed before being returned to their owners, wrote reports, and (best of all) had long discussions with the Queen. The outcome was that at the end of the two years the filing cabinets in the Palace Office were bulging with information, which the Queen intended should be available to those interested enough to ask for it.

Some chiefs were concerned lest the genealogies copied by the Tonga Traditions Committee were standardized, and their own particular version suppressed. Indeed a letter in the Palace Office by Elizabeth to a Ha'apai chief mentions "corrections" that the Queen would send him. But stories of genealogy books being destroyed and of "deprived lineages" seem to be apocryphal.

While this was happening in the Nuku'alofa office, other members of the committee, such as Ula Matatoa, went into the villages and collected local stories. Ve'ehala (Leilua) and Tupou Posesi Fanua gained their knowledge of local information from these activities.

The Queen herself wrote accounts of customs, one collection of her writings being typed and bound as *Ko e Tohi 'a 'Ene 'Afio ko Kuini Salote Tupou* (The Book of Her Majesty) and the other collection, known as *Ko e Ngaahi Tohi 'a 'Ene 'Afio 1958–59* (*The Writings of Queen Sālote 1958–59*) being filed among the Tonga Traditions Committee papers. In these writings and in her discussions with Elizabeth, the Queen shared some part of her extensive knowledge. For the Queen, knowledge was useless unless it was shared, and the very purpose of the Tonga Traditions Committee was to pass down knowledge to later generations. The Queen had high hopes of the whole venture, and expressed her satisfaction in her speech at the Closing of Parliament on 5 September 1959:

> One further thing which deserves your attention is the Tonga Traditions Committee, which was established as the result of a motion of Parliament in 1950 [*sic*]. The work of this committee is progressing satisfactorily. I wish that all Tongans should realize the importance of a full knowledge of our customs and traditions. Research into the social past of a people is not a Tongan characteristic only but rather the characteristic of an enlightened community. The customs of a people are its heritage and the possession of a complete knowledge of their customs will enable them to modify those customs to meet the demands of modern progress along lines most beneficial to their well-being. It is the aim of this committee to stimulate among the Chiefs and People of our land a desire to hold on to what is best in our customs. It is our duty to support the work of the Tonga Traditions Committee for the benefit of Tonga and its people.[10]

It was at this time people said that "The Queen is our Lo'au now", meaning that she was the one who explained everything about the past and set down the way in which Tonga should proceed. In addition to her own written accounts of custom, the Queen believed it was important to make a record of the *taumafa kava* (royal *kava* ceremony), which had once belonged to the Tu'i Tonga title and now belonged to the Tu'i Kanokupolu. The importance of the *taumafa kava* was that chiefs took their places in the circle and drank *kava* in the order based on tradition and amended by the Queen. The order demonstrated the pre-eminence not only of the Tupou dynasty, but of the Tu'i Kanokupolu title itself, and affirmed the relationship of all other titles to this supreme title. It was a setting out, in visual form, of the established political and social order of Tonga. It was solemn and dignified and had sacred and symbolic connotations.

In 1959 the Queen decided that there should be a major *taumafa kava*, that the whole event should be referred to as "the Lo'au", and that it should be filmed. Elizabeth and James Spillius arranged for David Attenborough of the British Broadcasting Corporation (BBC) and his cameraman Geoffrey Mulligan to come to Tonga. It was intended that a copy of the film would be deposited with the Tonga Traditions Committee as a record for future participants and scholars, both *papālangi* and Tongan. From this long film Attenborough would edit a 30-minute programme for BBC television.

In a note on the Lo'au, Elizabeth commented: "Her Majesty would like all of the Kauhala 'Uta [Tu'i Tonga chiefs] not just the Kauhala Lalo [Tu'i Kanokupolu chiefs] to come." That is, she wanted not only the chiefs whose titles were related to the Tu'i Kanokupolu, but the more ancient titles, formerly appointed by the Tu'i Tonga, to acknowledge her as their supreme chief. The

Tonga Traditions Committee (that is, the Queen) wanted the film to record every detail of a *taumafa kava*, starting with the arrival and seating of hundreds of chiefs (for all would be invited), who would come from all over the kingdom.

In a letter to Marian Smith, Secretary of the Royal Anthropological Institute, James Spillius said: "Attending, let alone filming, a kava ceremony of this sort in Polynesia is not an easy matter . . . The ceremony is sacred, and it is only natural that the participants should feel some uneasiness about revealing it to outsiders . . . Already there are misgivings about filming the taumafa kava at all . . . Fortunately the Queen wishes it and it is being done."[11] In a letter to David Attenborough, James emphasized the importance of understanding the ceremony, otherwise "all you would get on your film would be the Queen sitting in a large circle of men and everybody being served a cup of kava".[12]

Attenborough and Mulligan were royal guests. A house, car, food, servants, and introductions were provided for them. But shortly before the filming began, one of the nobles, Veikune (Lala), a former suitor of Princess Fusipala, died. He was a chief of high rank and a relative of the royal house, so the Queen herself had to ensure that the appropriate ceremonies were observed before, during, and after the burial. The ordering of such ceremonies was part of the proper ordering of society, for each person had to play their part and make the appropriate presentations to acknowledge the relationships between families. The Queen could not deputize these duties to anyone else.

Although her attention was distracted by Veikune's funeral, the ordering of the *taumafa kava* was also of great importance to the Queen. Day-to-day instructions were sent by the Queen through Ve'ehala, but she intended a more personal input. Although she rarely received *papālangi*, a royal audience was arranged for the two who were to carry out such an important task. Forty years later, Attenborough remembered that: "We had to wait several evenings in one of the verandahs of the Palace before we were admitted; and, of course, we had to be properly garbed in mats, approach on our hands and knees, and exit backwards so as not to turn our back on her. The conversation concerned exactly how we were planning to film the *taumafa kava* ceremony."[13]

Diagrams published in Gifford's *Tongan Society* of the 1918 circle and the post-1945 diagram in Bain's *Official Record of the Royal Visit to Tonga* show relatively few participants. By contrast, hundreds of titleholders and their *kau matāpule* attended in 1959, the diagram being published in Sione Lātūkefu's *The Tongan Constitution*. The undertaking was extremely difficult, for although there were "rehearsals", the fact is that the ceremony is different every time it is performed:[14] participants attempt to upstage each other in different ways, there are discussions between *kau matāpule* about the procedure, and members are publicly chastised by *kau matāpule* for such misdemeanours as wearing spectacles. In 1959 some of the minor titleholders were unsure of their places, which added to the confusion. There were several *pongipongi* making up the

Lo'au, but the event recorded on film was a re-enactment of the *pongipongi* of the Queen's nephew Vaea ('Alipate Tupou), son of Vīlai Tupou. The ceremony took more than four hours.

The first stage was that of preparation prior to the Queen's formal entrance. People moved around and talked before seeking out their places. Some *kau matāpule* ensured that the seating was correct and only those entitled were there. When the titled chiefs, representatives of vacant titles, and *kau matāpule* took their places, cross-legged, they formed a single continuous line, all facing inwards, beginning and ending at the Queen's shelter. The Queen's shelter at the Palace end of the Mala'e Pangai marked the head of the circle, the *tou'a*, where the *kava* mixer and his helpers sat in a group, being at the opposite end. The circle was nearly 100 metres across. Except for the Queen, all the participants were in full sunlight, for protocol forbade them to cover their heads in the royal presence. The size of a circle depends on the number of people present, and an equal number of presenters may sit behind the *kava* mixer. Those who sat behind the *kava* bowl included a few important titled chiefs (who for historical reasons did not sit in the Tu'i Kanokupolu circle). One of these was the Crown Prince, by virtue of his Tungī title. Some untitled chiefs also sat near by.

While the chiefs were still assembling, green *kava* and food (known as *ngāue*, literally, "work") was brought and laid out within the circle. The food consisted of pigs, yams, fish, and other types of food baked in an earth oven. Each type was assigned a place and acknowledged by the presiding *matāpule*. Large roots of *kava* and huge pigs were dragged in by many men chanting a work song. The *kava* was placed at the front.

Everyone was silent as the Queen (the only woman to sit in the circle) arrived and took her place on the pile of mats and bark cloth in her shelter. She wore one of her historic fine-mats beautifully tied with *kafa* (rope), as may be seen in one of the photographs in this book, to show the importance of the occasion for her. Once the Queen had taken her seat, the ceremony began. From this time no one could stand or enter the circle except to carry out specific functions, such as bringing, counting, or removing food, or to take the *kava* from the *tou'a* to a designated person in the circle.

The women then came and spread out the mats and bark cloth so they could be admired, and then folded them again. This *koloa* was presented to the Queen by Vaea's people and was later distributed by her or someone on her behalf. The women were thanked for their work.

Formal thanks were intoned by the Queen's two chief *matāpule*, Motu'apuaka and Lauaki. Lauaki had the greater role at funerals, and Motu'apuaka took the chief role at a ceremony such as this *taumafa kava*. One of the *matāpule* asked for someone from outside of the circle to come and see that the baked foods were in their proper places and to lift the coverings so they could be seen. Then two men from outside the circle came and counted the numbers in each category of food, shouting out the numbers. Motu'apuaka chanted the thanks, and his musical voice (he was a noted singer) adding much to the impressiveness of this stage of the ceremony. Like the *koloa* brought by the women, the food was distributed later.

The *matāpule* then ordered that one of the pieces of *kava* be taken to the *kava* bowl, where it was broken into pieces with a stick. While this was going on Motu'apuaka ordered men to come from the *tou'a* to make a path through the baked foods so that he could see the *kava* bowl. One of the pieces of *kava* was then pounded very slowly by a stone in the hand hitting it on a much larger stone, using highly stylized movements. When the pounding was finished, the broken *kava* was put into the bowl, and the pounder called out to Motu'apuaka that the *kava* had been pounded. Motu'apuaka then gave orders for water to be added and for mixing to begin. The mixing involved very elaborate and elegant movements, similar to the movements of a Tongan dance.[15] Motu'apuaka gave orders for some fibres from the hibiscus plant to be put in to act as strainers. Very elaborate, exaggerated, and elegant movements were again used by the mixer in the process of straining.

While the *kava* was being strained, certain *matāpule* made formal speeches. After the speeches, one of the men on the right and left of the mixer called out that the *kava* was ready. Several men then brought a large cooked pig to the front of the shelter where the Queen was sitting, and cut it up. The liver, the back, and some yams were placed in front of the Queen. This was her relish. Then portions were given to all the chiefs and *kau matāpule* in the circle. None of the participants ate his relish. Instead, certain persons came up from outside the circle to take away each chief's relish. First the Queen's relish was taken, usually by a "foreigner", but in this case it was taken by one of the descendants of Mumui, the first Tu'i Kanokupolu to live in Nuku'alofa. After the Queen's relish was taken, the titled chiefs and the *kau matāpule* in the circle called out for designated people to come and take theirs.

People from outside the circle then came and removed all the food so the inside of the circle was completely clear and ready for the serving of the *kava*. The chiefly woman chosen to serve the Queen's *kava*, 'Eva Ve'ehala, daughter of 'Ulukālala-Ata (Ha'amea) and wife of Ve'ehala (Leilua), came forward, and the mixer of the *kava* used the hibiscus fibres to fill the cup, which was a highly polished half of a coconut shell. 'Eva then stood in front of the *kava* bowl while men on the right and left of the mixer chanted, "The *kava* has been lifted!"

Motu'apuaka then called out: "Bring it here to Tupou!" The Queen brought her hollowed hands together once in a loud sound like a clap, and 'Eva walked up the middle of the circle with the cup of *kava*. All the circle was silent while the cup was carried towards the Queen and she drank from it. This moment was the most dramatic part of the entire ceremony because it affirmed that Queen Sālote was supreme.

Queen Sālote had changed the order of seating, putting Tu'ipelehake on her right next to Motu'apuaka, and he was the second to be served.[16] His name was too sacred to be called, nor did he clap. He was served in silence. After the Queen and Tu'ipelehake, the chiefs and *kau matāpule* were served in the order predetermined by the Queen. Serving took a long time, for when each title was called, the titleholder (or the person representing the title in the circle) had to respond by bringing his hollowed hands together in a single clap. Only then did the server begin the long journey from the *kava* bowl to the person for whom the cup was intended. When everyone had been served, it was announced that the ceremony had ended. The Queen departed, the bowl was taken away, and the participants dispersed.

Even though the film had been carefully planned, it was not certain that it would show what the Queen wanted. With hundreds of participants, little rehearsal, and only one cameraman (who had to remain outside the circle), the ceremony could appear only as confused movement. Elizabeth reported in a letter to Tu'ifua Carrick about the Lo'au: "I thought we would never finish. And the place was full of hou'eiki and matāpules from Vava'u and Niuafo'ou and Ha'apai and Niuatoputapu. For weeks no one talked about anything but *taumafa kava* and Lo'au. Anyway, it was lots of fun and a lot of work."[17]

After Attenborough and Mulligan left Tonga, the Queen decided that she should have described the significance of the *kava* in detail on the film. An invitation for Attenborough to return came too late, for he was now on his way back to England. The Spilliuses suggested that the editing should await their own return to London the following year. So the film was put into storage in the BBC studios in Ealing. While Attenborough was filming in Madagascar, the vault in which the film was stored was flooded and the film damaged. Enough was salvaged to make a half-hour television programme entitled *Royal Tonga*, but the grand enterprise had come to naught (as far as the chief actors were concerned).

The Spilliuses left Tonga in 1960. Elizabeth eventually published some articles and a book out of her Tongan research (see Selected Bibliography), but her other legacy is the collection of records in the Palace Office. She would deposit her own copies and other papers in the Library of The University of Auckland in 1983.

After the Spilliuses' departure in 1960, the Tonga Traditions Committee continued, but at a much slower pace. Elizabeth had reminded Queen Sālote of the wealth of material relating to Tonga in the Mitchell Library in Sydney, and during a visit to Sydney in 1961–62, the Queen rounded up a group of Tongan students – Ve'ehala (Leilua) and Epeli Hau'ofa among them – to copy extracts from missionary records. The Queen personally supervised the exercise, and Epeli Hau'ofa recalls that if one of the students stopped writing, the Queen would urge her or him to continue. Her assumption was that all was worth copying. What a wealth of material she would have acquired if photocopiers and microfilming cameras had been available at the time! The outcome of the library visit was disappointing. A combination of an unfamiliar language (to students and typist alike) and handwritten copy led to a typed volume of dubious accuracy being lodged with the Tonga Traditions Committee.

The Queen needed a historian or anthropologist as the permanent royal archivist, and she encouraged Sione Lātūkefu to study history in Australia for that reason. When she was undergoing medical treatment in New Zealand in the early months of 1965, she invited him to come and visit her so she could convey to him important information about her royal ancestors. She gave him an extended interview on 19 March 1965, an indication of how important the preservation of traditions was to her. Lātūkefu was awarded his PhD in History at the Australian National University in Canberra in 1967, but circumstances led to his going to Papua New Guinea instead of returning to Tonga.[18]

Preservation of traditions by means of records is one thing, but traditions can truly survive only if practised. In pre-contact Tonga there were the equivalent of guilds to which belonged the most proficient in their art: orators, navigators, fishermen, dancers, designers of patterns for bark cloth, weavers, undertakers, poets, boatbuilders, and so on. Some of these arts were superseded by modern skills, such as in boatbuilding. Others used new materials. As we have already seen, Queen Sālote herself was a notable orator, and her inspiring oratory was much admired. In the last chapter we saw how the practical arts of women were encouraged, such as weaving, the making of bark cloth, baskets, and so on. Many skills were passed from parent to child, and practitioners taught traditional arts in the schools. Children learned to dance and to practise other arts at a very young age, both in school and with their village group.

The Queen cared deeply about the treasures of the royal family, supervising their airing and storing, and making sure that the appropriate pieces were given away on the right occasion. The Queen was also acclaimed as an extremely gifted poet.[19] The earliest poem by her that can be dated with any certainty was *Loka Siliva*, written when she was in her teens. She may have learned the art from Tupou II, also a poet. Queen Sālote spent many hours perfecting the words of her poems, and she invited groups of musicians to come to the Palace in the evenings to work with her. They often stayed until the early hours of the morning. Poetry that was set to music consisted of love songs (both happy and sad), laments for deaths of chiefs and those close to her, lullabies for her grandchildren, and songs written especially for the accompaniment of dance, such as *lakalaka* and *mā'ulu'ulu*. Love songs (*hiva kakala*) were often used as accompaniment to the solo dance for a woman, the *tau'olunga*.

Superficially the Queen's songs were about historical and mythical personages, natural features, flowers and birds, but these are *heliaki* (indirect references or metaphors), intended to evoke in the mind of the listener remembrances of chiefs and events connected to the subject of the poem. The leader of a singing group and the director of the dance were expected to understand the meaning of the lyrics, but the singers themselves often did not understand them. In 1962 Queen Sālote wrote a more straightforward song to commemorate the endurance of those Tongans who had been wrecked on Minerva Reef, survived for 102 days, and effected their own rescue. The song is called *Ko e Tuai-kae-pau*, the name of the boat that was wrecked, and the first of four verses reads:

Vakai e Tohi Māhina
Fā 'o e fitu e ono ua
Folau na kuo fusi taula
'I he taulanga Nuku'alofa
Tu'u fua ai e kāpasa
Fakatele he Maka-o-'Oa
Kae fatu si'ono taumu'a
Tofikulu e 'Aotealoa
Seuke! Tāpinga-'a-maama
Ko 'eta fononga ta'e'iloa.

Behold the days of the calendar
Fourth of the seventh, sixty-two
Yonder voyage pulling up anchor
At the port of Nuku'alofa
Compass braced to give direction
Fishing lines to be cast at *Maka-o-'Oa*
The destination was charted
Heading for Aotearoa
Ah, but the ways of the world!
How unknown is our journey! [MT]

Or the more complex poem written for Tu'ipelehake, *'Ofa mei Pelehake* (also known as *Mavae Folau*). It is one of the most popular songs for Tongan singing groups today. The first of three verses is as follows:

Matangi ake matangi hifo
'O fepaki tu'u 'i hoku loto
He siale tafa he siale moto
Heilala 'anau mama'o
Ne longo e tau 'a Lupeoko
Tavake ni kuo siu mama'o.

Winds rise, winds fall.
They stand discordant in my heart.
The *siale tafa* the *siale moto*
The *heilala* longs for the distance.
The flight of pigeons falls silent
The tropic bird is seeking fish from afar. [MT]

Heliaki in poetry was not only the most skilful of games, in which only a few practitioners excelled, but also a display of the most inspired erudition. So erudite, in fact, that very few people now understand the references, even in the most popular of the songs.

Queen Sālote's poetry can be dramatic; for example, in the *lakalaka* called *Sangone* (her explication of an old myth about links between Sāmoa and Tonga), which was first performed on the Queen's fiftieth birthday, she sets a scene of Nature reacting strongly to the raising of the shell of the turtle Sangone:

Ne'ine'i hako mei he tonga
Tapa ē 'uhila mei lulunga
He na'e mana ē Feingakotone
Fakahake ē 'uno 'o Sangone.

No wonder the gales blew from the south
Lightning flashed from the west.
The Feingakotone thundered
For Sangone's shell was brought forth. [MT]

In modern times, high-ranking chiefs rarely dance in public, although they did so on special occasions, to show their respect and love for the Queen, for whom the dance was performed. Queen Sālote herself may have danced in honour of Tupou II, but once she became Queen she did not dance in public. She was nevertheless an expert in dance, and knew all the movements that comprised the dances. According to Konai Helu Thaman, the Tongan poet, when she was living in the women's hostel at 'Atalanga the Queen would demonstrate the movements to the young dancers, so they would learn to perform all the nuances with the utmost gracefulness.

Queen Sālote appropriated dance formerly performed for the Tu'i Tonga to be the property of the Tu'i Kanokupolu in the same way as she appropriated the *taumafa kava* of the Tu'i Tonga. The *me'elaufola* so often danced for the Tu'i Tonga had been transformed into the *lakalaka* of the Tu'i Kanokupolu, at the instigation, it is said, of Tuku'aho, father of Tungī Mailefihi, who lived in the village of Tatakamotonga, next to the Tu'i Tonga's village of Lapaha. To this day, when dancing their *lakalaka*, the people of Tatakamotonga wear black in memory of Tuku'aho.[20] The *'otuhaka* (seated part of the *fa'ahi'ula*) of the Tu'i Tonga became the new *mā'ulu'ulu* of the Tu'i Kanokupolu. The *eke* became the *sōkē*; the *tau'olunga* supplanted the *ula*.

Just as the transfer of the *taumafa kava* of the Tu'i Tonga to the Tu'i Kanokupolu was a sign of the latter's ascendancy, so the presentation of dances by the chiefs and their people before the Queen was a subtle recognition of supremacy of the Tu'i Kanokupolu over the descendants of the Tu'i Tonga. The *taumafa kava* of the Tu'i Kanokupolu was derived from the *taumafa kava* of the Tu'i Tonga; it is not identical. The *me'etu'upaki* and *fa'ahi'ula* are still associated with the descendants of the Tu'i Tonga in Lapaha, while the near-relations of these dances (the *lakalaka* and *mā'ulu'ulu*) are associated with the Tu'i Kanokupolu. After the last Tu'i Tonga died in 1865, no new words, music, or choreography were written for the Tu'i Tonga's dancers. It must have been a pleasing moment for the Queen when the Lapaha people eventually came to perform their Tu'i Tonga dances for her, for not only was her descent from the Tu'i Tonga being recognized, but also her inheritance of the Tu'i Tonga *mana*.

As already stated, Futa Helu has pointed out that many of the songs of Queen Sālote have references to stories about the Tu'i Tonga and to natural features and flowers associated with the Tu'i Tonga. Thus the Queen reminded people of her Tu'i Tonga heritage.[21] In her poetry the Queen also reminded the hearers of the descent of her sons not only from three royal lines, but also from Vava'u and Ha'apai lines, as in the poems 'Takafalu' (?1936), 'Maile' (?1938), and 'Kalauni' (1942).[22]

To Tongans, the important things about dances were not only the beauty of the performance but also the honouring of the highest chief by lower-ranking chiefs. When the Queen sent the words for a *lakalaka* to a village, they became the property of that village, and could be performed only by the people of that village, rather like an opera exclusively belonging to an opera company.[23] Most of the great celebrations of Queen Sālote's time were marked by dozens of dances, some specially written for the occasion, some being written on an earlier occasion for that village. Some dances are so famous that rehearsals to attain perfection could take many months, and their performance very special. In the last years of Queen Sālote's reign there were her fiftieth and sixtieth birthdays in 1950 and 1960, the celebration of the half-century since the ratification of the Treaty of Friendship with Great Britain in 1951, the opening of the Centenary Church in September 1952, the centenary of the Edict of Emancipation in 1962, and the celebration of Queen Sālote's reign in July 1965 (when it exceeded in length that of Tupou I). On the occasion of the Queen's sixtieth birthday, for example, there were so many villages wanting to perform dances for the Queen that the overflow was sent to perform at Tu'ipelehake's house (Fatai) and at the British Residency. Performances of *lakalaka* sometimes began before daylight and could continue well into the night.

Some of the famous village dance groups were known by special names. The group belonging to the village of Lapaha (descendants of the Tu'i Tonga) was known as the Lomipeau (named for a legendary canoe); the Kolomotu'a group was 'Ikale (Eagle), the Kolofo'ou group Laione (Lion), the Kanokupolu group Fola'osi (after the bark cloth they always wore when dancing), and the Kolovai group Milolua (the mixing of *kava*). Queen Sālote wrote nine *lakalaka* for the Lomipeau group alone.

Although individual poems are often difficult to interpret, the themes are constant. The *lakalaka* begins with an introduction that begs the indulgence of the chiefs, especially the royal family. Then follows praise of the royal family and the chiefly system, declaration of the singers' love of Tonga and allegiance to the established political and social order. References to legends and folklore from the remote and more recent past may be genealogical references or may be metaphors for something that occurred in the past or is happening in the present. There are references to flowers (which have their own hierarchical ranking) and to landscape that should remind the listeners of legendary or historical associations. Surprisingly, considering her Christian faith and the example of Tupou II's anthems, the Queen wrote no religious songs – or at least none is known.

When they appeared before the Queen, the dancers were so positioned as to demonstrate the social order of their village. Side by side in the centre of first line of the *lakalaka* stood the highest-ranking woman and highest-ranking man (*vāhenga*). They could be members of the local noble's family, or could be drawn from the village itself. Kaeppler records that there may be several contenders in some villages for the position of *vāhenga*, and the next position, that of *ta'ofi vāhenga*. When the dancers appeared before the Queen, she sometimes changed the *vāhenga*, using her own knowledge of genealogies. Tongilava noted (for example, prior to the 1945 celebration) that dance groups came to the Palace for the Queen to inspect before they were allowed to dance for her honoured guests. He also noted when schoolchildren came to perform for the Queen. No matter how many people were present, the performance was in truth a performance for an audience of one, the Queen herself. This did not mean that the Queen wished to be the sole specialist. She appreciated and encouraged the gifts of musicians, choreographers, and dancers, but she was the final arbiter.

At a time when Queen Sālote appeared to be in semi-retirement, appearing rarely in public, she was actually tirelessly working for causes that had commanded her attention ever since her accession. One can see in the *taumafa kava* of the Lo'au in 1959 and in the many celebrations (and the songs written and dances performed) that the focus of Queen Sālote's attention was not only on the glorification of the Tupou dynasty but also on the stability of Tongan society. These events demonstrated her success in moulding the public and private face of Tonga, in setting standards for chiefs and commoners alike, and making a place – albeit a small place – for Tonga in the world. But her endeavours had a higher motive: the preservation of the past in order to strengthen the future, not only of the chiefs, but also of all of the people of her kingdom; and, above all, the perpetuation of Tongan identity.

CHAPTER NINETEEN

"The Sun has Fallen"
"Ko e La'a e kuo Tō"

Mapaki e fā ka 'oku kei 'alaha hono tu'unga
(The flower of the pandanus has fallen, but its fragrance lingers on)[1]

FOLLOWING QUEEN SĀLOTE'S VISIT TO London in 1953, the British Agent & Consul to Tonga described Queen Sālote's standing in her own kingdom.

> The authority and prestige of the Queen is universally accepted . . . she is regarded as the ultimate authority . . . her subjects have almost unrestricted access to her and she decides in person many disputes amongst them. Her wishes to the majority of Tongans have much greater authority than any formal law, and to serve her in any manner whatever is regarded as the greatest honour. She is feared but also loved by her people. This is due in part to the fact that she understands her people and knows most of them personally.[2]

The Queen's health, however, was a source of anxiety. She had sought medical advice in Sydney in the 1930s (chapter 11). In 1945 she went to Auckland for a minor operation (tonsils?), and in 1947 she had all her teeth removed. During the 1947 visit, she rented the top flat at 24 St Stephen's Avenue, Parnell, belonging to a Mrs Moir. By the 1950s accommodation was a greater problem, for the Queen now travelled with a larger retinue, which might include daughters-in-law and grandchildren. The visits of Tupouto'a-Tungī to New Zealand on business were also frequent.

In 1952 Tupouto'a-Tungī arranged for the purchase by the government of Tonga of a house for the use of the royal family in Auckland. The house chosen was a single-storey, 13-room house, built by Sir James Gunson in 1910, and later acquired by the Nathan family, from whom the government of Tonga purchased it for £15,000. The house, at 183 St Andrew's Road, Epsom, was on a hill, with three and a half acres of grounds in which there were trees that were to grow spectacularly in the years that followed.[3] Epsom was the suburb Sālote had known as a pupil at the Anglican Diocesan School for Girls.

The property was renamed 'Atalanga. William Garfield Bagnall (Minister for Finance 1919–39) and his wife, Lilla, were caretakers from 1952 until 1955. Bagnall died in 1957, and Mrs Bagnall moved to a house nearby (at 13 Golf Road, Epsom) and continued to act as social secretary during the Queen's visits.

As far as the Queen was concerned, the purchase was also for Tongans in New Zealand. In the early 1950s there were very few Tongan families in Auckland. Secondary students from Tonga boarded at the colleges or with Methodist families, many of these arranged by Rev. A. H. Scrivin, General Secretary of the Board of Missions of the Methodist Church. Later in the 1950s and especially in the 1960s there was an increasing number of tertiary students in Auckland. A hostel (named Va'epopua) was built on 'Atalanga land for Tongan young men who were studying at tertiary institutions, and later a hostel for young women. The purpose of these hostels was to provide not only accommodation but also a focus for the Tongan community, even when no member of the royal family was in residence. When members of the royal family were at 'Atalanga, the students were added to the entourage that had accompanied the royal family from Tonga, thus reinforcing familiar rituals in a strange country.[4] The Queen kept a close watch on the students, and soon knew which were doing well with their studies, and which were having difficulties; which were working hard, and which were distracted by the entertainments of their new environment. Queen Sālote really enjoyed giving advice! The Queen's personal interest in them encouraged the students to persevere. Further, she tried to ensure that they remained Tongan in spite of their Western education and experiences.

'Atalanga became a refuge for the Queen from the heat and humidity of the summer months in Tonga and also from the many official demands that were made upon her in Tonga and endless requests for personal favours. There were also the organizing of her many committees and church groups, sponsorship of people who were gifted, writing Bible studies and speeches, supplying ideas for the church newspaper, urging on those who were flagging in their endeavours, keeping an eye on marriages, not only of the aristocracy but of church ministers and educated Tongans, attending to correspondence and (after her visit to England in 1953) demands from *papālangi* who came to Tonga especially to see her, and were disappointed when they found that she rarely appeared in public, even more rarely gave audiences, and almost never entertained in the *papālangi* way, at least not in Tonga. The Queen needed the periods of rest in Auckland.

The Queen's life at ‘Atalanga resembled that of a member of the British upper class. Although her royal status was recognized by the New Zealand government and by those who met her officially or informally, she had few royal duties to perform. In Auckland she attended concerts and plays, gave afternoon teas and garden parties, and was herself entertained at official functions, church occasions, and at social events in people's homes. Groups of Maori came to visit her, bringing food in the Polynesian way. Foremost among these were the Waikato people, with whom she had a longstanding friendship. On Sundays she attended the Epsom Methodist Church at Greenwood's Corner, where she was treated as was appropriate to her rank. The congregation (coached by Mrs Bagnall) rose to their feet as the Queen entered the church and remained standing at the end of the service until she had departed. In Tonga the Queen had an elevated seat in any church she visited, near the pulpit, where she could observe all the members of the congregation as well as being seen by all. At Epsom a place was reserved for her near the back, jealously guarded by Mrs Bagnall, who sat near by. (After the Queen's death, Mrs Bagnall sat in the Queen's chair each Sunday until her own death in 1983.)

Although servants and others of inferior rank entered her presence on their knees, sat on the floor, and did not speak until spoken to, the Queen was not as strict about social distinctions in New Zealand society as she was in Tonga. Members of the Epsom congregation were invited to garden parties to which the ‘Atalanga gardeners were also invited. Local dignitaries and academics of the University came to afternoon tea or met her at dinner parties. The household expanded, for by 1959 she had 10 grandchildren (Figure 19.1), and the Queen took some of the younger ones to Auckland with her on visits. ‘Atalanga became home for the older ones when they came to school. As the Queen commented in a letter to Sau Faupula: "I am very fond of being with children" (17 April 1941). However, she did believe in discipline, and advocated frequent corporal punishment, commending Princess Mata‘aho for beating her daughter, Pilolevu, on the soles of her feet. The quieter lifestyle in Auckland also gave the Queen opportunities to reflect, and it was in a quiet room at the back of the house, overlooking the garden, that she was able to refine the words of her poetry.

Queen Sālote was much saddened by the sudden death of her half-brother Vīlai Tupou, who died in tragic circumstances on 14 December 1954, while attempting to save the life of a member of his household who had been electrocuted.[5] She was also saddened by the death of Sau Faupula on 27 May 1960. Sau had been attending to church business in Sydney, when he had a heart attack at a railway station.

The Queen herself visited Sydney several times, staying at George Brown College, at Haberfield, when the students were absent. Mrs Bagnall recalled one visit when they stayed at the Australia Hotel, in Sydney, and the Queen asked her to share her bedroom, for not only was the Queen accustomed to her women sleeping near by, but she wanted to share her pleasure at the lights of the city. During these Sydney visits the Queen took the opportunity to confide in Rodger Page her concerns about the future of Tonga.[6] She was still anxious to prepare the Crown Prince for the responsibilities of kingship. He was the best of her premiers, she said, but she felt that when he was king he would become impatient with the reluctance of his ministers to embrace change.[7]

A nurse (Tala'inga Luani) was listed in the Queen's entourage in her 1957 visit to Auckland.[8] In the mid 1950s the Queen was diagnosed as having late-onset diabetes, and photographs show a gradual change in her appearance.[9] The Chief Medical Officer in Tonga (Dr W. A. E. Robertson) recommended that she should have a full-time nurse, but it was not until 1964, when the Queen had lost weight and her eyesight had deteriorated, that she agreed to have a nurse to supervise her diet and to care for her on a full-time basis. It was typical of the Queen that she already knew a Tongan nurse who would suit her: Moala Simiki, one of the daughters of Rev. S. Tonga Simiki, a minister of the Free Wesleyan Church. Moala returned from nursing training in Australia and immediately took up her duties at the Palace on 14 December 1964 dressed in her professional white uniform, which she wore for the remainder of her time at the Palace, at Fatai, and at 'Atalanga.

Looking after the Queen was not easy for Moala because of the many *tapu* that surrounded royalty. Like the old Tu'i Tonga, the Queen and her possessions could not be touched by others. This made a medical examination and treatment problematic. For example, Moala told me how difficult it was for her when the Queen asked for her hair to be cut. She had to forget her Tongan upbringing and remember only the training she had received in the Sydney hospital. The Queen's hair was cut.

On 4 January 1965 the Queen left Tonga on the government boat the *Aoniu*, then flew from Nadi in Fiji to Auckland on 7 January. Cancer of the lung and bone was diagnosed, but there were hopes that treatment would prolong her life. On 21 April some lumps and a fingernail were removed, and the subsequent blunt report by the doctor upset the Queen very much. There was a change of doctor, and the Queen had deep-ray treatment, although it was now clear that little could be done. The Queen's thoughts were back in Tonga, and she was worried and depressed after the mail came. On 15 May Queen Sālote and her entourage returned to Tonga and she was photographed looking much thinner, wearing glasses, and using a walking stick.

Rodger Page died in Sydney on 1 July 1965, and his ashes were returned to Tonga so they could be interred in the grave of his wife, Hannah, who had died in Tonga in 1939. As Rodger Page's ashes were interred, the Queen ordered her car to drive slowly past the Mala'e 'Aloa (the chiefs' burial ground), and when the proposed inscription for the grave was brought to her, she crossed out the chiefly word for burial and substituted the royal word *telio*.[10]

On 24 July the Queen left the Palace and moved to Fatai, the home of Tu'ipelehake and Princess Melenaite, where it was easier to manoeuvre her wheelchair. On 30 July there was a public holiday to celebrate the fact that Queen Sālote had ruled the kingdom for 47 years, 3 months, and 25 days, thus exceeding in length that of her celebrated ancestor Tupou I by 1 month and 11 days. The Queen returned to the Palace just for the day, so the thousands of schoolchildren who marched through the Palace grounds could wave to her as she sat on a couch on the verandah. Villages brought their *lakalaka*, and dancing went on all day. It was during this time that Queen Sālote wrote (with other women) the prayers for the Women's World Day of Prayer that were used in many countries in March 1967.

Prince Tupouto'a-Tungī and Prince Tu'ipelehake urged the Queen to return to New Zealand for further treatment, even though it was clear from her physical condition that such treatment was unlikely to help her. On 19 October, she was carried up the stairs of the Palace for the last time, so she could make her preparations for departure. On 22 October Queen Elizabeth II of England appointed Queen Sālote a Grand Commander of the Order of St Michael and St George, Dame Grand Cross, First Class (GCMG), the first woman in the British Empire to receive this honour.

On 31 October the Queen received the Sacrament of the Lord's Supper at the Palace from four ministers of the Free Wesleyan Church: Rev. George Harris, who was the royal chaplain as well as President of the Free Wesleyan Church, Rev. Dr S. 'Amanaki Havea (Secretary to the Conference of the Church), Rev. Lātū Puloka, and Rev. Kaivai Heimuli. After receiving the Sacrament the Queen spoke to them:

> I thank you for coming to me now because you know I am about to leave for New Zealand. I do not know what will happen, but it makes no difference. I have realized that the time may be short and my thoughts have dwelt upon the approaching event. I want you, the leaders of the Church, to know that all is well, all preparations have been made, and not just recently or in a hurry. Long ago I committed my life to Christ. My readiness is not my doing, I trust in the redeeming work of Jesus. Whenever the call comes I am ready to answer to my name. My family and nation and the Government are left. If I have done anything useful for them, it is the Lord's doing. I am not anxious or fearful. On the contrary, I have peace and joy in believing. My Lord is with me. This is my strength, my blessing, and I give you my assurance that it will remain with me to the end.[11]

This speech shows that the Queen was aware of her forthcoming death, and that she faced it patiently and without fear.

On 4 November, at the personal request of Queen Elizabeth II, the New Zealand government sent an Argosy aircraft to take Queen Sālote on the first stage of her journey to Auckland. Silent crowds sat beside the 21-kilometre road to Fua'amotu airport to witness the departure of the Queen. Everyone knew she was dying, and that they would not see her again, but this could not be said openly. The Queen was photographed at Fua'amotu airport, seated in her wheelchair, prior to going on board.

The government of the United Kingdom sent a larger, Britannia plane to take the Queen from Fiji to Auckland. The government of Tonga had requested that there be no official reception in Fiji, but Paddy Macdonald, Acting Governor of Fiji, flew from Suva to Nadi and stood on the roof of one of the terminal buildings to observe from a distance that the transfer went smoothly.[12] Accompanying the Queen were Moala Simiki, Tanginitopa Matoto (her maid), and Sela Vea (her cook). Sister Beryl Hazlemore, who had been matron at Vaiola Hospital, joined the 'Atalanga household to help with the nursing.

On 17 November Tupouto'a-Tungī, Tu'ipelehake, Princess Melenaite, Lepa Kupu (the Queen's uncle), and her ADC Ngalumoetutulu Kalanivalu arrived in Auckland. By this time the Queen's weight was a very much reduced 15 stone. The Queen had some deep-ray treatment, but the cancer was too deeply into the bone and lungs for treatment to be effective. "You can never choose a better time to go [than] when everyone is here," she told her daughter-in-law, Princess Melenaite. "When the new year comes, we'll start with new things."

Tupouto'a-Tungī had been on an extended business trip around the world and visited Auckland on his way back to Tonga. He left Auckland on 21 November.[13] Tu'ipelehake proposed returning on 24 November, but was persuaded to remain by the Queen and Princess Melenaite. On 12 December, the Queen collapsed and was moved from 'Atalanga to Aotea Hospital in Ranfurly Street, Auckland. She rallied a little on the following day, but collapsed again and died at 12.15 a.m. on the morning of Thursday 16 December 1965. Tu'ipelehake and Princess Melenaite were present. Tupouto'a-Tungī and Princess Mata'aho had left Tonga on 14 December, but their plane was delayed and they did not reach the hospital until two hours after the death of the Queen.

Tongans with shortwave radios heard the news during the early hours of 16 December, before it was officially announced from the Tonga radio station at 10 a.m. Immediately black clothing and mourning mats were prepared by the whole population. People who were *liongi* (closely related and of inferior rank on that occasion) wore large ragged mats and either cut their hair or wore it unkempt. They would be responsible for preparation of the food for the highly ranked mourners during the mourning period. Also on 16 December the new

King was proclaimed during his absence and a six months' mourning period determined. The Deputy Premier, Mahe 'Uli'uli Tupouniua, met with Ve'ehala to discuss "the preparations that must be done".

In Auckland the Queen's body was embalmed by an undertaker, Sibuns of Newmarket, and (as she had requested) dressed in a simple white cotton nightgown. The body was removed to Government House in Auckland on 17 December, attended by members of the royal family. From 18 until 20 December, there was a lying-in-state in the ballroom of Government House (now part of The University of Auckland), and 4000 people came to pay their respects to the Queen. Banks of flowers flanked the kauri coffin, which stood on a bier covered with a purple cloth, with the standard of Tonga draped over the foot of the coffin. Throughout the time of the lying-in-state the 'Atalanga household and the 800 members of the Tongan community kept vigil at the foot of the coffin, praying and singing hymns during the night, but silent when outsiders were present. The only sound louder than the quiet hymn singing was when a group of Waikato Maori led by Princess Piki came and held a *tangi* (formal crying) for the Queen.

On Saturday 18 December the new King, Queen Mata'aho, and the younger grandchildren returned to Tonga, while Tu'ipelehake and Princess Melenaite and the older grandchildren waited to accompany Queen Sālote on her final journey to Tonga. On 20 December Queen Sālote's body was escorted to Whenuapai airport, where a Hercules aircraft of the Royal New Zealand Air Force flew her, members of the royal family, and the Queen's personal staff to Tonga. A Maori *haka* marked her departure. It was a remarkable scene, with black-clothed Tongans wrapped in large waist-mats seated on the rain-soaked tarmac, the sun gleaming fitfully in a leaden sky while the coffin was carried aboard.

A hearse met the plane at Fua'amotu airport, the ground covered with bark cloth to receive the Queen in death as she had been received in life. It took two hours to drive the 21 kilometres from the airport to the Palace, while black-clad mourners sat weeping silently by the roadside. The body lay in state in the Royal Chapel from 20 December until the funeral on 23 December. The making of bark cloth, dancing, and singing (other than hymns), even weeding of gardens, were prohibited during the whole period of mourning. On the nights of the 20th, 21st, and 22nd, the ceremony of *takipō* was observed: groups of people sat just beyond the circumference of the Palace walls, each group burning a torch over clean sand onto which the sparks fell. At sunrise, the King's only daughter, Princess Pilolevu, gave the order for the torches to be extinguished.

During the week following Queen Sālote's death, the new King had invited heads of state from all over the Pacific to attend the funeral. Rev. Dr A. Harold Wood (then living in Melbourne) was invited to give the funeral oration, and was accompanied to the graveside by Rev. D. S. 'Amanaki Havea, Rev. S. Tonga

Simiki, and Rev. George Harris. The burial would be a Christian one, but many of the ceremonies connected with the burial were according to Tongan custom. While the Christian ceremony was suitably humble and thankful, everything about the Tongan ceremonies proclaimed the Queen's high rank, some of the ceremonies (such as the *fakapō teau* – hundred nights) formerly being reserved for the Tu'i Tonga.

The male and female chiefs who were the *liongi* had forebears who had been brothers to Queen Sālote's female ancestors, and were themselves direct descendants of the royal lines. Thus Kalanivalu-Fotofili (descended from the Kalanivalu who was brother to the Queen's great-grandmother), and Vaea (son of her half-brother Vīlai Tupou), and Ratu Sir Edward Cakobau (half-brother to the Queen) were all *liongi*. There was no *fahu* (person of higher rank) because the Queen's father and paternal grandfather had no sisters. More importantly, the Queen's *mana* was so high that no one would dare claim to outrank her.

Although the Auckland undertaker already mentioned had prepared the Queen's body for burial, there was a group of royal undertakers, the 30 members of the Ha'a Tufunga (the attendants for a royal funeral), to ensure that all the Tongan ceremonies were properly carried out, and they were housed in a specially built shelter in the Palace grounds. Gifts of food were brought to the Palace and received with full ceremony, then used to feed the mourners. Ve'ehala chose 23 of the named fine-mats to be brought from the royal collection to surround the coffin in the Royal Chapel.[14]

The *kauala* (catafalque) was constructed by the orders of the Ha'a Tufunga. On 23 December it was covered with mats and bark cloth and 200 men from Kolomotu'a and Kolofo'ou (the western and eastern sections of Nuku'alofa) carried it one kilometre to the grave at Mala'e Kula, where the Queen would be buried beside Tungī Mailefihi. Because the *kauala* was very heavy, the carriers changed over at short intervals. The casket was covered with the flag of Tonga, symbol of the independence that Sālote had so skilfully preserved. Two of her *kau matāpule*, Lauaki (head of the Ha'a Tufunga) and Tākapu, sat on the *kauala* beside the coffin. As the coffin was carried out of the Chapel, the bell began to toll, and a 65-gun salute was fired on the Mala'e Pangai, one for each year of the Queen's life. The Queen's Secretary recorded that "chiefly tears and commoner tears flowed – yes, and those of foreigners".

Along the route of the procession, from the Palace and along Tu'i Road to the Mala'e Kula, mourners sat silently, dressed in black and waist-mats except for the schoolchildren, who wore their uniforms. The royal procession was led by a guard of honour consisting of members of the Royal Guards and the Tonga Defence Force, the Police Band, and the four ministers of the Free Wesleyan Church. Then came the *kauala*, escorted by high-ranking chiefs, and followed by members of the royal family, including princes Tāufa'āhau and 'Uluvalu (eldest sons of Queen Sālote's sons) carrying her British Orders on cushions.

Then followed the representatives of foreign governments and Tongan dignitaries.

The service was conducted by Rev. George Harris, the President of the Free Wesleyan Church. Since the music played by the Police Band and the hymns sung by the crowds were of European origin, they were considered not to break the *tapu* that required silence. In his oration, Harold Wood touched the hearts of the listeners when he said: "Our Queen showed her interest and affection to men, women, and children, irrespective of family or church affiliation. It was astonishing that she knew the names of so many of her people and their special needs. Tonga was like a family because she was the mother of all her people."

The service concluded with a hymn that had meant a lot to Queen Sālote since the death of Tungī Mailefihi 24 years earlier. It was inspired by Isaiah 32:2, and she had quoted it in a letter to Sau after Tungī's death.

> Mālō kuo u ʻilo ia
> ʻI heʻete mei pongia
> Lele, hoku ʻatamai
> ʻO ke unga pe ki ai.
>
> Thanks be that I have known Him
> When I was almost fainting
> My understanding runs to Him
> And takes shelter.[15] [DR]

After the service, the burial began. The interment itself could not be witnessed by anyone except the Haʻa Tufunga, so women held up large mats around the burial place, and also a piece of bark cloth 150 metres long around the whole tomb for the 20 minutes during which the stone was removed from the vault of Tungī Mailefihi and the Queen was interred. Mats and bark cloth were placed inside the tomb to receive the casket. Once the casket was correctly placed beside that of Tungī Mailefihi, the stone cover of the vault was replaced and sand piled on the grave. Then the mats and bark cloth surrounds were lowered, and senior girls of Queen Sālote College placed floral wreaths around the grave. The whole ceremony took three hours.

All of the Haʻa Tufunga remained at the grave or the Palace until the *fakapō teau* was completed, and some remained for the full six months of mourning. The Haʻa Tufunga could not touch food for the first part of the mourning period, so members of their families had to remain with them in order to prepare their food and to feed them, which meant about 300 people living at the Palace for the first part of mourning. Relations connected to the Queen through Tupou II lived in temporary houses built at Fatai, the home of

Tu'ipelehake; those connected through Queen Lavinia lived in temporary shelters at the home of Kalanivalu-Fotofili, because of the Queen's descent from that family; and those connected on Tungī's side were at Mapu-'a-fuiva, just outside the Palace gates.

The funeral required massive amounts of food, not only to feed the mourners who remained at the grave or at the Palace or other places, but for the ceremonies that marked the continuance of the social order. Everyone in the kingdom was involved in the presentations of food, for villagers brought food to the chiefs of the village, who took it to higher chiefs, who brought it to the Palace.

Presentations marked the different stages of the mourning period. Soon after the funeral there were presentations by the major divisions of chiefs: first, those chiefs descended from Tu'i Kanokupolu (Ha'a Ngata and Ha'a Havea), then those descended from the Tu'i Ha'atakalaua (Ha'a Vaea and Ha'a Lātūhifo), and lastly from the Tu'i Tonga chiefs (Kauhala 'Uta). In the *taumafa kava* that followed each presentation, the new King was called by his new title, Tupou, for he would be known as His Majesty Tāufa'āhau Tupou IV. The presence of the chiefs at the ceremony indicated that they accepted him as their new ruler. In each of the ceremonies, women of high rank presented the first cup of *kava* to the new King.[16] Although the King would not be installed in the Tu'i Kanokupolu title until July 1967, these ceremonies signified that he was the royal successor.

Tu'ipelehake, the King's brother, was present in the *taumafa kava* that followed the presentations of the Kauhala 'Uta, as was Kalanivalu-Fotofili. Tu'ipelehake's title was second only to that of the King, and he was presented with the second cup (in silence). Tu'ipelehake's rank would now be fully recognized, for he, like the new King, would be addressed in the royal language formerly reserved for Queen Sālote, and he would be addressed as 'Eiki Hā'ele (Royal Chief) and Tu'i Fale Ua (Ruler of the Second House).

Pending the appointment of a full Cabinet, the new King appointed Tu'ipelehake as his Premier, Minister for Foreign Affairs, Education, Agriculture, and Works; Mahe 'Uli'uli Tupouniua as Deputy Premier and Minister for Finance; and Laufilitonga Tuita as Minister for Lands, Health, and Chair of the Niuafo'ou Evacuation Committee.[17]

At Mala'e Kula, scaffolding was erected to hold the grave decorations during the mourning period. These decorations were frequently renewed, and were presented at the Palace before being taken to the tomb. The new King went himself to the island of Tofua in February to supervise the collection and transportation of the special small black volcanic stones, which would be laid on the grave in the last of the burial rites, known as the *hifo kilikili*. For this ceremony on 14 June 1966 the decorations of *sisi* and sweet-smelling flowers were provided by the people of Ha'apai. On the highest horizontal piece of the scaffolding the letters G.B.E., G.C.V.O., and G.C.M.G. were clearly picked out. Equally elaborate decorations were provided by Tu'ipelehake's people to surround the whole area of the tombs during the ceremony.

Since February the 500 sacks of stones brought from Tofua had been sorted by size by women's groups. On the evening of Monday 13 June all 30 members of the Ha'a Tufunga and 300 of their relatives gathered at the Mala'e Kula, and at 4 a.m. on 14 June they began washing the stones in seawater in large wooden bowls. At 10 a.m. a procession of 300 high-ranking women brought baskets, lined with mats and holding bottles of sweet-smelling oil, which had earlier been presented at the Palace. The King, Queen Mata'aho, Tu'ipelehake, Princess Melenaite, and the royal grandchildren arrived at 11 a.m. Once oiled, the stones were carried in baskets to the steps leading up to the grave, where the Ha'a Tufunga spread them on top of the sand on the grave as directed by Lauaki, head of the Ha'a Tufunga. When all was done, Lauaki reported to the King that the ceremony was complete. Kioa, the King's *matāpule*, responded. Enormous presentations of food and *kava* to the Ha'a Tufunga followed at the Palace. The period of mourning ended at midnight on the night of 15 June, when a brass band played. On the following morning four of the royal grandchildren beat bark cloth with mallets, signalling that bark cloth could again be made (that is, that all work and sound could be resumed). No woman wanted to be the first to begin to work, so the silence continued for some time.

Even though the commencement of the preparations for the coronation of the new King on 4 July 1967 marked another end to the mourning period, there remained a strong feeling of the spirit of Queen Sālote still guiding and guarding Tonga.

What was it about Queen Sālote that made her a remarkable person and ruler? And what was the legacy she left Tonga?

The mythology of a beloved monarch that surrounds Queen Sālote's name has concealed her human qualities and obscured her very real political achievements. Sālote achieved her great *mana* by intelligent manipulation and (as she admitted in a rare moment) by "hard work . . . strong character, and kindness".[18] She did indeed have a strong character, and also worked very hard while maintaining that appearance of security that does not require effort to sustain it. Her "kindness" was benevolence, although she could be scathing, particularly of those who did not do their duty or whose moral character was dubious.

Queen Sālote had no power in the sense of military might – or force in any form – to persuade Tongan people to accept her leadership and her points of view. And, although from the time of her accession she had the trappings of royalty and was referred to in the royal or sacred language that had once distinguished the ancient Tu'i Tonga from his subjects, it would be through her own efforts that she eventually acquired the *mana* of the sacred ruler for herself and her heirs.

Throughout her reign, the Queen's achievements were due to her intelligence and the sheer force of her personality; that is, her ability to inspire confidence and loyalty and to influence opinion and behaviour among the Tongan people. Her authority was personal, not inherited or dependent upon her status. Some chiefs resented her accession to power as well as the ascendancy of the Tupou dynasty, and winning over these dissident chiefs was no easy task, for the centralizing of government implied loss of their former independence. By a system of rewards and promise of benefits, Sālote gradually won over the chiefs of high rank and great influence, and compensated the lesser chiefs with local official positions.

The goals that distinguished Sālote's career were, first of all, personal survival, then securing the future of her dynastic line. Convinced that God that chosen the Tu'i Kanokupolu (and in particular the Tupou dynasty) to rule Tonga in the place of the Tu'i Tonga, she was not deterred by human opposition. She was able to distinguish between personal attacks and antagonism arising from ancient controversies, and this bred a realistic response whenever her opponents attempted to undermine her position. Queen Sālote used the rules of Tongan traditional society to sustain her power, and changed the rules when they did not fit her purpose, most notably making the Tu'i Kanokupolu chiefs those from whom rank and privilege were derived instead of the more ancient Tu'i Tonga line.

"Truth is what the chief says, and history is what the highest chief says."[19] Sālote's history was not fiction, but the outcome of a lifetime of study, which was (as with many historians) interpreted through her own experience. Queen Sālote became the fountainhead of all knowledge about Tonga's past and present, about ritual and genealogy, about the appropriate roles of women and men in society. When Tongan and *papālangi* scholars quoted Queen Sālote as a source, it was increasingly with the intention of putting an end to further discussion. When she rewrote the history of her own dynasty, she did so selectively. For example, she made a hero of her great ancestor Tupou I, portraying him as the pinnacle of Christian virtues and patriotism, ignoring the dark side of the character and the violent means he used to elevate the Tu'i Kanokupolu title and to dominate his enemies. Significantly, Sālote did not attempt to rehabilitate her predecessor, Tupou II (although she loved him), because none could deny the divisiveness of his rule. Tupou I had united

Tonga and Tupou II had divided it, so the first was admired and the memory of the second faded.

It is a Eurocentric view that in the nineteenth and twentieth centuries *papālangi*, especially "missionaries" (the most abused term in Pacific historiography), had greater power in Tonga than the local chiefs. Throughout the two centuries, Tongans found certain things about European material culture very attractive, and they used their own methods of owning these; but to say that Europeans shaped Tonga's destiny prior to 1965 is to underestimate the ability of the Tongans themselves to make choices, to ignore much of what they were offered, and to transform much to their own design.

Queen Sālote's own choices in relation to the *papālangi* were clear: acceptance of alliances with the British representatives and with "loyal" missionary confidants, and a rejection of the values of those traders of the Beach who sought to reshape both political priorities and the economy of the country. Rejection of the impositions of *papālangi* legal men generally proved to be beyond her power, but her determination to respect the Constitution and Law ultimately worked to her advantage.

"The Friendship of Great Britain is Tonga's dearest possession",[20] said the Queen, expressing her gratitude for the assistance of High Commissioners and Agent & Consuls who came to annex but remained to praise and assist. Far from finding the British alliance irksome, Queen Sālote made a virtue out of necessity, and came sincerely to believe that Britain protected Tonga from the fate of those Pacific nations that had been colonized by other European powers. Her assumption that the British representatives who waited upon her in her kingdom had Tonga's best interests at heart was self-fulfilling. Furthermore, the threat of British interference was useful in keeping the refractory Tongan chiefs in line.

While notably dispensing advice to others, Queen Sālote had the ability to distinguish between good advice and bad advice offered to her and to know whom she could trust and whom she could not trust. She could evaluate events in larger terms than the personal or the short-term and she did not allow temporary setbacks to discourage her from her larger purposes.

These qualities imply a choice of allies. In Tongan social and political life, the key relationship is between the sister and brother who together rule the prime social unit, the *kāinga*. The sister determines the destiny of the group and is the ultimate authority on social relationships, and the brother governs the land and its produce. Thus it was fortunate that the chief chosen by Tupou II to be Sālote's consort was not only willing to operate within these traditional parameters, but had a passion for the land exceeded only by his loyalty to the Queen and the commitment to his sons as future leaders of the nation. The Queen and her consort adopted the traditional functions of the sister–brother of the traditional hierarchy, aiming at creating a *kāinga* of the whole nation.

The dual leadership of Queen Sālote and Tungī Mailefihi lasted for 23 critical years in Tonga's history.

"The Nobles are the curse of the country," said Dr James Egan Moulton in the early years of the century,[21] but for Sālote to admit that they rather than traders of the Beach were her real enemies would have alerted observers to the compromises that she had to make in order to gain the support of the nobles, mainly by permitting them to assume almost complete control of the land. At all costs she was determined to conceal the conflict between herself and those chiefs who sought to regain their independence from the central government. Her repeated pleas in speeches to Parliament for "peace and unity" suggest that she did not feel as secure as she pretended to *papālangi* observers. In a country where impartiality and neutrality were unknown, Sālote was simply being realistic when she interpreted the opposition of hostile chiefs as occasioned by political ambition rather than adherence to an alternative set of principles.

Queen Sālote was aware that many chiefs were not worthy of their high position in Tongan society, and her response was to encourage, regardless of rank, those who showed ability, were personally loyal to her, and were willing to work for the benefit of others and for the kingdom as a whole. She was not unaware of the needs of the common people. In 1919 – following the great influenza epidemic – she established a Department of Health and encouraged the reorganization of the Department of Education. The law provided for free and compulsory education, and she put the law into practice. Granted she did not achieve much in the way of social justice for the poorest of her subjects, but governors do not have as much power to change their world as those beneath them believe. The compromises that Sālote made, particularly in confirming the privileges of the highest chiefs, were not of her choosing, but in order to achieve what she believed to be a greater good.

Sālote ensured that the heirs of nobles and capable persons of lesser rank had the opportunity not only for education at home, but for overseas training. She had the reputation of knowing everything that happened in the kingdom, and chiefs and commoners besieged her, asking her to arbitrate in disputes, long before they approached the government or the law courts.

The second half of Queen Sālote's reign was characterized by dual leadership very different from that with her consort. Anxious that the Crown Prince should learn the duties of leadership, she appointed him Premier when he was only 31 years of age, and only hinted that she did not totally agree with his policies of modernization, nor with his Eurocentric view that the male is superior to the female.

Sālote had a strong Christian faith, which appears ultra-conservative to modern eyes, but it gave her a sense of God's presence in times of trouble. Even before she was freed of many of her duties in the last two decades of her reign by the premiership of the Crown Prince, she gave much time to establishing networks within the church and to giving instruction by means of Bible study and prayer. Nor was she sectarian in her behaviour. She ignored the demarcation between churches, which had been determined by political allegiance, and welcomed all who worked for the welfare of the people in whichever church. In the 1950s she founded a number of organizations, church and secular, that would help ordinary folk to cope with the growing intrusiveness of the outside world.

Sālote's ability to see things the way they were arose from a humility that was not inconsistent with her sense of high destiny, neither of which clouded her intelligent assessment of situations. She was similarly able to combine a sincere Christian faith with very traditional methods of getting her own way. She looked for a revival of faith among the Tongans, but did not encourage changes in the hierarchy or structure of the church. Although she encouraged sincerity and honesty as Christian virtues, the notion that the church should be the conscience of the nation simply did not occur to her.

Parliament did not change significantly during her reign. Its Tongan name *Fale Alea* (Speaking House) sums up its function and lack of relevance. Suggestions from Agent & Consuls that members of Parliament should be allowed a greater role in government were ignored. Taking on the rhetoric of her day, Sālote extolled democracy (in a country where there was none) as a political system, and decried communism (which at its best had something in common with the mutuality of traditional Tongan ideals). Perhaps Sālote succeeded too well in her aims of "peace and unity", for dissenting voices were generally silenced. In short, she discouraged that healthy public debate that allows a country to adapt to its own times.

The second half of Sālote's reign was one of personal acclamation. They were the golden years, when Queen Sālote's *mana* was such that the chiefs and people competed to outdo each other in carrying out her slightest wish. Sālote loved to celebrate events that enhanced the reputation of the Tupou dynasty. The most significant of these were the celebration of the centenary of Tupou I in 1945, the investitures when British honours were bestowed upon her (demonstrating the recognition of the outside world), and the great Lo'au of 1959, when hundreds of chiefs from all over Tonga came to signify their total acceptance of her as the highest chief by taking their places in her *taumafa kava*.

Perhaps Sālote rewrote not only Tonga's past but her own present; but this was not simply self-aggrandizement. In her last years, Queen Sālote could see Tongan values being eroded by economic considerations, and she attempted to reinforce those customs in Tongan society that would strengthen the Tongan sense of identity, such as "love, respect, and mutual helpfulness".[22] She was largely successful in preserving Tongan pride, for Tongans were not demoralized as were many colonized Pacific Islanders, nor (at least, not while the Queen was alive) did they mindlessly adopt foreign ways. In the words of the linguist Melenaite Taumoefolau, Queen Sālote provided "shade" for her people. It was this "shade" that enabled them to survive and which preserved their identity in a time of challenge.

What then was Queen Sālote's legacy to Tonga? When she became Queen there were among her subjects some who remembered the last years of the civil wars that had devastated the whole group of islands that were Tonga. The ancient dynastic quarrels that lay behind those wars could be settled only by the emergence of a centralized government led by a strong and just ruler. To her elder son she left the legacy of a secure throne and a loyal brother, and to both sons the *mana* of descent from three powerful royal lines.

To her people Sālote left the peace and unity she had so often extolled as her major goal. During her lifetime she attained by thoughtful planning what was possible for the well-being for the people rather than chasing impossible dreams of economic wealth. She was aware that women of high and middle rank, who had a privileged place in Tongan society, were losing ground because of the intrusion of the masculine ideology of *papālangi*, and she encouraged women to hold to their former dignity as well as taking their places beside men in the modern world. The Queen also realized the importance of continuity, and she ensured the preservation of the knowledge of Tonga's past and of Tongan language and culture.

The Queen prepared for retirement long before her people would let her go. Her speech at the Closing of a session of Parliament that overflowed from 1954 to 1955, has a feeling of a rallying cry and also a sense of handing over to others the struggle for the well-being of Tonga and its people.

> We are about to disperse and once again I urge the chiefs and people to fresh efforts in the maintenance of peace, the education of the young, the distribution of land and the furtherance of the general welfare of the community. Let us not look to Government to do all for us, but rather that each should carry out that which forms his legitimate obligations, for the real proof of that patriotism which has so often been stated in the Legislative Assembly is doing of one's rightful duty.[23]

Since the death of Queen Sālote in 1965, Tonga has been struggling with the forces of modern economics; so much so that change seems to be spinning out of control, and Tonga survives only because about 40 per cent of its people live overseas. The danger is that in the rush to be rich and to be "modern", Tongans will lose the very sense of identity that has protected them and enabled them to cope with challenges from the outside world. There is also a demand among commoners for political change, and for the people to have a greater say in the affairs of the kingdom.

Throughout this book I have spoken of Queen Sālote's *mana* as something she achieved. That is, I have used the word *mana* in its more modern meaning of "reputation", but it also retains it older meaning of superhuman or supernatural power. It was not so much that the Queen herself would respond, but that the supernatural *mana* was a force that was out of the control of the person who possessed it. I visited Tonga in 1974, nine years after the Queen's death, and received a very strong impression that for the Tongans the Queen was still present, and even the mention of her name could result in a manifestation of her supernatural presence. Although her memory has faded since then, and the younger people of Tonga know little about her, they owe Queen Sālote gratitude for her commitment to the preservation of the kingdom and dedication to the welfare of her people.

Glossary

For plural forms, see "Notes on Tongan Spelling and on Chiefly Titles", pp.xiii. Note that the fakau'a *has been ignored in determining the sequence.*

bark cloth – made from the bark of the paper mulberry (*hiapo*). Uncoloured it is *tapa*, with painted brown or black designs it is *ngatu*.

'eiki – (1) chief (rank derived from blood descent, especially descent from the Tu'i Tonga line, and especially through women); *hou'eiki* (plural) – aristocracy; *'eiki si'i* – lesser chiefs. (2) Anyone whose rank is superior in comparison with another, who is thereby lower (*tu'a*). See also *fie'eiki* and *nōpele*.

fa'ēhuki – lit. "support mother", a relative on the mother's side who accompanies the bride or bridegroom to the Tongan wedding ceremony (*tu'uvala*).

fahu – a person whose relationship to an individual is such that she/he may demand support and favours; usually descended from an eldest sister of father or male ancestor (e.g. father's father's eldest sister's child). In ceremonies a *fahu* is chosen from among those eligible to be the recipient of the major part of the presentations. See also *mehekitanga*.

faka'apa'apa is often translated as "respect". It is the respect a person of inferior status pays to anyone of superior status, within the family – such as a father or sister – or within society at large.

fakalēlea – on the night before the wedding the bridegroom's people go to the bride's house. Originally designed to prevent the bride from running away.

fakatapu – preface to a speech, expressing the speaker's respects to those present. For example, "*Tapu mo hou'eiki*" (My respect to the chiefs).

fānau – children, family, those with whom one has a special emotional tie. Queen Sālote referred to the Kolomotu'a *kāinga* as her *fānau*.

fatongia – work without reward for the benefit of a person of higher rank, usually the hereditary estateholder on whose estate one is living. Cf *kavenga*.

fau – bark of the hibiscus, used as a strainer in *kava* ceremony; used also to make *sisi* (see below).

fie'eiki – snobbish, pretending to or aspiring to higher rank. Not necessarily pejorative when applied to a high chief.

fihu – a fine, soft, whitish mat; a *fihu palavalu* is folded so that it fans out when the wearer moves.

fonua – land-and-people, i.e. the land plus the people living on it; the nation. Cf *kelekele*.

ha'a – clan group or lineage; a group of chiefs whose ancestors are said to have been *tehina* (younger brother) or *foha* (son) to the leading titleholder of the *ha'a*. Tungī belonged to the Ha'a Havea, and the Ha'a Ngata were the original supporters of the Tu'i Kanokupolu. The *ha'a* of the Tu'i Tonga was called *sina'e*, and ones of foreign origin called *fale* (e.g. Fale Fisi – House of Fiji). The Ha'a Tufunga are the royal undertakers. *Ha'a* may be used for other groups.

hā'ele – the regal word for "go" or "walk", was used only for Queen Sālote during her reign. The Tu'ipelehake (grandfather of Queen Sālote) was known as the 'Eiki Hā'ele, to remind people of his regal status. After Queen Sālote's death, the Tu'ipelehake (son of Queen Sālote) was the 'Eiki Hā'ele and Tu'i Fale Ua (Ruler of the Second House).

Hahake (Eastern) District. Particularly the Eastern District of Tongatapu where the Tu'i Tonga people lived and Tungī and Tu'ipelehake have their estates.

hala – connection or route, presentation at a funeral of a high chief by a relative.

hau – political or secular ruler who protected and provided for the sacred ruler (Tu'i Tonga). The peak of a *hau*'s achievements was often marked by his marriage to a woman of the Tu'i Tonga family, and of his sisters or daughters to the Tu'i Tonga.

heliaki – metaphor, used extensively in poetry.

hereditary estateholders – the 30 *kau nōpele* (nobles) and six *kau matāpule ma'u tofi'a* (*matāpule* with estates) appointed by Tupou I (two more *nōpele* being appointed by Tupou II and one more by Queen Sālote). Tupou I did not intend hereditary estateholders to be landowners (the Constitution stated that he owned all the land), but to be trustees, who were granted a small portion of their estates as personal holdings and required to distribute the remainder of their estates to the people. However, the hereditary estateholders behave like landowners.

hiapo – the paper mulberry. See bark cloth.

Hihifo (Western) District. Tupou I "instructed Tungī to proceed to Hihifo on Tongatapu and draw a line from Masilamea to Fāhefa and that was the Hihifo boundary. The instruction when they defined these boundaries was that all chiefs holding land there will be discontinued and 'Ahome'e, Ata, and Vaha'i will receive the Hihifo district."

hopi – "hops", home-brew. Widely made for sale during World War Two to the US troops.

hou'eiki – see *'eiki*.

kafa – rope made of coconut fibre or human hair used to tie the *ta'ovala* around a person's waist.

kāinga – originally used of people living in a place under the leadership of a chief, it came to mean a group of relatives under the leadership of a chief, whether they live together or not. More than a family and less than a tribe, the nearest English equivalent is "extended family". An individual will belong to the *kāinga* of her/his mother and also to the *kāinga* of her/his father, who nurture and rule her/him respectively. *Kāinga lotu* means people of the same church.

kauala – catafalque used in the funeral of a person of high rank to carry the body to the grave.

Kauhala 'Uta – the chiefly titleholders appointed by the Tu'i Tonga. The Kauhala Lalo were the chiefly titleholders appointed by the Tu'i Ha'atakalaua and Tu'i Kanokupolu.

kaukau tama – a form of adoption, in which a lower-ranking person provides for a person of superior rank.

kava – a plant, the root of which is pounded (in earlier times it was chewed) and made into a drink by infusion with water in a *kava* bowl made of hard wood. The pieces of root are removed by a strainer made of *fau* (fibre from the hibiscus). The drinking of *kava* is surrounded by ritual, but the complexity of the ritual varies according to the occasion and the people taking part. *Faikava* – any social circle formed around a *kava* bowl to drink and converse; *'ilo kava* – the kava circle of a chief of rank; *taumafa kava* – ceremonial *kava* circle presided over by the Tu'i Tonga until

1865, and by the Tu'i Kanokupolu thereafter, who adopted many features of the sacred *kava* ceremony of the Tu'i Tonga. *Taumafa kava* was used when Queen Sālote presided over a *kava* circle, while *'ilo kava* was used when Tungī Mailefihi, the princes, Princess Fusipala, or other chiefs presided. Holders of active and representatives of almost extinct chiefly titles may be seen when they take up their positions in the *taumafa kava* circle of the Tu'i Kanokupolu.

kavenga – burden or load, the duty owed by the people to the chief of their *kāinga*; said to be voluntary. Cf *fatongia*.

kelekele – the soil. Cf *fonua*.

kie hingoa – fine-mats of such quality and historic importance that they have individual names.

kiekie – girdle or waistband worn by women.

koka – *Bishovia javanica*. A dye is extracted from the bark and used for painting *tapa*. A *koka'anga* is a co-operative (*kautaha*) of women getting together to make or stain *tapa*. Hence the name of the house Fai-'a-koka (making of *koka*).

koloa – women's durable wealth, consisting of mats, bark cloth, perfumed oil, and (in the case of chiefs) rare and precious objects used in gift exchanges and for presentations. Women produce *koloa*, men produce food.

Kōmiti Tala Fakafonua – Tonga Traditions Committee.

lakalaka – a dance for women and men. It is accompanied with a song. Queen Sālote wrote *ta'anga* (the poetry) and worked with groups on the music for *lakalaka*.

Langa Fonua 'a e Fefine Tonga – "an organization for building up of land by the women of Tonga" or "nation-building by women" of which Queen Sālote was both founder and first President.

langi – terraced graves of great chiefs of Tu'i Tonga descent.

Lapaha – part of Mu'a that is the chief village of the ranking descendant of the Tu'i Tonga. The other part of Mu'a is Tatakamotonga, the chief village of Tungī.

liongi – certain categories of people who are of inferior *kāinga* rank to the corpse at a funeral, and who carry out menial tasks connected with the funeral, such as cooking, typically from the maternal *kāinga* of the corpse, but including brothers of a female. A *liongi* wears a very large, ragged mat, the size depending on the closeness of the relationship to the deceased, and the hair of the *liongi* women is either worn untied and dishevelled or cut short. Cf *fahu*.

Lo'au – the name for a chief who in legend appears when there are difficulties and resolves situations or reconstructs Tongan society. In one legend about Pulotu, Lo'au organizes the search for people who have offended Langi, the daughter of Havea Tu'ipulotu; in another he appears as the father of Nua, wife of the Tu'i Tonga Momo; in another he devises the *kava* ceremony. The event when the *taumafa kava* was recorded in 1959 was called the Lo'au, and Queen Sālote was referred to as "our Lo'au".

mala'e – field, an open space used for any communal purpose, such as the major *taumafa kava*, celebrations, *fono*, football. For example, the Mala'e Pangai, beside the Palace. The Mala'e Kula (Red Field) was named after a celebration, in 1883 or 1885, when everyone wore red.[1] The Mala'e Kula became a royal cemetery of the Tu'i Kanokupolu in 1893 when Tupou I was buried there. The Mala'e 'Aloa is the chiefly cemetery in the Kolomotu'a section of Nuku'alofa. See also Pangai.

mana – reputation of a chief of high rank, derived from her/his ascribed rank and her/his achievements; supernatural quality of chiefs. Cf *tapu*.

matāpule – a man appointed by a chief to carry out duties, including ceremonial duties, on her/his behalf, and given a title that often suggested the duties. Six *kau matāpule ma'u tofi'a* were appointed hereditary estateholders by Tupou I in 1882 (but without separate representation in Parliament). The Ha'a Tufunga (lit. "tribe of carpenters") were the *kau matāpule* who were royal undertakers. The following is a description by Elizabeth Bott Spillius: "The *kau matāpule* are the ceremonial attendants of chiefs. Their distinguishing feature is that they all have the right to serve the *kava* (*tufa*), which no chief can do. They also give and receive gifts of food on behalf of the chief. A village without a *matāpule* cannot present gifts of food to the Palace, for example. They have to borrow a *matāpule* from somewhere else. Traditionally, the *kau matāpule* have no political power except as informal advisers to their chiefs."

matua tauhi fonua – lit. "old people who look after the land-and-people"; older males close to the head of the *kāinga*.

mā'ulu'ulu – a sitting dance, originally from Sāmoa.

mehekitanga – the female within the paternal *kāinga* towards whom an individual owes the greatest respect. She is the eldest sister of the father or eldest sister of the father's father. The descendants of the *mehekitanga* may claim special privileges. See also *fahu*.

molumalu – the quality considered by men to be appropriate for women, meekness, submissiveness.

Mu'a – *see* Lapaha.

ngatu – see bark cloth.

nōpele – lit. "noble"; 30 chiefs were appointed as hereditary estateholders by Tupou I, two by Tupou II, and one by Queen Sālote Tupou III, according to the provisions of the Constitution of 1875. Until 1915 all nobles sat in Parliament. Unlike the titles of traditional chiefs, the titles of nobles were passed on by the law of primogeniture. Cf *matāpule*. See also hereditary estateholders.

'ofa – usually translated as "love", *'ofa* has a range of meanings, encompassing the emotions someone of lower rank is required to feel towards someone of higher rank, such as loyalty and fear.

Pangai – originally "centre" or "root". Pangai was later used for meeting places with special associations with the Tu'i Kanokupolu. For example, Mala'e Pangai (the open space beside the Palace), and numerous tracts of land throughout Tonga.

papālangi – persons of European descent; white person; white people; the lands from which white people come. The term *fakapapālangi* is used for those Tongans who live a *papālangi* lifestyle.

pongipongi – lit. morning or early in the day. The word also means a ceremony in which presentations are made to the chief e.g. after a wedding or funeral. Also used for the ceremony when the people of a newly appointed chief bring presentations to the appointing chief. For example, after the Crown Prince was appointed Tungī, the people living on the Tungī lands brought presentations to Her Majesty, Queen Sālote, as Tungī's *pongipongi* on 8 December 1945.

sisi – a skirt made of fibres of the hibiscus, with a decorated waistband. Now worn only in dances. *Sisi* are also used to decorate graves, cars, etc.

takipō – an all-night watch with fires around the Palace between the death and burial of a member of the royal family.

ta'ovala – piece of mat tied around the waist with a piece of rope (*kafa*) made of coconut fibre or human hair. The *ta'ovala* is worn as a sign of respect for people of higher rank. Mats of superior quality are worn to mark an important occasion such as a wedding, and of inferior quality (coarse and ragged) to indicate humility or unworthiness, such as the mat worn by a *liongi* (see above) at a funeral. See also *kie hingoa*.

tapa – see bark cloth.

tapu – sacred, secret, forbidden. An individual of higher rank is *tapu* to a person of lower rank. An object (e.g item of food) may be *tapu* because of its association with a person who is *tapu*. The negative aspect of *tapu* (prohibition) directs the behaviour of individuals of lower rank. The highest-ranking person (Queen Sālote) was *toputapu* (sacred and holy); the Bible is the *Tohi Tapu* (sacred book). Cf *mana*.

Tatakamotonga – *see* Lapaha.

tau'atāina – free. For example, Siasi Uēsiliana Tau'atāina 'o Tonga (Free Wesleyan Church of Tonga). Tau'atāina was a *kava* club founded by HRH Tu'ipelehake in Tongatapu in the 1940s and in Vava'u in 1954. The Edict of Emancipation of 1862 is called the Tau'atāina.

taumafa kava – see *kava*.

tau'olunga – dance for solo female performer, originating in Sāmoa.

tofi'a – estate; land controlled by a chief, from which he formerly assigned land for the use of his chiefly supporters. The hereditary estateholders appointed by the terms of the Constitution (*kau nōpele* and *kau matāpule ma'u tofi'a*) continued to hold personal estates (*fakatofi'a*) – nearly 10 per cent of all land – but were required to distribute the remainder among the adult males living on the estate. *See also* hereditary estateholders.

tonga – south. Tongatapu – Sacred Tonga.

tou'a – the place in the *kava* circle opposite the presiding chief where the *kava* maker and his/her assistants sit.

tu'a – of inferior rank to another.

Tu'i – paramount ruler of a specific piece of land. The sacred ruler the Tu'i Tonga had once been the ruler of all Tonga. The Tu'i Ha'atakalaua was the ruler of descendants of Takalaua. The Tu'i Kanokupolu was originally the ruler of the Hihifo (Western) District of Tongatapu (Kanokupolu "flesh of 'Upolu" indicating the title's connection with Sāmoa). Tu'ipelehake was the ruler of the place known as Pelehake, and Tu'iha'ateiho the ruler of the place known as Ha'ateiho, and so on.

tu'uvala – a traditional wedding ceremony, where the *kāinga* of the bride and the *kāinga* of the groom exchange *koloa* and food, signifying their recognition of the alliance between the two *kāinga* (many *kāinga* in the case of a high chief). The bride and groom and their attendants wear magnificent mats. A *kava* ceremony is part of the *tu'uvala*. Queen Sālote said that such a ceremony was the equivalent of modern marriage, and made the offspring legitimate – a definition recognized in legal title cases in modern times.

uho taha – lit "one cord"; half-brothers with the same mother but different father. *Uho tau* – fighting brothers; half-brothers with the same father but different mother. The *uho taha* were expected to be allies, and the *uho tau* were expected to be rivals.

vāhenga – the woman of highest rank in the *lakalaka*, who stands next to the man of highest rank, who is the male *vāhenga*.

vala – clothing, which may consist of mats and bark cloth; a *vala tupenu* is a piece of cloth worn by women from waist to ankle, and by men from waist to calf, in addition to an over-dress (*kofu*) for women and shirt for men.

Who's Who

See pages xv–xvi for English origin of some names; also List of Abbreviations, page 321.

AFUHA'AMANGO. Vava'u family. **Tēvita Ula Afuha'amango** (died 5 Feb. 1925), father of Queen Takipō and one of the chiefs promised a noble title and estates by Tupou II. Tēvita Manu-'o-pangai Afuha'amango, member of Parliament 1924–28. **'Unga Afuha'amango**, member of Parliament 1930–41, and one of the instigators of the impeachment of five Ministers of the Crown in 1940. **Samisoni Puli'uvea Afuha'amango,** born 22 Aug. 1888 at Vava'u. Younger brother of 'Unga and first cousin of Queen Takipō. Member of Parliament 1942–45, 1948–59. Charged with defamation of Queen Sālote in 1924; with defamation of the Premier, Ata, in 1946; with sedition in 1957. In 1957 much comment was caused when the Queen sent food to him in jail. Also suspended from Parliament for assault and for contempt. Died *c.*1961.

'AHOME'E (TĒVITA MANU-'O-PANGAI). Entered Public Service in 1919. Appointed to title 30 June 1936; Governor of Ha'apai 1946–52, 1955–60; Governor of Vava'u 1952–55; Minister for Police 1960. Married **Heu'ifanga** (daughter of Veikune), who died Dec. 1996. Their daughter Halaevalu Mata'aho married Tupouto'a-Tungī in 1947. 'Ahome'e died Mar. 1961, aged 62.

'AKAU'OLA (SIOSATEKI FALETAU). One of the six *matāpule ma'u tofi'a*. He held the title 'Akau'ola from 8 Dec. 1932 until his death on 10 Nov. 1954. He served in the New Zealand forces during World War One, and was a Liutenant-Colonel of the Tonga Defence Force during World War Two. He was Governor of Vava'u (1936–39); Minister for Police (1939–52). Died 10 Nov. 1954.

'ALIPATE MAFILE'O. Son of Sūnia Mafile'o and Fane Tupou Vava'u, therefore brother to Mele Siu'ilikutapu and uncle to Tungī Mailefihi. Died 19 Oct. 1932.

'AMELIA FAKAHIKU-'O-'UIHA (last Tamahā). Daughter of the Tu'i Tonga Fefine Nanasipau'u and Tu'iha'ateiho (Haveatungua). Chief wife of TK Tuku'aho (d.1799). Baptised a Wesleyan. Died 1852.

ANGA-'AE-FONU. Daughter of Old Lavinia and Inoke Fotu, hence great-aunt to Queen Sālote on her mother's side. Fonu married Laifone, who was Queen Sālote's great-uncle on her father's side. Anga-'ae-fonu reputedly "adopted" Queen Lavinia when she was a child.

ARMSTRONG, ARTHUR L. British Agent & Consul to Tonga 1937–43. Born 11 Sept. 1888. Cadet in Fiji Service from April 1915. Transferred to WPHC Nov. 1937, just before appointment to Tonga. On leave from 16 June until 30 Sept. 1941 and retired June 1943. Died 11 Nov. 1973. His wife, **Margaret**, ran First Aid classes, and wrote reminiscences of her time in Tonga.

ATA (SOLOMONE ULA). Born *c.*1883. Appointed to title Ata on 12 Nov. 1904. Attended Newington College (1896–1902). Lifetime friend of Tungī Mailefihi. A chief of the Ha'a Ngata

Motu'a, the holder of the Ata title had the right to speak directly to the TK. Minister for Lands 1925–41. Premier July 1941 to 30 Nov. 1949. Awarded OBE on 11 Aug. 1948. Died 27 March 1950. No legitimate children, and Ata title went to 'Ulukālala (Ha'amea). A new line was formed when HM Tāufa'āhau Tupou IV appointed as Ata his youngest son, 'Aho'eitu, on 4 Jan. 1982.

BAGNALL, WILLIAM GARFIELD. Born 1882. Came to Tonga 1904 as salesman. Appointed to government 1905 by HC; Treasurer and Minister for Finance 1919–39. Married **Lilla** (b.1888), daughter of Henry Riechelman, in 1908. One son. Bagnalls were caretakers of royal residence 'Atalanga in Auckland 1952–55. Bagnall died 17 July 1957; Mrs Bagnall died 11 Feb. 1983. Mrs Bagnall was social secretary for Queen Sālote.

BAIN, KENNETH. Secretary to Government 1953–56.

BAKER, SHIRLEY. As Wesleyan Missionary (1860–79), won confidence of Tupou I, and became his political adviser. Dismissed by church in 1879 for his involvement in politics. Appointed Premier by Tupou 1880. Deported 1890 by the HC. Died in Ha'apai 16 Nov. 1903. Daughter **Ku Baker** (a nurse) lived in Ha'apai until 1950s.

BLAMIRES, GWEN. Headmistress of the Kolisi Fefine (Girls' Division of Tupou College) 1927–33.

BLANC, Bishop J. F. Born in Toulon, France, on 26 March 1872. Ordained 1895. Consecrated Bishop of Tonga 29 June 1912 and Vicar Apostolic 13 April 1937. Prolific writer and translator. Editor of *Taumu'a Lelei*, the Catholic newspaper, and author of a history of Tonga. Retired 1952. Died in Tonga 1962.

BROWN, A. RADCLIFFE. Director of Education from Jan. 1918 to Oct. 1919. Sometimes confused with a Mr Burns, who was Acting Director in 1916.

BROWNLEES, JOHN K. Barrister-at-law. Secretary to Government from 2 Oct. 1941, and appointed in 1942 Judge of Land Court, Chief Police Magistrate, and Legal Adviser to Government. Retired 20 Aug. 1947.

CAKOBAU, Ratu Sir EDWARD. Half-brother of Queen Sālote. Son of **Adi Litia Cakobau** and Tupou II of Tonga. Born 21 Dec. 1908 at Bau. Adi Litia's father was Ratu Timoci Tuvanuvanua, and Ratu Timoci's father was the Cakobau who "ceded" Fiji to Britain. Adi Litia's mother was Tupoutu'a, of the Veikune family of Vava'u, Tonga. Edward visited Tonga for the first time in 1934, where he was nicknamed Tungī Fisi in recognition of his high rank. Teacher, then company commander in the 3rd Battalion of the Fiji Military Forces in World War II, when he fought in the Solomons. Awarded MC for gallantry in action 1944. Attended first post-war Administrative Service Course, Oxford, 1946–48. Served in Malaya campaign (1952–54). Administrator in Fiji Service. Appointed Roko Tui Tailevu in 1955. Deputy Prime Minister following independence in 1970. *Liongi* at the funeral of Queen Sālote. Died 27 June 1973.

CAKOBAU, Ratu Sir GEORGE. Born 6 Nov. 1912. Descended in the male line from the Cakobau of 1874. Second cousin of Edward Cakobau. Educated at Newington College. Mother was Adi Torika, from chiefly house of Cakaudrove. Entered Fiji Civil Service in 1936. Served in the Fiji Military Services 1942–44. Represented Fiji at coronation of Queen Elizabeth II 1953. Installed 1959 as the Vunivalu of Bau. Governor-General of Fiji 1973–83. Died 25 November 1989.

CAMPBELL, W. TELFER. British Agent & Consul to Tonga, 1909–12.

COCKER family. Joshua and Elizabeth Cocker came to Tonga in 1859 or 1860. Appointed Vice-Consul *c.*1862. Cocker descendants intermarried with the Riechelmanns, another long-established family, and with other *papalāngi* and Tongans who were traders or held appointments in the government.

COLLOCOTT, Rev. E. E. V. Born in Australia 7 June 1886. Wesleyan missionary (1911–23) at Ha'apai and Tongatapu. Principal of Tupou College (Nuku'alofa and Nafualu). Amateur anthropologist, who recorded an enormous amount of information, much of which he passed on to his friend E. W. Gifford.

COODE, E. J. British Commissioner & Consul to Tonga, 1959–62, 1963–July 1965.

FALEOLA, TONGA. Leading anti-unionist. Member of Parliament 1930–37.

FAUPULA, Rev. SAU. Born *c.*1909. Captain of Tupou College 1928, tutor then Head Tutor 1929–60. Gained LTh 1933. Married in 1936 'Asinate Kavapalu (sister of Nānisi Helu), who died on 19 Feb. 1941 (3 children), and **Manu Puloka** in 1956 (one child). Confidant of Queen Sālote. Died 27 May 1960 in Sydney.

FAVELL, Rev. HAROLD ALBERT. Born in England *c.*1878, In charge of the Anglican Mission in Tonga, 1929–46. Died April 1955.

FERGUSON, DOROTHY. Born 13 Feb. 1907. Taught at Wesleyan "European School" 1927–30, and kept diary.

FĪNAU, MOLITONI FISI'IHOI. Born 1881. Son of Tēvita Fīnau (who assisted J. E. Moulton with translation of Bible) and Mele Havea. Educated at Tupou College (?–1895) and Newington College (1896–1902). Locally trained lawyer, longest serving MP 1919–65. Claimed, unsuccessfully, Tu'ivakanō title on behalf of his son **Lupeti** (d.1979). Died 1 Dec. 1965.

FOTOFILI. **Fotofili (Siosiua)** (d.17 Oct. 1936) married to **Afā** (d.20 April 1926), sister of Sioeli Pangia. Their son, **Sēmisi** (born *c.*1911), was one of the suitors of Fusipala. He married **Sisilia Tu'itavake** (June 1932). When Sioeli Pangia died on 29 May 1935, Sēmisi was appointed a noble with the new title Kalanivalu on 31 May 1935 (*pongipongi* on 10 July 1935). After the death of his father (17 Oct. 1936), Sēmisi was trustee for the title of Fotofili for his son, but took the title himself on 1 Nov. 1955. Died 6 Jan. 1968. His son, **Ngalumoetutulu**, who became Kalanivalu-Fotofili in 1968, was ADC to Queen Sālote.

FUSIPALA (1). Daughter of Tēvita 'Unga, son of Tupou I. Married Tu'ipelehake (Fatafehi) in 1870. Mother of Tupou II. For three months after her brother Laifone died, she was heir to the title of TK. Died Sept. 1889.

FUSIPALA (2). Half-sister of Queen Sālote. Born 26 July 1912. Went to Auckland in Dec. 1920, and attended Diocesan School for Girls June 1921 to Dec. 1924. Attended Methodist Ladies' College, Melbourne, mid-1926 to the Dec. 1928. Died in Sydney 21 April 1933.

GARVEY, RONALD (later Sir Ronald). Born 4 July 1903. In Tonga as representative of the WPHC 10–24 Aug. 1939, and compiled report on Tongan government. Governor of Fiji and Consul-General for the Western Pacific 1952–58.

GOODACRE, GEORGE. Born 16 June 1902, in Auckland, NZ. Came to Tonga 1926 and filled various posts in Treasury. Minister for Finance 1950–61. Married Rita Riechelmann.

GORDON-KIRGAN, Rev. ROBERT. Born 23 Nov. 1886. President of Free Church 1927–c.1930.

GRANT, H. E. W. British Agent & Consul to Tonga 1913–16.

GRIBBLE, Rev. CECIL FRANK. Born 12 June 1903. Principal of Tupou College 1939–43, then Director of Education and Principal of the Teachers' Training College 1943–46. General Secretary of the Board of the Methodist Overseas Missions (1949–72), Sydney, Australia. Died 6 Sept. 1995.

HAFOKA, HAVILI. Son of Hafoka and Tōkanga (sister of Sione Havea). Recorder of traditions for Tonga Traditions Committee. Member of Parliament 1936–38. Inherited the Hafoka title of ʻEua.

HALAEVALU MAILE. Born 26 July 1899. Great-granddaughter of last TT. Daughter of Tisiola and Sipu (Minister for Lands 1911–18, died in Sāmoa 19 Sept. 1918). All her brothers and sisters died in influenza epidemic of 1918. She lived in Old Tungī's house, Latai, Nuku'alofa, with his widow ʻEsetia, and was companion of Sālote. Eloped with Maile Mataele. Died 1988. Her eldest son is **Tuʻilatai (Joe) Mataele**.

HALAEVALU MATAʻAHO (1). High-ranking daughter of TK Tupoutoʻa and Tupou ʻAhomeʻe (daughter of Tamahā Lātūfuipeka). Married Tuʻihaʻateiho (*c.*1823) and TT Laufilitonga (*c.*1827). When pregnant by Laufilitonga, returned to Haʻapai, where she brought up her twin children, Lavinia and Kalanivalu, with the support of her half-brother Tāufaʻāhau (later Tupou I).

HALAEVALU MATAʻAHO (2). Daughter of Heuʻifanga and ʻAhomeʻe. Born 29 May 1926. Married Crown Prince Tupoutoʻa-Tungī on 10 June 1947, and had one daughter and three sons.

HARRIS, Rev. GEORGE. Born 31 July 1900. Wesleyan missionary in Tonga 1926–34. President of the Free Wesleyan Church and royal chaplain 1962–69.

HAVEA, SIONE. Teacher and historian. Born 23 July 1869 in Angahā, Niuafoʻou. Suffered persecution as Old Wesleyan in the 1880s. Graduated Tupou College 1889. Head Tutor of Tupou College 1902–42 (with some years in parish appointments). He was a genealogist and writer of history, providing much material for Collocott and others (e.g. Collocott & Havea 1922). A notable publication was his *Koe Havea* (Tupou College magazine) 1941, in which he wrote a number of biographies of the chiefs, including those of Queen Sālote and Tungī Mailefihi. Died 24 Feb. 1942. By his first wife, Mele, his sons **Mānoa** was member of Parliament 1936–42, and Minister for Police 1962–71, and **Paula** served as missionary in the Solomon Islands throughout World War Two. By his second wife, Lakai, he had a son **Sione ʻAmanaki Havea**, born 6 Jan. 1922, who was the second Tongan to graduate from a university. ʻAmanaki became the second Tongan president of the Free Wesleyan Church of Tonga. Also daughters, ʻUngatea and **Nusi**.

HELU, NĀNISI. Born Nānisi Kavapalu. Married Tungī Mailefihi's *matāpule* Helu. Confidante of Queen Sālote.

HOAMOFALEONO. Daughter of the chief Maʻafu, and mother of Tāufaʻāhau Tupou I (by TK Tupoutoʻa).

HORNE, WILLIAM KENNETH. Chief Justice 1925–28. Born in 1883, in England, educated at Manchester Grammar School. Called to the Bar (Gray's Inn) in 1913. Arrived in Tonga on the *Tofua* on 27 Sept. 1925, and was sworn in on 2 Oct. Left Tonga for Gambia on 26 Nov. 1929.

HOWARD, A. E. S. Acting British Agent & Consul to Tonga 1933–34.

HUNTER, DAVID B. Judge of the Supreme Court, Judge of the Land Court, Chief Police Magistrate, 20 March 1954 until 31 Dec. 1963.

HUNTER, HAMILTON. British Agent & Consul to Tonga 1901–9.

HUTSON, Sir EYRE. High Commissioner for the Western Pacific, April 1925 – April 1929.

HYNE (HEIN), RAGNAR. Born 16 Feb. 1893. Appointed Director of Education and Principal of Government College Jan. 1920. Called to Bar (Queensland) Dec. 1924. Practised law in Tonga from 1925. Appointed Secretary to the Premier June 1932; Chief European Police Magistrate Jan. 1933; Acting Chief Justice and Judge of the Land Court Jan. 1935. Appointed Chief Justice from June 1936.

Left Tonga for legal appointments in the British Solomons Islands Protectorate in March 1938. Later appointed Chief Justice of Fiji.

IM THURN, Sir EVERARD. High Commissioner for the Western Pacific, October 1904 – August 1910.

JACKSON, Sir HENRY. High Commissioner for the Western Pacific, September 1902 – March 1904.

JOHNSON, C. W. TREVOR. British Agent & Consul 1943–49. Born 10 November 1893. Arrived in Tonga 30 June 1943, retired 23 March 1949. Very musical.

KAHO brothers. (1) **Polutele Kaho**, born 25 Dec. 1869, Minister for Police 1905–12, Premier (1912–23). Appointed **Tu'ivakanō** on 27 Jan. 1912. Resigned as Premier on 20 June and died 4 Aug. 1923. (2) **Siosiua Kaho** was Chief Justice 1904, MP 1915–19, 1921–23, and, after he inherited the noble title Tu'ivakanō (appointed 4 Aug. 1923), representative of the nobles in Parliament (1924 intermittently until 1953). Died 9 April 1959. (3) **Sioape Kaho**, born 1877 or 1878, was Minister for Police 1919–39, MP 1942–7, 1951–53. Died 1959. Sioape's second wife was Muimui (see below). (4) **Manase Kaho**, MP 1918–25, died in 1925. (5) **Fe'iloakitau Kaho** (born 17 May 1882), tutor at Tonga (Government) College. Fe'iloakitau's daughter, **Tupou Posesi Fanua** (1912–), is well known for her knowledge of traditions and her translations of Tongan poetry.

KAHO, MUIMUI. Born 1893. Daughter of Tae Manusā and Tēvita Ula Afuha'amango; sister of Queen Takipō. Muimui married Sioape Kaho, no children. Died June 1974.

KALANIVALU. (1) Personal name of "eldest" son of the last TT; twin brother of Old Lavinia. Appointed noble in 1875 with some of the TT lands as his estates. Succeeded by his son Sioeli Pangia (see below), for whose successor the noble title Kalanivalu was created. (2) *See* FOTOFILI.

KALAUTA, SIOSAIA. Son of Old Lavinia and great-uncle to Queen Sālote. Mayor of Neiafu. Died 27 April 1946.

KALOLAINE. Great-grandmother of Queen Sālote; mother of Tōkanga, who was mother of Queen Lavinia.

KRONFELD, GUSTAV. Born in Germany. A trader in Sāmoa and Vava'u. Married a Sāmoan woman, and they had seven sons and two daughters. Moved to Auckland c.1890. Princess Sālote lived in his house, 'Oli Ula, Eden Crescent, Auckland, for three years (1910–12). He closed his trading business at the outbreak of World War One, but thereafter had interests in the Pacific Trading Company, Auckland. Died 24 April 1924.

KUPU, LEPA. Grandson of Old Lavinia and uncle to Queen Sālote. He was in Auckland when she died.

KUPUAVANUA, 'ASIPELI (known as KUPU). Son of Old Lavinia and Inoke Fotu. Married Tōkonga. Father of Queen Lavinia and therefore grandfather of Queen Sālote.

LAIFONE. Son of Tēvita 'Unga, and his heir after the death of Wellington Ngū. Died 6 June 1889. Married Anga-'ae-fonu, daughter of Old Lavinia, but they had no children. Died 6 June 1889.

LANGI, MOTEKIAI TAUKOLO. Son of Free Church minister. Member of Parliament 1915–23. Leader among the anti-unionists 1923–24.

LĀTŪFUIPEKA (Tamahā). One of the great female ancestors from whom the highest chiefs are descended.

LAUAKI. Once a *matāpule* of the TT, now a *matāpule* of the TK. Head of Ha'a Tufunga, the royal undertakers.

LAUFILITONGA. Born *c.*1798 (according to John Thomas). His mother was Tupou Veiongo, daughter of TK Mumui. Installed as TT 1827. Among his many wives were Lātūniua (daughter of Tamahā Lātūfuipeka), Lupepau'u, later (1834) married to Tupou I, and Halaevalu Mata'aho, sister of Tupou I. Laufilitonga converted to Catholicism 1848 (baptised 1851). Died 9 Dec. 1865.

LAVINIA (MĀHANGA) VEIONGO (*māhanga* = "twin"), referred to by Queen Sālote as "Old Lavinia". Daughter of TT Laufilitonga and Halaevalu Mata'aho (half-sister of Tupou I), her twin brother was Kalanivalu. Great-grandmother of Queen Sālote. By 'Isileli Tupou, she had a daughter, Tupou Moheofo, mother of Vīlai Tupou. By Inoke Fotu of the Veikune family, she had a number of children. Old Lavinia was one of the prime movers in arranging the marriage of Tupou II to her granddaughter Lavinia. Said to be the last surviving of TT Laufilitonga's children and to be over 80 years of age when she died on 7 April 1907. Buried in the *langi* Paepae-'o-Tele'a.

LAVINIA VEIONGO (Queen). Born 9 Feb. 1879. Her father ('Asipeli Kupuavanua) was son of Old Lavinia. Married Tupou II on 1 June 1899. Mother of Queen Sālote. Died 24 April 1902.

LEEFE, R. BECKWITH. British Vice-Consul to Tonga, Feb. 1887 – Feb. 1901.

LOSALINE FATAFEHI. Granddaughter of TT Laufilitonga, her grandmother Lātūniua being the daughter of Lātūfuipeka (the great Tamahā). Taught genealogies by the last Tamaha ('Amelia Fakahiku-'o-'Uiha), and taught Sālote in turn.

LOWE, ALBERT GEORGE. New Zealander. Solicitor and barrister, appointed Legal Adviser and Secretary to the Premier 9 March 1938, with limited right of private practice, and Acting Chief Justice 13 May 1938 until 8 June 1938. Left Tonga *c.* June 1940.

LUKE, Sir HARRY. High Commissioner for the Western Pacific, Sept. 1938 – July 1942.

LUPEPAU'U. Her father was Makamalohi, son of the daughter of the Tu'i Tonga Fefine Nanasipau'u, and her mother from the 'Ulukālala line. Married when very young to TT Laufilitonga. From 1834 was wife of Tāufa'āhau Tupou I. Baptised by Wesleyans and took the name Sālote (after Queen Charlotte of Britain). She had two sons by Tāufa'āhau: Tu'uakitau (1839–42) and Vuna (1844–62). Lupepau'u died 8 Sept. 1889. In 1941 the Kolisi Fefine was renamed Queen Sālote College in her honour.

MĀ'ATU. Chiefs of Niuatoputapu. Mā'atu (Kivalu) married Tae Manusā, and became the father of 'Ofa-ki-Vava'u, **Mā'atu (Pānuve)**, known as "The Whip", died 22 June 1923, and **Mā'atu (Ma'afu-'o-tu'itonga)** died 12 Oct. 1934, and after lying-in-state at Pālesi (the "round house" in the Palace grounds) was buried in Loamanu, Lapaha (tomb of Mulikiha'amea). Both brothers opposed Queen Sālote in Parliament. Title left vacant from 1934 until Tupou IV appointed his second son, 'Alaivahamama'o, to the title (a new line) on 27 Sept. 1979.

McKAY, Rev. A. E. President of the Free Wesleyan Church and royal chaplain 1946–56.

McOWAN, ISLAY. Acting British Agent & Consul to Tonga 1912–13. British Agent & Consul to Tonga 1917–26. Born 4 April 1871. Took up appointment as Agent & Consul in August 1917. Although initially concerned about the Queen's youth and inexperience, he was quickly won over as a wholehearted supporter by her intelligence and willingness to be guided by him as representative of the British Government. He understood that the issue in the Queen's attempt to reunite the churches in 1923–24 was one of national unity. Having advised her to appoint additional *papālangi* members to her Privy Council in 1919, he subsequently supported her against recalcitrant *papālangi* members. He had legal and administrative ability, sound judgement, and strong but sympathetic character. Queen Sālote regretted his transfer, 30 June 1926. Died 4 April 1938.

MANU, Rev. SETALEKI. First president of the reunited Free Wesleyan Church 1924–25. Died 27 Oct. 1933.

MARK, Rev. YIM SANG. Minister of the Church of England in Tonga, 1902–28. Died 20 Nov. 1964 in Los Angeles.

MASTERTON, JOHN McLEAN. Held various government appointments. Defended the government ousted by Im Thurn in 1904/05. Married daughter of Rev. J. B. Watkin. Sometimes appointed British Vice-Consul (but never Acting Consul) when Agent & Consul was on leave. Died in Tonga 4 May 1931.

MATEIALONA. Grandson of Tupou I, born 1852. Educated at Tupou College and in Auckland. Disinherited by the Constitution of 1875 and Lands Act of 1882. One of the exiles to Fiji 1887–90. Married **Sela Kata Nau**, sister of Rachel Tonga. Close associate of his cousin Tu'ipelehake (Fatafehi), and supporter of Tupou II's marriage to Queen Lavinia. Premier 1905–12, Governor of Ha'apai 1897–1905, 1918–24, Minister for Lands 1924–25. His was the only new noble title created by Queen Sālote. He was appointed Tupouto'a on 5 Jan. 1921 (*pongipongi* 22 June 1921). Died 15 Sept. 1925. Buried Mala'e 'Aloa.

MATEKITONGA. (1) *c.*1826–1877, father of 'Ulukālala (S.F.M.). (2) An illegitimate son of Tu'ipelehake (Fatafehi) by a woman called Fīnau. He was thus a half-brother of Tupou II and uncle to Sālote and Fusipala.

MAUDE, H. E. Acting British Agent & Consul to Tonga 1941. He and his wife, **Honor**, represented Queen Sālote at the funeral of Tungī Mailefihi.

MELE SIU'ILIKUTAPU. Mother of Tungī Mailefihi. Daughter of Sūnia Mafile'o, great chief of Kolomotu'a, by high-ranking Fane Tupou Vava'u. *Fahu* at Tu'ipelehake's funeral 1912. Leader of the Ako Angelo. Married Tuku'aho, son of Old Tungī. Tungī Mailefihi was her only child. Died 29 July 1921, and buried in the Mala'e 'Aloa. Her two full brothers were 'Alipate Mafile'o and **Sione Lamipeti**; her half-brothers were **Maealiuaki** and **Tu'itavake**. Lamipeti, Maealiuaki, and Tu'itavake were among the exiles to Fiji of 1887–90.

MELENAITE TUPOU MOHEOFO. Daughter of Inoke S. Veikune and Lavinia (daughter of Afā and Fotofili). Born 13 Nov. 1924. Educated at Ravenswood Methodist School for Girls. Married Tu'ipelehake (Fatafehi) 10 June 1947. Had six children, all four daughters marrying nobles. Died 16 March 1993.

MITCHELL, Sir PHILIP. High Commissioner for the Western Pacific, July 1942 – Oct. 1944.

MOODY, ROBIN N. New Zealand barrister. Born 1883. Appeared for A. D. Cameron in the second and third cases relating to the Tonga Ma'a Tonga Kautaha (Tonga for the Tongans Co-operative or TMTK) 1910–11. Unofficial legal adviser of Tupou II. In Tonga for four months in 1924 in order to represent the anti-unionists in their court cases. Wrote the Constitution of the Free Church of Tonga in 1928. An obituary appeared in the *Auckland Star* on 2 Jan. 1937.

MOTU'APUAKA. A *matāpule ma'u tofi'a* and major actor in the *taumafa kava*, attendant of the TK, with estates in the Western District.

MOULTON, Rev. Dr JAMES EGAN. Born 1841 in England. Wesleyan missionary to Tonga in 1865–88, 1896–1906. Founded Tupou College 1866 to train young men as ministers and teachers; accepted women students in 1870. With the assistance of Tēvita Fīnau, Moulton translated the Bible into Tongan. Wrote many hymns known by heart to most Tongans. Died in Sydney 9 May 1909.

Buried Gore Hill, NSW. Greatly loved by his students, whose personal loyalty to Moulton caused many to suffer persecution in the 1880s. His son **James Egan Moulton** (the younger), was born in Nuku'alofa 18 April 1869. Entered ministry 1896. Served in Tonga 1893–1903.

MUIMUI. *See* KAHO, MUIMUI

MUMUI. First TK to live in Nuku'alofa. Died 1797. Father of TK Tuku'aho (murdered 1799).

MURRAY-AYNSLEY, C. M. Born *c.*1894. Called to the Bar (Inner Temple 1920). Took up appointment as Chief Justice of Tonga in Jan. 1931. Appointed [Acting] Judge of Land Court 1933. Took 7 months' leave Jan. 1934, returning Oct. 1934. Departed in Nov. 1934 for new appointment in Granada.

NEILL, JAMES SCOTT. Born 19 Nov. 1889 in Belfast. Educated at Trinity College, Dublin. Joined Fiji Service in 1914, became barrister-at-law in 1921. Co-opted as legal member of the Privy Council of Tonga Sept. 1924. British Agent & Consul to Tonga 1927–28, 1929–33, 1934–37. Very capable, and of particular assistance in the drafting and consolidation of laws, which had been neglected since 1903. During time as Consul to Tonga was seconded to other duties or on leave for a total of nearly four years. Attaché for Queen Sālote during her visit to England in 1953. Died 3 Oct. 1958.

NGŪ (Wellington Ngū). Grandson of Tāufa'āhau Tupou I, son of Tēvita 'Unga, and his heir. Born 3 Aug. 1854, died 11 March 1885.

NICOLSON, HORACE EVANDER. Minister for Finance 1939–49.

NOTT, C. R. H. British Commissioner & Consul to Tonga from Sept. 1954 until March 1957.

'OFA-KI-VAVA'U. Daughter of Tae Manusā and Mā'atu (Kivalu). The majority of chiefs supported her as a bride for Tupou II, who preferred Lavinia. 'Ofa died of tuberculosis Dec. 1901, and was buried at Mala'e 'Aloa.

PAGE, Rev. RODGER. Born 17 Oct. 1878, Grafton, NSW. Chairman of the Wesleyan Mission 1908–24; President of the Free Wesleyan Church and royal chaplain 1925–46. Friend and confidant of Queen Sālote, he translated some of her speeches into English, and wrote official and private letters for her. Page's wife, Hannah, died in 1939, was given a chiefly funeral by Sālote and Tungī, and buried at the Mala'e 'Aloa. Page was also the confidant of British Agent & Consuls, who appreciated his knowledge of Tonga and his discretion. After he retired (1946), Page visited Tonga in 1947 for the royal wedding and in 1950 for the moving of the old church to make way for the Centenary Church. Page died on 1 July 1965, and on Sālote's instruction his ashes were interred in the Mala'e 'Aloa.

PEARSON, COLIN BATEMAN. Born 1890. Chief (European) Magistrate 1928–32.

PENNEFATHER, C. E. de F. Acting British Agent & Consul to Tonga 1921–22.

REID, A. C. (Archie). British Commissioner & Consul to Tonga March 1957–March 1959, July 1965–70. Negotiated revision of Treaty of Friendship 1958.

RICHARDSON, P. A. Secretary to the Government, Judge of Land Court, Chief Police Magistrate, and Legal Adviser to Government from 20 Aug. 1947.

RIECHELMANN family. H. W. Riechelmann came to Tonga in 1877, and married Miss Cocker. Their children intermarried with other residents of Tonga.

ROBERTS, H. S. Judge of the Supreme Court, Judge of the Land Court, Chief Police Magistrate, from 1963 until 1976.

RODGERS, Bishop JOHN HUBERT. Born in Wallaceville, New Zealand, 9 Oct 1915. Ordained 15 Dec. 1940. Arrived in Tonga 23 Feb. 1941. Consecrated Roman Catholic Bishop of Tonga Feb. 1954. Retired 1972. Died in Auckland 1997.

RODWELL, Sir CECIL. High Commissioner for the Western Pacific, Oct. 1918 – Jan. 1924.

ROWLANDS, DILYS. Born 18 Jan. 1908. Principal of Queen Sālote College 1945–68. Closely associated with Queen Sālote in Kaluseti and other church organizations, also Vice-President of Langa Fonua 'a e Fefine Tonga.

RUSSELL, W. E. Acting British Agent & Consul to Tonga 1928–29.

SĀLOTE LUPEPAU'U. *See* LUPEPAU'U.

SĀLOTE MAFILE'O PILOLEVU (1). Born *c.*1824. Daughter of Tāufa'āhau Tupou I and Fīnau Kaunanga. Baptised with father and two brothers (Tēvita 'Unga and Siosaia) on 7 Aug. 1831. Married Tu'ipelehake (Filiaipulotu) in 1839. Exiled to Fiji 1887–90 because of her refusal to join Tupou I's Free Church. Died 18 Sept. 1891. Queen Sālote Tupou III was named after this great-grandmother.

SĀLOTE MAFILE'O PILOLEVU (2). Born 13 March 1900. Married Tungī Mailefihi 19 Sept. 1917. Succeeded father on his death on 5 April 1918. Installed TK on 9 Oct. 1918. Crowned Queen 11 Oct. 1918. Had three sons: Tāufa'āhau, Tuku'aho (d. 1936), and Sione Ngū. Invested with DBE 8 Sept. 1932, GBE Dec. 1945, GCVO 19 Dec. 1953, GCMG Oct. 1965. Died in Auckland, 16 Dec. 1965, and buried in the Mala'e Kula, Nuku'alofa, 23 Dec. 1965.

SCOTT, GEORGE. Born in Hobart, Tasmania, on 18 April 1877. Arrived Tonga 1900. Married Kalo Lolohea (daughter of Siosiua and Sila Lolohea) on 25 Jan. 1906. Appointed Chief European Clerk, Premier's Department, 20 March 1913; Judge of the Land Court 1923–32; occasional Acting Chief Justice 1915–37 (when Chief Justice absent from Tonga). Died in Tonga 5 Feb. 1938.

SECOMB, Rev. HOWARD and JANET. Missionaries to Tonga 1950–63. Janet daughter of Rev. Dr A. Harold and Dr Olive Wood.

SIAKI LOLOHEA. A chief of Ha'apai. Unsuccessfully claimed a title Tupou II promised his father, Iki Lolohea. Member of Parliament 1915–30. Leading anti-unionist, 1923–24. Joined 'Ulukālala's "Church of the Chiefs" in 1928. District Officer in Ha'apai. Married three times. Died 24 June 1952.

SIOAPE KAHO. *See* KAHO brothers.

SIOELI PANGIA. Son of Kalanivalu (and 'Ungatea), son of TT Laufilitonga and Halaevalu Mata'aho (sister of Tupou I). Sioeli succeeded to the hereditary estates of his father, but had no title. Died 29 May 1935. He had no legitimate children, and was succeeded by Sēmisi, the son of his sister (Afā), who took the name Kalanivalu as his title. Sioeli was buried in *langi* Paepae-'o-Tele'a.

SIU'ILIKUTAPU. *See* MELE SIU'ILIKUTAPU.

SKEEN, ROBERT LOWIS. Born in New Zealand 1862. Admitted to the Bar in NZ in 1885. Practised law in Sāmoa 1889–1901 and Tonga 1901–5. Appointed Chief Justice of Tonga Jan. 1905. Died in Auckland (while on leave) on 16 Dec. 1915.

SMITH-REWSE, G. B. Acting British & Consul to Tonga 1916–17.

SPILLIUS, JAMES and ELIZABETH. James Spillius was a Canadian social anthropologist who arrived in Tonga on 31 March 1958 to act as a consultant to the World Health Organisation Environmental Sanitation Project, investigating village water supplies. He undertook a social survey of Tongatapu villages. **Elizabeth Bott Spillius**, also an anthropologist, was appointed co-ordinator of the Tonga Traditions Committee 1958–60. This appointment involved lengthy discussions on Tongan traditions with Queen Sālote. James and Elizabeth left Tonga in May 1960. Elizabeth's subsequent publications were under the name Elizabeth Bott.

STRONGE, HERBERT CECIL. BA Trinity College, Dublin. Prior to appointment in Tonga, served in the West Indies. Chief Justice of Tonga from 1 July 1917. Went on eight months' leave in 1919, and again in 1923. He left Tonga on 6 May 1925 for appointment in the Bahamas.

STUART, WILLIAM HEMMING. Chief Justice 1938–40. Born *c.*1884 in South Africa. Called to the Bar (Middle Temple) 1909. Practised in South Africa 1909–38. Took up appointment as Chief Justice of Tonga 8 June 1938. Came with a reformist zeal and divided the community. Departed from Tonga for British Guiana Oct. 1940 where he was second puisne judge; transferred to Tanganyika 1943; retired from Colonial Service 1948.

SŪNIA MAFILE'O. Great chief of Kolomotu'a (son of Ulakai, brother of TK Tupouto'a). Grandfather of Tungī Mailefihi. Died between 1893 and 1899. Although he was not made a noble, many of his descendants married nobles.

TAE MANUSĀ. Daughter of Tupou 'Ahau (d.1867), sister of Old Tungī (Halatuituia). Tae married (1) Mā'atu (Kivalu) 2 March 1875, and their children were 'Ofa-ki-Vava'u (d.Dec. 1901), Mā'atu (Panuve, d.1923), Mā'atu (Ma'afu-'o-tu'itonga, d.12 Oct. 1934, and buried in Loamanu, Mu'a); (2) Tēvita Ula Afuha'amango, and their children were Vika Kaufusi, Takipō, Muimui. Tae invited Bishop Willis to come and establish the Church of England in Tonga. Died on 5 July 1931.

TAKIPŌ (Queen). Born 1 March 1893. Daughter of Tae Manusā and Tēvita Ula Afuha'amango. Married Tupou II on 11 Nov. 1909. Mother of two daughters, one dying in infancy and the other being Princess Fusipala. After the death of Tupou II, Takipō lived at Finefekai. Died in influenza epidemic, 26 Nov. 1918, and buried at the Mala'e 'Aloa.

TAPA, Dr SIONE. Born 30 Oct. 1923. Graduated from Otago Medical School 1954. Married Tangakina, daughter of noble Nuku. Later Minister for Health.

TĀPUAKA, HENA. One of the confidantes of Queen Sālote. Her mother was Toa from Kolomotu'a and her father was Tāpuaka.

TĒVITA 'UNGA. Born *c.* 1824, son of Tāufa'āhau Tupou I. Baptised 7 Aug. 1831. After death of sons with Sālote Lupepau'u, Tupou I named 'Unga and his descendants his heirs. First Premier of Tonga (1876–79). Died 18 Dec. 1879 in New Zealand. Buried at 'Uiha, Ha'apai.

THOMPSON, MARY. Headmistress of Kolisi Fefine 1934–44, then headmistress of Siu'ilikutapu College, Vava'u.

TŌKANGA. Her father was Fotofili and her mother was Kalolaine. Married 'Asipeli Kupuavanua. Mother of Queen Lavinia. Died 11 April 1929. Buried in Mala'e 'Aloa.

TONGA, RACHEL (LESIELI TONGAMOHENOA). Born Lesieli Kata Nau, 1 Oct. 1851. First woman graduate of Tupou College 1871. Married Rev. Tēvita Tongamohenoa, and both assisted with the translation of the Bible by Dr J. E. Moulton. She and Tēvita refused to join Tupou I's Free Church in 1885. Tēvita died 1901, and thereafter Rachel lived with her sister **Sela** (d. 5 June 1921), who was the wife of Mateialona, later appointed to the noble title Tupouto'a. From 1907 until Sālote went to school in New Zealand at the end of 1909, Rachel was a foster mother to Sālote. She lived at Talakaepau, opposite the Palace, from 1924 until her death on 4 Aug. 1928.

TONGILAVA, SIONE FILIPE. Born 2 April 1874. Private Secretary to the HM Tupou II 1905–18, and to HM Queen Sālote 1918–51. He was 76 when he retired on 1 March 1951. Died 14 June 1965, and was accorded a state funeral.

TOUTAIOLEPO, TĒVITA TU'IPULOTU. Born 26 Sept. 1910. Educated at Tupou College and Newington College (1928–32). He was known as a special friend of Princess Fusipala. After his return to Tonga he became an interpreter and translator in the Justice Department. Died 17 Jan. 1966.

TU'IFUA CARRICK. Born 2 Sept. 1903. Daughter of Veikune and sister of Heu'ifanga. Married Mervyn Douglas Carrick 1 July 1935. Lived in London for many years. Died in Tonga 1995.

TU'IHA'ATEIHO (HAVEA). Born 6 Feb. 1898. Descended from Tamahā. Educated in Australia. One of the suitors for Princess Fusipala. Married Leafā, a Sāmoan chiefly woman, in 1933. Died 4 Feb. 1962. No sons, so succeeded by a brother. He had two aunts, Fusipala (d.21 Sept. 1942) and Sālote Maumau Taimi (d.23 Feb. 1944), who were referred to as the *ongo ta'ahine* because of their high rank. Sālote Taimi was a leader of the Ako Angelo.

TU'IPELEHAKE. Tu'i Fale Ua (Ruler of the Second House) and 'Eiki Hā'ele. The ancestor of the title of Tu'ipelehake was said to be the divine half-brother of the first TT. The last TT (Laufilitonga d.1865) gave his *toputapu* to Tu'ipelehake (Fatafehi), son of his half-brother (**Filiaipulotu**), who married Tupou I's daughter, Sālote Mafile'o Pilolevu, in 1839. **Tu'ipelehake (Fatafehi)** (1), was born 2 July 1842, brought up in Sāmoa, and married his cousin, Fusipala, in 1870, their son Tāufa'āhau becoming Tupou II in 1893. Tu'ipelehake was known as the 'Eiki Hā'ele, a term formerly reserved for the TT. Some said he was the rightful TT and TK. Died on 20 Nov. 1912. Tungī Mailefihi the trustee from *c.*1918–41. **Tu'ipelehake (Fatafehi)** (2) was born on 7 Jan. 1922, and christened **Sione Ngū Manumataongo**. Queen Sālote sent him for his earliest instruction to Rachel Tonga. He attended the Wesleyan "European School" in Nuku'alofa, then Tupou College (Nafualu). After three years (1938–40) with a private tutor (Rev. H. A. Sharp) in Auckland, he attended Newington College for two years (1941–42), where he distinguished himself in football, and then Gatton Agricultural College, Queensland, for one year (1943), returning to Tonga in Jan. 1944. On 22 Sept. 1944 he was appointed Tu'ipelehake retrospectively from 7 Jan. 1943 (his 21st birthday) (*pongipongi* 14 July 1945). With his title came the name Fatafehi, and the honorifics 'Eiki Hā'ele and Tu'i Fale Ua, but he did not use these in his mother's lifetime. On 10 June 1947 he married Melenaite Tupou Moheofo, by whom he had six children (she died 16 March 1993). From late 1959 he lived at Fatai (formerly the home of Mele Siu'ilikutapu, mother of Tungī Mailefihi). His government appointments included Agriculture Visiting Officer (1 July 1944), Member of the Copra Board (20 Feb. 1946), Treasurer of the Centenary Memorial Committee (21 Feb. 1946), Chief Inspector under Diseases of Plants Act 1916 (8 July 1948), Governor of Vava'u (1949–52), Governor of Ha'apai (17 June 1952 – 1953), Minister for Lands and Health (20 July 1953 – Dec. 1965), Deputy Premier (11 Jan. 1965). He was appointed Premier to succeed his brother in Dec. 1965, a post he held until 1991. After retirement, he spent part of each year at 'Atalanga, in Epsom, Auckland.

TUITA, LAUFILITONGA. Born 29 Aug. 1920. One of the heirs to a noble title who won a scholarship (from Tupou College) to Wesley College, Auckland. Married Fatafehi, eldest daughter of Vīlai Tupou. Succeeded to title Tuita in 1972.

TU'IVAKANŌ. For holders of this title, *see* KAHO brothers.

TUKU'AHO (1). Father of Tungī Mailefihi. Born 1858. He was appointed Premier in 1890, but was dismissed by Tupou II on 22 Nov. 1893. Died of a heart attack 1897. Tuku'aho was *fahu* to Tupou II.

TUKU'AHO (2). Second son of Sālote and Tungī. Born 5 Nov. 1919. Died 28 April 1936. The grandchildren of Sālote were given Tuku'aho as a family name in remembrance of this Tuku'aho.

TUNGĪ (HALATUITUIA). Grandfather of Tungī Mailefihi. Descendant of the Tu'i Ha'atakalaua line. In 1853 he married Tupou I's sister's daughter ('Ana Seini Tupou Veihola), by whom he had a son, Tuku'aho. In 1885 Tupou I named Tungī his heir if Tēvita 'Unga's children died without legitimate heirs. Tungī's son, Tuku'aho (d.1897), predeceased him, and Tungī died in June 1900. The personal name Tungī became a title when his grandson was appointed in 1909.

TUNGĪ MAILEFIHI. Born 1 Nov. 1887 at Fatai, Nuku'alofa. Known as Uiliami (William) Tupoulahi until he was appointed Tungī in 1909. Attended Newington College, Sydney, from 1896, but had to return to Tonga on the death of his father, Tuku'aho, in 1897. Visited England in 1911 to attend George V's coronation. Married Princess Sālote on 19 Sept. 1917. Governor of Vava'u 1912–18. Minister for Lands 1918–23. Appointed Premier 21 June 1923. Invested with CBE 28 July 1937. Died 20 July 1941. The title was vacant from 1941 until Queen Sālote's eldest son was appointed Tungī on 28 March 1945. Tupou IV retained the Tungī title after he became TK.

TUPOU I (also known as Tāufa'āhau and King George). His birth date is sometimes given as 1797, because of a legend that he witnessed the sacking of the *Port-au-Prince* in 1806. However, John Thomas ("Tongatapu" n.d. p.179–82) estimated his age at about 13 when he fought beside his father at Pea in 1817. Peter Turner estimated his age at about 16 when his father died in 1820 (Peter Turner's Papers, A1506, Mitchell Library). His father was Tupouto'a, who held the title of TK, and his mother was Hoamofaleono, daughter of Ma'afu of Vainī. Baptised in 1831 along with three of his children (Sālote, Tēvita 'Unga, and Siosaia) and took the name Siaosi (George) as his baptismal name. In 1834 he married Lupepau'u, who had previously been one of the wives of the TT, and she took the name Sālote (Charlotte) after Queen Charlotte. Attempted to distribute land among people from 1830s. Installed as TK 4 Dec. 1845. Prior to this time he proclaimed laws in Ha'apai and Vava'u. Once he became TK he proclaimed a series of laws that were intended to apply to the whole of Tonga: 1850, 1862 (including the Edict of Emancipation), and 1875 (the Constitution). Attempted to reform Tongan society by abolishing many of the customs (*fatongia*, *fahu*, and *tapu*) by means of which inferiors were exploited by superiors. He outlived children and grandchildren who had been named in the line of succession. Died 18 Feb. 1893. His great-grandson Tāufa'āhau Tupou II succeeded him.

TUPOU II (Tāufa'āhau). Born 18 June 1874. Inherited title of TK through his mother, Fusipala, daughter of Tēvita 'Unga, who was son of Tupou I. His father was Tu'ipelehake (Fatafehi), son of Sālote, only daughter of Tupou I. Became King on the death of Tupou I, and was crowned on 17 March 1893 and installed in the TK on 21 March 1893. Married Lavinia on 1 June 1899, and she was the mother of Sālote. Married Takipo on 11 Nov. 1909, and she was the mother of **'Onelua** (died in infancy) and Fusipala. He was a musician, his anthem "Matapā 'o 'Iteni" written for eight parts being especially popular. He died on 5 April 1918.

TUPOU 'AHOME'E. Daughter of Tamahā Lātūfuipeka, mother of Halaevalu Mata'aho (1).

TUPOU MOHEOFO (1). Only woman known (before Queen Sālote) to hold the title of TK. Daughter of TK Tupoulahi, sister of TK Tu'ihalafatai, and wife of TT Paulaho. She was installed as the twelfth TK, and deposed by Tuku'aho, later the fourteenth TK. Tupou Moheofo fled to Vava'u with Paulaho *c.* 1784, where she probably died.

TUPOU MOHEOFO (2). Daughter of Old Lavinia, and therefore *mehekitanga* to Queen Lavinia. Mother of Vīlai Tupou by Tupou II. She had a daughter (Sālote) by Tu'i Cakau, and another daughter (Vāhoi) by Siale 'Ataongo, son of Henelē Ma'afu-'o-Tu'itonga, son of the TK Aleamotu'a. Tupou Moheofo died in the influenza epidemic, on 24 Nov. 1918. Vāhoi married Veikune (Fotu).

TUPOU, VĪLAI. *See* VĪLAI TUPOU.

TUPOUNIUA, MAHE 'ULI'ULI. Born 20 July 1927. Third Tongan to take university degree: B.Comm. 1953. First Tongan appointed Minister for Finance, 4 Feb. 1961. Deputy Premier Dec. 1965. Married 'Elenoa, daughter of noble 'Ahome'e.

TUPOUTO'A. Personal name of the father of Tupou I, who was appointed TK (*c.*1807–20), but (according to John Thomas, confirmed by Queen Sālote) was not recognized as such by all the districts of Tonga. Married Tupou 'Ahome'e, daughter of the Tamahā Lātūfuipeka. The noble title of Tupouto'a was created for Mateialona in 1921, and after his death in 1925, the title was vacant until Queen Sālote's eldest son was appointed Tupouto'a on 6 July 1936. His eldest son was appointed Tupouto'a on 4 May 1966.

TUPOUTO'A-TUNGĪ (Siaosi Tāufa'āhau Tupoulahi). Eldest son of Queen Sālote and Tungī Mailefihi. Born 4 July 1918. Attended Newington College 1933–37, University of Sydney 1938–42, graduating BA and LLB. First Tongan university graduate. Appointed to title Tupouto'a on 6 July 1936 (*pongipongi* 21 Jan. 1938), and title Tungī on 28 March 1945 (*pongipongi* 8 Dec. 1945). Appointed Minister for Education 1 Feb. 1943, Minister for Health 6 Nov. 1944, Premier 1 Dec. 1949. Succeeded his mother, as Tāufa'āhau Tupou IV, on 16 Dec. 1965; coronation on 4 July 1967, and installation as TK on 6 July 1967.

'ULUKALALA (SIAOSI FĪNAU MĪSINI). Born *c.*1865. His ancestors 'Ulukālala-'i-Ma'ufanga (d.1797) and 'Ulukālala-'i-Feletoa (d.1809), grandson and great-grandson of TK, invaded but did not conquer Tongatapu. 'Ulukālala (Tuapasi) appointed Tāufa'āhau his successor as Tu'i Vava'u in 1833, when his son **Matekitonga** (*c.*1826–1877) was only a child. Matekitonga gave his son the names **Siaosi Fīnau Mīsini-tuitui-'o-Vava'u** (George Fīnau Sewing-machine-of-Vava'u) in the hopes that he would sew up all of Vava'u – or perhaps all of Tonga. Tungī Mailefihi's mother's mother was sister of Matekitonga, which made Tungī *fahu* to him. His lands were in Vava'u, and he was twice Governor of Vava'u 1890–1904, 1905–06. In 1915 Tupou II appointed him a Minister Without Portfolio and Speaker of Parliament, appointments he held until his death on 10 Nov. 1938.

'ULUKALALA-ATA (HA'AMEA). Born 15 Aug. 1891. Son of 'Ulukālala (Siaosi Fīnau Mīsini) and Tapukitea of the Ata family. Educated at Uruoa Mission School, Longburn, Palmerston North, New Zealand. Contender for the hand of Sālote and Princess Fusipala. Married Tuna, daughter of the noble Vaea, in Aug. 1934, but had no legitimate children. Governor of Ha'apai 1924–28, Governor of Vava'u 1928–29, 1939–50. Minister for Police 1951–60. Appointed 'Ulukālala 11 Nov. 1938 (*pongipongi* 16 Dec. 1938). Succeeded to the title Ata in 1950. Died 12 Sept. 1960. His daughter 'Eva married the noble Ve'ehala (Leilua). A new line was formed when Tāufa'āhau Tupou IV appointed his youngest son 'Ulukālala on 4 July 1987.

'UNGA, TĒVITA. *See* TĒVITA 'UNGA.

VAEA. Noble title. Vaea (Tava) was deprived of his title in 1885 because he remained an Old Wesleyan against the wishes of Tupou I. **Vaea (Siosaia Pau'uvale Loloa'atonga)** had two daughters: (1) **Tupou Seini** (born c. 1888), who married Vīlai Tupou on 18 March 1919 and had eight children, and (2) **Tuna**, who married Ha'amea (later 'Ulukālala-Ata) in Aug. 1934, but had no children. Old Vaea died in 1939, and the eldest son of Vīlai and Tupou Seini, **'Alipate** (b.15 May 1921), was appointed Vaea on 16 May (from 14 Aug.) 1942. He attended Wesley College, Auckland (1938–41) and served in the Royal New Zealand Air Force (1942–45). He served the Queen as ADC (1953–58), then Governor of Ha'apai 19 Sept. 1960–68. Tupou IV appointed him first Tongan High Commissioner to London (1969–72), Baron Vaea 1970, Minister for Labour, Commerce, and Industries (1972–91), Premier (1991–).

VALU. The title of the chief of the village of 'Utulau in the Central District of Tongatapu. When Queen Sālote created the new noble title of Tupouto'a for Mateialona, Valu (also an Old Wesleyan) agreed to give up his land to add to the estates of the Tupouto'a title. Valu continued to be the chief of 'Utulau, although subordinate to Tupouto'a. Rev. Dr S. 'Amanaki Havea is of this family.

VE'EHALA. **Feleti Vī** was installed in this noble title on 29 June 1922, so was probably born *c.*1901. Deprived of his title (against the Queen's wishes) in 1927. Very musical. Married **Simoa** on 15 Jan. 1924. Their son, **Leilua Vī**, born 23 March 1925, educated at Tupou College, Tonga, and Wesley College (scholarship for heirs to noble titles) and Auckland Grammar School, New Zealand. Was appointed Ve'ehala on 23 March 1946, and appointed Keeper of the Public Record (1948–53) and Secretary to the Tonga Traditions Committee (1950–68). Ve'ehala (Leilua) died 26 Nov. 1986.

VEIKUNE. Tupou II created this noble title for **Siosateki Tonga** in 1903. Siosateki (Premier) and his son Fotu (Treasurer) were deported to Fiji in 1904 by (HC) Sir Everard Im Thurn, and returned in 1906. **Fotu** succeeded Siosateki in 1913, and died 17 Mar. 1951. **Lala** (b.28 Sept. 1908) was a suitor of Princess Fusipala; married 'Ofa (daughter of Sioape Kaho) 28 July 1942; appointed Veikune 18 Mar. 1951; died 15 Mar. 1959. Queen Lavinia, Edward Cakobau, and the brides of Prince Tupouto'a-Tungī and Prince Tu'ipelehake were descended from the Veikune family.

VIKA KAUFUSI, eldest daughter of Tae Manusā (therefore sister of Queen Takipō and Muimui Kaho). Married Fulivai. Died 8 Aug. 1947.

VĪLAI TUPOU. Born 1898. Illegitimate son of Tupou II and Tupou Moheofo, both of whom died in 1918. Married Tupou Seini, daughter of the noble Vaea, on 18 March 1919, by whom he had eight children. Sālote appointed Vīlai her ADC in 1923. In 1924 she sent him to Fiji for training, and two years later appointed him captain of the Royal Guards. Vīlai died on 14 Dec. 1954. *See also* VAEA.

VUNA. Son of Lupepau'u and Tupou I, was Tupou's heir, but died at age 18 (1862), and his brother at age 3 (1842). The name Vuna was given to an illegitimate son of Tupou II.

WALLACE, ALEXANDER BROOKE. Born 24 May 1880. Chief Surveyor 1911 – Jan. 1919. Minister for Works Jan. 1919 – Nov. 1928.

WATKIN, Rev. JABEZ BUNTING. Born on 31 March 1837, in Lifuka, Ha'apai, where his parents were missionaries. His father was forced to resign from the ministry in that same year. JBW entered the ministry in 1863, and came to Tonga as a missionary in 1866. When Tupou I set up his Free Church in 1885, he appointed JBW as President, a position JBW held until his death. A source of grievance was that the Methodist Church of Australasia removed JBW's name from its list of ministers when JBW accepted the appointment as President of the Free Church. His daughter married J. M. Masterton. There were two sons: Howard and Fred. JBW died on 23 Jan. 1925.

WESTON, Q. V. L. Acting British Commissioner & Consul to Tonga 1959.

WILLIS, Bishop ALFRED. Born c.1834. Arrived in Tonga June 1902 in response to petition of supporters of Tae Manusā and 'Ofa-ki-Vava'u. Bishop of the Church of England in Tonga. Died in England on 14 Nov. 1920.

WINDRUM, J. E. Born 5 June 1895. Joined Fiji service 19 March 1921. Appointed British Agent & Consul to Tonga 25 March 1949 until Sept. 1954. Mrs Windrum accompanied Queen Sālote to coronation of Queen Elizabeth II in 1953.

WOOD, Rev. Dr A. HAROLD. Born 4 May 1896 in Geelong, Australia. Principal of Tupou College 1924–37. Arrived in Tonga 8 May 1924, in time to stand in for barrister Richard Crompton in the Land Court case in June 1924. Well known for his *History and Geography of Tonga*, written as a textbook (in English and Tongan) for Tupou College 1932, and used in Tongan schools for many years. First editor of *Koe Tohi Fanogonogo*, the newspaper of the Free Wesleyan Church, and began training theological students at Tupou College in the 1930s. He died 27 Aug. 1989. His wife, **Olive** (born 12 June 1892), a medical doctor and teacher at Tupou College, occasionally gave medical advice to the Queen. She died 3 March 1976.

WOODGATE, Rev. RONALD and RUTH. Australian Methodist missionaries. Ron Woodgate was Principal of Tupou College (Toloa) 1947–50, and then Principal of Sia'atoutai Theological College (Nafuala) 1951–60. Their daughter **Helen** married **Rev. Siupeli Taliai**.

Notes

Abbreviations

A&C	Agent & Consul
ANU	Australian National University, Canberra, Australia
ATL	Alexander Turnbull Library, Wellington, New Zealand
BCT	British Consul, Tonga (files)
CMO	Chief Medical Officer
CO	Colonial Office
COCP	Colonial Office Confidential Print
DR	(translated by) Dilys Rowlands
encl.	enclosure
FOCP	Foreign Office Confidential Print
FWC	Free Wesleyan Church (of Tonga)
GCI	General Correspondence Inwards (files)
HC	High Commissioner (of Western Pacific)
HMSO	His/Her Majesty's Stationery Office
JPH	*Journal of Pacific History*
JPS	*Journal of the Polynesian Society*
MOMC	Methodist Overseas Mission Collection
MT	(translated by) Melenaite Taumoefolau
PIM	*Pacific Islands Monthly*
PMB	Pacific Manuscripts Bureau
POP	Palace Office Papers
PPSEAWA	Pan Pacific and Southeast Asian Women's Association
QS	Queen Sālote
SAH	(translated by) Rev. Dr S. 'Amanaki Havea
SofSCol	Secretary of State for Colonies
SPO	South Pacific Office
TDF	Tonga Defence Force
TF	(translated by) Toa Fīnau
TFB	(translated by) Tilisi Faupula Bryce
TGG	*Tonga Government Gazette*
TH	Tu'i Ha'atakalaua
TK	Tu'i Kanokupolu
TM	Tungī Mailefihi
TMTK	Tonga Ma'a Tonga Kautaha
TT	Tu'i Tonga
VSL	Victoria State Library, Melbourne, Australia
WPHC	Western Pacific High Commission

Chapter 1: Her Mother's Daughter

1. British Vice-Consul R. B. Leefe to HC, 2 June 1899, WPHC:GCI F3/12/99. The original may have been *tama* (child) of Queen Lavinia, not "son", as Leefe reported.
2. Pers. comm. 'Ana Fusipala 1974, Tupou Posesi Fanua 1976. Lambert, *A Doctor in Paradise*, pp.201–2, estimated that there were 40 persons staying at the Palace.
3. Tongan society was divided into chiefs and commoners. Among the chiefs there were aristocrats, nobles and *matāpule*

ma'u tofi'a (the two latter categories being hereditary estateholders) and lesser chiefs, who were important in their localities. See chapters 2 and 7 for further explanations.

4. Tungī was his personal name (used as a title by his successors) and distinguished from them by the name Tungī (Halatuituia) or Tungī Vaivai (Old Tungī). Tungī was named in the line of succession in 1885. *TGG* 2:35 (2 Dec. 1885) 1. See also Bott Spillius, "Discussions", p.354, where Queen Sālote explains that Tungī was son of the daughter of the sister of TK Tuku'aho, and therefore *fahu* to Tupou I.
5. 'Ofa was supported by most of the Tongatapu chiefs (particularly those known as the Ha'a Havea and Ha'a Ngata), and by ambitious chiefs such as 'Ulukālala and Polutele Kaho (chapter 2). Bott Spillius papers, Box 17, notebook XIV.
6. Tu'ipelehake and Mateialona were grandsons of Tupou I. Old Lavinia is sometimes referred to as Lavinia Māhanga ("twin"), because she had a twin brother, Kalanivalu. Lavinia was also supported by the following chiefs: Tu'iha'ateiho, all of the chiefs of the Fale Fisi, Ma'afu, and Veikune. Ibid.
7. Ibid.
8. Queen Sālote listed *koloa* as one of the three considerations in choosing a bride. The others were the chiefly rank of the woman, and the economic support her family could bring (The Writings of Queen Sālote, section IX, "The marriages of the chiefs"). An example was the marriage of Kupuavanua (Lavinia's father – known as Kupu) to Tōkanga, which was arranged by his sisters because Tōkanga had a *palavalu* and other *koloa*. Ibid. Pers. comm. Kakala Taumoefolau 1997. Some of the Tu'i Tonga fine-mats came from Sāmoa and were of very high quality.
9. Leefe to HC, 2 June 1899, WPHC:GCI F3/12/99. Much of the story of the politicking over the King's marriage is drawn from this letter. I am also indebted to Halaevalu Maile, Kakala Taumoefolau, and Tupou Posesi Fanua for additional details.
10. "King Taufa, Lord of Isles", pp.447–8.
11. A photograph in the *Auckland Weekly News* of 30 June 1899 shows the *papālangi* guests assembled on the front verandah of the Palace.
12. The 'Ulukālala chiefs had a claim to the Tu'i Kanokupolu title. Bott Spillius, "Discussions", pp.353–4. The list of guests given by the *News* was not exhaustive.
13. Pers. comm. Halaevalu Maile 1977.
14. Thomson, *Savage Island*, pp.152, 159–60, 163–4; Geil, *Ocean and Isle*, pp.102–3, 104, 142.
15. Campbell, Diary, 27 and 31 Aug. 1902; Donald, *In Some Sense*, pp.19, 57 et seq.
16. Much of the detail of Sālote's early life comes from Bott Spillius, "Discussions", pp.57, 344–6, 348, 352–4, 355, 359–60, 362–3. Rev. Dr S. 'Amanaki Havea prepared a questionnaire for the Queen some months before her death, and he kindly allowed me to see the Queen's responses. See also Fusitu'a, "King George Tupou II", pp.73–85 passim. Also pers. comm. 'Ana Fusipala 1974, Nānisi Helu 1976, Halaevalu Maile 1977, 1981, 1985.
17. Pers. comm. Tupou Posesi Fanua 1976.
18. [Seddon], *The Right Hon. R. J. Seddon's … Visit*, pp.15–61.
19. *Western Pacific Herald* 4 May (p.2), 5 Nov. 1901 (p.4); 3 Jan. (p.2), 31 Jan. 1902 (p.3); Campbell, Diary, 3 Sept. 1902. Also Fusitu'a, "King George Tupou II", pp.101, 108. 'Ofa's grave may still be seen at Mala'e 'Aloa.
20. This date is recorded in the Diary of Sione Filipe Tongilava, the King's Private Secretary, on 25 Apr. 1902.
21. Tongilava recorded the progress of Queen Lavinia's illness in his diary of 1902. The funeral and monument were described in *Western Pacific Herald* 20 May (p.5), 28 May (p.2), 20 June (p.2) 1902 and 26 Feb. (p.6), 22 Apr. (p.2) 1904.
22. Sālote told this story in the last year of her life to her nurse, Moala Simiki, who told me in 1974. I have not been able to trace this hymn.
23. Anga-'ae-fonu married Laifone, son of Tēvita 'Unga (see chapter 2), and lived with him in Vava'u until his death in 1889. They had no children. Bott Spillius, "Discussions", p.353; pers.

comm. HRH Nanasipau'u Tuku'aho 1996.

24. When referring to the King laughing and eating, Old Lavinia used the words *kokō* (squealing of a pig) and *fafa'o* (an abusive word for "eat"). Bott Spillius, "Discussions", pp.362–3.
25. Im Thurn, Diary, 8 Jan. 1905.
26. Crosby, Diary, 24 June 1910, records the burial place. *Cyclopedia* (1907) 58, also records the date of her death, saying she was the last surviving child of Laufilitonga, and was over 80 years of age. Paepae-'o-Tele'a means "Gravestones of [Tu'i Tonga] Tele'a". Lapaha was the part of Mu'a associated with the Tu'i Tonga, and was the ancient capital of Tonga, in the Eastern District of Tongatapu.
27. One of these playmates was her mother's sister's child, 'Ana Fusipala (interviewed 1974), and another was Vaine, daughter of the *matāpule* Tu'uhetoka.
28. The most derogatory term was *te'e* (excrement), and was commonly used by Palace people to refer to Sālote's attendants.
29. Pers. comm. Ve'ehala (Leilua) 1977.
30. Bott Spillius, "Discussions", pp.344, 359–60.
31. The bark of the *koka* tree (*Bishovia javanica*) is used to make a stain for painting bark cloth. *Fai-'a-koka* means to make a *koka* dye. It is sometimes spelt *Fale-'a-koka*, meaning house of *koka*.
32. Im Thurn, Diary, 5 Jan. 1905.
33. Rev. Dr James Egan Moulton, who founded Tupou College in 1866, translated the Bible with the assistance of Rachel and her husband, Rev. Tēvita Tongamohenoa.
34. Bott Spillius, "Discussions", p.146.
35. These chiefs were descended from Ulakai, brother of Tu'i Kanokupolu Tupouto'a (father of Tupou I). Gifford, *Tongan Society*, p.92. Tupou I had not appointed any of these chiefs as nobles, which was sufficient reason for grievance.
36. *Takipō* is the ceremony of lights performed after the death of a very high chief. Takipō was born on 1 Mar. 1893, just after the *takipō* for Tupou I.
37. Fusitu'a, "King George Tupou II", pp.173–4; Crosby, Diary, 1910. The annual salary voted by Parliament to the King was £2000, and he had rents from properties and gifts from his subjects.
38. See "Who's Who" in this volume and obituary in *Fiji Times* 10 Apr. 1924, p.7.
39. Pers. comm. 'Ana Fusipala, Moala Simiki 1974.
40. Letter from Sam Kronfeld to Lilla Bagnall, 21 Feb. 1974, in possession of author.
41. Pratt, "Report of a Visit", 1922. In the letter to Lilla Bagnall (see above), Sam Kronfeld says Princess Sālote was confirmed, together with his sister Mina, by Bishop Crossley, at St Paul's Church, in June 1911.
42. Princess Sālote to Tupou II, 14 Aug. 1911, POP. In spite of this letter, Sālote was obviously very fond of the Kronfeld family, and kept up a lifelong friendship with the Kronfeld children. [Davidson], *Traditional Arts of Pacific Island Women*, p.20, shows the fine-mat that the Queen sent to cover the coffin of Mina Kronfeld.
43. I am indebted to Beverley Williamson, Diocesan School for Girls, for information about Sālote's time at this school (letters dated 25 Jan. and 3 Feb. 1974), and for putting me in touch with several of Queen Sālote's contemporaries – Sister Dismas Wilson, letter to author, 17 July 1974; Mrs Avis Thomson (Perry), letter to the author, n.d. [1974].
44. Sālote's early reading included *Hereward the Wake*, a tale of the siege of Troy, Charles and Mary Lamb's *Tales from Shakespear*, and Florence Louisa Barclay's *The Rosary*. Bott Spillius, "Discussions", pp.353, 354 . See item in Palace Cuttings Book, "A Queen at Home" [1953], re the gym classes.
45. Letter in POP.
46. Tupou II to M. E. Pulling, 14 Mar. 1915, copy in POP.

Chapter 2: Ancestors and Antecedents

1. Gifford, *Tongan Society*, p.50, suggests c.1470.
2. Gifford, *Tongan Society*, p.86.
3. Hence the name Ha'a Ngata for the titles associated with the Tu'i Kanokupolu.

4. The names George and Charlotte are said to have been chosen because they were the names of George III of England and his queen.
5. London Missionary Society missionaries had come on the famous voyage of the *Duff* in 1797. Three (and a beachcomber helper) were murdered, and the remainder left in January 1800. A Wesleyan enterprise (1822–23) could not be established, so the coming of Christianity is dated from the coming of John Thomas and John Hutchinson on 28 June 1826.
6. Tupou advocated land reform as early as 1833 (P. Turner, Journal, 30 Apr. 1833, quoted by Lātūkefu, *Church and State*, p.99), and repeated the theme in his law codes of 1839, 1850, 1862, and the Constitution of 1875.
7. *Matāpule ma'u tofi'a* means a *matāpule* (ceremonial attendant) with an estate. In everyday discourse the term "nobles" usually includes *matāpule ma'u tofi'a*. The exception is in Parliament, where the nobles represent only themselves.
8. The grandfather of Tu'ipelehake (Fatafehi) had married both Tupou Veiongo (daughter of Tu'i Kanokupolu Mumui) and Lātūholeva (daughter of the Tamahā Lātūfuipeka).
9. Fatafehi did not relinquish all privileges. He was always referred to as the 'Eiki Hā'ele (which may be loosely translated as "the great chief") and Tu'i Fale Ua (Ruler of the Second House), and his *kava* ritual resembled that of the Tu'i Tonga.
10. An account by Elia Malupō is quoted in Gifford, *Tongan Society*, p.59. The mere fact of installation in Vava'u instead of Lapaha, Tongatapu, makes the ceremony somewhat doubtful.
11. Lātūkefu, "Conversations" ("Tu'i Pelehake"); The Writings of Queen Sālote, section I ("The Ha'as of Tonga").
12. 'Unga is said to have arranged the marriage between his daughter, Fusipala, and Tu'ipelehake. "Tu'ipelehake had a better claim than 'Unga, and in fact the Tu'ipelehake had many supporters in Tonga" and "'Unga's illegitimacy would go against him". Queen Sālote in Bott Spillius, "Discussions", p.353.
13. The line of succession was Tēvita 'Unga (d.1879), then 'Unga's sons, Wellington Ngū (d.1885) and Laifone (d.1889), then 'Unga's daughter, Fusipala (d.1889). Tupou I's 1889 will is specific: "Since Fusi is dead, who should have succeeded Laifone, then Tāufa'āhau should inherit." Copy of Will in FWC papers.
14. Some of the chiefs planned that the kingdom would be divided once again into districts, each with its hereditary independent chief: Mā'atu in the Niuas, 'Ulukālala in Vava'u, Tungī in Hahake, and to recall Henelē Ma'afu (son of the Tu'i Kanokupolu Aleamotu'a) from Fiji. Lātūkefu, "Conversations" ("Koe Vavakovi 'i he Constitution"). See also Bott Spillius, "Discussions", pp.355–6.
15. Bott Spillius, "Discussions", pp.353, 355.
16. Whitcombe, "Tonga Tabu", p.31.
17. Thomson, *Diversions*, pp.144–6. Thomson does not mention Tāufa'āhau as one of the group, but Queen Sālote does. Bott Spillius, "Discussions", p.354.
18. Bott Spillius, "Discussions", p.355.
19. Letter Book, POP. I am indebted to H. G. Cummins for a copy of this letter. See also Bott Spillius, "Discussions", p.355, where Sālote speaks of the letter.
20. Tu'ipelehake (Fatafehi) was not an Old Wesleyan, but his mother was. Mateialona was a staunch Old Wesleyan.
21. Tuku'aho was appointed Premier after the deportation of Shirley Baker in 1890 by Sir John Thurston, High Commissioner for the Western Pacific. Rutherford, *Shirley Baker*, p.168. See also Bott Spillius, "Discussions", p.357.
22. Fusitu'a, "King George Tupou II", p.23.
23. Bott Spillius, "Discussions", pp.355, 356, 358.
24. Fusitu'a and Rutherford, "George Tupou II", pp.173–4.
25. Fusitu'a, "King George Tupou II", pp.24, 31, 34.
26. Parliament, Privy Council, and Cabinet were set up by the Constitution of 1875. Lātūkefu, *Constitution*, ch.4 and appendix A.
27. "King Taufa, Lord of Isles", pp.447–8.
28. After the deportation of Tupou I's Premier, Shirley Baker, in 1890, Basil Thomson was appointed by the British for one year to assist Tuku'aho, whom they had appointed Premier. Rutherford, *Shirley Baker*, ch.11.

29. Thomson, *Savage Island*, p.174.
30. Thomson, *The Scene Changes*, p.223. Copies of the proclamation in English and Tongan, dated 19 May 1900, are in FWC papers.
31. HC to SofSCol, 15 Aug. 1902, COCP *Australia 182*, item 4. This COCP contains correspondence relating to the signing of the Supplementary Agreement to the Treaty of Friendship of 1905.
32. *Methodist*, 29 Feb. 1896, p.4. Dr J. E. Moulton to Egan Moulton, 25 Mar. 1904, Letter Book, FWC papers.
33. Leefe to Seddon, 5 June 1900, quoted in Cummins, *Sources of Tongan History*, pp.505–7; Hunter to HC, 23 Jun. 1902, same to same, 13 Jan. 1903, WPHC:GCI 2/00; CO 225/67, quoted by Kennedy, "Britain and the Tongan Harbours", p.264.
34. Hunter to HC, 6 June 1903, WPHC:GCI 2/00.
35. Reported in ibid.
36. Ibid. Veikune's estates were Holonga (from his wife) and Longamapu (from his mother), Kanatea (part of Kupu's land). Bott Spillius, "Discussions", p.364.
37. Bott Spillius, "Discussions", p.358. Although the 'Ulukālala chiefs outranked the Veikune chiefs, Old Lavinia had married Inoke Fotu of the Veikune family instead of Matekitonga (father of 'Ulukālala (S.F.M.)), which may have been the origin of the quarrel.
38. Hunter to HC, 13 Jan. 1903, WPHC:GCI 2/00.
39. Im Thurn, Diary, 7 Jan. 1905.
40. Petition of the foreign residents of Nuku'alofa, n.d. COCP *Australia 182*, encl. 2 in item 14.
41. Suggestions of foreign residents, COCP *Australia 182*, encl. 1 in item 14.
42. Petition of the foreign residents of Nuku'alofa, n.d. COCP *Australia 182*, encl. 2 in item 14.
43. Hunter to HC, 6–9 June 1903, WPHC:GCI 2/00.
44. 1000 Tongans died of measles in 1893. Tupou II to SofSCol, 20 June 1903, COCP *Australia 182*, item 16.
45. Dr J. E. Moulton to Egan Moulton, 25 Mar. 1904, Letter Book, FWC Papers.
46. SofSCol to HC, 14 Oct. and 25 Nov. 1904, COCP *Australia 182*, items 30, 36.
47. The records of interviews and copies of correspondence are in COCP *Australia 182*. See also HC to SofSCol, 28 Jan. 1905, ibid., item 54, and Im Thurn, "Report", encl. in item 62. Veikune (Siosateki) and Fotu lived comfortably in Suva until their return in 1906.
48. Im Thurn, "Report".
49. Bott Spillius, "Discussions", p.349; pers. comm. Tupou Posesi Fanua 1974, Fa'ahivalu Taumoepeau 1976, Halaevalu Maile 1977.
50. 'Ulukālala was appointed by Thomson in 1890 and dismissed in 1904, reappointed in 1905 and dismissed in 1906. Thomson, *Diversions*, pp.169–71; *TGG* 18:4 (7 June 1904) 1; FOCP 8933, annex. F, 2 Jan. 1905; *TGG* 20:2 (6 Feb. 1906) 1.
51. Im Thurn, Diary, 7 and 20 Jan. 1905. The *sulu* is the Fijian wrap-around garment worn from the waist down. It is shorter than the Tongan *vala*.
52. Bott Spillius, "Discussions", p.347.
53. Mateialona to HC, 6 Apr. 1905, WPHC:GCI F3.
54. *TGG* 21:7 (20 May 1907) 1; HC to SofSCol, 10 May 1907, WPHC:GCI 279/06.
55. Tupou II to SofSCol, 21 Mar. 1905 (drafted by Thomas Cotter, an Auckland lawyer), COCP *Australia 182*, item 65; Hunter to HC, 30 Mar. 1905, FOCP 8933, encl. 8 in item 15.
56. Bott Spillius, "Discussions", p.356; Tongilava, Diary, 20 Nov. 1912.
57. Those known to have been promised ennoblement by the King were 'Alipate Mafile'o, son of Sūnia Mafile'o, the great aristocrat of Kolomotu'a; Sione Tupou Mateialona, Premier and grandson of Tupou I; S. A. Sipu, a chief living in Kolomotu'a; Iki Lolohea, a Ha'apai chief; Tēvita Tapueluelu, a Vava'u chief, who represented 'Ulukālala during his many absences; S. F. Tafolo; Tēvita Ula Afuha'amango, a Vava'u *matāpule* and father of Queen Takipō; and Siosiua Kaho, brother of Polutele Kaho and erstwhile Chief Justice of Tonga (Figure 2.4). Tupou II to Campbell, 28 May 1910, BCT 1/3.
58. Reports of the proceedings of Parliament, *TGG* 5 (6 July 1909) 6–7; "Notes

of a private interview with the King of Tonga", 15 Sept. 1911, BCT 1/43/69; *TGG* 12 (15 July 1912) 83–4 et seq.

59. Cameron, "Memoirs"; Lavaka, "Tonga Ma'a Tonga Kautaha"; Rutherford, "Tonga Ma'a Tonga Kautaha".
60. Many files of WPHC:GCI and BCT for 1910–12 are concerned with the TMTK and its aftermath. See especially correspondence in WPHC:GCI 1855/11; correspondence of May and June 1912, POP; *TGG* 12 (15 July 1912) 108–9. See also H. W. Just to Campbell, 22 June 1912, WPHC:GCI 1632/12.
61. Scott to "Hanny", 28 Oct. 1904, POP. There are several typed copies of Scott's letter in POP, suggesting it was widely read.
62. COCP *Australia 182*, encl. in item 35; C. H. Hart-Davis to HC, note on cover of WPHC:GCI 110/13.
63. I am indebted to Lily Goodwin for a copy of this waltz.
64. Siosaia Falevatu named Polutele Kaho in a confession dated 27 June 1905. I am indebted to Penny Gregory for a copy of this letter. Pers. comm. Ve'ehala (Leilua) 1977. Bott Spillius, "Discussions", p.347.
65. Tu'ivakanō to Tupou II, 30 Oct. 1914, WPHC:GCI 2990/14 argues the case for the reform.
66. Mā'atu (Pānuve) was relieved of his appointments as Governor of Niuatoputapu, Judge of the Land Court, and magistrate on the insistence of Grant and Smith-Rewse. The HC commented on Mā'atu's "drinking and beating". *TGG* 20 (31 Aug. 1916) 129; Smith-Rewse to HC, 27 Oct. 1916, BCT 7, misc. 103; HC to Smith-Rewse, 3 Nov. 1916, HC to Smith-Rewse, 3 Nov. vol. 1916–17. See also McOwan to HC, 27 Aug. 1920, BCT 1/19.
67. Smith-Rewse to HC, 8 Jan. 1917 (paras 3 and 13), BCT 7/II/104.
68. Smith-Rewse to HC, 8 and 20 Jan. 1917 (para. 11 (d)), BCT 7/II/104.

Chapter 3: A Dynastic Marriage

1. Queen Sālote said a bridegroom was chosen for his title (which implied possession of land) and for the economic support he could give the girl's family. The Writings of Queen Sālote, section IX ("The marriages of the chiefs").
2. Tungī did not even have the full support of the people on his estates prior to his installation in the title. Pers. comm. HRH Princess Nanasipau'u Tuku'aho 1996.
3. Sālote's account of the years 1915–17 are constructed from Bott Spillius, "Discussions" and pers. comm. 'Ana Fusipala 1974 and Tupou Posesi Fanua 1974, 1976–77.
4. Sālote to Tupou II, 6 Dec. 1913 (in care of 'Ēseta Fusitu'a); Bott Spillius, "Discussions", p.340.
5. Bott Spillius, "Discussions", pp. 57, 345, 355, 368.
6. Smith-Rewse to HC, 4 Apr. 1917, BCT 1/43/85.
7. Among the dignitaries voicing their concerns were the Catholic Bishop Blanc, Rev. Rodger Page of the Wesleyan Mission, and Mateialona. The events were narrated by Smith-Rewse in letters to HC of 13 Apr., BCT 1/19; 14 Apr., BCT 1/43/85; 5 May, WPHC:GCI 1208/17; 7 May 1917, WPHC:GCI 1209/17; and enclosures within this correspondence.
8. Watkin to HC, 7 May 1917, WPHC:GCI 1211/17.
9. Clauses 45 and 46 of the Constitution, in *Laws 1903*.
10. See chapter 2 for earlier rumours of the ambitions of Tu'ivakanō (Polutele).
11. Domenika was of Ata's family. She never married, and when Tungī died, she walked from Kolovai to Nuku'alofa, and the Queen looked after her. Pers. comm. Tupou Posesi Fanua 1976, Ve'ehala (Leilua) 1976, Halaevalu Maile 1977.
12. Tungī Mailefihi arrived in Nuku'alofa on 10 June by the *Talune*. Tongilava, Diary, 10 June 1917.
13. Tongilava, Diary, 9 June 1917.
14. Tongilava, Diary, June entries; correspondence in POP.
15. *Fiji Times*, 19 Oct. 1917.
16. The bridesmaids were Halaevalu (daughter of Sipu), Simoa (daughter of Tuita), 'Ānau (Tungī's cousin), Luseane and Lavinia (daughters of Fotofili), Tu'ifua (daughter of Veikune), and Princess Fusipala. Pers. comm. Halaevalu Maile 1977.

17. Sione Lātūkefu, "Conversations" ("Paea 'i Ma'opo'opo"), says *Kie Vela* was one of the mats Queen Sālote wore for her wedding. The other one could have been *Hau-'o-Momo* or *Laumata-'o-Fainga'a*.
18. Gifford, *Tongan Society*, p.229. A portion of the list of the *koloa* brought to the Palace exists in POP, and a photocopy appears as an appendix in E. Wood-Ellem, "Queen Sālote Tupou III and Tungī Mailefihi".
19. Bott Spillius, "Discussions", p.342. 'Ulukālala was descended from Matekitonga (male side), while Tungī was descended from Matekitonga's sister, Fane Tupou Vava'u (female side).
20. McOwan to HC, 25 Sept. 1917, BCT 1/43/85.
21. The Book of Her Majesty, no pagination.
22. Sione Havea, *Koe Havea*, 1941. Most of the information about Mailefihi's childhood and youth is from this publication.
23. Crosby, Diary, 1910.
24. Pers. comm. Halaevalu Maile 1977.
25. Im Thurn, Diary, 16 Jan. 1905; *Missionary Review*, Jan. 1913, p.14.
26. Tovi married Kato'one, half-sister of Fusipala, mother of Tupou II.
27. Tungī did not forget those who befriended him in his youth. Halaevalu Maile (pers. comm. 1977) said that when Tungī became a noble he gave his noble's salary and permanent tenancy of Latai to his grandfather's widow. This house was demolished after Halaevalu's death in 1988.
28. Sione Havea, *Koe Havea*, 1941.
29. *Methodist Recorder*, cutting in Rodger Page Scrapbook, n.d.; Collocott, "King Taufa, Lord of Isles", p.442; Sione Havea, *Koe Havea*, 1941; Basil Thomson to Tupou II, 1 Aug. 1912 (letter in care of 'Eseta Fusitu'a).
30. *Missionary Review*, Jan. 1913, p.14.
31. McOwan to HC, 22 June 1912, WPHC:GCI 1855/11.
32. J. E. Moulton (the younger) to Rodger Page, 1 Nov. 1912, FWC papers; Blanc, Diary, 31 Aug. 1912. Blanc later revised his opinion of Tungī: see Blanc, Diary, entries for 1924 and chapter 8.
33. Both of these letters are in POP.
34. The incident of which he complained occurred on 16 Mar. 1917. Record of Inquiry, Aug. 1917, POP.
35. Tungī was descended from TK Mumui's daughter, Halaevalu Kovi, while Sālote was descended from Halaevalu Kovi's full brother, TK Tuku'aho. Halaevalu Mata'aho (daughter's daughter of the Tamahā Lātūfuipeka) was Tungī's father's mother's mother. Sālote was descended from Halaevalu, but also from Halaevalu's half-brother Tupou I. See figures 3.2 and 3.3.
36. Collocott, "King Taufa, Lord of Isles", p.442.
37. *TGG* 25 (20 Nov. 1917) 163, 5 (4 Feb. 1918) 21.
38. Cowan to Premier, 29 May 1917, third report on health of the King, WPHC:GCI 1495/17; *Premier's Report 1917*, p.4; McOwan to HC, 12 Apr. 1918, WPHC:GCI 1016/18.
39. Pers. comm. Halaevalu Maile 1977.
40. Tungī Mailefihi to Sālote, 25 Feb. 1918, POP.

Chapter 4: The First Year of a Reign

1. McOwan to HC, 12 Apr. 1918, WPHC:GCI 1016/18.
2. Bott Spillius, "Discussions", p.348.
3. Tongilava, Diary, 5–9 Apr.; McOwan to HC, 12 Apr. 1918, WPHC:GCI 1016/18; *TGG* 11 (6 Apr. 1918) 1.
4. Bott Spillius, "Discussions", pp.244–5.
5. Bott Spillius, "Discussions", p.245, describes Sālote as "chief *liongi*", but she would not have undertaken the menial tasks expected of *liongi*. Halaevalu Maile (pers. comm. 1977) says Sālote's hair was not cut; indeed no Tongan could touch her head, because it was now *tapu*.
6. Queen Sālote explained that the chiefs appointed by the Tu'i Tonga (Kauhala 'Uta) brought presentations because the Tu'i Kanokupolu was now the *only* king (i.e. there was no Tu'i Tonga or Tu'i Ha'atakalaua). In earlier days *only* the *ha'a* (alliances of chiefs) related to the Tu'i Kanokupolu would have brought presentations to the funeral of the Tu'i Kanokupolu. Bott Spillius, "Discussions", p.151.
7. Tongilava, Diary, 20 Nov. 1912, 15 Apr.

1913; *Recorder*, 2 May 1918, pp.5, 6; Tongilava, Diary, Apr.–Oct. passim; McOwan to HC, 12 Apr. 1918, WPHC:GCI 1016/18; Bott Spillius, "Discussions", pp.151, 184, 244–5.
8. Bott Spillius, "Discussions", p.245.
9. McOwan to HC, 12 Apr. 1918, WPHC:GCI 1016/18.
10. HC to McOwan 24 Apr., SofSCol to HC, 18 July, HC to McOwan, 24 Oct. 1918, BCT 1/43/85.
11. McOwan to HC, 14 May 1918, BCT 1/19.
12. McOwan to HC, 12 Apr. 1918, WPHC: GCI 1022/18, and 11 and 14 May 1918, BCT 1/19.
13. In Tongilava, Diary, 1917, there are frequent references to the King's borrowings and repayments. In 1918 he refers to regular repayment of "Queen's debts", which I assume are really the King's, and a regular £25 a month for the renovation of the Palace. The loan of 14 Oct. 1918 was also repaid at £50 a month. See also "Koe Tohi Paaga 'a 'Ene 'Afio ko Kuini Salote Tubou kamata i Epeleli 1918" in POP.
14. Tongilava, Diary, 8 Nov. 1919. Tupou II had appointed Sione Filipe Tongilava as his Private Secretary in 1905. Tongilava retired in 1951, aged 76, and he died some months before Sālote, in 1965. See obituary in *Chronicle* 18 June 1965.
15. Queen Sālote to J. B. Watkin, 5 May 1921, FWC papers. The Queen borrowed £340 from the government in October 1922, which she repaid at the rate of £80 a month for four months, and the remainder in the fifth month. Tongilava, Diary, 20 Oct. 1922.
16. *TGG* 25 (7 Nov. 1918) 173, 10 (3 June 1919) 60, 12 (5 Aug. 1924) 89, 18 (11 Nov. 1924) 121. Wood, Diary, 4–5 Dec. 1924. Tongilava reported on 25 Nov. 1925 that Queen Sālote sent £3170 to the monumental mason, presumably a final instalment.
17. Tongilava, Diary, 4–8 Oct. 1918.
18. Bain, *Royal Visit*, p.36; Tongilava, Diary, 9 Oct. 1918.
19. In former days the Queen and chiefs would have eaten the food (*fono*), but a "stranger" took the Queen's portion, and the chiefs' portions were also taken by other persons.
20. *Recorder*, 22 Jan. 1919, p.1.
21. Gifford, *Tongan Society*, pp.95–8. The diagram of the *kava* circle reproduced in Gifford (p.96) was almost certainly given to him by Collocott, and the Queen confirmed that this was the circle of her installation (Bott Spillius, "Discussions", p.252). Ve'ehala was represented by a trustee of the title. The names of lesser chiefs were not recorded. The *kava* circle reproduced in Kenneth Bain, *Royal Visit*, p.37, and dated 1918, was given to him many years later by "someone in the Lands Department", and was not the circle of 1918, because the title Tupouto'a (which appears there) was not created until 1921 (after being vacant from 1925 until 1936, the title Tupouto'a was bestowed upon the Crown Prince). The title Tu'ipelehake also appears in Bain's diagram, so the circle must be post 1945, when the youngest prince was appointed to that title (which had been vacant since 1912).
22. Tongilava, Diary, 13 and 14 Oct. 1918.
23. By contrast, there was no loss of life in American Sāmoa, where quarantine regulations were enforced. The *Talune* had earlier visited Western Sāmoa, where the loss of life was 20–25 per cent of the population. The census of 1911 gave the population of Tonga as 22,000.
24. Collocott, "King Taufa, Lord of Isles", pp.459–61 passim.
25. Bott Spillius, "Discussions", pp.248–50 passim.
26. *Recorder*, 22 Jan. 1919.
27. McOwan to HC, 23 Dec. 1918, WPHC:GCI 12/19. His first report on the epidemic was made on 25 Nov. WPHC:GCI 2774/18.
28. Dated 3 Jan. 1919, copy in WPHC:GCI 132/19.
29. McOwan to Queen Sālote, 9 Dec. 1918, BCT 1/6.
30. Lambert, *A Doctor in Paradise*, pp.202, 211–2, 381. Native Medical Practitioners had previously been trained in the Fiji Medical School, set up in 1888.
31. Bott Spillius, "Discussions", p.84.

Chapter 5: At Home at the Palace

1. Bott Spillius, "Discussions", p.84.
2. Bott Spillius, "Discussions", p.246; Bott

Spillius papers Box 17, notebook XIV. Lambert *A Doctor in Paradise*, p.200, records that the "doctor" had no medical qualifications and did not know what to do; that is, he did not repair the tears that occurred during the birth.

3. Tupou Seini was older than Vīlai, 31 years to his 20 years. Pers. comm. Halaevalu Maile 1977. See also *Western Pacific Herald* 15 July 1904, p.2.
4. Tongilava, Diary, passim. The first birthday was celebrated rather than the birth, because infant mortality was so high. Pers. comm. Dr Olive Wood 1974.
5. The letter is in POP.
6. McOwan to HC, 14 Nov. 1923, BCT 1/19.
7. Bott Spillius, "Discussions", pp.300–1.
8. Bourne, *Out of the World*, p.109.
9. Pers. comm. Halaevalu Maile 1977. Tiliti was educated in New Zealand.
10. Smith-Rewse to HC, 8 Jan. 1917, BCT 7/II/104; Tongilava, Diary, 1 Nov. 1922.
11. The language is not completely different, but certain words would be used to indicate the person referred to or addressed. For example *hā'ele* (royal), *me'a* (superior or chiefly), and *'alu* (inferior or commoner) all mean "to go". Pronouns do not differentiate between male and female, and the same Tongan names are used for females and males, although there are words for man (*tangata*) and woman (*fefine*). I am indebted to Melenaite Taumoefolau for conversations about language. See also Taumoefolau, "Language as an Indicator of Rank in Tonga".
12. Bott Spillius, "Discussions", pp.365–6. Tongilava used royal language for the princes, but I have been assured that this was not the custom.
13. Taumoefolau, "Language as an Indicator of Rank".
14. Tu'iha'ateiho referred to himself as the Queen's "male slave" in a letter of 16 Aug. 1919; Lauaki referred to Malupō as "a miserable floating coconut shell", Bott Spillius, "Discussions", p.171.
15. R. F. Millar & Co. (agents for the Tongan Government) to Tungī, 31 Mar., Tu'ivakanō to Queen Sālote, 15 May, Queen Sālote to Tu'ivakanō, 21 May 1923, POP.
16. Rachel Tonga, Diary, 5 Feb. and 7 May 1924.
17. Rachel Tonga, Diary, 12 Aug. and 10 Sept. 1924.
18. This school was established by Rodger Page in 1910 at the request of *papālangi* who wanted their children to be taught in English. The school was variously located in a room in the Wesleyan Mission House, in the Victoria Memorial Hall, and in a building on the old Tupou College site. Collocott, "King Taufa, Lord of Isles", pp.439–40.
19. Ferguson, Diary.

Chapter 6: The British Connection

1. Queen Sālote's speech at the Opening of Parliament, 13 June 1922, *TGG* 20 (13 July 1922) 93.
2. McOwan to Queen Sālote, 23 May (quoting HC), POP; Queen Sālote to McOwan, 5 June 1918, WPHC:GCI 1623/18.
3. McOwan compared the situation of Tonga with that of the Federated Malay States and Protected States of India. McOwan to HC, 30 Jan. 1925, WPHC:GCI 328/25, pp.6, 7. See also David McIntyre, "Techniques of Informal Empire", in *The Frontier in Perspective*, ed. W. D. Wyman and C. B. Kroeber. Madison, Wis.: University of Wisconsin Press, 1965, pp.364–8.
4. Queen Sālote's speech at the Opening of Parliament, 3 July 1925, in *TGG* 10 (18 Aug. 1925) 52.
5. Collocott, "King Taufa, Lord of Isles", p.450.
6. COCP *Western Pacific 3*, correspondence and encl. in item 16, esp. McOwan to HC, 20 Oct. 1917, and HC to McOwan, 3 Apr. 1918.
7. R. Greene to HC, 13 June 1921, note on cover of WPHC:GCI 1-12/21; HC to Shuchburgh (Colonial Office), 25 Aug. 1933, WPHC:GCI 342/33.
8. Inquiry of 21, 24, and 31 Aug. 1917, BCT 1/13; *TGG* 29 (17 Dec. 1917) 185. M. F. Fīnau was at this time a supporter of Tu'ivakanō, although he later became a strong supporter of Tungī.
9. McOwan to HC, 15 May 1918, WPHC:GCI 1221/18; Stronge to Acting Premier, 20 Aug. 1918, BCT 1/7;

pers. comm. Halaevalu Maile (daughter of Sipu) 1977. Halaevalu told me that Sipu was a friend to Tungī in his youth, giving him money before he came into his inheritance (see chapter 3).

10. *TGG* 29 (17 Dec. 1917) 185, 19 (16 Aug. 1918) 99, 1 (8 Jan. 1919) 2; J. D. Wall to Tu'ivakanō, 31 Oct. 1918, BCT 1/4.
11. *TGG* 12 (8 Apr. 1911) 1, 15 (17 July 1915) 121, 17 (16 July 1917), 5 (4 Feb. 1918) 21, 3 (21 Jan. 1919) 9. See also correspondence in BCT 1/43/92, for 1918 in BCT 1/4, and WPHC:GCI 1008/21.
12. For example, McOwan to HC, 4 Sept. 1924, WPHC:GCI 1804/25. Decisions made by the Queen and Agent & Consul together were recorded in correspondence.
13. Pers. comm. A. H. Wood 1976.
14. Burnett, *Summer Isles of Eden*, p.68; Humphrey, *Loafing Through the Pacific*, p.27. These two visitors must have associated with different members of the *papālangi* community.
15. Tongilava, Diary, 1918 passim. McOwan, "Memorandum on the Constitution of Tonga and the Working of Article III of the Treaty of Friendship with Tonga and the Supplementary Agreement of 1905", 15 June 1925, COCP *Western Pacific 3*, encl. no.3 in item 18.
16. McOwan to HC, 30 Jan. 1925, WPHC:GCI 328/25.
17. McOwan to HC, "Memorandum".
18. Allen, *Stewart's Handbook*, 1922 ed., pp.103–7. Of the 571 *papālangi*, 295 lived on the main island, Tongatapu. There were 219 adult males (108 of whom were described as "young") and 159 adult females (86 of whom were described as "young"), 99 male children and 94 female children. *TGG* 27 (30 Oct. 1921) 137.
19. Im Thurn, Diary, 26 July 1905.
20. Smith-Rewse to HC, 8 Jan. 1917, BCT 7/II/104.
21. Bishop Willis died during a visit to England in 1920, and the Church of England was then in charge of Rev. Yim Sang Mark.
22. Thomson, *Diversions*, p.45.
23. Smith-Rewse to HC, 17 Nov. 1916, and Tu'ivakanō to McOwan, 24 Sept. 1917, BCT 1/19; *Premier's Report 1918*, p.8; Neill to HC, 22 Feb. 1928, WPHC:GCI 775/28.
24. This was the case with the Wesleyan missionaries, who came from Australia. The Rev. J. B. Watkin was paid by the Free Church.
25. Tremblay, *When You Go to Tonga*, p.207. See also *Marist Missions* 10:2 (1954) p.61.
26. Harkness to Pratt, 17 June 1922, Methodist Church Archives, Christchurch, NZ.
27. Pratt, Diary, 26 Aug. 1922.
28. On 24 July 1916 Parliament heard a petition from Watkin, Blanc, and Page that (i) the age of consent be raised to 14 years, and (ii) the age for marriage be reduced to 14 years. Parliament voted to raise the age of consent from 10 to 12 years, and reduce the legal age for marriage from 16 to 15 years. The legal age for marriage appears to have remained at 16 years. *TGG* 22 (18 Sept. 1916) 141–2. In 1918 there was a petition from the Free Church and Wesleyan Synod and 30 *papālangi* residents asking for complete prohibition on the sale of alcohol. Eighty *papālangi* signed a contrary petition. In Parliament seven MPs supported the churches' petition, while nine opposed it. *TGG* 25 (7 Nov. 1918) 173, 174.
29. The story told in Fanua, *Malō Tupou* (pp. 10–14), is true, except that the protagonist was not Mr Brown himself, but his predecessor, a Mr Burns. See Smith-Rewse to HC, 8 Jan. 1917 (p. 9), BCT 7/II/194; *Premier's Report 1917*.
30. McOwan to HC, 6 Dec., WPHC:GCI 3116/20; also McOwan to Queen Sālote, 24 Aug., BCT 1/6 and McOwan to HC, 27 Aug. 1920, BCT 1/19.
31. *Western Pacific Herald* 31 Jan., 28 and 31 Mar., 4 and 7 Apr. 1905 (pp.6, 5, 6, 3, 3, respectively).
32. W. Telfer Campbell to HC, 27 Nov. 1911, BCT 7 misc. 18.
33. R. Greene to HC, 13 June 1921, note on cover of WPHC:GCI 1012/21.
34. Smith-Rewse to HC, 13 Apr. 1917, BCT 1/19; notes of interview between HC and Tu'ivakanō, Suva, 4 Sept. 1918, BCT 1/7; Tongilava, Diary, 25 June 1920; *Premier's Report 1920*, p.4.
35. McOwan to HC, 26 Apr. 1924, WPHC:GCI 1069/24.

36. McOwan to HC, 4 Mar. 1921, BCT 1/19; correspondence in WPHC:GCI 3206/20; HC to Acting Consul Pennefather, 14 Sept. 1921, HC to A&C vol. 1921.
37. Scott was secretary to the Lands Committee set up by the Privy Council on 14 July 1922 under Tungī as Minister for Lands. Report, 22 Nov. 1922, FWC papers. None of the 14 recommendations of the committee suggested that Scott would have the powers he claimed after his appointment was confirmed in 1923.
38. *Report of the Judge of the Land Court 1925*, J11/26, Box 26/3, ATL.
39. Wall to HC, 25 Mar. 1925, WPHC:GCI 1079/25; McOwan to HC, 5 May 1925, BCT 1/19; Hutson, "Memorandum", in Hutson to McOwan, 7 Aug. 1925, COCP *Western Pacific 3*, encl. in item 19, also WPHC:GCI 1079/25; Acting HC (Fell) to McOwan, 27 Aug. 1924, WPHC to A&C vol. 1923–24.
40. McOwan to Tungī, 1 May 1925, copy in WPHC:GCI 1012/25; Neill, *Ten Years in Tonga*, p.25.
41. McOwan to HC, 4 Sept. 1924, WPHC:GCI 1804/24.
42. McOwan to HC, 5 May (see also 13 June) 1925, BCT 1/19.
43. Queen Sālote to HC, 8 Mar. 1926, WPHC:GCI 22/1/11.

Chapter 7: Aristocrats, Nobles, and Lesser Chiefs

1. Bott Spillius, "Discussions", p.30.
2. Mā'atu (Pānuve) died in 1923 and was succeeded by his brother, Mā'atu (Ma'afu-'o-tu'itonga), who was in Parliament from 1930 until his death in 1934.
3. McOwan to HC, 27 Aug. 1920, BCT 1/19.
4. Islay McOwan to HC, 8 Aug. 1918, WPHC:GCI 2142/18.
5. *TGG* 26 (1 Dec. 1920) 1; Tongilava, Diary, 2 July 1920; Tu'ivakanō to McOwan, 26 June 1920, BCT 1/41; McOwan to HC, 6 Dec. 1920, WPHC:GCI 3116/20.
6. McOwan to HC, 6 Dec. 1920, WPHC:GCI 3116/20.
7. Tongilava, Diary, 24 and 25 June 1920.
8. *TGG* 26 (1 Dec. 1920) 146.
9. *TGG* 23 (17 Sept. 1920) 131–2.
10. In her speech at the Opening of Parliament on 12 July 1921, Queen Sālote again referred to troubled countries, where the people "cry out for Equal Distribution of Wealth and to be free from all obedience to established authority". *TGG* 24 (1 Sept. 1921) 118.
11. McOwan to Queen Sālote, 24 Aug. 1920, BCT 1/6.
12. "Notes of interview between the High Commissioner and representative Nobles and members of the Legislative Assembly", encl. in McOwan to HC, 6 Dec. 1920, WPHC:GCI 3116/20.
13. McOwan to HC, 6 Dec. 1920, WPHC:GCI 3116/20.
14. "Notes of interview between the Queen and HC", 23 Nov. 1920, WPHC:GCI 3117/20.
15. Ibid. As a consequence of the Queen's request, the British government blocked the issuing of visas to Mormons wishing to enter Tonga. Correspondence in WPHC:GCI 2532/19, 3117/20; Passport Act, no. 10 of 1922, ss. 7, 8, 9. In 1924 these sections were repealed by a vote of 12 to nine. *TGG* 14 (20. Aug. 1924) 101. *Ninety-seventh Semi-Annual Conference of the Church of Jesus Christ of the Latter Day Saints 3–5 October 1926*, pp.101–3. The issue was raised again in 1946. Correspondence in SPO 41/13.
16. HC to SofSCol., 21 Jan. 1921, WPHC:GCI 3117/20.
17. *TGG* 20 (13 July 1922) 95.
18. For the Matafonua grant, see Smith-Rewse to Tupou II, 31 May 1917, POP; Smith-Rewse to HC, 5 June 1917, BCT 1/19; Tongilava, Diary, 4 July 1918. For the Matahau grant, see Tongilava, Diary, 14 Mar. and 18 Apr. 1921; Pennefather to HC, 6 Oct. 1921, and note on cover of WPHC:GCI 2638/21. For Tu'ivakanō's resignation and death, see McOwan to HC, 11 June 1923, BCT 1/19; *TGG* 13 (1 June 1923) 87 and 15 (29 June 1923) 91.
19. Tēvita Polutele Kaho had inherited the Tu'ivakanō title through his mother, and it was passed to his brother Siosiua. (See Figure 2.4.) Siosiua had been promised a title by Tupou II. Tupou II to Campbell, 28 May 1910, BCT 1/3.
20. Siaki Lolohea to Queen Sālote, 12 Aug.

1918, POP.

21. Collocott, "King Taufa, Lord of Isles", p.441.
22. Mateialona was appointed Tupouto'a on 21 Jan. 1921, and his estates gazetted in 1923. The lands were 'Utulau in Tongatapu, Nomuka and Lofanga in Ha'apai, and Taoa in Vava'u. *TGG* 1 (13 Jan. 1921) 4 and 18 (27 July 1923) 99. See also Bott Spillius papers, Box 17, notebook XIV, and Rachel Tonga, Diary, 19 June, 2 and 16 Aug. 1924. On 4 July 1924 the 'Utulau people came to dance for the sixth birthday of the Crown Prince, Tāufa'āhau, and then came and danced for Tupouto'a.
23. Bott Spillius, "Discussions", p.144. 'Ulukālala was of the Ha'a Ngata Tupu, distinct from the Ha'a Ngata Motu'a of the Western District of Tongatapu.
24. Tongilava, Diary, 15–30 Sept. 1925.
25. Bott Spillius, "Discussions", p.339.
26. Pers. comm. A. H. Wood 1974; Ve'ehala (Leilua) 1977.
27. Pers. comm. Rev. Dr S. 'Amanaki Havea 1974. See also Blanc, Diary, 20 May 1925.
28. Notes in Premier's minute paper MP 104/35, POP.
29. Bott Spillius, "Discussions", p.302.
30. Tongilava, Diary, 11–25 Apr. 1929.
31. Pers. comm. A. H. Wood 1974.
32. Bott Spillius ("Discussions", pp.56, 67) commented on the great number of elopements when she was in Tonga.
33. Bott Spillius, "Discussions", p.58.
34. Gifford, *Tongan Society*, p.176. When Acting Consul in 1912–13, McOwan had made a similar observation. McOwan to HC, 26 Feb. 1913, BCT 1/43/69.
35. Lātūkefu, *Constitution*, p.77.
36. Watkin to Queen Sālote, 7 Mar., Tu'ivakanō to Watkin, 24 Apr. 1922, copies in Minutes of Conference of FWC, 1922, FWC papers. This incident was cited as evidence of customary right to land in the Land Court case of June 1924 (see below).
37. Sione Havea, *Koe Havea*, 1941.

Chapter 8: God and Tonga Are My Inheritance

1. Tradition has it that at the time of the Emancipation (Tau'atāina) in 1862, when Tupou I gave Tonga to God, he proposed three possible mottos: *Ko e 'Otua mo Tonga ko hoku tofi'a* (God and Tonga are my inheritance), which was chosen; *Ko Tonga mo'unga ki he loto* (The mountain of Tonga is the mind/heart), which became the motto of Tupou College, founded in 1866; and *Tonga ma'a Tonga* (Tonga for the Tongans), which became the motto of Government College, founded in 1882.
2. Queen Sālote in a speech opening the meeting of nobles and ministers of the Free Church in the Royal Chapel, 10 Sept. 1923, POP.
3. Watkin to J. H. Fletcher, 15 Jan. 1885, copy in FWC papers. Becoming head of a new church is tantamount to resignation from the old, but Watkin complained that he was expelled from the Methodist Church of Australasia although his intention was to keep the new church true to Methodism. See Watkin to Rev. M. A. Rugby Pratt, 23 Oct. 1921, Methodist Church Archives, Christchurch.
4. See Thomson, *Diversions*, pp.88–90, for comments on Watkin and Free Church clergy in 1890. Watkin was said to have "used the language of disaffection" at Vava'u and warned not to meddle in politics; while the Free Church clergy were described as "the most self-satisfied and insubordinate body of ecclesiastics in the world".
5. *TGG* 27 Jan. 1898, 1; Tupou II to Watkin, 16 Aug. 1899, FWC papers. However, in reply to a query from Watkin in 1911, Tupou II said that the church was *NOT* the state church, although he wished it was. Watkin to Tupou II, 24 Mar., Tupou II to Watkin, 25 Mar. 1911, FWC papers.
6. Correspondence between Mā'atu (representing the nobles) and Watkin and Harkness, encl. in Smith-Rewse to HC, 30 June 1917, WPHC:GCI 1770/17 and BCT 7/II/115. The Conference met annually, while each District (for example, Ha'apai, Vava'u) was headed by a superintendent minister, and met quarterly.
7. Ibid. and legal file in FWC papers, including Crompton's Questions for Witnesses and notes by A. H. Wood on

these questions and on "Effect of the Blue Book", and his closing address to the Land Court, June 1924, FWC papers.

8. Blanc, Diary, 9 Apr. 1924. See also R. N. Moody's opening address in the Land Court, 10 June 1924, as recorded in the notes of the Judge of the Land Court (George Scott), FWC papers.
9. Queen Sālote to Watkin, 5 May 1920, item 10 in file of legal exhibits, FWC papers.
10. Watkin to Queen Sālote, 2 June 1920, item 11 in ibid.
11. Five nobles and four chiefs to Queen Sālote, Aug.–Sept. 1922, encl. A in Queen Sālote to ?, 23 May 1923, BCT 1/3. The noble Vaea brought the petition on 6 Oct. 1922, and Queen Sālote sent it to Watkin for comment. Tongilava, Diary, 6 and 7 Oct. 1922.
12. Queen Sālote to chiefs, 22 May 1923, BCT 1/3. The language of the letter suggests that Queen Sālote sought legal advice while on holiday in New Zealand (see chapter 5).
13. The nobles Vaea, Fohe, Ve'ehala, Nuku, [Tu'iha'ateiho] Havea, Tuita, Lavaka, and the chiefs T. Hokafonu, I. Ma'u, A. Taungahihifo, S. Tovi, T. Ma'afukala'a, S. Matekitonga, P. Havili, V. Lausi'i, V. Uhu'ia to Queen Sālote and Privy Council, 31 July 1923, BCT 1/3. This letter also bears the marks of legal advice.
14. Tongilava, Diary, 27 Apr.–22 May 1922 passim; Blanc, Diary, 11 Apr. 1924. An account by Mordaunt, *The Venture Book*, p.129, may refer to this occasion. Rugby Pratt recorded another occasion when Watkin was carried ashore in Ha'apai by 60 men and three women. Pratt, Diary, 24 Aug. 1922.
15. In the 1921 census, only 5235 of a Tongatapu population of 10,379 were Free Church (many of the remainder being Roman Catholics, others Old Wesleyans), whereas they were 5058 of a total population of 6154 in Ha'apai, and 4881 of a total population of 6121 in Vava'u. *TGG* 27 (3 Oct. 1921) 136 and 138.
16. Only nobles who were members of the Free Church attended. A copy of the minutes of the meeting of 10 Sept. are in POP, and of 14 Sept. in the FWC papers. Thirty-five nobles, chiefs, and ministers attended the meeting of 10 Sept.; the list for 14 Sept. is incomplete.
17. Pers. comm. Nānisi Helu 1976.
18. Petition of Chiefs, 31 July 1923, BCT 1/3; minutes of 10 and 14 Sept. 1923; McOwan to HC, 1 Oct. 1923, BCT 1/19.
19. Crompton address to Privy Council, 5 Sept. 1924, BCT 1/43/60.
20. Auditors' reports for Tongatapu, 31 Oct., incomplete copy; for Vava'u, 26 Nov.; for Ha'apai, 26 and 29 Nov. and 12 Dec. 1923, POP. Queen Sālote to Watkin, 20 Nov., Watkin to Queen Sālote, 23 Nov. 1923, items 18 and 19 in files of legal exhibits, FWC papers; Crompton's Questions to Witnesses; Pratt to W. A. Sinclair, 12 Oct. 1923, Methodist Church Archives, Christchurch; McOwan to Acting HC, encl. in 29 Sept. 1924, WPHC:GCI 2263/24.
21. McOwan to HC, 12 Nov. 1923, WPHC:GCI 2915/23; Blanc, Diary, 3 and 7 Apr. 1924; McOwan to HC, encl. in 29 Sept. 1924, WPHC:GCI 2263/24; Wood, Diary, 28 May 1924. See also *Fiji Times*, 8 Nov. 1919, Palace Office cuttings book, POP.
22. Rodger Page to J. G. Wheen, 29 Sept. 1923, MOMC, now in Mitchell Library, Sydney.
23. Queen Sālote to Page, 19 Oct., and Page to Queen Sālote 26 Oct. 1923, in legal file, FWC papers.
24. The Wesleyan Mission was a District of the Conference of the Methodist Church of Australasia. It was the tardiness of the Australasian church to allow Tonga its own Conference that had provoked the 1885 split.
25. Legal file, FWC papers.
26. McOwan to HC, 12 Nov. 1923, BCT 1/19.
27. Watkin to Queen Sālote, 8 Jan. and 11 Feb. 1924, FWC papers.
28. Tongilava, Diary, 18–21 Feb. 1924; extract from the minutes of the meetings, and amended Constitution, FWC papers.
29. Watkin to Samisoni, 14 Mar. 1924, FWC papers. Samisoni was possibly Samisoni Puli'uvea Afuha'amango.

30. Tongilava, Diary, 22 and 31 Mar.; Queen Sālote to Watkin, 22 Mar. 1924, FWC papers.
31. Blanc, Diary, 15 Mar., Tongilava, Diary, 12 Mar., Watkin to Samisoni, 14 Mar., M. T. Langi to Watkin, 25 Mar., Sioape Kaho to Queen Sālote, 25 Mar., Queen Sālote to Sioape Kaho, 1 Apr., Sioape Kaho to Queen Sālote, 3 Apr. 1924, POP. The Queen believed that Langi was a prime mover among the anti-unionists.
32. McOwan to Acting HC, encl. in 29 Sept. 1924, WPHC:GCI 2263/24.
33. Puli'uvea was charged with defamation on 17 and 19 Mar. Stronge acquitted him on 5 June 1924.
34. Blanc, Diary, 8 Apr., 23 and 25 May, 11, 12, 21 and 25 June 1924.
35. Queen Sālote and Watkin at meeting of 10 Sept. 1923, also fifth motion moved by Vaea. See also Wood, Diary, 6 June 1925.
36. Mordaunt, *The Venture Book*, pp.146–7.
37. Neill to HC, 22 Feb. 1928, WPHC:GCI 775/28.
38. The census of 1921 stated that there were 132 *papālangi* adherents of the Wesleyan Mission and 100 *papālangi* adherents of the Free Church. *TGG* 27 (3 Oct. 1921) 138.
39. Petition from Free Church members 14 Apr., Petitioners to Masterton, 28 Apr., Masterton to Tungī, 28 Apr. (twice), 1 and 6 May, Tungī to Masterton, 30 Apr., 2 May (twice), 7 May, Masterton to Acting HC, 7 May, Acting HC to McOwan, 11 May, WPHC:GCI 1069/24; McOwan to Acting HC, 26 Apr., WPHC:GCI 1069/24 and encl. in 29 Sept. 1924, WPHC:GCI 2263/24.
40. McOwan to HC, encl. in 29 Sept. 1924, WPHC:GCI 2263/24.
41. Blanc, Diary, 6 and 9 Apr. 1924.
42. McOwan to HC, 29 Sept. 1924, WPHC:GCI 2263/24.
43. Blanc, Diary, 15 Apr. 1924; Stronge to HC, 25 May 1924, WPHC:GCI 1069/24.
44. I am indebted to the Moody family for information about R. N. Moody and his career. See also obituary in *Auckland Star* 2 Jan. 1937.
45. Blanc, Diary, 31 Mar. and 1 Apr. 1924.
46. Wood, Diary, 31 May 1924; pers. comm. 1976.
47. *Fiji Times* 3 July 1924. "Old Resident" referred to the protagonists as "Free Church" and "Wesleyans", although it is clear from other sources that the rival groups were unionist and anti-unionist factions within the Free Church. See also Wood, Diary, 17 July 1924.
48. Tongilava, Diary, 15 Apr.; Blanc, Diary, 16 Apr.; Wood, Diary, 24 May; Stronge to Acting HC, 25 May 1924, WPHC:GCI 1069/24; McOwan to HC, 18 July 1924, WPHC:GCI 1798/24.
49. Tongilava, Diary, 15 Apr. 1924, says Tungī, Tupouto'a, and 'Ulukālala went to Mu'a to see the Queen. Blanc, Diary, 16 Apr. 1924, says Vaea, Fohe, 'Ahome'e, and Ma'afu went. See also Wood, Diary, 24 May 1924.
50. Queen Sālote to Watkin, 9 Apr. 1924, legal file, FWC papers; Stronge to HC, 25 May 1924, WPHC:GCI 1069/24; McOwan to Acting HC, encl. in 29 Sept. 1924, WPHC:GCI 2263/24.
51. Watkin's evidence in Land Court case, Scott's notes, FWC papers.
52. Queen Sālote to Watkin, 17 Apr. 1924, POP.
53. Queen Sālote to Watkin, 22 Apr. 1924; Minutes of the Conference, 1924, FWC papers.
54. "The Facts which the Queen gave to the Conference of the Free Church, held in Nuku'alofa in April 1924", file of legal exhibits, FWC papers.
55. Queen Sālote to Watkin, 24 Apr. 1924, file of legal exhibits, FWC papers. The Conference dismissed the 27 ministers who left with Watkin, and appointed 12 new ministers on 28 Apr. Minutes of Conference, 1924, FWC papers; McOwan to Acting HC, encl. in 29 Sept. 1924, WPHC:GCI 2263/24; Wood, *Overseas Missions of the Australian Methodist Church*, vol.1, p.221.
56. Nobles and Chiefs of Tonga to Robert Crompton, 24 Apr. 1924, FWC papers; Wood, Diary, 2 and 8 May; Tongilava, Diary, 8 May 1924.
57. Stronge to Acting HC, 25 May 1924, WPHC:GCI 1069/24.
58. Stronge to Acting HC, 25 May 1924, WPHC:GCI 1069/24.
59. Page to Wheen, 26 May 1924, evidence of A. M. Sanders, in Land Court case,

Scott's notes, FWC papers.

60. Blanc, Diary, 15, 20 and 21 Apr., Scott to Page, 14 Apr., Page to Scott, 16 Apr. 1924, FWC papers; Wood, Diary, 21 June 1924; Crompton, appeal case, Sept. 1924, BCT 1/43/60.
61. McOwan to Acting HC, 26 Apr. 1924, WPHC:GCI 1069/24.
62. Tongilava, Diary, 26 May 1924.
63. McOwan to HC, 13 June 1925, BCT 1/19.
64. McOwan to Acting HC, 15 Sept. 1924, 2261/24, WPHC:GCI.
65. McOwan to Acting HC, 18 July 1924, WPHC:GCI 1798/24.
66. Wood had worked as a clerk in the law courts in Sydney while studying for a law degree. He had not completed the degree when he applied to be a candidate for the ordained ministry of the Methodist Church. Just prior to the Land Court case both Page and Wood enrolled as lawyers to practise in the Tongan courts. Pers. comm. A. H. Wood 1974.
67. Pers. comm. A. H. Wood 1974.
68. McOwan to Acting HC, encl. in 29 Sept. 1924, WPHC:GCI 2263/24.
69. Scott's notes; Wood's notes "Effect of the Blue Book", FWC papers.
70. Wood, Diary, 21 June 1924.
71. Blanc, Diary, 21 June 1924.
72. McOwan to Acting HC, 18 Aug. 1924, WPHC:GCI 2081/24.
73. Moody to Queen Sālote, 14 Aug. 1924, WPHC:GCI 2081/24. The letter of 25 June (ibid.) was in similar vein.
74. *New Zealand Herald*, 3 Sept. 1924, p.12.
75. McOwan to Acting HC, encl. in 29 Sept. 1924, WPHC:GCI 2263/24.
76. Stronge to Queen Sālote, 26 July 1924, BCT 1/3. See also correspondence in WPHC:GCI 1798/24 and 1069/24, BCT 1/3, 1/6, 1/19 and 1/43/60.
77. Stronge to Queen Sālote, 5 Aug. 1924, BCT 1/3.
78. Queen Sālote to Stronge, 5 Aug. 1924, BCT 1/43/60.
79. Wood, Diary, 5 and 6 Aug.; Stronge to McOwan, 6 Aug., Stronge to Moody, 28 Aug. 1924, BCT 1/43/60.
80. Acting HC to McOwan, 7 and 8 Aug., and McOwan to Acting HC, 8 Aug. 1924, WPHC:GCI 1798/24.
81. Wood, Diary, 15, 20 and 29 Aug.; Moody to Queen Sālote, 14 Aug., WPHC:GCI 2081/24; McOwan to Acting HC, 18 Aug., BCT 1/19; same to same, encl. in 29 Sept., WPHC:GCI 2263/24; Tongilava, Diary, 24 Aug. 1924; Moody to Scott, 8 Oct. 1926, BCT 1/43/60; Acting HC to SofSCol., 5 Sept. 1924, WPHC:GCI 2081/24. Moody had been in Tonga for four months.
82. For accounts of the Appeal, see report of proceedings, BCT 1/43/60; Crompton's submission to the court, Sept., FWC papers; Tongilava, Diary, and Wood, Diary, 1–12 Sept.; McOwan to Acting HC, 12 Sept., BCT 1/43/60 and WPHC:GCI 2081/24; same to same, 15 Sept., WPHC:GCI 2261/24; same to same, encl. in 29 Sept., WPHC:GCI 2263/24; excerpt from Stronge's Judgment of 11 Sept., *TGG* 10 (27 May 1927) 47–51; Neill, *Ten Years in Tonga*, pp.21–3; Blanc, Diary, 20 Oct. 1924. *Daily Guardian*, 22 Sept. 1924, called the Appeal a "glorious farce".
83. Tongilava, Diary, 1 Sept. 1924.
84. McOwan to Acting HC, 15 Sept., WPHC:GCI 2261/24; Wood, Diary, 11 Sept. 1924; Neill, *Ten Years in Tonga*, p.23; Rachel Tonga, Diary, 11 Sept., also entries of 10 June and 20 Dec.; Tongilava, Diary, 21 Sept. 1924.
85. Tongilava, Diary, and Rachel Tonga, Diary, 24 Jan. 1925; pers. comm. Ve'ehala (Leilua) 1976.
86. HC to Queen Sālote, 7 Aug. 1925, BCT 1/6; *TGG* 12 (21 Aug. 1925) 69–70; Wood, Diary, 7 Aug. 1925.
87. "A Message from Her Majesty Queen Salote Tubou to her people", *TGG* 12 (21 Aug. 1925) 67–8.
88. Correspondence in BCT 1/19 and 1/2/24; HC to McOwan, 29 Dec. 1924, BCT 1/43/60.
89. McOwan reported that £2000 was collected to pay for Ellis's trip to London, and Moody was paid a retainer of £400 per annum until the end of 1927. McOwan to Acting HC, 16 Dec. 1924, BCT 1/42/60; Neill to HC, 22 Feb. 1928, WPHC:GCI 775/28. See also Moody to Scott, 8 Oct. 1925, BCT 1/43/60.
90. Tongilava, Diary, 15 Aug.; Clerk of the Chief Justice to Clerk of the Privy

Council, 15 Sept., POP; Moody to Scott, 12 July, Moody to committee of the Free Church, 20 Apr., Moody to Siaki Lolohea, 14 June, Moody to Scott, 12 July 1928, BCT 1/43/60; Bott Spillius papers, Box 17, notebook XIV, and "Discussions", pp.300, 302.

91. Page to Tungī, 7 Jan., Stronge to Tungī, 16 and 20 Jan., Tungī to McOwan, 11 Feb. 1925, BCT 1/4; Crompton opinion, 9 Sept. 1926, FWC papers; Page to Cabinet, 5 and 18 Jan., Tungī to Page, 20 Jan., Page's petition to Privy Council, 26 Jan. 1927, BCT 1/43/61; Crompton to Page, 28 Jan. 1927, FWC papers. Correspondence between Crompton, Ellis, and McOwan, 14 and 15 Sept. 1924, FWC papers and BCT 1/2/24.
92. Campbell, *Island Kingdom*, p.161.
93. Wood, Diary, 28 and 30 May 1924.
94. Tongilava, Diary, passim. In Bible Cricket, the young people of the village are divided into two teams, which are alternatively given questions about a chapter of the Bible that they have studied.
95. When the Queen visited Ha'apai c.1925, Siaki Lolohea came to the Queen and apologized for his part in the church troubles: "he literally howled, it was said that he could be heard a quarter of a mile away! . . . He was trying to get some land . . . after his submission . . . the Queen felt she had to give him the land." A. H. Wood, letter to author, 6 Dec. 1976. Lolohea's daughter confirmed that he had a "big piece of land". Pers. comm. Fane Lolohea 1993.
96. Walter Lawry had set up a Wesleyan mission in 1822 at Mu'a, but Thomas and Hutchinson set up the continuing mission in 1826.
97. Pers. comm. Rev. Dr S. 'Amanaki Havea 1974. Tongilava significantly used the word *fata* (the platform on which the Tu'i Tonga was carried) when referring to the Queen's car.
98. George Minns, *Spectator*, 19 Jan. 1927.

Chapter 9: Problems With Judges

1. Speech at the Opening of Parliament, *TGG* 21 (10 Sept. 1926) 218.
2. McOwan to Acting HC, encl. in 29 Sept. 1924, WPHC:GCI 2263/24.
3. Tungī to McOwan, 21 Aug., encl. in McOwan to HC, 22 Aug. 1925, WPHC:GCI 1517/25. The Representation in Courts Bill 1924 prohibited representation in court by *papālangi* lawyers, which would have affected the appeal in the church case. The Queen pointed out that such a Bill was in conflict with proposed amendments to the Treaty of Friendship (1927). Tungī to McOwan, 21 Aug. encl. in McOwan to HC, 22 Aug. 1925, WPHC:GCI 1517/25.
4. McOwan to HC, 13 June 1925, BCT 1/19.
5. HC to Queen Sālote, recorded in "Notes of an Interview", 6 Aug. 1925, COCP *Western Pacific 3*, encl. in item 25.
6. HC to SofSCol., 13 Aug. 1925, and "Notes of an Interview", 6 Aug. 1925, COCP *Western Pacific 3*, item 25 and encl.
7. HC to SofSCol., 13 Aug. 1925, COCP *Western Pacific 3*, item 25.
8. Wall to SofSCol., 25 Mar. 1925, copy in WPHC:GCI 1079/25. McOwan wrote comments in the margin of this copy.
9. HC to SofSCol., 14 Aug. 1925, COCP *Western Pacific 3*, item 18; Wall to Queen Sālote, 12 Aug., Tungī to Queen Sālote, 25 Nov. 1925, POP; McOwan to HC, 29 Nov. 1925, WPHC:GCI 1079/25 and SPO 38/12/2.
10. In his report for 1927, Agent & Consul Neill reported that the Queen "was not happy with certain of her European ministers". Neill to HC, 22 Feb. 1928, WPHC:GCI 775/28. Wall was retired in 1931 (see below).
11. Horne to Queen Sālote, 30 Oct. 1925, POP.
12. The correspondence relating to Ata's appointment is as follows: Horne to Queen Sālote, 17 Oct., Queen Sālote to Horne, 20 and 22 Oct., Horne to Queen Sālote, 5 Nov., Queen Sālote to Ata, 13 Nov. 1925, Wallace to Queen Sālote, 2 Feb., Queen Sālote to Horne, 3 Feb., 'Ulukālala to Queen Sālote, 24 Feb., Ata to Queen Sālote, 3 Mar., Queen Sālote to HC, 6 Mar. 1926, POP. Also Crompton to Tongilava, 9 Dec. 1925,

Crompton to Page, 4 Mar., Queen Sālote to Privy Council, 5 June 1926, FWC papers.

13. Queen Sālote to HC, 6 Mar. 1926, POP.
14. Crompton to Page, 4 Mar. and Queen Sālote to Privy Council, 5 June 1926, FWC papers; Queen Sālote to HC, 6 Mar. 1926, POP. Queen Sālote's speech at the Opening of Parliament, 14 June 1926 in *TGG* 21 (10 Sept. 1926) 218. M. F. Fīnau moved that the words "with the consent of the Privy Council" be deleted from s. 9 of the Law of 1903. This was passed with 15 votes in favour out of a possible 23 (if all members and Ministers were present). *TGG* 25 (18 Oct. 1926) 235, 237.
15. Queen Sālote to Horne, 3 Feb. 1926, POP.
16. Gifford, *Tongan Society*, pp.132–43; Powles, "Persistence of Chiefly Power", p.308.
17. Stronge to Queen Sālote, 14 Nov. 1918, POP.
18. The nobles in the 1921 Parliament were Tu'ivakanō, Tungī, Tupouto'a (Mateialona), Veikune, Vaea, Ata, Fotofili, Malupō, Tu'iha'angana, Tu'i'afitu, Fulivai. *TGG* 31 (1 Nov. 1921) 157.
19. Scott's Judgment in *Tēvita 'Uluilakepa v. Fulivai*, 15 Oct. 1924, [1963] 2 *Tongan Law Reports* 10–12, gives a brief account of the rival claims. See also encl. in Queen Sālote to Privy Council, Apr. 1926, BCT 1/6.
20. McOwan's "Notes on the Chief Justice's Memorandum", n.d. [Apr.? 1926]; Horne to McOwan, 11 May 1926, FWC papers.
21. See chapter 8 and *Report of the Judge of the Land Court 1925*, J11/26, Box 26/3, ATL.
22. Horne to McOwan, 11 May 1926, FWC papers.
23. Horne apparently wrote a memorandum of the subject, but no copy was found. McOwan replied with "Notes on the Chief Justice's Memorandum", n.d., and Horne replied to McOwan on 11 May 1926, FWC papers.
24. The Writings of Queen Sālote, Section VI ("Different duties").
25. These views of Queen Sālote were expressed in her letter to the Privy Council of Apr. 1926, in McOwan's "Notes" (see above), and expanded upon in her discussions with Elizabeth Spillius in 1958–59. Bott Spillius, "Discussions", pp.170–80 passim.
26. McOwan to Queen Sālote, 14 Apr. 1926, BCT 1/6.
27. Clause 70 of the Constitution prevented "representatives of the people" from voting on matters that affected the nobles.
28. Tongilava, Diary, 11 June 1926.
29. Queen Sālote said that Sioape encouraged chiefs to lodge claims in the court. Bott Spillius, "Discussions", p.173.
30. HC to Queen Sālote, 26 June 1926, WPHC:GCI 988/26; Tongilava, Diary, 30 June 1926.
31. Bott Spillius, "Discussions", pp.51, 180.
32. Queen Sālote to HC, 13 Apr. 1926, WPHC:GCI 1056/26.
33. *TGG* 19 (11 July 1922) 89. The correspondence relating to Feleti Vī: Crompton to Page, 23 July, FWC papers; Sioape Kaho to Queen Sālote, 1 Sept., Queen Sālote to Sioape Kaho, 1 Sept. 1926, POP.
34. *TGG* 17 (17 July 1923) 84.
35. Queen Sālote to Sioape Kaho, 1 Sept. 1926, POP.
36. Horne to Queen Sālote, 17 Dec., Queen Sālote to Feleti Vī, 24 Dec. 1926, POP.
37. The Queen gave £450 to start off the fund in January 1938. Tongilava, Diary, 24 Jan. and 29 Apr. 1938. Leilua went to Wesley College, Auckland, 1941–44, then entered the Tongan Civil Service. He was appointed to the title of Ve'ehala in 1946. *TGG* 12 (6 Nov. 1944) 101, and 14 (11 Dec. 1947) 131; Tohi Fakanofo, POP.
38. Annual Report of the Chief Justice 1926. The evidence is recorded in MP J18/26, ATL.
39. The Agreement Between Great Britain and Tonga was signed by Queen Sālote on 12 Aug. 1927 and ratified on 7 Nov. 1928, COCP *Western Pacific 3*, encl. in item 15; also encl. in items 13 and 14. Also Neill to HC, 22 Feb. 1928 WPHC:GCI 775/28; same to same, 31 July 1931, WPHC:GCI 2271/31.
40. Russell to HC, 2 Mar. 1929, WPHC:GCI 689/29; same to same, 11

Mar. 1929, WPHC:GCI 912/29. See also Powles, "Persistence of Chiefly Power", pp.296–307 passim for powers of the Minister for Lands. In 1928 most of the work of the Land Court was concerned with trustee applications, and Scott suggested that the Land Court be abolished and its work done by the Supreme Court. A similar proposal was made in the Privy Council in 1929. Note of Privy Council resolutions attached to MP 78/29, Box 29/24, ATL.

41. Powles, "Persistence of Chiefly Power", p.323.
42. Neill to HC, 5 Sept. 1927, WPHC:GCI 2628/27.
43. *TGG* 1 (26 Jan. 1928) 3.
44. Neill to HC, 22 Feb. 1928, WPHC:GCI 775/28.
45. Powles, quoted by Lātūkefu, *Constitution*, pp.80–1.
46. Neill to HC, 22 Feb. 1928, WPHC:GCI 775/28.
47. Neill commended Horne in his annual report for 1927. Neill to HC, 22. Feb. 1928, WPHC:GCI 775/28.
48. This was an outcome of the 1927 amendment of the Treaty of Friendship. W. E. Russell (Acting Agent & Consul), to Queen Sālote, 5 July 1928, POP; *TGG* 25 (15 Nov. 1928) 151 and 27 (23 Dec. 1932) 164.
49. Hyne to Tungī, 6 Jan., Acting HC to Neill, 3 June, Queen Sālote to Neill, 5 June 1936, 28 Dec. 1937, BCT 1/43/92.
50. Neill to HC, 1 Aug. 1932, WPHC:GCI 2608/32.
51. Neill to HC, 31 July 1931, WPHC:GCI 2271/31.
52. In his first annual report to the HC, Neill commented on "inordinate" delays. Neill to HC, 22 Feb. 1928, WPHC:GCI 775/28.
53. The proceedings of the 1928 Parliament were summarised in *TGG* 20 (28 Sept. 1928) 1. See also Russell to HC, 22 Oct. 1928, WPHC:GCI 3055/28; HC to SofSCol., 19 Nov. 1928, vol. 1928.
54. Tongilava, Diary, 13 July 1928.
55. Horne to Page, 18 May 1928, FWC papers; Queen Sālote to Russell, 10 Oct. 1928, WPHC:GCI 3055/28.
56. Neill had drawn attention to waste in the Public Works Department. Neill to Tungī, 7 June 1927, copy in WPHC:GCI 1787/27; Queen Sālote to Russell, 19 Oct. 1928, WPHC:GCI 1787/27.
57. HC to Russell, 8 Nov. 1928, WPHC:GCI 3055/28; HC to SofSCol., COCP *Western Pacific 3*, item 29.
58. *TGG* 18 (26 Aug. 1929) 1.
59. HC to SofSCol., 29 Nov. 1928, vol. 1928.
60. Neill to HC, 31 July 1931, WPHC:GCI 2271/31.
61. Neill to HC, 31 July 1931, WPHC:GCI 2271/31.
62. Tongilava, Diary, Aug., 1–6 Sept. passim, 7–10 and 13 Sept. 1932; Wood, Diary. 7–10 Sept. 1932: HC to SofSCol., 14 Sept. 1932, WPHC:GCI 2808/32; *PIM* 3:2 (Sept. 1932) 7, 3:3 (Oct. 1932) 34–5.
63. HC to SofSCol., 14 Sept. 1932, WPHC:GCI 2808/32.
64. See, for example, *PIM* 6:1 (Aug. 1935) 5, 6:5 (Dec. 1935) 33, 12:10 (May 1942) 40; *Sydney Morning Herald* 31 July 1935; *Fiji Times* 10, 11 and 16 Oct. 1935.

Chapter 10: The Queen's Sister: Princess Fusipala

1. Bott Spillius, "Discussions", p.365.
2. The Writings of Queen Sālote, section IX ("The marriages of the chiefs"), explains the factors considered when arranging a chiefly marriage.
3. Queen Sālote's reminiscences about Fusipala are recorded in Bott Spillius, "Discussions", pp. 296–7, 361–2, 365–8. Some of Fusipala's contemporaries wrote short biographies of her in which the recurring refrain was "you must not blame her". I am indebted to Manu Faupula for copies of the biographies, and to Rev. Dr S. 'Amanaki Havea for the translations. I am also indebted to Tupou Posesi Fanua for her personal memories of Fusipala, and to Nānisi Helu and Miss Elsie Scholes for additional information.
4. There are various kinds of adoption in Tonga. The form of adoption of Fusipala by Polutele was *kaukau tama*. See Glossary.
5. Mrs Bagnall took Fusipala to Auckland and bought clothes for her. Lilla Bagnall to Queen Sālote, 23 Dec. 1920, POP. See accounts from the school dated 22

Sept. 1921 and 18 Jan. 1923 in POP; also account from Milne & Choyce, 29 Sept. 1921, POP.

6. Dr W. H. Fitchett to Queen Sālote, 11 Dec. 1926, POP.
7. Elsie Scholes to author, n.d. [1974].
8. The children referred to were Ha'amea's illegitimate children. I am indebted to Penny Gregory for a copy of this letter and that of 19 Aug. 1927.
9. A. H. Wood to J. W. Burton, 12 Dec. 1927, MOMC, now in Mitchell Library, Sydney.
10. Biography of Fusipala by Sau Faupula, translated by Rev. Dr S. 'Amanaki Havea.
11. References to intimate letters and secret love suggest that Tēvita was the author of an anonymous article in *PIM* 4:3 (Oct. 1933) 9–10, published after Fusipala's death; Bott Spillius, "Discussions", p.362. Tupou Posesi Fanua says that she also wrote poems for him: pers. comm. 1977.
12. Biography of Fusipala by Sau Faupula, translated by Rev. Dr S. 'Amanaki Havea.
13. Wood, Diary, 17 Dec. 1931.
14. Pers. comm. Tupou Posesi Fanua, 1976.
15. Neill to HC, 22 Apr. 1930, COCP *Western Pacific 3*, item 22.
16. Pers. comm. Halaevalu Maile 1977.
17. Wood, Diary, 10 Aug. 1931, recorded the announcement of the engagement.
18. Pers. comm. Halaevalu Maile 1977, who believed Fusipala would have married Lala if Muimui had not intervened.
19. Tongilava, Diary, 13 Feb. and 24 Oct. 1932. Tongilava wrote *me'a* (chiefly word for "go") then added *hola* ("fled") in red ink. Wood, Diary, 14 Feb. 1932, records that Sēmisi Fotofili was courting Fusipala against the Queen's wishes, and that Fusipala had "been taken" to the home of her aunt, who did not want her to marry Lala Veikune.
20. Lala was the son of Vāhoi, daughter of Tupou Moheofo. Lala's mother was therefore the half-sister of Vīlai on the mother's side.
21. Queen Sālote blamed Muimui for stirring up trouble with the families of rejected suitors. Bott Spillius, "Discussions", pp.366–7.
22. Bott Spillius, "Discussions", p.367; Tongilava, Diary, 8–10 June 1932; pers. comm. Halaevalu Maile 1977. The Tongan ceremony was at Sēmisi's house on the Beach Road at Fongoloa, in Kolofo'ou.
23. Fusipala to Tongilava, 8 Mar. 1932, POP.
24. Pers. comm. Halaevalu Maile 1977; Tupou Posesi Fanua 1976.
25. Matekitonga was an illegitimate half-brother of Tupou II. Tongilava, Diary, 24 Oct. 1932; Fanua "Conversations".
26. Bott Spillius, "Discussions", pp.367, 368; pers. comm. Rodger Page the younger, 1976. Fusipala's relations included Adi Litia Cakobau, mother of her half-brother Edward.
27. Pers. comm. 1994.
28. HC to SofSCol., 31 Dec. 1932, WPHC:GCI 3439/32; Wood, Diary, 28 Nov. 1932.
29. Obituary in *Chronicle* 21 Jan. 1966, p.3.
30. Nusipepa, daughter of Sione Havea, accompanied the Wood family to Australia, and was staying with Dr Olive Wood and the children at Pymble. She died of tuberculosis on 14 Oct. 1935.
31. The letter was written in English. Only the last two pages were found in POP, so the date is unknown.
32. Lupeti Fīnau won the first place. Wood, Diary, 14 Nov. 1932; Annual Report, Tupou College, 1932, BCT 1/43/95.
33. They arrived in Sydney on the *Aorangi* on 27 Jan. 1933. *Methodist* 2:2 (4 Feb. 1933) 6.
34. Cables were sent from Sydney about Fusipala's illness and death. Tongilava, Diary, 28 Feb. and 21 Apr. 1933. Wood reported that her death was due to tubercular peritonitis. Diary, 1 Mar. 1933. A three-month period of mourning began on 21 Apr. Neill to HC, 26 Apr. 1933, WPHC:GCI 1260/33.
35. Biography of Fusipala by Sau Faupula; Marc T. Greene, "A Princess's Home-coming", *Auckland Star*, 3 June 1933.
36. Fanua, "Conversations".
37. See "Lament of Princess Melenaite Tupou Moheofo, wife of HRH Tu'ipelehake, at the death of Ratu Edward Cakobau", *Faikava* no.3, pp.3–7.
38. 'Ulukālala (S.F.M.) was married several times and had many children by

different women. Ha'amea's mother was Tapukitea, sister of a former holder of the noble title of Ata.

Chapter 11: The Queen's Consort: Tungī Mailefihi

1. Neill to HC, 31 July 1931, WPHC:GCI 2271/31.
2. It was generally agreed by my informants that Tungī had a daughter, whose Tongan mother brought her up in Fiji. The daughter was known as Adi Loa, and she married a Tongan boxer named Naufahu, but they had no children. She divorced Naufahu and died in Fiji in the 1970s.
3. A phrase used by Thomson, *Diversions*, p.92.
4. Tungī and his tenants, 5 Jan. and Tu'ivakanō to McOwan, 4 Feb. 1918, BCT 1/4. The second plan met with the wholehearted approval of the Consul. Neill to Tungī, 18 July 1931; Tungī to Queen Sālote, 20 May 1938, Premier's Papers 9 and 40, VSL.
5. A. G. Slocombe to Tungī, 9 July 1935, POP.
6. Pers. comm. Tavi (Preben Kaufmann) 1976. Selling food was a new thing in Tonga. Yams in particular had a sacred quality, and it was scandalous to sell them.
7. Pers. comm. Halaevalu Maile 1977; Rev. Dr S. 'Amanaki Havea 1974. Tungī's debts were repaid by the Queen after his death. Tongilava, Diary, passim.
8. Correspondence in WPHC:GCI 1537/36.
9. Neill to HC, 8 June 1936 (paras 12–14), WPHC:GCI 2063/36.
10. Neill, *Ten Years in Tonga*, pp.25, 26.
11. Tongilava, Diary, and Wood, Diary, 19 July–1 Aug. 1933.
12. The Banno brothers came to Tonga in about 1921 and set up stores throughout the group. Neill to HC, 31 July 1931, WPHC:GCI 2271/31, and 1 Aug. 1932, WPHC:GCI 2608/32.
13. *TGG* 17 (6 Sept. 1933) 107.
14. Bott Spillius papers, Box 17, notebook XIV. Only the 1924 miscarriage was recorded in diaries, but informants have referred to a miscarriage c.1920 and another in 1923, one of the latter being of a daughter. One miscarriage was at Faka'osikato, on the island of Ha'afeva, Ha'apai, and the child was buried at Falefakauo. Pers. comm. Halaevalu Maile 1977; Nānisi Helu 1976; Rev. Dr S. 'Amanaki Havea 1974; HRH Nanasipau'u Tuku'aho 1998.
15. Meleane Fatafehi and Fetutuki 'One'one were the two women. The royal party left Tonga on 13 July 1935.
16. Article by "Eriki", cutting in Rodger Page Scrapbook.
17. There were proposals for a civic reception given by the Lady Mayoress on 31 July, a lunch at Government House on 1 Aug., and a reception by the Premier's wife on 6 Aug., all prior to the Queen entering hospital.
18. Queen Sālote to Sau Faupula, 31 July, 12 and 17 Aug., 1 and 13 Sept. 1935.
19. Prince Tāufa'āhau to Queen Sālote, 12 Dec. 1933, POP.
20. Queen Sālote to Sau Faupula, 13 Sept. 1935.
21. *Fiji Times*, 16 Oct., pp.4, 8; *Sydney Morning Herald*, 26 Oct., p.17; *PIM* 6:5 (Dec. 1935) 33; Rodger Page Scrapbook, p.49.
22. Tongilava, Diary, 16–30 Oct. 1935.
23. Tāufa'āhau, quoted in *PIM* 6:10 (May 1936) 4; Bott Spillius, "Discussions", p.362; pers. comm. Ve'ehala (Leilua) 1976, Rev. Dr S. 'Amanaki Havea 1977.
24. Wood, Diary, entries in Mar. and Apr. 1936.
25. Tongilava, Diary, Jan.–Apr. 1936 passim; Wood, Diary, Mar.–Apr. 1936 passim.
26. Wood, Diary, 1 May 1936; Bott Spillius, "Discussions", pp.308, 343.
27. The lament was first published in *Koe Tohi Fanogonogo* vol.8, no.1 (July 1936). Since the Queen had left for Sydney late in May, the lament must have been written soon after Tuku'aho's death.
28. Bott Spillius papers, Box 17, notebook XIV.
29. Neill to HC, (telegram) 26 May, (letter) 29 May 1936, WPHC:GCI. Tongilava, Diary, 28 May 1936, records a Privy Council meeting at which 'Ulukālala was appointed Regent.
30. Correspondence in WPHC:GCI 1537/36. The protocol of the High Commissioner receiving the Queen in

full uniform had been established by the Colonial Office in 1935.

31. Queen Sālote to Sau Faupula, 10 Sept. 1936.
32. King, *Te Puea*, pp.196–7, 227–9.
33. *New Zealand Herald*, 5 Oct. 1936, pp.3, 4.
34. Tongilava, Diary, 23 Dec. 1936 and 21 Jan. 1938; Wood, Diary, 14 Jan. 1937.
35. Tongilava, Diary, 9 Feb. 1938.
36. *Kalanuvalu* [sic] *(noble) v. Minister for Lands* [1963] 2 *Tongan Law Reports* 40–4; the witness was not named in the judgment.
37. Tungī on 11 Oct. 1938, *TGG* 22 (7 Nov. 1938) 160. The English translator used the word "king" at the end of the first sentence. In Tongan the word would have been *tu'i*, which is not a gender-specific word.
38. The Speech of Her Majesty Queen Sālote Tubou, 11 Oct. 1938, ibid.
39. *PIM* 9:3 (Oct. 1938) 16.
40. McOwan to Parliament, 24 July 1918, BCT 1/6; Tungī to McOwan, 5 Aug. 1918, BCT 1/4; *TGG* 18 (16 Aug. 1929) 1; Neill to HC, 22 Apr. 1930, WPHC:GCI 1352/30; *PIM* 2:6 (Jan. 1932) 5, 8:12 (July 1938) 30; *Premier's Report 1940* p.2.

Chapter 12: The Chief Justice Plays the Champion

1. Armstrong to HC, 28 July 1940, BCT 1/43/92.
2. Ronald Garvey, 5 Sept. 1939, WPHC 661(s)39, hereinafter referred to as Garvey Report.
3. Tungī to Armstrong, 19 Aug. 1939, WPHC 170(s)39.
4. Armstrong to HC, 9 June 1941, WPHC:GCI 5297/40.
5. Report on Prisons, Tungī to Hyne, 28 Sept. 1937, and Tungī to Queen Sālote, 26 Oct. 1938, VSL; Garvey Report, para. 37; Armstrong to HC, 9 June 1941, WPHC:GCI 5297/41. McOwan had criticized Sioape as early as 1923. McOwan to Queen Sālote, 6 Dec. 1923, BCT 1/6; Tungī to McOwan, 15 July 1924, BCT 1/4.
6. Armstrong to HC, 22 July 1939, BCT 1/9.
7. HC to Armstrong, 25 Mar. 1938, BCT 1/43/92.
8. Stuart to HC (personal), 18 Jan., Armstrong to Vaskess, 3 Jan. 1939, extract copy in SPO 1017/38; Armstrong to HC, 7 May 1939, WPHC 170(s) 39.
9. Garvey Report, app. xviii; pers. comm. Cecil Gribble 1976.
10. Tongilava, Diary, 26 July and 19 Aug. 1938.
11. Dalby, *Cocker Connection*, p.63.
12. Pers. comm. Lilla Bagnall 1974, 1976.
13. Tungī to Stuart, 22 Oct. 1938, PP41, VSL; Garvey Report, paras 20, 21.
14. Armstrong to Vaskess (WPHC), 3 Jan., Armstrong to HC, 10 and 18 Jan. 1939, SPO 1017/38; correspondence in BCT 1/43/92; Stuart's memoranda, Jan., 17 May and 13 June 1939, BCT 1/43/92; Garvey Report, para. 16.
15. Garvey Report, para. 21.
16. A half-caste man was charged with attempting to intoxicate and rape a woman who was the mistress of one of the *papālangi* of the Beach. Tungī to Queen Sālote, 26 Oct. 1938, PP41, VSL; Tungī to Armstrong, 6 June 1939, copy in WPHC:GCI 2354/39; Garvey Report, para. 21 and app. v.
17. Stuart to Tungī, 23 Mar. 1939, Box 59/11, ATL; Armstrong to HC, 7 May 1939, WPHC 170(s)39.
18. Garvey Report, para. 1–8.
19. Armstrong to HC, 7 May 1939, WPHC 170(s)39.
20. Memoranda I–III of Chief Justice Stuart, encl. in Stuart to HC, 19 May 1939, WPHC:GCI 2354/39.
21. Maude, *Kingdom of Tonga* (Report on the Civil Service), pp.20–1.
22. Garvey Report, para. 30.
23. Dora Parsonage to Armstrong, 3 Aug. 1939, WPHC 661(s)39.
24. Armstrong to HC, 8 May 1939, WPHC 170(s)39; Dora Parsonage to Armstrong, 3 Aug. 1939, WPHC 661(s)39.
25. Armstrong to HC, 1 July 1939, BCT 1/43/92.
26. HC to Armstrong, (telegram) 24 July, Armstrong to HC, 27 July 1939, BCT 1/43/92 and WPHC 170(s)39.
27. Stuart to HC, 18 Jan. 1939, SPO 1917/38; Armstrong to HC, 7 May 1939, WPHC 170(s)39; same to same, 1

July 1939, BCT 1/43/92; Stuart to Sir Grattan Bushe, 22 Aug. 1939, in Garvey Report, app. xvii.

28. Governor-General of New Zealand (Viscount Galway) to HC, 18 Nov. 1939, WPHC 170(s)39.
29. The Queen's reply, 19 Mar. 1939, BCT 1/43/92. See also Garvey Report, para. 4.
30. Garvey Report, app. ix; copy of Bill in WPHC 661(s)39.
31. Stuart to HC, 5 June 1939, BCT 1/43/92.
32. Queen Sālote to HC, 5 June, Queen Sālote to Armstrong, 4 July 1939, BCT 1/43/92.
33. Preliminary inquiry, 20 Apr. 1939, BCT 4/IV/11; Stuart's judgment on Palu case, 5 May 1939, BCT 1/43/92.
34. Feleti Vī's statement, 7 June, Queen Sālote to HC, 5 June, Armstrong to HC, 29 June 1939, BCT 1/43/92.
35. Queen Sālote to HC, 5 May, Armstrong to HC, 7 May 1939, WPHC 170(s)39.
36. Stuart to Sir Grattan Bushe, 22 Aug. 1939, in Garvey Report, app. xvii.
37. Memorandum II of Chief Justice Stuart, encl. in Stuart to HC, 19 May 1939, WPHC:GCI 2354/39; Armstrong to HC, 1 July 1939, BCT 1/32/92. Ve'ehala (Leilua) told me that Stuart "promised to make his supporters nobles", pers. comm. 1976.
38. Luke to SofSCol., 22 May 1939, BCT 1/43/92.
39. Statement of Feleti Vī, 7 June 1939, BCT 1/43/92; Armstrong to HC, 1 July 1939, WPHC:GCI 2354/39.
40. Queen Sālote to Armstrong, 4 July 1939, BCT 1/43/92. See also Stuart to Tungī, Tungī to Queen Sālote, 2 June 1939, POP; Armstrong to HC, 26 June and 6 July 1939, SofSCol. to Assistant HC, 8 July 1939 WPHC 170(s)39.
41. Sir Cosmo Parkinson to HC, 27 May 1939; SofSCol. to HC, (telegram) 8 July 1939, WPHC 170(s)39.
42. Address-in-Reply, *TGG* 24 (26 Oct. 1939) 131–2. The drafting committee consisted of Stuart, the nobles Vaha'i, Lavaka, and Tu'ilakepa, and "representatives of the People" S. Mataele and I. Pulu. These Tongans were identified as supporters of Stuart and Kaho in Garvey Report, app. xxvi. Other supporters of Stuart in Parliament were said to be Tu'ivakanō (Siosiua), Tuita ('Isileli), Tēvita Vī, 'Unga Afuha'amango, and Taniela Tonga. Ibid. We cannot take the list too seriously, although some were members of the "Reactionary Party".
43. Stuart to Sir Grattan Bushe, 22 Aug. 1939, copy in Garvey Report, app. xvii. See also *TGG* 15 (21 June 1940) 117.
44. Mataele to HC, 8 Mar. 1939, WPHC:GCI 1315/39.
45. *PIM* 10:12 (July 1940) 27.
46. Stuart to Sir Grattan Bushe, 22 Aug. 1939, copy in Garvey Report, app. xvii.
47. Garvey Report, app. xix.
48. *TGG* 15 (21 June 1940) 111–20; HC to Armstrong 2 Aug., HC to Queen Sālote, 8 Aug., BCT 1/43/92; HC to Armstrong, 8 Aug. 1939, HC to Garvey, 8 Aug. 1939, WPHC 170(s)39.
49. See also Queen Sālote to HC, 24 Aug. 1939, BCT 1/43/92 and WPHC 170(s)39.
50. Pers. comm. Sir Ronald Garvey 1979.
51. Speech at the Closing of Parliament, 8 Sept. 1939, in *TGG* 24 (26 Oct. 1939) 133.
52. Queen Sālote to HC, 24 Aug. 1939, WPHC 170(s)39.
53. Garvey Report, paras 1–3.
54. Garvey Report, para. 8.
55. Garvey Report, para. 40.
56. Garvey Report, paras 36–41.
57. Garvey Report, para. 23.
58. Garvey Report, para. 42.
59. Garvey Report, para. 32.
60. HC to Queen Sālote, 30 Aug. 1939, WPHC 170(s)39.
61. Queen Sālote to HC, 15 Nov. 1939, WPHC 170(s)39.
62. *TGG* 20 (4 Sept. 1940) 178–9. A summary of the events of the 1940 Parliament were reported in ibid. and *TGG* 1 (10 Jan. 1941) 2. Notes of the proceedings of the impeachments were taken by Stuart, PP141, VSL.
63. Wartime Contingencies Bill, copy in WPHC 170(s)39. See also Queen Sālote to HC, 18 July, Armstrong to HC, 28 July 1940, BCT 1/43/92 and WPHC 170(s)39.
64. Tungī to Queen Sālote, quoted in Queen Sālote to HC, 18 July 1940, WPHC 170(s)39.

65. Ibid.
66. Armstrong to HC, 3 Jan. 1939, WPHC:GCI 1017/38; same to same, 7 May 1939, WPHC 170(s)39; Armstrong to Luke, 28 July 1940, BCT 1/43/92.
67. Armstrong to Luke, 28 July 1940, BCT 1/43/92. Stuart had no authority to issue ammunition. So unpopular was Stuart in some quarters that 26 *papālangi* said they were desirous of serving in the Tonga Defence Force, "provided His Honour the Chief Justice shall not at any time have control of or power over this Force". Armstrong to Luke, 15 Sept. 1939, BCT 1/43/92.
68. HC to SofSCol., 15 Aug. 1940, WPHC 170(s)39.
69. Armstrong to HC, 24 Oct. 1940, WPHC 170(s)39.
70. HC to SofSCol., 10 July 1942, WPHC 170(s)39; pers. comm. A. C. Reid 1974. Stuart was transferred in November 1943 to Tanganyika, and retired on 20 August 1948.
71. Armstrong to HC, 6 July 1942, WPHC 170 (s)39.

Chapter 13: The Greatest Loss of All

1. Queen Sālote to Rev. Sau Faupula, 28 July 1941.
2. HC to Agent & Consul (J. E. Windrum), 1952, BCT 4/1/3.
3. It is not clear when Tungī Mailefihi was appointed Colonel-in-Chief. 'Akau'ola was a *matāpule ma'u tofi'a* title and Siosateki Faletau his name before he was installed in the title. ('Akau'ola reverted to Major when Colonel Bagnall arrived from New Zealand in February 1941 to take command of the of the Force.)
4. *TGG* 26 (24 Nov. 1939) 146, 147.
5. In October 1939 Captain J. S. Rennie and Sergeant-Major G. Stevens were seconded from the Fiji Defence Force, *TGG* 23 (23 Oct. 1939) 128; Sergeant-Major Latimer in Mar. 1940. Hornabrook, "New Zealand", p.20. In October 1941 four captains and four sergeant-majors were seconded from New Zealand. SF 66/1 (WPHC), also known as "Tonga 1939–45", MP 199/46/10, in ATL, referred to hereinafter as Report SF 66/1.
6. Report SF 66/1.
7. Armstrong to C. S., [15 Sept. 1944], WPHC:GCI 499/44.
8. Fanua, "Conversations". The words sound more like Fanua's speech than the Queen's.
9. Margaret Armstrong, "Reminiscences".
10. Hornabrook, "New Zealand", pp.36, 40.
11. Hornabrook, "New Zealand", p.116.
12. Armstrong to C. S., [15. Sept. 1944], WPHC:GCI 499/44.
13. Pers. comm. Rev. Dr S. 'Amanaki Havea 1974.
14. Queen Sālote to Armstrong, 17 Sept. 1940, POP.
15. Fanua, "Conversations".
16. £5450 was raised for the Red Cross; £7400 for other war funds, including £1525 for the TDF Comforts Fund.
17. Informants about the events of the weekend were Harry and Honor Maude, Ve'ehala (Leilua), 'Etina Havea, and Saiatua Lavulo.
18. The marriage, postponed because of Tungī's death, never took place.
19. Uiliami Tufui reported that at midday someone saw a man in a tree in which lived devils who bring sudden death. The man jumped from the tree holding a branch and ran into Tungī's house. Pers. comm. 1976.
20. The room was thereafter *tapu* until seawater was sprinkled after the removal of the body.
21. Pers. comm. Nānisi Helu 1976.
22. I am indebted to Mary Page for a copy of a letter Rodger Page wrote to his son, another Rodger, dated 23 September 1939, describing the illness, death, and funeral ceremonies for Hannah Page.
23. The other love song is *Loto ne kafo he mausa he fā* (How the heart hurts as the pandanus's fragrance . . .).
24. The gladiolus was a popular flower of the time.
25. Maude to Luke (personal), 31 July 1941, WPHC:GCI 3311/41.
26. Collocott, "King Taufa, Lord of Isles", pp.441–2.

Chapter 14: America Invades Tonga

1. At the Closing of Parliament, 29 June 1942, *TGG* 17 (2 Sept. 1942) 138.

2. Armstrong to Queen Sālote, 9 Dec. 1941, MP 110/41, POP, records that the decision to declare war on Japan was made at a Privy Council meeting on 8 Dec. 1941.
3. The Kolisi Fefine was renamed Queen Sālote College in 1941 (*Koe Tohi Fanogonogo* Dec. 1940, p.3). Mrs Thompson returned in time to re-open the school on its own site in February 1943.
4. Report SF 66/1. In 1994 I visited the site of the house, and found only concrete stumps remained near a most beautiful beach. Part of the cave had fallen during an earthquake.
5. Tongilava, Diary, entries for 3 and 12 Mar., 18, 20, and 29 Apr., 9 May and following days 1942; US Government, "History of Tongatabu", pp.18, 34, 43; Report SF 66/1. See also C. J. Weeks, "The United States Occupation of Tonga", pp.399–426.
6. "History of Tongatabu", p.132. New Zealand and the United Kingdom paid the first amount. Hornabrook, "New Zealand", p.16.
7. Pers. comm. Siupeli Taliai 1997.
8. Sir Harry Luke was Governor of Fiji as well as HC. Liongi was the Free Wesleyan Church minister in Fua'amotu.
9. Pers. comm. Cecil Gribble 1976.
10. Hornabrook, "New Zealand", p.56.
11. Captain Benjamin Tate Perlman to Queen Sālote and to Ata, 31 July 1942, MP 143/42, ATL, thanking them for flowers and sympathy. The bodies of American servicemen were reburied in American Sāmoa on 18 Sept. 1945. "History of Tongatabu", chronology and pp.112–13.
12. Armstrong to C. S., [15 Sept. 1944], WPHC:GCI 499/44; Margaret Armstrong, "Reminiscences".
13. "History of Tongatabu", p.4.
14. Queen Sālote to Sau Faupula, 8 May 1942. 'Ahio (the name is a chiefly title) held a large piece of land near by.
15. Weeks, "Occupation", p.407.
16. Series B, Box 43/1, MP 2/43, ATL; Priday, *Coconut Square*, pp.34–5.
17. Pers. comm. Futa Helu 1997.
18. The *Sumner* was in Tonga in January or March, or from January to March, Hornabrook, p.46; pers. comm. Cecil Gribble 1976; "History of Tongatabu", chronology; Report SF 66/1.
19. "History of Tongatabu", pp.42–3; Tongilava, Diary, 26 May 1942; Margaret Armstrong, "Reminiscences"; pers. comm. Cecil Gribble 1976.
20. Speech made by Agent & Consul to Parliament, *TGG* 3 (22 Mar. 1946) 18. The businessman Willy Cocker gave £2000 towards the first plane. Queen Sālote to Armstrong, 17 Sept. 1940, POP.
21. Armstrong to C. S., [15 Sept. 1944], WPHC:GCI 499/44.
22. Pers. comm. Bishop Rodgers 1994.
23. *Pacific Islands Year Book*, 6th ed. (Sydney 1950), p.114.
24. *TGG* 17 (2 Sept. 1942) 138.
25. The following is based on my conversations with Joe Mataele (1995), Fanua (various dates) and "Conversations", and Saiatua Lavulo (1994).
26. Pers. comm. Saiatua Lavulo 1994. See also Priday, *Coconut Square*, p.32; Lindstrom & White, *Island Encounters*, pp.30, 120.
27. Ata to Lockwood, 22 Oct., Lockwood to Ata, 23 Oct. 1942, Series B, Box 42/10, MP 142/42, ATL.
28. Queen Sālote to Sau Faupula, 24 May 1942.
29. Same to same, 13 Sept. 1942 [DR].
30. Series B, Box 43/1, MP 2/43; Box 43/12, MP 165/43; Box 43/3 MP 30/43; Box 43/1, MP 10/43, ATL; pers. comm. Tupou Posesi Fanua 1976 and Kakala Taumoefolau 1995.
31. "Report of Superintendent G. D. Hill relative to Murder of Tongans at Fuamotu [*sic*]", 31 Mar. 1943, including "Diary of Action Taken", MP 30/45/43, ATL.
32. Queen Sālote to Sau Faupula, 23 Mar. 1943.
33. Same to same, 23 July 1943.
34. Hornabrook, "New Zealand", pp.59, 66, 88.
35. The agreement between the New Zealand and Tongan governments resembled that between Tonga and the US government. New Zealanders continued to be seconded to the Tonga Defence Force. Series B, Box 43/12, MP

156/43, ATL. See also Hornabrook, "New Zealand", pp.59ff; pers. comm. Joe Mataele 1995. Priday, *Coconut Square*, p.34, said the New Zealanders were "Scottish", i.e. careful with their money.

36. Hunt had expected that the Americans would leave equipment for New Zealanders ("History of Tongatabu", p.134). The few New Zealand vehicles constantly broke down (Hornabrook, p.42), prompting the summary of the situation by Joe Mataele: "Their wheels fell off" (pers. comm. 1995).
37. Hornabrook, "New Zealand", p.82.
38. Hornabrook, "New Zealand", p.43.
39. Hornabrook, "New Zealand", p.105.
40. Pers. comm. Halaevalu Maile 1977.
41. "History of Tongatabu", pp.181–2.
42. Ibid. p.177; pers. comm. Bishop Rodgers 1994.
43. Pers. comm. Bishop Rodgers 1994. Details about the "Cigarette Raid" and its aftermath are from "History of Tongatabu", pp.166–201 (the official historian quotes Hodsdon's own account and argues that it was self-serving and unreliable). See also CMO to Premier, 25 Aug., Ata to Johnson, 4 Oct. 1944, MP 218/44/12, ATL; Weeks, "Occupation", pp.399–426.
44. Margaret Armstrong, "Reminiscences".
45. Hornabrook, "New Zealand", pp.103–4. Their complaints were: (1) the Union Jack was flown over their camp instead of the flag of Tonga; (2) Tongan officers did not have enough say in policy-making in the camp; (3) when TDF men returned from the Solomons, those who had remained in Tonga were not given transport to attend the feast.
46. Tongilava, Diary, 23 and 25 July 1943; Hornabrook, "New Zealand", p.79. Although Taliai was a commoner, Tongilava used the chiefly word *pekia* when referring to his death.
47. Report SF 66/1; Armstrong to C. S., [15 Sept. 1944], WPHC:GCI 499/44; citations in *TGG* 6 (16 May 1944) 42.
48. A Japanese submarine shelled Pago Pago in January 1942. *Pacific Islands Year Book*, 5th ed. (Sydney 1944) p.16.
49. *TGG* 15 (20 Dec. 1945) 129, 18 (2 Dec. 1953) 194.
50. "King Taufa, Lord of Isles", p.474.
51. Hornabrook, "New Zealand", pp.56, 112. The sophisticated drugs that would be so effective against tuberculosis in the 1950s were not available during the war. The X-ray machine the Americans left behind was in use for another 15 years. The CMO had doubtless attempted to discourage the Tongan practice of relatives sleeping beside sick people, but 47 doctors and 52 nurses saying the same thing must have had an effect.
52. Cecil Gribble to John Burton, 14 July 1944, MOMC 316, Mitchell Library, Sydney.
53. Pers. comm. Helen Taliai 1996.
54. Reports of the Justice Department, 1955 and 1961, New Zealand and Pacific Collection, Library of The University of Auckland.
55. "Report on the Social Survey of Villages of Tongatapu, 13th September 1959", app. A, p.13, Bott Spillius papers, Box 16, folder 1.
56. In 1940 copra had fetched £12 a ton; in 1945 it was £27 a ton. After the war an agreement with the UK guaranteed continuing high prices. Exports, which largely consisted of copra, had been worth £56,459 in 1938, but were worth £263,544 in 1946, and £1,624,301 in 1964. See *Pacific Islands Year Book* 6th ed. (Sydney 1950) p.109, 11th ed. (Sydney 1972) p.131.

Chapter 15: Mother and Sons

1. The Writings of Queen Sālote, section VII ("Showing Respect").
2. Queen Sālote to Sau Faupula, 25 June 1943.
3. Queen Sālote at the Closing of Parliament, 11 Aug. 1948, *TGG* 12 (8 Sept. 1948) 128.
4. Queen Sālote to Sau Faupula, 10 Dec. 1942, 8 Feb. 1943.
5. HC to SofSCol., 15 Dec. 1941, WPHC to SofSCol, vol. 1941.
6. The Chief Justice of Fiji was designated Chief Justice of Tonga, but did not sit in Parliament or in the Privy Council, except when the latter was sitting as a Court of Appeal. This Chief Justice came to Tonga less frequently than intended. Only the first three men who

held the office of Secretary to Government (John K. Brownlees, P. A. Richardson, and Atwell Lake) had legal qualifications.

7. *TGG* 1 (2 Feb. 1943) 1, 13 (11 Dec. 1944) 107.
8. *TGG* 1 (2 Feb. 1943) 1, 2 (3 Mar. 1943) 7.
9. Tongilava, Diary, 9 Apr. 1943.
10. R. J. Harrison reported having four *papālangi* and one Tongan teacher at Tonga High School when he was principal. *PIM* 22:11 (June 1952) 85.
11. Published by Leighton's, Auckland, 1946.
12. The Writings of Queen Sālote, section VI ("Different Duties").
13. Tu'ipelehake was Acting Governor from January to July 1949, then Governor from 1 September. *TGG* 1 (16 Feb. 1949) 2, 11 (12 Oct. 1949) 123.
14. Tupouto'a-Tungī to Cecil Gribble, 8 Oct. 1948, MOMC 510, Mitchell Library; *PIM* 21:4 (Nov. 1950) 7.
15. There are three stages in the bestowal of a title. First, the Queen writes to tell the person that she appoints him to the title (*tohi fakanofo*). Second, the chief takes his place at the first opportunity in the *kava* circle and is called by his title for the first time – that is, his *ha'a* recognizes him. The third step is when the new titleholder's people (at his instigation) bring presentations to the Queen on his behalf: consisting of food, *kava*, *koloa*, and dances. The interval between the second and third step varies. A *matāpule* does not always bring a *pongipongi*, but many do, and a *matāpule ma'u tofi'a* should always do so.
16. The Fijian chiefs stayed at 'Otualea during the double wedding 18 months later, and I am assuming that this was their place in 1945 also.
17. Information about the evacuation of Niuafo'ou and subsequent events has been taken from [Rogers], *The Fire Has Jumped*; from *Marist Moments*, Lent 1949; and sources cited below.
18. Kalanivalu did not take the title Fotofili when his father died in 1936, reserving it for his son. However, he was installed as Fotofili in 1957, and then known as Kalanivalu-Fotofili.
19. On 2 June 1947, Siosiua Mafile'o (clerk to the Queen's Secretary) recorded food being purchased so a soup could be made for these people. This was during the preparations for the double wedding of the princes.
20. Speech on 26 June 1947, printed in *TGG* 12 (12 Sept. 1947) 109–10.
21. Tongilava, Diary, 15 May, 15 and 24 June, 14 July 1948.
22. Pers. comm. Ruth and Ron Woodgate 1997.
23. "'Eua Niuafo'ou People", Bott Spillius papers, Box 17, notebook 1.
24. Immediately after his accession H.M. Tāufa'āhau Tupou IV appointed a cabinet of three: the Premier; the Deputy Premier and Minister for Finance; and the Minister for Lands, Health and Chair of the Niuafo'ou Evacuation Committee. *Chronicle* 7 Jan. 1966, p.2.
25. Pers. comm. Halaevalu Maile 1977; Bott Spillius papers, Box 17, notebook XIV.
26. Pers. comm. Halaevalu Maile 1977, Saiatua Lavulo 1994.
27. Pers. comm. Joe Mataele 1995.
28. Pers. comm. Adrienne Kaeppler 1993; commentary of a film on the wedding of Princess Pilolevu, *Ko e Ta'ane*, made by Brigham Young University, Laie, Hawai'i, 1976.
29. Bott Spillius papers, Box 17, notebook XIV; pers. comm. Bott Spillius to author, 10 Jan. 1980.
30. Tupouto'a-Tungī went to Auckland 9–27 October 1944 and 3 June–10 July 1948 to seek medical advice.
31. The price of copra rose from £22.85 per ton in 1945 to £66 per ton in 1951 and £90 per ton in 1960.
32. Letters of the Premier 1961–63, Box 42/12, ATL.
33. According to Kenneth Bain, in the three years 1953–56, Tupouto'a-Tungī spent 18 months travelling overseas. Bain, *The Friendly Islanders*, p.105.
34. *PIM* 25:8 (Mar. 1955) 140; also 26:2 (Sept. 1955) 97–9; 28: 12 (July 1958) 101.
35. Puli'uvea's daughter and son-in-law were caretakers of royal estates in Ha'apai. Puli'uvea said he was preparing a feast for the Queen's visit to Vava'u at the time of his arrest. Pers. comm. Mileti Helu (formerly Ahaha'amango).

36. The only *papālangi* minister, the Minister for Finance, retired at age 60 or 65, but Tongan ministers continued if requested by the Queen.
37. *PIM* 25:11 (June 1955) 131, 25:12 (July 1955) 123, 26:1 (Aug. 1955) 15.
38. Agent & Consul to HC, 16 Nov. 1954, BCT 6 s4/1/7 – vol. 1.
39. Report of Agent & Consul, 15 June 1962, BCT 6 s4/1/7. It was possible to get overseas radio programmes, and Tonga set up its own radio station in 1961.
40. James Spillius, "Interim Report on Anthropological Aspects of the Work of the ES Project in Tonga, January 1959", Bott Spillius papers, Box 16, folder 1, p.34.

Chapter 16: At the Coronation of Queen Elizabeth II

1. In a co-educational school in Tonga visited by a young ballet company in the 1990s, the male half of the audience had to leave during the performance because they could not witness such "indecency" before their "sisters".
2. Bott Spillius, "Discussions", p.358.
3. A cutting from the column "London Day By Day" June 1953, given to me by Brian Bell, of Ngongotaha, New Zealand, in 1994.
4. The mantle and shoes that Queen Sālote wore on that day were exhibited in the 1990s at the Tonga National Centre, Nuku'alofa.
5. Neill, *Ten Years in Tonga*, p.202. For Neill's account of the Coronation visit and subsequent tour of Scotland and Ireland, see ibid. pp.201–11.
6. Kitione Lave was a Tongan heavyweight boxer, who was 18 years old at this time.
7. A *fuatanga* stencil for a piece of bark cloth was made to commemorate what Queen Sālote wore at the coronation of Queen Elizabeth II. The design included a *lave'i tavake* (a hair ornament of tail feathers of the Tropic Bird) and *kahoa puleoto* (a necklace of a *puleoto* shell strung on human hair). Pers. comm. Adrienne Kaeppler 1993.
8. *TGG* 1 (15 Jan. 1954) 1–2.
9. Queen Sālote's speech at the Opening of Parliament, 15 June 1961, *TGG* 9 (13 Oct. 1961) 159.
10. Pers. comm. A. C. Reid 1974.
11. Tonga Defence Force Act 1952, and *TGG* 18 (2 Dec. 1953) 194.
12. Pers. comm. A. C. Reid 1974. The text of the revised treaty was published in *TGG* 9 (28 Aug. 1958) 110–13.
13. Queen Sālote in speech at the Closing of Parliament, 24 Sept. 1958, *TGG* 10 (9 Oct. 1958) 120–1.
14. Queen Sālote in Speech at the Opening of a Special Session of Parliament, 20 Feb. 1959, *TGG* 5 (8 May 1959) 61.

Chapter 17: Changing Roles

1. In a letter to Father Tremblay, 21 July 1953, telling him of her travels and meeting with the Pope, the Queen said she was preparing to retire to her house in Ha'apai. Provincial Archives, Marist Fathers, Framlingham, Mass., USA (per favour of Dr Hugh Laracy). She said the same thing to Rodger Page (pers. comm. Mary Page 1976). See also Quentin Weston to Sir Kenneth Maddocks, 10 Oct. 1959, A. C. Reid to Sir Kenneth Maddocks, 12 Oct. 1959, BCT 6.PF S-1; Bott Spillius papers, Box 17, notebook XIV.
2. Queen Sālote to Sau Faupula, 20 July 1938.
3. Maamaloa (Long Light) was a building on the Tupou College site in Nuku'alofa. When Tupou College moved from Nafualu to Toloa the Maamaloa was taken there and used as the school chapel. The old church was used as a primary school until it was blown down by hurricane Isaac in 1982.
4. *Ko e Tohi Fanongonongo*, Dec. 1940.
5. The saying is "starve a fever and feed a cold". Pers. comm. Kakala and Melenaite Taumoefolau 1994.
6. Pers. comm. Dilys Rowlands 1997; *PIM* 25:3 (Oct. 1954) 151.
7. [Taufe'ulungaki], "Elimination of Discrimination", paragraph 3.1.4, p.63.
8. Report of Minister for Health 1956.
9. Dilys Rowlands and Liu Tongilava attended the PPSEAWA conference in Manila in 1956, and a group of women attended the 1960 conference in

Australia, although not as members. It was during the Australian conference that the invitation was issued to PPSEAWA to hold its next meeting (1964) in Tonga.

10. In 1959 the Queen was President and Princess Mata'aho and the wife of the British Agent & Consul were Vice-Presidents of PPSEAWA; the Queen was President, and Princess Melenaite, Dilys Rowlands, and the high-ranking Leafā (wife of Tu'iha'ateiho) were Vice-Presidents of Langa Fonua; the Queen was head of the Women's Health Committees. The positions of secretary and treasurer were held by lower-ranking women. Sister Fatafehi Mataele did a great deal to keep the Women's Health Committees going.
11. James Spillius, Quarterly Report to World Health Organization, 15 Sept. 1959, app.A, p.14, Bott Spillius papers, Box 16, folder 1.
12. See James, "Rank overrules everything".
13. Queen Sālote's speeches at the Opening and Closing of Parliament, 14 June and 7 Sept. 1956, in *TGG* 13 (19 Oct. 1956) 169–71.
14. See Walsh, "Nuku'alofa, Tonga", pp.54–60; Report of British Agent & Consul, 20 Dec. 1962, 27 Aug. 1963, Dec. 1963 BCT 6 s4/1/9 – vol.2; *Chronicle* 11 (28 Aug. 1964) 3; speeches by Tupou IV at the Opening and Closing of Parliament in 1967, *TGG* 10 (31 Oct. 1967) 141–2.
15. Queen Sālote's speech at the Closing of Parliament, 14 Oct. 1965, in *TGG* 13 (26 Oct. 1965) 214–15.
16. Bott Spillius papers, Box 13. Tu'ifua Carrick was a daughter of Veikune and Vāhoi, and aunt to Princess Mata'aho. The Queen wanted Elizabeth to write a comprehensive history, and Elizabeth's book *Tongan Society at the Time of Captain Cook's Visits* was a partial fulfilment of that expectation.

Chapter 18: Reconstructing Tradition

1. *Tongan Society*, p.68, quoting a manuscript by Old Tungī.
2. The Writings of Queen Sālote, section I ("The Ha'as of Tonga").
3. In Rodger Page Scrapbook, 13 June [1936].
4. The Writings of Queen Sālote , sections VII ("Showing respect"), XIV ("Costumes"), XV ("What was worn").
5. HRH 'Ulukālala-Lavaka-Ata, address at the opening of the conference of the Tongan History Association, 28 Jan. 1997.
6. Bain, *Royal Visit*, p.36; pers. comm. Kakala Taumoefolau 1995.
7. Queen Sālote to Sau Faupula, 19 Nov. 1936.
8. Queen Sālote's speech at the Closing of Parliament 24 Aug. 1949, *TGG* 4 (21 Feb. 1950) 33–4.
9. Comments appended to questionnaire devised by Rev. Dr S. 'Amanaki Havea, and answered by the Queen, 1965.
10. *TGG* 12 (21 Sept. 1959) 157.
11. Dated 12 Sept. 1959, but not sent. Bott Spillius papers, Box 13.
12. 17 Apr. 1959, Bott Spillius papers, Box 13.
13. Sir David Attenborough to author, 10 Mar. 1995.
14. What follows is based on Elizabeth Bott Spillius's descriptions of the 1959 *taumafa kava*, in Bott Spillius papers, Box 13.
15. See Kaeppler, "Structured movement systems in Tonga" for a description of the stylized movements used by the *kava* maker.
16. The Writings of Queen Sālote, section II ("The Ha'as"), says that "Only very recently during the time of Queen Salote Tupou . . . the Tu'i Fale Ua [Tu'ipelehake] was made second".
17. Dec. 1959. Bott Spillius papers, Box 13, folder 3.
18. Lātūkefu tells the story in his "The Making of the First Tongan-born Professional Historian".
19. I have drawn on the publications of Adrienne Kaeppler (see Bibliography) for the descriptions below.
20. In 1938 Sir Harry Luke wrote (*South Seas Diary*, p.34) that this was done in memory of Tuku'aho. Nowadays, the wearing of black is deemed also to be in memory of Tungī Mailefihi.
21. Pers. comm. Futa Helu, Oct. 1994.
22. Quoted by Māhina, "Tongan Traditional History", pp.192–209.

23. Songs and dances were also written for schools, such as the Queen Sālote College *mā'ulu'ulu*. In 1998 there was much discussion about Lapaha dances being performed by other groups.

Chapter 19: "The Sun Has Fallen"

1. *Ko e Kalonikali* (Tongan edition of *Chronicle*), 17 Dec. 1965, p.2, used *punakaki* instead of *mapaki*.
2. J. E. Windrum to HC, 8 Aug. 1953, BCT 6:2/6/4. The letter is based on notes by Dorothy Crozier in ibid.
3. *PIM* 23:3 (Oct. 1952) 21.
4. When the author visited one of the royal princesses in 'Atalanga in 1974 the attendant who brought afternoon tea entered and left the room on her knees. On another visit in 1995, no afternoon tea was served as the guests included a Tongan who could not eat in the royal presence.
5. Bain, *Friendly Islanders*, chapter 16.
6. Pers. comm. Mary Page 1976.
7. Bott Spillius papers, Box 17, notebook XIV.
8. A. C. Reid to Secretary of External Affairs (Wellington), 25 July 1957, CO 1009/455.
9. The following account of the Queen's illness, death, and funeral are from Rev. Dr A. H. Wood (orator at her funeral), her private nurse Moala Simiki, Saiatua Lavulo, Konai Helu Thaman, A. C. Reid, Kaeppler, "*Me'afaka'eiki*", issues of the *Chronicle* and other periodicals, Dec. 1965 and early months of 1966.
10. Pers. comm. A. H. Wood 1974, and inscription on grave at Mala'e 'Aloa.
11. Dr Havea wrote down the words and they were quoted by Rev. Dr A. H. Wood during his funeral oration, 23 Dec. 1965. *Ko e Tohi Fanongonongo*, Jan. 1966.
12. Pers. comm. Paddy Macdonald 1976.
13. Tupouto'a Tungī had been on a business trip to the USA, Europe, and Japan and came to New Zealand before returning to Tonga. *TGG* 17 (21 Dec. 1965) 249.
14. The fine-mats in the royal collection had been carefully labelled under the Queen's instruction. At this time the labels were removed, and never replaced. The names of the 23 used near the coffin were listed. Pers. comm. Adrienne Kaeppler 1994.
15. In the New Revised Standard Version the verse reads: "Each will be like a hiding place from the wind, a covert from the tempest, like streams of water in a dry place, like the shade of a great rock in a weary land."
16. These were Lātūniua 'Ahome'e (sister of Queen Mata'aho), Nanasipau'u Vaea (eldest granddaughter of Vilai Tupou), Melenaite Faletau, and HRH Princess Siu'ilikutapu (eldest daughter of Tu'ipelehake). *Chronicle* 7 Jan. 1966, p.2.
17. Ibid.
18. Bott Spillius, "Discussions", p.84.
19. Wood-Ellem, "Queen Sālote Tupou and Tungī Mailefihi", p.9.
20. Queen Sālote's speech at the Opening of Parliament, 13 June 1922, *TGG* 20 (13 July 1922) 93.
21. Reported in Hunter to HC, 6 June 1903, WPHC:GCI 2/00.
22. *TGG* 23 (17 Sept. 1920) 131–2.
23. *TGG* 3 (12 May 1955) 25.

Glossary of Tongan Words

1. Siotame Tupou gave the date as 1883 when a witness in the Niukapu case on 30 October 1937, but in the Tohi Hohoko 'a O. F. Veikune, p.79, the date is given as 1885. Churchward, *Dictionary*, p.254 also gives the date as 1885.

Selected Bibliography

See list of Abbreviations, p.321.

1. Archives and periodicals

Armstrong, Margaret, n.d. "Reminiscences of Life in Tonga". Photocopy of TS. Auckland Institute and Museum Library MS 867.

Blanc, J. F., Diary, 1912–16, 1924–34 (in French). Archives of the Catholic Church of Tonga, Nuku'alofa, translated by author. (Volume 1916–24 missing from archives.)

Bott Spillius papers. New Zealand and Pacific Collection, Library of The University of Auckland, A265. *See also* Tonga Traditions Committee papers, Palace Office; Bott, Elizabeth; Spillius, Elizabeth; Spillius, James (below).

Cameron, A. D., n.d. "Extract from Memoirs 1901–1947". Unpublished TS in possession of Mrs T. Stairmand, Sydney.

Campbell, Helen Fahnestock, 1902. Excerpts from Diary of Helen Fahnestock Campbell, wife of Dr Clarence Campbell and mother of Helen Gordon Campbell (born 1895). TS copy in POP.

Catholic Church papers, now on Pacific Manuscripts Bureau microfilm, especially Bishop Blanc's Diary (see above).

Chronicle (Tongan edition: *Ko e Kalonikali*). Nuku'alofa, 1964– .

Collocott, E. E. V. Papers at the Bernice P. Bishop Museum, Honolulu; Alexander Turnbull Library, Wellington; Mitchell Library, Sydney. Especially "King Taufa, Lord of Isles", MS case 5, MS TO 4.4 in Bernice P. Bishop Museum, Honolulu.

Crosby, E. E., Diary and other papers. MOMC 579, Mitchell Library, Sydney.

Faikava: a Tongan Literary Journal (Tonga), issues 1–10, 1978–83.

Fanua, Tupou Posesi, "Conversations with Garth Rogers", Auckland, 1974. Now part of the Wendy Pond Collection of Audio-tapes, Asia–Pacific Archive of the School of Music, Victoria University, Wellington, New Zealand.

Ferguson, Dorothy, Diary, 1927–30. Methodist Archives, Auckland, New Zealand.

Fiji Times, Suva.

Fiji Times and Herald, Suva.

Free Wesleyan Church papers (FWC papers) as read in Mission House, 1974 and 1976.

Hafoka, S. Havili, n.d. Writings of Havili Hafoka for the Tonga Traditions Committee. TS copies in Tonga Traditions Committee papers, Palace Office, Nuku'alofa; Bott Spillius papers, New Zealand and Pacific Collection, Library of The University of Auckland, A265, box 11, folder 6.

Im Thurn, Sir Everard. Diary (1905–6). Royal Anthropological Institute Library, MSS 219, 220, 221. Microfilm in Division of Pacific and Asian History, ANU.

Koe Boobooi 1875–1877, Nuku'alofa. Facsimile volume printed by authority of Her Majesty in Council 1964. (Translation by Tupou Posesi Fanua in POP.)

Ko e Makasini ko e Lo'au (April 1959). Nuku'alofa: Government Printing Office.

Koe Tohi Fanogonogo (from 1943 *Ko e Tohi Fanongonongo;* Newspaper of the Free Wesleyan Church). Nuku'alofa, 1927–.

Ko e Tohi Māhina 'a e Pule'anga Tonga (Annual calendar of the Tongan Government).
Lātūkefu, Sione. "Conversations with Queen Sālote, March 1965". Photocopy in possession of author.
Methodist, Sydney.
Methodist Church of New Zealand, Archives in Auckland and Christchurch.
Methodist Overseas Mission Collection (MOMC), Mitchell Library, Sydney.
Missionary Review, Sydney.
Moore, Gweneth H. An anecdotal "tale" of her life (1922–1976), 1988. Copy in possession of author.
Native Medical Practitioner, Suva.
New Zealand Herald, Auckland, New Zealand.
Pacific Islands Monthly, Sydney.
Page (Rodger) papers. (1) Scrapbook [of newspaper cuttings]. Division of Pacific and Asian History, ANU. (2) Letters from Queen Sālote to Page; Rodger Page's letter to his son of 23 Sept. 1939 describing the death of Hannah Page; and photographs. In possession of Mary Page. (3) Notes by Page; genealogies; conversations with Queen Salote; and poetry. ATL 1058/1.
Palace Office Papers (POP). Including Tonga Traditions Committee papers; Palace Office Cuttings Book; genealogies; and other. Nuku'alofa.
Pratt, M. A. Rugby, "Diary of a Visit to Tonga 18 August–4 September 1922". Methodist Church Archives, Christchurch, New Zealand.
– "Report of a Visit Paid by the Rev. M. A. Rugby Pratt of the N.Z. Methodist Conference to the Free Church of Tonga, 1922". TS copy in Methodist Church Archives, Christchurch, New Zealand.
Queen Sālote. *Koe Tohi Hohoko 'a Kuini Salote Tupou* (Genealogy Book of Queen Sālote Tupou). TS copy in POP, n.d.
– *Koe Tohi 'a 'Ene 'Afio ko Kuini Salote Tupou* (The Book of Her Majesty). TS copy in POP, n.d.
– *Ko e Ngaahi Tohi 'a 'Ene 'Afio 1958–59* (The Writings of Queen Sālote). TS copies (some with translations) in POP; also in Bott Spillius papers (box 11, folder 2), n.d.
I. Ko e Ngaahi Ha'a 'o Tonga (The Ha'as of Tonga).
II. Ko e Ngaahi Ha'a (The Ha'as).
III. Ko e Pongipongi 'o e Hingoa (The confirmation of the title).
IV. Ko e Talatupu'a 'oe Kava mo Lo'au (Legends of Kava and Lo'au).
V. Ko e Tanaki'anga 'oe Fonua (Assemblages of the people).
VI. Ko e Ngaahi Fatongia Kehekehe (Different duties).
VII. Ko e Faka'apa'apa (Showing respect).
VIII. Ko e Kāinga Faka-Tonga (Relationships).
IX. Ko e Ta'ane 'a Hou'eiki (The marriages of the chiefs).
X. Ko e Hisitolia 'oe Ngaahi Kie (The record of the fine-mats).
XI. Ko e Ngaahi Faiva Faka-Tonga (Tongan entertainments).
XII. Ko e Me'akai (Food).
XIII. Ko e Fānau (Family).
XIV. Ko e Vala (Costumes).
XV. Ko e Teuteu (What was worn).
– The songs and poems of Queen Sālote. Collection in possession of the author (publication anticipated).
– Diary of Visit to Britain to attend the Coronation of Queen Elizabeth II (in Tongan), 1953. TS copy in POP.
– "Conversation with Kuini Salote, at George Brown College, 17.1.56", in Collocott papers, ATL, 1956.
– "Respect" (an address to the Langa Fonua 'a e Fefine Tonga, 1956).
– Questionnaire on her life prepared by Rev Dr S. 'Amanaki Havea. In possession of Dr Havea, 1965.
Recorder [of Patriotic League], Nuku'alofa.
Spectator, Melbourne.
Spillius, Elizabeth, "Discussions of Tongan Custom 1958–59 [between] Her Majesty Queen Salote Tupou, the Hon Ve'ehala, Kolofau, Nua." TS in Tonga Traditions Committee papers, Palace

Office; also in New Zealand and Pacific Collection, Library of The University of Auckland, A265.
Sydney Morning Herald, Sydney.
Taumoefolau, Melenaite. "Language as an Indicator of Rank in Tongan Society". Paper given at seminar at The University of Auckland, July 1990.
– "Women in Tonga: cruelty and hierarchy, past and present". Women's Studies seminar given jointly with Elizabeth Wood-Ellem, July 1994.
Thomas, John. "Tongatabu or the Friendly Islands", n.d. Holograph MS, Library of the School of Oriental and African Studies, University of London. Cited as Thomas, "Tongatabu".
Tonga Government Gazette, Nuku'alofa.
Tonga Traditions Committee papers. Including typed copies of genealogies of (1) Losaline Fatafehi; (2) Tuituiohu; (3) 'Ulukālala-i-Mala'e-'Aloa (1910); (4) Queen Sālote (1958, copied 1960); (5) Queen Sālote (copied 1962); (6) Fielakepa (copied 1960); (7) Veikune (copied 1959); (8) Amelia Becker (copied 1961); (9) Afu Ha'amango (copied 1960); (10) S. Tu'iketei Pule (copied 1963); (11) Havea Tu'i Ha'ateiho (1900–12); (12) 'Etueni Tupou (1921, copied 1959); (13) Afu-Kaipo'uli (Hansen); (14) Sepuita Hala'api'api (1930, copied 1963); and (15) Tupou I.
Tongamohenoa, Lesieli [Rachel Tonga], Diary, 6 January 1924–30 April 1925. Incomplete holograph MS in POP.
Tongilava, Sione Filipe, Diary, 1917–22, 1924–38, 1940–9. Holograph MSS in POP.
Tupou College, 1941. *Koe Havea. Koe Makasini 'oe Koliji ko Tubou Nafualu. Koe Jiubeli koe ta'u 'e 75 1866–1941* (Magazine of Tupou College, Nafualu, the 75th jubilee issue 1866–1941), Nuku'alofa. The 1941 issue includes little biographies of people associated with the College, written by Sione Havea. Translations by Rev. Dr S. 'Amanaki Havea in possession of author.
Western Pacific Herald, Suva.
Western Pacific High Commission Gazette, Suva.
Western Pacific Archives. Formerly in Suva, now in Foreign and Commonwealth Office, Milton Keynes, England. Some of the earlier years of these records are on microfilm.
Whitcombe, J. D. "Tonga Tabu", n.d. TS in Division of Pacific and Asian History, ANU.
Wood, A. H., Diary, 1924–37. Holograph MS (shorthand and long-hand) in possession of author.

2. *Books, articles, and theses*

Allen, P. S. *Stewart's Handbook of the Pacific Islands.* Sydney: McCarron, Stewart & Co., 3rd ed. 1912; new ed. 1922.
'Api Fo'ou College 1886–1961. Nuku'alofa, n.d.
Attenborough, David. *Quest in Paradise*. London: Lutterworth Press, 1960.
Bain, Kenneth R. *The Official Record of the Royal Visit to Tonga 19th–20th December 1953*. London: Pitkin, 1954.
– *The Friendly Islanders: a story of Queen Salote and her people*. London: Hodder & Stoughton, 1967.
– *The New Friendly Islanders*. London: Hodder & Stoughton, 1993.
Beaglehole, Ernest & Pearl. *Pangai: village in Tonga*. Wellington: Memoirs of the Polynesian Society no. 18.
Beaglehole, J. C (ed.). *The Journals of Captain James Cook on His Voyages of Discovery*. Cambridge University Press for Hakluyt Society, vols 3 & 4, 1967, 1974.
Blamires, Gwen. *Little Island Kingdom of the South*. London: Arthur H. Stockwell, n.d.
Blanc, J. F. *A History of Tonga or Friendly Islands* (translated from Tongan by C. S. Ramsay). California: Vista [1934].
Bolitho, Hector. "Queen Salote's Second Kingdom", *Queen* 28 Oct. 1958, pp.70–1.
Bott, Elizabeth. "Power and Rank in the Kingdom of Tonga", *JPS* 90:1 (1981) 7–81.
– with the assistance of Tavi. *Tongan Society at the Time of Captain Cook's Visits: discussions with Her Majesty Queen Sālote Tupou*. Wellington: Polynesian Society Memoir No. 44, 1982.
Bott, Elizabeth & Edmund Leach. "The Significance of Kava in Tongan Myth and Ritual", in *The Interpretation of Ritual: essays in honour of A. I. Richards*, ed. J. S. La Fontaine. London: Tavistock Publications, 1972. *See also* Bott Spillius papers; Spillius, Elizabeth.

Bourne, Pamela. *Out of the World*. London: Geoffrey Bles, 1935.
Burnett, Frank. *Summer Isles of Eden*. London: Sefton, Praed, 1923.
Campbell, I. C. *Island Kingdom: Tonga Ancient and Modern*. Christchurch, New Zealand: Canterbury University Press, 1992.
Churchward, C. M. *Tongan Grammar*. London: Oxford University Press, 1953.
– *Tongan Dictionary*. London: Oxford University Press, 1959.
– "Honorific Language in Tongan", *Bible Translator* 14:4 (1963) 407–40.
Collocott, E. E. V. "The Speech of Niua Fo'ou", *JPS* 31:124 (1922) 185–9.
– "Marriage in Tonga", *JPS* 32:4 (1923) 221–8.
– "Kava Ceremonial in Tonga", *JPS* 36:1 (1927) 21–7.
– *Tales and Poems of Tonga*. Honolulu: Bernice P. Bishop Museum Bulletin no.46, 1928.
– *Ko e Ta'u 'e Teau*. London: Siasi Uesiliana Tau'atāina 'o Tonga, 1972 [1926].
Collocott, E. E. V. and Sione Havea. *Proverbial Sayings of the Tongans*. Honolulu: Bernice P. Bishop Museum Occasional Paper no.8:3, 1922.
Constitution and Laws of the Free Wesleyan Church of Tonga 1924. Nuku'alofa: Government Printer (in English and Tongan) 1924.
Constitution of Tonga. Published in Lātūkefu *Constitution* and *Laws 1903* (1907).
Cook, James. *See* Beaglehole, J. C.
Crocombe, Ron. "Protocole dans le Pacifique: le roi de Tonga à l'église", *Journal de la Société des Océanistes* 28:35 (1972) 169–72.
Crozier, Dorothy. "Problems Seen in Tonga", *Australia's Neighbours* series 3, no. 2, 1952.
– "Obituary: H.M. Queen Salote of Tonga", *JPS* 75:4 (1966) 401–3.
Cummins, H. G. *Sources of Tongan History: a collection of documents, extracts and contemporary opinions in Tongan political history 1616–1900*, compiled and arranged by H. G. Cummins. Nuku'alofa: H. G. Cummins, 1972.
– "Missionary Chieftain: James Egan Moulton and Tongan society 1865–1909". PhD thesis, ANU, 1980.
Cyclopedia of Samoa, Tonga, Tahiti, and the Cook Islands. Suva: Cyclopedia Company of Fiji, 1907.
Dalby, Mark. *The Cocker Connection*, London: Regency Press, 1989.
[Davidson, Janet.] *Traditional Arts of Pacific Island Women*. Wellington: Museum of New Zealand, 1994.
[Dineen, T. B.] *Dineen's Commercial Directory and Tourists' Guide to the Pacific Islands*. Sydney: Dineen, 1903–04.
Donald, Stephen. *In Some Sense the Work of an Individual: Afred Willis and the Tongan Anglican Mission 1902–1920*. Hibiscus Coast (New Zealand): Colcom Press, 1955.
Düring, Kurt. *Pathways to the Tongan Present*. Nuku'alofa: Government Printing Dept., 1990.
Fanua, Tupou Posesi. *Malō Tupou: an oral history* (as told to Lois Wimberg Webster). Auckland: Pasifika Press, 1996.
Fusitu'a, 'Ēseta Fulivai. "King George Tupou II and the Government of Tonga". MA thesis, ANU, 1976.
Fusitu'a, 'Ēseta & Noel Rutherford. "George Tupou II and the British Protectorate", in *Friendly Islands*, ed. Noel Rutherford. Melbourne: Oxford University Press, 1977.
Geil, W. E. *Ocean and Isle*. Melbourne: Wm T. Pater, 1902.
Gifford, E. W. *Tongan Place Names*. Honolulu: Bernice P. Bishop Museum Bulletin no.6, 1923.
– *Tongan Society*. Honolulu: Bernice P. Bishop Museum Bulletin no.61, 1929.
Great Britain: Colonial Office (annual). *Annual Report on Tonga*. London: HMSO.
– *Colonial Office List*. London: HMSO.
– *Correspondence 27 June 1902 to 26 May 1906 Relating to Affairs in Tonga*. COCP *Australia 182*. Cited as COCP *Australia 182*. *See also* Im Thurn.
– *Correspondence (1914–33) Relating to Affairs in the Tongan Islands Protectorate. Western Pacific 3*. Cited as COCP *Western Pacific 3*.
Great Britain: Foreign Office. *Correspondence Respecting the Affairs of Tonga: January–June 1905*. FOCP 8933.
Grimshaw, Beatrice. "Tonga and its Queen", *ABC Weekly* 8 April 1944.
Gunson, N. "The *Hau* Concept of Leadership in Western Polynesia", *JPH* 14:1–2 (1979) 28–49.

– "Sacred Women Chiefs and Female 'Headmen' in Polynesian history", *JPH* 22:3 (1987) 139–72.
Guthrie, Margaret W. *Misi Utu: Dr D. W. Hoodless and the development of medical education in the South Pacific*. Suva: Institute of Pacific Studies, University of the South Pacific, 1979.
Hau'ofa, Epeli. "The Pangs of Transition: kinship and economy in Tonga", *A New Zealand Journal of Sociology* 14:2 (1978) 160–5.
Havea, Sione. Biographies of Queen Sālote and Tungī Mailefihi and others in the jubilee edition of *Koe Havea* (magazine of Tupou College). Nuku'alofa: Tupou College, 1941.
Helu, Futa. "Fahu", *Chronicle* 11:51 (15 May 1975) 4.
– "Thinking in Tonga", in *Thinking: the expanding frontier*. Philadelphia: Franklin, 1982.
Henley, Sir Thomas. *A Pacific Cruise: musings and opinions on island problems*. Sydney: John Sands, 1930.
Herda, P. S. "Hierarchy and the Prerogative of History-making", in *Tonga and Samoa: images of gender and polity*, ed. Judith Huntsman. Christchurch, New Zealand: Macmillan Brown Centre for Pacific Studies, University of Canterbury, 1995.
Herda, P., J. Terrell and N. Gunson (eds). *Tongan Culture and History*. Papers from the first Tongan History Conference, held in Canberra 14–17 January 1987. Canberra: Department of Pacific and Southeast Asian History, Research School of Pacific Studies, ANU, 1990.
Hornabrook, Judith S. "New Zealand and the Tonga Defence Force 1939–1945". MA thesis, Victoria University, Wellington, 1951.
Humphrey, S. K. *Loafing through the Pacific*. Garden City: Doubleday, 1927.
Im Thurn, Sir Everard. "Report on Tongan Affairs" published in COCP *Australia 182*, as encl. in item 62, 15 March 1905. *See* Great Britain: Colonial Office (COCP *Australia 182*).
James, K. E. "'Rank overrules everything': hierarchy, social stratification and gender in Tonga", in *Tonga and Samoa: images of gender and polity*, ed. Judith Huntsman. Christchurch, New Zealand: Macmillan Brown Centre for Pacific Studies, University of Canterbury, 1995.
Kaeppler, Adrienne L. "Sunday in Tonga", *Delphian Quarterly* 49:4 (1966) 8–11, 15.
– "Folklore as expressed in the dance in Tonga", *Journal of American Folklore* 80:316 (1967) 160–8.
– "Rank in Tonga", *Ethnology* 10:2 (1971) 174–93.
– "*Me'afaka'eiki*: Tongan funerals in a changing society", in *The Changing Pacific: essays in honour of H. E. Maude*, ed. Niel Gunson, pp.174–202. Melbourne: Oxford University Press, 1978.
– "Structured Movement Systems in Tonga", in *Society and the Dance: the social anthropology of process and performance*, ed. Paul Spencer, pp.25–33. Cambridge: Cambridge University Press, 1985.
– "The Production and Reproduction of Social and Cultural Values in the Compositions of Queen Sālote of Tonga", in *Music, Gender, and Culture*, ed. Marcia Herndon and Susanne Ziegler (International Council for Traditional Music, ICTM Study Group on Music and Gender), pp.191–219. Wilhelmshaven: Florian Noetzel Verlag, 1990.
– "Poetics and Politics of Tongan Laments and Eulogies", *American Enthnologist* 20:3 (1993) 474–501.
– *Poetry in Motion: studies of Tongan dance*. Tonga: Vava'u Press, 1993.
– "Poetics and Politics of Tongan Barkcloth", in *Pacific Material Culture: essays in honour of Dr. Simon Kooijman*, ed. Dirk Smidt, Pieter ter Keurs and Albert Trouwborst. Mededelingen van het Rijksmuseum voor Volkenkunde 28, pp.101–21. Leiden: National Museum of Ethnology, 1995.
– "The Paradise Theme in Modern Tongan Music", in *The Essence of Singing and the Substance of Song . . . essays in honour of Catherine Ellis*, ed. Linda Barwick, Allan Marett, & Guy Tunstill, pp.159–83. Sydney: University of Sydney, 1995.
Kavaliku, S. Langi. "An Analysis of 'Ofa in Tongan Society: an empirical approach". BA Honours thesis, Harvard University, 1961.
Kavapalu, Helen. "Becoming Tongan: an ethnography of childhood in the Kingdom of Tonga". PhD thesis, ANU, 1991. *See also* Morton, Helen.
Kennedy, P. M. "Britain and the Tongan Harbours 1898–1914", *Historical Studies* 13:58 (1972) 251–67.
King, Michael. *Te Puea: a biography*. Auckland: Hodder & Stoughton, 1977.
Lambert, S. M. *A Doctor in Paradise*. London: J. M. Dent, 1941.
Lātūkefu, Sione, "Tonga after Queen Salote", *JPH* 2 (1967) 159–62.
– *Church and State in Tonga: the Wesleyan Methodist Missionaries and political development 1822–1875*. Canberra: ANU Press, 1974.
– *The Tongan Constitution: a brief history to celebrate its centenary*. Nuku'alofa: Tonga Traditions Committee, 1975.

– "The Making of the First Tongan-born Professional Historian", in *Pacific Islands History: Journeys and Transformations*, ed. Brij Lal. Canberra: Journal of Pacific History, Research School of Pacific Studies, ANU, 1992.
Lavaka [Gregory], Penelope A. "The Limits of Advice: Britain and the Kingdom of Tonga, 1900–1970". PhD thesis, ANU, 1981.
– "The Tonga Ma'a Tonga Kautaha: a watershed in British–Tongan relations", *Pacific Studies* 4:2 (1981) 142–63.
Lindstrom, Lamont & Geoffrey M. White. *Island Encounters: black and white memories of the Pacific War*. Washington & London: Smithsonian Institution Press, 1990.
Luke, Sir Harry. *From a South Seas Diary 1938–1942*. London: Nicholson & Watson, 1945.
– *Queen Salote and Her Kingdom*. London: Putnam, 1954.
– *Islands of the South Pacific*. London: Harrap, 1961.
McArthur, Norma. *Island Populations of the Pacific*. Canberra: ANU Press, 1967.
MacQuarrie, Hector. *Friendly Queen*. London: Heinemann, 1955.
Māhina, 'Okusitino. "The Tongan Traditional History *Tala-ē-Fonua*: a vernacular ecology-centred historico-cultural concept". PhD thesis, ANU, 1992.
Marcus, George E. *The Nobility and Chiefly Tradition in the Modern Kingdom of Tonga*, Wellington: Polynesian Society, 1980.
Martin, John/William Mariner. *An Account of the Natives of the Tonga Islands in the South Pacific Ocean* . . . 3rd ed. 2 vols. Edinburgh: Constable, 1827.
Maude, Alaric. "Tonga: equality overtaking privilege", *Land Tenure in the Pacific*, ed. R. Crocombe. Melbourne: Oxford University Press, 1971.
Maude, H. E. *Kingdom of Tonga: report on the public service with recommendations for reorganization*. Suva: Government Press, 1942.
Mordaunt, Elinor. *The Venture Book*. London: John Lane, 1926.
Morton, Helen. *Becoming Tongan: an ethnography of childhood*. Honolulu: University of Hawai'i Press, 1996.
Moulton, J. E. [the younger]. *Moulton of Tonga*. London: Epworth Press, 1921.
Moyle, Richard. *Tongan Music*. Auckland: Auckland University Press, 1987.
Neill, J. S. *Ten Years in Tonga*. London: Hutchinson, 1955.
Ninety-seventh Semi-Annual Conference of the Church of Jesus Christ of the Latter Day Saints 3–5 October 1926. Salt Lake City, Utah.
Nuku'alofa Club 1914–1964. Nuku'alofa: Government Printer, 1964.
Orange, J./George Vason. *An Authentic Narrative of Four Years' Residence at Tongataboo, one of the Friendly Islands in the South Sea*. London: Longman, Hurst, Rees & Orme, 1810.
Pacific Courts and Justice. London: Commonwealth Magistrates Association; Suva: Institute of Pacific Studies, University of the South Pacific, 1977.
Pacific Islands Yearbook. Sydney & Suva: Pacific Publications, 1932, 1942, 1944, 1950, 1956, 1959, 1968, 1972.
Powles, C. G. "The Persistence of Chiefly Power and its Implications for Law and Political Organisation in Western Polynesia". PhD thesis, ANU, 1979.
Priday, H. E. L. *The War from Coconut Square: the story of the defense of the island bases of the South Pacific*. Wellington: A. H. & A. W. Reed, 1945.
Ritchie, J. & J. *Growing Up in Polynesia*. Sydney: Allen & Unwin, 1979.
Rogers, Garth. "Kai and Kava in Niuatoputapu: social relations, ideologies and contexts in a rural Tongan community". PhD thesis, University of Auckland, 1975.
– "The Father's Sister is Black: a consideration of female rank and power in Tonga", *JPS* 86:2 (1977) 157–82.
[Rogers, Garth (ed.)]. *The Fire Has Jumped: eyewitness accounts of the eruption and evacuation of Niuafo'ou, Tonga*. Suva: Institute of Pacific Studies, University of the South Pacific, 1986.
Rosendahl, Jorgen. *The Happy Lagoons: the world of Queen Salote* (trans. from the Danish by Eiler Hansen and J. F. Burke). London: Jarrolds, 1961.
Royal Tonga. Film made by David Attenborough and Geoffrey Mulligan, 1960, for the British Broadcasting Corporation.
Rutherford, Noel. *Shirley Baker and the King of Tonga*. Melbourne: Oxford University Press, 1971.

– (ed.) *Friendly Islands: a history of Tonga*. Melbourne: Oxford University Press, 1977.
– "Tonga Ma'a Tonga Kautaha: a proto-co-operative in Tonga", *JPH* 16:1 (1981) 20–41.
Scarr, Deryck. *Fragments of Empire: a history of the Western Pacific High Commission 1877–1914*. Canberra: ANU Press, 1967.
[Seddon, R. J.] *The Right Hon. R. J. Seddon's (the Premier of New Zealand) Visit to Tonga . . . May 1900*. Wellington: New Zealand Government Printer, 1900.
Spillius, Elizabeth. *Tonga 5: a brief study of mother–child relationships in Tonga, May–October 1958*. WHO Regional Office for the Western Pacific, 1960. *See also* Bott, Elizabeth; Bott Spillius papers.
Spillius, James. Quarterly reports to World Health Organization on Environmental Sanitation Project. Nuku'alofa: 1959–60.
– *Tonga: assignment report*. Nuku'alofa: World Health Organization, 1961.
Taliai, Siupeli. "Tupou College and the Education of Women", in *Tongan Culture and History: papers from the 1st Tongan History Conference held in Canberra 14–17 January 1987*, ed. P. Herda, J. Terrell, and N. Gunson. Canberra: Department of Pacific and Southeast Asian History, Research School of Pacific Studies, ANU, 1990.
Tamahori, Maxine J. "Cultural Change in Tongan Bark-cloth Manufacture". MA thesis, The University of Auckland, 1963.
[Taufe'ulungaki, 'Ana.] "Conference on UN Convention on the Elimination of All Sorts of Discrimination Against Women: overview paper". Nuku'alofa, 4 January 1991.
Taumoefolau, Melenaite. "Is the Father's Sister Really Black?", *JPS* 100:1 (1991) 91–9.
Thompson, E. M. *Tonga*. Prepared for the Methodist Young Women's Missionary Movement of Victoria, Melbourne: Spectator Publishing, n.d.
Thomson, Basil, 1894. *The Diversions of a Prime Minister*. Edinburgh & London: Wm Blackwood & Sons, 1894.
– *Savage Island: an account of a sojourn in Niué and Tonga*. London: John Murray, 1902.
– *The Scene Changes*. New York: Doubleday, Doran, 1937. British edition published in 1939 by Collins (London).
Tonga Chamber of Commerce. *Rules and Constitution of the Tongan Chamber of Commerce*. Suva: G. L. Griffiths, 1887.
– President's Annual Report, 1930, 1931, 1932. TS copies in ATL.
Tonga Council of Churches. *Land and Migration: papers presented at Seminar . . . in Nuku'alofa on September 22 to September 26 1975*, ed. Siosiua H. Fonua. Cyclostyled, n.p.
Tonga Government. Annual Reports of government departments, available in ATL; Palace Office, Nuku'alofa; New Zealand and Pacific Collection, Library of The University of Auckland, New Zealand.
– *Koe Tuutuuni maae Koliji Toga 1900: Toga maa Toga* (The Regulations of Tonga College 1900: Tonga for the Tongans). Nuku'alofa: J.Vaka, 1900.
– *The Law of the Government of Tonga 1903*. Auckland: Brett Printing, 1907. (Cited as *Laws 1903*.)
– *A Revised Edition of the Law of Tonga* . . . Nuku'alofa: C. S. Summers, Government Printer, 1929.
– *Tonga Law Reports*. Nuku'alofa: Government Printer: 3 vols. Vol. 1: *Cases decided in the Supreme Court of Tonga 1908–1959*, ed. D. B. Hunter, 1963. Vol. 2: *Reports of Land Court Cases 1923–1962/Privy Council Decisions 1924–1961*, ed. D. B. Hunter, 1963. Vol. 3: *Land Court Cases and Privy Council Decisions 1962–1973*, ed. H. S. Roberts, 1974.
– *The Law of Tonga* . . . London: Sweet & Maxwell, 1967.
Tremblay, E. A. *When You Go to Tonga*. Derby, New York: Daughters of St Paul, Apostolate of the Press, 1953.
[Tremblay, E. A.] *Under the Southern Cross in Tonga-Tabu*. Melbourne: Advocate Press, 1929.
Tu'inukuafe, K. L. "Overseas-trained Tongans and their contribution to the modern development of Tonga". MA (Ed.) thesis, The University of Auckland, 1976.
Tu'ipelehake of Tonga, HRH Prince, 1953. "Tongan Customs" *Transactions of the Fiji Society* 5:3 (1953) 47–50.
Tupouto'a-Tungī, *Koe Tohi Tu'ungafasi 'ae Kolisi Tonga*. Auckland: Leighton's, 1946.
United States Government. "History of Tongatabu", n.d. Command History, Advanced Navy Base microfilm NRS II–465.
Vason, George. See Orange, J./George Vason.

Walsh, A. C. "Nuku'alofa, Tonga: a preliminary study of urbanization and immigration". MA thesis, Victoria University, Wellington, 1964.
– *Nuku'alofa: a study of urban life in the Pacific Islands*. Wellington: A. H. & A. W. Reed, 1972.
Weeks, C. J. "The United States Occupation of Tonga, 1942–45: the social and economic aspect", *Pacific Historical Review* 56:3 (1987) 399–426.
White, Geoffrey M. & Lamont Lindstrom (eds). *The Pacific Theater: island representations of World War II*. Melbourne: Melbourne University Press, 1990.
Willis, Alfred. *Letter from Bishop Willis and Report for 1908 of the Anglican Church in Tonga*. London: Wm Cole, 1909.
Wood, A. H. *A History and Geography of Tonga*. Nuku'alofa: Government Printer, 1932.
– *Overseas Missions of the Australian Methodist Church*. Vol 1: *Tonga and Samoa*. Melbourne: Aldersgate Press, 1975.
Wood, A. H. & E. Wood-Ellem. "Queen Sālote Tupou III", *Friendly Islands*, ed. Noel Rutherford. Melbourne: Oxford University Press, 1977.
Wood-Ellem, Elizabeth. "Queen Sālote Tupou III and Tungī Mailefihi: a study of leadership in twentieth-century Tonga (1918–41)". PhD thesis, University of Melbourne, 1981.
– "Sālote of Tonga and the Problem of National Unity", *JPH* 18:3 (1983) 163–82.
– "Queen Sālote Tupou of Tonga as Tu'i Fefine", *JPH* 22:4 (1987) 209–27.
– "Chief Justices of Tonga 1905–40", *JPH* 24:1 (1989) 21–37; also in *Tongan Culture and History*, ed. P. Herda, J. Terrell, and N. Gunson. Canberra: Department of Pacific and Southeast Asian History, Research School of Pacific Studies, ANU, 1990.
– "Customary Landholding in Tonga after the 1875 Constitution", in *Dangerous Liaisons: essays in honour of Greg Dening*, ed. Donna Merwick. Melbourne: History Department, University of Melbourne, 1994.
– "Queen Sālote and the Dual Mandate Policy", in *Emerging from Empire?: decolonisation in the Pacific*, ed. Donald Denoon. Canberra: Division of Pacific and Asian History, Research School of Pacific and Asian Studies, ANU, July 1997.
– "Behind the Battle Lines: Tonga in World War II", in *Echoes of Pacific War*, ed. Deryck Scarr, Niel Gunson and Jennifer Terrell. Canberra: Target Oceania, 1998.

Index

Unless otherwise indicated, the relationships are to Queen Sālote. For abbreviations, see page 321. The fakau'a *(glottal stop) has been ignored in alphabetical sequence. Titleholders are identified by title with their personal names in parentheses; other persons are identified by personal names only (if there was no family name), or by family and personal name (if the person had a family name at the time).*